P9-CFV-675

ETHICAL DILEMMAS AND DECISIONS IN

Criminal Justice

tenth EDITION

JOYCELYN M. POLLOCK
TEXAS STATE UNIVERSITY—SAN MARCOS

 CENGAGE

Australia • Brazil • Canada • Mexico • Singapore • United Kingdom • United States

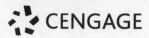

Ethical Dilemmas and Decisions in Criminal Justice, Tenth Edition
Joycelyn M. Pollock

Product Director: Marta Lee-Perriard

Product Manager: Carolyn Henderson-Meier

Content Developer: Katie Seibel/Shelley Murphy

Product Assistant: Megan Nauer

Sr. Marketing Manager: Mark Lindton

Manufacturing Planner: Rebecca Cross

Intellectual Property Analyst: Jennifer Bowes

Intellectual Property Project Manager: Nick Barrows

Art Director: Helen Bruno

Cover Image Credit: iStockPhoto.com/ MarekPiotrowski
Tetra Images/Getty Images

Cover and Internal Designer: Pam Verros

Production Management, and Composition: Lumina Datamatics, Inc.

© 2019, 2017 Cengage Learning, Inc.

Unless otherwise noted, all content is © Cengage.

ALL RIGHTS RESERVED. No part of this work covered by the copyright herein may be reproduced or distributed in any form or by any means, except as permitted by U.S. copyright law, without the prior written permission of the copyright owner.

For product information and technology assistance, contact us at
Cengage Customer & Sales Support, 1-800-354-9706.

For permission to use material from this text or product,
submit all requests online at **www.cengage.com/permissions.**
Further permissions questions can be e-mailed to
permissionrequest@cengage.com.

Library of Congress Control Number: 2017952407

Student Edition:
ISBN: 978-1-337-55849-5

Loose-leaf Edition:
ISBN: 978-1-337-56093-1

Cengage
200 Pier 4 Boulevard
Boston, MA 02210
USA

Cengage is a leading provider of customized learning solutions with employees residing in nearly 40 different countries and sales in more than 125 countries around the world. Find your local representative at **www.cengage.com.**

To learn more about Cengage platforms and services, visit **www.cengage.com.** To register or access your online learning solution or purchase materials for your course, visit **www.cengagebrain.com.**

Printed at CLDPC, USA, 05-22

To Greg and Eric, as always

About the Author

 **Joycelyn M. Pollock** received her Ph.D. in Criminal Justice from the State University of New York, Albany. She also obtained a J.D. from the University of Houston, and passed the Texas Bar in 1991. She has retired from university teaching and is a University Distinguished Professor, Emeritus from Texas State University. She continues to be involved in training and consulting in criminal justice.

The first edition of *Ethics in Crime and Justice: Dilemmas and Decisions* was published in 1986 and continues to be one of the leading texts in the field. Dr. Pollock has published over 15 separate books, many with multiple editions, including *Crime and Criminal Justice in America, 3rd Ed.* (2016); *Morality Stories, 3rd Ed.* (with Michael Braswell and Scott Braswell, 2016); *Criminal Law, 11th Ed.* (2016); *Women's Crimes, Criminology and Corrections* (2015); and *Prisons and Prison Life: Costs and Consequences, 2nd Ed.* (2014).

She has delivered training to police officers, probation officers, parole officers, constables, correctional administrators, and other groups in the areas of sexual harassment, ethics, criminology, ethical leadership, and other subjects. She has taught at the Houston Police Academy, the Bill Blackwood Law Enforcement Management Institute, and the California Department of Corrections and Rehabilitation Leadership Institute, and has been a guest speaker for the International Association of Policewomen, the Texas Juvenile Justice Association, and the Southwest Legal Institute, among other groups. In 1998, she was awarded a Fulbright Teaching Fellowship to Turku School of Law in Turku, Finland. She was also a recipient of a Senior Scholar Justice award from the Open Society Institute. The Academy of Criminal Justice Sciences has honored her with the Bruce Smith Award for outstanding contributions to the field of criminology and the ACJS Fellows Award for contributions to criminal justice research.

Brief Contents

Contents

PART IV	CORRECTIONS	329

Chapter 11   The Ethics of Punishment and Corrections   329

Chapter 12   Discretion and Dilemmas in Corrections   365

Chapter 13   Correctional Professionals: Misconduct and Responses   399

Chapter 14   Making Ethical Choices   432

Preface

The first edition of this book was published in 1986, thus this 10th edition marks over 30 years the book has been used in criminal justice and training classrooms. When I first wrote the book, there were very few textbooks for a course covering criminal justice ethics. Now there are probably a dozen, so I appreciate that readers continue to find value in this one. Over the years, the book has been shaped by current events, reviewers' comments, and the many individuals who have provided feedback. I want to thank every person who has contacted me through e-mail, letters, or personally at conferences. I welcome and appreciate all feedback. Please continue to let me know what you think and help me make the book better and more accurate.

Since the first edition, this text has provided the basic philosophical principles necessary to analyze ethical dilemmas, and it has also included current news events to show that these are not simply "ivory tower" discussions. Each edition has incorporated recent news, sometimes requiring updates even as the book goes to press. The book also identifies themes that run through the entire system, such as discretion and due process. In each edition, I have tried to improve the coverage and structure of the book without changing the elements that work for instructors.

The last edition captured the rise of the "Black Lives Matter" movement, increasing attention to wrongful convictions, and presidential commutations of drug offenders sentenced under mandatory minimums. This edition has had major news to cover as well. Our recent presidential election has led to changes within the Department of Justice, "sanctuary city" resolutions, and the federal turnabout on the use of private prisons, among other major events or policy changes that affect criminal justice organizations. As with prior years, it is difficult not to devote more space to law enforcement than courts or corrections, since the troubles there seem to receive greater coverage by both the academic and popular press. In some areas, a discussion in the last edition has been expanded and updated, such as prosecutorial misconduct, the Rikers Island jail scandal, and halfway house scandals in New York City and Philadelphia. Systemic issues such as use-of-force training, mandatory minimums, the lack of indigent defense, and mass imprisonment continue to be covered in this book as ethical issues, although legal and policy factors are covered as well.

This edition retains the basic structure of devoting three chapters each to police, courts, and corrections with four introductory chapters. Instructors will find only minor changes in the chapter learning objectives and study questions, making for an easy transition in terms of adapting course material to the new edition. Several of the Walking the Walk boxes have been changed, removing some to make way for individuals involved in recent events. The focus of revisions has been, as always, on covering new academic work and current news that is relevant to ethics. The changes are described in more detail below.

New to This Edition

- **Chapter 1: Morality, Ethics, and Human Behavior**—The chapter introduction has been rewritten, replacing a summary of current events with a more personal approach as to why we study ethics. A list of ethical issues and ethical dilemmas has been added as examples. The discussion about Governor Ryan was shortened and current news on a Florida prosecutor refusing to use the death penalty was inserted as another example of a person who had discretion to make a decision regarding what is only an ethical issue for the rest of us. A current controversy over the emoluments clause of the Constitution is included as an example of conflict of interests. The In the News box was updated to the current TRANSPARENCY INTERNATIONAL corruption index. The Ethical Issue box was changed, dropping the discussion of the "fast and furious program" to one dealing with the current issue of whether the Department of Justice should abandon the use of consent decrees to force change in law enforcement agencies. One of the Ethical Dilemmas at the end of the chapter was changed to the current issue regarding city council choices to declare sanctuary city status.

- **Chapter 2: Determining Moral Behavior**—The introductory news story about the "crookedest cop" in Florida was removed, as was the Ethical Issue box in this chapter, allowing the discussion of ethical systems to begin much earlier and reducing the length of the chapter. A short application of each ethical system was added to help readers learn how to apply the systems. The Walking the Walk box was replaced with one about Ana Mari Cauce, the president of the University of Washington, and her decision regarding the First Amendment. The In the News box was expanded with the recent attempted elimination of office of congressional ethics.

- **Chapter 3: Justice and Law**—This chapter updated the CEO salary box to 2016 figures. The In the News box on a CEO increasing workers' wages to $70,000 was updated with new information. The discussion on minimum wage has been updated with current news and studies. The discussion about Obamacare has been updated to include legal challenges as well as the current attempts by Congress to repeal it. The section on procedural justice has been updated with new research. Updated numbers on the NATIONAL REGISTRY OF EXONERATIONS and INNOCENCE PROJECT information has been added. Two older In the News boxes were removed, leaving three in the chapter. The Gallup poll on race has been updated. There is an expanded and updated section on race with new news stories and academic studies. New academic sources have been used for the discussion on restorative justice. Two of the end-of-chapter Ethical Dilemmas have been changed to more current topics.

- **Chapter 4: Becoming an Ethical Professional**—The section on biological influences on behavior has been rearranged and rewritten for greater clarity, with the discussion of oxytocin enlarged with new sources. The In the News box on Hidalgo County was replaced with one on the Wells Fargo scandal in the organizational influences subsection. The In the News box on Jon Burge has been expanded with new articles. The Ethical Issue box was replaced with one about sanctuary cities. In the leadership discussion, information on transformational leadership and applications to ethical employees has been added. Also added is new research on procedural justice and correctional leadership. The Walking the Walk box was replaced with one focusing on former Chief David Brown of Dallas. A new study question was added on organizational justice.

- **Chapter 5: The Police Role in Society**—The Learning Objectives were changed to include one that specifies knowledge about police history eras and the Ferguson effect. Then, the section "Future of Policing" was retitled as "Future of Policing and the Ferguson Effect," and now includes an expansive discussion of the concept and research about the Ferguson effect. The In the News box about good acts by police officers has been expanded with a new item. The discussion about military veterans in policing has been expanded in the "warrior–guardian" section. The number of police officers killed over the years has been added. There is now an expanded discussion of Crisis Intervention Team (CIT) training and dealing with mentally ill. The section on research on procedural justice in policing has been expanded, and includes new research that ties into the concepts of legitimacy of policing and the social contract. In the section on earlier police research, two of three police typologies (Muir & Brown) were deleted and one study question was changed as a result. Current events were added to make the revised discussion of duty/discretion topical. Dated references to McAnany and Davis were deleted as they are no longer necessary to the discussion of discretion. The references to Gallup polls and perceptions of police were moved out of the conclusion and into the discussion of public perceptions and procedural justice. The intelligence-led policing section was reduced and some information was moved to Chapter 14. The Baltimore police officer scandal was updated to include the acquittals of the officers and dropping drug cases associated with them. New information on the 1033 program and consent decrees by Department of Justice was included in the appropriate sections. The discussion of police subculture was reduced with old sources consolidated. A new In the News box on San Francisco police was added.

- **Chapter 6: Police Discretion and Dilemmas**—There is an updated and expanded discussion of public perceptions of law enforcement racism and disproportional shootings of blacks. Old research has been condensed throughout the chapter. The Walking the Walk box has been changed to one focusing on a former officer who helps other officers deal with shootings. There is a greatly expanded discussion of asset forfeiture. New data have been added to the discussion of stop and frisk. The discussion of officers dying in the line of duty was removed to avoid repetition from Chapter 5. The In the News box about the Boyd shooting was replaced with one about the Reid interrogation method. The In the News box on the stashhouse stings has been updated.

- **Chapter 7: Police Corruption and Responses**—A dated In the News box was replaced with one about a Portland officer whistleblower. Other In the News boxes were changed to more current events or updated with new information, for example, Baltimore acquittals of charged officers. There are expanded sections on body cameras, early warnings, consent decrees, and civilian review. The sections describing individual cases of misconduct in various cities have been reduced. There is an expanded discussion in the Ethical Issue box dealing with disciplinary action secrecy, and the Ethical Issue box was moved to immediately after police misconduct databanks for better flow. The section on consent decrees was moved to the societal responses section and there is a new discussion of recent societal changes under that subsection. There is an added section describing new legislation and the President's Task Force recommendations. One end-of-chapter Ethical Dilemma and one study review question were changed.

- **Chapter 8: Law and Legal Professionals**—The Walking the Walk box was removed and replaced with one about former Attorney General Comey. The asset forfeiture In the News box was removed since the topic was covered in Chapter 6. The discussion on indigent defense was moved from Chapter 9 to this chapter. New In the News boxes include one on laws criminalizing homelessness, and one on lawsuits against states because of underfunding indigent defense programs. There is a new, full discussion of the "criminalization of poverty" (bail, fines, fees, etc.). The discussion on marijuana legalization has been updated. There is a new section on courtroom workgroups.

- **Chapter 9: Discretion and Dilemmas in the Legal Profession**—The section on asset forfeiture was substantially reduced with much of the discussion, including the key term and margin definition, moving to Chapter 6 where there is a fuller discussion. The Ethical Dilemma box was removed to reduce chapter length. Several dated In the News boxes were replaced with current news items, for example, the ACLU defending an alt-right group, the Oakland jailhouse informant scandal, and the Brock Turner sentencing. Other current news was included in relevant discussions, including an ethical complaint against the attorney for Jody Arias, updated salary figures for prosecutors, and Justice Ginsburg's comment about President Trump as a potential conflict of interest issue. A section on jailhouse informants was moved from Chapter 10 and consolidated with the existing discussion in this chapter.

- **Chapter 10: Ethical Misconduct in the Courts and Responses**—The chapter introduction was changed by reducing the Clarence Brandley section and adding several additional summaries of wrongfully convicted individuals. New In the News boxes were added, including one of a defense attorney accused of witness tampering, and the District Attorney Seth Williams' indictment (Philadelphia). There was a new study of prosecutorial misconduct added. The In the News box on prosecutorial misconduct was changed, shortening the old story and adding a new one. New In the News boxes were added on judicial misconduct including sexual exploitation of defendants, and one on a California law making Brady violations a felon. Updated court cases on prosecutorial immunity were added. The Walking the Walk box was replaced with one on Kenneth Thompson, the late District Attorney from Brooklyn.

- **Chapter 11: The Ethics of Punishment and Corrections**—The chapter introduction on the philosophy of punishment has been shortened. All statistics concerning imprisonment and other correctional supervision have been updated. The information on supermax prisons is no longer in its own section; the discussion has been shortened to focus on supermax prisons as an example of a type of punishment. The discussion of private corrections has been expanded and updated. The discussion of capital punishment has been slightly shortened but new Supreme Court cases were added. The In the News box on Riker's Island jail has been updated. The In the News box on President Obama's commutations of drug offenders was updated with the final numbers. New In the News boxes were added on raising the age of responsibility in New York, adding monitors to review private prisons in Michigan, and the conviction of the former head of corrections, Chris Epps, in Mississippi.

- **Chapter 12: Discretion and Dilemmas in Corrections**—The discussion of the scandal in New Jersey and New York City surrounding halfway (sober) houses was enlarged with a new investigation in Philadelphia. There is an updated discussion of California's response to *Brown v. Plata*. The PREA survey has been updated. New In the News boxes are included on a New York same-sex prison sexual abuse case, and violence in North Carolina prisons. The In the News box on the Denver jail has been updated. There are several new academic sources added to the section on correctional treatment professionals' ethics. The Walking the Walk box was removed and replaced with one on Dr. Eric Reininga, a whistleblower in California.

- **Chapter 13: Correctional Professionals: Misconduct and Responses**—There are several new In the News boxes, including one on an investigation of correctional officers in Georgia. The sections on California prisons and the Los Angeles jail have been updated with current news. The sections in the last edition on misconduct in corrections departments in Texas and Mississippi were deleted. The section on misconduct in the New York corrections system has been expanded with new information, as was the section on the Florida corrections system. New news on scandals in the parole systems in Utah and Missouri were added. There is a new discussion of procedural justice research in corrections as a response and solution to misconduct.

- **Chapter 14: Making Ethical Choices**—There is an updated discussion and listing of terrorist events in the last several years. The missiles fired at the Syrian airbase in retaliation for the chemical weapon attack was used as an example of a natural law justification. Some of the sections on the aftermath of 9/11 have been shortened. The numbers held at Guantanamo have been updated. There is a new In the News box regarding the Senate report on torture that has been suppressed by the current administration. The discussion of Mitchell and Jessen, the two psychologists who have been described as the architects of waterboarding, has been updated with a current link to a video deposition where they defend their actions. Academic articles on law enforcement working with Muslim communities as counterterrorism efforts are referenced. A new In the News box on new surveillance technology was added, along with an expanded discussion of surveillance technology.

Features

There are several boxed features found in *Ethical Dilemmas and Decisions in Criminal Justice, 10th Ed.*, which highlight and provide real-world examples of key concepts and issues.

IN THE NEWS This feature has been present since the earliest editions of this book. Each chapter presents news items that relate to the discussion. In every edition, some of the news stories are kept, but most are cycled out to make room for current events. Examples in this edition include:

Jon Burge and his "midnight crew"

Commutations of drug offenders by President Obama

Chris Epps' conviction (former head of corrections for Mississippi)

Brock Turner sentencing

QUOTE AND QUERY Another longtime feature of the book, these boxes offer some classic and current quotes meant to illustrate a point or issue from the chapter's discussion. There is a query following the quote that spurs the reader to think about the quote in the context of the discussion.

WALKING THE WALK Introduced in the sixth edition, these boxes describe individuals who display ethical courage. This feature proved to be so popular that every chapter now has one and this edition has replaced some of the older ones with new descriptions of individuals faced with ethical dilemmas.

ETHICAL DILEMMA Each chapter features a dilemma, followed by an extended analysis of the dilemma under law, policy, and ethics. The feature makes explicit the focus of the book, illustrated by its title, *Ethical Dilemmas and Decisions*.

ETHICAL ISSUE Introduced in the ninth edition, these boxes present a current issue or policy in policing, courts, or corrections, and like the Ethical Dilemma boxes, provide an extended analysis of the issue under law, policy, and ethics. The addition of these issues boxes in some chapters shows how issues can be analyzed in a similar way to personal dilemmas.

Pedogogical Aids

In addition to the boxed features, *Ethical Dilemmas and Decisions in Criminal Justice, 10th Ed.*, has several pedagogical aids designed to enhance student learning and comprehension.

KEY TERMS Key terms are bolded and defined when they first appear in the text, and are included at the end of the chapter for student review.

STUDY QUESTIONS These end-of-chapter questions identify important points and concepts in the chapter and can be used for test reviews or test questions.

WRITING/DISCUSSION QUESTIONS These end-of-chapter questions cover more abstract concepts and are designed to provide an opportunity to employ critical thinking skills in a writing or discussion exercise.

ETHICAL DILEMMAS These end-of-chapter dilemmas are designed to be representative of what criminal justice professionals might face in the field. Many of the dilemmas describe true incidents and have been provided by police officers, probation officers, lawyers, and other criminal justice professionals. Others have been gleaned from news events or the media.

LEARNING OBJECTIVES Chapter-opening learning objectives preview the key content in each chapter for the reader.

CHAPTER REVIEW At the end of each chapter, the chapter objectives are presented again, but there is also a short summary of content. These reviews summarize the key content of the chapter for the reader.

▌ Ancillaries

A number of supplements are provided by Cengage Learning to help instructors use *Ethical Dilemmas and Decisions in Criminal Justice* in their courses and to aid students in preparing for exams. Supplements are available to qualified adopters. Please consult your local sales representative for details.

For the Instructor

ONLINE INSTRUCTOR'S MANUAL The manual includes learning objectives, a detailed chapter outline (correlated to PowerPoint slides), lecture notes, assignments, media tools, ethical dilemmas, and classroom discussions/activities. The learning objectives are correlated with the discussion topics, student activities, and media tools.

ONLINE TEST BANK Each chapter of the test bank contains multiple-choice, true/false, completion, and essay questions to challenge your students and assess their learning. It is tagged to the learning objectives that appear in the main text, references to the section in the main text where the answers can be found, and Bloom's taxonomy. Finally, each question in the test bank has been carefully reviewed by experienced criminal justice instructors for quality, accuracy, and content coverage.

CENGAGE LEARNING TESTING, POWERED BY COGNERO The Test Bank is also available through Cognero, a flexible online system that allows you to author, edit, and manage test bank content as well as create multiple test versions in an instant. You can deliver tests from your school's learning management system, your classroom, or wherever you want.

ONLINE LECTURES Helping you make your lectures more engaging while effectively reaching your visually oriented students, these handy Microsoft PowerPoint˚ slides outline the chapters of the main text in a classroom-ready presentation. The PowerPoint slides are updated to reflect the content and organization of the new edition of the text, are tagged by chapter learning objectives, and feature some additional examples and real-world cases for application and discussion.

For the Student

Mindtap Criminal Justice

With MindTap™ Criminal Justice for *Ethical Dilemmas and Decisions in Criminal Justice*, you have the tools you need to better manage your limited time, with the ability to complete assignments whenever and wherever you are ready to learn. Course material that is specially customized for you by your instructor in a proven, easy-to-use interface keeps you engaged and active in the course. MindTap helps you achieve better grades today by cultivating a true understanding of course concepts and with a mobile app to keep you on track. With a wide array of course-specific tools and apps—from note taking to flashcards—you can feel confident that MindTap is a worthwhile and valuable investment in your education.

You will stay engaged with MindTap's You Decide career-based decision-making scenarios and remain motivated by information that shows where you stand at all times—both individually and compared to the highest performers in class. MindTap eliminates the guesswork, focusing on what's most important with a learning path designed specifically by your instructor and for your Ethics course. Master the most important information with built-in study tools such as visual chapter summaries and integrated learning objectives that will help you stay organized and use your time efficiently.

Acknowledgments

The staff members at Cengage have been integral to the development of this edition. They are Carolyn Henderson Meier, Senior Product Manager; Katie Seibel, Content Developer; and Mark Linton, Senior Marketing Manager. Thanks also to Pradhiba Kannaiyan, Senior Project Manager at Lumina Datamatics, and Manish Kumar, Senior Copy Editor.

I also wish to thank those individuals in the field who have e-mailed me with questions and suggestions for the book and hope that they continue to do so. Most importantly, I thank my husband, Eric Lund, for all that he does.

—**Joycelyn Pollock**
jpl2@txstate.edu

Morality, Ethics, and Human Behavior

1

mediaphotos/Getty Images

Learning Objectives

1. Explain the difference between ethical issues and ethical dilemmas.

2. Give examples of how discretion permeates every phase of the criminal justice system and creates ethical dilemmas for criminal justice professionals.

3. Explain why the study of ethics is important for criminal justice professionals.

4. Define the terms *morals*, *ethics*, *duties*, *supererogatories*, and *values*.

5. Describe what behaviors might be subject to moral/ethical judgments.

Ethics is the study of right and wrong. Cheating may be efficient for the individual but it is judged as wrong and unethical.

Ethical judgments permeate our lives. You employ ethical analysis when you decide to utter a white lie to get out of doing something you don't want to do or when you call in sick on a beautiful, sunny day. Being honest in your interactions with others is a generally recognized duty; therefore, these decisions can be judged as wrong. Small decisions about behavior are often made without thinking of the ethical implications of these choices, but they form our character.

In this text, we will explore ethical decision making. More specifically, we explore the ethical dilemmas and issues within the criminal justice system. Every day one can pick up a newspaper or read news from other media outlets that present ethical issues or describe individuals who have made choices that are subject to ethical judgments. Some decisions affect very few people—as our decision to call in sick when we don't want to go to work. However, depending on the person and the decision, thousands or even millions of people might be affected. The decisions of criminal justice professionals almost always affect others.

The criminal justice system can be examined using political, legal, organizational, or sociological approaches; however, in this book, we shift the lens somewhat and look at the system from an ethics perspective. Asking whether something is legal, for instance, is not necessarily the same as asking whether something is right.

Ethical discussions in criminal justice focus on *issues* or *dilemmas*. **Ethical issues** are broad social questions, often concerning the government's social control mechanisms and the impact on those governed. These issues can be subject to legal analysis and/or ethical analysis since the two are related but not the same. The following is a list of a few current issues in the field of criminal justice that can be subject to ethical analysis:

ethical issues
Difficult social or policy questions that include controversy over the "right" thing to do.

- Decriminalizing recreational marijuana
- Reversing mandatory minimum laws for drug crimes
- Abolishing the death penalty
- Using private prisons
- Requiring police officers to carry their own liability insurance
- Instituting civilian review boards to advise police departments
- Instituting deportation against "Dreamers" ("Deferred Action for Childhood Arrivals" Act recipients)
- Cities adopting "Sanctuary City" resolutions
- Instituting conviction review task forces in prosecutors' offices
- Requiring mandatory DNA collection for all misdemeanant arrestees.

The typical individual does not have much control over these issues. If one is a political or organizational leader, it is possible that it is within that person's discretion to decide some ethical issues, but generally, these choices are decided by political action or deliberation by many people.

ethical dilemmas
Situations in which it is difficult for an individual to decide, either because the right course of action is not clear or because the right course of action carries some negative consequences.

While ethical issues are broad social questions or policy decisions, **ethical dilemmas** are situations in which one person must decide what to do. Either the choice is unclear or the right choice will be difficult because of the costs involved. Every one of us has faced ethical dilemmas. Our dilemmas involve our jobs and our interactions with others. Criminal justice professionals face dilemmas arising from the choices they are faced with during their employment. Dilemmas of criminal justice professionals include the following:

- A police officer's decision whether to ticket a traffic violator or not
- A police officer's decision to tell a supervisor that her partner has an alcohol problem
- A sheriff's decision how to advise a mayor and city council regarding budgetary priorities
- A defense attorney's decision to take a case or not
- A prosecutor's decision on whether and what to charge
- A probation officer's decision on whether to file a violation report on a probationer

At times, one's belief regarding an ethical issue gives rise to an ethical dilemma. In 2000, George Ryan, then governor of Illinois, declared a moratorium on use of the death penalty in his state when at least five individuals on death row were exonerated with DNA evidence. One of his last acts as he left office in 2003 was to commute the sentences of all 160 prisoners on death row to life without parole. Unlike most of us, Governor Ryan's position meant he could do something about his belief regarding the death penalty.

A more current example is Orange County, Florida, State Attorney Aramis Ayala who refused to pursue the death penalty against a cop killer. In fact, she reportedly has expressed her intent to *never* pursue the death penalty because of continued constitutional challenges to Florida death penalty sentences and the cost. After she refused to recuse herself, Governor Rick Scott signed an executive order that removed her from the case and appointed another prosecutor. He then took 23 other death penalty cases away from her and assigned them to prosecutors in neighboring counties. There are some who want her removed from her position as state attorney because of her refusal; however, others argue that the governor has no legal authority to interfere. Ayala has contested the action and the case is before the Florida Supreme Court (Evans, 2017; Rohrer, Stutzman, and Lotan, 2017). This case can be analyzed legally: it is unclear whether her position gives her the lawful authority to unilaterally reject the death penalty for all cases. It is also a legal question whether the governor has the legal authority to remove her from a case in her jurisdiction because she is an elected official and does not meet any legal definition of impeachment. It is also an ethical dilemma when an elected prosecutor does not believe in the death penalty. Does she have an ethical duty to reject it or an ethical duty to pursue it because it is the law of the state? Would it make a difference if her position regarding the death penalty was clear and publicized before the election and voters elected her anyway? These cases clearly show how law and ethics are intertwined, but resolving the legal questions doesn't always resolve the ethical dilemma.

In this book, ethical *issues* and ethical *dilemmas* will be analyzed. As you will see, the approach taken in both types of analysis is similar. Throughout the book, we approach decision making using the framework of applying, *law*, *policy*, and then *ethics*. In each chapter, there will be at least one ethical issue or ethical dilemma that will be presented and analyzed. You will see that tools of ethical reasoning are necessary for a good analysis. It is for this reason that we must first explore the foundations of ethics.

Why Study Ethics?

Although the decisions faced by professionals associated with the criminal justice system—ranging from legislators who write the laws to correctional professionals who supervise prisoners—may be different, they also have similarities, especially in that these professionals all experience varying degrees of **discretion**, authority, and power. If decisions were totally bounded by legal rules or policy regulations, then, perhaps, there would be less reason for ethical analysis; however, the greater role discretion plays in a profession, the more important is a strong grounding in ethics.

discretion The authority to make a decision between two or more choices.

Legislators have the power to define certain acts as illegal and, therefore, punishable. They also have the power to set the amount of punishment. Public safety is usually the reason given for criminalizing certain forms of behavior. In other cases, legislators employ moral definitions for deciding which behaviors should be illegal. "Protection of public morality" is the rationale for some laws, including those involving drugs, gambling, and prostitution. While judges invalidate laws that run afoul of state and/or federal constitutions, legislators still have a great deal of discretion in setting the laws that we must live by. There is sometimes no consensus on laws, especially those that concern private behavior. For instance, several years ago, some states had laws recognizing same-sex marriages and other states had laws that prohibited them. In *Obergefell v. Hodges*, 576 U.S. ___, 2015, the Supreme Court held that all states must license and recognize same-sex marriages, eliminating any contradiction between states. How do legislators decide what behaviors to criminalize? How do judges determine whether such laws violate fundamental rights? We explore these questions in more detail in Chapter 3, which covers the concept of justice, and in Chapter 8, which begins our discussion of the law and legal professionals.

Part of the reason that legislators are not held to very high esteem in this country is that we perceive that their discretion is unethically influenced by lobbyists and personal interests rather than the public good. The 2010 movie *Casino Jack and the U.S. of Money* is based on former lobbyist Jack Abramoff, who ended up in prison for his notorious dealings with legislators. Our current political discussions often focus on inappropriate influences on legislative decision making, and conflict-of-interest laws are designed to prevent or at least minimize the ability of special interest groups to purchase legislative favor.

Police officers, who enforce the laws created by legislators, also have a great deal of discretionary power. Most of us, in fact, have benefited from this discretion when we receive a warning instead of a traffic ticket. Police officers have the power to deprive people of their liberty (through arrest) and the power to decide which individuals to investigate and perhaps target for undercover operations. They also have the power to decide that lethal force is warranted. In the United States, we enjoy constitutional protections against untrammeled police power, and police act as the guardians of the law, not merely enforcers for those in power. In Chapters 5–7, the ethical use of police discretion is discussed in more detail.

Prosecutors probably face the least public scrutiny of all criminal justice professionals—which is ironic because they possess a great deal of discretion in deciding whom and how to prosecute. They decide which charges to pursue and which to drop, which cases to take to a grand jury, how to prosecute a case, and whether to pursue the death penalty in homicide cases. Although prosecutors have an ethical duty to pursue justice rather than conviction, some critics argue that at times their decision making seems to be influenced by politics or factors other than the goal of justice.

Defense attorneys have ethical duties similar to prosecutors in some ways; however, they also have unique duties to their client. After deciding whether to take a case or not, they decide whether to encourage a client to agree to a plea deal, what evidence to utilize and how to try the case, and whether to encourage a client to appeal.

Judges possess incredible power, typically employed through decisions to deny or accept plea bargains, decisions regarding rules of evidence, and decisions about sentencing. Chapters 8–10 explore the ethical issues of legal professionals in the criminal justice system.

Finally, correctional officials have immense powers over the lives of some citizens. Probation officers make recommendations in presentence reports and violation reports that affect whether an individual goes to prison. Prison officials decide to award or take away "good time," and they may punish an inmate with segregation; both types of decisions affect the individual's liberty. Correctional officers make daily decisions that affect the life and health of the prisoners they supervise. Parole officials decide when to file a violation report and make other decisions that affect a parolee as well as his or her family members. In short, all correctional professionals have a great deal of discretion over the lives of those they control. The ethical issues and dilemmas of correctional professionals are discussed in Chapters 11–13.

Although the professionals discussed face different dilemmas, they also share the following common elements:

- *They each have discretion—that is, the power to make a decision.* Although the specific decisions are different, they all involve power over others and the potential deprivation of life, liberty, or property.

- *They each have the duty of enforcing the law.* Although this concept is obvious with police, it is also clear that each of the professionals mentioned has a basic duty to uphold and enforce all laws; they serve the law in their professional lives. You may have heard the phrase "we are a nation of laws, not men." What this means is that no one is supposed to be above the law, no matter how powerful, and no one is supposed to take the law into their own hands, no matter how clear the guilt.

- *They must accept that their duty is to protect the constitutional safeguards that are the cornerstone of our legal system—specifically, due process and equal protection.* Due process protects each of us from error in any governmental deprivation of life, liberty, or property. We recognize the right of government to control and even to punish, but we have certain protections against arbitrary or unlawful use of that power. Due process protects us against such abuses. We also expect that the power of our government will be used fairly and in an unbiased manner. Equal protection should ensure that what happens to us is not determined by the color of our skin, our gender, our nationality, or the religion we practice. Laws are for everyone, and the protection of the law extends to all of us. Although a fair amount of evidence indicates that different treatment does exist, the ideal of equal protection is an essential element of our legal system and should be an operating principle for everyone working in this system.

- *They are public servants.* Their salaries come from the public purse. Public servants possess more than a job; they have taken on special duties involving the public trust. Individuals such as legislators, public officials, police officers, judges, and prosecutors are either elected or appointed guardians of the public's interests. Arguably, they must be held to *higher standards* than those they guard or govern. Temptations are many, and, unfortunately, we find examples of *double standards*, in which public servants take advantage of their positions for special favors, rather than higher standards of exemplary behavior.

The Josephson Institute (2005), which is heavily involved in ethics training for corporations and public agencies, identifies the ethical principles that should govern public servants: public service (treating the office as a public trust), objective judgment (striving to be free from conflicts of interest), accountability (upholding

🗨 IN THE NEWS | *Public Corruption*

Transparency International compiles a list of countries ranked by the perception of corruption by public officials. For years, the countries perceived as least corrupt have usually been Scandinavian. In 2016, Denmark was ranked as the least corrupt with a score of 90, followed by New Zealand, Finland, Sweden, Switzerland, and Norway.

Canada was ranked in the ninth place with a score of 82, and the United Kingdom came in twelfth with a score of 81. The United States appears as the eighteenth least corrupt country with a score of only 74. Not surprisingly, the most corrupt countries, according to this perception index, include Somalia, South Sudan, and North Korea.

Source: Transparency International, 2017.

open decision making), democratic leadership (observing the letter and spirit of the law), and respectability (avoiding the appearance of impropriety). Unfortunately, as the In the News box indicates, we are not so sure our public servants represent these qualities.

Currently, there is a raging controversy over President Trump's business interests, as well as those of his advisors and family members, because of the possibility that personal business interests will be promoted over the public interest. This is new territory for public concern because there hasn't been a president in recent memory whose business interests have been so potentially subject to such conflict. The Emoluments Clause refers to a paragraph in Article I of the Constitution, which reads in part, ". . . no Person holding any Office of Profit or Trust under them, shall, without the Consent of the Congress, accept of any present, Emolument, Office, or Title, of any kind whatever, from any King, Prince, or foreign State." The definition of emolument includes a salary, fee, or any type of profit from employment or office. Some have argued that this clause prohibits the president from profiting in any way from foreign investors or customers, which means the prohibition of any business deal with foreign investors, or any profit from foreign states who pay Trump enterprises such as golf courses or hotels. For example, potentially problematic business would be foreign governments that rent office space in Trump buildings or foreign representatives who rent rooms at Trump hotels. A small government watchdog agency, Citizens for Responsibility and Ethics in Washington, has filed a lawsuit, arguing that the Emolument Clause is being violated. Critics argue that it was designed to prohibit gifts, not business dealings, and, furthermore, the watchdog agency has no "standing," meaning they are not the appropriate party to file the lawsuit because they cannot show injury (Fahrenthold and O'Connell, 2017). It is unclear how this issue will be resolved at this point; however, it represents what has always been a concern with local, state, and national politicians. Public servants at any level may serve their personal self-interest through their public office rather than promote the public good. There are continuing efforts taken to guard against self-dealing by public officials.

QUOTE & **QUERY**

Part of what is needed [for public servants] is a public sense of what Madison meant by wisdom and good character: balanced perception and integrity. Integrity means wholeness in public and private life consisting of habits of justice, temperance, courage, compassion, honesty, fortitude, and disdain for self-pity.

Source: Delattre, 1989b: 79.

? Do you believe that this is asking too much of our public servants?

BOX 1.1 \ Areas of Ethical Concern for Criminal Justice Professionals

Relationships with	Ethical concerns
Public/Clients	Sexual exploitation/coercion, bribery, rudeness, racial discrimination, and negligence
Agency/Organization	Overtime fraud, theft, rule-breaking, and low work ethic
Peers/Coworkers	Sexual or racial harassment, cover-ups, retaliation, gossip, and taking undue credit

Ethical issues for professionals in the justice system include relationships with citizens, with their agency, and with each other. Box 1.1 illustrates the different areas of ethical concern.

Felkenes (1987: 26) explained why the study of ethics is important for criminal justice professionals:

1. Professionals are recognized as such in part because [a] "profession" normally includes a set of ethical requirements as part of its meaning . . . . Professionalism among all actors at all levels of the criminal justice system depends upon their ability to administer policy effectively in a morally and ethically responsible manner.

2. Training in ethics helps develop critical thinking and analytical skills and reasoning abilities needed to understand the pragmatic and theoretical aspects of the criminal justice system.

3. Criminal justice professionals should be able to recognize quickly the ethical consequences of various actions and the moral principles involved.

4. Ethical considerations are central to decisions involving discretion, force, and due process that require people to make enlightened moral judgments.

5. Ethics is germane to most management and policy decisions concerning such penal issues as rehabilitation, deterrence, and just deserts.

6. Ethical considerations are essential aspects of criminal justice research.

We also could note that individuals who ignore ethics do so at their peril. They may find themselves sliding down a slippery slope of behaviors that threaten their career and personal well-being. Even if their actions are not discovered, many people suffer from a moral crisis when they realize how far their actions have strayed from their moral ideals. We can summarize this discussion with these three basic points:

1. We study ethics because criminal justice is uniquely involved in coercion, which means there are many and varied opportunities to abuse such power.

2. Almost all criminal justice professionals are public servants and, thus, owe special duties to the public they serve.

3. We study ethics to sensitize students to ethical issues and provide tools to help identify and resolve the ethical dilemmas they may face in their professional lives.

Defining Terms

morals Principles of right and wrong.

ethics The discipline of determining good and evil and defining moral duties.

The words **morals** and **ethics** are often used in daily conversation. For example, when public officials use their offices for personal profit or when politicians accept bribes from special interest groups, they are described as unethical. When an individual does a good deed, engages in charitable activities or personal sacrifice, or takes a stand against wrongdoing, we might describe that individual as a moral person. Often, the terms *morals* and *ethics* are used interchangeably. This makes sense because both come from similar root meanings. The Greek word *ethos* pertains to custom (behavioral practices) or character, and the term *morals* is a Latin-based word with a similar meaning. As Box 1.2 shows, the inquiry into how to determine right and wrong behavior has perplexed humans for thousands of years. Philosophers through the ages owe much to the great Greek philosophers who discussed what the "good life" meant.

Morals and Ethics

Morals and morality refer to what is judged as good conduct. Immorality refers to bad conduct. We would judge someone who intentionally harms a child for his own enjoyment or someone who steals from the church collection plate as immoral. Some of us disagree on whether other behaviors, such as abortion, capital punishment, or euthanasia, are immoral. How to resolve such questions will be the subject of the next chapter.

The term *ethics* refers to the study and analysis of what constitutes good or bad conduct (Barry, 1985: 5; Sherman, 1981: 8). There are several branches, or schools, of ethics:

- *Meta-ethics* is the discipline that investigates the meaning of ethical systems and whether they are relative or are universal and are self-constructed or are independent of human creation.
- *Normative ethics* determines what people ought to do and defines moral duties based on ethical systems or other means of analysis.
- *Applied ethics* is the application of ethical principles to specific issues.
- *Professional ethics* is an even more specific type of applied ethics relating to the behavior of certain professions or groups.

While these definitions of ethics refer to the *study* of right and wrong behavior, more often, in common usage, *ethics* is used as an adjective (ethical or unethical) to refer to behaviors relating to a profession, while *moral* is used as an adjective to describe a person's actions in other spheres of life. Most professions have codes of conduct that describe what is ethical behavior in that profession. For instance, the medical profession follows the Hippocratic Oath, a declaration of rules and principles of conduct for doctors to follow in their daily practices; it dictates appropriate behavior and goals.

Even though professional ethics restricts attention to areas of behavior relevant to the profession, these can be fairly inclusive and enter into what we might consider the private life of the individual. For instance, psychiatrists are judged harshly if they engage in romantic relationships with their patients. These rules usually are included

BOX 1.2 \ Socrates, Plato, Aristotle, and the Stoics

Socrates (469–399 BCE)

Socrates associated knowledge with virtue. He believed that bad acts are performed through ignorance. The wisest man was also the most virtuous. He believed that all people acted in a way to serve their own interests, but some people, because they were ignorant, pursued short-term happiness that would, in the long run, not make them happy. True happiness could come only from being virtuous, and virtue comes from knowledge. Thus, Socrates believed his role was to strip away self-deception and incorrect assumptions; hence, the so-called Socratic method of questioning a person's beliefs. The concept of *eudaimonia* is translated as happiness, but it is much more than that and is sometimes translated as flourishing. Self-actualization, to borrow Abraham Maslow's term, might be similar to the Greek concept of *eudaimonia*, the idea that one's happiness involved the pursuit of excellence and virtue.

Plato (423–347 BCE)

Plato was a student of Socrates. In fact, it is his writings that are the source for what we know about Socrates's ideas. Because his writings were largely in the form of dialogues, with Socrates as the main character in many of them, it is hard to distinguish Socrates's ideas from Plato's. Another difficulty in summarizing Plato's ideas about ethics is that he undertook a wide-ranging exploration of many topics. His writings included discussions of ethical and political concepts as well as metaphysical and epistemological questions. In *The Republic*, he, like Socrates, associates virtues with wisdom. The four virtues he specifically mentions are wisdom, courage, moderation, and justice. Three of the virtues are associated with the three classes of people he describes as making up society: the rulers (wisdom), the soldiers (courage), and the merchants (moderation since they pursue lowly pleasures). Justice is the idea that each person is in the place they should be and performs to their best ability. Plato also discussed the concept of *eudaimonia*, mentioned above, which can be considered self-completion or self-actualization. A good life would be one that fit the nature of the person—that is, moderation for the merchant class, courage for the *soldier*, and wisdom for leaders. There is, of course, the need for all virtues in every life to some degree.

Aristotle (384–322 BCE)

Aristotle was a student of Plato. Aristotle did not believe, as did Socrates, that bad behavior came from ignorance. He believed some people had weak wills and did bad things knowing they were bad. The idea of *eudaimonia* is part of Aristotle's discussions of what it means to live a good life. Again, this concept, although translated as happiness, has more to do with flourishing or self-actualization. The good life is one devoted to virtue and moderation. The so-called Golden Mean was choosing actions that were moderate and between two extremes. For instance, courage was the virtue, whereas the deficiency of courage was cowardice and the excess of courage was foolhardiness. Generosity is the mean between stinginess and wastefulness, and so on. Aristotle's virtue theory is discussed more fully in the next chapter.

Stoics (Third Century BCE, Includes Zeno, Seneca, and Epictetus)

The Stoic philosophical school is associated with the idea that man is a part of nature and the essential characteristic of man is reason. Reason leads to virtue. Virtue and morality are simply rational action. While Plato divided people into the three classes of leaders, soldiers, and everyone else, the Stoics simply saw two groups: those who were rational/virtuous and those who were irrational/evil. They perceived life as a battle against the passions. They argued that people should not seek pleasure but should seek virtue, because that is the only true happiness. Moreover, they should seek virtue out of duty, not because it will give them pleasure.

For further information, go to:

Stanford Encyclopedia of Philosophy: http://plato.stanford.edu; and the Internet Encyclopedia of Philosophy: www.iep.utm.edu

in codes of ethics for these professions. When private behavior affects professional decision making, it becomes an ethical issue, such as when school bus drivers abuse drugs or alcohol, or when scientists are paid to do studies by groups who have a vested interest in a particular outcome.

The private life of public servants is especially scrutinized. President Clinton's affair with intern Monica Lewinsky almost ended his presidency, and not just because he lied about it in the congressional investigation. Anthony Weiner's political career as a U.S. congressman was over after it was revealed he "sexted" (sent a sexually suggestive picture) to a woman, who reported it to the press. When he attempted a political comeback in a run for mayor of New York City in 2013, more sexting by Weiner was revealed under the pseudonym of "Carlos Danger." Such behavior, while a gift to late-night comics, is tragically inexplicable behavior for a serious public servant. Most recently, the video that exposed President Trump's comments regarding how he could sexually accost women embarrassed his supporters and solidified opposition among his detractors. It was relevant to his position as the leader of the country arguably because it represented his character, and character affects professional judgments.

In professions involving the public trust, such as politics, education, and the clergy, there is a thin line between one's private life and public life. Citizens assume that if one is a liar and cheat in one's private life, then that also says something about how they would make decisions as a public servant. If one displays extremely poor judgment and disrespect for one's family in private life, arguably he or she is not a good fit for public office. There is the other argument, however, that while President Clinton was an adulterer, he accomplished great things as president. The same argument might be applied to President Trump—specifically, that his private behavior is no barometer of how successful he might be as president.

What about police officers, prosecutors, and judges? They are also public servants. Should their private behavior, such as extramarital affairs, accumulating debt, or using illegal substances after work concern us? We will explore these issues in the chapters to come.

For our purposes, it does not make a great deal of difference whether we use the formal or colloquial definitions of *morals* and *ethics*. This text is an applied ethics text, in that we will be concerned with defining behaviors as right and wrong (specifically, those of criminal justice professionals). It also is a professional ethics text, because we are concerned primarily with professional ethics in criminal justice.

Duties

duties Required behaviors or actions, that is, the responsibilities that are attached to a specific role.

The term **duties** refers to those actions that an individual must perform to be considered moral. For instance, everyone might agree that one has a duty to support one's parents if able to do so, one has a duty to obey the law (unless it is an immoral law), and a police officer has a moral and ethical duty to tell the truth on a police report. Duties are what you must do to meet the responsibilities of your role.

supererogatories Actions that are commendable but not required in order for a person to be considered moral.

Other actions, considered **supererogatories**, are commendable but not required. A good Samaritan who jumps into a river to save a drowning person, risking his or her own life to do so, has performed a supererogatory action. Those who stood on the bank receive no moral condemnation, because risking one's life is above and beyond anyone's moral duty. Of course, if one can help save a life with no great risk to oneself, a moral duty does exist in that situation.

Police officers have an ethical duty to get involved when others do not. Consider the 2001 attack on the World Trade Center. One of the most moving images of that tragedy was of police officers and firefighters running toward danger while others ran away. Indeed, this professional duty to put oneself in harm's way is why we revere and pay homage to these public servants. Many civilians also put themselves in harm's way in this and other disasters, and because they have no professional duty to do so, they can be said to be performing supererogatory actions.

There are also **imperfect duties**, general duties that one should uphold but do not have a specific application as to when or how. For instance, most ethical systems support a general duty of generosity but have no specific duty demanding a certain type or manner of generosity. Another imperfect duty might be to be honest. Generally, one should be honest, but, as we will see in Chapter 2, some ethical systems allow for exceptions to the general rule.

imperfect duties
Moral duties that are not fully explicated or detailed.

Values

Values are defined as elements of desirability, worth, or importance. You may say that you value honesty; another way of saying it is that one of your values is honesty. Others may value physical health, friendships, material success, or family. Individual values form value systems. All people prioritize certain things that they consider important in life. Values only become clear when there is a choice to be made—for instance, when you must choose between friendship and honesty or material success and family. Behavior is generally consistent with values. For instance, an individual who is a workaholic, choosing to spend more time at work than with family and endangering their health with long hours, stress, and lack of exercise, may believe that they value family, but their actions indicate that they value financial or career success more. Others place a higher priority on religious faith, wisdom, honesty, and/or independence than financial success or status. Of course, our values are constantly being balanced. If one chooses to get an advanced degree, some family time is sacrificed for the benefit of future opportunities. The point is that we don't really know what our values are until we must choose between them. Consider the values in Box 1.3. Which, if any, do you believe are more important than others? Do you ever think about the values by which you live your life? Do you think that those professionals who are caught violating laws and/or ethical codes of conduct have a clear sense of their value system?

values   Judgments of desirability, worth, or importance.

BOX 1.3 \ Values Exercise

Achievement	Altruism	Autonomy	Creativity
Emotional well-being	Family	Health	Honesty
Knowledge	Justice	Love	Loyalty
Physical appearance	Pleasure	Power	Recognition
Religious faith	Skill	Wealth	Wisdom

Arrange these values in order of priority in your life. What life decisions have you made that have been affected by the ordering of these values? Did you think of them directly when making your decision?

Values as judgments of worth are often equated with moral judgments of goodness. We see that both can be distinguished from factual judgments, which can be empirically verified. Note the difference between these factual judgments:

"He is lying."
"It is raining."

and these value judgments:

"She is a good woman."
"That was a wonderful day."

The last two judgments are more like moral judgments, such as "Lying is wrong" or "Giving to charities is good." Facts are capable of scientific proof, but values and moral judgments are not.

Some writers think that value judgments and moral judgments are indistinguishable because neither can be verified. Some also think that values and morals are relativistic and individual. In this view, there are no universal values; values are all subjective and merely opinions. Because they are only opinions, no value is more important than any other value (Mackie, 1977).

In contrast, others believe that not all values are equal and that some values, such as honesty, are always more important than other values, such as pleasure. In this view, values such as charity, altruism, integrity, knowledge, and responsibility are more important or better than the values of pleasure or wealth. You may value personal pleasure over charity or honesty, but to someone who believes in universal values, you would be wrong in this view. This question is related to a later discussion in Chapter 2 concerning whether ethics are relative or absolute.

As stated earlier, values imply a choice or a judgment. If, for instance, you were confronted with an opportunity to cheat on an exam, your values of success and honesty would be directly at odds. Values and morals are similar, although values indicate the *relative* importance of these constructs, whereas morals prescribe or proscribe behavior. The value of honesty is conceptually distinct from the moral rule against lying.

In the United States, success is defined almost exclusively by the accumulation of material goods, not by doing good deeds. Ours is a capitalist country and so it is not surprising that the value system that seems to be pervasive in our culture places money over charity, service, or family. There are those who oppose this cultural message—the tiny house movement, the living simply subculture, and others who actively resist the "more is better" mantra are examples.

An explicit value system is part of every ethical system, as we will see in Chapter 2. The values of life, respect for the person, and survival can be found in all ethical systems. Certain values hold special relevance to the criminal justice system and those professionals who work within it. These include privacy, freedom, public order, justice, duty, and loyalty.

Making Moral Judgments

We make moral or ethical judgments all the time: "Abortion is wrong." "Capital punishment is just." "It's good to give to charity." "It's wrong to hit your spouse." "You should put in a day's work for a day's pay." "You shouldn't take credit for someone else's work."

These are all judgments of good and bad behavior. We also make choices, knowing that they can be judged as right or wrong. This chapter began with the question of whether you should call in sick to enjoy a beautiful day. You may have done so even while agreeing it is wrong. Other behavioral choices come up frequently that can be judged as moral or immoral, unethical or ethical. Should you give back extra change that a clerk gave you by mistake? Should you tell a friend that her husband is having an affair even though he asked you not to tell? Should you cut and paste sections of Wikipedia into your term paper? Should you fudge the facts on your resume to bolster your chance of getting a job? Should you take longer on a project than necessary to not get more work assigned? These are all ethical decisions in that they can be judged as right or wrong.

Not all behaviors involve questions of ethics. Acts that can be judged as ethical or unethical, moral or immoral, involve four elements: (1) acts (rather than beliefs) that are (2) human and (3) of free will (4) that affect others.

1. *Act*. First, some act must have been performed. For instance, we are concerned with the *act* of stealing or the *act* of contributing to charity, rather than an idle thought that stealing a lot of money would enable us to buy a sailboat or a vague intention to be more generous. We are not necessarily concerned with how people feel or what they think about an action unless it has some bearing on what they do. The intention or motive behind a behavior is an important component of that behavior in some ethical systems; for instance, in ethical formalism (which we will discuss in Chapter 2), one must know the intent of an action to be able to judge it as moral or immoral. However, one also must have some action (not merely a thought) to examine before making a moral judgment.

2. *Only human acts*. Second, judgments of moral or ethical behavior are directed specifically to human behavior. A dog that bites is not considered immoral or evil, although we may criticize pet owners who allow their dogs the opportunity to bite. Nor do we consider drought, famine, floods, or other natural disasters immoral even though they result in death, destruction, and misery. The devastating earthquakes that hit Haiti in 2010, Nepal in 2015, and Ecuador in 2016 are not considered immoral, although individuals who could have helped victims and did not might be. Philosophers widely believe that only humans can be moral (or immoral) because of our capacity to reason. Because only humans have the capacity to be good—which involves a voluntary, rational decision and subsequent action—only humans, of all members of the animal kingdom, have the capacity to be bad.

    What about actions taken by animals? There are those who argue that some mammals show moral traits, if not moral sensibilities. Shermer (2004: 27–28), for instance, recognizes a premoral sense in animals, including shame or guilt in dogs, food sharing in bats, comforting and cooperative behaviors in chimpanzees, life-saving behaviors in dolphins and elephants, and defending behaviors in whales. He argues that mammals, especially apes, monkeys, dolphins, and whales, exhibit attachment and bonding; cooperation and mutual aid; sympathy and empathy; direct and indirect reciprocity; altruism and reciprocal altruism; conflict resolution and peacemaking; deception and deception detection; community concern and caring about what others think; and awareness of and response to the social rules of the group.

    Does this mean, then, that these mammals can be considered moral or immoral? Although perhaps they may be placed on the continuum of moral awareness closer to humans than other species, one could also argue that they do not possess the rationality of humans. They do not, as far as we know, freely choose to be good or bad (another necessary element for moral judgments).

3. *Free will.* In addition to limiting discussions of morality to human behavior, we usually further restrict our discussion to behavior that stems from free will and free action. Moral culpability is not assigned to persons who are not sufficiently aware of the world around them to be able to decide rationally what is good or bad. The two groups traditionally exempt from responsibility in this sense are the young and the insane, similarly to what occurs when ascribing legal culpability.

   Arguably, we do not judge the morality of their behavior because we do not believe that they have the capacity to reason and, therefore, have not freely chosen to be moral or immoral. Although we may chastise a two-year-old for hitting a baby, we do so to educate or to socialize, not to punish, as we would an older child or adult. We incapacitate the violent mentally ill to protect ourselves, but we consider them sick, not evil. This is true even if their actual behavior is indistinguishable from that of other individuals we do punish. For example, a murder may result in a death sentence or a hospital commitment, depending on whether the person is judged to be sane or insane, responsible or not responsible.

4. *Affects others.* Finally, we usually discuss moral or immoral behavior only in cases in which the behavior significantly affects others. For instance, throwing a rock off a bridge would be neither good nor bad unless you could possibly hit or were aiming at a person below. If no one is there, your behavior is neutral. If someone is below, however, you might endanger that person's life, so your behavior is judged as bad.

All the ethical issues and dilemmas we will discuss in this book involve at least two parties, and the decision to be made affects at least one other individual in every case. It is difficult to think of an action that does not affect others, however indirectly. Even self-destructive behavior is said to harm the people who love us and who would be hurt by such actions.

Indeed, even a hermit living alone on a desert island may engage in immoral or unethical actions. Whether he wants to be or not, the hermit is part of human society; therefore, some people would say that even he might engage in actions that could be judged immoral if they degrade or threaten the future of humankind, such as committing suicide or polluting the ocean. We sense that these elements are important in judging morality when we hear the common rationale of those who, when judged as doing something wrong, protest, "But nobody was hurt!" or "I didn't mean to."

One's actions toward nature also might be defined as immoral, so relevant actions include not only actions done to people but also those done to animals and to the environment. To abuse or exploit animals is defined by some people as immoral. Judgments are made against cockfighting, dog racing, laboratory experimentation on animals, and hunting. The growing area of environmental ethics reflects increasing concern for the future of the planet. The rationale for environmental ethics may be that any actions that harm the environment affect all humans. It also might be justified by the belief that humankind is a part of nature—not superior to it—and part of natural law should be to protect, not exploit, our world.

Thus far, we know that morality and ethics concern the judgment of behavior as right or wrong. Furthermore, such judgments are directed only at voluntary human behavior that affects other people, the earth, and living things. We can further restrict our inquiries regarding ethics to those behavioral decisions that are relevant to one's profession in the criminal justice system. Discussions regarding the ethics of police officers, for instance, would concern issues such as the following:

- Whether to take gratuities
- Whether to cover up the wrongdoing of a fellow officer
- Whether to sleep on duty

Discussions regarding the ethics of defense attorneys might include the following:

- Whether to devote more effort to private cases than appointed cases
- Whether to allow perjury
- Whether to attack the character of a victim to defend a client

Of course, these actions affect other people, as do most actions taken as a professional. In this text, we will present some of the unique issues and dilemmas related to each area of the criminal justice system. It is important, first, however, to explore the means available for analyzing and evaluating the "right" course of action.

Analyzing Ethical Issues and Policies

"Critical thinking skills" has become an overused and abused term in education, but the core idea of critical thinking is to be more cognizant of facts as opposed to concepts, assumptions, or biases and the use of objective reasoning to most effectively reach a decision or understand a problem. Paul and Elder (2003) explain that all reasoning is based on assumptions, points of view, and data or evidence, but reasoning is shaped by concepts and ideas that affect our interpretations of the data, which then lead us to conclusions that give meaning to the data. To be a critical thinker, one must ask these types of questions:

- What information am I using?
- What information do I need to settle the question?
- Is there another way to interpret the information?
- What assumption has led me to my conclusion?
- Is there another point of view I should consider?
- What implication or consequence might be the result of this conclusion?

In each of the discussions throughout the book that subject issues or policies to an ethical analysis, critical thinking will be required. One of the most important elements of critical thinking is to separate facts from concepts and identify underlying assumptions. In the issue we will analyze below, we will use only general concepts concerning right and wrong because ethical systems will not be covered until Chapter 2. In all analyses, we will begin by determining if there is any relevant law, then if there are relevant policies, and, finally, ethical principles will be applied.

ETHICAL ISSUE

Should Attorney General Jeff Sessions "pull back" on federal investigations of police departments?

During his confirmation hearings, Attorney General Sessions indicated his lack of enthusiasm for the Department of Justice's (DOJ) numerous "pattern and practice" investigations of police departments across the country. At the end of the Obama administration, there were 14 jurisdictions that had monitored consent decrees or settlements in place. The latest reports were of Baltimore and Chicago. Both of these reports detailed a troubling pattern of use of force, discriminatory use of discretion, lack of clear directives over body cameras and tasers, and/or other problematic elements of police departments. The DOJ's report has typically resulted in a legal settlement detailing what steps were needed with a monitor put in place to see that changes were made. The Attorney General made comments on March 1, 2017 reported by various news outlets that indicated he would not be seeking consent decrees or settlements: "We need to help police departments get better, not diminish their effectiveness, and I'm afraid we have done some of that . . . . So we're going to pull back on this" (referring to the consent decrees) (Byrne, Wilber, and Hinkel, 2017). While some police unions have applauded the stand, advocates strongly oppose any pullback. They argue that consent decrees have led to better policing, lasting change, and best practices for all police departments. Objective research on their effectiveness is mixed (Arthur, 2017; Walker, 2017).

Law

The 1994 Violent Crime Control and Law Enforcement Act allowed the Department of Justice to investigate "patterns and practices" of local and state law enforcement agencies to determine whether there was a pattern of civil rights violations. If the investigation proved abuse, there could be a settlement or consent decree that would be agreed upon by all parties and approved by a federal judge. If the agency refused, DOJ could sue. This law remains in place so the DOJ has the legal authority to institute investigations and obtain settlement agreements. The attorney general has the discretion to order such investigations—or not.

Policy

The choice to utilize the DOJ's power to force change in police departments is a policy decision. Under President Bush, the attorney general performed on average less than one per year, with none begun between 2005 and 2008. Attorneys General Holder and Lynch, under President Obama, performed about three per year.

Ethics

Attorney General Sessions is utilizing a cost-benefit rationale when he points to the risk that these investigations and settlement orders result in decreased morale among police officers with an increased unwillingness to conduct proactive policing. He associated the spike in violent crime in Chicago and other cities to this negative outcome. We need facts to determine if these DOJ interventions result in overall good outcomes or negative outcomes. We also need to know if there are other alternatives that could improve police departments without the attendant costs of the consent decrees. It is also important to note where these facts come from because advocacy groups on both sides have strong opinions and their presentation may not be purely unbiased. An ethical analysis would look at "stakeholders" who are affected (police officers, administrators, citizens, members of minority groups, taxpayers, arrestees, and so on). Would "pulling back" result in worse outcomes for these groups? Would it result in better outcomes for some and worse outcomes for others? Is there any evidence that such settlements resulted in decreased (or increased) crime?

In order to more fully analyze the ethics of this policy choice, we need to know more about consent decrees (which will be discussed more fully in Chapter 7) and more information about ethical systems (which will be discussed in Chapter 2).

█ Analyzing Ethical Dilemmas

Recall that an ethical dilemma is when an individual is faced with at least two courses of action and the decision is difficult. In applied ethics texts, various authors set out the steps to take when facing ethical dilemmas. For instance, Ruggiero (2001) advises us to (1) study the details of the case, (2) identify the relevant criteria (obligations, ideals, and consequences), (3) determine possible courses of action, and (4) decide which action is the most ethical. This approach is very like the one we will use throughout the book when analyzing ethical dilemmas, detailed in the steps below:

1. *Identify the facts.* Make sure that one has all the facts that are known—not future predictions, not suppositions, not probabilities.

2. *Identify relevant values and concepts.* Concepts are things that cannot be proven empirically but are relevant to the issue at hand. Understand that your concepts and values may affect the way you interpret the facts. For instance, the issue of abortion not only revolves around the value of life, but it is also a concept in that there is no agreement of when life begins or ends (although there are provable facts regarding the existence of respiration, brain activity, and other body functions). Many arguments surrounding ethical issues are really arguments about concepts that cannot be proven (e.g., "life").

3. *Identify all possible dilemmas and then decide what is the most immediate dilemma.* Identifying all dilemmas can help us see that sometimes one's own moral or ethical dilemma is caused by others' actions. For instance, a police officer's ethical dilemma when faced with the wrongdoing of a fellow officer is a direct result of that other officer making a bad choice.

4. *Decide what is the most immediate moral or ethical issue facing the individual.* This is always a behavior choice, not an opinion. For example, the moral issue of whether abortion should be legalized is quite different from the moral dilemma of whether I should have an abortion if I find myself pregnant. Obviously, one affects the other, but they are conceptually distinct.

5. *Resolve the ethical or moral dilemma by using an ethical system or some other means of decision making.* (Ethical systems will be discussed in Chapter 2.)

ETHICAL DILEMMA

You are a correctional officer working the late-night shift. Your sergeant and another officer from the day shift come onto the tier where you are working and ask you to open an inmate's cell. After you do so, they enter the cell. Then you hear a series of grunts, cries, and moans. They leave, muttering about how the inmate has been taught a lesson. You believe that you have been a party to an assault, but you say nothing. The next night you find out that the inmate did not report the incident, nor did any other inmate. You believe that if you come forward and report what you saw, you will be severely ostracized. You may not be believed (especially if the inmate doesn't back you up). You might even lose your job. What would you do?

Law

Correctional officers, like police officers, have the legal authority to use physical force to defend themselves or others, or to subdue an inmate. Legally, they can only use the reasonable force necessary to accomplish their goal (which is usually stopping a fight, removing an inmate from a cell, or moving an inmate to segregation). Obviously, if this was a case of going into a cell for the express purpose of a retaliatory beating, then it would constitute either simple or aggravated assault and the officers involved could be prosecuted. The correctional officer has a legal duty to protect inmates and might be an accessory after the fact if he lies about the incident, or be subject to some charge of obstruction if

(*continued*)

there is an investigation, or malfeasance of office for not coming forward.

Policy

Every correctional facility has express policies regarding the use of force. Usually a sergeant or lieutenant must give approval of the use of force, usually a use-of-force report must be written, and, usually, there are procedures in place for a medical professional to check the inmate after the use of force to make sure there are no serious injuries. Obviously, there is no policy that would allow retaliatory uses of force. Thus, what happened was a clear violation of policy.

Ethics

Understanding the law and policies related to the event does not necessarily resolve the ethical dilemma. Thus, we move to an ethical analysis as detailed above:

1. This officer must make sure that he has all the facts. Was the inmate hurt? Did his injuries occur during the time the two other officers were in his cell? Is the officer sure that no one reported it? Would the inmate come forward if he believed that someone would testify against the other two officers, or would he deny the assault (if there was one)? What other facts are important to know? Remember that facts are those things that can be proven; however, this does not necessarily mean that the individual facing the dilemma knows what the facts are.

2. The officer might examine the relevant values. In this situation, one can identify duty, legality, honesty, integrity, safety, protection, loyalty, self-preservation, and trust. Are any other values important to resolve the dilemma? Concepts that may affect this dilemma include things like just punishment—if one feels that prison as punishment is not enough, then that concept will affect the way this dilemma is perceived.

3. Several ethical dilemmas come into play here. The first is whether the other officers should have entered the prisoner's cell. There is probably an earlier issue involving whatever the prisoner did to warrant the visit. There is obviously the dilemma of whether the officer should have let off-duty officers into the cell in the first place. Finally, there is the dilemma of what the officer should do now that he believes an injustice may have taken place.

4. The most immediate dilemma for the officer is whether to come forward with the information.

5. To resolve the dilemma, it is helpful to work through Chapter 2 first because one way to resolve ethical dilemmas is to decide on an ethical system. If the officer was a utilitarian, he would weigh the costs and benefits for all concerned in coming forward and in staying quiet. If he followed duty-based ethics (ethical formalism), he would find the answer once he determined his duty.

It is important to note that very often the ethical thing to do is clear once you identify the relevant law and/or policy. Although there are instances where the law or policy itself is unethical, in most situations, if something is illegal, it is also unethical. Most individuals who engage in public corruption know that they are violating the law, but they do it anyway. There is no ethical dilemma involved when a police officer decides whether to steal from a burglary site or a prosecutor decides to hide exculpatory evidence; these acts are illegal and wrong and the individual knows they are wrong. We use ethical analysis when the right thing to do is not clear. Why someone chooses to behave in an illegal or unethical way is the subject of Chapter 4.

Another type of dilemma is when you know what is the right thing to do, but doing it comes at great cost. The clearest example of this situation is the so-called blue curtain of secrecy that refers to police officers covering up the wrongdoing of peers. Those who do not and, instead, come forward and testify against a fellow officer typically face social ostracism and, sometimes, worse retaliation. It should also be noted that the same phenomenon exists in other professions to some degree. Whistleblowers may lose their job or be blacklisted from their profession. Thus, sometimes it is fairly easy to apply ethical analysis to determine the right thing to do but extremely difficult to do it when there are great costs.

WALKING THE WALK

Scott Waddle was the captain of the USS *Greenville* in 2001, a former Eagle Scout whose career in the navy saw a steady progression of successes resulting in his command of the *Greenville*. A tireless promoter of the navy and the giant submarine he captained, Waddle sent autographed pictures of the sub to schoolchildren, and he enthusiastically participated in the "distinguished visitor" program, which allowed civilians to accompany the submarine crew on cruises.

During one of these public relations cruises, on February 9, 2001, the submarine captain gave the order for an "emergency blow," a maneuver in which the submarine comes up out of the depths at great speed, breaking the surface of the water like a breaching whale before settling back onto the surface. In a tragic accident, the probabilities of which boggle the mind, the submarine came up under a Japanese trawler carrying students and their teachers as well as a crew. The submarine smashed it to bits and sent the crew and passengers who survived the initial impact into the ocean. The accident killed nine people and cost more than $100 million in damages and compensation costs.

The ensuing investigation and testimony determined that the person in charge of the radar deferred to Waddle's visual inspection of the surface and didn't tell him of a sonar contact that was within 4,000 yards. Waddle and other officers who manned the periscope had scanned the surface too quickly and missed the small ship in the turbulent swells. Testimony indicated that after the crash Waddle grimly kept the crew focused and instructed them over the intercom, "Remember what you saw, remember what happened, do not embellish. Tell the truth and maintain your dignity."

Against his lawyer's advice, Waddle gave up his right to silence in the military tribunal that was held to assess whether to court-martial him. He was reported to have said, "This court needs to hear from me—it's the right thing to do." In his testimony, he refused to shift responsibility to others and accepted all blame for the accident. He said, "I'm solely responsible for this truly tragic accident, and for the rest of my life I will have to live with the horrible consequences."

A father of one of the victims was sitting in the room when Waddle testified, and his anger was overcome by Waddle's tearful apology. Waddle ultimately accepted a letter of reprimand that ended his career with the navy. Then he went to Japan to apologize to the victims' families personally.

In the aftermath of his decision to testify and not fight to keep his career, Waddle reported that he considered suicide, but he moved past his shame and guilt. Today he gives speeches on the experience and advises others of the importance of dealing with failure honestly, one of which was to a Boy Scout awards ceremony in Chattanooga, Tennessee. Speaking to the 500 attendees, he said that the values of honesty and responsibility he learned in Scouting helped him make the decisions he did during the aftermath of the accident.

Sources: Hight, 2005; Putman, 2008; Thomas, 2001.

Conclusion

In this chapter, we distinguished ethical issues or policies and ethical dilemmas. We explained why a study of ethics is especially important to criminal justice professionals. It also was noted that not all behaviors would be subject to ethical judgments—only those that are performed by humans who are acting with free will and that affect others. We also defined the terms *morals* and *ethics* as both relate to standards of behavior. Professional ethics deals with only those behaviors relevant to one's profession. We make ethical judgments (what we consider right and wrong) using rationales derived from historical and traditional ethical systems. These ethical systems will be described in Chapter 2.

The most important thing to remember is that we all encounter situations where we must determine the ethical or moral course of action. In the Walking the Walk boxes, present in each chapter, we will offer real-life examples of individuals who faced ethical dilemmas. In many of these situations, the easier decision would have been to avoid responsibility, transfer blame, hide behind rationalizations, or refuse to stand up for what is right. By becoming aware of those who uphold ethics in their professional decision making, we can honor them for doing what is right.

This chapter closes with a chapter review and study questions to answer in class or in a journal. These can be helpful to check your understanding of the issues. These are followed by writing/discussion exercises, which have no right or wrong answers and can be the basis for classroom discussions or individual writing assignments. Finally, ethical dilemmas are presented to encourage the reader to practice ethical analysis.

Chapter Review

1. **Explain the difference between ethical issues and ethical dilemmas.**

    Ethical issues are broad social or policy questions, while ethical dilemmas are situations in which one person must make a decision that can be judged as right or wrong, and where what is right is difficult to decide or is hard to do for some other reason.

2. **Give examples of how discretion permeates every phase of the criminal justice system and creates ethical dilemmas for criminal justice professionals.**

    Discretion can be defined as the power and authority to choose one of two or more alternative behaviors. At each stage of the criminal justice system, professionals have such discretion: legislators make decisions regarding the creation of laws, police make decisions on the street in their enforcement of those laws, prosecutors make decisions about which arrests to formally prosecute, judges make decisions about which evidence to allow, and correctional professionals make decisions that affect the lives of offenders.

3. **Explain why the study of ethics is important for criminal justice professionals.**

    First, we study ethics because criminal justice is uniquely involved in coercion, which means there are many and varied opportunities to abuse such power. Second, almost all criminal justice professionals are public servants and, thus, owe special duties to the public they serve. Finally, we study ethics to sensitize students to ethical issues and provide tools to help identify and resolve the ethical dilemmas they may face in their professional lives.

4. **Learn the definitions of the terms *morals*, *ethics*, *duties*, *supererogatories*, and *values*.**

    The terms *morals* and *ethics* come from Greek and Latin words referring to custom or behavioral practices. Morals refer to what is judged as good conduct. Ethics refers to the study and analysis of what constitutes good or bad conduct. Duties are obligatory acts (by law, practice, or morals). Supererogatories are those acts that go above and beyond duties. Values are statements of worth or importance.

5. **Describe what behaviors might be subject to moral/ethical judgments.**

   Behaviors that can be adjudged under moral criteria are those that are acts (not thought) committed by humans (not animals) of free will (not by those judged as incompetent) and that affect others.

Study Questions

1. Define a public servant and why public servants should be especially sensitive to ethical issues.
2. Discuss Felkenes's reasons for why it is important for criminal justice professionals to study ethics.
3. Define *morals, ethics, values, duties, supererogatories, imperfect duties, meta-ethics, normative ethics,* and *applied ethics.*
4. What are the four elements that specify the types of behaviors that are judged under ethical criteria? Which groups traditionally have been exempt from legal and moral culpability? Why?
5. What are the steps in analyzing an ethical dilemma?

Writing/Discussion Exercises

1. Write an essay about (or discuss) a difficult ethical dilemma that you faced. What was it? What were the options available to you? Who was affected by your decision? Were there any laws, rules, or guidelines that affected your decision? How did you make your decision?
2. Write an essay about (or discuss) whether public servants should be held to higher standards than the rest of us. Touch on the following questions in your response: Should we be concerned about a politician who has extramarital affairs? Drinks to excess? Gambles? Uses drugs? Abuses his or her spouse? What if the person is a police officer? A judge? Should a female police officer be sanctioned for posing naked in a men's magazine, using pieces of her uniform as "props"? Should a probation officer socialize in bars that his or her probationers are likely to frequent? Should a prosecutor be extremely active in a political party and then make decisions regarding targets of "public integrity" investigations of politicians?
3. Write an essay about (or discuss) the issue of the medical use of marijuana. What do medical studies indicate regarding whether it is necessary or the best medical alternative for certain patients? What do critics argue in their opposition to the medical use laws? If you or a loved one were suffering and someone told you that marijuana could ease your pain, would you violate the law or not? Why?

Key Terms

discretion	ethical issues	morals
duties	ethics	supererogatories
ethical dilemmas	imperfect duties	values

ETHICAL DILEMMAS

Situation 1

A rich businessman's daughter, Patty, had the best of everything all her life. Her future would have included college, a good marriage to a successful young man, and a life of comparative luxury—except that she was kidnapped by a small band of radical extremists who sought to overthrow the government by terror, intimidation, and robbery. After being raped, beaten, and locked in a small, dark closet for many days, continually taunted and threatened, she was told that she must participate with the terrorist gang in a bank robbery; otherwise, she and her family would be killed. During the robbery, a bank guard was shot.

Was her action immoral? What if she had killed the guard? What if the terrorists had kidnapped her mother or father, too, and told her if she didn't cooperate, they would kill her parents immediately? What would you have done in her place? (Readers might recognize this dilemma as the Patty Hearst case. In 1974, the Symbionese Liberation Army, a terrorist group, kidnapped the daughter of Randolph Hearst, the tycoon of a large newspaper chain. Her subsequent capture, trial, conviction, and prison sentence have been portrayed in books and movies and provide ripe material for questions of free will and legal and moral culpability.)

Situation 2

You are taking an essay exam in a college classroom. The test is closed book and closed notes, yet you look up and see that the person sitting next to you has hidden under his blue book a piece of paper filled with notes, which he is using to answer some questions. What would you do? Would your answer change if the test was graded on a curve? What if the student were a friend? What would you do if the student was flunking the course and was going to lose the scholarship he needed to stay in school? What about a situation of plagiarism? Would you turn in a student if you knew he or she had turned in a plagiarized paper? Why or why not? If someone cheats in school, isn't it likely that he or she will be less honest as a criminal justice professional?

Situation 3

You are selected for a jury in a trial of a 64-year-old mother who killed her two adult sons. The two men had Huntington's disease, a degenerative brain disease, and were institutionalized. They were certain to die and would endure much pain and suffering before they expired. The defendant's husband had died from this same disease, and she had nursed him throughout his illness until his death.

The defendant took a gun into the nursing home, kissed her sons good-bye, and then shot them both through the head. She was arrested for first-degree murder. The prosecutor informs you that there is no "mercy killing" defense in the law as it is written.

If you were on the jury, how would you decide this case? What punishment does she deserve? (See "Justice Tempered with Mercy," by K. Ellington, *Houston Chronicle*, January 30, 2003, 10A. The prosecutor accepted a plea of guilty to assisting suicide.)

Situation 4

You are completing an internship with a juvenile probation agency and truly have enjoyed the experience. Although working with the kids is challenging, you see many rewards in the job, especially when you sense that you are reaching a client and making a difference. Mr. Childers, the probation officer with whom you work, is less optimistic about the kids and operates in a strictly by-the-book legalistic manner. He is burned out and basically does his job without getting too involved. Although you respect him, you know you would approach the clients differently if you were to be hired full-time.

One weekend, you are out with friends in a downtown bar frequented by college students. To your surprise, you see Sarah, a 16-year-old probationer, dancing. In watching her, you realize that she is drunk and, in fact, is holding a beer and drinking it while she is dancing with a man who is obviously much older than she is. You go over to her, and she angrily tells you to mind your own business and immediately leaves with the man. Later she comes back into the bar and pleads with you to keep quiet. She is tearfully apologetic and tells you that she already has had several violations of her probation and at the last hearing was told that if she has one more violation, she will be sent to a juvenile detention center. You know that Sarah has been doing much better in school and plans to graduate and even go to college.

On Monday morning, you sit in Mr. Childers' office. What should you tell him?

Situation 5

You are on a county commissioners' court and there has been an action committee that recommends the county adopt a "sanctuary" status that would prohibit the county sheriff from holding individuals who are the subject of detainers from ICE. Detainers are not warrants, and some jurisdictions have been sued for holding people on the document since it has no legal force. On the other hand, your sheriff advises you that there is a possibility that federal money will be withheld that has been used to hire five new deputies for an enhanced "saturation patrol" designed to address downtown burglaries and robberies that are affecting businesses. What is the ethical decision? What criteria should county commissioners use to determine the right thing to do?

Determining Moral Behavior

2

VASILIS VERVERIDIS / 123RF

Socrates was one of the earliest "ethicists," along with Plato and Aristotle.

Our principles of right and wrong form a framework for the way we live our lives. But where do these principles come from? Before you read on, answer the following question: if you believe that stealing is wrong, why do you believe this to be so? You probably said:"Because my parents taught me" or "Because my religion forbids it," or maybe "Because society cannot tolerate people harming one another." Your answer to this question is an indication of your **ethical system**. Ethical systems provide the answer to the question of why something is wrong or right.

C. E. Harris (1986: 33) used the term *moral theories or moral philosophies* instead of *ethical systems* and defined them as a systematic ordering of moral principles. To be accepted as an ethical system, the system of principles must be internally consistent, must be consistent with generally held beliefs, and must possess a type of "moral common sense." Baelz (1977: 19) further described ethical systems as having the following characteristics:

- *They are prescriptive.* Certain behavior is demanded or proscribed. They are not just abstract principles of good and bad but have substantial impact on what we do.

Learning Objectives

1. Define deontological and teleological ethical systems, and explain ethical formalism and utilitarianism.

2. Describe how other ethical systems define what is moral—specifically, ethics of virtue, natural law, religion, and ethics of care.

3. Discuss the argument as to whether egoism is an ethical system.

4. Explain the controversy between relativism and absolutism (or universalism).

5. Identify what is good according to each of the ethical systems discussed in the chapter.

- *They are authoritative.* They are not ordinarily subject to debate. Once an ethical framework has been developed, it is usually beyond question.

- *They are logically impartial or universal.* Moral considerations arising from ethical systems are not relative. The same rule applies in all cases and for everyone.

- *They are not self-serving.* They are directed toward others; what is good is good for everyone, not just for the individual.

ethical system
A structured set of principles that defines what is moral.

We don't consciously think of ethical systems, but we use them to make judgments. For instance, we might say that a woman who leaves her children alone to go out drinking has committed an immoral act. That would be a *moral judgment*. Consider that the moral judgment in any discussion is only the tip of a pyramid. If forced to defend our judgment, we would probably come up with some rules of behavior that underlie the judgment. Moral rules in this case might be as follows:

"Children should be looked after."
"One shouldn't drink to excess."
"Mothers should be good role models for their children."

But these moral rules are not the final argument; they can be considered the body of the pyramid. How would you answer if someone forced you to defend the rules by asking "why?" For instance, "Why should children be looked after?" In answering the "why" question, one eventually comes to some form of ethical system. For instance, we might answer, "Because it benefits society if all parents watched out for their children." This would be a utilitarian ethical system. We might have answered the question, "Because every parent's duty is to take care of their children." This is ethical formalism or any duty-based ethical system. Ethical systems form the base of the pyramid. They are the foundation for the moral rules that we live by.

The ethical pyramid is a visual representation of this discussion. In Figure 2.1, the moral judgment discussed above is the tip of the pyramid, supported by moral rules

---

FIGURE 2.1 The Ethical Pyramid

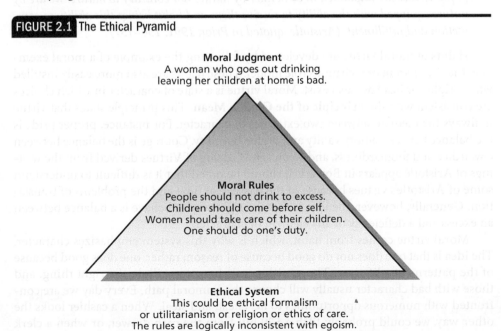

Moral Judgment
A woman who goes out drinking
leaving her children at home is bad.

Moral Rules
People should not drink to excess.
Children should come before self.
Women should take care of their children.
One should do one's duty.

Ethical System
This could be ethical formalism
or utilitarianism or religion or ethics of care.
The rules are logically inconsistent with egoism.

on which the judgment is based. The moral rules, in turn, rest upon a base, which is one's ethical system. We will discuss the ethical systems in roughly chronological order, beginning with Aristotle and the ethics of virtue.

The Ethics of Virtue

The question of what it means to be a good person is an ancient one. We will begin our discussion of ethical systems with Aristotle. As you read in Chapter 1, Socrates associated virtue with knowledge. Ignorance led to bad behavior because if one was rational and wise, he or she would know what virtue was and behave accordingly. Socrates and Plato identified four virtues: wisdom, fortitude, temperance, and justice. Recall that Plato associated these virtues with the three classes of citizens: leaders (wisdom), soldiers (fortitude or courage), and all others (temperance). Justice was the virtue associated with one doing the duties of one's role. Aristotle disagreed with the idea that bad behavior occurred only through ignorance and argued that there were people who chose to behave in ways that were not virtuous. In *Nicomachean Ethics*, he answers the **ethics of virtue** question, "What is a good person?" Aristotle believed that to be good, one must do good. Virtues that a good person possesses include thriftiness, temperance, humility, industriousness, and honesty. Aristotle believed that **eudaimonia** was the goal of life. The word can be translated as "happiness," but another translation is "flourishing." The meaning of this word does not mean simply having pleasure, but also living a good life, reaching achievements, and attaining moral excellence.

Aristotle defined virtues as "excellences." He distinguished intellectual virtues (wisdom, understanding) from moral virtues (generosity, self-control). To possess the moral virtues is not sufficient for "the good life"; one must also have the intellectual virtues, primarily "practical reason." Aristotle believed that we are, by nature, neither good nor evil, but become so through training and the acquisition of habits:

> [T]he virtues are implanted in us neither by nature nor contrary to nature: we are by nature equipped with the ability to receive them and habit brings this ability to completion and fulfillment. (Aristotle, quoted in Prior, 1991: 156–157)

Habits of moral virtue are developed by following the example of a moral exemplar, that is, a parent or a virtuous role model. These habits are also more easily instilled when "right" or just laws also exist. Moral virtue is a state of character in which choices are consistent with the **principle of the Golden Mean**. This principle states that virtue is always the median between two extremes of character. For instance, proper pride is the balance between empty vanity and undue humility. Courage is the balance between cowardice and foolhardiness, and so on. The Catalog of Virtues derived from the writings of Aristotle appears in Box 2.1. It should be noted that it is difficult to understand some of Aristotle's virtues because of the passage of time and the problems of translation. Generally, however, the idea is that the right way to behave is a balance between an excess and a deficiency of any element of character.

Moral virtue comes from habit, which is why this system emphasizes character. The idea is that one does not do good because of reason; rather, one does good because of the patterns of a lifetime. Those with good character will do the right thing, and those with bad character usually will choose the immoral path. Every day we are confronted with numerous opportunities to lie, cheat, and steal. When a cashier looks the other way, we could probably filch a $20 bill from the cash drawer, or when a clerk

ethics of virtue The ethical system that bases ethics largely upon character and possession of virtues.

eudaimonia The Greek term denoting perfect happiness or flourishing, related to the way to live a "good life."

principle of the Golden Mean Aristotle's concept of moderation, in which one should not err toward excess or deficiency; this principle is associated with the ethics of virtue.

BOX 2.1 \ Catalog of Virtues

Courage (balance between cowardice and foolhardiness)
Temperance (balance between self-indulgence and asceticism)
Liberality (balance between meanness and too generous)
Munificence (similar to liberality; balance between stinginess and being profligate)
Magnanimity (balance between being vain and being petty)
Proper ambition (balance between being without ambition and having too much)
Good temper (balance between being quick to anger and not showing anger when warranted)
Truthfulness (balance between unnecessary truths and lying)
Wittiness (balance between being a bore and being a clown)
Friendliness (balance between obsequiousness and being unfriendly)
Modesty (balance between being too humble and too boastful)
Righteous indignation (balance between being envious and being spiteful)

Source: *Nicomachean Ethics*, Aristotle. Adapted from: www.cwu.edu/~warren/Unit1/aristotles_virtues_and_vices.htm.

---

gives us a $10 bill instead of a $1 bill by mistake, we could keep it instead of handing it back. We don't because, generally, it does not even occur to us to steal. We do not have to go through any deep ethical analysis in most instances when we can do bad things, because our habits of a lifetime dictate our actions.

Somewhat related to the ethics-of-virtue ethical system are the Six Pillars of Character promulgated by the Josephson Institute of Ethics (2008). The Six Pillars of Character echo Aristotle's virtues. They include the following:

1. *Trustworthiness.* This concept encompasses honesty and meeting one's obligations. Honesty means to be truthful, forthright, and sincere, and the pillar also involves loyalty, living up to one's beliefs, and having values.

2. *Respect.* This pillar is like the second portion of the categorical imperative of Ethical Formalism, which will be discussed subsequently. The concept admonishes us to treat each person with respect and not as a means to an end. The idea is also like the Golden Rule in Christianity.

3. *Responsibility.* This means standing up for one's choices and being accountable. Everyone has a moral duty to pursue excellence, but, if one fails, the duty is to take responsibility for the failure.

4. *Fairness.* This concept involves issues of equality, impartiality, and due process. To treat everyone fairly doesn't necessarily mean to treat everyone the same, but rather, to apply fairness in one's dealings with everyone.

5. *Caring.* This pillar encompasses the ideas of altruism and benevolence. It is like the ethics of care, which will be described later in the chapter.

6. *Citizenship.* This includes the duties of every citizen, including voting, obeying the law, being a good steward of the natural resources of one's country, and doing one's fair share.

One difficulty with the ethics of virtue is in judging the primacy of moral virtues. For instance, in professional ethics, there are often conflicts that involve honesty and loyalty. If both are virtues, how does one resolve a dilemma in which one virtue must be sacrificed? Another difficulty is that it is not a system that provides an analysis of what to do in each dilemma. If one is truly perplexed as to what the right course of action should be, this system does not help much in that it basically concludes that a virtuous person will act virtuously. The ethics of virtue probably explains more individual behavior than other ethical systems because most of the time, if we have developed habits of virtue, we do not even think about the possible bad acts we might do. However, when faced with a true dilemma—that is, a choice where the "right" decision is unclear—the ethics of virtue does not provide any equation or approach to find the right answer.

Aristotelian virtue ethics certainly influenced later thinkers, but as the timeline displayed in Box 2.2 shows, other ethical systems eclipsed this older system for centuries. More recently, Alasdair MacIntyre (1991), a contemporary philosopher, has done much to resurrect virtue ethics. He defines virtues as those dispositions that will sustain us in a quest to live a good life. MacIntyre (1999) also seems to endorse an ethics-of-care approach because he discusses virtue as necessary to care for the next generation. He sees life as one of reciprocal indebtedness and emphasizes networks of relationships. This language is like the ethics of care, which will be discussed in a later section of this chapter.

Faced with the ethical dilemma presented in Situation 1 at the end of this chapter, how will the ethics of virtue help us decide what to do when our friend steals? One would look to the virtues (trustworthiness, respect, responsibility, fairness, caring, and citizenship). It seems clear that these virtues are more consistent with stopping the theft and firing the friend. One cannot be trustworthy or responsible and allow theft to occur.

Natural Law

natural law The idea that principles of morals and rights are inherent in nature and not human-made; such laws are discovered by reason but exist apart from humankind.

The **natural law** ethical system holds that there is a universal set of rights and wrongs that is like many religious beliefs, but without reference to a specific supernatural figure. Originating most clearly with the Stoics, natural law is an ethical system wherein no difference is recognized between physical laws—such as the law of gravity—and moral laws. Morality is part of the natural order of the universe. Further, this morality is the same across cultures and times. In this view, Christians simply added God as a source of law (as other religions added their own prophets and gods), but there is no intrinsic need to resort to a supernatural figure because these universal laws exist quite apart from any religion (Buckle, 1993; Maestri, 1982).

The natural law ethical system presupposes that what is good is what is natural, and what is natural is what is good. The essence of morality is what conforms to the natural world; thus, there are basic inclinations that form the core of moral principles. For instance, the preservation of one's own being is a natural inclination and thus is a basic principle of morality. Actions consistent with this natural inclination would be those that preserve one's own life, such as in self-defense, but also those that preserve or maintain the species, such as a prohibition against murder. Other inclinations are peculiar to one's species—for instance, humans are social animals; thus, sociability is a natural inclination that leads to altruism and generosity. These are natural and thus moral. The pursuit of knowledge or understanding of the universe might also be recognized as a natural inclination of humans; thus, actions that conform to this natural inclination are moral.

The Greek philosophers recognized natural law, but we also see it clearly in later writings, such as St. Augustine, who is attributed with a famous quote: "An unjust law

BOX 2.2 \ Timeline of Ethics	
Socrates (469–399 BCE)	
Plato (429–347 BCE)	
Aristotle (384–322 BCE)	Virtue theory
St. Augustine (354–430)	Natural law
	Religion
St. Thomas Aquinas (1225–1274)	Religion
John Locke (1632–1704)	Social contract
Adam Smith (1723–1790)	Egoism
Immanuel Kant (1724–1804)	Ethical formalism
Jeremy Bentham (1748–1832)	Utilitarianism
John Stuart Mill (1806–1873)	Utilitarianism
Ayn Rand (1905–1932)	Egoism
John Rawls (1921–2002)	Ethical formalism+ Utilitarianism
Alasdair MacIntyre (1929–)	Neo-virtue theory
Nel Noddings (1929–)	Ethics of care

is no law at all." This concept refers to the idea that if man's law contradicts the law of nature, then it is not only wrong, it may not even be considered law. St. Thomas Aquinas, in *Summa Theologiae*, distinguished natural law from God's law, and placed reason at the epicenter of the natural law system: "Whatever is contrary to the order of reason is contrary to the nature of human beings as such; and what is reasonable is in accordance with human nature as such" (Aquinas as cited in Buckle, 1993: 165).

Natural law theory defines good as that which is natural. The difficulty of this system is identifying what is consistent and congruent with the natural inclinations of humankind. How do we know which acts are in accordance with the natural order of things? Who determines what are the natural laws? Natural law has been employed to restrict the rights and liberties of groups of people; for instance, historically, the so-called natural superiority of whites was used to support and justify slavery, and the "natural" role of women as childbearers restricted their employment opportunities. Today, natural law is sometimes employed to oppose same-sex marriage with the argument that the only natural marriage is between heterosexuals joined together for procreation. Proponents of same-sex marriage argue that humans are naturally sociable and there is a natural human need for bonding, noting that many heterosexual marriages are for reasons other than procreation, but that does not make them unnatural. The fundamental problem with this ethical system is: how does one know whether a moral rule is based upon a true natural law or a mistaken human perception?

Applying natural law to the ethical dilemma of a friend stealing from an employer (Situation 1 at the end of this chapter), the natural need for sociability is why loyalty to friends is such a strong force, even when they do wrong. In this case, this natural law of sociability explains why we feel torn between our friend and our employer, but reason dictates that social relationships are bound by trust. Therefore, honesty and fair dealings are always prioritized over other values.

Religion

St. Augustine and St. Thomas Aquinas described natural laws, but they were also Christian theologians who placed morality and ethics into the discussion of sin. Religion provides moral guidelines and directions on how to live one's life. For instance, Christians and Jews are taught the Ten Commandments, which prohibit certain behaviors defined as wrong. The authority of **religious ethics**, in particular Judeo-Christian ethics, stems from a willful and rational God. For believers, the authority of God's will is beyond question, and there is no need for further examination because of His perfection. The only possible controversy comes from human interpretation of God's commands. Indeed, these differences in interpretation are the source of most religious strife.

> **religious ethics** The ethical system that is based on religious beliefs of good and evil; what is good is that which is God's will.

Religious ethics is, of course, much broader than simply Judeo-Christian ethics. Religions such as Buddhism, Confucianism, and Islam also provide a basis for ethics because they offer explanations of how to live a "good life" and address other philosophical issues, such as "What is reality?" Pantheistic religions—such as those of primitive hunter-gatherer societies—promote the belief that there is a living spirit in all things and tend not to be as judgmental as religions we are more familiar with, such as Christianity, Judaism, or Islam. A religion must have a willful and rational God or god figure before there can be a judgment of right and wrong, thus providing a basis for an ethical system. Those religions that do have a god figure consider that figure to be the source of principles of ethics and morality.

It is also true that of the religions we might discuss, many have similar basic moral principles. Many religions have their own version of the Ten Commandments. In this regard, Islam is not too different from Judaism, which is not too different from Christianity. What Christians recognize as the Golden Rule predates Christianity, and the principle can be found in all the major religions, as well as offered by ancient philosophers:

- Christianity: "Do unto others as you would have them do unto you."
- Hinduism: "Do naught to others which, if done to thee, would cause thee pain: this is the sum of duty."
- Buddhism: "In five ways should a clansman minister to his friends and familiars . . . by treating them as he treats himself."
- Confucianism: "What you do not want done to yourself, do not do unto others."
- Judaism: "Whatsoever thou wouldst that men should not do unto thee, do not do that to them."
- Isocrates: "Do not do to others what would anger you if done to you by others."
- Diogenes Laërtius, *Lives of the Philosophers:* "The question was once put to Aristotle how we ought to behave to our friends; and his answer was, 'As we should wish them to behave to us.'"

- The Mahabharata: "This is the sum of all true righteousness, deal with others as thou wouldst thyself be dealt by. Do nothing to thy neighbor which thou wouldst not have him do to thee hereafter." (Reiman, 1990/2004: 147; Shermer, 2004: 25)

A fundamental question discussed by philosophers and Christian religious scholars is whether God commands us not to commit an act because it is inherently wrong (e.g., "Thou shalt not kill"), or whether an act acquires its "badness" or "goodness" solely from God's definition of it. Another issue in Western religious ethics is how to determine God's will. Some believe that God is inviolable and that positions on moral questions are absolute. This is a legalist position. Others believe that God's will varies by time and place—the situationalist position. In this position, situational factors are important in determining the rightness of any action. Something may be right or wrong depending on the circumstances (Borchert and Stewart, 1986: 157). For instance, lying may be wrong unless it is to protect an innocent, or stealing may be wrong unless it is to protest injustice and to help unfortunates. Some would say that it is impossible to have an *a priori* knowledge of God's will because that would put us above God's law: we ourselves cannot be "all-knowing." Thus, for any situation, if we are prepared to receive God's divine commands, we can know them through faith and conscience. This discussion has focused on Christianity; therefore, Box 2.3 briefly describes some of the other major world religions.

Barry (1985: 51–54) wrote that human beings can "know" God's will in three ways:

1. *Individual conscience.* An individual's conscience is the best source for discovering what God wants one to do. If one feels uncomfortable about a certain action, it is probably wrong.
2. *Religious authorities.* These authorities can interpret right and wrong for us and are our best source if we are confused about certain actions.
3. *Holy scriptures.* The third way is to go directly to the Bible, Quran, or Torah as the source of God's law. Some believe that the written word of God holds the answers to all moral dilemmas.

Strong doubts exist as to whether any of these methods are true indicators of divine command. Our consciences may be no more than the products of our psychological development, influenced by our environment. Religious authorities are, after all, only human, with human failings. Even the Bible seems to support contradictory principles. For instance, advocates of capital punishment can find passages in the Bible that support it (such as Genesis 9:6: "Whoever sheds the blood of man, by man shall his blood be shed"), but opponents to capital punishment argue that the New Testament offers little direct support for execution and has many more passages that direct one to forgive, such as Matthew 5:38–40: "Offer no resistance to injury. When a person strikes you on the right cheek, turn and offer him the other."

The question of whether people can ever know God's will has been explored through the ages. St. Thomas Aquinas (1225–1274) believed that human reason was sufficient not only to prove the existence of God but also to discover God's divine commands. Others believe that reason is not sufficient to know God and that it comes down to unquestioning belief, so reason and knowledge must always be separate from faith. These people believe that one can know whether an action is consistent with God's will only if it contributes to general happiness, because God intends for us to be happy, or when the action is done through the *Holy Spirit*—that is, when someone performs the action under the influence of true faith (Borchert and Stewart, 1986: 159–171).

BOX 2.3 \ Overview of Major World Religions

Judaism

Judaism is older than Christianity or Islam, with the Torah, rather than the Bible, as its foundational text. As with Christianity and Islam, there are various movements or divisions under Judaism, but, generally, Judaism incorporates a monotheistic belief in God with recognized prophets, including Abraham and Moses. Judaism teaches that Jesus was not the Messiah or son of God (like Islam) and not a prophet (unlike Islam) because of disagreements with Jewish teachings. The definition of what is good in Judaism comes from the Torah, the Talmud, and religious authorities. Judaism's definitions of goodness lie in virtues and religious faith. Believers are exhorted to lead a righteous life that includes helping the needy. Virtues include benevolence, faith, and compassion. The Jewish version of the Golden Rule is: "What is hateful to you, do not do unto others." Falsehoods, unkind actions, stealing, and revenge are wrong. Shalom (peace) is the path one should live one's life by which could equate to pleasantness and kindness in dealings with others.

Islam

One of the newest, yet largest, religions is Islam. Like Christianity, this religion recognizes one god, Allah. Jesus and other religious figures are recognized as prophets, as is Muhammad, who is the last and greatest prophet. Islam is based on the Quran, which is taken much more literally as the word of Allah than the Bible is taken by most Christians. There is a great deal of fatalism in Islam: *Inshallah*, meaning, "If God wills it," is a prevalent theme in Muslim societies, but there is recognition that if people choose evil, they do so freely. The five pillars of Islam are (1) repetition of the creed (*Shahada*), (2) daily prayer (*Salah*), (3) almsgiving (*Zakat*), (4) fasting (*Sawm*), and (5) pilgrimage (*Hajj*).

Another feature of Islam is the idea of the holy war. In this concept, the faithful who die defending Islam against infidels will be rewarded in the afterlife (Hopfe, 1983). This is not to say that Islam provides a legitimate justification for terroristic acts. Devout Muslims protest that terrorists have subverted the teachings of Islam and do not follow its precepts, one of which is never to harm innocents.

Buddhism

Siddhartha Gautama (Buddha) attained enlightenment and preached to others how to do the same and achieve release from suffering. He taught that good behavior is that which follows the "middle path" between asceticism and hedonistic pursuit of sensual pleasure. Essentials of Buddhist teachings are ethical conduct, mental discipline, and wisdom. Ethical conduct is based on universal love and compassion for all living beings. Compassion and wisdom are needed in equal measures. Ethical conduct can be broken into right speech (refraining from lies, slander, enmity, and rude speech), right action (abstaining from destroying life, stealing, and dishonest dealings, and helping others lead peaceful and honorable lives), and right livelihood (abstaining from occupations that bring harm to others, such as arms dealing and killing animals). To follow the "middle path," one must abide by these guidelines (Kessler, 1992).

Confucianism

Confucius taught a humanistic social philosophy that included central concepts such as *Ren*, which is human virtue and humanity at its best, as well as the source of moral principles; *Li*, which is traditional order, ritual, or custom; *Xiao*, which is familial love; and *Yi*, which is rightness, both a virtue and a principle of behavior—that is, one should do what is right because it is right. The *doctrine of the mean* exemplifies one aspect of Confucianism that emphasizes a cosmic or natural

(continued)

order. Humans are a part of nature and are included in the scheme of life. Practicing moderation in one's life is part of this natural order and reflects a "way to Heaven" (Kessler, 1992).

Hinduism

In Hinduism, the central concept of *karma* can be understood as consequence. Specifically, what one does in one's present life will determine what happens in a future life. The goal is to escape the eternal birth/rebirth cycle by living one's life in a moral manner so that no bad karma will occur (Kessler, 1992). People start out life in the lowest caste, but if they live a good life, they will be reborn as members of a higher caste, until they reach the highest Brahman caste, and at that point, the cycle can end. An early source for Hinduism was the Code of Manu. In this code are found the ethical ideals of Hinduism, which include pleasantness, patience, control of mind, refraining from stealing, purity, control of the senses, intelligence, knowledge, truthfulness, and non-irritability (Hopfe, 1983).

To summarize, the religious ethics system is widely used and accepted. The authority of the god figure is the root of all morality; basic conceptions of good and evil or right and wrong come from interpretations of the god figure's will.

Going back to the dilemma of whether to go along with a friend who steals, using Christianity as an ethical system, one need look no further than the Ten Commandments to see clear direction that stealing is wrong. Letting someone do it under your supervision would make you complicit.

Ethical Formalism

Ethical formalism is a deontological system. A **deontological ethical system** is one that is concerned solely with the inherent nature of the act being judged. If an act or intent is inherently good (coming from a good will), it is still considered a good act even if it results in adverse consequences. The philosopher Immanuel Kant (1724–1804) wrote that the only thing that is intrinsically good is a *good will*. On the one hand, if someone does an action from a good will, it can be considered a moral action even if it results in adverse consequences. On the other hand, if someone performs some activity that looks on the surface to be altruistic but does it with an ulterior motive—for instance, to curry favor or gain benefit—that act is not judged as "good" just because it results in good consequences. Only if an act springs from a good will can we say that it is truly good.

Kant believed that moral worth comes from doing one's duty. Just as there is the law of the family (father's rule), the law of the state and country, and the law of international relations, there is also a universal law of right and wrong. Morality arises from the fact that humans, as rational beings, impose these laws and strictures of behavior upon themselves (Kant, trans. Beck, 1949: 76). Kant was a Christian, but he also believed that what is good could be discovered through pure reason.

Kant distinguished hypothetical from categorical imperatives. **Hypothetical imperatives** are commands that designate certain actions to attain certain ends. An example is, "*If* I want to be a success, *then* I must do well in college," or "*If* I want people to like me, *then* I must be friendly." By contrast, a **categorical imperative** commands action that is necessary without any reference to intended purposes or consequences. The "imperative of morality" needs no further justification

ethical formalism The ethical system espoused by Kant that focuses on duty; holds that the only thing truly good is a good will, and that what is good is that which conforms to the categorical imperative.

deontological ethical system The study of duty or moral obligation emphasizing the intent of the actor as the element of morality, without regard to the consequences of acts.

hypothetical imperatives Statements of contingent demand known as if-then statements (if I want something, then I must work for it); usually contrasted with categorical imperatives (statements of "must" with no "ifs").

categorical imperative The concept that some things just must be, with no need for further justification, explanation, or rationalization for why they exist (Kant's categorical imperative refers to the imperative that you should do your duty, act in a way you want everyone else to act, and don't use people).

(Kant, trans. Beck, 1949: 76).The following constitute the principles of Kant's categorical imperative of morality (Bowie, 1985: 157):

- *Act only on that maxim through which you can at the same time will that it should become a universal law.* In other words, for any decision of behavior to be made, examine whether that behavior would be acceptable if it were a universal law to be followed by everyone. For instance, a student might decide to cheat on a test, but for this action to be moral, the student would have to agree that everyone should be able to cheat on tests.

- *Act in such a way that you always treat humanity, whether in your own person or that of any other, never simply as a means but always at the same time as an end.* In other words, one should not use people for one's own purposes. For instance, being friendly to someone so that you can use her car is using her as a means to one's own ends. Even otherwise moral actions, such as giving to charity or doing charitable acts for others, would be considered immoral if done for ulterior motives such as self-aggrandizement.

- *Act as if you were, through your maxims, a lawmaking member of a kingdom of ends.* This principle directs that the individual's actions should contribute to and be consistent with universal law. However, the good act must be done freely. If one is compelled to do a good act, the compulsion removes the moral nature of the act. Only when we freely choose to abide by moral law and these laws are self-imposed rather than imposed from the outside are they a reflection of the higher nature of humans.

A system such as ethical formalism is an *absolutist system*—if something is wrong, it is wrong all the time, such as murder or lying. To assassinate evil tyrants such as Adolf Hitler, Saddam Hussein, or Osama Bin Laden might be considered moral under a teleological system, more fully discussed below as concerned with consequences, because ridding the world of dangerous, evil people is a good end. However, in the deontological view, if the act and intent of killing are wrong, then killing is always wrong; thus, assassination must be considered immoral in all cases, regardless of the good consequences that might result. This absolute judgment is criticized by those who argue that there are sometimes exceptions to any moral rule such as "one should not lie." In a well-known hypothetical, Kant argued that if someone asked to be hidden from an attacker in close pursuit and then the attacker asked where the potential victim was hiding, it would be immoral to lie about the victim's location. This seems wrong to many of us. However, Kant argued that an individual cannot control consequences, only actions; therefore, one must act in a moral fashion without regard to potential consequences. In the example, the attacker may not kill the potential victim, the victim may still be able to get away, or the attacker may be justified. The victim may have even left the place you saw them hide and move to the very place you offer to the attacker as a lie. Also, to not say anything is an option to lying. The point is that no one person can control anything in life, so the only thing that makes sense is to live by the categorical imperative, which does not justify lying.

Kant also defended his position with semantics—distinguishing untruths from lies with the explanation that a lie is a lie only when the recipient is led to believe or has a right to believe that he or she is being told the truth. The attacker in the previous scenario or an attacker who has one "by the throat" demanding one's money has no right to expect the truth; thus, it would not be immoral not to tell this person the truth. Only if one led the attacker to believe that one was going to tell the truth and then did not would one violate the categorical imperative. To not tell the truth when the attacker doesn't deserve the truth is not a lie, but if one intentionally and deliberately sets out to deceive, then that is a lie—even if it is being told to a person who doesn't deserve the truth (Kant, ed. Infield, 1981).

This ethical framework follows simply from the beliefs that an individual must follow a self-imposed moral law and that one can use reason to determine right actions because any action can be evaluated by using the principles just listed. Criticisms of ethical formalism include the following (Maestri, 1982: 910):

- *Ethical formalism seems to be unresponsive to extreme circumstances.* If something is wrong in every circumstance regardless of the good that results or good reasons for the action, good people might be judged immoral or unethical.

- *Morality is limited to duty.* One might argue that duty is the baseline of morality, not the highest aspiration of it. Further, it is not always clear where one's duty lies. At times one might face a dilemma where two duties conflict with each other.

- *The priority of motive and intent over result is problematic in some instances.* It may be seriously questioned whether the intention to do good, regardless of result or perhaps with negative result, is always moral. Many would argue that the consequences of an action and the actual result must be evaluated to determine morality.

Other writers present variations of deontological ethics that do not depend so heavily on Kant (Braswell, McCarthy, and McCarthy, 2002/2007). The core elements of any deontological or duty-based ethical system are the importance placed on intention, and the use of a predetermined set of principles to judge morality rather than an evaluation of the consequences of an act.

We can apply ethical formalism to our dilemma of the friend who steals by, first, looking at duty. One's duty as a manager certainly would include stopping your friend from stealing and firing her because of her dishonesty. Applying the categorical imperative, the first premise states that your desired action should be acceptable as a universal law. Allowing employees to steal cannot be a universal law, but stopping stealing from happening should be universal. The second is to not use people. In this case, it seems as if she is using you much more than you would be using her by stopping her from stealing. The third premise of the categorical imperative states that your action must be done only because of the inherent morality of it to be moral, not some ulterior purpose. You would have to stop her because it was the right thing to do, not because you were afraid of being caught in order for your action to be moral.

WALKING THE WALK

Ana Mari Cauce is the president of the University of Washington (UW). In February 2017, a firestorm occurred when she would not step in to stop Milo Yiannopoulos from speaking on the university campus. Yiannopoulos is a controversial writer and speaker. Formerly an editor at Breitbart News (an "alt-right" news website), he speaks against feminism, Islam, LBGT rights, and political correctness. He has been variously associated with neo-Nazi and far-right conservative groups even though he is gay. Invited to campus by a conservative student group, a strong opposition emerged to try and prevent him from speaking. President Cauce was asked to cancel the event. She had the power to do so; however, she refused. Her position was that the First Amendment was more important than the hateful

(continued)

speech that Yiannopoulos was sure to deliver. Opponents called her "collaborator" and "appeaser," and said she was complicit in any violence that might occur. Her position was that "hateful" speech was not "hate" speech. Hate speech may be criminalized, but it must include a threat; hateful speech may be offensive, it may disgust, it may lead to anger, but it is not illegal, and it doesn't justify censorship. The jurisprudence on the First Amendment is very clear that only if there is a clear and imminent danger can offensive speech be stopped, and there wasn't clear and imminent danger, so her decision was not to cancel the speech.

Unfortunately, there was violence at the UW speech, and a shooting left one man injured. A speech scheduled for University of California (UC) at Berkeley a few weeks later was canceled after altercations between protestors and others outside the event. Thus, Cauce was criticized for letting him speak, and the authorities of UC Berkeley were criticized for stopping him from speaking. Reasonable people can see both sides.

President Cauce, however, probably has no regrets for her decision to stand up for the First Amendment.

Once offensiveness becomes the barometer of what speech to censor, where does that stop and who gets to decide what is offensive? She holds more right, perhaps, than many of the rest of us to object to hateful speech—her brother was killed by Ku Klux Klan (KKK) members in a protest in 1979.

The ethical dilemma of whether to support the right of hateful speakers is an echo of the infamous Skokie, Illinois, march in 1978. The KKK planned to march in an area of town filled with Holocaust survivors and the town attempted to prevent it. The KKK was defended, surprisingly, by the American Civil Liberties Union (ACLU), and the Supreme Court upheld the right of the KKK to march in *National Socialist Party v. Skokie*, 432 U.S. 43, 1977. Why would the ACLU defend the KKK? Because civil liberties belong to all of us, and First Amendment rights do too, regardless of how offensive the message is. In that march, there were hundreds more who came to demonstrate against the KKK than the marchers themselves. Not censoring offensive speech does not mean one should not object to it.

Source: Westneat, 2017a.

Utilitarianism

utilitarianism The ethical system that claims that the greatest good is that which results in the greatest happiness for the greatest number; major proponents are Bentham and Mill.

teleological ethical system An ethical system that is concerned with the consequences or ends of an action to determine goodness.

Utilitarianism is a teleological ethical system. A **teleological ethical system** judges the consequences of an act. Even a bad act, if it results in good consequences, can be defined as good under a teleological system. The saying "the end justifies the means" is a teleological statement. Jeremy Bentham (1748–1832), a major proponent of utilitarianism, believed that the morality of an action should be determined by how much it contributes to the good of the majority. Bentham argued that human nature seeks to maximize pleasure and avoid pain, and a moral system must be consistent with this natural fact.

The "utilitarian doctrine asserts that we should always act to produce the greatest possible ratio of good to evil for everyone concerned" (Barry, 1985: 65). That is, if one can show that an action significantly contributes to the general good, then it is good. In situations where one must decide between a good for an individual and a good for society, then society should prevail, despite the wrong being done to an individual. This is because the utility or good derived from that action generally outweighs the small amount of harm done to the individual (because the harm is done only to one, whereas the good is multiplied by the many). For instance, if it could be shown that punishing an innocent person would be an effective deterrent to crime, the wrong done to that person by this unjust punishment would be outweighed by the good resulting for society. This example shows how the individual sometimes is sacrificed for the good of the many. However, if citizens found out about the injustice and lost respect for the authority of the legal system, that would be a negative effect for all concerned, illustrating the problem of trying to predict outcomes in utilitarianism.

Although utilitarianism is quite prevalent in ethical reasoning, there are some serious criticisms of it:

- *All "pleasures" or benefits are not equal.* Bentham did not judge the relative weight of utility. He considered pleasure to be a good whether it derived from vice, such as avarice or greed, or from virtue, such as charity and kindness. Later utilitarians, primarily John Stuart Mill (1806–1873), believed that utilities (benefits) had different weights or values. In other words, some were better than others. For instance, art offers more utility for society than alcohol even though both may bring utility/benefit to individuals, altruism carries more benefit than pleasure, and so on. But who is to determine which is better? Determining what is good by weighing utilities makes sense, but the actual exercise is sometimes very difficult.

- *The system presumes that one can predict the consequences of one's actions.* In the well-known "lifeboat" dilemma, five people are in a lifeboat with enough food and water only for four. It is certain that they will survive if there are only four; it is also certain that they will all perish if one does not go overboard. What should be done? Under ethical formalism, it would be unthinkable to sacrifice an innocent, even if it means that all will die. Under utilitarian ethics, it is conceivable that the murder of one might be justified to save the others. But this hypothetical situation points out the fallacy of the utilitarian argument. In real life, it would not be known whether any would survive regardless of the decision. The fifth might be murdered and five minutes later a rescue ship appears on the horizon. The fifth might be murdered, but then the remaining four be eaten by sharks. Only in unrealistic hypothetical situations does one absolutely know the consequences of one's action. In real life, one never knows if an action will result in a greater good or ultimate harm.

- *There is little concern for individual rights in utilitarianism.* Ethical formalism demands that everyone must be treated with respect and not be used as a means to an end. However, under utilitarianism, the rights of one individual may be sacrificed for the good of many.

Utilitarianism has two forms: act utilitarianism and rule utilitarianism. The basic difference between the two can be summarized as follows: in **act utilitarianism**, only the basic utility derived from one action is examined. We look at the consequences of any action for all involved and weigh the units of utility accordingly. In **rule utilitarianism**, one judges that action by the precedent it sets and the long-term utility of the rule set by that action.

On the one hand, act utilitarianism might support stealing food when one is hungry and has no other way to eat because the utility of survival would outweigh the loss to the victim of the theft. On the other hand, rule utilitarianism would be concerned with the effect that the action would have if made into a rule for behavior: "Any time an individual cannot afford food, he or she can steal it" would contribute to a state of lawlessness and a general disrespect for the law. Such a rule would probably not result in the greatest utility for the greatest number. With rule utilitarianism, then, we are concerned not only with the immediate utility of the action but also with the long-term utility or harm if the action were to be a rule for all similar circumstances. Note the similarity between rule utilitarianism and the first principle of the categorical imperative. In both approaches, one must judge as good only those actions that can be universalized.

act utilitarianism
The type of utilitarianism that determines the goodness of a particular act by measuring the utility (good) for all, but only for that specific act and without regard for future actions.

rule utilitarianism
The type of utilitarianism that determines the goodness of an action by measuring the utility of that action when it is made into a rule for behavior.

In summary, utilitarianism holds that morality must be determined by the consequences of an action. Society and the survival and benefit of all are more important than any individual. Something is right when it benefits the continuance and good health of society. Rule utilitarianism may be closer to the principles of ethical formalism because it weighs the utility of such actions after they have been made into general laws of behavior, and this premise is very similar to "act in such a way as to will it to become a universal law," the first part of Kant's categorical imperative. The difference between ethical formalism and rule utilitarianism is that the actions themselves are judged right or wrong depending on the motives behind them under ethical formalism, whereas utilitarianism looks to the long-term consequences of the prescribed rules to determine their morality.

Returning to the dilemma of the friend who steals, weighing the benefit of stopping her or not from stealing, you must consider every potential consequence, including your own feelings of guilt. The benefit to her would be counterweighed by the loss to your employer, and, therefore, act (and rule) utilitarianism would not support letting her take the items. Weighing the benefit of firing her or not is a bit more equivocal. Firing her would be a disutility (negative) to her, a benefit to your employer, and probably to you as well in that you wouldn't have to worry about her stealing again, but there is also the negative consequence to you in that you'll probably lose a friend. Applying rule utilitarianism would result in firing her (because the long-term rule of firing thieves is more palatable made into a rule for all future incidents), but act utilitarianism might support warning her and letting her continue in the job if the loss of her friendship was more negative than the positive of not having to worry about her stealing again. Act utilitarianism can sometimes justify things for this one person, this one time, that we couldn't justify if made into a rule for the future. Note that such concepts as duty don't play into this ethical reasoning—only the positive and negative consequences of each behavior choice.

The Ethics of Care

ethics of care The ethical system that defines good as meeting the needs of others and preserving and enriching relationships.

The **ethics of care** is based on human relationships and needs. The ethics of care has been described as a feminine morality because women in all societies are the childbearers and consequently seem to have a greater sensitivity to issues of care. Noddings (1986: 1) points out that the "mother's voice" has been silent in Western, masculine analysis: "One is tempted to say that ethics has so far been guided by Logos, the masculine spirit, whereas the more natural and perhaps stronger approach would be through Eros, the feminine spirit."

The ethics of care is founded in the natural human response to care for a newborn child, the ill, and the hurt. There are similarities in the ethics of care's idea that morals derive from natural human impulses of compassion and Jean-Jacques Rousseau's (1712–1778) argument that it is humans' natural compassion that is the basis of human action and the idea that morality is based in emotion rather than rationality, that is, "What I feel is right is right, what I feel is wrong is wrong" (Rousseau, as cited by Ruggiero, 2001: 28).

Carol Gilligan's work on moral development in psychology identified a feminine approach to ethical decision making that focused on relationships and needs instead of rights and universal laws. The most interesting feature of this approach is that while a relatively small number of women emphasized needs over rights, no men did. She attributed this to Western society, in which men and women are both socialized to Western ethics, which are primarily concerned with issues of rights, laws, and universalism (Gilligan, 1982).

Applying the ethics of care does not necessarily lead to different solutions, but perhaps to different questions. In an ethical system based on care, we would be concerned with issues of needs rather than rights. Other writers point to some Eastern religions, such as Taoism, as illustrations of the ethics of care (Gold, Braswell, and McCarthy, 1991; Larrabee, 1993). In these religions, a rigid, formal, rule-based ethics is rejected in favor of gently leading the individual to follow a path of caring for others. In criminal justice, the ethics of care is represented to some extent by the rehabilitative ethic rather than the just-deserts model. Certainly the "restorative justice" movement is consistent with the ethics of care because of its emphasis on the motives and needs of all concerned, rather than simply retribution. In personal relationships, the ethics of care would promote empathy and treating others in a way that does not hurt them. In this view, meeting needs is more important than securing rights.

In their text, Braswell and Gold (2002) discuss a concept called **peacemaking justice**. They show that the concept is derived from ancient principles, and it concerns care as well as other concepts: "Peacemaking, as evolved from ancient spiritual and wisdom traditions, has included the possibility of mercy and compassion within the framework of justice" (2002: 25). They propose that the peacemaking process is composed of three parts: connectedness, caring, and mindfulness:

> **peacemaking justice**   An ancient approach to justice that includes the concepts of compassion and care, connectedness, and mindfulness.

- *Connectedness* refers to the interrelationships we all have with one another and all of us have with the earth.
- *Caring* refers to Noddings' concept that the "natural" inclination of humans is to care for one another.
- *Mindfulness* involves being aware of others and the world in all personal decision making (Braswell and Gold, 2002: 25–37).

To summarize, the ethics-of-care approach identifies the needs of all individuals in any ethical situation and attempts to maximize them. It is different from utilitarianism, however, in that one person cannot be sacrificed for others. Also, there is an attempt to resolve situations through human relationships and a sense that decisions should come from compassion rather than attention to rights or duties.

The ethics of care would support not seeing the dilemma of the thieving friend as a binary choice of stopping her or not, and/or firing her or not. Caring for one's friend would certainly involve not allowing her to make such a bad choice; but the ethical thing to do might involve doing more, for example, showing her why what she wanted to do is harmful and helping her learn from the experience. There would also be attention to need: does she need the clothes because of poverty? If so, the resolution would be different than if the theft was just due to greed. You still wouldn't let her steal, but you would try and help her meet her needs in some other way.

▌ Egoism: Ethical System or Not?

Egoism postulates that what is good for one's survival and personal happiness is moral. The extreme of this position is that all people should operate on the assumption that they can do whatever benefits themselves. Others become solely the means

> **egoism**   The ethical system that defines the pursuit of self-interest as a moral good.

to ensure happiness; there is no recognition of the rights of others under this system. For this reason, some have rejected egoism as an ethical system entirely, arguing that it is fundamentally inconsistent with one of the elements ("they are not self-serving") (Baelz, 1977).

psychological egoism The concept that humans naturally and inherently seek self-interest, and that we can do nothing else because it is our nature.

Psychological egoism refers to the belief that humans are naturally egoists and that it would be unnatural for them to be any other way. All species have instincts for survival, and self-preservation and self-interest are merely part of that instinct. Therefore, it is not only moral to be egoistic, but it is the only way we can be, and any other explanations of behavior are mere rationalizations. In behaviors that appear to be altruistic, such as giving to charity or volunteering, the argument goes that these acts provide psychic and emotional pleasure to the individual and that is why they do them, not for some other selfless reason. Even though acts such as running into a burning building or jumping into a river to save victims seem altruistic, psychological egoists believe that these acts occur because of the personality makeup of individuals who derive greater pleasure from being considered heroes, or enjoy the adrenalin rush of the dangerous act, more than the feeling of security derived from staying on the sidelines.

enlightened egoism The concept that egoism may appear to be altruistic because it is in one's long-term best interest to help others in order to receive help in return.

Enlightened egoism is a slight revision of this basic principle, adding that each person's objective is long-term welfare. This may mean that we should treat others as we would want them to treat us to ensure cooperative relations. Even seemingly selfless and altruistic acts are consistent with egoism because these acts benefit the individual by ensuring reciprocal assistance. For instance, if you help your friend move when he asks you to, it is only because you expect that he will help you when you need some future favor. Under egoism, it would be not only impossible but also immoral for someone to perform a completely selfless act. Even those who give their lives to save others do so perhaps with the expectation of rewards in the afterlife. Egoism completely turns around the priorities of utilitarianism to put the individual first, before anyone else and before society as a whole; however, because long-term interests often dictate meeting obligations and helping others, enlightened egoists might look like altruists.

Adam Smith (1723–1790), the "father" of free enterprise, promoted a type of practical egoism, arguing that individuals pursuing their own personal good would lead to nations prospering as well. Capitalism is based on the premise that everyone pursuing self-interest will create a healthy economy: workers will work harder to get more pay; owners will not exploit workers too badly because they might quit; merchants will try to get the highest price for items, whereas consumers will shop for the lowest price; and so on. Only when government or liberal do-gooders manipulate the market, some argue, does capitalism not work optimally. Nietzsche is associated with egoism, as is Ayn Rand (1905–1982), who is perhaps the best-known modern writer/philosopher associated with egoism. She promoted both psychological egoism (that humans *are* naturally selfish) and ethical egoism (that humans *should be* self-interested). Libertarians utilize Rand's writings to support their view of limited government and fierce individualism.

Most philosophers reject egoism because it violates the basic tenets of an ethical system. Universalism is inconsistent with egoism, because to approve of all people acting in their own self-interest is not a logical or feasible position. It cannot be right for both you and me to maximize our own self-interests because it would inevitably lead to conflict. Egoism would support exploitative actions by the strong against the weak, which seems wrong under all other ethical systems. However, psychological egoism is a relevant concept in natural law (self-preservation is natural) and utilitarianism (hedonism is a natural inclination). But if it is true that humans are *naturally* selfish and self-serving, one can also point to examples that indicate that humans are also altruistic and self-sacrificing. One thing seems clear: when individuals are caught doing illegal acts, or acts that violate their professional codes of ethics, or acts that harm others, such as those described in the In the News box, it is usually only egoism that can justify their behavior.

Other Methods of Ethical Decision Making

Some modern writers present approaches to applied ethics that do not directly include the ethical systems discussed thus far. For instance, Krogstand and Robertson (1979) described three principles of ethical decision making:

- The **imperative principle** directs a decision maker to act according to a specific, unbending rule.
- The **utilitarian principle** determines the ethics of conduct by the good or bad consequences of the action.
- The **generalization principle** is based on this question: "What would happen if all similar persons acted this way under similar circumstances?"

> **imperative principle** The concept that all decisions should be made according to absolute rules.

> **utilitarian principle** The principle that all decisions should be made according to what is best for the greatest number.

> **generalization principle** The principle that all decisions should be made assuming that the decision would be applied to everyone else in similar circumstances.

IN THE NEWS | Ethics Committees

Ethics committees/commissions that monitor the behavior of politicians seems like a good idea, but not everyone appreciates their value. Two news stories in the last several years illustrate the issue:

Governor Andrew M. Cuomo of New York set up a commission in July 2013 to investigate corruption, but reports indicated that commission members almost immediately began receiving pressure from the Governor's Office to divert their attention away from some people. In response to criticism, the governor explained that he had the right to monitor and direct the work of a commission he had created. Then, he abruptly disbanded the commission halfway through its proposed 18-month life. An investigation by the U.S. Attorney's Office concluded that no laws had been broken by the governor in doing so.

One of the first acts of the U.S. House of Representatives in 2017 was to vote on a bill (119–74) during a closed-door meeting that gutted an ethics watchdog agency by placing the independent Office of Congressional Ethics (OCE) under the control of the very lawmakers who might be investigated. The argument was that the OCE took anonymous complaints and some lawmakers had been wrongly accused. Critics argued that the independent, bipartisan agency was put in place after widespread corruption was exposed in 2008. Once the vote was made public, the strong criticism that resulted, including a tweet from President Trump scolding them for bad optics, forced the House to rescind the vote, at least temporarily.

Source: Rashbaum and Kaplan, 2015; Walsh, Raju, and Collinson, 2017; Weiser, 2016a.

These should sound familiar because they are, respectively, religious or absolutist ethics, utilitarianism, and ethical formalism. Ruggiero (2001) proposes that ethical dilemmas be evaluated using three basic criteria. The first principle is to examine one's obligations and duties and what one has promised to do by contract or by taking on a role (this is like ethical formalism's focus on duty). The second principle is to examine moral ideals such as how one's decision squares with prudence, temperance, justice, honesty, compassion, and other ideals (this is like Aristotle's ethics of virtue). The third principle is to evaluate the act to determine if it would result in good consequences (this is utilitarianism).

Close and Meier (1995: 130) provide a set of questions more specific to criminal justice professionals and sensitive to the due process protections that are often discarded in a decision to commit an unethical act. They propose that the individual decision maker should ask the following questions:

1. Does the action violate another person's constitutional rights, including the right of due process?

2. Does the action involve treating another person only as a means to an end?

3. Is the action illegal?

4. Do you predict that your action will produce more bad than good for all persons affected?

5. Does the action violate department procedure or professional duty?

The simplest test is the so-called front page test. This ethical check asks us to evaluate our decision by whether we would be comfortable if it was on the front page of the newspaper. Public disclosure is often a good litmus test for whether something is ethical or not.

Using Ethical Systems to Resolve Dilemmas

As discussed in Chapter 1, if confronted with an ethical dilemma, one can follow a series of steps to come to an ethical resolution:

1. *Identify the facts.* Identifying all relevant facts is essential as a first step. Sometimes individuals facing a dilemma do not know all the facts, and sometimes the decision to find the facts is an ethical dilemma unto itself.

2. *Identify relevant values and concepts.* One's values of duty, friendship, loyalty, honesty, and self-preservation are usually at the heart of professional ethical dilemmas.

3. *Identify all possible moral dilemmas for each party involved.* Recall that this was to help us see that sometimes one's own moral or ethical dilemma is caused by others' actions. Usually one's ethical dilemma is prefaced upon others' ethical (or unethical) decisions.

4. *Decide what is the most immediate moral or ethical issue facing the individual.* This is always a behavior choice, not an opinion.

5. *Resolve the ethical or moral dilemma by using an ethical system or some other means of decision making.*

ETHICAL DILEMMA

Detective Russell Poole was a Robbery–Homicide Division investigator with the Los Angeles Police Department (LAPD). In 1998, he was assigned an investigation regarding the alleged beating of Ismael Jimenez, a reputed gang member, by LAPD officers, and a suspected cover-up of the incident. In his investigation, he uncovered a pattern of complaints of violence by the anti-gang task force in the Ramparts Division. Gang members told Poole and his partners that several officers harassed them, assaulted them, and pressured them to provide untraceable guns. The beating occurred because Jimenez would not provide the officers with a gun. An investigation of Officer Rafael Perez, a member of the anti-gang task force, led to Poole concluding that several of the officers in the division were "vigilante cops." He requested that the investigation proceed further.

After Poole informed his superiors of what his investigation had uncovered, Bernard Parks, the LAPD chief at the time, ordered Poole to limit his investigation solely to the Jimenez beating. Poole prepared a 40-page report on the Jimenez case for the district attorney's office, detailing the pattern of complaints, alleged assaults, and other allegations of serious wrongdoing on the part of the Rampart officers. Poole's report never reached the district attorney's office because his lieutenant, enforcing the chief's orders, replaced his detailed report with a two-page report written by the lieutenant and another supervisor. Poole knew that in not providing the district attorney's office with all the information he uncovered, he could be charged with obstruction of justice, and the report provided so little information that the officer probably would not even be charged. Poole's lieutenant then asked him to put his name on the report.

Following the steps of analysis above, it is important for Poole to know all the facts that are relevant; for instance, if his superiors were telling him to avoid exposing the other wrongdoing because of an ongoing larger federal investigation, that would be an important fact to know to determine why he was being told to mislead the prosecutor. Concepts and values at issue include duty, loyalty, legality, and integrity. Regarding the third step, Poole's dilemma was created by the unethical/illegal acts of the police officers and the acts of his superiors. His immediate dilemma is whether to sign the misleading report.

Law

It is possible that obstruction of justice charges could be brought if it was concluded that anyone was intentionally misleading prosecutors as to the amount and quality of evidence against any suspect.

Policy

It is important in a hierarchical organization for subordinates to follow the orders of superiors. However, it is also important that any organization reward and not punish those who live up to high ideals of honesty and mission. Obviously, Poole would be following formal policies to cooperate with the district attorney's office to pursue criminal convictions when warranted. Often in organizations there are formal and informal policies. Informal policies may act to obstruct the formal goals of the organization; in this case, there was a concerted effort to suppress the Rampart Division investigative findings.

Ethics

Poole reported that he never considered putting his name on a report he knew was wrong. His superiors, coworkers, and colleagues described him as "professional," "hard working," "loyal, productive, thorough, and reliable," "diligent," "honest," and "extremely credible." He was known as a first-rate investigator and trusted by the district attorney's office to provide thorough and credible testimony. In other words, his habits in his professional life were directly contrary to participating in a cover-up. From all accounts, Poole represented many of Aristotle's virtues.

Natural law and religious ethics do not give us clear answers to Poole's dilemma. However, ethical formalism does in that Kant's categorical imperative can be applied to his choice to sign or not sign the report. This dilemma illustrates that sometimes duties conflict: in this case, his duty to follow the law conflicted with his duty to obey his superiors. The first part of the categorical imperative is to act in such a way that you would agree should be universal. Not exposing or pursuing evidence of corruption would not be an action that we would want universalized, so signing the doctored report fails the first part of the categorical
(continued)

imperative. The second part of the imperative is to not treat others as a means to an end. It seems clear that Poole's superiors were attempting to use him to further their goals. Their behavior, then, violates this part of the imperative. If Poole does mislead the prosecutor by signing, then he is violating this imperative as well. The last portion of the imperative is that in order to be moral, behavior must be autonomous and freely chosen. If Poole were frightened or pressured into doing something, then the action would not be moral regardless of what it was. If, for instance, he believed that the district attorney would find out and come after him for falsifying a legal document, then he might not sign it, but it would not be because of a good will and, therefore, could not be considered a moral act.

Applying utilitarianism to Detective Russell Poole's dilemma, it seems clear that his superiors were engaged in damage control. They did not want a scandal, especially considering that it had not been that long since the Rodney King incident. By suppressing evidence of further wrongdoing, they probably assumed that they could keep the information from the public and deal with it internally. Applying the utilitarian ethical system to Poole's dilemma requires determining which choice (to sign or not to sign) results in the greatest benefit to all (society, the department, his peers, and Poole himself).

Did the greatest benefit lie in exposing the corruption or trying to hide it?

Actually, the attempt to suppress the actions of the Ramparts Division officers was unsuccessful anyway. A year after Poole refused to sign the report that protected Officer Rafael Perez, Perez was prosecuted for stealing a large amount of cocaine from the evidence room. In a plea arrangement, he told investigators from the district attorney's office the whole story of the Ramparts Division officers, leading to the biggest scandal in LAPD's history. This illustrates one of the problems with utilitarianism: if people sacrifice their integrity for what they consider is a good cause, the result may be that they lose their integrity and still do not achieve their good cause.

Under the ethics of care, individual needs should be considered to determine the best course of action. Unfortunately, sometimes individuals' needs are not met even when they do the right thing. Detective Poole knew what the right course of action was. He also knew that he would pay a price for doing it. In fact, after he refused to sign the report he was transferred to a less prestigious position and denied a promotion. He was vilified and treated as a traitor by some officers when he went public with his evidence of a cover-up. Ultimately, he resigned from the LAPD.

Source: Boyer, 2004; Golab, 2000.

▌Relativism, Absolutism, and Universalism

Ethical relativism describes the position that what is good or bad changes depending on the individual or group, and that there are no moral absolutes. Relativists believe that what is right is determined by culture and/or individual belief and that there are no universal laws. Absolutism, as previously discussed, is the position that, if something is wrong, it is always wrong. Universalism is a similar concept in that it is the position that what is considered wrong is wrong for all people for all time and if one wants to perform a certain act, one would have to agree that anyone else should be able to do it as well.

One may look to anthropology and the rise of social science to explain the popularity of moral relativism. Over the course of studying different societies—past and present, primitive and sophisticated—anthropologists have found that there are very few universals across cultures. Even those behaviors often believed to be universally condemned, such as incest, have been institutionalized and encouraged in some societies (Kottak, 1974: 307). Basically, **cultural relativism** defines good as that which contributes to the health and survival of society. Hunting and gathering societies that must contend with harsh environments may hold beliefs allowing for the euthanasia of burdensome elderly, whereas agricultural societies that depend on knowledge passed down through generations may revere their elderly and accord them an honored place in society.

cultural relativism
The idea that values and behaviors differ from culture to culture and are functional in the culture that holds them.

Cultural relativists recognize that cultures have very different definitions of right and wrong, and moral relativists argue that there are no fundamental or absolute definitions of right and wrong. In opposition to this position, absolutists argue that just because there may be cultural norms endorsing such things as cannibalism, slavery, or having sex with six-year-olds, the norms do not make these acts moral and there are absolute rights and absolute wrongs whether we agree with them or not.

Although cultural relativism holds that different societies may have different moral standards, it also dictates that individuals within a culture conform to the standards of their culture. Therein lays a fundamental flaw in the relativist approach: if there are no universal norms, why should individuals be required to conform to societal or cultural norms? If their actions are not accepted today, it might be argued, they could be accepted tomorrow—if not by their society, perhaps by some other.

An additional inconsistency in cultural relativism as a support for moral relativism is the prohibition against interfering in another culture's norms. The argument goes as follows: because every culture is correct in its definitions of morality, another culture should not step in to change those definitions. However, if what is right is determined by which culture one happens to belong to, why then, if that culture happens to be imperialistic, would it be wrong to force cultural norms on other cultures? Cultural relativism attempts to combine an absolute (no interference) with a relativistic "truth" (there are no absolutes). This is logically inconsistent (Foot, 1982).

Cultural relativism usually concerns behaviors that are always right in one society and always wrong in another. Of course, what is more common is behavior that is judged to be wrong most of the time, but acceptable in certain instances. As examples: torture is wrong except possibly against terrorism; lying is wrong except when one lies to protect another.

Even absolutist systems may accept some exceptions. The **principle of forfeiture** associated with deontological ethical systems holds that people who treat others as means to an end or take away or inhibit their freedom and well-being forfeit the right to protection of their own freedom and well-being (Harris, 1986: 136). Therefore, people who aggress first forfeit their own right to be protected from harm. This could permit self-defense (despite the moral proscription against taking life) and possibly provide justification for lying to a person who threatens harm. Critics of an absolutist system see this exception as a rationalization and a fatal weakness to the approach; in effect, moral rules are absolute *except* for those exceptions allowed by some "backdoor" argument.

Relativism allows for different rules and different judgments about what is good. Proponents argue that it promotes tolerance. Universalists argue that if moral absolutes are removed, subjective moral discretion leads to egoistic (and nationalistic) rationalizations. They would argue that things like the Holocaust, slavery, the slaughter of Native American Indians, the Armenian genocide, Japanese-American internment, the Bataan Death March, and torture in Abu Ghraib and Guantanamo happen

QUOTE & **QUERY**

The "Gestalt Prayer" of humanistic psychotherapist Fritz Perls:

I do my thing and you do your thing.

I am not in this world to live up to your expectations.

And you are not in this world to live up to mine.

You are you, and I am I, and if by chance we find each other, it's beautiful.

If not, it can't be helped.

Source: Dolliver, 1981.

? Is this a statement consistent with egoism? Do you believe that we should not judge each other? Are there absolute wrongs that cannot be ignored?

principle of forfeiture The idea that one gives up one's right to be treated under the principles of respect for persons to the extent that one has abrogated someone else's rights; for instance, self-defense is acceptable according to the principle of forfeiture.

because people promoting what they consider to be a good end (security or progress) do not apply absolute rules of morality and ethics and, instead, utilize relativism: it is okay for me to do this to you, at this time, because of what I consider to be a good reason, but you can't do it to me.

Toward a Resolution: Situational Ethics

situational ethics
The philosophical position that although there are a few universal truths, different situations call for different responses; therefore, some action can be right or wrong depending on situational factors.

Situational ethics is often used as a synonym for *relativism*; however, if we clarify the term to include certain fundamental absolute elements, it might serve as a resolution to the problems inherent in both an absolutist and a relativist approach to ethics. Recall that relativism, on the one hand, is criticized because it must allow any practice to be considered "good" if it is considered good by some people; therefore, even human sacrifice and cannibalism would have to be considered moral—a thoroughly unpalatable consequence of accepting the doctrine. Absolutism, on the other hand, is also less than satisfactory because we all can think of some examples when the "rule" must be broken. Even Kant declined to be purely absolutist in his argument that lying isn't really lying if told to a person who is trying to harm us. What is needed, then, is an approach that resolves both problems.

moral pluralism
The concept that there are fundamental truths that may dictate different definitions of what is moral in different situations.

Hinman (1998) resolves this debate by defining the balance between absolutism and relativism as **moral pluralism**. In his elaboration of this approach, he stops short of an "anything goes" rationale but does recognize multicultural "truths" that affect moral perceptions. The solution that will be offered here, whether one calls it situational ethics or some other term, is as follows:

1. There are basic principles of right and wrong.
2. These principles can be applied to ethical dilemmas and issues.
3. These principles may call for different results in different situations, depending on the needs, concerns, relationships, resources, weaknesses, and strengths of the individual actors.

Situational ethics is different from relativism because absolute laws are recognized, whereas under relativism there are no absolute definitions of right and wrong. What are absolute laws that can be identified as transcendent? Natural law, the Golden Rule, and the ethics of care could help us fashion a set of moral absolutes that might be general enough to ensure universal agreement. For instance, we could start with the following propositions:

- Treat each person with the utmost respect and care.
- Do one's duty or duties in such a way that one does not violate the first principle.

These principles would not have anything to say about dancing (as immoral or moral), but they would condemn human sacrifice, child molestation, slavery, and a host of other practices that have been part of human society. Practices could be good in one society and bad in another. For instance, if polygamy was necessary to ensure the survival of society, it might be acceptable; if it was to serve the pleasure of some by using and treating others as mere objects, it would be immoral. Selling daughters into marriage to enrich the family would never be acceptable because that is not treating them with respect and care; however, arranged marriages might be acceptable if all parties agree and the motives are consistent with care.

This system is not too different from a flexible interpretation of Kant's categorical imperative, a strict interpretation of rule-based utilitarianism, or an inclusive application of the Golden Rule. All ethical systems struggle with objectivity and subjectivity, along with respect for the individual and concern for society. Note that egoism does not pursue these goals and that is why some believe it cannot be accepted as a legitimate ethical system. Interestingly, situational ethics seems to be entirely consistent with the ethics of care, especially when one contrasts this ethical system with a rule-based, absolutist system. In the ethics of care, you will recall, each individual is considered in the equation of what would be the "good."

Conclusion

Ethical systems provide the guidelines or principles to make moral decisions. Box 2.4 summarizes the key principles of these ethical systems. It can happen that moral questions are decided in different ways under the same ethical system. For instance, if facts are in dispute, two people using utilitarianism may "weigh" the utilities of an act differently. Capital punishment is supported by some because of a belief that it is a deterrent to people who might commit murder; others argue it is wrong because it does not deter (this is an argument about facts between two utilitarians). Others believe that capital punishment is wrong regardless of its ability to deter (this would be an argument by those following a religious ethics system or ethics of care). Most arguments about capital punishment get confused during the factual argument about the effectiveness of deterrence. "Is capital punishment wrong or right?" is a different question than "Does capital punishment deter?"

Another thing to consider is that none of us is perfect; we all have committed immoral or unethical acts that we know were wrong. Ethical systems help us to understand or analyze morality, but knowing what is right is no guarantee that we will always do the right thing. Few people follow such strong moral codes that they *never* lie or *never* cause other people harm. One can condemn the act and not the person. The point is that just because some behaviors are understandable and perhaps even excusable does not make them moral or ethical. Another point is that few people consistently use just one ethical system in making moral decisions. Some of us are fundamentally utilitarian and some predominantly religious, but we may make decisions using other ethical frameworks as well.

BOX 2.4 \ The Major Ethical Systems

Ethics of virtue. What is good is that which conforms to the principle of the Golden Mean.
Natural law. What is good is that which conforms to the natural laws of the universe.
Religion. What is good is that which conforms to God's will.
Ethical formalism. What is good is that which conforms to the categorical imperative.
Utilitarianism. What is good is that which results in the greatest utility for the greatest number.
Ethics of care. What is good is that which meets the needs of those concerned.
Egoism. What is good is that which benefits me.

Finally, it should be noted that while philosophical discussions typically emphasize the differences between these ethical systems, in most cases where individuals face a dilemma about the right thing to do, the ethical systems agree. For instance, the first dilemma at the back of this chapter asks: should you report your friend for stealing from the store where you both work? Under ethics of virtue, the virtuous person would not condone or participate in theft. Even Aristotle said that a friend who is a scoundrel is more scoundrel than friend and deserves no loyalty. Under natural law, theft violates trust, which is one of the building blocks of society itself; therefore, it is unnatural to steal (except perhaps in life-threatening circumstances) and unnatural to condone stealing. Religion would obviously condemn the act and encourage stopping it since we are instructed that we are "our brother's keepers." Ethical formalism would look to your duty as a manager and apply universalism to determine that it was necessary to stop the stealing by reporting it. Utilitarianism would weigh the benefits and determine that it was not beneficial to anyone except your friend to allow her to get away with the theft. Finally, ethics of care would be concerned for your friend as well and would perhaps arrive at a solution where she might be persuaded to return the item and quit the job without undergoing any public retribution. Only egoism might support keeping quiet if it meant losing a friend; however, even enlightened egoism might support reporting the friend, since she might turn around and use the incident against you later.

Ethical systems are more complex to apply than they are to explain. For instance, utilitarianism is easy to understand, but the measurement of utility for any given act is often quite difficult. Ethical formalism says to "do one's duty," but it does not help us when there are conflicting duties. The ethics of care emphasizes relationships but is vague in providing the steps necessary to resolve ethical dilemmas. More applied approaches utilize steps one can take to resolve ethical dilemmas, such as the "front page" test (exposing the decision to outside scrutiny). Whether morals are relative or absolute has been debated throughout time. The concept of situational ethics is offered to reconcile the question as to whether ethics are universal or not, and it is also true that in many ethical dilemmas, these systems arrive at the same answer as to what is the right thing to do.

Chapter Review

1. **Define deontological and teleological ethical systems and explain ethical formalism and utilitarianism.**

   A deontological ethical system, like ethical formalism, is one that is concerned solely with the inherent nature of the act being judged. If an act or intent is inherently good (coming from a good will), it is still considered a good act even if it results in bad consequences. A teleological ethical system, like utilitarianism, judges the consequences of an act. The saying "the end justifies the means" is a teleological statement. Kant's ethical formalism defines good as that which conforms to the categorical imperative, which includes the universalism principle, the idea that we shouldn't use people, and the stricture that we must do our duty through a free will be considered moral. Utilitarianism, associated with Jeremy Bentham, defines good as that which contributes to the greatest utility for the greatest number.

2. **Describe how other ethical systems define what is moral—specifically, ethics of virtue, natural law, religion, and the ethics of care.**

   Under the ethics of virtue, goodness is determined by the virtues. Those who possess such virtues will make the right decision when faced with a moral dilemma. Under natural law, good is determined by what is natural. Moral rules are like other natural laws, such as gravity. Even if humans have not discovered these moral rules, or disagree about what they are, they still exist. Under Judeo-Christian religion, what is good is determined by God's will. One can know God's will through one's religious leaders or the Bible. The ethics of care is based on the emotions of relationships. Caring is the basis of this morality.

3. **Discuss the argument as to whether egoism is an ethical system.**

   Egoism is not considered by many to be an ethical system because it is self-serving and logically inconsistent. It doesn't make sense to have a universal rule that everyone should pursue self-interest, because our self-interests will inevitably conflict. Proponents of ethical egoism also believe in psychological egoism, the idea that we are, by nature, purely self-interested. Under this view, we are egoists and, therefore, to pursue our self-interest is good.

4. **Explain the controversy between relativism and absolutism (or universalism).**

   Absolutist ethics allow no exceptions to moral rules for exceptional circumstances. Relativism seems to allow individuals to define anything as morally acceptable, even abhorrent acts like slavery. The compromise is situational ethics, which propose a very few absolute rules that will support different decisions in different circumstances.

5. **Identify what is good according to each of the ethical systems discussed in the chapter.**

   Under *ethics of virtue*, what is good is that which conforms to the principles of Golden Mean. Under *natural law*, what is good is that which conforms to the natural laws of the universe. Under *religion*, what is good is that which conforms to God's will. Under *ethical formalism*, what is good is that which conforms to the categorical imperative. Under *utilitarianism*, what is good is that which results in the greatest utility for the greatest number. Under *ethics of care*, what is good is that which meets the needs of those concerned. Under *egoism*, what is good is that which benefits me.

Study Questions

1. What are the elements of any ethical system, according to Baelz? What are the three parts of the ethical pyramid?

2. What are the three parts of the categorical imperative? What is the difference between act and rule utilitarianism?

3. What are the three ways to know God's will? What are the Six Pillars of Character?

4. What are Krogstand and Robertson's three principles of ethical decision making?

5. Explain the differences between situational ethics and relativism.

Writing/Discussion Exercises

1. Write an essay on (or discuss) the ethical systems applied to the following situations:
    a. In the movie, *Sophie's Choice,* a woman is forced to choose one of her children to send to the gas chamber. If she does not decide, both will be killed. How would ethical formalism resolve this dilemma? How would utilitarianism resolve it?
    b. There is a continuing debate over whether the United States had to bomb Hiroshima and Nagasaki at the end of World War II. Present the arguments on both sides. Now consider this: are they utilitarian arguments, ethical formalist arguments, or some other?

2. Write an essay on (or discuss) the basic nature of humans. Are we basically altruistic? Basically egoistic? Include in this essay responses to the following and examples to support your answer: what are the "natural" inclinations of human beings? Do you think most people do the right thing out of habit or out of reason?

3. Write an essay on (or discuss) whether ethics and morals are relative or absolute. Are there absolute moral truths, or is morality simply an individual's definition of right and wrong? Should everyone have the right to decide which behaviors are acceptable for them? Should all cultures have the right to decide what is right? If you believe there are absolute definitions of right and wrong, what are they?

Key Terms

act utilitarianism	ethics of virtue	principle of the Golden
categorical imperative	eudaimonia	Mean
cultural relativism	generalization principle	psychological egoism
deontological ethical	hypothetical imperatives	religious ethics
system	imperative principle	rule utilitarianism
egoism	moral pluralism	situational ethics
enlightened egoism	natural law	teleological ethical system
ethical formalism	peacemaking justice	utilitarianism
ethical system	principle of forfeiture	utilitarian principle
ethics of care		

ETHICAL DILEMMAS

Situation 1
You are the manager of a retail store. The owner of the store gives you permission to hire a fellow classmate to help out. One day you see the classmate take some clothing from the store. When confronted by you, the peer laughs it off and says the owner is insured, no one is hurt, and it was under $100. "Besides," says your acquaintance, "friends stick together, right?" What would you do?

Situation 2
You are in a lifeboat along with four others. You have enough food and water to keep only four people alive for the several weeks you expect to be adrift until you float into a shipping lane and can be discovered and rescued. You will all perish if

the five of you consume all the food and water. There is the suggestion that one of you should die so the other four can live. Would you volunteer to commit suicide? Would you vote to have one go overboard if you choose by straws? Would you vote to throw overboard the weakest and least healthy of the five? If you were on a jury judging the behavior of four who did murder a fifth to stay alive, would you acquit them or convict them of murder? Would your answer be different if the murdered victim was your son or daughter?

Situation 3

You aspire to be a police officer and are about to graduate from a criminal justice department. Your best friend has just been hired by a local law enforcement agency, and you are applying as well. When you were freshmen, you were both caught with marijuana in your dorm room. Although you were arrested, the charges were dismissed because it turned out that the search was illegal. The application form includes a question that asks if you have ever been arrested. Your friend told you that he answered no because he knew this agency did not use polygraphs as part of the hiring process. You must now decide whether to also lie on the form. If you lie, you may be found out eventually, but there is a good chance that the long-ago arrest will never come to light. If you don't lie, you will be asked to explain the circumstances of the arrest, and your friend will be implicated as well. What should you do?

Situation 4

You have a best friend who has confessed a terrible secret to you. Today the man is married and has two children. He has a good family, has a good life, and is a good citizen. However, 14 years earlier he killed a woman. A homeless person was accused of the crime but died before he could be tried and punished. Nothing good can come of this man's confession. His family will suffer, and no one is at risk of being mistaken as the murderer. What would you advise him to do? (Some may recognize this dilemma as coming from Dostoyevsky's *The Brothers Karamazov*.)

Situation 5

You are working in internal affairs, and in the course of another investigation, you discover disturbing evidence regarding the police chief's son, who is also an officer in the department. Several informants have confided in you that this individual has roughed them up and taken their drugs, yet you find no record of arrest or the drugs being logged in the evidence room. When you write your report, your sergeant tears it up and tells you that there is not enough evidence to justify an investigation and for you to stick to what you are told to do. What would you do? What would you do if the chief calls you into his office the next day and offers you a transfer to a high-status position that will lead to a promotion?

Justice and Law

Pool/Getty Images

Justice Neil Gorsuch, in his confirmation hearing in March 2017, swore that he would administer justice in a fair and unbiased manner if he were confirmed as a Supreme Court Justice.

Learning Objectives

1. Describe the three themes included in the definition of justice.

2. Define Aristotle's distributive and corrective justice.

3. Distinguish between substantive justice and procedural justice, including how procedural justice impacts wrongful convictions and perceptions of racial discrimination.

4. Explain the concept of restorative justice and the programs associated with it.

5. Describe civil disobedience and when it may be appropriate.

It may seem strange that an ethics book has a chapter on justice, but the concept of justice is integrally related to ethics and, obviously, especially relevant in a discussion of ethical issues related to criminal justice professionals. Professionals in the criminal justice system serve and promote the interests of law and justice, so before we explore the ethical issues and dilemmas that confront them, this chapter begins with a discussion of justice itself.

Many of the major philosophers and ethicists frame their discussion of ethics around the concept of justice. For instance, Michael Sandel (2009), a popular Harvard professor, has an ethics course, book, and website titled *Justice: What's the Right Thing to Do*? His approach places ethical questions within the context of justice. This juxtaposition of justice and ethics is consistent with ethical formalism to the extent that moral duties derive from rights. For instance, a child has a right to be cared for, which creates a moral duty for parents. Other potential rights are more controversial; for instance, does one have a right to healthcare? Does one have a right to be told the truth in all situations? Injustice occurs when rights are denied, thus, discussions of justice and ethics overlap.

Lucas (1980: 3) argued that justice "differs from benevolence, generosity, gratitude, friendship, and compassion." Justice is not something for which we should feel grateful, but rather, something upon which we have a right to insist. Justice should not be confused with "good." Some actions may be considered good, but not demanded by justice. For instance, the recipients of charity, benevolence, and forgiveness do not have a right to these things; therefore, it is not an injustice to withhold them. Although the idea of need is important in some discussions of justice, it is not the only component or even the primary one; that is why ethical formalism (which focuses on duty) is more consistent with justice than the ethics of care (which focuses on need). It is important to understand that what is *just* and what is *good* are not always the same. The current controversies over healthcare and homelessness are examples of this distinction. In an ideal society, all people would have healthcare and a place to live whether they could afford these things or not. To meet that need would be good, but do they have a *right* to healthcare and a home? While some believe that every single person has a human right to basic healthcare and shelter, others believe that there is no such right and, while it is a good thing to meet these needs, there is no duty to do so, therefore it is not unjust when society does not provide them.

People can be described as displaying unique combinations of generosity and selfishness, altruism and self-interest. Some writers insist that the need for justice arises from the nature of human beings and that we are not naturally generous, open-hearted, or fair. On the one hand, if we were to behave all the time in accordance with those virtues, we would have no need for justice. On the other hand, if humans were to always act in selfish, grasping, and unfair ways, we would be unable to follow the rules and principles of justice. Therefore, we uphold and cherish the concept of justice in our society because it is the mediator between people's essential selfishness and generosity. In other words, justice is the result of a logical and rational acceptance of the concept of fairness in human relations.

Any discussion of justice includes at least three continuing themes: fairness, equality, and impartiality. **Fairness** is related to equal treatment. Parents ordinarily give each child the same allowance unless differences between the children, such as age or duties, warrant different amounts. Children are sensitive to issues of fairness long before they grasp more abstract ideas of justice. No doubt every parent has heard the plaintive cry, "It's not fair—Johnny got more than I did" or "It's not fair—she always gets to sit in the front seat!" What children are sensing is unequal and, therefore, unfair treatment. The concept of fairness is inextricably tied to equality and impartiality.

Equality refers to equal shares or equal treatment as well. There is a predisposition to demand equity or equal shares for all, or equal shares for similar people. The concept of equality is also present in retributive justice in the belief that similar crimes should be punished equally ("equal justice for all"). In contrast to the concept of equal shares is the idea of needs or deserts; in other words, we should get what we need or, alternatively, what we deserve by status, merit, or other reasons.

Impartiality is also related to the concept of equal treatment. At the core of our system of criminal justice is the theme of impartiality. Our symbol of justice represents, with her blindfold, impartiality toward special groups and, with her scales, proportionally just punishments. Impartiality implies fair and equal treatment of all without discrimination and bias. It is hard to reconcile the ideal of "blind justice" with taking individual circumstances into consideration when determining culpability or punishment. Most would argue, individual differences and circumstances should be

fairness The condition of being impartial, the allocation of equal shares or equal opportunities.

equality The same value, rights, or treatment between all in a specific group.

impartiality Not favoring one party or interest more than another.

IN THE NEWS | *Too Big to Jail?*

Law professor Brandon L. Garrett, author of a recent book *Too Big to Jail*, analyzed 303 nonprosecution and deferred prosecution agreements with corporations from 2001 to 2014. Individuals were charged in only 34 percent of the cases that involved all types of white-collar and corporate crimes. Only 42 percent of those charged received any jail time. This is even though companies paid huge fines and admitted criminal culpability; for example, Siemens paid over $1.6 billion for bribery, Pfizer paid $2.3 billion for bribing doctors, and Tyson Foods paid a $4 million fine for bribery. Prosecutors explain that they would like to prosecute executives, but it is harder to prove cases of individual culpability. Critics argue that top executives are unlikely to be prosecuted because of other reasons.

Source: Garrett, 2014; Stewart, 2015.

taken into consideration—if not during a finding of guilt or innocence, then at least when sentencing occurs. If the blindfold of Lady Justice signifies no special treatment for the rich or the powerful, then it must also signify no special consideration for the young or desperate, or for any extraordinary circumstances in a criminal case. The In the News box illustrates that those who believe the justice system treats white-collar criminals differently than other criminals may be right.

Origins of the Concept of Justice

justice The quality of being impartial, fair, and just; derived from the Latin justitia, concerning rules or law.

Justice originated in the Greek word *dike*, which is associated with the concept of everything staying in its assigned place or natural role (Feinberg and Gross, 1977: i). This idea is closely associated with the definitions of justice given by Plato and Aristotle.

Plato associated justice with maintaining the societal status quo. Justice is one of four civic virtues, the others being wisdom, temperance, and courage (Feibleman, 1985: 173). In an ordered state, everyone performs his or her role and does not interfere with others. Each person's role is the one for which the individual is best fitted by nature; thus, *natural law* is upheld. Moreover, it is in everyone's self-interest to have this ordered existence continue because it provides the means to a good life and appropriate human happiness.

In Aristotle's conception of justice, the lack of freedom and opportunity for some people—slaves and women, for instance—did not conflict with justice, if the individual was in the role for which, by nature, he or she was best suited. In other words, those with the highest intellect should be given schooling, those who were musical should be the musicians in society, and those with qualities that were suited to servitude should be slaves. Aristotle lived in a time where slavery was an accepted practice and people believed that slaves were different in aptitude and character from free men. Even Aristotle recognized that injustice may occur when someone placed into slavery, for instance, a vanquished enemy, might not be "naturally" suited to slavery. Aristotle associated justice with the law; if a person violated the law, he would be considered unjust. However, he didn't view justice solely as a function of law. A person's dealings with others in all areas of life determined whether he could be considered just or unjust.

Distributive Justice

Aristotle distinguished between two types of justice: distributive justice and corrective justice. **Distributive justice** concerns what measurement should be used to allocate society's resources; for instance, this type of justice would include issues such as affirmative action, welfare, free schooling, and other goods and opportunities, and how society distributes them among its members. **Corrective justice** concerns unfair advantage or undeserved harm between people. Justice demands remedies or compensations to the injured party.

> **distributive justice**   Justice that concerns what measurement should be used to allocate society's resources.

The concept of the appropriate and just allocation of society's goods and interests is one of the central themes in all discussions of justice. The goods that one might possess include the following:

- Economic goods (income or property)
- Opportunities for development (education or citizenship)
- Recognition (honor or status)

> **corrective justice**   Justice that concerns when unfair advantage or unjust enrichment occurs (either through contract disputes or criminal action) and what the appropriate remedy might be to right the wrong.

If there was enough of everything (goods, opportunity, and status) for everyone, issues of distributive justice are less likely to arise. Two valid claims to possession are *need* and *desert* (Raphael, 1980). Different writers have presented various proposals for deciding issues of entitlement.

Lucas (1980: 164–165) identified distributions based on need, merit, performance, ability, rank, station, worth, work, agreements, requirements of the common good, valuation of services, and legal entitlement. The various theories can be categorized as egalitarian, Marxist, libertarian, or utilitarian, depending on the factors that are emphasized (Beauchamp, 1982):

- *Egalitarian theories* start with the basic premise of equality or equal shares for all.
- *Marxist theories* place need above desert or entitlement.
- *Libertarian theories* promote freedom from interference by government in social and economic spheres; therefore, merit, entitlement, and productive contributions are given weight over need or equal shares.
- *Utilitarian theories* attempt to maximize benefits for individuals and society with a mixed emphasis on entitlements and needs.

CEO compensation, as shown in Box 3.1, is, on average, 200 times that of average worker's compensation. Is that fair, or is that just compensation for reaching the pinnacle of one's career? Interestingly, one study found that companies with the highest paid executives have lower average profits for shareholders than the companies with lower average executive pay (Adams, 2014). Thus, evidence doesn't seem to support a merit-based argument for such compensation differences.

The Economic Policy Institute found that CEO pay rose from 20 times that of average worker pay in 1965 to almost 296 times average worker pay in 2013. Compensation for executives includes base pay, bonuses, perquisites, and grant-date value of stock options. Equilar, a compensation computing company, reported that average CEO salary in 2014 was around $14.3 million, an increase of about 5 percent from 2013. Companies dispute the calculation of executive compensation and salary ratios, arguing that stock options are not really compensation until they are realized

BOX 3.1 \ Annual CEO Salaries—2016		
Dara Khosrowshahi	Expedia	$94.6 million
Leslie Moonves	CBS	$56.4 million
Philippe P. Dauman	Viacom	$54.1 million
Mark V. Hurd	Oracle	$53.2 million
Safra A. Catz	Oracle	$53.2 million
Frank J. Bisignano	First Data	$51.6 million
Leonard S. Schleifer	Regeneron Pharmaceuticals	$47.5 million
Robert A. Iger	Walt Disney	$43.5 million
Sandeep Mathrani	General Growth Properties	$39.2 million
Howard M. Lorber	Vector Group	$37.0 million

Note: Different sources have different lists of highest paid executives due to differences in computing stock options and other compensation sources.

Source: Equilar.com, 2017.

(Morgenson, 2015). In 2010, Congress included in the Dodd–Frank law a requirement that companies disclose the CEO–worker pay ratio each year. Evidently, this requirement was largely ignored by American businesses. More recently, plans are underway in Congress to repeal the law.

Egalitarian distribution systems would pay people equally, or at least equal people doing equal work would get paid equally. There is very little debate that men and women, for instance, should be paid equal salaries if they do the same work. In *Ledbetter v. Goodyear*, 550 U.S. 618, 2007, Lilly Ledbetter lost her equal pay case because the Supreme Court agreed with her company that she should have brought the suit earlier even though she was not aware of the pay discrepancy. Congress, in response, passed the Lilly Ledbetter Equal Pay Act (Pub.L.222-3. S. 181); this redefined the statute of limitations for filing an equal protection claim to start tolling when a person finds out about the disparity.

Even though gender disparate pay in equal jobs is clearly wrong, when jobs are not the same, it is more difficult to determine fairness. Obviously, few would agree that workers in all jobs and all professions should be paid the same amount of money. Some jobs require more schooling, and some demand more responsibility and involve greater stress. Questions of worth are difficult. Should a kindergarten teacher be paid more than a truck driver? Should a police officer be paid less than a social worker? How should you weigh the value of different professions?

Marxist distribution systems propose that we pay people based on need. In that case, a person with two children would earn more than a person with no children. Libertarian advocates would be appalled at that system and argue that vast disparities in economic remuneration are acceptable and should be left to the free market. High salaries promote competition and competition promotes quality, therefore if a CEO or athlete earns a salary that is extremely disproportionate to anyone else, it must be because they have a skill or talent that the rest of us are willing to pay for.

🖥 IN THE NEWS | *Sharing the Wealth*

Dan Price, the founder of Gravity Payments, ignited a media firestorm in April 2015 when he made an announcement that he would raise all 120 employees' salaries to $70,000—even clerks, customer service representatives, and salespeople. The company processes credit card payments, and to increase his employee's minimum pay, Price, who started the company at the age of 19, cut his own $1 million salary to $70,000. He said he was doing so because of an article he read describing a social science study that discovered people's emotional well-being was affected by salaries less than $75,000,

but that salaries over that amount did not contribute proportionally to happiness. A year after he increased salaries, the average salary was $72,000 compared to $48,000 before the move. The publicity evidently was good for business—the company boasted a doubling of profit as well as increased happiness and retention of employees. Effects on workers are reported as including a shorter commute time (workers evidently could afford to move closer to downtown Seattle), and having more babies (the birthrate among employees increased 10-fold after the pay increase).

Source: P. Cohen, 2015; Murray, 2016.

Even if one subscribed to a libertarian approach, how should salary be calculated? Should workers be paid based on their production or as a salary? If so, how would one pay secretaries, teachers, or customer service workers, whose production is more difficult to measure? How would one pay police officers—by the number of arrests? Thus far, we have discussed only salaries, but in the workplace other goods are also distributed, such as promotions, merit increases, job postings, desirable offices, and parking places. How should these "perks" be awarded if production isn't easily measured?

Utilitarian systems of distribution would allow economic disparities if they contributed to the greater good. For instance, doctors should make more money than many other workers because it is difficult to become a doctor and not many people would go through with it unless there were some rewards to look forward to. Also, doctors contribute to the greater good by curing the sick and injured and help the economic prosperity of the society by keeping people healthy, thus it benefits all of us that the compensation is sufficient to keep adequate numbers of people interested in medicine as a profession.

Minimum pay laws can be justified under a utilitarian system, but not a libertarian one. Federal minimum wage is $7.25 per hour but states can set their own wage laws and many have set minimum wages higher than the federal law. About 28 states have higher minimum wage laws than the federal rate. The highest wage laws are $11.50 for the District of Columbia and $11 for Washington and Massachusetts (United States Department of Labor, 2017). The argument for increasing minimum pay is not just need. The utilitarian argument is that more money in workers' pockets improves the economy since low-income workers spend a greater percentage of their income on consumable goods than do those at the top of the socioeconomic ladder. The raise in pay goes straight back to the economy and the boost is good for everyone. However, opponents argue that it is not good for everyone because when business owners have to pay workers more, they hire fewer workers so the number of jobs goes down, or they give workers fewer hours, making it just as difficult to make ends meet. Recent research supports this finding, at least in Seattle, when it raised the minimum wage to $13 per hour although other studies find the opposite effect (Scheiber, 2017).

Just distribution of other goods in society is also problematic. There are perennial arguments over how much people should receive in entitlement programs, such as food stamps and TANF (Temporary Assistance for Needy Families). The principle of need is the rationale we use to take from the financially solvent, through taxes, and give to those who have little or nothing. There is always resentment over this redistribution because of the belief that some people choose not to work and take advantage of governmental "hand-outs."

The issue of universal healthcare has become a divisive controversy in this country. In July 2012, the Supreme Court upheld the legality of the Patient Protection and Affordable Care Act, colloquially referred to as "Obamacare" (*National Federation of Independent Business v. Sebelius*, 567 U.S. 519, 2012). In *King v. Burwell*, 576 U.S. ___, 2014, opponents challenged the use of subsidies, but the Supreme Court ruled in favor of the healthcare law again. In the winter of 2017, an attempt to repeal and replace the law by the Republican majority in the House of Representatives was unsuccessful, and the Senate's version did not fare much better, but efforts continue to repeal or drastically dismantle the Affordable Care Act. Criticism comes from both sides of this philosophical debate. From the right, there is the belief that government should not be involved in providing health insurance (it may be a good, but it is neither a duty of government to provide it nor a right of the government to demand individuals purchase insurance). From the left, there is the belief that the government should be providing universal healthcare, not health insurance subsidies.

The national debate over this issue echoes the opposition over Franklin Delano Roosevelt's "New Deal" to get the country out of the Great Depression. The creation of the Civilian Conservation Corps, Social Security, Medicaid, and Medicare was met with vigorous opposition from conservatives and libertarians, and legally challenged. Opponents argued that the programs were an extreme government overreach, while proponents argued that there was a need for a governmental safety net for the most vulnerable among us, such as the aged. Today, these programs have come to be integral parts of American's financial well-being. Regarding the current controversy over healthcare, whether the federal government has the legal authority to mandate everyone buy insurance is a *legal* question; whether a government-run health system is more efficient or effective than the private market is an *empirical* question; however, whether everyone *deserves* to have basic healthcare is a philosophical and moral question.

Another good to be distributed in society is opportunity. There is a compelling argument that although the *ideal* of education is that everyone in this country has equal access to educational opportunities; the *reality* is that, because of unequal tax bases, school districts are not equal and distribute the opportunity of education unequally. States struggle with how to fund poor school districts, and "Robin Hood" laws, which take from rich districts to subsidize poor districts, are bitterly opposed by parents, who move to a district specifically for the resources it provides students. Washington, Kansas, and Texas are or have been recently in litigation over school funding. Generally, the right to adequate education is found in state constitutions. Legal and political arguments exist over the parameters of the state's obligation to provide funding, the definitions of adequacy, and the source for school funding.

There are also perennial arguments about charter schools and voucher systems with some arguing for choice and parental control, and others arguing that the basis of a democracy is a well-funded public school system. The nomination and confirmation of Betsy DeVos as President Trump's Secretary of Education was controversial, partly because she did not have a background as an educator, but, also, because of her ardent support for private school vouchers. This option to school funding would allow parents to receive vouchers (or tax credits) to apply toward tuition at private schools. Opponents argue that the financial assistance given to parents who place their children in private schools takes away from public school budgets, which are stretched woefully thin as it is, and distributed to families who don't need the financial help. Proponents argue that parents should not be forced to place their children in poorly performing public schools and there are private school choices that would be better for children, perhaps especially high-risk children, because of smaller class sizes and individualized assistance.

John Rawls' theory of justice is perhaps the best-known modern conception of justice. He elegantly combines utilitarian and rights-based concepts in his theory of distributive justice. Basically, he proposes an equal distribution unless a different distribution would benefit the disadvantaged. Rawls believes that any inequalities of society should be to the benefit of those who are least advantaged (Rawls, 1971: 15):

- Each person is to have an equal right to the most extensive total system of basic liberties compatible with a similar system of liberty for all.

- Social and economic inequalities are to be arranged so that they are both reasonably expected to be to everyone's advantage and attached to positions and offices open to all (except when inequality is to the advantage of those least well-off).

So, for instance, Rawls may argue for a purely objective hiring scoring system except when one gives extra points for those who are least well-off, and tax rebates that are equally distributed, except if they are a bit more favorable for those in the lower income brackets. Rawls uses a heuristic device that he calls the **veil of ignorance** to explain the idea that people will develop fair principles of distribution only if they are ignorant of their position in society, for they just as easily may be "have-nots" as "haves" (Rawls, 1971: 12). Thus, justice and fairness are in everyone's rational self-interest because, under the veil of ignorance, one's own situation is unknown, and the best and most rational distribution is the one that is most equal to all.

Rawls' theory of justice has been criticized. First, some argue that the veil of ignorance is not sufficient to counteract humanity's basic selfishness: given the chance, people would still seek to maximize their own gain, even if doing so involves a risk (Kaplan, 1976: 199). Second, Rawls' preference toward those who are least well-off may be contrary to the good of society. Rawls states that "all social values—liberty and opportunity, income and wealth, and the bases of self-respect—are to be distributed equally unless an unequal distribution of any, or all, of these values is to the advantage of the least favored." This may be ultimately dysfunctional for society, for if those who are least well-off have the advantages of society preferentially, there will be no incentive for others to excel. Also, some argue that Rawls is wrong to ignore desert in his distribution of goods (Galston, 1980: 3).

Is distributive justice relevant to criminal justice? One application of distributive justice is the appropriateness of affirmative action in the hiring and promotion of police officers and other criminal justice professionals. Should your race give you an edge in hiring decisions? What if the profession is one, such as policing, that historically has been closed to minorities? Another issue that is related to distributive justice is how much to pay police officers or correctional officers compared to other

veil of ignorance
Rawls' idea that people will develop fair principles of distribution only if they are ignorant of their position in society, so to get objective judgments, the decision maker must not know how the decision would affect him or her.

professions. Most people believe that police are underpaid. If so, how much is a fair salary, and how does that salary compare to others, such as elementary school teachers? The criteria you use to determine these answers should have some basis in the distribution systems discussed earlier.

Finally, there is a connection between distributive justice and corrective justice, which will be discussed next. If it is true that socioeconomic status predicts criminal predisposition, should we care? Is it fair that poor people tend to end up in prison and those with more resources usually receive less punishment? Further, should we consider issues of distributive justice (i.e., what someone has by accident of birth) in any discussion of corrective justice (i.e., what people deserve when they commit a crime)? For example, is a rich person who embezzles from their employer equally culpable as a desperately poor individual who commits a theft? Reiman (2007) argues that economic power affects lawmaking, lawbreaking, enforcement, and punishment practices; literally, he argues that the rich get richer and the poor get prison under our system of justice. Clearly, distributive justice is an important concept in any discussion of the criminal justice system.

Corrective Justice

Recall that, in addition to distributive justice, Aristotle also described corrective justice, which is concerned with balancing unfair advantage. We will not discuss the types of issues relevant to civil law, such as contract disputes and other forms of business or consumer conflicts. We will concentrate, instead, on the concept of justice as it applies to determining guilt and dispensing punishment for criminal violations. As with distributive justice, the concepts of equality and desert, fairness and impartiality are important. Two components of corrective justice should be differentiated. **Substantive justice** involves the concept of just deserts, or how one determines fair punishment, and **procedural justice** concerns the steps we must take before administering punishment.

Substantive Justice

substantive justice Concerns just deserts—in other words, the appropriate amount of punishment for a crime.

procedural justice The component of justice that concerns the steps taken to reach a determination of guilt, punishment, or other conclusion of law.

Substantive justice refers to issues of inherent fairness in what we do to people in the name of justice. For instance, whether capital punishment is a fair punishment for the crime of murder is a substantive justice question. Many believe that the only just punishment is death because that is the only punishment equal to the harm caused by the offender. Others might say that life imprisonment is equitable and fair. Since the beginning of codified law, just punishment has been perceived as proportional to the degree of harm incurred. This was a natural outcome of the early, remedial forms of justice, which provided remedies for wrongs. For instance, for the early Greeks or Romans, the response to a theft of a slave or the killing of a horse involved compensation. The only just solution was the return or replacement of the slave or horse. This remedial or compensatory system of justice contrasts with a punishment system: the first system forces the offender to provide compensation to the victim or the victim's family, and the second apportions punishment based on the degree of harm suffered by the victim. They both involve a measurement of the harm, but in the first case, measurement is taken to adequately compensate the victim, and in the second it is to punish the offender. In a punishment-based system, the victim is a peripheral figure.

The state, rather than the victim, becomes the central figure—serving both as victim and as punisher. Two *philosophies* of substantive justice (or how to calculate appropriate punishment) can be identified: retributive justice and utilitarian justice.

Retributive Justice

The concept of **retributive justice** is one of balance. Justice demands that the criminal must suffer pain or loss proportional to what the victim was forced to suffer. A life for a life might be easy to measure, but most cases involve other forms of harm. How does one determine the amount of physical or mental pain suffered by the victim, or financial loss such as lost income or future loss, in most crimes? And if the offender cannot pay back financial losses, how does one equate imprisonment with fines or restitution?

> **retributive justice** The component of justice that concerns the determination and methods of punishment.

Historically, corporal and capital punishment were used for both property crime and violent crime. With the development of the penitentiary system in the early 1800s, punishment was more likely to be measured by the number of years of imprisonment rather than amounts of physical pain. However, a year in prison is hard to equate to any crime. How many prison years are equal to a burglary? How many prison years are equal to a drug offense? Research on prison adjustment indicates that a year in prison might be no more than mildly inconvenient for some, but for others, it might lead to suicide or mental illness (Toch, 1977).

In earlier systems of justice, the status of the victim was important in determining the level of harm and, thus, the punishment. Nobles were more important than free men, who were more important than slaves. Men were more important than women. Punishment for offenders was weighted by these designations of the worth of the victim. Although we have no formal system for weighing punishment in this way and have rejected the worth of the victim as a rationale for punishment (except in a few cases, such as assaulting a police officer or president), many believe that our justice system still follows this practice informally. People argue that harsher sentences are given when the victim is white than when the victim is black and when the victim is rich as opposed to poor.

📱 IN THE NEWS | *What Is a Just Punishment for Juvenile Murder?*

In *Roper v. Simmons*, 543 U.S. 551, 2005, the Supreme Court determined that execution for anyone who committed murder before the age of 18 was cruel and unusual and, thus, a violation of the Eighth Amendment. In 2010, the Supreme Court decided *Graham v. Florida*, 560 U.S. 48. The majority held that life without parole for a person who was under 18 when he committed a nonhomicide crime was also a violation of the Eighth Amendment. It was cruel and unusual to punish a juvenile in this way because of differences in the brain's maturity between juveniles and adults, and because capital punishment should be reserved for the "worst of the worst" and juveniles, because of their youth and probable capacity to change, would not meet that definition. In 2012, the Supreme Court consolidated two cases: juveniles Evan Miller and Kuntrell Jackson participated in murders when they were 14 and were sentenced to mandatory life without parole terms. In June 2012, the Supreme Court ruled that a mandatory life without parole sentence was a violation of the Eighth Amendment because the mandatory nature of the sentence did not allow for a consideration of the juvenile's youth and culpability (*Miller v. Alabama*, 567 U.S. 460, 2012). The next case that will appear before the Supreme Court will no doubt ask the question whether any life without parole sentence is legally acceptable for a juvenile killer. The justices decide these cases on legal grounds, but there is also the moral question—are juveniles less culpable, even for murder, than adults and should they receive less punishment?

Our system of justice has also rejected discriminations between offenders based on status, at least formally, but other distinctions in offenders' culpabilities are accepted. For instance, we don't hold juveniles fully responsible for their actions because they are considered less than rational. See the In the News box for the Supreme Court's treatment of juvenile culpability.

In Rawls' (1971) theory of justice, retributive punishment is limited in such a way as to benefit the least advantaged, similarly to the distributive justice scheme discussed earlier. In this philosophy of justice, the offender is punished until the advantage changes and the offender becomes the least advantaged. What is a just punishment for any offense should be considered using the veil of ignorance so one does not know whether one is the offender, the victim, or a disinterested bystander. Critics argue that Rawls' system would create a situation wherein an offender may victimize a large corporation or a well-off victim and still be more disadvantaged, dictating that no punishment is due him or her. Most of us would not countenance this definition of justice.

One other issue that must be addressed in any discussion of retributive justice is the concept of mercy. From the very beginnings of law, there has been the element of forgiveness or mercy, even though the offender deserves to be punished. Even tribal societies had special allowances and clemencies for offenders, usually granted by the king or chief. For instance, the concept of **sanctuary** allowed offenders respite from punishment if they were within the confines of church grounds. Benefit of clergy, dispensation, and even probation are examples of mercy by the court. However, it must be made clear that mercy is different from just deserts. If, on the one hand, because of circumstances of the crime, of the criminal, or of the victim, the offender deserves little or no punishment, then that is what he or she deserves, and it is not mercy to give a suspended sentence or probation. On the other hand, if an offender truly deserves the punishment, and is instead forgiven, then the individual has been granted mercy.

Murphy (1985/1995) proposes that retributive emotions derive from self-respect, that it is a healthy response to an injury to feel angry, resentful, and, yes, even vengeful. However, it is also acceptable to forgive and extend mercy to one's assailant if the forgiveness extends not from a lack of self-respect but rather from a moral system. For instance, he points out that many religions include the concept of "turning the other cheek" and extending mercy to enemies. Mercy is appropriate when the offender is repentant. Who has the right to extend mercy?

sanctuary
Ancient right based on church power; allowed a person respite from punishment if he or she was within the confines of church grounds.

Utilitarian Justice

As discussed above, retributive justice justifies punishment simply because the offender deserves it. However, **utilitarian justice** only supports punishment if it benefits society. Cesare Beccaria (1738–1794) and Jeremy Bentham (1748–1832) provided a utilitarian rationale for proportionality in punishment. Punishment should be based on the seriousness of the crime: the more serious the crime (or the greater the reward the crime offered the criminal), the more serious and severe the punishment should be to deter the individual from committing the crime. A utilitarian framework of justice would justify punishment based on deterrence.

Bentham's **hedonistic calculus**, for instance, is concerned with measuring the potential rewards of the crime so the amount of threatened pain could be set to deter people from committing that crime. The use of proportionality in this scheme is for deterrence, not balance. In a retributive system, we measure to determine the proportional amount of punishment to equalize the wrong; in a utilitarian system, we measure

utilitarian justice The type of justice that looks to the greatest good for all as the end.

hedonistic calculus Jeremy Bentham's rationale for calculating the potential rewards of a crime so that the amount of threatened pain could be set to deter people from committing that crime.

to determine the amount of punishment needed to deter. We see that under the utilitarian framework, there is no necessity for perfect balance. In fact, one must threaten a slightly higher degree of pain or punishment than the gain or pleasure that comes from the criminal act; otherwise, there would be no deterrent value in the punishment.

In some cases, retributive notions of justice and utilitarian notions of justice may conflict. If a criminal is sure to commit more crime, the utilitarian could justify holding him in prison as a means of incapacitation, but the retributive approach to just punishment would not hold anyone past the time "equal" to the crime. Deterrence is the primary reason to punish under a utilitarian system, but desert is the only determinant of a retributive system of justice. We subscribe to both utilitarian and retributive rationales for punishment. Amid any discussion of the costs and benefits of prison programs, diversion programs, or the correct punishment for different groups, the concept of desert is ever present.

Procedural Justice

We turn now to the procedure of administering punishment—our legal system. Law includes the procedures and rules used to determine guilt, decide punishment, or resolve disputes. It is important to keep in mind that justice and law are not the same thing. You might think of justice as the concept of fairness, while law is a system of rules.

The law is an imperfect system. Fuller (1969) explored the weaknesses of law and described ways that the procedure of law may fail to achieve justice. Generally, there is a tension between having no rules which would mean ad hoc decisions for each individual case, and a system of rules that is too stringent with no exceptions made for extraordinary circumstances.

The tension between rules and a conception of justice that is basically fundamental fairness is found in several Supreme Court cases. In 1993, the Supreme Court heard *Herrera v. Collins*, 503 U.S. 902, 1993. Herrera was convicted of killing two police officers. In an appeal, he argued that new evidence warranted a new trial because innocence should always be legitimate grounds for appeal, despite having exhausted all standard appeals. The Supreme Court majority issued a narrow holding that Herrera did not prove a constitutional violation by his actual innocence evidence. Some justices who concurred argued that there could be actual innocence evidence that would create a procedural right to rehear the case, but Justice Rehnquist wrote the opinion, and, in dictum argued there was no independent constitutional right for relief based on true innocence and the only recourse in a situation where evidence was discovered after appeals were exhausted was pardon or clemency. Justice Scalia, in his concurring opinion, wrote: "There is no basis, tradition, or even in contemporary practice for finding that in the Constitution the right to demand judicial consideration of newly discovered evidence of innocence brought forward after a conviction" (at 427).

In another case dealing with whether new evidence of innocence should trump legal rules, Justice Scalia wrote in a dissent that the Court had "never held that the Constitution forbids the execution of a convicted defendant who has had a full and fair trial but is later able to convince a habeas court that he is 'actually innocent,'" *In re Troy Anthony Davis*, 130 S. Ct. 1, 2, 2009. Especially considering the increasing number of wrongful convictions, the position that innocence is not protected by the Constitution or procedural due process is quite amazing, yet the Supreme Court has never established clearly that innocence trumps legal rules (Bazelon, 2015).

In *Holland v. Florida*, 530 U.S. 631, 2010, the Supreme Court did uphold fairness over rules in holding that the time for filing a federal habeas corpus petition could be extended by "equitable tolling" when the conduct of an attorney was sufficiently egregious to warrant the extension. Holland had lost two direct appeals and had one year to file a federal habeas corpus appeal. Despite his many pleas to his attorney to get an appeal in before the deadline, the attorney failed to do so. Because the deadline was missed, Holland was barred from filing a habeas petition appealing his death sentence. He filed his own *pro se* (without legal assistance) petition arguing that the deadline be waived because of the attorney's negligence. The Eleventh Circuit denied relief, but the Supreme Court held that courts must look at the totality of circumstances on a case-by-case basis to determine whether the deadline should be extended. Consistent with his opinion in prior cases, Justice Scalia dissented.

These cases show the tension between the fundamental fairness of considering "actual innocence" claims and following strict rules of law. Although a system of law is necessary for the ordered existence of society, it sometimes does not result in justice. "Moral rights" may differ from "legal rights," and "legal interests" may not be moral. Shakespeare's *The Merchant of Venice* (excerpted in the Quote and Query box) addresses many of the issues discussed. Here, the plea for mercy emphasizes the relationship between justice and mercy. Shylock's demand for the court's enforcement of his legal right (his pound of flesh) and the unwillingness of the court to deny it, despite the clear implication that it would be a tragedy, illustrate how law sometimes has little to do with justice. Then Portia's surprise argument—that because Shylock's contract mentioned only flesh and not blood, so no blood could be spilled, and thus Shylock is denied his compensation—is a superb illustration of the law's slavish devotion to technical rules over substance.

In our system of justice, **due process** exemplifies procedural justice. Our constitutional rights of due process (found in the Fifth, Sixth, and Fourteenth Amendments) require careful inquiry and investigation before punishment or forfeiture of any protected right can be carried out by the state. An individual has the right to due process whenever the government seeks to deprive that person of the protected rights of life, liberty, or property. Due process is the sequence of steps taken by the state that is designed to eliminate or at least minimize error. Procedural protections may include the following:

- Notice of charges
- Neutral hearing body
- Right of cross-examination
- Right to present evidence
- Representation by counsel
- Statement of findings
- Appeal

---

due process

Constitutionally mandated procedural steps designed to eliminate error in any governmental deprivation of protected liberty, life, or property.

QUOTE & **QUERY**

The quality of mercy is not strained;
It droppeth as the gentle rain from heaven
Upon the place beneath. It is twice blest;
It blesseth him that gives and him that takes.

. . .

It is an attribute to God himself,
And earthly power doth then show likest God's
When mercy seasons justice. Therefore, Jew,
Though justice be thy plea, consider this,
That, in the course of justice, none of us
Should see salvation. We do pray for mercy;
And that same prayer doth teach us all to render
The deeds of mercy. I have spoke thus much
To mitigate the justice of thy plea;
Which if thou follow, this strict court of Venice
Must needs give sentence 'gainst the merchant there.

Source: William Shakespeare, The Merchant of Venice, Act 4, Scene 1.

 What is the magistrate in this passage asking Shylock to do? How do you believe mercy should "season" justice? What would be procedural justice in this case? What would be substantive justice?

These protections do not eliminate deprivation or punishment, but they do result in more accurate and just decisions. Thus, if due process has been violated—by use of coerced confessions, tainted evidence, or improper police or court procedures—an injustice has occurred. The injustice does not arise because the offender does not deserve to be punished, but rather, because the state does not deserve to do the punishing, having relied on unfair procedures.

Procedural Justice Research

One of the most interesting and policy-relevant avenues of social science research in recent years is "procedural justice" research. This research is extremely relevant to our discussion here in that it illustrates the importance of procedural justice as it affects the legitimacy of the entire justice system. Thibaut and Walker (1975) conducted observations of courtroom settings and discovered some participants may not have been happy with the outcome, but they perceived the process as fair; in other words, the perception of the *process* (or procedures) of justice was distinct from perceptions of the *outcome*. From this research, two criteria were identified that must be present for the perception the process is fair (which has come to be known as "procedural justice"): voice (which refers to an individual's ability to have a say during the proceedings) and control (which is the ability or power to have some influence over the outcome).

Tyler (1990) and his colleagues took these concepts and carefully developed the measurement of perceptions of procedural justice, establishing the association between perceptions of procedural justice and perceived "legitimacy" (of the police or other criminal justice agency) (Sunshine and Tyler, 2003; Tyler, 1990/2006, 2003; Tyler and Fagan, 2008). Procedural justice has become more distinctly defined as including four elements: *voice* (allowing the citizen the chance to speak), *neutrality* (fairness in decisions), *respect* (using respectful language and not demeaning the citizen), and *trustworthiness* (the idea that the actions of the officer are for the public good; Tyler, 1990/2006; Tyler and Huo, 2002).

This growing body of research has established the relationship between procedural justice and citizens' satisfaction with police, their view that police power is legitimate, and even their willingness to comply with the law (Mazerolle, Bennett, Davis, Sargeant, and Manning, 2013). Research continues in this area to isolate, analyze, and validate the constructs of procedural justice and legitimacy (see, Gau, 2014; Rottman, 2007). For instance, elements of procedural justice appear to mitigate individuals' reactions to police searches (Jonathan-Zamir, Hasisi, and Margalioth, 2016). The impact of this research has provided law enforcement authorities with strategies for creating and maintaining public trust (Tyler, Goff, and MacCoun, 2015).

The application of procedural justice is not limited to compliance in police–citizen encounters on the street. Researchers have found that perceptions of procedural justice strongly predict booked arrestees' willingness to cooperate irrespective of their crime (White, Mulvey, and Dario, 2016). Research has found that the same process applies in prison; specifically, those who feel there is procedural justice are more likely to also perceive correctional officials as having legitimacy (Jackson, Tyler, Bradford, Taylor, and Shiner, 2010; Tyler, 2010). Research has also shown that ex-prisoners who perceived a higher level of procedural justice during their incarceration were less likely to recidivate (Beijersbergen, Dirkzwager, and Nieuwbeerta, 2016).

Concepts of procedural justice apply internally to organizations as well, although some researchers change the name of the concept to organizational justice. A growing body of research, using police officers and correctional officers for the most part, supports the idea that individuals in justice organizations who feel they are not treated fairly are less satisfied, more likely to quit, and more likely, perhaps, to treat others badly or engage in corrupt behaviors (De Angelis and Kupchik, 2007; Farmer, Beehr, and Love, 2003; Harris and Worden, 2014; Lambert, 2003; Lambert, Hogan, and Allen, 2006; Lambert, Hogan, and Griffen, 2007; Reynolds, 2015; Shane, 2012; Wolfe and Piquero, 2011). Recent research, for instance, finds that perceived internal procedural justice (organizational justice) of police officers is directly related to support for external procedural justice (interactions with citizens including voice, neutrality, respect, and trustworthiness). There was also an indirect relationship between internal procedural justice and trust in citizens (Van Craen and Skogan, 2017). The importance of treating people fairly and providing due process protections is a theme that runs not only through law but also through ethics. In the following two sections, we take a closer look at procedural justice by examining the evidence related to wrongful convictions and the presence of racism in the criminal justice system.

Wrongful Convictions

There is no greater example of injustice than an innocent person being convicted of a crime and spending years in prison, or, worse, being executed. One of the reasons that many people distrust our justice system is that there seems to be a small—but steady—stream of exonerations. Radelet, Bedau, and Putnam (1992) and Christianson (2004) provided early descriptions of innocent defendants who were wrongfully convicted. Now there is the National Registry of Exonerations, created by the University of Michigan and Michigan State law schools and the University of California–Irvine Newkirk Center for Science and Society. The registry gathers together all the known cases of false convictions or cases where convictions have been overturned because of egregious errors or misconduct in procedural justice. Currently 2,009 cases are in the registry. Almost half (47 percent) of all cases involve black defendants. About 40 percent were homicide cases. About half of the cases involved official misconduct (National Registry of Exonerations, 2017).

Innocence Project An organization (www.innocenceproject.org) staffed by lawyers and students who reexamine cases and provide legal assistance to convicts when there is a probability that serious errors occurred in their prosecution.

The **Innocence Project** was created by Barry Scheck and Peter Neufeld in 1992 at Cardozo Law School. Now Innocence Project sites exist across the country. The project is an affiliation of groups of lawyers, journalists, and, often, students in many states that identify cases where people may have been falsely convicted and there is DNA evidence still on file that could be used to prove or disprove their protestations of innocence. This organization has been pivotal in getting the wrongly accused off death row and freed from prison. On the website for this organization, there are brief summaries of the 349 individuals that have had their convictions overturned, including a description of what they were convicted of, the mistakes made, and sometimes the true perpetrator.

Studies of wrongful convictions should distinguish between true innocence and those cases where official misconduct or error requires a new trial, but the individual might still be guilty. Both types of cases may be counted in exoneration totals. Studies of these cases find that DNA is typically the method by which exoneration occurs. Elements that lead to wrongful convictions include false confessions (especially by the mentally ill, the mentally handicapped, and juveniles), defense lawyers' incompetence, and the suppression of exculpatory evidence. Other elements include false/mistaken eyewitness identification, invalid forensic science ("junk science"), informant/jailhouse informant perjured testimony, government misconduct, and bad lawyering (Acker and Redlich, 2011; Columbia Law School, 2002; Liptak, 2004). Schehr and Sears (2005) discuss **confirmatory bias**, which is when investigators focus on a suspect and ignore contradictory evidence. Examples of the types of official misconduct that lead to wrongful conviction will be further discussed in Chapter 10.

One important thing to consider is that in cases of true innocence, the actual perpetrator may go on to commit more crimes. Acker and Redlich (2011: 18) found that 49 rapes and 19 murders occurred because police and prosecutors focused on the wrong suspect.

Brandon Garrett's (2011) study of 250 exonerees found that 70 percent were minorities. Racial bias in wrongful convictions has been attributed to individual factors and structural factors. Structural factors include systemic bias against minorities in all institutions of society (political, economic, and social) that leads to different opportunities and treatment. Individual factors include racism, a higher rate of error in cross-racial identification, stereotyping, and lack of resources among minority defendants.

Several studies have used different sources to estimate wrongful convictions. Estimates range from 0.5 percent to 15 percent, depending on which sources were used. Inmate reports account for the higher figures, prosecutors' estimates offer the lowest. The average estimate is around 1–3 percent of all felony cases (Acker and Redlich, 2011; Krajicek, 2015;Poveda, 2001; Ramsey, 2007; Zalman, Smith, and Kiger, 2008). The Quote and Query box above presents two perceptions of the costs involved in wrongful convictions.

The state of Texas has the highest number of exonerations, including Clarence Brandley, Delma Banks, James Curtis Giles, Joyce Ann Brown, Michael Morton, and Cameron Todd Willingham. Randall Dale Adams, another freed inmate, was the subject of the documentary *The Thin Blue Line*. He was convicted in 1976 of killing a Dallas police officer who was actually killed by David Harris. Adams spent years in prison and on death row before finally being released (Hall, 2002; Kirchmeier et al., 2009). The case of Michael Morton, who spent almost 25 years in prison after being wrongfully convicted of killing his wife, has led to new legislation in Texas requiring prosecutors to open their files to defense attorneys.

The growing body of information on wrongful convictions illustrates the fact that procedural safeguards to minimize error and promote procedural justice can be put in place, but these rules and procedures can be subverted consciously or unconsciously by police and prosecutors who are pursuing a conviction.

> **confirmatory bias** Fixating on a preconceived notion and ignoring other possibilities, such as focusing on a specific suspect during a police investigation.

QUOTE & QUERY

Is it better for 100,000 guilty men to walk free rather than have one innocent man convicted? The cost-benefit policy answer is no.

Source: (prosecutor) Quoted in Liptak, 2004: 3.

No rate of preventable errors that destroy people's lives and destroy the lives of those close to them is acceptable.

Source: (law professor) Quoted in Liptak, 2004: 3.

? Do either of these statements represent ethical formalism? Which statement represents utilitarian thinking? Why does it have to be a choice between letting guilty people go free and punishing innocents?

Race, Ethnicity, and Justice

The major constructs of procedural justice research include *neutrality* (fairness in decisions) and *respect* (using respectful language and not demeaning the citizen). There is strong evidence that these two aspects of procedural justice are differentially experienced depending on what race or ethnic group you belong to.

There is a large difference in the perceptions of blacks and whites regarding the criminal justice system. In a combined Gallup Poll of 2011–2014, 59 percent of whites, but only 36 percent of blacks, had a great deal or a lot of confidence in the police. In the aggregated polls of 2014–2016, the percent of whites decreased slightly to 58 percent, and only 29 percent of blacks had a great deal of confidence in the police. In the 2011–2014 poll, about 59 percent of whites stated that the honesty and ethics of police officers was very high or high, compared with 45 percent of blacks. In the more recent results, 60 percent of whites, but only 28 percent of blacks believed that the honesty and ethics of police was very high or high. In the latest poll, 76 percent of blacks say that the justice system is biased against blacks, compared with 45 percent of whites (Newport, 2014, 2016).

The issue of race permeates the criminal justice system. A recent study by the National Registry of Exonerations found that blacks are about seven times more likely to be wrongfully convicted of murder than whites, accounting for a disproportionate share of exonerations. They also spent four years longer on death row than wrongfully convicted whites. Part of the reason for this disproportionality is that there is a much higher homicide rate in the black community; thus, it follows that the wrongfully accused would also be black. However, in the cases where the wrongfully convicted is black, there is a greater likelihood of official misconduct by police or prosecutors as compared with other factors identified in wrongful convictions (Gross, Possley, and Stephens, 2017; Martelle, 2017).

Studies show that there seems to be differences in the sentencing of blacks and whites unexplained by other sentencing factors (e.g., seriousness of charge and criminal history). Blacks are less likely to receive bail, and receive harsher plea offers (Kutateladze and Andiloro, 2014). Interestingly, one study showed that black judges gave black juvenile defendants 14 percent longer sentences than white juveniles (and white judges give white offenders longer sentences). Researchers speculated that judges could be reacting unconsciously sympathetically to same-race victims, it could be because of more familiarity with same-race offenders, or it might be because judges were worried about seeming prejudiced (Guo, 2016).

The shooting of Michael Brown in Ferguson, Missouri, in the summer of 2014 sparked the "Black Lives Matter" movement. Freddie Gray's death in Baltimore resulted in violent protests. Since that time, new scrutiny has been directed at police use of force, especially deadly force, and how blacks are disproportionally killed by police. In a study of 990 civilians killed by police officers in 2015, results indicated those from minority groups were significantly less likely than whites to have been attacking the officer(s) or other civilians, and that black civilians were more than twice as likely as white civilians to have been unarmed. The authors concluded that "implicit bias" was a factor, specifically an unconscious bias of police that blacks are more dangerous (Nix, Campbell, Byers, and Alpert, 2017). Anecdotes show this disparity, for example, a black man reaches into his car for his license and is shot (Levar Jones), but a white man carries an automatic rifle and revolver into a pizza restaurant, shoots several times, and is still taken into custody by police without injury (Edgar Welch). There is also the perception that when police do use lethal force against a black suspect, they are unlikely to be punished. In 2016, a jury deadlocked and a mistrial was declared in Michael Slager's trial despite a video showing Walter Scott running away when Slager shot him. We will discuss the very complicated issue of police use of force in Chapter 6.

Racial profiling studies continue to show that black drivers are more often stopped for minor traffic offenses, more likely to receive tickets rather than warnings, and more likely to experience auto searches (but there is less likely any contraband found in searches of black drivers than white drivers). Studies show that blacks are more likely to be arrested in traffic stops for resisting, and force is more likely to be used. Critics of these studies argue that the reason police officers stop blacks more often is because they are more likely to live in high-crime areas, and traffic stops are used as crime deterrence. There is little research to indicate that this policy does much to reduce crime, but it has a clear and negative effective on police–community relations (Baumgartner, Christiani, Epp, Roach, and Shoub, 2017; Gordon, 2015; Hart, 2017; Kauffman, 2015; LaFraniere and Lehren, 2015).

The disproportionate number of arrests that lead to lost jobs and tickets and citations resulting in fines and late charges when they can't be paid are creating a widespread "poverty-tax" on minorities wherein the criminal justice system differentially draws dollars from those least able to pay (Williams, 2015b). In one study of arrests in New York City in 2014, 43,000 people were arrested for minor infractions on public transportation (as minor as putting one's foot on the subway seat), but only 3,600 were white, who make up 37 percent of public transit riders. In the first six months of 2015, of 20,000 arrests, fewer than one in 10 arrestees were white. More recently, authorities have stated they will pursue civil remedies and citations rather than use arrests for minor infractions (Sunne, 2016). In a study of Charlotte, North Carolina, blacks were more likely to be arrested for small amounts of marijuana than whites. Surveys show about the same percentage of blacks and whites use marijuana; however, in Charlotte, with blacks comprising about one-third of the city, they accounted for 74 percent of those arrested or cited with possessing marijuana. Police officers had a choice to arrest or issue a citation and, in this period, there were 762 blacks arrested for possessing less than a half-ounce of marijuana and only 64 arrests of whites. Like all studies that show disparity, there may be factors other than racial discrimination that account for the difference. Police, in response to this study, argued that police officers are more likely to arrest dealers as opposed to users, which assumes, of course, that blacks are more likely to be dealers (Harrison, 2016).

Data on police complaints in Chicago show that although blacks make up 32 percent of Chicago's population, they filed 61 percent of all complaints since 2011, but their complaints about police misconduct resulted in disciplinary action less frequently than those filed by white residents. In complaints of unlawful searches, fully three-quarters of all complaints are made by black residents of Chicago; 72 percent of complaints regarding use of force are by black residents (Ehrenfreund, 2017).

It is difficult to extricate the effects of race from other factors such as living in a high-crime area and poverty. Arguably, the differential arrests, enforcement, and interaction patterns of police and minority citizens are because they are more likely to live in high-crime areas of the city where police feel more threatened and there is, indeed, more crime to enforce. Peterson (2012) reviewed neighborhood crime studies to show that blacks and other minorities are much more likely than whites to live in structurally disadvantaged neighborhoods, and it is these neighborhoods that contribute disproportionally to crime statistics. What they found was that crime rates in the few white neighborhoods that had similar levels of structural disadvantage to minority neighborhoods had similar crime levels. The perception of minorities, especially blacks, that police are unfair and untrustworthy is ominous, especially when we see that these perceptions are getting worse not better. It is probably not a coincidence that the cities where police–citizen relations are arguably the worst in the country are also the pockets where violent crime is increasing. Some argue that crime is increasing because of the criticism directed at police, federal consent orders, and resulting low morale resulting in less proactive policing. The other side would argue that low perceptions of police legitimacy increase retaliatory violence and lack of trust in police reduces the ability to solve crime. It is obvious that police can never solve crime on their own; employing empirically based procedural justice research and community policing models to improve police–citizen interactions in minority communities may be effective tools to address crime in those communities (Serpas and Brown, 2017).

▌Restorative Justice

What would a system of justice be like if the emphasis were on the victim's rights, needs, and compensation? In a system with a primary emphasis on the victim rather than the offender, money would be spent on victim services rather than prisons. It would be victims who would receive job skills training, not offenders. Some of the money that now goes to law enforcement and corrections would be channeled to compensation programs for victims of personal and property crimes. Victims would be helped even if their offenders were not caught. The major goal would not be punishment but service. Offenders would be peripheral figures; they would be required to pay restitution to victims, and punishment would occur only if they did not fulfill their obligation to their victims. Could such a system work? Would such a system provide better justice?

restorative justice An approach to corrective justice that focuses on meeting the needs of all concerned.

Although the restorative justice movement does not propose quite this level of radical restructuring, it does dramatically redesign the justice system and offers a new alternative to retributive justice. **Restorative justice** is a term used to describe programs that seek to move compensation back to center stage in the justice system, instead of retribution. A similar, but not identical, philosophy has been called "peacemaking justice" by Braswell and Gold (2002). Programs that require the offender to confront the victim and provide compensation, and programs that place the victim in the middle of the process of deciding what to do about the offender, can be categorized under the restorative justice rubric. The propositions of the movement are as follows (Van Ness and Strong, 1997):

1. Justice requires restoring victims, offenders, and communities who have been injured by crime.

2. Victims, offenders, and communities should have the opportunity to be a fully active part of the justice process.

3. Government should restore order, but the community should establish peace.

Roman and Grecian law was compensatory; only when the offender refused to provide compensation was physical punishment employed. Gradually, however, this compensation to the victim approach was relegated to civil law, and criminal law became almost solely concerned with punishment. In the 1970s, a trend toward "community justice" was part of the larger movement of community empowerment and development. Community justice boards or local justice committees were created as part of the justice system (Schweigert, 2002). Hallmarks of community justice models include the idea that justice should be informal, employ local leadership, and encourage community participation. The goal is to repair the harm and promote the health of the community, not simply punish the offender. Customs and traditions create the authority employed to resolve disputes (Schweigert, 2002). In community or restorative justice models, crime is viewed as a natural human error that should be dealt with by the community. Offenders remain a part of the community.

In retributive justice, the question is "Who did it?" while in restorative justice, the question is "What is the harm?" In retributive justice, the question is "Which laws were broken?" while in restorative justice, the question is "What needs to be done to repair the harm?" In retributive justice, the question is "What should the punishment be?" while in restorative justice, the question is "Who is responsible for this repair?" One recent author noted that today's field of restorative justice can be broadly differentiated into four key areas: (1) victim–offender mediation schemes; (2) conferencing based on the ancient concepts held by the Aboriginals in Australia and the Maoris in New Zealand; (3) peace circles, which were used by the First Nation people in Canada and some native U.S. Indian tribes; and (4) the realm of international crimes, such as crimes against humanity and war crimes (Weitekampa and Parmentier, 2016).

Victim–offender mediation (or victim–offender reconciliation programs) involves victims and offenders meeting and agreeing upon restitution. Reparative boards have community members (rather than justice officials) decide what should happen after a crime has been committed and an offender identified. It has been found that victims are more satisfied in restorative justice programs than with traditional sentencing (79 percent compared to 57 percent). Offenders were also more likely to successfully satisfy their restitution orders in such programs (Braithwaite, 2002: 71).

Community reparative boards are more commonly used with youthful offenders. They are also called youth panels, neighborhood boards, or community diversion boards, and they have been in use in some locales since the 1920s. These boards reemerged across the country in the mid-1990s. The goals are to involve the community, provide the opportunity for the offender to take responsibility for his or her actions, and facilitate the development of prevention (Braithwaite, 2002: 73). One recent study found that 31 states had restorative justice principles incorporated in juvenile justice legislation, with 20 of those states combining the principles of restorative justice with rehabilitation and accountability. Twenty states had legislation identifying and enabling specific restorative justice programs (Pavelka, 2016: 6–8).

Family group conferencing comes from the Maori tribal model and was made a part of national legislation in New Zealand in 1989. It includes conferences of offenders, victims, families, and interested or involved others to resolve the problem. Circle sentencing, a similar model, comes from the Navajos in North America. Everyone involved directly in a criminal offense sits in a circle and gets a turn to speak. The entire circle decides what should be done. The goal is not to respond only to the current offense but also to heal the community (Braithwaite, 2002: 76).

There are potential problems with, and some criticisms of, these types of programs (Braithwaite, 2002; Dzur and Wertheimer, 2002). For instance, victims may feel pressured to forgive before they are ready. Less due process may be given to offenders because the goal is not to punish; thus, issues of guilt or innocence may be unresolved. However, restorative justice seems to offer an alternative to our traditional retributive justice system that can be supported by ethics of care, utilitarianism, religion, and possibly other ethical systems. It is more akin to older systems of law that focused on compensation rather than punishment. While legal sanctions usually do not make the victim "whole" or change the offender, restorative justice attempts to do both.

Immoral Laws and the Moral Person

We have distinguished procedural justice from substantive justice and noted that justice is not the same as law. In other words, just because the legal rules have been followed does not necessarily mean that justice occurs. Nelson Mandela, for instance, was tried by a court of law before he was imprisoned, but that legal system was part of a brutal regime of oppression. In his trial, he argued that the process was illegitimate because it did not conform to principles of natural laws of justice. The Walking the Walk box describes his life.

What is the moral duty of individuals when laws and governmental edicts are themselves immoral? Examples might include the laws of the Spanish Inquisition in the fifteenth century that resulted in large numbers of people being tortured and killed for having dissenting religious beliefs, and the Nuremberg laws of Nazi Germany stripping Jewish citizens of their citizenship as well as later laws requiring Jews to give themselves up to be transported to concentration camps and often to their death. Examples in the United States might include the internment laws during World War II that forced U.S. citizens of Japanese descent to give up land and property and be confined in camps until the end of the war, and the Jim Crow laws that once forced blacks to use different doors and water fountains than whites.

WALKING THE WALK

Nelson Mandela was imprisoned in South Africa for 27 years. He began fighting apartheid in the 1940s. In 1964, he was convicted of sabotage and treason and sentenced to a life term of imprisonment for his activities in the African National Congress Party, which had been outlawed by the government. Throughout his decades in prison, he refused to compromise his position to gain his release, arguing that "only free men can negotiate." However, he did begin secret talks in the late 1980s when he was approached by the ruling white party leaders, who gradually came to the realization that apartheid could not continue as South Africa was in danger of being torn apart by race-based violence. Eventually, Mandela's reputation grew to worldwide proportions, and he was released in 1990. In 1991, he was elected president of the African National Congress when the ban against the political party was lifted. In 1994, black South Africans voted for the first time and Mandela was elected as president of a democratic South Africa, formally ending the era of apartheid. He was awarded the Nobel Peace Prize in 1993 along with Frederik de Klerk, the South African president who released him from captivity.

(continued)

After apartheid ended, Mandela was instrumental in averting a civil war between blacks and whites. There was a strong possibility that it might happen; small numbers of blacks began a pattern of violence toward those who had cooperated with the separatist government. "Necklaces" made of burning rubber were used to burn victims alive in a pattern of retaliation. This violence was condemned by Mandela and others, and, instead, Truth and Reconciliation panels were created. These panels brought out into the open the horrors of apartheid and the brutal system that developed to protect it, but promised amnesty for those who admitted their wrongdoing. The Truth and Reconciliation panels as well as earlier conciliatory gestures, such as Mandela congratulating the white rugby team during his only term (1994–1998) as president (memorialized in the movie *Invictus*), and his refusal to use his power to attack and punish the vanquished white ruling party, led to South Africa coming out of a brutal, repressive regime to a democracy with minimal civil strife.

Throughout his life, Mandela's principles served as the guiding light for his actions and, because of those actions, a whole country was changed.

Sources: Nelson Mandela Foundation website, www.nelsonmandela.org (accessed June 14, 2012); Bryson, 2010.

These laws are now thought of as immoral, but they were not considered so by many people at the time. Boss (2001) has described unjust laws as having the following characteristics:

- They are degrading to humans.
- They are discriminatory against certain groups.
- They are enacted by unrepresentative authorities.
- They are unjustly applied.

Martin Luther King Jr., Mahatma Gandhi, and Henry David Thoreau agreed with St. Augustine that "an unjust law is no law at all." Martin Luther King Jr. said "A just law is one that is consistent with morality. An unjust law is any that degrades human personality or compels a minority to obey something the majority does not adhere to or is a law that the minority had no part in making" (quoted in Barry, 1985: 3).

One example that meets the definition, perhaps, of an immoral law was the Japanese American internment during WWII. We can also analyze it using ethical systems. The religious ethical framework would probably not provide moral support for Japanese internment because it runs contrary to some basic Christian principles, such as, "Do unto others as you would have them do unto you." Ethical formalism could not be used to support this law because it runs counter to the categorical imperative that each person must be treated as an end rather than as a means, and violates the universalism principle. The principle of forfeiture could not justify the action because these were innocent individuals, many of whom were fiercely loyal to the United States. The only ethical framework that might be used to support the morality of this law is utilitarianism. Even under utilitarianism, however, we must be able to show that the total utility derived from the action outweighed the negative effect on those impacted. Did it save the country from a Japanese invasion? Did the benefits outweigh the harm to Japanese Americans?

Are there any laws today that might be considered immoral? Many argue that holding the detainees in Guantanamo for years without any due process is in violation of the Geneva Convention as well as U.S. law and has no ethical or moral justification. Defenders argue that our actions have been necessary and morally justified as self-defense. More recently, the Trump administration's ban on individuals from selected majority-Muslim countries has been criticized as immoral and illegal. The legality of

BOX 3.2 \ Civil Disobedience

1. It must be nonviolent in form and actuality.
2. No other means of remedying the evil should be available.
3. Those who resort to civil disobedience must accept the legal sanctions and punishments imposed by law.
4. A major moral issue must be at stake.
5. When intelligent men [*sic*] of good will differ on complex moral issues, discussion is more appropriate than action.
6. There must be some reason for the time, place, and target selected.
7. One should adhere to "historical time."

Source: Hook, quoted in Fink (1977: 126–127).

the action will be determined by the Supreme Court. The morality of the action can be analyzed using ethical systems—clearly the support offered is from the utilitarian ethical perspective; however, whether the harm is outweighed by the utility derived from the ban is arguable. Arguments have also been made from a rights perspective (e.g., "those outside the United States have no *right* to enter" or " those who already have a legally issued visa or have passed background checks have a *right* to be allowed in"). Unfortunately, actions that may seem reasonable when in the grip of fear, in retrospect, may not be legally or morally justifiable.

civil disobedience
Voluntarily breaking established laws based on one's moral beliefs.

Civil disobedience is the voluntary disobedience of established laws based on one's moral beliefs (See Box 3.2). Rawls (1971) defined it as a public, nonviolent, conscientious, yet political act contrary to law and usually done with the aim of bringing about a change in the law or policies of the government. Many great social thinkers and leaders have advocated breaking certain laws thought to be wrong. Philosophers believe that the moral person follows a higher law of behavior that usually, but not necessarily, conforms to human law.

Civil disobedience is unusual because most people tend not to challenge authority. The Milgram experiments are often used to show how easily one can command blind obedience to authority. In these experiments, subjects were told to administer shocks to individuals hooked up to electrical equipment as part of a learning experiment (Milgram, 1963). Unbeknownst to the subjects, the "victims" were really associates of the experimenter and faked painful reactions only when the subjects thought they were administering shocks. In one instance, the subject and the "victim" were separated, and the subject heard only cries of pain and exclamations of distress, then silence, indicating that the "victim" was unconscious. Even when the subjects thought they were harming the "victims," they continued to administer shocks because the experimenter directed them to do so and reminded them of their duty (Milgram, 1963).

Although it is always with caution that one applies laboratory results to the real world, history shows that individual submission to authority, even immoral authority, is not uncommon. Those who turned in Jewish neighbors to Nazis and those who participated in massacres of Native Americans in this country were only following the law or instructions from a superior authority. The point is that it is a rare individual who stands up to legal authority, even when he or she believes the law to be wrong.

Remember that civil disobedience occurs when the individual truly believes the law to be wrong and therefore believes that the enforcement of it or obedience to it would also be wrong. We are not referring to chronic lawbreaking because of immediate rewards. Indeed, most criminals have a conventional sense of morality. They agree with the laws, even though they break them. Even those gray-area laws that involve disagreement over the "wrongness" of the behavior are not proper grounds for disobedience unless one believes that the government is immorally oppressing certain people.

There is a widespread belief that law is synonymous with morality and that if one remains inside the law, one can be considered a moral person. Callahan (1982: 64) points out the following:

> *We live in a society where the borderline between law and ethics often becomes blurred. For many, morality is simply doing that which the law requires; a fear of punishment is the only motivation for behavior in some minimally acceptable way.*

We should always remember that law is considered the basement of morality; even if you never break a law that does not automatically make you a moral person. There are immoral acts that are not illegal, and once in a great while some laws are immoral. Before we conclude the chapter, a dilemma will be presented along with a discussion of how consideration of law, policy, and ethics would help us in determining the right thing to do.

ETHICAL DILEMMA

You are a prosecutor involved in a case concerning a brutal murder. No DNA evidence was uncovered at the scene and there were no witnesses. The state lab examiners are unable to match a boot print left at the scene to the suspect's boot, but you find an expert who is willing to testify to a match. You also discover your expert has been sanctioned in another state for overstating her qualifications and her testimony has been excluded in other states because it does not meet legal tests for admission of expert testimony. Would you share such information with the defense? Would you use this expert's testimony at all?

Law

In *Brady v. Maryland*, 373 U.S. 83, 1963, the Supreme Court held that due process required that prosecutors divulge any exculpatory information to the defense. Not doing so could result in a reversal of a conviction. For scientific evidence to be admitted, it must meet the "*Daubert* standard" in most states. This guidance came from the Supreme Court in *Daubert v. Merrell Dow Pharmaceuticals Inc.*, 509 U.S. 579, 1993. Before admitting scientific evidence, the *Daubert* standard requires the information to be proven relevant and reliable based on several criteria provided by the Court, including whether the findings were subject to peer review and whether the theory or method is accepted in the scientific community. The guidance still leaves a great deal of discretion to the judge in whether to admit expert testimony.

Policy

Since a National Academy of Science's 2009 report on forensic science, many in the criminal justice system are more skeptical of forensic testimony, especially in the areas where the examiner uses subjective judgment to determine whether a match exists between footprints, bite marks, or hair. That doesn't mean this type of evidence is not still being admitted, but it does mean that many district attorney offices are more careful now in the use of such testimony. Some offices may have policies that direct whether prosecutors can "shop" for experts or whether they must utilize only the state lab examiners. It is possible office policies exist that promote an "open file" approach where nothing in the case is hidden from defense. If that was the case, then the defense would know everything about the expert witness that the prosecutor knows. Most offices do not have open file policies, however.

(continued)

Ethics

Recall that the steps in making an ethical decision are to identify the facts, the concepts, the ethical dilemmas, the main dilemma, and then resolve it by applying an ethical system. In this case, the facts known to the prosecutor are that the boot print match has been made by one expert, but not by the state forensic examiner, and that there is information that calls into question the expert witness's credentials. The relevant concepts are justice, of course, but also professionalism, honor, and honesty. The two dilemmas are whether to use the expert witness testimony and whether to share the negative information with the defense counsel. The utilitarian ethical system would weigh up the costs and benefits of both sides. Since it is possible that any conviction that resulted might be overturned, it would serve the greater good to share the information if the testimony was used. It's possible that the greater good would also be served by not utilizing such problematic testimony, especially since the defense counsel would probably discredit the expert witness on the stand with the information provided. Ethical formalism would also probably not support utilizing such information since the system requires one to do one's duty and follow the categorical imperative. In this case, the prosecutor probably would not want to universalize the practice of using potentially discredited expert witnesses. The duty of a prosecutor is to seek justice, not a conviction; therefore, it is one's ethical duty to make sure that all the protections of due process occur in any prosecution.

Conclusion

In this chapter, we have explored the origins and components of justice. Typically, justice includes the concepts of fairness, equality, and impartiality. Justice was defined by Aristotle as being either distributive or corrective. Distributive justice concerns the allocations of goods and opportunities in society. Corrective justice is the central concern of the criminal justice system and can be further divided into substantive and procedural issues. Substantive justice is concerned with the fairness of what we do to offenders; procedural justice is concerned with the procedures that must be undertaken before punishment occurs. Research shows that people who perceive they are treated unfairly by justice professionals lose faith in the procedural justice of the system and are less likely to follow the law. The failings of procedural justice can be seen in wrongful convictions and the perceptions of minorities that criminal justice actors, especially those in law enforcement, act in a discriminatory manner. Restorative justice is a new approach that has ancient roots. It focuses attention on the victim rather than the offender. A special concern is when the legal system is unjust and immoral. Principles of civil disobedience allow us to provide guidance as to when a moral person might legitimately oppose a law.

Chapter Review

1. **Describe the three themes included in the definition of justice.**

   Most definitions of justice include the concepts of fairness (equal treatment), equality (equal shares), and impartiality (absence of bias). Justice acts to mediate our impulses of selfishness and fairness. Justice is distinguished from goodness.

2. **Define Aristotle's distributive and corrective justice.**

   Aristotle described two forms of justice: distributive justice (which concerns the fair distribution of goods and opportunities in society) and corrective justice (which concerns the fair resolution in controversies when unjust enrichment or unfair advantage occurs, either through civil or criminal wrongs).

3. **Distinguish between substantive justice and procedural justice, including how procedural justice impacts wrongful convictions and perceptions of racial discrimination.**

   Substantive justice concerns the inherent fairness of a law or punishment. One issue of substantive justice is fair punishment. Punishment can be supported by either retributive or utilitarian rationales. Procedural justice is concerned with the steps taken before punishment is administered. For instance, a substantive justice question would be "Is capital punishment just?" while a procedural justice question would be "What due process should apply before a decision of capital punishment is just?" Procedural justice research shows that when people are treated in conformance to justice concepts (voice, neutrality, equity, and dignity), they feel the entire justice system is more legitimate. When procedural justice is not followed, wrongful convictions are more likely to occur and groups of citizens (especially minorities) feel that justice professionals treat them unfairly.

4. **Explain the concept of restorative justice and the programs associated with it.**

   Restorative justice puts the emphasis on making the victim whole and maintaining bonds between the community, the victim, and the offender. Types of restorative justice programs include victim–offender mediation (or victim–offender reconciliation programs), reparative boards, family group conferencing, and circle sentencing.

5. **Describe civil disobedience and when it may be appropriate.**

   Laws that may be subject to civil disobedience must be immoral and unjust. For instance, they could be degrading, discriminatory, enacted by unrepresentative authorities, or unjustly applied. Civil disobedience must be nonviolent, there should be no other alternative, one must accept the legal consequences, and there should be a major moral issue at stake. If people of good will disagree on the matter, then civil disobedience is not appropriate.

Key Terms

civil disobedience	fairness	restorative justice
confirmatory bias	hedonistic calculus	retributive justice
corrective justice	impartiality	sanctuary
distributive justice	Innocence Project	substantive justice
due process	justice	utilitarian justice
equality	procedural justice	veil of ignorance

Study Questions

1. Explain how Plato and Aristotle associated status with justice.
2. Describe distributive and corrective justice. Identify how different systems under distributive justice would allocate the resources of society.
3. Describe Rawls' system of distributive and corrective justice.
4. Describe retributive and utilitarian rationales for punishment. Explain due process and how it fits with procedural justice. What are the elements of due process?
5. Describe some types of restorative justice programs. What ethical systems support restorative justice?

Writing/Discussion Exercises

1. Write an essay on (or discuss) how the government should distribute societal resources such as education and healthcare. How would you answer the argument of a couple who did not believe they should have to pay school taxes because they have no children? What about the argument that rich school districts should share their wealth with poor districts (keeping in mind that those who pay higher taxes in that district might have moved there because of the reputation of the school)? What are the arguments for and against universal healthcare?

2. Write an essay on (or discuss) the following issues under substantive and procedural justice:

   a. What is the proper punishment for a burglary, for a murder in an armed robbery, and for a million-dollar embezzlement? If you were being punished for a crime, would you rather receive a year in prison or 50 lashes? Why do we not use corporal punishment for criminal offenders? Do you think we should? Are there situations in our justice system where victims or offenders are treated differently than others because of who they are?

   b. An 87-year-old man living in Chicago is exposed as a soldier who took part in killing hundreds of Jewish concentration camp victims. U.S. extradition procedures are followed to the letter, and he is extradited to Israel to stand trial, as Israeli law determines that courts in Israel have jurisdiction over Nazi war crimes. Israeli legal procedure is followed without error, and he is convicted of war crimes and sentenced to death.

   c. Federal law enforcement agents determine that a citizen of another country participated in a drug cartel that sold drugs in the United States. A small group of agents goes to the foreign country, kidnaps the offender, drugs him, and brings him back to the United States to stand trial. Upon challenge, the government agents explain that, although these actions would have been unconstitutional and illegal against a citizen of the United States in this country, because they were conducted on foreign soil against a non-U.S. citizen, they were not illegal.

3. Write an essay on (or discuss) whether civil disobedience is ever justified. Discuss war protesters or antiabortion activists who are arrested for trespassing and so on. If you believe that civil disobedience might be justified, when and in what circumstances would it be acceptable?

ETHICAL DILEMMAS

Situation 1

Two individuals are being sentenced for the exact same crime of burglary. You are the judge. One of the individuals is a 20-year-old who has not been in trouble before and participated only because the other individual was his friend. The second person has a history of juvenile delinquency and is now 25. Would you sentence them differently? How would you justify your decision?

Situation 2

In your apartment building, your neighbors are a Hispanic family of a mother, father, and two sons. You do not know them well, but you say hello when you see any of them, and they seem pleasant. One day there is a commotion in the building and, asking around, you find out that the father and oldest son have been taken away by ICE because they are in this country illegally. You find out from other neighbors that only the youngest son, who is 12, is in the country legally because he was born here. During the next several days you find out that the father and son will most likely be deported. Several neighbors have organized to try and help them. They ask you to sign a petition, come to a rally in front of the federal courthouse and donate money for their legal defense. Would you agree to any of these actions? Why or why not?

Situation 3

You are serving on a jury for a murder trial. The evidence presented at trial was largely circumstantial and, in your mind, equivocal. During closing, the prosecutor argues that you must find the defendant guilty because he confessed to the crime. The defense attorney immediately objects, and the judge sternly instructs the jury to disregard the prosecutor's statement. Although you do not know exactly what happened, you suspect that the confession was excluded because of some procedural error. Would you be able to ignore the prosecutor's statement in your deliberations? Should you? Would you tell the judge if the jury members discussed the statement and seemed to be influenced by it?

Situation 4

You are a probation officer who must prepare sentencing recommendation reports for the judge. The juvenile defendant to be sentenced in one case grew up in a desperately poor family, according to school records. He had a part-time job in a local grocery store, stocking the shelves and providing general cleanup. The store owner caught him stealing meat. This is the second time he has been caught stealing food. The first time he shoplifted at the store, the deferred adjudication included his commitment to work for the store owner. He explained that he was trying to help his mother, who could not provide enough food for his family. In general, failure to succeed at deferred adjudication results in a commitment to a juvenile facility. What would you recommend to the judge?

Situation 5

You are an ardent liberal who believes that President Trump's election was tainted by Russian interference. You plan to participate in a march in Washington, D.C., to oppose the President and his policies. At the march, several individuals plan to jump the fence of the White House and stage a sit-in. You know that the planned activities will constitute trespass and you will be arrested. Would you participate? Why or why not?

Becoming an Ethical Professional

4

In all professions, young recruits look to their leaders, like Chief Art Acevedo of the Houston Police Department, for direction and guidance. Leaders dramatically affect the ethical climate of an organization.

AP Images/Yi-Chin Lee

Learning Objectives

1. Describe biological influences on ethical behavior.
2. Describe psychological theories that attempt to explain individual differences in behavior.
3. Describe research that addresses work group influences on behavior.
4. Explain organizational influences on behavior.
5. Explain the cultural and societal influences on ethical behavior.

In this chapter, we shift from the discussion of "What is ethical?" to "Why do some people act ethically and others act unethically?" Why people act the way they do has been the question for philosophers, religious scholars, psychologists, sociologists, psychiatrists, economists, and, more recently, criminologists. There is an obvious overlap between criminologists' question: "Why do people commit crime?" and the one we ask here: "Why do people commit unethical acts?" In some cases, when the unethical acts are also crimes, the question is the same.

The sections that follow very briefly explore influences on ethical decision making. We will approach this question in a way that is visually represented in Figure 4.1. Arguably, one's morals and value systems are well established by the time one enters the workforce; thus, a dishonest, egoistic employee will be more likely to choose unethical behavior when the opportunity exists than another employee who values honesty and lives by a strong moral code. The section on individual influences on ethical behavior will be the first and longest discussion in the chapter because we assume that, generally, an adult's character is well formed by the time they begin their

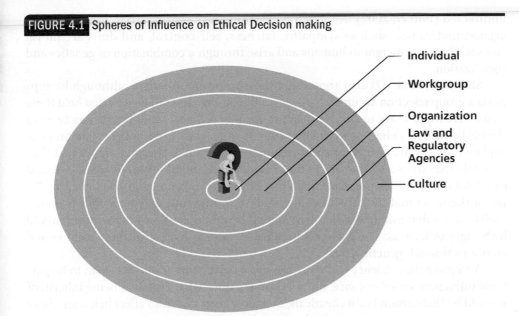

FIGURE 4.1 Spheres of Influence on Ethical Decision making

- Individual
- Workgroup
- Organization
- Law and Regulatory Agencies
- Culture

professional life. There is also evidence to indicate, however, that our ethical decision making can be influenced by external factors, even into adulthood. An employee can be influenced by peers in a micro-climate of a workgroup. In ethical scandals, it is often the case that the deviant behavior is limited to a small work group or division. Micro-climates can be created in even medium-sized organizations if they are isolated and unmonitored. An employee can also be influenced by larger organizational influences, for example, reward structures, training, and leadership. These factors play an important role in encouraging ethical behavior or facilitating unethical behavior. Finally, cultural and societal factors may influence the level of ethical behavior one finds in any given public service organization.

Individual Influences

Why do some people lie and others tell the truth in similar situations? Why do some people take advantage of others, while others never would? How does one develop from an amoral infant to a virtuous adult? These are fascinating questions, and we can only skim the surface of the vast amount of literature that exists on the subject, briefly discussing biological and psychological research that helps us understand moral development and ethical decision making.

Biological Factors

There has been a long research tradition of exploring genetic influences on behavior. Accumulated findings indicate that identical twins are more similar than fraternal twins in the presence of schizophrenia, autism, dyslexia, learning disabilities, gambling addictions, and criminality (Fishbein, 2000; Pinker, 2002). Genetics evidently plays a role in the presence of personality traits that may impact ethical decision making, including such differences as whether someone is introverted/extroverted, neurotic/stable, incurious/open to new experiences, agreeable/antagonistic, and conscientious/

undirected (Pinker, 2002). Although his position was controversial, Wilson (1993) argued that values, such as sympathy, fairness, self-control, and duty, are moral "senses" that are inherent in humans and arise through a combination of genetics and socialization.

Shermer (2004: 37) also argues that these traits are inherited, although he supports a group selection argument—specifically, eons ago human groups that held these traits were more likely to survive than groups that did not. In an interesting twist to the philosophical debate as to whether morals exist apart from humans (natural law explanations) or are created by them (relativism positions), Shermer argues that they are both: they transcend humans in the sense that our moral senses have been created by evolutionary factors that have taken place over the millennia; however, they are "of us" in the sense that they are human emotions, sentiments, and behaviors. Shermer (2004) states that asking why humans should be moral is like asking why we should be hungry or jealous. The answer is because we are hardwired for these feelings and emotions through genetic selection.

Accepting the evidence that there are some personality traits that seem to be partially influenced by inheritance, the question remains: what exactly is being inherited? It could be that certain brain chemicals, that have been shown to affect behavior, differ among individuals and the relative levels of these chemicals (or "receptors" that allow the brain to utilize the chemicals) may be inherited. Oxytocin, serotonin, and dopamine have been identified as related to nurturing, trusting, and prosocial attitudes and behaviors; while testosterone, cortisol, and epinephrine have been associated with aggression, anxiousness, and suspiciousness.

Paul Zak (2012), a neuroeconomist, focuses on the importance of oxytocin, going so far as to call it the "moral molecule." He argues that this hormone promotes human bonding and trust. Oxytocin stimulates uterine contractions in pregnant women and is released during the act of nursing an infant, but it is also released when people pet their dogs, have sex, or hug someone. The brain releases oxytocin in settings where there are feelings of trust and safety and this leads to greater feelings of trust, which promotes altruistic reciprocity.

Evidently some people have normal levels of oxytocin but few receptors in the brain, so they cannot feel the effects of it. These individuals are, according to Zak, "at best selfish and at worst psychopaths" (quoted in Haederle, 2010: 47). Testosterone is found to counteract the effect of oxytocin, and those who are administered testosterone are less likely to be generous and trusting and more likely to punish opponents (Zak, 2012). Another inhibitor to oxytocin reception is cortisol, which increases during perceived stress (Yong, 2012).

Others dispute the emphasis Zak has placed on morality and trust, arguing that exactly what oxytocin does to the brain is not well understood, but it has more to do with a general desire for sociability (Yong, 2012). Sometimes the administration of oxytocin in experimental conditions leads to trusting behaviors, as Zak found, but in other scenarios, oxytocin spurs in-group favoritism against out-group members and has resulted in dishonesty by subjects when the dishonesty benefits the in-group (Yong, 2014). It is possible that oxytocin simply increases a drive for social interactions. This improves trust in some situations, but could also spur bias and favoritism in others. Another possibility is that oxytocin increases our sensitivity to social cues. Those who are naturally sociable react with positive behavior; those who are anxious or antisocial do not (Yong, 2012).

The discovery of oxytocin and its effects have generated a great deal of research and speculation as to how brain chemistry influences moral judgment. Churchland (2011) is a neurophilosopher who explains how the hardwiring of the brain to promote bonding and empathy, primarily through the effects of oxytocin, is the fundamental building block of all moral reasoning. Churchland argues that morality originates in the neurobiology of attachment and bonding. Oxytocin is an evolutionary necessity to promote mother–infant bonding and can be the vehicle by which individuals experience care extended to others beyond one's own offspring. Recall from Chapter 2 that ethics of care basically argues this same principle, albeit without the biological explanation.

The neurotransmitter serotonin also seems to directly alter both moral judgment and behavior based on experimental research. Researchers enhanced serotonin in healthy volunteers and contrasted its effects with both a control and a placebo on tests of moral judgment utilizing a set of hypothetical moral dilemmas. Enhancing serotonin made subjects more likely to judge harmful actions as forbidden, and increased subjects' aversion to personally harming others. Findings provided evidence that serotonin could promote prosocial behavior by enhancing harm aversion, thereby directly affecting both moral judgment and moral behavior (Crockett, Clark, Hauser, and Robbins, 2010).

While oxytocin and serotonin have been examined for their role in prosocial judgments and behavior, testosterone has long been identified as being associated with aggression. Since men have more testosterone than women, studies that identify sex differences are probably not only measuring socialization differences between men and women but are also chronicling the effects of testosterone and other sex hormones. Over 70 studies examining sex differences in brain functioning found evidence that men are more likely to cheat, more antisocial, commit more serious types of offenses, and more often have serious childhood conduct disorders. There are also sex differences in delinquency, school performance, hyperactivity, impulsivity, and attention-deficit disorders (Ellis and Pontius, 1989; Emerson and McKinney, 2010; Hatamyar and Simmons, 2002; Lau and Haug, 2011; White, 1999).

In addition to brain chemistry, scientists have been studying the different parts of the brain and their relationship to moral judgment. One study showed that the brain seems to be hardwired for moral judgment. In the study, individuals were shown sequences where a victim was injured either accidentally or intentionally. The intentional harm sequence produced a response in the brain within 60 milliseconds in the right posterior superior temporal sulcus, followed within 180 milliseconds by a response in the amygdala and the ventromedial prefrontal cortex. However, when the harm sequence was accidental, there was no such response in the amygdala and ventromedial prefrontal cortex. The amygdala is associated with emotion and the ventromedial prefrontal cortex plays a critical role in moral decision making. Researchers conclude that the brain is "hardwired" to respond to harm with moral judgments which appear to emerge almost instantaneously from the emotional center of the brain (Harms, 2012).

In another study, subjects were given a moral dilemma involving a woman hiding from enemy soldiers with others in a cellar when her baby starts crying. When test subjects are asked to imagine what they would do in this situation, two areas of the subjects' brains light up in MRIs—the inferior parietal lobe, which is related to rational but impersonal thinking, and the amygdala, the part of the brain connected with emotion. Both parts of the brain showed activity. This indicates that moral decision making is both rational and emotional. Arguably, the subjects were reasoning that the solution was to smother the baby to save everyone (which is utilitarian reasoning), but the amygdala indicated there was a strong emotional response to this horrible solution (Vedantam, 2007). Other researchers have also accumulated findings that moral decision making seems to take place in the emotion centers (e.g., the amygdala) of the brain and the frontal lobes, an area responsible for rational thinking and conscience (Moll et al., 2005; Shermer 2004).

The frontal lobes of the brain seem to be implicated in not only reasoning but also feelings of empathy, shame, and moral reasoning. Phineas Gage was a railroad worker in the early part of the twentieth century and became a textbook celebrity when an accident resulted in an iron spike impaling itself into the frontal lobes of his brain. He miraculously recovered but changed from being a shy, soft-spoken, easygoing individual to one who was irascible, quick to anger, unpleasant, and quarrelsome (Pinker, 2002). The physical injury to his brain changed his personality. Individuals with frontal-lobe damage (like Phineas Gage) display characteristics that may be related to unethical behaviors, including increased impulsiveness, decreased attention span, tendency toward rude, unrestrained, tactless behavior, and a tendency to not be able to follow instructions, even after being able to verbalize what is required (Ellis and Pontius, 1989).

In another study, researchers compared those who had prefrontal lobe damage to those who had damage to other parts of the brain or no damage, and found that, when presented with a moral dilemma, those with prefrontal lobe damage had no difficulty applying utilitarian reasoning to moral judgments; however, they experienced no emotional aversion to harming individuals. That is, they readily concluded that the solution to problems such as the woman with the crying baby was to smother the baby, but experienced no conflict or emotional reaction, as would individuals without damage to that part of the brain (Koenigs et al., 2007). Other research also indicated that those with damage to the ventromedial prefrontal cortex, which is related to emotions, were unable to have any feelings regarding moral judgments (e.g., sympathy for others' pain and suffering or good feelings from altruism), although they were quite able to impersonally and coldly evaluate costs and benefits (Vedantam, 2007).

Researchers have found that when subjects performed altruistic acts, their behavior triggered the pleasure center of the brain, connected with food and sex. This indicates that altruistic moral behaviors are hardwired into humans' basic impulses. The argument of some researchers is that morality lies in empathy, which derives from the emotional center of the brain. They say that only much later in evolution did the reasoning area of the brain develop and become involved in moral decision making (Vedantam, 2007).

This is an interesting scientific discussion that seems to parallel the distinction between ethical systems seated in emotion compared to those based in rationality. Emotion-based ethical systems such as ethics of care utilize the premises and approach of earlier philosophers such as David Hume (1711–1776) who believed that moral decisions were ultimately emotional. This contrasts with rational, formulistic ethical systems, such as utilitarianism and ethical formalism, that

QUOTE & **QUERY**

Reason is, and ought only to be the slave of the passions, and can never pretend to any other office than to serve and obey them.

Source: David Hume, A Treatise of Human Nature (1739).

 What is David Hume saying in this quote? Does he believe that moral beliefs arise from one's heart or head?

presume that intellectual development is necessary for moral decision making and that ethical and moral decisions can be arrived at through reason.

When we look at other fields of study, there is a parallel contrast in that some theories are based on the idea that humans make decisions rationally, while others focus on emotional responses. For instance, rational-choice theories of crime argue that criminals choose to commit crime based on rationally weighing the opportunities and risks (see, Cohen and Felson, 1979), and theories in business ethics presume that employees look at financial stakes and detection risk (see, Tabish and Jha, 2012). These theories view the individual as rationally weighing risk and reward. Other explanations of behavior point to emotional or relationship-based decision making (see, social bond theory, Hirschi, 1969). Some theorists mix the two approaches in that shame or guilt is one of a number of perceived risks that are correlated with not committing the crime. Since, arguably, shame is an emotion based on relationships, this is an explanation that utilizes both rational and emotional motivations for behavior (see, Grasmick and Bursik, 1990). To complicate things further, other researchers have found that rational factors (risk of being caught and level of punishment) are only statistically significant in predicting crimes when moral norms are low (Kroneberg, Heintze, and Mehlkop, 2010).

Jonathan Haidt (2001) describes the relationship between emotions and rationality as a rider on an elephant, with the "elephant" representing the subjective, emotional component of humans' reactions to behavioral choices and the "rider" representing cognitive, rational, ethical decision making. The point of this discussion is that the rider can't control the elephant very well; in other words, emotional reactions and responses overwhelm rationality in many circumstances.

Others utilize different terminology to describe the same phenomenon: specifically, System 1 decision making (emotional, intuitive, and immediate), and System 2 decision making (rational, deliberate, and taking time to weigh various options) (Bazerman and Tenbrunsel, 2011). These researchers found that when workers are busy and stressed, they are more likely to make unethical choices because, possibly, the brain processes responsible for rationally deciding the correct action are already overloaded with other demands (Bazerman and Tenbrunsel, 2011). When individuals have time to reflect on their ethical choices after the fact, they often report that they wished they had done something different. Immediate decisions are influenced by biological instincts, emotional needs, and socialized values, and these influences are not necessarily operating at a conscious level. Thus, a worker may cheat on an expense voucher because of an emotional urge to get something they want and then create a post hoc rationalization for why it wasn't dishonest (e.g., "everyone does it" or "the company doesn't pay me enough").

Learning Theory

Learning theorists believe that children learn what they are taught, including *morals* and *values* as well as behavior. In other words, our beliefs about right or wrong and behavior are shaped by rewards and punishments, especially during our childhood. This learning can take place through modeling or by reinforcement. Note that criminology has also developed learning theory somewhat separately from what has occurred in psychology. Sutherland (1947), Burgess and Akers (1966), and then Akers (1998) have utilized learning theory to explain criminality.

modeling
Learning theory concept that people learn behaviors, values, and attitudes through relationships; they identify with another person and want to be like that person and pattern themselves after the "model."

reinforcement
Rewards.

In **modeling**, values and moral beliefs come from those whom one admires and aspires to identify with. It is no surprise that, when asked who has been important in their moral development, most people say it is their parents, because primary care-givers are the most significant people in life during the important formative years. Although we may not hold the same views and have the same values as our parents, they are influential in our value formation. Note the similarity of this description of moral growth to that of Aristotle's who believed that one became virtuous by following the example of virtuous people.

Another way learning takes place is through **reinforcement**. Behaviors and beliefs that are reinforced (either through material rewards or through more subjective rewards, such as praise) are repeated and eventually become permanent. In one experiment, children were told a hypothetical story in which an adult punished a neutral act, such as a child practicing a musical instrument. The children later defined that act as bad, despite the intrinsic neutrality of the action. This indicates the power of adult definitions and punishment in the child's moral development (Boyce and Jensen, 1978). Large gains in moral maturity (at least as measured by paper-and-pencil tests of expression of beliefs) can be achieved by direct manipulation of rewards for such beliefs (Boyce and Jensen, 1978).

Albert Bandura (born 1925) described how the successful use of rewards is related to the child's age. As the child matures, concrete rewards and external sanctions are replaced by symbolic and internal controls, such as one's conscience (Bandura, 1964). Eventually, Bandura described the individual as not simply a passive recipient of rewards, but rather, as an active participant in the construction and meaning of rewards (Bandura, 1969, 1971). In this view, individuals are active, not passive; self-reflective, not merely acted upon; and self-regulating, not merely controlled by external forces. Bandura's later work revolved around his development of the concept of self-efficacy and moral identity. **Self-efficacy** can be defined as the individual's feelings of competence, and this sense is developed by comparing the self to others. The idea of a **moral identity** is composed of *moral agency*, which involves intent, anticipation of consequences, and self-regulation; and *moral efficacy*, which is the belief that one can successfully decide to act in moral ways.

self-efficacy
Individuals' feelings of competence and confidence in their own abilities and power, developed by comparing self to others.

moral identity
Composed of *moral agency*, which involves intent, anticipation of consequences, and self-regulation; and *moral efficacy*, which is the belief that one can successfully decide to act in moral ways.

One's values are formed during childhood, perhaps through modeling and/or reinforcement. Recall from Chapter 1 that values and ethics are related. Milton Rokeach (1918–1988) developed a value survey that is still in wide use today. He proposed that there are terminal values which would be the preferences for one's ideal life: true friendship, mature love, self-respect, happiness, inner harmony, equality, freedom, pleasure, social recognition, wisdom, salvation, family security, national security, a sense of accomplishment, a world of beauty, a world at peace, a comfortable life, and an exciting life. There are also instrumental values, which are one's preferences for *how to live* one's life: cheerfulness, ambition, love, cleanliness, self-control, capability, courage, politeness, honesty, imagination, independence, intellect, broad-mindedness, logic, obedience, helpfulness, responsibility, and forgiveness (Rokeach, 1973).

Much research exists that evaluates the correlation between values and workplace behavior, although findings are mixed. Fritzsche (1995), for instance, found that value systems somewhat predicted types of wrongdoing in the workplace (e.g., bribery, conflict of interest, and product misrepresentation). For instance, he found that the values of wisdom and honesty were negatively related to lying, and independence was positively related to whistleblowing. The idea that different values affect different types of ethical behavior is an interesting finding and suggests the complexity of ethical decision making.

Kohlberg's Moral Stage Theory

Developmental theories propose that individuals mature physically, cognitively, and emotionally. Physical development—such as height and weight—can be charted by a pediatrician. Intellectual development is measured by a variety of intelligence tests and is charted against a normal curve of development. Emotional or social development also progresses at a predictable and normal pace, although it may be more difficult to measure. Social maturity is marked by the ability to empathize with others and a willingness to compromise one's desires with others' needs. An emotionally mature person balances individual needs with others' demands; however, that development might be stunted by negative environmental influences.

Jean Piaget (1896–1980) believed individuals go through stages of cognitive, or intellectual, growth that is related to their moral awareness. Piaget studied the rules that children develop in their play. Children move from egocentrism to cooperativeness as they learn to play with others; eventually organized play and sports teach children about roles and duties. Lawrence Kohlberg (1927–1987) carried on with Piaget's work and more fully described the stages that individuals pass through in moral development (Kohlberg, 1984).

Kohlberg's moral stages consist of three levels of moral reasoning, with two stages in each level (Kohlberg, 1976). According to Kohlberg and his colleagues, each stage involves qualitative differences in the way the individual sees the world. Cognitive development and moral development are integrated—that is, one must grow intellectually to achieve a higher moral stage. One cannot skip stages, they are hierarchical; however, some people will not advance to the highest stages (Hersh, 1979: 52).

At the *pre-conventional level*, the person approaches a moral issue motivated purely by personal interests. The major concern is the consequence of the action for the individual. Young children first start sharing when they perceive benefit to themselves, such as giving someone their doll in exchange for a game or a ball, or they grudgingly share because they fear punishment from an adult if they do not.

At the *conventional level*, people perceive themselves as members of society, and living up to role responsibilities is paramount in believing oneself to be good. Children enter this level when they can play with other children according to rules. Games and play are training grounds for moral development because they teach the child that there are defined roles and rules of behavior. For instance, a game of softball becomes a microcosm of real life when a child realizes that he or she is not only acting as self but also as a first baseman, a role that includes certain specific tasks. Children learn to submerge individual interest to conform to rules and role expectations.

At the *post-conventional level*, a person moves beyond the norms and laws of a society to determine universal good—that is, what is good for all societies. Few people reach this level, and their actions are observably different from the majority. For instance, Mahatma Gandhi might be described as having a post-conventional morality. He acted in accordance with his belief in a higher order of morality. At this level of moral development, the individual assumes the responsibility of judging laws and conventions. In Figure 4.2, the six stages are illustrated.

Kohlberg advanced the possibility of a seventh stage, which has been described as a "soft" stage of ethical awareness with an orientation of cosmic or religious thinking. It is not a higher level of reasoning, but is qualitatively different. According to Kohlberg, in this highest stage individuals have come to terms with questions such as "Why be just in a universe that is largely unjust?" This is a different question than the

developmental theories
Psychological theories that identify and chart individuals' normal growth phases in areas such as morality and emotional maturity.

Kohlberg's moral stages
Hierarchical moral development described as stages; each higher developmental stage is described as moving away from pure egoism toward altruism.

FIGURE 4.2 Kohlberg's Moral Stages

Pre-conventional Level: Egoistic	*Stage 1* has a punishment and obedience orientation. What is right is that which is praised; what is wrong is that which is punished. The child submits to an authority figure's definition and is concerned only with the consequences attached to certain behaviors, not with the behavior itself.
	Stage 2 has an instrument-and-relativity orientation. The child becomes aware of and is concerned with others' needs. What is right is still determined by self-interest, but the concept of self-interest is broadened to include those who are within the child's sphere of relationships. Relationships are important to the child, and he or she is attached to parents, siblings, and best friends, who are included in the ring of self-interest. There is also the emerging concept of fairness and a recognition that others deserve to have their needs met.
Conventional Level: Fitting into Society	*Stage 3* has an interpersonal concordance orientation. The individual performs conventionally determined good behavior to be considered a good person. The views of "significant others" are important to self-concept. Thus, individuals will control their behavior so as to not hurt others' feelings or be thought of as bad.
	Stage 4 has a law-and-order orientation. The individual is concerned not just with interpersonal relationships but also with the rules set down by society. The law becomes all-important. Even if the laws themselves are wrong, one cannot disregard them, for that would invite social chaos.
Post-conventional Level: Transcending Society	*Stage 5* has a social contract orientation. The person recognizes interests larger than current laws. This individual is able to evaluate the morality of laws in a historical context and feels an obligation to the law because of its benefits to societal survival.
	Stage 6 centers on universal ethical principles. The person who has reached this stage bases moral judgments on the higher abstract laws of truth, justice, and morality.

Source: Kohlberg, 1984.

---

definition of justice that forms the content of the other stages. In this stage, one sees oneself as part of a larger whole, and humanity as only part of a larger cosmic structure. This stage focuses on *agape*—a nonexclusive love and acceptance of the cosmos and one's place in it (Kohlberg, 1983; Power and Kohlberg, 1980).

Kohlberg has been criticized for focusing too much on the concept of justice, ignoring other aspects of morality. In fact, it is argued that the way he defines moral development is culturally biased, reflecting only Judeo-Christian concepts of morality. He has also been criticized for focusing too much on rational thinking as opposed to emotional aspects of morality (Levine, Kohlberg, and Hewer, 1985: 99). There has also been research that indicates the stages are not necessarily invariant or form a coherent explanation for people's moral beliefs (Bandura, 1991: 49; Boyce and Jensen, 1978).

Another criticism is that Kohlberg's research can be described as sexually biased because he interviewed only boys in early research. Carol Gilligan (1982, 1987), one of Kohlberg's students, researched an apparent sex difference in moral reasoning and proposed that women may possess a morality *different* from men. Most men, it seems, analyze moral decisions with a rules or justice orientation (stage 4), whereas many women see the same moral dilemma with an orientation toward needs and relationships (stage 3). Gilligan labeled this a *care perspective.* A morality based on the care perspective (which is like the ethics-of-care system described in Chapter 2) would be more inclined to look at how a decision affects relationships and addresses needs, whereas the justice perspective is concerned with notions of equality, rights, and universality.

In Gilligan's study, although both men and women raised justice and care concerns in responses to moral dilemmas, among those who focused on one or the other, men focused exclusively on justice, whereas half of the women who exhibited a focus did so on justice concerns and the other half on care concerns (Gilligan, 1987). She also found that male and female respondents alike could switch from a justice perspective to a care perspective (or back again) when asked to do so; thus, their orientation was more a matter of perspective than an inability to see the other side. What Gilligan points out in her research is that the care perspective completely drops out when one uses only male subjects—which is what Kohlberg did in his early research for the moral stage theory.

In later studies, researchers have found small or no differences between men and women using stage scoring. The type of ethical dilemma seems to be important with dilemmas involving interpersonal relationships bringing out care concerns more than others (Flanagan and Jackson, 1987; Jaffee and Hyde, 2000; Loo, 2003; Rothbart, Hanley, and Albert, 1986; Thoma, 1986; Walker, 1986). Other research has found that moral orientations showed no stability over time or circumstance (Jaffee and Hyde, 2000).

There also seems to be mixed evidence of any correlation between moral stage scores as measured by psychological tests and actual behavior (Lutwak and Hennessy, 1985). Almost all studies of moral development utilize measures of moral judgment derived from Kohlberg's research. The more involved method is to interview subjects and code their responses into Kohlberg's moral stages; however, this method is time-consuming and expensive, and therefore, paper-and-pencil tests have been developed. These so-called "**recognition tests**" require the subject merely to recognize and identify certain moral principles and agree with them. The most common is Rest's DIT (Defining Issues Test). Recognition tests may be less helpful in predicting behavior than "production" measures, which require the subject to reason through a dilemma and provide some rationale, but they have the advantage of cost effectiveness (Aleixo and Norris, 2000; Gavaghan, Arnold, and Gibbs, 1983).

recognition tests
Paper-and-pencil tests that measure an individual's ability to recognize and/ or agree with moral terms.

Using these measures of morality, research has been accumulating as to what attributes are associated with higher scores on ethical reasoning. Although findings seem to be mixed, some correlates include strength of religious belief (but not necessarily church attendance) and being female. Some research has also found older individuals have higher scores on measures of morality. In studies on college campuses, it has been found by some researchers that business students exhibit lower scores on measures of ethics than other majors. Some studies do find moral development scores and actions to be correlated (Ashkanasy, Windsor, and Trevino, 2006; Greenberg, 2002; Seiler, Frischer, and Ooi, 2010). Lau and Haug (2011), for instance, found that ethical beliefs were related to cheating in a college sample. In another study, "honesty scores" for people in three organizations were compiled from an attitudinal questionnaire about beliefs. It was found that the organization with the highest average honesty score had the least employee theft, and the organization with the lowest average honesty score had the most employee theft (Adams, 1981).

In contrast, other studies have found no correlation between ethical beliefs and behavior. In a study of clinical psychology students, only 37 percent indicated that they would do the ethically correct act that they identified as the correct response in an ethical dilemma (reported in Verges, 2010: 499). Many people can identify an ethical choice, but they do not necessarily follow through and do the right thing when faced with a dilemma. It is possible that the reason the gap exists between belief and behavior is the disjunction between System 1 (emotional, impulse-based) and System II (rational, deliberate) decision making described earlier. In the featured dilemma presented here, your decision may depend on whether you employ System 1 or System 2 thinking.

ETHICAL DILEMMA

You are a well-respected professional, successful in your field due to years of hard work. Your brother is a high-level mobster, responsible for perhaps dozens of murders and about to be indicted on felony counts of murder, extortion, and a range of other crimes. He also has been an informant for the FBI for over 10 years, providing them information that resulted in the arrests of his competitors. Right before he is arrested, he disappears. Now the FBI wants you to help them find him. You refuse. The fallout of your refusal threatens your reputation and livelihood. Would you cooperate to help catch him? Alternatively, change the scenario to a brother who is brilliant but seems to be increasingly disturbed. He then disappears. One day you see the newspaper has published a "manifesto" from the Unabomber, a mysterious figure who has sent 16 bombs through the U.S. mail, killing three people and injuring dozens. You recognize the letter as very probably written by your brother and have a strong suspicion that he is the Unabomber. Would you go to the FBI with your suspicions?

Law

There is no law that requires uninvolved relatives to help law enforcement catch their criminal siblings. If one has not aided, abetted, or encouraged crime, or assisted in a flight from justice, there is no legal duty to assist law enforcement's efforts to capture loved ones who are suspected of crimes.

Policy

Since these individuals are not deciding as employees of an organization, there are no policy issues involved.

Ethics

In both dilemmas, the values of loyalty and love are weighed against public safety and justice. The first scenario reflects the situation faced by William Bulger, who was president of the University of Massachusetts and forced to resign when he refused to help capture his infamous brother, James "Whitey" Bulger. The second is the dilemma of Ted Kaczynski's brother David, who did go to the FBI, an act that led directly to the capture of the Unabomber. These two brothers saw their ethical duties differently. Are there differences between the two situations that would lead to a different decision, or was it simply two different people resolving a similar dilemma in a different way? Our emotional reaction no doubt is "family first"; however, David Kaczynski's actions very probably saved lives. After rationally applying utilitarianism, it seems one would support sacrificing one's criminal brother for the safety and security of others. Ethical formalism would probably also support such actions. Ethics of care, on the other hand, would attempt to resolve the situation by trying to meet the needs of all, for instance, by brokering a deal for the brother to give up in return for something that was needed. This is what Kaczynski's brother attempted to do, possibly saving his brother from the death penalty.

Summary of Individual Differences

To summarize individual explanations of ethical decision making and behavior, we look, first, to evolutionary, genetic elements. The specific biological markers that have implications for morality include brain chemicals like oxytocin; with some even going so far as to call it the "moral molecule" (Zak, 2012). Individual differences in behavior are also explained through psychological theories; specifically learning theory and moral development theory. There is strong evidence that both rational and emotional components to decision making exist when one is faced with an ethical dilemma. There is mixed research as to whether individuals' beliefs and values predict their behavior. Research has found that people may believe the right thing to do is one thing and act in a different way entirely. Part of the reason for this may lie in external influences. Workgroup and organizational explanations will be discussed in the following section, and these must be considered in addition to individual explanations to better understand why people do what they do in the context of their profession.

▌ Workgroup and Organizational Influences

Most people agree that when a person enters the working world, their ethical and value systems are well established. It is also the case, however, that individuals sometimes behave in ways that are contrary to their belief systems and/or their belief systems may change when exposed to external influences. Bandura (2002) sees social and moral maturity as constantly changing and reacting to outside influences, including family, peers, and social institutions. These external influences affect our ethical decision making even into adulthood. In this section, we will focus specifically on the work group and organization.

Bandura believed that individuals developed their moral identity through reinforcement, the development of empathy, and strengthening one's self-regulatory ability (self-control). He argues, however, that this self-regulation can be "turned off," leading to inhumane acts, through cognitive restructuring via several different mechanisms. Many of these mechanisms are most powerful in a small group setting, which is why workgroup influences on ethical decision making must be examined. Bandura's mechanisms are described as follows (1990, 1991, 2002):

- *Moral justification.* This is an appeal to a higher or more important end to justify the wrong act (e.g., terrorists). Like utilitarianism, the idea here is that the end justifies the means.
- *Euphemistic labeling.* By using words that downplay the seriousness of actions, the true moral nature of such actions is ignored (e.g., sanitizing language, such as the term "collateral damage" for killing civilians in times of war).
- *Advantageous comparison.* This is an argument that the action may be wrong, but it isn't as bad as some other actions (e.g., "We've killed civilians but have never used chemical weapons against them").
- *Displacement of responsibility.* This argument basically removes the individual as a free-thinking agent of his or her own actions to deny culpability (e.g., "I was only following orders" or "I had to do it because the rules say so").

- *Diffusion of responsibility.* In this situation, the individual can redefine his or her responsibility for an action by diffusing it among several or many people (e.g., mob action, or the observation that "everyone is doing it").
- *Disregard or distortion of the consequences.* By misidentifying the consequences of one's actions, one can deny one's responsibility for harm (e.g., when a criminal says, "the insurance will take care of it," or a prosecutor excuses misconduct by a belief that all defendants are guilty).
- *Dehumanization.* Humans feel the most sympathy/empathy for those who are closest to us, and we feel the least for those who are most unlike us. Therefore, dehumanization strips the victim of any qualities of similarity that may create sympathy (e.g., the use of terms such as *gooks, slant-eyes, pigs, wetbacks,* and other dehumanizing references; in policing, there are many terms used to describe citizens in high crime neighborhoods, e.g., *mopes, thugs, and low-lifes*).

These should sound familiar to criminology students because they hold much in common with Sykes and Matza's (1957) techniques of neutralization, described as being used by juvenile delinquents to excuse or justify their delinquency. Techniques of neutralization included: the denial of responsibility (placing blame on the other party), the denial of injury (the action does not actually harm anyone), the denial of victim (the victim wasn't harmed or deserved it), the condemnation of the condemners (rejecting the judgers), and the appeal to higher authorities (end justifies the means thinking or loyalty to a deviant group).

Bandura argues that it takes a certain constellation of conditions to create human atrocities, not necessarily "monstrous" people (Bandura, 1991). Also, he purports that the shift to immoral acts and attendant justifications is probably gradual, not immediate. The important point to note is that inhibitions are lessened when there is social support for inhuman acts; that is, an individual in a workgroup that generates some of these mechanisms (e.g., dehumanization or moral justification) has a much stronger probability of engaging in unethical behavior than someone who does not have that influence. Bandura also noted though that external conditions are not all-powerful; the individual adapts and reinterprets them within his or her own internal cognitive processes (Bandura, 2002). In the In the News box below, the actions of Jon Burge and his subordinates can arguably be explained by Bandura's moral disengagement theory. The small work group led by Burge reinforced the idea that suspects were not deserving of the same level of care extended to peers and family; they were thugs and lowlifes who, if not guilty of the crime they confessed to, probably were guilty of something else. Also, the higher goal achieved supposedly was obtaining convictions.

Others besides Bandura have explained how individuals may engage in unethical behavior. Bazerman and Tenbrunsel (2011) present the concept of **bounded ethicality**. This refers to the cognitive structuring whereby decisions are interpreted using variables that do not include ethics; often in the context of a group decision-making process. For instance, in the infamous Ford Pinto case, where the automobile company's executives estimated that it would be less costly to pay a few wrongful death lawsuits than issue a recall, the decision making was purely economic without any consideration given to the morality of knowing some victims would die because of the faulty design. In some decision making, **ethical fading** occurs whereby the ethical ramifications of the decision choices may be addressed initially, but, over time, become removed from the decision-making process. These forces are incredibly powerful when operating as

bounded ethicality
This concept refers to the cognitive structuring whereby decisions are interpreted using variables that do not include ethics; for instance, companies evaluate decisions based only on economic factors rather than whether the action is moral.

ethical fading This concept refers to the situation whereby decision makers, who might have initially questioned whether an action was ethical or not, over time drop that element of the discussion and concentrate on other factors so that the decision is eventually made without taking into consideration whether it is ethical or not.

IN THE NEWS | Jon Burge and the Midnight Crew of Area 2

Back in the 1980s, former Commander Jon Burge in the Chicago Police Department and his "midnight crew" operated out of Area 2. They were applauded for quick clearances and confessions and no one paid much attention to the steady complaints that confessions were achieved through beatings, threats, and worse. Even defense attorneys had a hard time believing that in a police precinct, police officers would beat individuals so badly that they damaged internal organs. Some individuals described being choked to the point of unconsciousness, others were handcuffed to a hot radiator that burned skin. Still others were subjected to electric shocks and/or Russian Roulette.

Eric Caine, for instance, spent 25 years in prison for a 1986 double murder. Caine confessed after being hit so hard in the head that his eardrum was ruptured. His confession was eventually thrown out and prosecutors dropped the charges. Caine is one of a large group of defendants who were tortured by Burge and his men until they confessed to crimes. Some did commit the crimes they were accused of; but others did not and confessed only to stop the torture. Caine won a $10 million judgment in 2013.

Torture victim Darrell Cannon described how he was subjected to Russian Roulette and an electric cattle prod was used on his genitals. James Kluppelberg was another victim of Burge. He falsely confessed to stop being beaten, but immediately recanted. He was still convicted of an arson murder that killed 28-year-old Elva Luperio and her five children. He was eventually exonerated and freed after spending 24 years in prison.

Other detectives in Area 2 have also been associated with later exonerations, including former detective Kenneth Boudreau, who has been implicated in a dozen cases where confessions have been thrown out. Former sergeant Ray Guevara has been accused of beating suspects, falsely translating statements of Spanish-speaking suspects, and threatening witnesses with criminal charges if they did not say what he wanted them to say. In 2009, a federal jury awarded $21 million to Juan Johnson after finding Guevara intimidated and threatened witnesses to get them to testify against Johnson, who spent more than 11 years in prison until he was acquitted in a retrial. Guevara invoked his Fifth Amendment right in a retrial of Armando Serrano and Jose Montanez after a witness recanted and swore that Guevara intimidated him into falsely accusing the two. Chicago taxpayers also paid $12.3 million to Ronald Kitchen and Marvin Reeves, who spent more than two decades in prison for the 1988 murders of five because of their false confessions and the testimony of a jailhouse informant who lied. In this case, as in others, the city settled.

In 2006, a special prosecutor's report concluded that Burge and others in Area 2 had tortured criminal suspects for two decades. The investigation uncovered dozens of cases—some where the individuals were still in prison. Daniel Yellon, dean of Loyola Law School, was appointed by a federal judge to review over 100 cases for evidence of wrongful convictions connected to Burge.

Although city officials describe the scandal as a few deviant officers, others argue the corrupt and illegal activity was systemic. Former Mayor Richard Daley was the Cook County State Attorney and then mayor during the time that Burge and his Area 2 subordinates were operating. Some argue Daley was cognizant of the activity and even participated in a conspiracy to cover it up. Burge was convicted in 2010—but only of perjury and obstruction of justice for lying in a federal civil case. Since the statute of limitations for more serious charges had long run out, he could not be charged for any of the abuse that took place. He was sentenced to four years in federal prison, was released early for good behavior, and lives in the Tampa area. He still receives his $4,487 a month pension and won a court case when the city attorney tried to rescind it. It is estimated that he has cost the city more than $100 million and, because of the number of pending lawsuits as the wrongfully convicted win their release, that number will go much higher.

Mayor Rahm Emmanuel authorized a $5.5 million "reparations" fund to compensate Burge's victims. It was paid out in 2016 to 57 victims of Burge and his fellow officers. Each victim received up to $100,000, which is in addition to any civil judgment they receive. The city plans to provide other forms of compensation as well, including job training, free City College tuition, and psychological, family and substance abuse counseling. The city also has promised to create a "permanent memorial" about the abuse. The reparation came 44 years after the "first known instance" of torture by Burge and his midnight crew. According to the city attorney who negotiated the plan: "We do this not because it's required legally. It is not. We do it because we think it's the right thing to do—for the victims, their families, and the city." Mayor Rahm Emmanuel said "Reparations is not a necessity. But it is a moral compunction and a moral reckoning to right a wrong. There is no statute of limitations on that." Critics argue that the reparations are welcome but systemic problems in the police department still exist.

Sources: Black, 2015; Korecki, 2014; Meisner, 2013; Mills, 2015; Schmadeke, 2015; Shaw, 2014; Shelton, 2013; Spielman, 2013a; Spielman, 2013b; Spielman, 2016.

group influences and could account for the atrocities that were committed in the name of justice described in the In the News box about Jon Burge and his fellow detectives.

Another important concept Bazerman and Tenbrunsel (2011) discuss is "motivated blindness," which occurs when there are real and substantial pressures to ignore ethical issues. For instance, mortgage brokers who approved mortgages for people who could not afford them leading to the 2007–2008 recession, Arthur Anderson auditors who did not report Enron's creation of phony subsidiaries to hide debt, and fund managers who sent their client's money to Bernard Madoff's impossibly lucrative investment fund, which turned out to be a Ponzi scheme, all profited from ignoring the ethical red flags of their behavior. In 2014, schedulers at Veterans Administration hospitals and medical centers were found to be entering false data regarding the time it took to see a doctor because of supervisor pressure and incentives to stay within timelines. Even though it was taking veterans six months to see doctors, records showed only weeks (by changing the date of the request) to bolster the ratings of the facility. Similarly, teachers and administrators in Atlanta were convicted of felony tampering charges in 2015 due to their cheating on student test results, arguably because they would face negative consequences if their schools were found to be low achieving. In 2016, it was discovered that Volkswagen intentionally circumvented emission test requirements in the United States and eventually pleaded guilty to three felonies. The company will pay a $14.7 fine in addition to fixing or buying back 11 million vehicles (Muoio, 2017). In the In the News box, the Wells Fargo bank case adds yet another example of arguably good people who do bad things because of organizational pressures.

Motivational forces can operate on a micro-level within small work groups or within the whole organization. Formal incentives (such as bonuses and quotas) typically occur at an organizational level. Organizations that desire to improve ethical

---

IN THE NEWS | *Wells Fargo*

A scandal emerged in 2016 when it was discovered that Wells Fargo employees opened as many as 2.1 million accounts without customers' permission or knowledge. There was also a wide-spread practice of pushing fee-generating accounts on gullible patrons, especially the poor and elderly. The misconduct was prompted by purely goal-oriented leaders who set unrealistic sales goals and promoted a culture whereby it didn't matter how employees met those goals. Former CEO John Stumpf and the head of community banking Carrie Tolstedt have been forced out and will lose or pay back $75 million in bonuses. More than 5,000 low-level Wells Fargo employees were also fired due to the scandal. Evidence indicates that employees who called the company's ethics hotline were sometimes fired or otherwise punished, branch managers were warned 24 hours before internal auditors showed up, and some employees were ordered to shred documents and forge signatures during audits. Investigations have shown bank employees caused customers to miss deadlines for extending a promised interest rate, then charged those customers late fees. This scheme was in addition to the forged new-account scandal. The epicenter of the corrupt practices seems to have been in Los Angeles and Arizona, but practices were nation wide. The bank has refunded $3.2 million in fees that were charged on sham accounts; however, when some customers tried to sue, the bank argued that lawsuits were prohibited by the mandatory arbitration clauses connected to the opened accounts—even though they were fraudulent accounts opened in the customers' names without their consent. Surprisingly, the court agreed! Critics point to this move as evidence that Wells Fargo's corporate culture is still less than perfect in promoting ethical banking.

Sources: Colvin, 2017; Editorial Board, 2017.

decision making among workers need to review their reward systems. If unethical behavior is unintentionally rewarded by focusing only on numbers and quotas, then the culture becomes corrupt, as evidenced in the Wells Fargo scandal described in the In the News box. This concept is called "perverse incentives" and refers to the fact that if incentives are set up so that goals are more important than how one achieves them, then leaders should not be surprised when patterns of unethical behavior occur. Are organizational messages about the importance of ethics as powerful as the messages about goals? Are there compliance systems in place to monitor worker's behavior, not just measures of productivity? While compliance systems have multiplied in response to ethical scandals, ironically there is some indication, at least in business settings, that they may increase rather than decrease unethical behavior. The reason seems to be that compliance systems create the perception that it is a mere rule-breaking issue as opposed to one's moral identity that is impacted by unethical behavior in the workplace (Bazerman and Tenbrunsel, 2011).

Ethical Climate and Organizational Justice

A growing body of research explores the ability to measure the "ethical climate" of an organization. The Ethical Climate Questionnaire (ECQ) includes questions regarding respondents' perceptions of how they (and other workers) behave and/or believe regarding a range of ethical behaviors. Research shows that leadership, the reward structure, and organizational messages affect the ethical climate (Mulgan and Wanna, 2011; Victor and Cullen, 1987). Victor and Cullen (1988) discovered that there are significant differences in ethical climates even within one organization. These researchers identified theoretical scales indicating the primary vehicle of decision making as the following: self-interest, company profit, efficiency, friendship, team interest, social responsibility, personal morality, company rules/procedures, and laws/professional codes. They also identified three basic ethical orientations: egoism, benevolence (utilitarianism), and principle (ethical formalism). In their research, these theoretical scales were tested and results showed the strongest, most robust scales could be described as caring, law/code, rules, instrumental (egoism), and independence. They did find that strong differences emerged between companies in the ethical climate scores of employees. They also found that job level in organizations also showed significant differences in their ethical climate scores.

Other researchers have used the ECQ to find that ethical climate does affect decision making. In stores where employees' scores showed high levels of instrumentality (egoism), when given "what would you do?" scenarios, their behavior choices were more likely to be negative than those stores where employees scored lower on egoism. Stores where employees' aggregate scores were higher on caring, service, law/code, and independence showed lower negative behavior scores (Wimbush, Shepard, and Markham, 1997).

Research shows that a strong ethics program results in less pressure to perform unethical acts, less misconduct, and less retaliation against whistleblowers. In the National Business Ethics Survey, it was found that among the businesses with the strongest ethics programs, 30 percent of respondents reported seeing or participating in unethical behavior, but in the organizations with the weakest programs, fully 89 percent of employees reported seeing or participating in misconduct (Hopkins, 2013). Gardner (2007), among many others, reports that organizations that express and enforce a strong ethical code (e.g., product quality or fairness for the customer) are also likely to have ethical workers.

In any organization, there is the formal organizational culture (i.e., rituals, myths, symbols, anecdotes, and informal codes of conduct) and, usually, an informal subculture (i.e., subterranean values, language, and habits) that is sometimes in opposition to the formal culture. We will discuss the subculture of policing, for instance, in an upcoming chapter. The organizational culture (both formal and informal) can generate and reinforce ethical employee behavior by emphasizing values, identifying "heroes," and reinforcing behavior patterns that follow ethical guidelines (Jondle, Ardichvili, and Mitchell, 2014).

As mentioned in the last chapter, procedural justice refers to the belief that one is being treated fairly and with respect by justice professionals. In management science, the same concept is called organizational justice, which refers to the idea that workers feel they are being treated fairly in the organization. Perceptions of a lack of organizational justice lead to negative behaviors, and perceptions of organizational justice lead to positive employee behaviors, including what has been called organizational citizenship behaviors (OCB). These refer to employee discretionary behaviors that are not required but contribute to the health of the organization, like staying late to get a job done or going out of their way to help a client (Bateman and Organ, 1983; Katz, 1964). According to Tyler (2010/2011), these extra-role behaviors are normally not influenced through instrumental means, such as rewards and sanctions, and occur when the employee scores high on organizational commitment and organizational commitment is associated with perceptions of organizational justice.

While the vast bulk of organizational justice research has occurred in the private/profit sector, there has been research conducted in criminal justice organizations. Lambert (2003), for instance, in various studies with colleagues, found that distributive (outcome) and procedural justice perceptions had significant positive effects on job satisfaction of correctional workers, but only perceptions of procedural justice were related to organizational commitment (Lambert, Hogan, and Allen, 2006; Lambert, Hogan, and Griffin, 2007).

De Angelis and Kupchik (2007) found that when police officers perceived departmental investigations of citizen complaints were conducted in a fair and objective manner, they had a positive attitude toward the department, regardless of the outcome in the investigation. Shane (2012) found officers were more likely to perceive that the disciplinary process was fair when supervisory discretion was reduced by utilizing a disciplinary matrix for disciplinary outcomes. Reynolds and Hicks (2014), in a small, phenomenological study, found that unfair policies create perceptions of uncertainty among officers, making them question their status within the department; officers focused more on the fairness of procedures (procedural justice) rather than the actual outcome (distributive justice), and fair treatment was interpreted by the officers as the department could be trusted and that they were valued by the administration. Reynolds (2015) found that officers' organizational commitment behavior was associated with perceptions of fairness and organizational justice.

In a large ongoing study of police officers, various surveys have shown that organizational justice seems to be more commonly perceived in small- and mid-size police departments and there is more perceived unfairness and a lack of organizational justice in the largest police departments. Leaders, also, were perceived more positively in small rather than large departments (National Police Research Platform, 2017). This has implications, of course, for job satisfaction and organizational commitment behaviors and may shed some light on why major ethical scandals tend to occur in the largest police departments.

Farmer, Beehr, and Love (2003) found that both distributive (outcome) and procedural (interactional) perceptions of justice were positively related to officers' job performance, job satisfaction, and organizational commitment. Wolfe and Piquero (2011) found that officers who perceived that organizational procedures were fair were less likely to engage in police misconduct (measured by self-reports). In addition, favorable perceptions of organizational justice were related to a lower likelihood of adhering to the code of silence. Harris and Worden (2014) found that when officers perceived a disciplinary system as harsh or unfair, it led to negative police behaviors. This area of research is still developing and studies use a variety of measures for relevant constructs making synthesis of findings difficult.

Another issue with much of this research is that it measures the organization. It seems clear that a worker's beliefs and feelings about the organization as a whole is related to, but distinct from, his or her supervisor, peers, or small workgroup (Lavelle, Rupp, and Brockner, 2007). For instance, Reynolds (2015), in his study of organizational justice in police departments, suggests that officers' perceptions of the fairness of immediate supervisors are distinct from perceptions of the whole organization. As noted in the Jon Burge case described in the In the News box, the activities of the "Midnight Crew" in Area 2 evidently did not extend to other divisions in the city.

Ethics Training

The Enron fraud and bankruptcy scandal prompted the Sarbanes–Oxley Act of 2002 that held CEOs responsible for the actions of their employees. The Act spurred the emergence of ethics courses and compliance officers in business. The question is whether ethics training is effective. Kohlberg (1976) described the following as necessary for moral growth:

- Being in a situation where seeing things from other points of view is encouraged.
- Engaging in logical thinking, such as reasoned argument and consideration of alternatives.
- Having the responsibility to make moral decisions and to influence one's moral world.
- Being exposed to moral controversy and to conflict in moral reasoning that challenges the structure of one's present stage.
- Being exposed to the reasoning of individuals whose thinking is one stage higher than one's own.
- Participating in creating and maintaining a just community whose members pursue common goals and resolve conflict in accordance with the ideals of mutual respect and fairness.

Most professional schools today (in law, medicine, and business) require at least one class in professional ethics. Typically, these classes present the opportunity to examine the ethical dilemmas that individuals may encounter as members of that profession and help students discover the best way to decide ethical issues. Part of the task is to socialize new entrants to the values and codes of behavior of that profession.

Criminal justice ethics courses exist in college and university curriculums; indeed, this text is written for such a class. In law enforcement and corrections academy classes, ethics is part of the curriculum as well. According to Sherman (1982: 17–18), criminal justice ethics courses should "stimulat[e] . . . the moral imagination" by posing difficult moral dilemmas and encourage analytical skills and the tools of ethical analysis. Sherman also believed that such courses should elicit a sense of moral obligation and personal responsibility, and an understanding of the morality of coercion.

There are differences in focus and scope between ethics classes in a university or college environment and an ethics training course in a professional organization or academy. Are they effective in changing behavior? Most of the research focuses on business applications. Research also typically has only measured whether training results in a different level of moral beliefs—for instance, a higher moral stage score as measured by Rest's DIT or other paper-and-pencil test of ethical beliefs, not whether changes in behavior have occurred because of ethics training. It is obviously very difficult to study whether ethics training might influence actual behavior. Research to date has obtained mixed results, but findings indicate that training is more effective if it is longer (rather than shorter), involves participatory learning methods, and is tailored to the specific organization. It also seems to be the case that training has more impact on reasoning ability (Type II thinking) than on intuitive judgments of right and wrong (Type I thinking) (Jones, 2009; Seiler, Fischer, and Ooi, 2010). Sekerka (2009) found that ethics training can affect and shape organizational culture and contributes to a positive perception of organization by employees. Antes et al. (2009), after a meta-analysis of ethics training, report that the overall effectiveness of ethics instruction is modest. They report that training content should include ethical decision making, problem-solving, and ethical sensitivity, and stand-alone courses are more successful than attempting to insert ethics in other courses.

As noted, all the research reviewed thus far has occurred in business applications. The only studies of ethics training in law enforcement have been reviews of prevalence and content. Wyatt-Nichol and Franks (2010), using a survey of police chiefs, found that training was more often pre-service, mostly lecture and discussion, and usually four hours or less. The chiefs surveyed thought ethics training was important and believed that the focus should shift from rules to shared values and problem-solving. Ethics classes covered off-duty conduct, falsifying reports, excessive use of force, use of position for private gain, failure to report others' misconduct, providing false testimony, gifts and gratuities, and using police property for private use.

Skogan, Van Craen, and Hennessy (2014) noted that there was a paucity of rigorous academic evaluations of training in police academies in general, much less any attempt to measure the effect of ethics training. These researchers developed, implemented, and analyzed the effects of an eight-hour training session on procedural justice that was administered to Chicago police officers. A survey was developed to measure adherence to procedural justice concepts (neutrality, voice, respect, and trust). This study found that police officers who went through the training increased adherence to procedural justice concepts, except for trust. Researchers also found that those officers who went through the training showed an enduring difference in adherence to procedural justice concepts compared to those who had not gone through the training.

Rosenbaum and Lawrence (2012; also see Schuck and Rosenbaum, 2011) presented findings from an evaluation of a 20-hour training unit included in the traditional academy instruction. The researchers utilized a randomized control design with a control group of cadets going through traditional training and an experimental group exposed to the training. They were evaluated on both attitudinal measures and through a video assessment of their interactions with citizens. Results were mixed as to how well the training affected the officers' interactions with citizens using procedural justice concepts. The two studies described above were not involved with ethics training *per se*; however, procedural justice training does seem to be related to the concepts, values, and principles reflected in an ethics training course.

Recently, a police training program that has been instituted in New Orleans, Louisiana and Springfield, Massachusetts may be more effective than traditional ethics courses in changing behavior. "Ethical Policing is Courageous" (EPIC) was developed in New Orleans; a city that has had its share of ethical scandals, including the infamous Danziger Bridge incident after Hurricane Katrina where officers shot six unarmed people and then attempted to cover it up. The new training will eventually reach all 1,172 members of the department. The goal is to teach officers to intervene when they see fellow officers on the verge of unethical behavior. The curriculum was developed by New Orleans officers and outside experts based on the work of psychologist Ervin Staub on the bystander effect (the idea that people won't intervene if they think someone else is going to). His research also shows that groups grow more violent when observers remain passive.

In New Orleans, like in many police departments, there is a culture whereby cops don't often intervene when other cops go over the line. EPIC training is designed to socialize new and in-service officers that loyalty demands that they do. Training includes watching videos of the Kitty Genovese case (where a young woman was murdered and no one called the police because they didn't want to get involved), and psychological experiments about morality and authority. The goal is to help officers understand that reticence to intervene hurts the other officer and is not "ratting." In today's era of body cameras and smartphones, stepping in and stopping a fellow officer from doing something wrong can save him or her from disciplinary action, criminal charges or worse. Instructors ask if officers would intervene to stop their partner getting shot. Obviously, all officers answer in the affirmative, and so the next question is: why wouldn't they intervene to stop their partner from being fired?

The concept of intervention is not without critics. Some officers question whether intervening when a superior or senior officer is about to do something wrong may not go over well in reality. Others have argued that it is not easy to tell an over-stressed officer on the verge of misconduct to take a break and let others handle the situation when they are understaffed and racing from call to call (Robertson, 2016a).

The program is being replicated in Springfield, Massachusetts, starting with in-service officers, but slated to cover all officers by mid-2017. Unlike New Orleans, Springfield is not under any federal consent decree. However, there have been incidents where officers engaged in misconduct, while other officers did nothing. Police leaders realized that there was no element in training that dealt with the issue of what to do when other officers were engaging in misconduct. The other element of the training that might make it more palatable to officers is that there is a recognition that often misconduct occurs, not because of evil intent, but because of stress and heightened emotion. The importance of prevention and intervention to protect the errant officer through peer intervention make this program potentially effective in changing police culture (Glaun, 2016).

Leadership

If there is a culture of impropriety or a pattern of transgressions in any organization, we look to the leader for fault. The In the News box describes what sometimes happens when public servant leaders are perceived as deficient in running an ethical organization.

There are thousands of articles and books about leadership. Researchers identify, typologize, and deconstruct different types of leadership styles, for example, task-versus people-oriented leadership; participative, authoritarian, technocratic and charismatic leadership, and so on. We cannot do justice to leadership studies here, but it is important to note that the concepts of "authentic leadership" and "transformational leadership" seem to be very relevant to this discussion of ethical organizations. These leadership styles involve less social distance between leaders and employees, greater participation of employees, fairness, consistency and integrity, taking responsibility for one's actions, promoting ethical conduct, being concerned for others, and rewarding ethical conduct. Research has shown that leadership styles that incorporate these elements are associated with higher levels of job satisfaction and organizational commitment, satisfaction with supervision, extra effort, lower turnover intention, organizational citizenship behaviors, better overall employee performance, and reduction in cynicism toward organization (Bommer, Rich, and Rubin, 2005; Onorato and Zhu, 2015; Podsakoff, MacKenzie, and Bommer, 1996).

In one study, it was found that transformational leadership was correlated with higher stage moral reasoning (universality) of the leaders; however, "pseudo-transformational leadership" was not. Pseudo-transformational leaders were those who "talked the talk" but didn't "walk the walk" of transformational leadership—they did not fully invest in the principles of worker participation and empowerment. These leaders scored high in motivation but low in idealism; their motivation for leading workers was ego (Barling, Christie, and Turner, 2008).

IN THE NEWS | *Leaders and Scandals*

In October of 2014, Julia Pierson, the first female head of the Secret Service, stepped down after several scandals regarding the behavior of Secret Service agents became front-page news. Whistleblowers testifying to a Senate committee reported that Secret Service agents and managers engaged in sexual misconduct in 17 different countries. In recent years, advance team members preparing for President Obama's visit to Cartagena, Columbia, allegedly engaged in a night of heavy drinking and prostitution, others sent sexually explicit e-mails to a female agent, and two, after a night of drinking, drove into a traffic barrier during a bomb investigation. It was reported that supervisors averted the imminent arrest of the driver. The whistleblowers testifying to a congressional committee described an organization that seemingly tolerated a range of unethical behaviors, including heavy drinking, hiring prostitutes, having extramarital affairs with other agents, and sexual relationships with foreign nationals that were not properly reported.

In April of 2015, Michele Leonhart, the first female head of the Drug Enforcement Administration (DEA), stepped down for much the same reason when it was revealed that DEA agents had engaged in sex parties in Columbia paid for by drug cartel leaders. It was also revealed that some agents had received gifts of cash and guns from cartel affiliates and, during the parties, laptops and Blackberries with sensitive governmental information were left accessible to cartel members and potentially compromised.

Source: Johnson, 2015; Leonnig and Nakamaura, 2014.

In one study of leadership, the relationship between ethical leadership and worker helping behavior was moderated by the moral awareness of workers. The statistical relationship between individual and group-level perceptions of ethical leadership and measures of helping behavior was stronger when the moral awareness of workers was low. The relationship weakened when moral awareness of workers was higher. Thus, although ethical leadership relates positively to follower helping and courtesy, the strength of this relationship differs depending on the level of moral awareness in the work group (Kalshoven, Den Hartog, and De Hoogh, 2013).

The first thing to note is that for a leader to influence ethical behavior among employees, he or she, first, must act ethically. If a leader engages in unethical behavior, it is highly unlikely that ethical behavior of employees will be the result. Research has shown that the correlates of leaders who make unethical decisions include the following:

- They are very proactive and goal-oriented but not concerned about potential problems.
- They are self-directed and make their own decisions; not prone to take advice or seek input from others.
- They want to be in charge and have a high achievement orientation.
- They are likely to have their own rules and are willing to tell others to follow them or, they do not care about others or about rules at all.
- They have a low interest filter for people (Harshman and Harshman, 2008, p. 185).

Organizational leaders must not only act ethically themselves, they must also create an environment that encourages ethical behavior from everyone. This can be done by promoting ethical workers, rewarding morally courageous behavior, and providing clear and powerful organizational policies that emphasize worthwhile goals and honest means. Issues that could be examined in a discussion of ethical leadership include the practice of recruitment, training, discipline and reward structures, and evaluation of performance. Souryal (1992: 307) offers advice to leaders who would like to advance ethical decision making and emphasizes the importance of organizational support for ethical actions. Ethical leaders should do the following:

1. Create an environment that is conducive to dignified treatment on the job.
2. Increase ethical awareness among the ranks through formal and informal socialization.
3. Avoid deception and manipulation in the way officers are assigned, rewarded, or promoted.
4. Allow for openness and the free flow of unclassified information.
5. Foster a sense of shared values and incorporate such values in the subculture of the agency.
6. Demonstrate an obligation to honesty, fairness, and decency by example.
7. Discuss the issue of corruption publicly, expose corrupt behavior, and reward ethical behavior.

Metz (1990) offers a similar advice. He proposes that ethical administrators follow these steps:

1. Establish realistic goals and objectives.
2. Provide ethical leadership (meaning, set a moral tone by actions).

3. Establish formal written codes of ethics.
4. Provide a whistleblowing mechanism.
5. Discipline violators of ethical standards.
6. Train all personnel in ethics.

When top leaders take responsibility for their subordinates' behavior, they will lead and administer with greater awareness, interaction, and responsibility. Because of this responsibility, a supervisor or administrator must be concerned with how the workplace treats the worker, how the worker views the mission, and how the public views the organization. A strong ethical leader would have a personal relationship with subordinates—without showing favoritism. This personal relationship is the foundation of modeling, identification, and persuasive authority. Strong leadership involves caring and commitment to the organization. A strong leader is connected with others, but also has a larger vision, if you will, of goals and mission.

A contrary environment would be what Trautman (2008) describes as the "Corruption Continuum," which details how organizations can become corrupt through the actions of its leaders; specifically, (1) administrative indifference toward integrity, (2) ignoring obvious ethical problems, (3) creating a hypocrisy- and fear-dominated culture; all leading to (4) a survival-of-the-fittest approach by individual employees (who will commit unethical acts to protect themselves).

Schafer's (2010a, 2010b) research on police leadership supports these concepts. In a survey of police managers attending an FBI national academy career development course, survey respondents identified ineffective leaders as possessing five acts of commission: a focus on self, ego/arrogance, closed-mindedness, micromanagement, and capriciousness; and five acts of omission: poor work ethic, failure to act, ineffective communication, lack of interpersonal skills, and a lack of integrity (Schafer, 2010a). He also looked at what was considered effective leadership. The strongest factor emerged as honesty and integrity (37 percent identified that as the first element of good leadership; 2010b: 651). Integrity, along with a work ethic, communication skills, and caring for the needs of employees were the most commonly agreed elements of good leadership. Finally, leaders must never lose sight of the organizational mission; for public servants, the mission is public service.

Other researchers, in studies with correctional workers, conclude that training workers in procedural justice concepts so that they will interact more positively with clients/inmates is unlikely to be successful if organizational leaders do not practice procedural/organizational justice within the organization. Correctional workers who perceived their leaders as transformational were more likely to perceive the organization as having procedural (organizational) justice. The elements of organizational justice that was identified as important in perceptions were the ability to appeal grievances and have their voices heard. These researchers found that procedural justice elements needed constant reinforcement, and older officers were less likely to perceive procedural justice in the organization (Baker, Gordon, and Taxman, 2015).

Societal and Cultural Influences

Organizational culture is subject to external influences. External influences are both objective (e.g., laws and regulations that constrain the organization) and normative (public belief systems). We see these external influences operating in for-profit organizations as well as public service organizations such as those in criminal justice. Messages filter from the public to the organization in terms of what will be tolerated and what will not be; for instance, our popular media glorified the Wall Street values of money as the sole measure of success until the bankruptcy of Enron, at which time public pressure on Congress led to the Sarbanes–Oxley Act, which placed more accountability on CEOs, which, in turn, affected the internal culture of organizations. The crash of 2008 led to public pressure for banking regulations, and there was a new Consumer Protection Agency created (although the future of this agency is in doubt today).

In April 2017, when a passenger was injured while being dragged off an airplane by airport security personnel at the request of United Airlines personnel, the cellphone videos of the event went viral. At first the CEO of United Airlines excused the event, saying the passenger was belligerent and he stated that he stood behind his employees and their actions. However, as public sentiment grew more virulent, and other videos emerged, he changed his message and apologized. When social media began sharing other examples of poor treatment by United Airlines passengers in other circumstances, the organization had a public relations crisis. Eventually, United Airlines compensated all passengers on the airplane by refunding the price of their tickets. A lawsuit filed by the injured passenger will no doubt take longer to resolve. The CEO swore that no passenger would ever again be removed from an airplane because of overbooking. Industry observers noted that organizational culture does affect how employees treat customers/clients, and this incident may have been the trigger that will generate a concerted effort of cultural change in the organization. It's also clear that if change does occur, it was due to external pressure brought on by a media firestorm over one event.

The ethical issue box illustrates how law enforcement organizations are influenced by and must respond to larger social events, for instance, the immigration issue. The Michael Brown shooting in Ferguson, Missouri, in 2014 and the Freddy Gray death in Baltimore, Maryland, shortly afterward sparked a strong public backlash against police use of force, especially against minority men. The backlash took a violent turn when several police officers were ambushed and killed, supposedly in retaliation for the police killings of black men. The Walking the Walk box that follows highlights one chief who was hailed as a hero for his handling of the Dallas.

This external pressure on police organizations spurred leaders to improve training, tighten up use-of-force policies, and improve discipline systems. Public pressure has also spurred discussion of body cameras, citizen review panels, and special prosecutors. The Department of Justice began or continued numerous investigations that lead to consent orders or agreements with cities across the country designed to improve police policies. Outside legal actions and oversight do impact organizational culture and behavior, and, in turn, affect the individual behaviors of the professionals in the organization.

More recently, Attorney General Sessions has signaled that the Department of Justice is drawing back "pattern and practice investigations" and will be less likely to scrutinize individual police departments. The DOJ has even requested a federal court to not enforce an existing consent order that had already been agreed to by the city and police department (Baltimore). The external message now seems to be that police departments do not need to worry about the DOJ oversight over use-of-force policies or other issues. Attorney General Sessions has stated that he believes there has been too much interference in police matters and that there should be a priority on addressing violent crime increases in central cities rather than police practices. Interestingly,

ETHICAL ISSUE

Should Sheriffs and Police Chiefs Follow Sanctuary City Principles?

With the election of President Trump, the conflict over what to do with this nation's estimated 11 million immigrants who are here illegally has created ethical issues for law enforcement leaders. Many city council members across the country have espoused their allegiance to and sometimes have voted to declare their identity as sanctuary cities. Federal leaders, in turn, have vowed to withhold federal funds from jurisdictions that profess to be sanctuary cities and, indeed, Attorney General Sessions has stated he may attempt to rescind federal grant money already disbursed to some cities. However, no one seems to agree on what being a sanctuary city means, and many do not seem to understand the legal powers of sheriffs or police chiefs. Before we can analyze the ethical issue, we must be clear on terms. In this discussion, the definition of sanctuary city may not be equivalent to how your jurisdiction and news media have defined it.

Generally, there is a clear distinction between federal powers and state powers. Only the federal government has the right to enforce immigration law. Indeed, when Arizona attempted to pass a law several years ago that required their police officers to inquire as to immigration status and arrest illegal immigrants; this portion of the law was rejected by the Supreme Court as usurping federal powers (*Arizona v. United States*, 567 U.S. 387, 2012). Of course, state and local law enforcement can hold someone who has an outstanding federal warrant, just as they can hold a suspect for other jurisdictions when there is an outstanding arrest warrant. Warrants are issued by judges after probable cause has been established, so there is some degree of due process that has occurred.

During President G.W. Bush's administration, the Secure Communities program was established. This was a voluntary program whereby local law enforcement who arrested individuals on other grounds would hold those suspected of being in the United States illegally with only a detainer from immigration authorities. Detainers do not have the same legal authority as warrants and are not issued by judges; they are simply administrative requests from Immigration and Customs Enforcement (ICE) to hold the individual. During President Obama's administration, the Secure Communities program was rolled back because of concerns about due process. The

Priority Enforcement Program, instead, targeted only individuals who were involved in significant criminal offenses. In most of these cases, the individual would not have been released anyway, because of the seriousness of the charge. President Trump, however, has revived the Secure Communities program, prompting some cities and jurisdictions to declare themselves sanctuary cities; in effect, saying they will not participate and will not hold individuals on merely detainer requests.

Cities who have declared sanctuary city status promise not to allow police to question suspects, witnesses, or victims about their immigration status, nor contact ICE when they encounter someone here illegally. Some cities also incorporate promises to not withhold city services based on immigration status. As noted above, local police have never had the power to arrest someone on suspicion of an immigration violation; however, the main issue is what to do about individuals who are arrested for some other offense. Should the sheriff (who is typically the authority in charge of the jail, not the police chief) hold the individual past the time he or she would have released for the offense? For example, if a group of three men were arrested for public drunkenness and ordinarily would be released the next morning after posting bail or paying a fine; the issue becomes whether to hold one of them because he has no driver's license, cannot produce a social security card, and speaks Spanish. When jurisdictions proclaim themselves to be sanctuary cities, it typically means they will not hold that individual, nor contact ICE, nor (if ICE somehow finds out about the person and issues a detainer) hold the person on a detainer.

Law

Police chiefs serve at the pleasure of a mayor or city council so, as an executive, he or she is duty bound to carry out legal orders. A sheriff, on the other hand, is typically elected. He or she, as an elected official, has discretion to determine the nature of their duties if the decision does not run afoul of existing law. However, there is unsettled law in this area. A federal magistrate judge in Oregon concluded that county officials violated a woman's Fourth Amendment rights when they kept her in custody solely based on an immigration detainer (*Miranda-Olivares v. Clackamas County*, No. 3:12-cv-02317-ST, slip op., D. Or. April 11, 2014). In this case, the woman was arrested for violating a restraining order, the judge granted bail, but ICE had issued a detainer, so she was kept in jail. She was finally released roughly two weeks after she was judged guilty for the misdemeanor with a two-day jail sentence; evidently ICE never did initiate proceedings for removal. Other cases have also determined that detainers are mere requests, not lawful orders, for example, *Galarza v. Szalczyk*, No. 12-3991, slip op., 3d Cir. March 4, 2014. The Supreme Court has also determined that the Tenth Amendment's anti-commandeering principle prohibits the federal government from enlisting local police officials to help enforce federal law (*Printz v. United States*, 521 U.S. 898, 1997). Because they are mere requests and not lawful orders, counties may be liable for unlawful confinement. In the *Miranda-Olivares* case, the court held that the county was authorized to hold Miranda-Olivares while her criminal proceedings were ongoing, but holding her longer violated the Fourth Amendment. Sheriffs in several jurisdictions have pointed to these case decisions as a reason for refusing to honor detainer requests from ICE. For instance, Sheriff Sally Hernandez in Travis County, Texas (Austin) refused to honor detainer requests and, in response, Governor Abbott cancelled about $1.5 million in criminal justice grants to the county. Thus, law enforcement officials face either being sued for unlawful imprisonment or lose state or federal monies. San Francisco has filed a lawsuit against the federal government alleging there is no legal authority to rescind or refuse federal funds and other jurisdictions have joined the lawsuit. The legal argument is basically that the federal government cannot force jurisdictions to enforce unconstitutional detainers. There is a lot of money at stake. The Edward Byrne Memorial Justice Assistance Grant Program, administered by the Department of Justice, alone allocated $274.9 million in 2016 (Kopan, 2017; Ratcliffe, 2017).

Policy

Police chiefs typically are not in charge of jails, although in a few jurisdictions there is a county–city overlap so they might be. Generally, however, the sanctuary city conflict presented above lies with sheriffs. Sheriffs may take advice from city councils or county commissioners, but because they are elected officials, there is independence in decision making over this issue. County Commissioners have control over a sheriff's budget, but not over his or her decision to honor detainers.

Ethics

A sheriff or locality facing this issue often employs utilitarianism to support their decision to honor or not honor detainers. Utilitarianism supports actions that benefit the majority. One side would argue that it is to the benefit of most of us for immigration laws to be enforced. This side often points to the idea that illegal immigrants commit crimes and absorb resources that could be used for native-born or legal immigrant residents. While illegal immigrants lose in this equation, there are fewer of them than the rest of us, so the math is in favor of the majority. Utilitarianism would also justify participation by pointing to the threat of the loss of federal and/or state monies. Losing such funds hurts the jurisdiction and the many residents outweigh the few illegal immigrants who might suffer under the program, and even the few legal residents who might be held with no just cause because of error. Utilitarianism also is used as the ethical justification for sanctuary city policies by law enforcement. Many major chiefs and sheriffs argue that their primary role is to enforce criminal law and if they become agents for ICE, witnesses and victims will be less likely to talk to them. That hurts everyone because they are hampered in their ability to investigate and solve crimes. They also note that jail space is not free and ICE often does not come and pick people up, thereby taking up valuable jail cell space without reimbursing the county. Finally, they note that if the jurisdiction loses a civil rights lawsuit, as the jurisdiction did in the case described above, already stretched budgets must be decimated to pay damages and county residents receive fewer services.

Ethical formalism is dependent on one's perception of duty. If the duty of local law enforcement is perceived as protecting and serving and local crime control, then immigration enforcement does not fall within that purview; if there is a more generalized perception of "law" as including immigration law, then the duty extends to enforcement. Religion has also been used to support the sanctuary position, and, in fact, the idea of sanctuary (protection from civil law) historically comes from religion: think of the right of sanctuary in *The Hunchback of Notre Dame*. If someone stayed within the walls of the cathedral, they were protected from the king's law. Recall that under religion and ethics of care there is less emphasis on man's law and more universal principles of care. Ultimately, like many of the issues discussed in this text, well-meaning, reasonable people can apply ethical reasoning and reach different conclusions.

this has led to some mayors and police chiefs assuring their constituencies that they will continue to pursue compliance with the changes requested by the DOJ, even if the DOJ does not want them anymore. Clearly, this dramatic turnaround on the federal level will have an impact on the organizations in law enforcement and the culture within them. In each subsystem of the criminal justice system (police, courts, and corrections), we will examine individual, organizational, and systemic (cultural or societal) responses to unethical behavior (Mark, 2017).

WALKING THE WALK | A Quiet Man

Former Dallas Police Chief David Brown became a national figure on July 8, 2016, when five Dallas officers were shot and killed and seven others wounded by a sniper. The killings occurred during a peaceful "Black Lives Matter" march. During the panic and chaos, officers protected marchers although it was they who were the targets. Micah Johnson, a 25-year-old black man, was reportedly upset at the number of black men killed by police, so used an AR-15 to ambush police officers escorting the marchers. He was eventually cornered and police negotiated with him in a standoff that lasted for several hours. Finally, when it seemed as if he might have a bomb that could potentially injure many more people, police detonated a bomb-equipped robot and Johnson was killed. Shortly after the Dallas event, officers were shot in Georgia, Tennessee, and Missouri. Chief Brown became known in the tense days following the killing as a type of moral exemplar in how he handled the murders in what was the deadliest day for police since 9/11.

Grief-stricken, heartbroken, and overcome with the atrocity, Chief Brown displayed sincerity and a calm certainty that the department would get through the crisis as professionals. Asked how his officers would return to community policing after the shooting, he responded: "With steel resolve. Bravery and courage." He became a moral touchstone in what might have evolved into a dangerous city-wide schism between the black community and the police department. He did not downplay the critical nature of the events that gripped the country in the summer of 2016. Before the shootings of police officers, two black men had been killed in Louisiana and Minnesota. Before then, several killings had spawned the "Black Lives Matter" movement. President Obama's and others' efforts to address the seeming disproportionality of killings and uses-of-force against black men, in turn, galvanized police unions and others to argue there was a "war on cops." It was said that racial tensions among the police and minority communities

were at an all-time high. Even though Dallas was not the epicenter of the strained relations between police and minorities, there was a real possibility that the shootings would spark further conflict. As a black man, Chief Brown was forced into the role of negotiator, diplomat, and mediator between these two worlds. When asked how to bridge the gap between blacks and police, his answer was matter of fact and, in a way, profound: "I've been black a long time, so it's not much of a bridge for me." Indeed, his whole history has been bridging the divide between law enforcement and the black community.

Brown entered policing in 1983, he said, because of the crack epidemic of the early 1980s that devastated his community. He worked his way up the ranks of the Dallas Police Department as someone who was not afraid to criticize conventional wisdom and policing tactics. He served in management roles in both internal affairs and SWAT, directing it for seven years. He became Deputy Chief in 2003 and Chief in 2010.

Shortly after he was selected to become chief in 2010, his 27-year-old son, who suffered from mental illness, shot and killed a police officer and another man before being killed in a confrontation with the police. In his own grief, Brown nevertheless reached out to the families of the victims, met with them, and offered his apology and condolences. He experienced other losses: an academy classmate and former partner was killed in the line of duty, and Brown's younger brother was killed by drug dealers in Arizona.

He developed a reputation as an introspective leader, as a reformer and proponent of community policing that he attributed as instrumental in a steady 12-year decline of crime. In 2015, the city experienced its fourth lowest murder rate since 1930. He saw the most significant reduction in crime in the city's history, and, also, promoted increased diversity and education levels of officers. As leader, he was

(continued)

instrumental in reducing the number of officer-involved shootings by 40 percent. At 55, Brown was one of 20 black police chiefs among the 68 who are members of the Major Cities Chiefs Association. He has not been without critics, however. Before the shootings, the Black Police Association of Greater Dallas had called for his resignation, and the Dallas Police Association indicated their displeasure with his plans to put many officers on overnight shifts to curb rising crime. The unions accused him of being overbearing and inflexible.

Brown was universally commended for being calm in the aftermath of the killings. In his candid interviews, he publicly expressed the loss and pain of police officers by expressing his own deep grief and despair. He also acknowledged the pain of the community, especially the black community, who saw injustice. He challenged protesters, though, to solve the problems they protested by entering public service. He reportedly said: "We're hiring. Get off that protest line and put an application in. And we'll put you in your neighborhood, and we will help you resolve some of the problems you're protesting about." Applications reportedly tripled. In the many interviews after the shootings, he tried to make everyone understand the impossible demands placed upon police officers who were expected to handle social problems, such as the mentally ill and drug addicted, as well as everything from loose dogs to truants.

His public comments were evidence that he was a transformational leader who cared deeply about the men and women who served under him. In one interview, he said he was tempted to impose mandatory counseling because officers tended to pretend to be supermen and women, and not be able to say they needed help. Instead, he said, he tried to hug as many as he could, or shake their hand and tell them how grateful he was for their commitment and sacrifice. He spoke of how his Christian faith has helped him get through crises. He also had words for his fellow chiefs and law enforcement leaders, urging them to "put their careers on the line to make sure we do things right and not be so worried about keeping their jobs."

In September 2016, Brown announced his retirement after 33 years of policing. In 2017, it was announced that he would become managing director in the investigations and disputes division of Kroll, a company that deals with risk mitigation, investigations, compliance, cyber resilience, security, and incident response solutions.

Sources: ABC News, 2016; Fausset, Blinder, and Fernandez, 2016; Government Security News, 2017; Schuppe, 2016; Vargas, 2016.

Conclusion

This chapter shifted the focus from "What is ethical or moral?" to "Why do people act in ethical or unethical ways?" More specifically, we are interested in any findings that shed light on how to ensure that criminal justice professionals act ethically. Philosophers, religious scholars, biologists, psychologists, sociologists, and criminologists have all tried to explain why people do bad things. Biology, learning theory, and Kohlberg's moral stages were used to explain why people's ethical belief systems develop the way they do, but it was also noted that research finds that people's beliefs sometimes do not match their behavior. Philosophy, biology, and psychology all seem to be consistent in the theme that ethical decision making is both emotional and rational.

Research also shows that even adults can be influenced to change their beliefs and behavior given external influences. Bandura discusses moral disengagement and Bazerman and Tenbrunsel explain that bounded ethicality and ethical fading result in unethical behavior. It is probable that these forces are more powerful in small work groups. The organization can incentivize unethical behavior unwittingly by rewarding goals over methods. This leaves the question for organizations how to best ensure ethical behavior by professionals and other employees in the organization. It seems clear that training alone is not sufficient and must be combined with ethical leadership.

Ethical leadership is essential for the ethical organization. Ethical leaders owe a duty to their employees to take responsibility for their own behavior and to create an environment conducive to employees acting ethically, which includes open communication and the use of fair and appropriate discipline. Research on organizational justice shows how the concept is related to higher levels of job satisfaction, organizational commitment, and organizational citizenship behaviors.

While much of the research that has been done in management science applies to criminal justice organizations, we should never lose sight of the unique elements that make up the role of the criminal justice professional. How criminal justice professionals perform their job determines whether justice is a reality or an illusion. The greatest protection against corruption of power is a belief in and commitment to the democratic process and all it entails. If one desires a career in criminal justice, one must ask these questions:

Do I believe in the Constitution?
Do I believe in the Bill of Rights?
Do I truly believe in the sanctity and natural right of due process?

If a person views these protections as impediments, nuisances, or irrelevant, that person should not be a public servant.

In the next nine chapters, we examine the criminal justice system by allocating three chapters each to three areas of study: police, courts, and corrections. In Chapters 5–7, we will discuss ethics as they relate to policing in the United States. Chapters 8–10 are devoted to professionals in the court system. Chapters 11–13 explore the ethics of correctional professionals. In each set of three chapters, we begin in the first chapter (Chapters 5, 8, and 11) with some overarching issues that relate to the profession itself, the formal ethics and mission of the professions described in those chapters, and any occupational subcultures that exist. In the second chapter in each set (Chapters 6, 9, and 12), the focus is on the discretion inherent in the roles related to that set and the dilemmas related to such roles. Finally, in the third chapter in each set (Chapters 7, 10, and 13), the parameters and prevalence of corruption and misconduct are described, along with measures that have been suggested to reduce them.

Chapter Review

1. **Describe biological influences on ethical behavior.**

   Individual explanations of behavior include *biological theories*, which propose that we commit good or bad acts because of biological predispositions, which may be inherited or not. Attention has focused on brain chemicals, such as oxytocin, that influence behavior. Research indicates that both the rational and emotion centers of the brain are implicated in ethical choices. Biological sex differences may be an influence on men's and women's predisposition to crime and, also, unethical behavior.

2. **Describe psychological theories that attempt to explain individual differences in behavior.**

   Learning theory argues that our behavior is based on the rewards we have received in our past. Albert Bandura's more sophisticated social learning theory presents the individual as an active participant in adapting and interpreting the rewards of his or her environment. Lawrence Kohlberg's *moral stage theory* explains that people's behavior is influenced by the intellectual and emotional stage of development and that one reaches or does not reach higher stages of development based on environmental factors. Kohlberg's theory proposes a hierarchy of moral stages, with the highest stage holding the most perfect moral principles, which are universal. Carol Gilligan found that women were more likely to have a stage 3 relationship orientation to ethical judgments, while men were more likely to have a stage 4 "law-and-order" orientation.

3. **Describe research that addresses work group influences on behavior.**

Research indicates that adults can be influenced by peers and, especially, small groups in ethical decision making. Bandura's moral disengagement theory explained that individuals behaved ethically through self-regulatory mechanisms (conscience) but that these mechanisms could be "turned off" through cognitive restructuring using the following: moral justification (appealing to higher principles), euphemistic labeling (downplaying the seriousness of the act), making comparisons (arguing it isn't as bad as something else), displacing responsibility (arguing someone else is at fault), diffusion of responsibility (by acting in a mob), disregarding the consequences (acting in such a way to ignore the effect of one's action), and dehumanization (pretending one's victims are less than human).

4. **Become familiar with organizational influences on behavior.**

In addition to small work groups, the organization itself can also affect ethical decision making of individuals. Reward structures, leadership, and training all can either incentivize or discourage unethical behavior. Research on organizational justice indicates that employees who perceive they are being treated fairly are more likely to engage in organizational citizenship behavior. Research on training and ethics programs indicate that they can be successful in affecting the level of unethical behavior in the workplace.

5. **Become familiar with cultural and societal influences on ethical behavior.**

The public can affect the ethical climate of an organization in what messages organizational leaders and members receive as to what will be tolerated and what will not be. When the public places more value on winning than sportsmanship in sports, organizations are more likely to break rules; when the public reelects politicians convicted of criminal transgressions, the message is received that the rules don't matter; and, when political leaders say no changes are needed, no change will probably occur in patterns of police behavior. The public exerts power in pressuring legislators to enact laws and regulations, but also in the normative pressure displayed in public opinion.

Study Questions

1. Briefly explain how biological approaches might explain antisocial behavior. Explain modeling and reinforcement.

2. Explain Kohlberg's moral development theory. What problems do critics have with his theory? How does Carol Gilligan disagree with Kohlberg's stage theory?

3. Explain why behavior does not always conform with beliefs. Mention specifically bounded ethicality and ethical fading.

4. What necessary elements did Kohlberg identify for reaching higher moral stages?

5. Why is organizational justice important to citizens' perceptions of procedural justice? What are some standards that can be applied to good leadership? What advice do Souryal and Metz offer to those who desire to be good leaders?

Writing/Discussion Exercises

1. Develop an essay on (or discuss) the development of morality. Who has been the greatest influence on your moral development? Why? How? Why do you think people behave in ways that hurt other people? Have you ever done something you knew to be wrong? Why did you do it?

2. Develop an essay on (or discuss) the relationships between morality, moral/ethical teaching, and criminality. Do thieves have the same moral beliefs as others? Do they know that stealing is wrong? Can we successfully predict which individuals will perform unethical or immoral actions?

3. Develop an essay on (or discuss) what an ideal ethical organization would be. What would be the characteristics of leadership? Training? Employees? How does one create such an organization as a change agent if the existing organization is rife with corruption?

Key Terms

bounded ethicality	Kohlberg's moral stages	recognition tests
developmental theories	modeling	reinforcement
ethical fading	moral identity	self-efficacy

ETHICAL DILEMMAS

Situation 1

You are a prosecutor trying your first case. You are thrilled with how well it is going. Every objection you make is upheld, and every objection the defense makes is overruled. The judge shakes her head affirmatively every time you make a point and scowls and makes disparaging comments about and to the defense attorney. As the trial proceeds, you begin to see that it is going so well not because of your legal expertise, but rather, because the judge is obviously and seriously biased against the defense. You do not know if she simply does not like the defense attorney or if she does this in all the trials, but you do know that she is making it extremely difficult for the jury to ignore her and, thus, is violating the due process rights of the accused. Should you be grateful for your good luck and accept an easy conviction or make a stand against the judge's actions?

Situation 2

You are a police officer assigned to the juvenile division. For the most part, you enjoy your job and believe that you have sometimes even made a difference when the juvenile has listened to you and stayed out of trouble (at least as far as you knew). One day you are told repeatedly by your captain to pick up a juvenile, even though you don't think there is any probable cause to do so. This is the third time you have been ordered to pick him up and bring him into the station. You discover that the detectives are trying to get the juvenile to become an informant because he is related to a suspected drug dealer. Should you participate in the attempt to intimidate him or refuse to do so?

Situation 3

Your partner has been on the force 25 years, and you value her opinion greatly. However, you have noticed that she has become progressively more lethargic and unenthusiastic about the job. When dispatch asks for available cars, she won't let you respond. When you see accidents on the highway, she instructs you to go around the block so that you won't have to stop. Even when you receive calls, she tells you to advise dispatch that you are otherwise occupied. You believe that she has become burned out and isn't performing up to the standard that you know she is capable of. What, if anything, would you do about it?

Situation 4

You are a rookie police officer and are riding with a Field Training Officer (FTO). During your shift, the FTO stops at a convenience store and quickly drinks four beers in the back room of the store. He is visibly affected by the beers, and the smell of alcohol is noticeable. What should you do? What if the FTO had just written a favorable evaluation of you even though you should have received a reprimand for an improper disposition of a traffic accident?

Situation 5

You are a senior getting close to graduation and are taking too many classes during your last semester. You find yourself getting behind in class and not doing well on tests. One of the classes requires a 30-page term paper, and you simply do not have the time to complete the paper by the due date. While you are on the Internet one day, you see that term papers can be purchased on any topic. You ordinarily would do your own work, but the time pressure of this last semester is such that you see no other way. Do you purchase the paper and turn it in as your own?

The Police Role in Society   5

AP Images/Elaine Thompson

Learning Objectives

1. Describe the two different missions of law enforcement in a democracy.

2. Compare the current trends of policing to past historical eras.

3. Provide the justification for police power and the basic ethical standards that derive from this justification.

4. Identify the differences between the formal ethics of law enforcement and the values of the police subculture.

5. Describe recent research findings on the police subculture.

Officer Russ Hicks at the Washington State Criminal Justice Training Commission explains the "guardian" style of policing which emphasizes the idea that police are, fundamentally, the guardians of the Constitution.

A tsunami of scrutiny has battered law enforcement officers in the last several years. The Michael Brown shooting in Ferguson, Missouri in 2014 and the 2015 Freddie Gray killing in Baltimore, Maryland triggered the Black Lives Matter movement, negative media attention, and Department of Justice (DOJ) "pattern and practice" investigations leading to demands for reform. Allegations that officers use deadly force against African American men disproportionately and that, more pervasively, they discriminate against minorities, policing them differently than whites, have been the theme of intense scrutiny since 2014. These are not new concerns and we will address both issues in the next chapter.

President Obama has been perceived by a large contingent of law enforcement professionals as an enemy of police because of statements that could be taken as disparagement of all, unwillingness to defend police actions, an executive order that restricted the 1033 program (which will be discussed in a later section), and the large number of "pattern and practice" investigations undertaken by the DOJ under his administration. The President's Task Force on 21st Century Policing (https://cops.usdoj.gov/pdf/taskforce/TaskForce_FinalReport.pdf)

was created by President Obama and Attorney General Holder to examine a wide range of issues. Despite the presence of law enforcement leaders on the panel, along with academics and community advocates, the panel's findings were looked upon with distrust. The panel's recommendations were wide-ranging and covered issues that should be hard to disagree with, including the need for promoting health and emotional support for police officers who face incredibly stressful work environments. We will explore these findings in more detail in Chapter 7. In contrast, President Trump is perceived as an avid supporter of police, and his appointment of Attorney General Jeff Sessions has been interpreted as a signal of support. As noted in the last chapter, Attorney General Sessions has indicated he will dramatically restrict the number of federal investigations of individual police departments. Police reformers are dismayed that what they view as progress may now be undone by new political winds.

Police officers have felt attacked, misunderstood, wrongfully blamed, and unappreciated. Harsh scrutiny is directed at police actions. However, there is an important reason for such scrutiny. The police represent the "thin blue line" between disorder and order. They are also the personification of the power of the state. No other criminal justice professional comes under as much constant and public scrutiny—but no other criminal justice professional wields as much unfettered power and authority over the citizenry.

Police have the choice to arrest or not to arrest, to mediate or to charge, and in decisions to use deadly force, they even hold the power of life and death. If such power is used fairly, legally, and ethically, they are our protectors. If such power is used abusively, arbitrarily, and/or in corrupt ways, they become our oppressors. In nondemocratic countries, police are feared because they act with impunity to maintain those in power. In some areas of Mexico and South America, police are viewed as corrupted by the drug cartels; in other parts of the world, police are viewed as "owned" by oligarchs. Abusive power and economic corruption exist in the United States as well, although, not in pervasive patterns as in some other countries. No doubt the scrutiny police officers endure here helps to keep it that way.

In this chapter, we deconstruct the nature of policing and uncover some of the structural and historical precedents for current events. We first explore the dual mission of crime fighter and public servant and explain how the roles affect perceptions of duty and the way discretion is employed. The current debate over whether there is a "Ferguson effect" will be reviewed. The philosophical justification for police power is discussed, as well as the limits of such power. Codes of ethics followed by the informal, subcultural codes of behavior that also influence officer behavior complete the chapter.

Law enforcement in the United States is extremely decentralized and, because of this, it is difficult to get an accurate count of how many law enforcement officers exist. One recent federal report notes that sources vary but there were between 687,657 and 750,340 sworn officers and between 203,632 and 325,714 nonsworn law enforcement employees for a total in 2012 as high as 1,076,054 (Banks, Hendrix, Hickman, and Kyckelhahn, 2016). Even though there are a few extremely large police departments (New York City Police Department has over 34,000 officers), most police departments are very small with about 48 percent employing fewer than 10 officers. About 27 percent of all officers were members of a racial or ethnic minority in 2013, which is about double the percentage in 1987 (Reeves, 2015). Because of the large differences between departments, it is extremely difficult to have a conversation about "policing" in this country. Large city police departments are very different from departments in small

IN THE NEWS | *Above and Beyond...*

A recent news item described how Officer Katrina Culbreath of the Dothan Police Department was in court in May 2017 and heard a young woman plead guilty to fourth degree theft for shoplifting food for herself and her family. The officer asked the woman to come with her and the two went to a nearby grocery store where the officer purchased over $100 in food for the teenage mother. The two have had almost daily contact since and there is little doubt that the officer's actions have impacted this family.

These incidents are not rare. In the last edition of this book, the actions of two Seattle police officers, Jeremy Wade and Ryan Gallagher, were described. They purchased a set of twin beds for a poor family on their day off and with their own money, and then set up the "Beds for Kids Project," which enlists sponsors and conducts fundraisers to provide beds for children in need. The actions of these officers, and countless others across the nation, represent the side of policing that is not presented in the media as often as it should be.

Source: Heffernan, 2014; WHAS, 2017.

towns and suburban areas in informal culture, policies, and discipline systems. Unfortunately, when any agency is front page news because of ethical misconduct, the effects of such negative press affect all agencies.

As we discuss issues of law enforcement ethics in these chapters, it is important to remember that the vast majority of officers are honest and ethical. We focus on the few officers who abuse their position or forget their mission; however, this in no way should be taken as a criticism of the thousands upon thousands of officers who perform their job well, every day, in every city in the country. Nor should we forget the thousands of officers who go above and beyond the call of duty. Officers risk their lives to save victims, sacrifice their health, and take time away from family to address the needs and problems of the citizenry. We must focus on the actions of the deviant few to discover the elements of the profession that open the door to such behavior, but we should always remember that almost all officers are more typical of those described in the In the News box above.

Crime Fighter or Public Servant?

We will approach these chapters with an underlying premise that what drives individual decisions on the part of law enforcement officers and society's reactions to them is derived from a perception of the law enforcement mission. Two different missions—crime fighting and public service—can be identified as having quite different implications for decision making. We do not, of course, mean to say that these missions are necessarily contradictory or exclusive; however, it is important to note the history and present-day influence of these different roles.

Crime Control and Due Process Models

When one asks most people what the role of policing is in society, the response is some version of "catch criminals" or "fight crime." If one views police as crime control agents, the presumption is that criminals (who are different from the rest of us) are the enemy and police officers are the soldiers in a war on crime. This model is based on Herbert Packer's (1968) crime control model (which he contrasted with the due process model discussed next). According to Packer, the crime control model operates under the following principles:

1. Repression of criminal conduct is the most important function.
2. Failure of law enforcement means the breakdown of order.
3. Criminal process is the positive guarantor of social freedom.
4. Efficiency is a top priority.
5. Emphasis is on speed and finality.
6. A conveyor belt is the model for the system.
7. There is a presumption of guilt.

Police perception of their role as crime fighters will lead to certain decisions in their use of force, their definition of duty, and their use of deception and coercion. Public perception of the police mission as primarily crime fighting leads to a willingness to accept certain definitions and justifications of behavior: that drug addicts are unworthy of protection, that individuals who are beaten by police must have deserved it, that all defendants must be guilty, and so on. In most cases, police actions are rationalized or excused by the belief that people "get what they deserve."

If one views police as **public servants**, presumptions are different and include the idea that criminals are not so different from us and, in fact, may be our sons or daughters. As public servants, police officers serve all people and owe everyone the duty of civility and legality. Finally, there is the idea that police have limited ability to affect crime rates one way or the other because crime is a complex social phenomenon.

public servants
Professionals who are paid by the public and whose jobs entail pursuing the public good.

Under Packer's (1968) due process model, the following principles stand out in contrast to those in the crime control model:

1. There is a possibility of error.
2. Finality is not a priority.
3. There is insistence on prevention and elimination of mistakes.
4. Efficiency is rejected if it involves shortcuts.
5. Protection of process is as important as protection of innocents.
6. The coercive power of the state is always subject to abuse.

Packer's original model of due process that he contrasted with his crime control model is somewhat different from our description of the public service mission. Rather than just an emphasis on rights as in the due process model, under the public servant model proposed here, law enforcement is perceived as "owned" by all people, so service is foremost. Police must respond to all constituencies, including groups that may be less supportive of the police than white middle-class communities. It is an enlarged view of the police officer role in society. Rather than simply catching criminals, officers are perceived to be crime preventers, peace keepers, and service providers.

A perception of the police officer as public servant implies a much more restrictive view of the use of force and police power. The utilitarian idea that the "end" (crime control) justifies almost any "means" is rejected in favor of an approach that is more protective of due process and equal protection. In the public service mission, law enforcement, above all, protects the rights of every citizen and—only in this way—escapes the taint of its historical role as a tool of oppression for the powerful.

The crime control model of policing is related to a "war on crime" mentality, with police officers seen as the warriors on the front line. Military and war imagery is, arguably, not appropriate in civil police settings in democracies; however, some have observed that law enforcement in this country has become increasingly "militarized," even as crime rates have declined. Peter Kraska (an academic researcher) and Radley Balko (a journalist) are the two most prolific researcher/writers who have identified and discussed this trend. Kraska (1999, 2001, 2007; Kraska and Cubellis, 1997; Kraska and Kappeler, 1997; Kappeler and Kraska, 2014) has, for decades, noted the increasing number of Special Weapons and Tactics (SWAT) teams even while the crime rate declined dramatically, the use of SWAT teams for nonhostage situations (e.g., execution of search warrants), military imagery and training, and the merging of police officer/soldier role-sets.

Balko (2013a & b) described the origins of the SWAT model in Los Angeles. Now there are thousands of such squads in the United States (no one knows how many) conducting tens of thousands of raids each year. These units use military tactics, including flash-bang grenades and battering rams. They are dressed in camouflage or black uniforms, often masked, and heavily armed. Because the crime rate is half what it was in the 1980s, there is concern that they are being used for increasingly inappropriate operations, such as licensing and gambling raids when there is no evidence that police officers will be met with force. An ACLU study found that 79 percent of SWAT team deployments were for executing a search warrant, and only 7 percent of deployments were for hostage, barricade, or active shooter scenarios (Peralta and Eads, 2015).

Balko (2013a) also focused on the dangers of the rise in the use of no-knock warrants and the dubious constitutional analysis extended by the Supreme Court in approving of heavily armed state agents bursting into private homes without announcing their presence. Balko provides shocking examples where homeowners have been shot by police or have ended up in prison for shooting police officers whom they believed were armed intruders. Some of these raids were conducted on the wrong house against completely innocent homeowners; others were to execute arrest or search warrants for minor and/or nonviolent crimes. Cases where SWAT raids resulted in needless death include Katherine Johnston, a 92-year-old woman killed in Atlanta in 2006; Alberto Sepulveda, an 11 year old accidentally shot by a California SWAT officer in 2000 (Balko, 2013a); and Aiyana Stanley-Jones, a 7 year old shot in a Detroit raid where the SWAT team used a flash-bang grenade and an officer accidentally discharged his weapon (Abbey-Lambertz, 2015).

Another element of the militarization of police is the growing number of ex-military who join police departments. It is reported that one in five police officers have a military background, returning from Afghanistan, Iraq, or other deployments. Just 6 percent of the population at large has served in the military, but almost 20 percent of police officers are veterans. These veterans bring discipline and important skill-sets to police departments, but they also bring a warrior mentality that may be inappropriate for civil engagement if it is not redirected. More troubling is the number of veterans who return with varying symptoms of PTSD, which may include flashbacks, blackouts, and waking nightmares (Weichselbaum and Schwartzapfel, 2017).

There is no conclusive research on whether police officers who have a military background are quicker to use force or more likely to use deadly force than those officers without a military background. According to records of the Albuquerque Police Department, of the 35 fatal shootings by police between January 2010 and April 2014, 11 fatal shootings—or 31 percent—were by military veterans, numbers that indicate veterans are disproportionally involved in shootings (Weichselbaum and Schwartzapfel, 2017). Other anecdotal evidence, however, supports the idea that military-trained officers are calmer in the face of danger, and more secure in their defensive skills, allowing them to put off using physical tactics when engaging with a vocal and noncompliant individual (Pollock and Strah, 2017).

Balko (2014) explains that officers today are socialized by their training and culture to be suspicious of all citizens and to be constantly wary of danger. He points to the shooting of Levar Jones by former South Carolina state trooper Sean Groubert after pulling him over for a seatbelt violation, and the shooting of John Crawford in a Walmart because he was carrying a BB rifle. Balko notes that Jones and Crawford were shot most probably because police officers were acting in conformance with their socialization that every black man is a potential threat and every day has a high probability of death—despite the falseness of these perceptions. Officers experience in-service "active shooter training," they see videos of officers killed in the line of duty, and they are exposed to a mindset that policing is getting more dangerous. The risk of a traffic stop resulting in a shooting incident is about 1 in 4.6 million stops and the average risk is more like 1 in 10 million, but police officers are trained that traffic stops may result in violent shootouts (Balko, 2014).

Balko also was one of the first to draw attention to the 1033 program under which local police departments could receive military equipment no longer needed as the military ratcheted down its presence in Afghanistan and Iraq. Local departments now own armored vehicles, aircraft, and even grenade launchers (Apuzzo, 2014). President Obama issued an executive order restricting some of the types of military equipment (tracked armored vehicles, weaponized aircraft, and high-caliber weapons) from being distributed to local police departments under the 1033 program and requiring local departments to return some equipment (Peralta and Eads, 2015; Tau, 2014). Grovum (2015) reported that before the executive order, law enforcement in Florida, for instance, received 47 mine-resistant vehicles, 36 grenade launchers, and more than 7,540 rifles. In Texas, there were 73 mine-resistant vehicles and a $24.3 million aircraft. Many law enforcement leaders were livid when they had to return armored vehicles, bayonets, and other equipment. They pointed to the 14 killed in San Bernardino, the hostages taken at a Planned Parenthood clinic in Colorado Springs in 2015, and the 50 killed at the Orlando nightclub in 2016 as instances reflective of the need for military-grade defensive weapons (Hall and Brasier, 2015; Williams, 2016a). This, perhaps more than anything else, led to a perception that President Obama was not supportive of law enforcement. President Trump has indicated he will rescind President Obama's executive order restricting the distribution of military weaponry (Fraternal Order of Police, 2017).

In contrast to the described warrior approach to policing, is the guardian approach. There has been a growing national movement toward the "guardian" model of policing. The warrior approach views police as soldiers engaged in a battle. The emphasis is on danger and force. The guardian model, however, sees the officer as primarily a protector of the citizenry, but also of democratic values. In academy training, the warrior mindset of power, control, battle, and survival is deemphasized. There is a greater focus on values such as service and protection of democratic values

(Rahr and Rice, 2015). The guardian model is consistent with deescalation and implicit bias training, Crisis Intervention Team (CIT) training, increased accountability and citizen involvement in oversight, and community engagement programs. A Vera Institute of Justice found that 34 states and Washington, D.C. passed at least 79 laws in 2015 and 2016 (compared to only 20 in the three-year period before) directed at police, including: requiring policies that limited use of force (e.g., chokeholds); prohibiting racial profiling; requiring better use of force training, cultural sensitivity, and bias-free policing training; prohibiting profiling solely based on race, ethnicity, gender, national origin, language, religion, sexual orientation, gender identity, age, or disability; requiring yearly CIT training; requiring the use of body cameras; and, improving accountability in cases of police misconduct. Some states also passed "Blue Alert" systems that improved a coordinated public response when a police officer was killed or wounded (Vera Institute of Justice, 2017).

What type of policing do we want: crime fighters or public servants? Those who value the crime-fighter/warrior role are more tolerant of police error in use of force incidents and "over-policing." Those who believe that police should emphasize their public servant/guardian role are much less tolerant of inappropriate uses of power. Police officers, too, tend to perceive one role as dominant over the other and this perception shapes their daily behavior. These two models are better understood if we take a brief look at the history of law enforcement in the United States.

History of Policing: From Public Servant to Crime Fighter

Kappeler, Sluder, and Alpert (1984/1994) have discussed the early origins of law enforcement as a model of service. Police were involved in social service activities: they ran soup kitchens, provided lodging for indigents, and spurred moral reform movements against cigarettes and alcohol. Of course, early law enforcement personnel were also involved in social control and employed utilitarian violence—that is, they acted as the force for power holders in society and were union busters and political-machine enforcers. Such force was frequently used against immigrants, labor organizers, and the poor (Alpert and Dunham, 2004; Harris, 2005). Researchers note that early law enforcement even used undercover agent provocateurs in the 1800s, placing them in anarchist groups to incite violence to justify using official violence against protesters. Two incidents of this are the 1874 Tompkins Square riot, where 7,000 were injured, and the Haymarket incident in 1886 (Donner, 1992).

Early police departments also were marred by frequent graft and other forms of corruption. Crank (2003), for instance, discusses how police were involved in local political machines. They stuffed ballot boxes and coerced votes. Their graft was widely tolerated because of their meager salaries. Donner (1992) called this the "dialectic of the bargain," referring to police pursuing and harassing dissenter groups in exchange for the power holders' toleration of police corruption.

The move toward police "professionalism," starting in the 1920s, was spurred by several factors, one of which was to improve the image of police as *objective* enforcers of the law rather than enforcers for whomever happened to be in power. In effect, there was a real or perceived shift of police loyalty from political bosses to the law itself (Fogelson, 1977; Kappeler et al., 1994). Part of this transformation involved the idea that police were crime fighters—professional soldiers in the war on crime—a concept that implies objectivity, professional expertise, and specialized training. This role deemphasized the social service role and ultimately led to policing characterized by detachment from the community being policed instead of being a part of that community. In this new role, police were proactive rather than simply reactive to public demands (Crank and Caldero, 2000/2005; Payne, 2002).

Even though the professional crime fighter role of the police officer has been well established for more than 70 years, we can see remnants of the legacy of both the early political enforcer role and the public service role. Some continue to see the police as enforcers for those who hold financial and political power and point to their continuing role in investigating and monitoring dissident groups. The so-called Red Squads in some police departments infiltrated and spied on organizations believed to be sympathetic to socialism from the 1930s to the 1960s (Donner, 1992). Then, in the 1960s and 1970s, police turned their attention to antiwar groups and others that expressed opposition to the government. At one point, the Chicago police department had files on 117,000 individuals and 14,000 organizations (Donner, 1992), and J. Edgar Hoover kept his secret files on many Americans, including Martin Luther King, Jr., who, arguably, was no threat to this nation's security. These activities led to the Church Committee's (headed by Senator Frank Church) 1975–1976 investigation of the government's "spying" on Americans and subsequent stringent wiretapping laws and legal decisions that ruled such activities were improper infringements on citizens' privacy rights (Donner, 1992). After 9/11, these laws were viewed as impediments in the efforts to find who was responsible and guard against another terrorist attack, and the Patriot Act and other laws have removed some restrictions to law enforcement surveillance actions. We will discuss more current counterintelligence activities of law enforcement agencies in Chapter 14.

Police are still sometimes seen as enforcers for the powerful in society, especially when public protests become unruly. Examples of this include the mass arrests during the Republican convention in 2004; a 2007 protest in support of illegal immigrants in Los Angeles that resulted in injuries to demonstrators when LAPD officers used rubber bullets and batons; the Occupy protests that began in 2011 and continue sporadically in various cities; the Ferguson and Baltimore protests in 2014 and in 2015; and, the arrests of protesters at the Republican convention in 2016. The arrest of journalists during the Ferguson riots has raised issues of improper use of police authority to control the media (Stewart, 2016).

In other countries, the image of police as corrupt and serving the interests of the powerful is much more pronounced. Semukhina and Reynolds (2013) discuss the widespread distrust of police in Russia along with a short history of their role vis-à-vis the citizenry and the state. Before the fall of the Iron Curtain, police were viewed as the enforcers for the totalitarian government. When the government loosened its hold on Russian society (perestroika), organized crime filled the void and police were perceived as tools of powerful crime figures (Wendle, 2009). In every failed state, law enforcement loses public trust when it becomes a tool for the powerful instead of neutral enforcers of civil law.

The historical social service role of police was resurrected in the **community policing** movement that reached the height of its prevalence in the late 1990s. Community policing involves having officers develop closer relationships with community leaders to help them solve some of the social problems that are believed to be associated with the development of disorder and crime. In community policing initiatives,

community policing   A model of law enforcement that creates partnerships with the community and addresses underlying problems rather than simply enforcing the law.

police officers were involved in cleaning up parks and graffiti, helping to raze abandoned houses, helping to start youth programs, setting up storefront locations to improve communications with community members, and having community meetings to listen to what citizens think are the problems of the community (National Institute of Justice, 1992; Skogan and Wycoff, 1986).

While community policing was endorsed nationally by federal agencies such as the National Institute of Justice and the Bureau of Justice Assistance, individual police officers across the country were less enthused about the concept. Several researchers described patrol officers' resistance to community policing models and explained that such efforts were viewed as trading in the crime fighter role for a much less esteemed social worker role. However, even those who resisted the community policing model admitted that the role of law enforcement has always included community relations and community service. For instance, a recent Police Foundation study on the benefits of foot patrol was consistent with the tenants of community policing without using the terminology (Cowell and Kringen, 2016).

While some aspects of the community policing approach have been institutionalized, observers note that 9/11 led to a retrenchment in policing and a return to more traditional crime fighting elements (Brown, 2007; Murray, 2005). Harris (2005) noted that 9/11 led to sweeping reforms that changed the face of federal law enforcement and influenced changes in state and local law enforcement as well. In fact, the warrior approach described above illustrates this shift and many police officers today have spent their entire career in a post 9/11 policing world. If training has emphasized the warrior approach, it may be simply reflecting the national posture in response to terrorism and the realization that law enforcement is our first line of defense against internal and external threats. The more recent shift to guardian policing may signal a return-to-center position, acknowledging that police should not be trained and socialized to expect that every person is a likely enemy and the community a battlefield.

It is important to have some historical perspective on shifts in policing rhetoric and tactics. The riots of the 1960s served as the impetus to hire minority and female officers and create public information units within police departments. The counterintelligence and undercover activities of police departments in the 1970s spurred strict controls of surveillance tactics. The heyday of the drug war in the 1980s with "Miami Vice" policing in many cities, including freewheeling narcotics units, and the much publicized beating of Rodney King, led to the community policing efforts in the 1990s. Then 9/11 pushed policing back to a traditional war model. Moving too far toward militarization with the overuse of SWAT units and the deterioration of relationships with minority neighborhoods has led to advocating the guardian approach (by police leaders), pattern and practice investigations (by federal overseers), and civil rights movements (by communities targeted by heavy-handed policing efforts). Policing has always reflected and reacted to historical eras and political shifts.

The Future of Policing and the "Ferguson Effect"

Today, preventive policing, problem-solving policing, predictive policing, and intelligence-led policing exist in a confused mix of approaches and terminology. Problem-solving policing arises naturally out of community-based policing whereby neighborhood problems are identified and dealt with, often in partnership with community members. Predictive policing focuses on sophisticated data gathering and analysis; geographic analysis is used to identify where criminal events are likely to occur based on where offenders have struck in the past. Intelligence-led policing is a managerial philosophy whereby data analysis and intelligence are used for objective decision making designed for crime prevention (Ratcliffe, 2008). The approach emphasizes the use of confidential informants, offender interviews, analyzing incident reports and calls for service, surveillance, and community sources of information. Today, policing, at least in major cities, is proactive (rather than merely reactive) and highly sophisticated in the use of crime analysis (Carter and Phillips, 2013). Larger cities, such as New York and Los Angeles, have intelligence gathering that rivals the sophistication of the federal government (Moore, 2014).

Whether police continue to move toward the guardian model or there is a major retrenchment back to the warrior mentality remains to be seen. The approach of the President's Task Force on 21st Century Policing was that police should acknowledge "the role of policing in past and present injustice and discrimination" and take steps to restore public trust and confidence (President's Task Force on 21st Century Policing's, 2015:12). Civil lawsuits, federal consent decrees, collaborative reform, and memorandums of agreement have led to police departments keeping better use of force and stop-and-frisk records, offering training in deescalation, CIT, and implicit bias, and reviving community policing concepts such as community engagement projects. However, there is also strong resistance to the theme that there is something wrong with policing that needs to be fixed, or that police are systemically biased.

Some police leaders and others argue that national scrutiny and criticism has led to such a strong anti-police bias that it has endangered police (FBI, 2017). According to this view, the constant focus on the few "bad apples" in policing arguably has created public antipathy and hostility to the point where it is harder for police to do their job and it has led to a dramatic increase in ambush-style killings of officers. Certainly, the five officers—Brent Thompson, Patrick Zamarripa, Michael Krol, Michael Smith, and Lorne Ahrens—ambushed and killed in Dallas in July 2016 while on duty at a peaceful "Black Lives Matter" protest escalated the concern that policing was under attack. An annual report by the nonprofit National Law Enforcement Officers Memorial Fund (2017) indicated that 64 officers were killed by gunfire in 2016, a 56 percent increase from the 42 officers killed by guns in 2015. The average since 2004 has been 55 police deaths annually. It is important to have some historical context. In 2011, 73 officers were killed in gunfire, the most in any year in the past decade; however, in 1973, 156 police officers were killed by gunfire and the 1970s averaged about 140 officer deaths per year. These are not rates per 1,000, so the 1973 number would have been from a much smaller total number of police officers in the country. Note that these are deaths by gunfire only; there is about an equal number of additional deaths due to traffic accidents.

A recent study released by the FBI (2017) examined the 64 officers killed in 2016, reporting that 86 percent of the assailants had prior criminal histories, and 56 percent were known to the local police or sheriffs' department. Diagnosed mental health issues existed in 18 percent of the cases and was indicated as a contributing factor in 40 percent of the shootings. About 60 percent of the assailants had a history of drug use, and almost a third were confirmed to have been under the influence at the time of the shooting. Forty-eight percent of the assailants were white, 36 percent were black, 14 percent were Hispanic, and 2 percent were Alaska Native. About 28 percent had expressed a desire to kill law enforcement. The remainder were attempting to resist going to jail or prison. The report then offers some findings from interviews with police officials; specifically, that law enforcement not only felt that their national political leaders were against them, but that public disrespect allowed assailants to become more emboldened to question, resist, and even kill law enforcement officers. This "chill wind" has led to "de-policing" where officers engaged in life or death struggles have chosen not to use their weapons because of a fear of being a scapegoat for forces against law enforcement. This summary of the perceptions of law enforcement officials was not accompanied by any methodological notes so it is unknown how many were interviewed, whether there was random sampling or there were any objective facts to support such perceptions.

One academic study disputes the conclusion that killings of law enforcement officers have been influenced by the events following Ferguson. Maguire, Nix, and Campbell (2016), using time series analysis, and national data regarding officer killings concluded that there was no statistical relationship between the events after the Ferguson riots and police killings.

While the number of firearm-related deaths is down dramatically from the 1970s, and there may not be any statistical relationship over time between events and the number of police killings, there has been a recent increase in the number of ambush style attacks. There had already been five ambush-style shooting by March of 2016 and the July 2016 killings of five law enforcement officers in Dallas was the single deadliest incident for law enforcement since 9/11; therefore, despite the gradual downward trend, it is understandable why police officers may feel under attack.

Another current discussion concerns the so-called "Ferguson effect" or "YouTube effect" and de-policing. Some distinguish the concepts; however, the idea is that intense public scrutiny and hostility have made police officers so demoralized that they have reduced their self-initiated activities and no longer engage in proactive activities such as engaging in suspicious individuals on the street. This, then, has led to spikes in crime and homicides (Davis, 2016; MacDonald, 2015). Beginning in 2015, major news outlets began reporting on big-city crime spikes. Eventually the Washington Post, New York Times, NPR, CNN, the BBC, USA Today, Reuters, Time, and other major news outlets had "crime spike" stories. Other news outlets and think tanks, for example, New York Daily News, Brennan Center, and Marshall Project, argued that the spike was not related to de-policing because it was not nationwide, nor was it connected to any pervasive crime increase. Further, there was no strong evidence for "de-policing" other than a dramatic drop in arrests for minor crimes, citations for violations, and investigative stops in some cities. Whether these constituted a troubling de-policing trend that led to violent crime increases or a return to a less aggressive style of policing called for more research (Rosenfeld, 2015, 2016).

One study, using survey data from 567 officers, found that negative publicity did lead to feelings of being less motivated and a perception of less self-legitimacy (Nix and Wolfe, 2015). There has also been one study that found arrests dropped significantly in Baltimore after the Freddie Gray incident with an accompanying rise in crime. Another study found that cities that agreed to federal consent decrees (with arguably subsequent changes in policing tactics) experienced temporary crime increases (Gross, 2016). However, New York City dramatically reduced stop-and-frisks and continues to experience declining crime rates, although when individual neighborhoods are examined, the findings are more complicated (Rosenfeld and Fornango, 2017). The research question is extremely difficult to study because crime rates are generated by citizens calling in crime reports. If they do not trust police, they will not call and crimes do not get counted. If trust increases, citizens will be more likely to report crimes, leading to what appears to be a crime increase. It could also be the case that it is not "de-policing" that is causing the crime spikes, but a lack of trust in scandal-ridden police departments leading to retaliatory and vigilante homicides.

In the most recent and comprehensive study of police attitudes, a Pew Research Center study, using the National Police Research Platform data from 8,000 officers, revealed that about 66 percent of police officers say the deaths of black Americans during encounters with police are isolated incidents, not a sign that law enforcement is characterized by systemic bias; however, 60 percent of the general population did believe there was a broader problem between police and minority communities. Most officers reported that high-profile deaths have made their job harder. More than 7 in 10 say officers are less likely to stop and question suspicious people, roughly three-quarters agreed that fellow officers report they are more reluctant to use force when necessary, and more than 9 in 10 agreed that fellow officers have grown more worried about their safety. This study shows a wide gulf in perception between police officers and members of the public, but there is also a divide between black officers and other officers. While 72 percent of white and Hispanic officers agreed that blacks killed in police altercations are isolated incidents, a majority of black officers say those deaths a sign of broader problems between police and black citizens. About 92 percent of white officers say the country has made the changes needed to achieve equality between black and white citizens, compared with only 29 percent of black officers. Six in 10 white and Hispanic officers alike agreed their department's police had a positive relationship with the black community, but only 32 percent of black officers agreed (Clement and Lowery, 2017; Pew Research Center, 2017). What this study reveals is that there is no national consensus on whether there is a current problem with policing, much less agreement on approaches to improve policing. With this backdrop, we now turn to the elements of police power and discretion.

Power and Discretion

Klockars (1984) describes police control as consisting of the following elements: **authority** (the unquestionable entitlement to be obeyed), **power** (the means to achieve domination), **persuasion** (signs, symbols, words, and arguments used to induce compliance), and **force** (physical domination and control). Any police officer at any time might have the need or opportunity to exercise one of these four different types of domination, from unquestioned authority to physical force. Individual officers have a great deal of discretion in what type of power to use in any given situation. **Discretion** can be defined as having the authority to choose between two or more courses of behavior.

Why does law enforcement have the right to employ these types of control? "We give it to them" is the easy answer. Police power is a governmental right invested in federal, state, and local law enforcement agencies. It means that these organizations, unlike almost any other except perhaps the military, have the right to control citizens' movements to the point of using physical and even deadly force to do so.

authority Unquestionable entitlement to be obeyed that comes from fulfilling a specific role.

power The right inherent in a role to use any means to overcome resistance.

persuasion The use of signs, symbols, words, and arguments to induce compliance.

force The authority to use physical coercion to overcome the will of the individual.

discretion The authority to make a decision between two or more choices.

social contract
The concept developed by Hobbes, Rousseau, and Locke in which the state of nature is a "war of all against all" and, thus, individuals give up their liberty to aggress against others in return for safety.

Cohen and Feldberg (1991) developed a careful analysis of, and justification for, police power and proposed that it stems from the **social contract**. Thomas Hobbes (1588–1679) and John Locke (1632–1704) created the concept of the social contract to explain why people have given up liberties in civilized societies. According to this theory, each citizen gives up complete liberty in return for societal protection against others. Complete freedom is given up in return for guaranteed protection. Police power is part of this *quid pro quo*: we give the police these powers to protect us, but we also recognize that their power can be used against us.

This general idea has corollary principles. First, each of us should be able to feel protected. If not, we are not gaining anything from the social contract and may decide to renegotiate the contract by regaining some of the liberties given up. For instance, vigilante movements arise when the populace thinks that formal agents of social control do not protect them, and isolationist groups "opt out" of most traditional societal controls because they believe that they can create a better society.

Second, because the deprivations of freedoms are limited to those necessary to ensure protection against others, police power should be circumscribed to the minimum necessary to meet the goals of protection. If police exceed this threshold, the public rightly objects.

Third, police ethics are inextricably linked to their purpose. If the social contract is the basis of their power, it is also the basis of their ethics. Cohen and Feldberg (1991) propose five ethical standards that can be derived from the social contract:

- Fair access
- Public trust
- Safety and security
- Teamwork
- Objectivity

Law enforcement, if it is lawful, objective, and professional, is part of the foundation of a stable government and a hallmark of democratic societies. Banks (2014) points out the elements of democratic policing include the following:

- Responsiveness
- Accountability
- Defense of human rights
- Transparency

She discusses how the convergence of police and military is seen when regime protection eclipses public safety even if military dictatorships are replaced with elected governments. Other impediments to a free society include toleration for corruption in public offices, lack of political commitment to police reform, patterns of patronage, and rule by fiat. Pino and Wiatrowski (2006) argue that democratic policing includes the rule of law, legitimacy (consent of the governed), transparency, accountability, and subordination to civil authority.

Recall the concept of procedural justice described in Chapter 3. Research shows that people are more likely to view law enforcement as legitimate if their experience includes the elements of procedural justice: voice, neutrality, respect, and trustworthiness. Voice refers to when people can express themselves and police officers listen to them. Neutrality is the concept of equity; specifically, that police officers do not discriminate and treat everyone equally. Respect is when citizens feel that they are being treated with respect (even those who have committed a crime). Trustworthiness is the idea that individuals trust police to do the right thing and act within the law. These elements echo the hallmarks of democratic policing cited above. As noted in Chapter 3, research has shown that those who have higher scores on perceived procedural justice have greater satisfaction with police and are more likely to see police power as legitimate and comply with police commands.

One important aspect of trusting the police is the likelihood that people will call police when they are victimized or know of a crime. In one study, it was found that after public disclosure of police officer misuse of force (e.g., a video of a beating or a police shooting), calls to 911 drop significantly. Since these events often involve black men, it is not surprising that calls from black neighborhoods decreased more dramatically. The decline in calls represents a severe breach in the social contract that exists between citizens and the criminal justice system. Arguably, community members do not trust that law enforcement acts within the law for the public's best interest; public apologies and even holding the participating officers accountable may not easily repair that trust (Lantigua-Williams, 2016).

Communities can increase perceptions of procedural justice by training police to interact with citizens in a less authoritarian manner and provide training on deescalation and implicit bias. Public perceptions of police misconduct influence the public's trust in the police and the recognition of police as agents of legal and moral authority (Tyler, 1990; Tyler and Wakslak, 2004). Scandals and videos of poor behavior from one department unfortunately resonate across the country and affect public perception of all police officers (De Angelis and Wolf, 2016). Today, police officers in departments that haven't had any negative incidents recite examples of individuals in the most benign interactions ask them "Who are you going to beat up today?" (Pollock and Strah, 2016). The most influential factors on public attitudes about police misconduct are personal experiences of self, family and friends, neighborhood characteristics, and media coverage (Miller and Davis, 2007). It should also be noted that positive videos of police behavior also go viral. A video of Gainesville, Florida police officer Bobby White, responding to a noise complaint, playing basketball with the teenagers in his uniform and duty belt before gently admonishing them to hold down the noise had over 4 million views. A video of a female Washington, D.C. officer who responded to a street disturbance between two groups of teen girls resolving the situation by staging an impromptu dance-off with one of the girls also went viral. Other videos exist of officers playing football or engaging in random acts of kindness with residents and are, arguably, just as powerful as the other type of videos that show officers displaying bad behavior (Jonsson, 2016). Officer Casey Jones of the Spokane Police Department has been known to strum his banjo, play with street performers, and pop wheelies on his bicycle during his patrols of downtown Spokane. He exemplifies a different type of policing that also ends up on cellphone videos (see at http://www.khq.com/clip/12769349/hometown-heroes-officer-casey-jones). He is definitely not alone, and many officers across the country are not afraid to show a bit of vulnerability over sport or musical skill to humanize their interactions with others.

Citizens' trust in police accountability measures (e.g., citizen review boards and police discipline) matters too. De Angelis and Wolf (2016) found that in a study of respondents in a western city, satisfaction with police accountability was a strong, consistent predictor of satisfaction with local police, even after controlling for other important variables, such as race/ethnicity and community context.

The Gallup Poll has measured respect for police since 1965. In a 2010 poll, 57 percent of Americans, when asked about a profession's honesty and integrity, rated police as "high" or "very high." This is down from about 68 percent in 2001, but up from 1995 when only 41 percent of the population rated police integrity and honesty as high or very high (Jones, 2010). In the 2014 poll, 48 percent and, in 2016, 56 percent of respondents rated police integrity and honesty as high or very high. In 2016, respect for police surged to 76 percent of Americans having a great deal or quite a lot of respect for police (Gallup, 2015a, 2017a). Note this stands in stark contrast to the perception that police are facing widespread public hostility.

Discretion and Duty

Law enforcement professionals have a great deal of discretion regarding when to enforce a law, how to enforce it, how to handle disputes, when to use force, and so on. Every day is filled with decisions—some minor, some major. Discretion allows officers to choose different courses of action, depending on how they perceive their duty. **Duty** can be defined as the responsibilities that are attached to a specific role. In the case of police officers, myriad duties are attached to their role; however, there is a great deal of individual variation in how officers perceive their duty and, in a few cases such as those detailed in the In the News box, officers shirk their duties.

> **duty** Required behavior or action, that is, the responsibilities that are attached to a specific role.

One way researchers have described how discretion is utilized is through typologies of police. For instance, Wilson (1976), in one of the classic typologies, described policing styles as follows:

- The *legalistic* style of policing is described as the least amenable to discretionary enforcement. Officers enforce the law objectively without making exceptions.

- The *watchman* style describes police who define situations as threatening or serious depending on the groups or individuals involved, and act accordingly.

- The *caretaker* style treats citizens differently, depending on their relative power and position in society. Some people get breaks, others do not.

Patrol officers are the most visible members of the police force and have a duty to patrol, monitor, and intervene in matters of crime, conflict, accident, and welfare. Patrol officers possess a great deal of discretion in defining criminal behavior and deciding what to do about it. Studies indicate that police do not arrest in many cases where they legally could. For instance, Terrill and Paoline (2007) found that officers in their sample made arrests in less than a third of the cases where an arrest was legally possible. The decision to arrest was influenced by seriousness of the offense, the city (there were two cities in their sample), whether they were responding to a citizen call for service, suspect resistance, suspect disrespect, and suspect intoxication. What is clear from many studies focused on police discretion is that police do not arrest, nor do they ticket, in every case where they have a legal right to do so.

Discretion also comes into play when the officer is faced with situations that have no good solutions. Many officers agonize over family disturbance calls where there are allegations of abuse, or when one family member wants the police to remove another family member. Other calls involve elderly persons who want police to do something

⬛ 🗨 IN THE NEWS | *Nonfeasance of Duty*

In New Orleans, five detectives and their two supervisors in a special victims' unit were investigated for not doing their job investigating child abuse and sexual assault cases. An Inspector General's report prompted the department to transfer the identified detectives to other units during the internal investigation that ensued. The report detailed a pattern of discounting victim reports, misclassifying crimes, and leaving cases uninvestigated. In one case, detectives knew a toddler had tested positive for a sexually transmitted disease and detectives did not pursue an investigation. In another, a child complained of sexual abuse and a registered sex offender was living in the home, yet the detectives did nothing.

The report also described a "culture of indifference" toward rape victims, which seems to have been present since at least 2009, when a Time-Picayune investigation found that the NOPD classified 60 percent of rape reports as "miscellaneous" with no follow-up. In 2010, it was found that there were at least 800 backlogged rape kits in storage, untested. The investigation found that there were at least 53 outstanding DNA matches that NOPD detectives failed to follow-up on to start the process of finding the suspects. The Inspector General's investigators found the detectives had misclassified 46 percent of 90 rapes they investigated.

The NOPD has evidently had a longstanding reputation for problematic rape investigations, and victims reported that detectives did not believe them or did not seem to care about their victimization. The report described one detective who told people that

nonconsensual sex with an intoxicated victim should not be a crime and in 11 of those cases she was assigned, only one was presented to the DA. In several other cases, detectives never sent rape kits to the state police lab for testing even though victims' injuries were documented and evidence was collected by hospital nurses.

The absence of oversight and pervasiveness of the problem prompted some observers to note that it was a systemic problem, not just individual officers or their supervisors. The Inspector General's report indicated that the detectives wrote no investigative reports for 86 percent of the 1,290 sexual-assault or child abuse calls they were assigned from 2011 to 2013. In 65 percent of the cases reviewed by the Inspector General's investigators, detectives classified the cases as "miscellaneous" incidents that did not merit any documentation at all. In over half of the cases where there was an initial incident report, there was no supplemental follow-up report. Only 105 of the total number of cases were presented to the district attorney's office and only 74 were prosecuted, but only after the DA's office did their own investigation.

In 2016, it was reported that improvements had been made in training, policies, and accountability measures. New Orleans Police Department has been under a consent decree with an outside monitor who agreed that the unit was much improved. NOPD hired an additional three civilian investigators and three social workers to work with detectives in the unit, and had received a $1 million grant from the federal government to process the backlog of rape kits.

Source: Lipinski, 2016; Martin, 2014.

---

about the "hoodlums" in the neighborhood, homeless people with young children who are turned away from full shelters, and victims of crime who are left without sufficient resources with which to survive.

A very problematic call is when family members call concerned about a mentally ill person. Observers note that in 1955, at the peak of hospitalization, there were 558,992 in-patient beds in state hospitals in the United States for people with severe mental illness; however, in 2005, there were only 50,509 and the number has fallen even more since that time. It is a strange reality that 10 times as many people being treated for mental illness are in jails or prisons rather than in hospitals (Yakin, 2015).

In these cases, officers often face extremely difficult decisions, which sometimes result in violence when the mentally ill person attacks the officers or won't put down a weapon (Finn and Stalens, 2002; Wells and Schafer, 2006). Many cases have been described in the media where officers are called to help with a mentally ill person and end up killing the individual. CIT training teaches officers how mental illness presents itself, how to deescalate and communicate with a mentally ill person, and the resources available in the area that can be utilized. Training may include visits to facilities housing mentally ill and roleplaying so that officers can learn how to respond to those in active psychotic states. Training may be only 8 hours in a basic academy class, but advanced training is usually 40 hours. The President's Task Force on 21st Century Policing recommended that CIT be a part of both recruit and in-service training for all officers. Officers who have undergone the training explain that it helps them interact with all people in crisis, not only those suffering from mental illness (Pollock and Strah, 2016).

Generally, the command language and intimidating approach of police officers is extremely counterproductive when an individual is in mental distress and can lead to violence. The mentally ill may not respond to commands to drop their weapon, for instance, and officer training emphasizes neutralizing any threat. The result sometimes can be tragic. In situations where lethal force is used, such force is almost always legally justified; however, the actions of the officer leading up to the threat may have exacerbated the situation rather than helped to avoid the need for the use of force. The LAPD has an approach that has been described as a national model whereby the department partners with the county's Mental Health Department and employs officer–clinician teams on patrol and also provides clinician support for solo officers in addition to having all officers undergo CIT training (Beck, 2016; Yakin, 2015).

Police officers also frequently respond to domestic disputes. One officer may ascertain that departmental policy or law does not dictate any action if no party is seriously injured and no one wants to press charges. However, another officer might take a shaken and distraught victim to a shelter, drive her to a relative's home, or wait with her until friends or family members arrive. Historically, law enforcement's response to domestic violence was noninterference, with the perception that domestic violence was not a crime control matter unless it involved injury amounting to felony assault. Mandatory arrest policies generated in the 1980s served to push police officers to be more likely to arrest, but even today, victims of domestic abuse often feel that law enforcement is not responsive. For instance, a $1.1 million judgment was upheld against the Federal Way, Washington, police department in 2013 by the daughters of a murdered woman. The victim had obtained an antiharassment order against her abusive husband, and the police officer served the order on the husband in the home with the wife present, leaving the husband there with her without making any attempt to ensure her safety. She was stabbed shortly after the officer left (Clarridge and Sullivan, 2013).

In the next two sections, we will look at how individual officers are influenced by both the formal ethics of the agency and the informal culture that exists. These two sources arguably promote somewhat different views of the mission, values, and ethical actions for individual officers, and these views affect how they utilize their discretion.

Formal Ethics for Police Officers

A professional code of ethics exists for most professions. For instance, doctors pledge allegiance to the Hippocratic Oath, lawyers are taught their professional code of responsibility, and psychiatrists subscribe to the code promulgated by their professional organization. In fact, having a professional code of ethics seems to be part of the definition of a profession, along with some form of self-regulation (Sykes, 1989).

A code of ethics helps engender self-respect in individual officers; pride comes from knowing that one has conducted oneself in a proper and appropriate manner. Further, a code of ethics contributes to mutual respect among police officers and helps in the development of an *esprit de corps* and common goals. Agreement on methods, means, and aims is important to these feelings. As with any profession, an agreed-upon code of ethics is a unifying element. A code can help define law enforcement as a profession, for it indicates a willingness to uphold certain standards of behavior and promotes the goal of public service, an essential element of any profession.

Police officers generally pledge an oath upon graduation from an academy, and many police agencies have adopted a code of ethics. Other agencies accomplish the same purpose by a value or mission statement that identifies what values are held to be most important to the organization. These documents may be mere wall hangings, forgotten once an officer has graduated from the academy, or they might be visible and oft-repeated elements in the cultures of the agencies, known by all and used as guides for behavior by administrators and officers alike. Recent research indicates that codes of ethics are more effective in influencing behavior when they are familiar to the members of the organization and when they are written and are perceived as useful. The code must be in the "fabric" of the organization and part of the socialization. Principles of the code must be strictly enforced (Klaver, 2014).

The Law Enforcement Code of Ethics

The International Association of Chiefs of Police (IACP) promulgated the Law Enforcement Code of Ethics and the Canons of Police Ethics, and many departments have used these or adapted them for their own agencies. More recently, the IACP has endorsed the Oath of Honor (displayed in the Quote and Query box). This oath, developed by a committee of the IACP, is offered as a shortened version encapsulating the contents of the code of ethics.

The IACP code or other codes of ethics for law enforcement have at least four major themes. The principle of justice or *fairness* is the single most dominant theme in the law enforcement code. Police officers must uphold the law regardless of the offender's identity. They must not single out special groups for different treatment. Police officers must not use their authority and power to take advantage, either for personal profit or professional goals. They must avoid gratuities because these give the appearance of special treatment.

A second theme is that of *service*. Police officers exist to serve the community, and their role appropriately and essentially concerns this idea. Public service involves checking on the elderly, helping victims, and, in the community service model, taking a broad approach to service by helping the community deal with problems such as broken street lights and dilapidated buildings.

Still another theme is the *importance of the law*. Police are protectors of the Constitution and must not substitute rules of their own. Because the law is so important, police not only

---

QUOTE & QUERY

IACP Oath of Honor

On my honor,
I will never betray my badge,
my integrity, my character,
or the public trust.
I will always have
the courage to hold myself
and others accountable for our actions.
I will always uphold the Constitution,
my community, and the agency I serve.

Source: International Association of Chiefs of Police, 2008.

? Does this oath emphasize a crime fighter or public service mission?

must be concerned with lawbreakers, but also their own behavior must be totally within the bounds set for them by the law. In investigation, capture, and collection of evidence, their conduct must conform to the dictates of law.

The final theme is one of *personal conduct*. Police must uphold a standard of behavior consistent with their public position. This involves a higher standard of behavior in their professional and personal lives than that expected from the general public. "Conduct unbecoming" is one of the most often cited discipline infractions and can include everything from committing a crime to having an affair or being drunk in public (Bossard, 1981).

The emphasis on service, justice for all groups, and higher standards for police behavior is consistent with the public service mission more so than the crime fighting mission. One might also argue that while the code promotes a public servant ideal, police are, for the most part, socialized and rewarded for actions consistent with the crime fighter role.

The Police Subculture

Research has long described an occupational culture that is at odds with the formal ethics and values of the police organization, as well as the larger society. Scheingold (1984) described the factors that lead to the extreme nature of the police subculture:

- Police typically form a homogenous social group.
- They have a uniquely stressful work environment.
- They participate in a basically closed social system.

Paoline (2003) also described how certain elements of the law enforcement environment create elements of the subculture. He described a framework whereby the occupational environment creates coping mechanisms and outcomes. The perception of danger leads to suspiciousness. The duty to employ coercive authority leads to "maintaining the edge" (which refers to the idea of officers always being in control over their surroundings). Supervisor scrutiny leads to a lay-low or "cover-your-ass" (CYA) approach to performance. Finally, role-ambiguity is related to investing in the crime-fighter orientation. Social isolation and loyalty are described as outcomes of the environment officers work in.

Themes and Value Systems

In one of the classic pieces of research on the police subculture, Van Maanen (1978) discussed how police operate with stereotypes of the people with whom they come into contact. The individual who does not recognize police authority is "the asshole." Other names for this type of person include creep, animal, mope, rough, jerk-off, clown, and wiseguy. The idea is the same—that some individuals are troublemakers, not necessarily because they have broken the law, but rather, because they do not recognize police authority. Others have identified the same concept in terms such as bad guy, punk, idiot, knucklehead, terrorist, and predator (Herbert, 1996). Herbert further points out the problem whereby officers are so quick to identify these types of individuals as threats to safety that they may overgeneralize and identify, for instance, everyone living in a neighborhood in the same way.

Themes that run through descriptions of police subculture include:
Loyalty toward peers is paramount
Them-us feelings toward the public (and administrators)
Respect (thus, the crime of POPO or "pissing off a police officer")
The end justifies the means thinking to catch the bad guy
The importance of the use of force (even in response to disrespect)
Priority of crime calls over others
Cynicism (the idea that everyone is weak or corrupt) and suspicion
The priority of adventure/machismo/excitement
The idea that the police are the good guys overcoming evil
Source: (Crank, 1998; Herbert, 1996; Scheingold, 1984; Sherman, 1982.)

Zhao, He, and Lovrich (1998) found that police exhibited similar value preferences across time (comparing 1961 to 1997) and across place. In their study, they found that police rated equality significantly lower than did the public and, in general, were more conservative than the general public in their viewpoint. Crank and Caldero (2000/2005) also have discussed the values of police, reporting on other research showing that police officers place less emphasis on independence and more emphasis on obedience.

The Cop Code

Many authors present versions of an informal code of conduct that new officers are taught through informal socialization that is quite different from the formal code of ethics described above. Reuss-Ianni (1983) presented the most complete "cop code" that included principles to watch out for partners, never "give up" another cop, be aggressive, don't implicate any other cop, and don't leave work for other cops. The informal code also specified conduct indicating that management was not to be trusted: protect your ass, don't make waves, keep out of the way, don't do the bosses' work, and don't trust the bosses (Reuss-Ianni, 1983).

What is obvious is that the informal code of behavior, as described above, is different from the formal principles as espoused by management. Some principles of the informal code directly contradict the elements in formal codes of ethics. Scheingold (1984) described the police subculture as no more than an extreme of the dominant U.S. culture and argued that it closely resembles a conservative political perspective. In other words, we all agree with certain elements of the police value system and, if the general public is less extreme in its views, it is only because we have not had a steady diet of dealing with crime and criminal behavior as have the police.

Police Culture and "Noble Cause"

Noble-cause corruption refers to the utilitarian concept that the "end" of crime fighting justifies "means" that might otherwise be illegal, unethical, and/or against rules or regulations (such as "testilying" [lying on an affidavit or the witness stand], or planting evidence). Arguably, the police culture, at least in some locales, endorses or tolerates this type of activity (Cooper, 2012; Crank and Caldero, 2005; Moskos, 2009). Klockars (1983) presented us with a type of noble-cause corruption in the "Dirty Harry problem" (from the Clint Eastwood movie), asking whether it was ethically acceptable for a police officer to inflict pain on a suspect in order to acquire information that would save an innocent victim.

McDonald (2000) offers a detailed study of the practice of "testilying," which includes reordering facts, adding details, or omitting information. It is also referred to as shading, fluffing, firming up, or shaping and occurs in sworn affidavits for arrest or search warrants, in reports, or in testimony. In McDonald's (2000) study of one police department, he found that testilying was more likely to occur when there was a differential emphasis on the goal (crime control) over means. McDonald noted that, in his sample, police perceived that some prosecutors "wink at" deception or encourage it to get a win. Studies have shown that about 60 percent of rookies support mild lies to achieve a conviction (Crank and Caldero, 2000). As described in the In the News box, testilying was only one portion of the problems exposed in the San Francisco Police Department.

IN THE NEWS | *Testilying, Texting, and Use of Force in San Francisco*

The San Francisco Police Department became embroiled in a long-running scandal when, in 2011, police officers were caught lying on official reports and affidavits in support of arrest warrants. A wide-ranging investigation uncovered dozens of cases where officers' statements were proven to be untrue. The district attorney dismissed charges in dozens of cases and asked the FBI to investigate. The U.S. Attorney's office also reportedly dismissed 137 cases. Eventually, in 2015, one detective was found guilty of four federal counts of conspiring to carry out illegal searches and violating the civil rights of the occupants. Another was acquitted.

In another case, Sgt. Ian Furminger and Officer Edmond Robles were convicted of charges related to stealing money and property seized during searches in 2009. Their convictions included conspiracy to violate civil rights, wire fraud, and theft from a federally funded program. The actions of the officers resulted in the dismissal of 119 drug and attempted robbery cases of people who had been arrested by the involved officers. In the investigation and trial of former sergeant Ian Furminger, text messages between him and other officers were received by the U.S. Attorney's office and released publicly in March of 2015. The text messages were racist and included derogatory language toward members of the public and police colleagues, including offensive terms such as "nigger," "rag head," and "beaner." The text messages discussed lynching African Americans and proposed that African Americans "should be spayed." Other texts denigrated gays, Mexicans, and Filipinos. A judge eventually ruled the officers could not be fired because the department had waited too long to discipline them.

The exposure of the messages led to the creation of an investigative panel by District Attorney George Gascon in May of 2015. Their review included roughly 3,000 criminal cases over the last 10 years that were potentially tainted by the 14 involved officers. The Blue Ribbon Panel on Transparency, Accountability and Fairness in Law Enforcement (http://sfblueribbonpanel.com/) was led by three retired judges and the investigation was carried out by eight teams of attorneys, all of them working on a pro-bono basis. The group found that San Francisco officers were more likely to search black and Hispanic people without consent than any other group, but less likely to find any contraband on them. Other findings included: the department lacked oversight that could help uncover racial bias; data collection on stops and use of force was only on paper (not computerized) making it impossible to track; officer discipline was weak; the department lacked staffing for data analysis or policy development; and there was no oversight body. The Blue Ribbon Panel identified a "good old boy club" atmosphere and police culture as key issues to be addressed. Panel members noted that the police union attempted to prevent officers from speaking to panel investigators. The union president labelled the panel as a "kangaroo court" and biased, calling the report "divisive."

The department had also been involved in two problematic shootings. In December of 2015, 26-year-old Mario Woods was shot more than 20 times as he stumbled down a sidewalk with a knife in his hand. Also, in 2015, 45-year-old Luis Gongora, a homeless transient, was shot within 30 seconds after officers stopped him. He also had a knife. Both shootings were criticized with arguments that officers did not need to use deadly force.

(continued)

The department seemed to be moving in a good direction with deescalation training and community engagement efforts pushed by Chief Greg Suhr. Then, in May of 2016, a police sergeant fatally shot an unarmed black woman. That shooting led to protests and eventually calls for federal intervention. The woman was in a car suspected stolen and she drove away from police officers then crashed into a utility vehicle. Officers fired one shot into the car killing her and no weapon was found.

Because of the shooting, Police Chief Greg Suhr was asked to resign. Appointed in 2011, Suhr was a 30-year veteran of the force and had the backing of the police union. He had maintained support through the two previous controversial police shootings and the texting scandal, but the mayor indicated that he felt the police department had lost the confidence of the minority community and named as acting police chief Toney Chaplin, 47, a deputy chief overseeing the department's professional standards and principled policing bureau.

A U.S. Department of Justice study released in 2016 echoed the results of the Blue Ribbon Panel. They concluded that the San Francisco Police Department used disproportionate force on people of color, and stopped and searched them more often than it did whites. The study looked at 548 use of force cases between May 2013 and May 2016, finding 37 percent of force cases involved African Americans, and 9 of 11 killed were black. Federal officials made 272 separate recommendations for reform in the report, including better training with batons to nonfatally subdue suspects with knives. The study found that the department did not properly investigate officer use of force incidents, did not keep "complete and consistent officer-involved shooting files," and did not use current technology and tools to identify patterns of misconduct. The study also found that black and Latino drivers were more likely to be pulled over than white drivers, but "less likely to be found with contraband." The department was not transparent about officer discipline, completing only one investigation into the deadly use of force during the three-year period. It was also found that police officers properly categorized the type of force used on only 5 of the over 500 cases.

A revised use-of-force policy had already been approved that emphasizes de-escalation and prohibits practices such as the carotid choke hold and shooting at moving vehicles. The mayor's office released a statement indicating monies had been budgeted for increased implicit bias and cultural competency training, investments in body cameras, and deescalation training.

Source: Albarazi, 2015; Bay City News, 2016; Cheever, 2015; Green, Egelko, Lyons, and Allday, 2016; Lamb, 2015; Queally and Mozingo, 2016; Williams, 2015a.

McDonald (2000) found that the reasons given for testilying were that legal technicalities made their job impossible to do, and the belief that the offender was guilty. Officers in large agencies were more likely to use testimonial deception, as were police officers who perceived their jurisdiction as having high crime and officers who believed there were too many legal technicalities. Alexander (2013) opines that pressure for numbers does act as an incentive to lie. Police officers today, she writes, are evaluated solely by their productivity and this demand eclipses any other mission or value of police work. Federal grants based on drug confiscation levels, asset forfeiture, and quotas all create pressure to make arrests and/or seizures.

Crank and Caldero (2000) would argue that the motivation is not quotas, but the noble cause of getting an offender off the street, even if it means employing a "magic pencil"—that is, making up facts on an affidavit to justify a warrant or to establish probable cause for arrests. Arguably, they are inclined to behave this way because we hire those who have a strong desire to protect, train, and socialize them to internalize the value of

QUOTE & QUERY

Police officer perjury in court to justify illegal dope searches is commonplace. One of the dirty little not-so-secret secrets of the criminal justice system is undercover narcotics officers intentionally lying under oath. It is a perversion of the American justice system that strikes directly at the rule of law. Yet it is the routine way of doing business in courtrooms everywhere in America.

Source: Peter Keane, a former San Francisco police commissioner, in an article in The San Francisco Chronicle, *quoted in Alexander, 2013.*

 Is lying in official reports ever justified?

"catching the bad guys," and then put them in situations where their values dictate doing whatever it takes to "make the world safe." Ironically, exposure leads to the dismissal of hundreds of cases and the inability of officers involved to be police officer witnesses because their credibility has been destroyed. Alexander (2013) and others present depressing numbers of these incidents across the country.

The occupational subculture of policing is not supportive of egoistic corruption like bribery or abuse of authority, such as when officers engage in sexual misconduct, but it may be supportive of "catching the criminal—whatever it takes." If we want to change this attitude, we must address it directly.

Police Culture, Loyalty, and the Blue Curtain of Secrecy

code of silence The practice of officers to not come forward when they are aware of the ethical transgressions of other officers.

blue curtain of secrecy Another name for the code of silence.

Another element of the police code is absolute loyalty to other officers, even if it means not coming forward to expose a wrongdoer. Variously described as the **code of silence**, **blue curtain of secrecy**, or other terms, it refers to the subcultural code of "Don't give up another cop" (Skolnick, 2001). This phenomenon has been recognized in academic literature, first-person accounts by former officers, and even cited in court holdings (e.g., *Jones v. Town of E. Haven*, 493 F. Supp. 2d 302 [D. Conn. 2007]). It should also be noted that a code of silence is present in other occupations and groups as well, even when members engage in incompetent or corrupt activities.

The book *Serpico* (Maas, 1973) describes how Frank Serpico became a whistleblower against the NYPD officers who were involved in the "pad" (graft). He was shot in a drug raid and believes that fellow officers conspired to kill him. He went on to testify against corruption but never again was a NYPD cop and his name is used as an epithet by many NYPD officers today. In the Quote and Query box, Serpico's statement to the Knapp Commission illustrates the problem of police loyalty when officers are willing to cover up corruption. The later statement indicates that nothing much had changed in the decades between the Knapp Commission and the Mollen Commission.

QUOTE & QUERY

The problem is that the atmosphere does not yet exist in which honest police officers can act without fear of ridicule or reprisal from fellow officers. . .

Source: Frank Serpico, Knapp Commission, 1971, as reported in Hentoff, 1999.

Cops don't tell on cops. . . . [I]f a cop decided to tell on me, his career's ruined. . . [H]e's going to be labeled as a rat.

Source: Police officer testimony, Mollen Commission, 1992, as reported in Walker, 2001.

 How would you create an atmosphere in a police department wherein officers would feel more comfortable reporting the misdoings/criminality of other officers? Or would you even want to?

These quotes are old but still resonate today. In fact, Frank Serpico is involved in the case of Adrian Schoolcraft, a cop who exposed the quota system of his precinct by secretly taping his watch commander and then handing the tapes over to a journalist. In retaliation, he was hounded and intimidated. Police officials even orchestrated his involuntary commitment in a mental hospital. In his $50 million lawsuit against the city, the NYPD, and the hospital, the hospital's defense was that the involuntary commitment was warranted because he appeared paranoid (Brown, S. 2015). One might note, however, that when your superiors and coworkers appear at your apartment and forcibly take you to a mental hospital, there may be legitimate reasons for your paranoia. Schoolcraft settled with the city for $600,000, but the lawsuit against the hospital continues (Goodman, 2015).

Quinn (2005) argues that good officers are sucked into the corrupt cover-ups because of the nature of policing. Every officer does something wrong, and the most common mistake, perhaps, is using too much force. When coworkers cover for the officer, the officer who made the mistake is indebted and trapped in a situation where the officer thinks he or she must do the same. Weisburd and Greenspan (2000) discovered that, although 80 percent of police officers did not think that the code of silence was essential for police trust and good policing, fully two-thirds reported that a whistleblower would encounter sanctions. Further, more than half agreed that it was not unusual for police to ignore improper conduct on the part of other officers, and 61 percent indicated that police officers do not always report even the most serious violations/crimes of other officers. In another study using hypotheticals, about one-third of officers responded that they would not report an incident depicting a clear case of excessive force. In this study, newer officers, supervisors, and those with many years of experience were more likely to report other officers, while those least likely to report were mid-career officers (Micucci and Gomme, 2005).

The code of silence can be considered on a continuum where observing and not coming forward is on one side of the continuum, representing a passive position toward the misconduct of others. More serious actions occur when officers actively lie to supervisors, or perjure themselves in the effort to cover up wrongdoing. The most serious forms of cover-up are when officers involve themselves in manufacturing evidence or intimidating witnesses. These actions can lead to serious consequences. Recently, three longtime Chicago police officers were indicted for felony conspiracy, official misconduct, and obstruction of justice for their actions after the 2014 shooting of Laquan McDonald, the 17-year-old that was shot by Officer Jason Van Dyke. They allegedly filed false reports saying McDonald approached Van Dyke and swung a knife at the officer before he was shot, and did not interview at least three witnesses whose accounts of events would have conflicted with the official police version. The dash cam video of the shooting was suppressed for about a year, but finally released under court order showing the teenager walking away when shot by Van Dyke. He was indicted in late 2015 for murder and awaits trial. Their actions were taken, allegedly, to protect Van Dyke from being investigated and charged. A special prosecutor said that, "The indictment makes clear that it is unacceptable to obey an unofficial code of silence." One of the newly indicted officers was a detective assigned to investigate the shooting, another was Van Dyke's partner, and the third was one of the officers at the scene. Two are no longer with the police department. They each face up to 10 years in prison if convicted (Davey and Smith, 2017).

ETHICAL DILEMMA

You are approached by internal affairs to make a statement concerning what you saw concerning an alleged beating that occurred in a patrol car before the suspect was taken up to the jail for booking. You did see the two officers use their flashlights to hit the suspect on the head and shoulders. As they dragged the man out of the car they told you that he had been kicking at them through the grille and vomited all over the back of the patrol car. The suspect ended up being admitted to the hospital with a skull fracture. What would you do?

Law

The relevant law at issue is perjury if you lie on the witness stand or in a formal, legal document. Official oppression or obstruction of justice is sometimes also used as a charge against officers who do not tell the

(continued)

truth in official investigations if proof exists that they are lying about what they saw. Generally, those who merely say nothing are internally sanctioned or fired rather than criminally prosecuted; however, if they are actively involved in a cover-up, more serious charges can be filed. On the other hand, it is difficult to prove the opposite when an officer makes a statement that he didn't see anything.

Policy

Recall that the IACP Code of Ethics specifically dictates that officers who are aware of wrongdoing have the duty to do something about it. All police departments have value statements, mission statements, or codes of ethics that support exposing wrongdoing of fellow officers, but, generally, subcultural codes oppose any form of whistleblowing or "ratting" on a fellow officer.

Ethics

Teleological ethical rationales are concerned with the consequences of an action. Egoism may support not coming forward because it may not be in one's best interest. An officer might say, "I don't want to get involved," "I don't want to go against everyone," or "It's the sergeant's (or lieutenant's or captain's) job, not mine." These are all egoistic reasons for not coming forward. Utilitarian reasons to keep quiet also look at the consequences (or utility) of the action, but do so to measure the utility for all. "The end justifies the means" thinking, described above as noble-cause corruption, may conclude that protecting the officers is more beneficial to the ends of justice, at least in the short term. The loss of a skilled police officer—even though that officer may have committed some form of misconduct—is a loss to society. One may believe that the harm to the police department in exposing the deviance of one officer is greater than the harm to society created by what that officer did, or that there is greater utility in stopping the officer quietly without making the issue public. For any of these arguments to be legitimate, the utility of not exposing the wrongdoing must outweigh the utility for everyone if the wrongdoing was exposed.

There are also teleological arguments for coming forward. Egoism may dictate that an individual has to come forward to protect himself from being accused of wrongdoing. The police officer may also endure such a crisis of conscience or fear of being punished that he

or she can attain peace of mind only by "coming clean." Utilitarian arguments for coming forward exist as well. The harm that comes from letting the individual carry on his or her misdeeds or not forcing the individual to a public punishment may be greater than the harm that would come from the scandal of public exposure. This is especially true if one is forced to either tell the truth or lie; in this case, the harm to police credibility must be considered. Recall that procedural justice research shows that low trust in policing leads to perceptions of illegitimacy. It is definitely a net loss if community members feel that police officers are not held to the same standards as the rest of us when they commit a crime.

Recall that deontological arguments look at the inherent nature of the act. Arguments against exposing other officers include the idea that one's duty is to the police force and one's fellow officers so one should protect them from exposure. Arguments for coming forward are much stronger, including the argument that a police officer has a sworn duty to uphold the law. Also, one cannot remain silent in a particular situation unless one could approve of silence in all situations (Kant's categorical imperative), and one must do one's duty, which involves telling the truth when under an oath (Wren, 1985). It should be noted that, in general, deontological ethics support whistleblowing because it is a higher duty to uphold the law than it is to defend one's fellow officers.

When one considers whether to come forward to expose the wrongdoing of others, external moral philosophies, such as utilitarianism, are rarely articulated. What tends to be the impetus for covering up for other officers is an internal mechanism—loyalty. While the prime motivator for coming forward and/or truth-telling is personal integrity and duty, the individual often feels great anguish and self-doubt over turning in or testifying against friends and colleagues. That is understandable because "a person's character is defined by his commitments, the more basic of which reveal to a person what his life is all about and give him a reason for going on" (Wren, 1985: 35). Loyalty is a difficult concept that others have written about extensively; it can be a vehicle of both ethical and unethical behavior (Fletcher, 1993).

Loyalty in police work is explained by police officers' dependence on one another, sometimes in life-or-death situations. Loyalty to one's fellows is part of the *esprit de corps* of policing and is an essential element of a healthy department. Richards (2010) describes how it is part of the socialization process of the academy and infused in the rituals, routines, symbols, stories, and rites of the informal culture. If things go well in this process, an individual officer will view fellow officers as family and feel a sense of duty toward all members of the same family.

Ewin (1990) writes that something is wrong if a police officer doesn't feel loyalty to fellow officers. Loyalty is a personal relationship, not a judgment. Therefore, loyalty is uncalculating. We do not extend loyalty in a rational way or based on contingencies. Loyalty to groups or persons is emotional, grounded in affection rather than reflection (Ewin, 1990).

The application to policing is obvious. If police officers feel isolated from the community, their loyalty is to other police officers and not to the community at large. If they feel oppressed by and distrust the police administration, they draw together against the "common enemy." To address abuses of loyalty, one would not want to attack the loyalty itself because it is necessary for the health of the organization. Rather, one would want to encourage loyalty beyond other officers to the department and to the community. Organizational permeability rather than isolation promotes community loyalty, just as the movement toward professionalism promotes loyalty to the principles of ethical policing rather than to individuals in a particular department.

Wren (1985) believes that police departments can resolve the dilemma of the individual officer who knows of wrongdoing by making the consequences more palatable—that is, by having a fair system of investigation and punishment, by instituting helping programs for those with alcohol and drug problems, and by using more moderate punishments than dismissal or public exposure for other sorts of misbehavior. This is consistent with the ethics of care, which is concerned with needs and relationships.

Delattre (1989a) handled the problem differently, but came to somewhat similar conclusions. He turned to Aristotle to support the idea that when a friend becomes a scoundrel, the moral individual cannot stand by and do nothing. Rather, one has a moral duty to bring the wrongdoing to the friend's attention and urge him or her to change. If the friend will not, then he or she is more scoundrel than friend, and the individual's duty shifts to those who might be victimized by the person's behavior. We see here not the ethics of care, but rather, a combination of virtue-based and deontological duty-based ethics. Souryal (1996, 1999b) argued that personal loyalties often lead to unethical actions and that loyalty to values or organizations has a stronger ethical justification. The informal practice of punishing individuals who come forward is an especially distressing aspect of loyalty and the police culture. Individual police officers have been ostracized and have become the target of a wide variety of retaliatory gestures after "ratting" on another officer. Reports include having equipment stolen, threats made to the officer and his family members, interfering with radio calls and thereby jeopardizing hissafety, scrawling the word "rat" on her locker, putting cheese or dead rats in her locker, vandalizing his patrol car, or destroying his uniform.

Administrators are often the ones who retaliate against whistleblowers, telling the accused officer who informed on them, or supporting implicitly or explicitly the retaliation against the officer who came forward. Instead of rewarding officers who expose wrongdoing, administrators sometimes punish them by administrative sanctions, transfers to less desirable positions, or poor performance reports. This retaliation is not just true of law enforcement agencies. Sanctions against whistleblowers are so common that most states and the federal government now have laws designed to protect whistleblowers.

Police Culture Today

Our descriptions of the police culture date back more than 40 years and so a legitimate question is whether modern police officers subscribe to the same set of values and whether the "cop code" still exists. Arguably, the subculture and the values described above may be breaking down in police departments today. Several factors contribute to the possible weakening of the subculture:

- *Increasing diversity* of police recruits has eliminated the social homogeneity of the workforce. Many diverse groups are now represented in police departments, including African Americans, Hispanics, people of other ethnicities, women, and college-educated recruits. These different groups bring elements of their own cultural backgrounds and value systems into the police environment.

- *Police unions*, with their increasing power, formalize relationships between the line staff and the administration. Subcultural methods for coping with perceived administrative unfairness are giving way to more formal rather than informal means of balancing different objectives of management and line staff.

- *Civil litigation* has increased the risk of covering for another officer. Although police officers may lie to internal affairs or even on a witness stand to save a fellow officer from sanctions, they may be less likely to do so when large monetary damages may be leveled against them because of negligence and perjury.

One might add that many of the authors who described the police culture did so in the 1970s and 1980s, during a time of great social change when the Supreme Court recognized groundbreaking due process protections. Older police officers who had not been socialized to give *Miranda* warnings or obtain search warrants were understandably slow to adapt to the new order. Today's recruit officers were born after the *Miranda* warning was institutionalized as a standard arrest element and have never known a time when police did not need a search warrant. Today's recruit is also more likely to have been exposed to community policing and its tenets of community–police partnership and other progressive police practices through television, education, or other means. Thus, for younger police officers, these due process protections may be seen as normal and expected elements of the job rather than barriers to good police work.

However, even recent research shows that there is still some support among even recruits for certain aspects of the informal value system of the police subculture. Phillips (2013) in a small and nonrepresentative, but interesting, study of academy recruits showed that there was already some predisposition to harbor the informal occupational value of not reporting a fellow officer for an inappropriate use of force.

There is also no doubt that the police subculture varies from department to department. Size, regional differences, and management may influence the strength of the subculture. The makeup of the department, its relationship with the community, and training may also influence the type of occupational culture found in any department.

Research shows that the subculture is not monolithic and the commitment to various elements of the subculture vary by demographics of officers, the type of department,

⎙ IN THE NEWS | *Protecting Whistleblowers*

News stories across the country indicate that officers who violate the blue curtain of secrecy may still face informal sanctions by both peers and supervisors.

A Baltimore officer who reported a fellow officer for beating a handcuffed suspect in 2012 endured months of retaliation leading to a federal lawsuit. He said he and fellow officers chased a drug suspect who kicked in the door of an apartment and was captured. The homeowner was a girlfriend of another officer and this officer arranged for the suspect to be returned to the scene and then beat him requiring a trip to the hospital. No one came forward to report the incident except Joseph Crystal. Afterward, he was threatened by supervisors, reassigned, and given

confusing, against policy, or misleading orders which he believed were attempts to "set him up." He said that other officers refused to back him up on the streets, even during a foot chase. He alleged that a detective once pulled up alongside his police car and asked if he was "having a cheese party. I know rats like cheese." He was told no one wanted to ride with him, and he was told to go find a different agency. He quit the Baltimore Police Department and filed a lawsuit, winning a settlement of $42,000.

Evidently no officer was ever punished for the incidents described by Crystal. The officer, Anthony Williams, who beat the suspect, was convicted of assault and battery and served a 45-day jail sentence and returned to the force.

Source: Broadwater, 2016; Krayewski, 2014; Smith, 2014.

---

and other factors (Paoline, 2003; Paoline, Myers, and Worden, 2000). Greene et al. (2004) examined attitudinal data from a sample drawn from the Philadelphia police department. A series of questions measured their attitudes toward ethics and some elements of the police culture. More than half of the officers thought gratuities were acceptable, directives sometimes needed to be subverted to make an arrest, would not report a fellow police officer even if they knew of misconduct, and would extend professional courtesy to other officers (ignore minor violations of the law). The majority of officers did not support testilying, exaggerating probable cause, or "street justice."

Research continues to support the idea that there is a police culture, albeit one that is more fragmented and weaker than in earlier decades (Caldero and Larose, 2001; Conti, 2006; Crank, Flaherty, and Giacomazzi, 2007; Loftus, 2010; Murray, 2005).

Regarding the "blue curtain of secrecy," research indicates that this practice may be breaking down. Barker (2002), for instance, reported on some research indicating that the addition of minorities and women has led to a less homogenous force and a weaker subcultural norm of covering up wrongdoing, as evidenced by the proliferation of complaints against fellow officers. Barker notes that there were more than 30 cases in Los Angeles where officers were the primary witnesses against other officers. Rothwell and Baldwin (2007a & b) found that police respondents were *more* likely to report misdemeanors and felonies of their fellow officers than were civilian employee respondents in other agencies. These researchers also found that reporting was positively related to the agency having a mandatory reporting policy. The other factor associated with reporting misconduct of fellow officers was supervisory status. Other researchers have found that police officers were more likely to report wrongdoing of other officers if it involved acquisition of goods or money (except for gratuities) rather than excessive force or bending rules (Gottschalk and Holgersson, 2011; Westmarland, 2005). In the Walking the Walk box, the experiences of one officer who exposed wrongdoing are described.

WALKING THE WALK

Walter Harris is a big, quiet man, a college football star, and an ex-NFL football player. He joined the Bloomington police department in 1991 and was doing well, but decided to join the Detroit Police Department. He was quickly tagged to join the mayor's executive protection unit (EPU), and was an executive protection officer for Detroit mayor Dennis Archer until 2001, when Kwame Kirkpatrick was elected. Harris stayed on the detail after Kirkpatrick became mayor but began to notice changes in the EPU. The new mayor immediately appointed two patrol officers to head the unit, promoting them above seasoned commanders. Harris later found out that one of these officers had been in trouble before, but somehow the trouble had been swept under the rug. The other was a boyhood friend of the mayor.

Harris was uncomfortable with some of the new patterns of behavior, including eating and drinking with the mayor while on duty, and a lax manner toward protection protocols. Part of the problem was the mayor, who liked to go into bars to drink, and it became increasingly apparent to Harris that the mayor was also engaged in an extramarital affair with his administrative assistant and probably other women.

As time went on, Harris became more and more uncomfortable with the behavior of the EPU leaders and the mayor himself. On at least one occasion, the mayor had his protection officers drive him to a rendezvous with a woman in an apartment building, and he sometimes disappeared from the mayor's mansion, taking one of the cars himself, and leaving his protection officers behind. Due to a number of troubling incidents, Harris decided he had to quit.

Another officer had already quit and had gone to internal affairs about the problems with the EPU, including some officers padding their overtime records and drinking on duty. Harris was asked to back up this officer's allegations; the other officer had already filed a whistleblower suit, alleging retaliation for his speaking out.

Harris had a dilemma. If he supported this officer's allegations, he could be targeted for retaliation; if he didn't, he'd be going against everything he believed in. From the beginning of his law enforcement career he had avoided any hint of corruption; he had even turned down offers from officers when he first joined the force to fudge arrest reports to make himself look better. He told the truth, backing up

the other officer, and immediately began getting phone calls where the caller would hang up. He believed he was being followed by other police, and there were three separate incidents that he thought were attempts to set him up. The last was when he and his partner were told by the duty officer to take a call of a robbery, and he discovered the car they had been assigned had no camera in it. He insisted on a camera and by the time his angry superior put one in, they were still expected to go to the scene, which was strange because the dispatcher should have sent another patrol unit by then, but the call evidently hadn't been dispatched to another unit. They took the complaint from an individual in a car with several other people and thought no more of it until they were called in because of a report that Harris had robbed the complainant. This was the third citizen complaint that was completely unfounded and, if he hadn't insisted on the camera, or his partner hadn't walked to the car and taken the complaint so the man couldn't even describe Harris, he would have been facing very serious charges with very little ability to defend himself. He realized his vulnerability as a patrol officer and immediately took a stress leave, then fought with the departmental psychologist, who seemed to be committed to putting him back on the street despite what his personal doctor advised. This tenuous situation went on for months, until his family was threatened. Harris then realized that his whistleblowing had endangered his family and they moved in the middle of the night back to Bloomington, where his previous chief was happy to have him back.

The whistleblower case eventually ended Mayor Kirkpatrick's term of office, exposing him as a liar and a corrupt politician. He ended up in federal prison. When the case finally went to trial, Harris returned to Detroit to testify. His testimony was instrumental in setting the foundation for the hundreds, if not thousands, of text messages that the mayor had sent to his administrative assistant. Since they had lied on the stand about their affair, the text messages were evidence of perjury. Harris and the others won their case, although Harris did not even recover the costs involved in abandoning his house in Detroit and moving to Bloomington. However, if he had it to do over again, he would—because it was the right thing to do.

Sources: Harris, 2011.

Generally, police, like any occupational group, are socialized to some type of informal value system that guides and provides a rationale for decision making. This value system may be as—or in some cases, more—influential than the police rulebook or code of ethics. It is also true that the police culture is not now, or perhaps never was, as monolithic as early writers indicated and the strength of it is affected by the size of the department and other variables.

Conclusion

In this chapter, we have identified two "missions" of law enforcement: crime fighting and public service. Examining the history of policing, we see that these two approaches seem to gain dominance in cycles. Currently, we have witnessed a recent ascendency of the "guardian" or public service model, but with the election of President Trump and the appointment of Attorney General Sessions, we may see a retrenchment to the warrior/crime fighting model.

We looked at the parameters of police discretion and how researchers have drawn typologies to describe the way individual police officers navigate their multifaceted role by emphasizing certain duties over others. Officers' discretion is controlled and guided by both the formal ethics and the informal culture of law enforcement officers. The police subculture is not monolithic and may be different from when the early researchers described it. There does seem to be some continued support for what has been called "noble-cause corruption" and "the blue curtain of secrecy." Throughout this discussion and the chapters to follow, the mission and role of police as crime fighters or public servants is a pervasive theme. Whereas the formal code of ethics emphasizes the public servant role of law enforcement, the informal subculture emphasizes the crime fighter role.

The public expects the police to live up to the crime fighter role, but also expects more. The public expects the police to be problem solvers and supermen (and superwomen). From noisy neighbors to incest, we expect the police to have the answers to our problems—to be the one-stop shop for solving problems. The surprising thing is that the police do so well at this impossible task.

Chapter Review

1. **Describe the two different missions of law enforcement in a democracy.**

    The two missions of law enforcement are crime fighting and public service. Under the crime fighting mission, criminals are the "enemy," and fundamentally different from "good" people. Police are the "army" that fights the enemy, and various means that might otherwise be illegal or against the rules are excused or justified because of the importance of the mission of crime fighting. Under the public service mission, police are seen as serving the needs of all the public. This role is more expansive than the crime fighter role and includes other types of public service. Furthermore, it involves the idea of public service to all people, not just law-abiding "good" citizens.

2. **Compare the current trends of policing to past historical eras.**

The crime fighter and public service missions have cycled several times as dominant themes in policing. Most recently, the "war on drugs" led to community policing and the "warrior" model that rose after 9/11 has been supplanted in some departments with the "guardian" model in response to the perceived extreme militarization and overuse of force, especially against minority communities. The backlash has been proponents arguing the "Ferguson effect" has led to de-policing and crime spikes. Thus, we may see a retrenchment back to a crime fighter role.

3. **Provide the justification for police power and the basic ethical standards that derive from this justification.**

The social contract is the basis of police power in a democratic society. We basically give up some rights in return for protection (by police). Part of that agreement is that they have the right to utilize power in order to protect the populace against aggressors. The social contract is also the basis of police ethics. Cohen and Feldberg (1991) propose five ethical standards that can be derived from the social contract: fair access, public trust, safety and security, teamwork, and objectivity.

4. **Identify the differences between the formal ethics of law enforcement and the values of the police subculture.**

Formal law enforcement ethics promote the principles of fairness, service, the importance of the law, and upstanding personal conduct. The police subculture, on the other hand, has been described as endorsing stereotyping ("assholes"), absolute loyalty to colleagues (blue curtain of secrecy), the use of force for those who don't respect police authority, and noble-cause corruption (testilying and other bad "means" to achieve the good "end" of convicting criminals).

5. **Describe recent research findings on the police subculture.**

In a research study, two-thirds reported that a whistleblower would encounter sanctions, more than half agreed that it was not unusual for police to ignore improper conduct on the part of other officers, and 61 percent indicated that police officers do not always report even the most serious violations/crimes of other officers. About 60 percent of rookies support mild lies to achieve a conviction. However, substantial variation exists among officers in their cultural views, according to survey studies. Current researchers conclude that the police culture is not monolithic and is perhaps more fragmented today than in the past.

Study Questions

1. What are Klockars's descriptions of police authority, power, persuasion, and force?
2. Describe Wilson's typologies of police, and explain how each might use discretion.
3. Describe the elements of the formal code of ethics, and contrast them with the values of the police subculture.
4. Describe the elements of the police subculture.
5. Explain why some people think the police subculture is breaking down.

Writing/Discussion Exercises

1. Write an essay on (or discuss) discretion in policing. In this essay, define discretion, give examples, and discuss unethical and ethical criteria for the use of discretion. Find newspaper articles illustrating police use of discretion. Analyze the officer's use of discretion in relation to the ethical systems described in earlier chapters.

2. Write an essay on (or discuss) community policing and whether it is likely to reduce or to encourage unethical actions by police officers. Utilize current research to illustrate whether or not community policing is growing or declining in popularity.

3. Write an essay on (or discuss) the two perceptions of the police officer—crime fighter or public servant. Consider various police practices and innovations as supporting one or the other role.

Key Terms

authority	discretion	power
blue curtain of secrecy	duty	public servants
code of silence	force	social contract
community policing	persuasion	

ETHICAL DILEMMAS

Situation 1

As a patrol officer, you are only doing your job when you stop a car for running a red light. Unfortunately, the driver of the car happens to be the mayor. You ticket her anyway, but the next morning you get called into the captain's office and told in no uncertain terms that you screwed up, because of an informal policy extending "courtesy" to city politicians. Several nights later, you observe the mayor's car weaving erratically across lanes and speeding. What would you do? What if the driver were a fellow police officer? What if the driver were a high school friend?

Situation 2

There is a well-known minor criminal in your district. Everyone is aware that he is engaged in a variety of crimes, including burglary, fencing, and drug dealing. However, you have been unable to make a case against him. Now he is the victim of a crime—he reports that he is the victim of theft and that his neighbor stole his riding lawnmower. How would you treat his case?

Situation 3

You are completing an internship with a local police agency. The officers you ride with are great and let you come along on everything they do. One day, the officer you are riding with takes you along on a drug raid. You are invited to come in when the house is secure, and you observe six young men sitting on two sofas in the living room. The officers are ransacking the house and asking the young men where they have hidden the drugs. Four of the youths are black and two are white. One of the officers walks behind the sofa where the black youths are sitting and slaps each one hard on the side of the head as he walks past. He ignores the two white youths sitting on the other sofa. You are shocked by his actions, but you know that if you say anything, your chance of being hired by this agency will be very small. You desperately want a good recommendation from the officers you ride with. What would you do?

Situation 4

You are a police officer in New Orleans. During the flood following Hurricane Katrina, you are ordered to patrol a section of the downtown area to prevent looting. The water is waist high in some places, and sections of blocks are, for the most part, inundated with floodwater. You come upon one shop where the plate glass window has been broken, and about a dozen people are coming out of the shop with clothing in their arms. The stores' contents will be written off anyway by the owners and covered by insurance. Should that make a difference in your decision? What if the store was in an area of the city that wasn't flooded and the contents were not ruined? What if the people said they were desperate and didn't have any clothes because their belongings were under water? What if the items being taken were televisions and other electronics?

Situation 5

You and your partner have been working together for more than five years. He has seen you through the serious illness of your young child, and you have been there for him during his divorce. After the divorce, though, you have become increasingly anxious about him. He is obviously not taking care of his health, he drinks too much, and he has been consistently late to roll call. Now you can smell alcohol on his breath during the day and suspect that the ever-present cup of coffee he carries has more than a little whiskey in it. You've tried talking to him several times, but he just gets angry and tells you to mind your own business. Today, when the two of you responded to an accident scene, a witness drew you aside and said, "Aren't you going to do something about him?" pointing to your partner. Unfortunately, you knew what she meant, for he was literally swaying, trying to keep his balance in the hot sun. To make matters worse, he insists on driving. What would you do?

Police Discretion and Dilemmas

6

Spencer Platt/Getty Images

Makeshift memorials honor officers Brent Thompson, Patrick Zamarripa, Michael Krol, Michael Smith, and Lorne Ahrens who were ambushed and killed in Dallas in July 2016 while on duty at a peaceful "Black Lives Matter" protest.

Learning Objectives

1. Evaluate evidence that law enforcement officers perform their role in a discriminatory manner.
2. Present information concerning the prevalence of and factors associated with the use of force by police officers.
3. Enumerate predictors associated with the use of excessive force.
4. Discuss the ethical issues involved in proactive investigations.
5. Discuss the ethical issues involved in reactive investigations.

In this chapter, we will focus on how police officers utilize their discretion. Recall that discretion is the power to make a choice of action from several alternatives. Even the youngest and newest patrol officer has an awesome power over the rest of us. While most police officers are respectful of those they encounter and abide by the law; if they do not, there is little immediate recourse; if you refuse or resist, you may be subject to physical force. If a police officer insists you stop your car, you must. If they ask to search your car, you may say no, but they can then make you wait a "reasonable" amount of time for a drug-sniffing dog or arrest you for a minor traffic violation. If an officer insists you sit down on the curb, you must; if he insists you leave the area, you must; and, in a few troubling cases across the country, if an officer insists you submit to a body cavity search on a public street, people do; as described in the In the News box. Officers who conduct unconstitutional searches may be punished later and victims may receive large settlements (paid by the taxpayers, not the offending officers); however, the fact remains that, at that moment, the individual officer's power is supreme. The fact that unreasonable and/or illegal applications of such power are more likely to be visited upon the poor and disenfranchised in this country is a truism that should not be ignored. Police officers don't police Wall Street like they police Watts; perhaps if they did, we would see a stronger reaction to police abuse of power. Those few officers who do abuse their power make it much harder for most officers who use their discretion wisely, ethically, and for the good of the community.

Most ethical dilemmas that police officers face derive from their powers of discretion. Muir (1977) describes moral dilemmas of the police officer as frequent and unavoidable, always unpopular with some groups, usually resolved quickly, dealt with alone, and involving complex criteria. Police officers are trained in the law and they know departmental policy, but that still leaves a wide range of possible alternatives when arriving on any scene. Should they pull over a driver who forgot to signal? Should they ask a group of black youths clustered in a park entrance what they are doing? What should they do when a driver refuses to comply to an order to produce his license? An officer makes hundreds if not thousands of decisions a week. We discussed police officer discretion in the last chapter, but in this chapter, we will focus on discretion as it relates to three topics: race and ethnicity, the use of force, and investigative practices. Each of these topics has been the source of controversy.

IN THE NEWS | *That Can't Happen Here, Can It?*

One suspects that most people, if told that police officers performed searches of peoples' genitals on the side of the road in full public view, would not believe it. Unfortunately, it has happened—more than once, in more than one state. In Texas, two women filed a federal lawsuit against the Texas Department of Public Safety troopers after they were subjected to a "cavity search" during a traffic stop. They were pulled over for tossing cigarette butts out of the window of their vehicle. The trooper believed he smelled marijuana coming from the vehicle and performed a consensual search of the vehicle finding nothing. He then called for a female trooper, who, after putting on gloves, used her fingers to search their anuses and vaginas, using the same latex glove on both women. The search was performed on the side of the road in full view of other passing vehicles. The women settled their lawsuit for $185,000. However, a similar search also happened near Houston. Two women were stopped for speeding by a state trooper who called for a female trooper to search the women for drugs. These women also claimed that the trooper used the same gloves on both women and that

they were groped in full view of passing traffic. Drug paraphernalia was found in the car, but no drugs were found. Newspaper reports indicate that, in the second case, the female trooper was fired and the male trooper was suspended over the incident.

One shouldn't think it could only happen in Texas either. Many similar searches were reputedly performed against black men in inner-city neighborhoods in Milwaukee between 2008 and 2013; 60 people have claimed such encounters on public streets in full view of witnesses. The police chief blamed the behavior on "overzealous" policing, but eventually one officer, Michael Vagnini, pleaded guilty to four felonies and is serving 26 months in prison and three others pleaded to misdemeanors. A larger number of officers were investigated for impeding the inquiry and/or lying; however, none were charged or disciplined. One of the victims received a half-million-dollar settlement from a disgusted jury that sent a strong message that such humiliation and degradation would not be accepted even to further the mission of drug enforcement.

Source: Barton, 2014; CBSDFW.com, 2012; McNally, 2014; NBC.com, 2013.

Discretion and Discrimination

When individuals have discretion, individual prejudices and perceptions of groups such as women, minorities, and homosexuals can influence their decision making. Officers' views of the world affect the way they do their job. If these views include prejudicial attitudes toward groups, and such prejudices affect decisions, those groups may not receive the same protections as "good" citizens. It is also true that we are all subject to implicit bias; subconscious biases that we are not even aware of but that may affect decision making (Staats, Capatosto, Wright, and Contractor, 2015). The point is not that police officers are more prejudiced than the rest of us; it is that their special position creates the possibility that their prejudices could cause a citizen to be treated differently than others. This becomes even more of a problem when the law enforcement agency's occupational culture reinforces prejudicial views. Essentially, when police act on prejudices while performing their jobs, discrimination takes the form of either enforcing the law differentially or withholding the protections and benefits of the law. As the In the News box illustrates, some police officers may express extremely negative stereotypes of certain groups. Administrators cannot take the chance that such views may translate into differential enforcement of the law.

In this section, we will examine the evidence as to whether blacks are treated differentially, always with the recognition that one cannot discuss the 17,000 police agencies in the country as a monolithic unit. We will also focus specifically on racial profiling. Finally, we will examine the evidence as to whether blacks are more likely than whites to be shot by police officers.

A Racial Divide

Historically, law enforcement has been involved in slave patrols, enforcing white power in late-nineteenth-century and early-twentieth-century race riots, and, more recently,

IN THE NEWS | *Off the Record?*

In several police departments around the country, embarrassing and troubling exposure of texts and e-mails between officers have occurred that call into question the ability of police officers to police all citizens fairly. San Francisco's texting scandal came about after a prosecutor obtained racist and homophobic messages sent during 2011 and 2012. An investigation ensued and some officers resigned and others were fired. Similar patterns of racist messaging or forwarded jokes have taken place in Ferguson, Missouri, exacerbating the tensions there; Edison, New Jersey; Seattle, Washington; Baton Rouge, Louisiana; and Miami Beach and Fort Lauderdale, Florida. In the Miami Beach case, after racist jokes and texts were exposed, prosecutors reviewed more than 100 cases for evidence of bias. In the Fort Lauderdale incident, prosecutors dropped 11 felony and 23 misdemeanor cases of the involved officers. In that case, officers made a video featuring Ku Klux Klan imagery.

Some argue that the Internet is full of racist, sexist, homophobic rants. Since the messages were private, officers have a First Amendment right to say anything they want, if they do not act in a discriminatory manner. The reality is that police officers do not have the same freedom on social media as the rest of us, if they can be identified as an officer. Some officers have been fired for what they post on their Facebook page because racist, homophobic, or sexist commentary can be defined as conduct unbecoming an officer.

Sources: Robles, 2015a; Williams, 2015a; Wood, 2015.

⌨ IN THE NEWS | No Charges for Officer, but Systemic Racism in Ferguson, Missouri

Officer Darren Wilson was no-billed by a grand jury after the Michael Brown shooting, and some individuals took that to mean that the charges of racism in Ferguson were unfounded until the Department of Justice completed their investigation and released their report. The report documented widespread discriminatory practices directed toward the black community. The report put into context the violent reaction of the community to the Brown shooting, explaining that there had been years of distrust and resentment because of illegal and unethical practices by the police and justice officials in the town and county. Some of the findings indicated that the city depended on revenue generated from fines and late charges, differentially paid by the poor community. Late charges increased rapidly so that a traffic fine might end up costing thousands and inability to pay would result in jail. African Americans constituted 67 percent of the population but accounted for 93 percent of arrests and all arrests for resisting arrest were of black citizens between 2012 and 2014. Officers were encouraged to make arrests to generate revenue rather than public safety.

Source: Berman, 2015.

using the legal force inherent in the institution of law enforcement to intimidate and abuse civil rights protestors in the 1960s. It should also be strongly emphasized that the charge of racism is not limited to law enforcement, but rather has been leveled against the whole legal system. The system of laws and punishment, the courts that administer the laws, and the corrections system that makes decisions regarding the liberties of those convicted have all been described as agencies that systematically and pervasively discriminate against minority groups. Police, in this view, are just one element in systematic, even institutional, racism. The In the News box describes the Department of Justice report of Ferguson, Missouri, after the Michael Brown shooting, which details problems that go well beyond the police department.

Most studies indicate that blacks express more distrust of police than whites or Hispanics. In the latest Pew Research Center public opinion report (Morin and Stepler, 2016), there were dramatic differences between the perceptions of whites and blacks regarding police performance. Figure 6.1 shows the percentage of respondents who answered with "excellent" or "good" when asked how police do in the following areas:

- Protecting people from crime
- Using the right amount of force for each situation
- Treating racial and ethnic groups equally
- Holding officers accountable when misconduct occurs

The Pew study also showed that while 79 percent of blacks felt the recent shootings of blacks reflected a larger problem between police and the minority community, only 54 percent of whites felt the killings reflected a larger issue (Morin and Stepler, 2016). Hispanics generally fall between whites and blacks in their view of police. In another study, two in three Hispanics fear police use of excessive force, and 18 percent reported that they had friends or family members who had suffered police brutality (Planas, 2015).

Studies show that civil rights complaints against police are correlated positively to the percentage of minorities in the population (Holmes, 2000), that more than twice as many lower-class African Americans as whites report disrespectful language or

FIGURE 6.1 | Public Perception of Police Performance

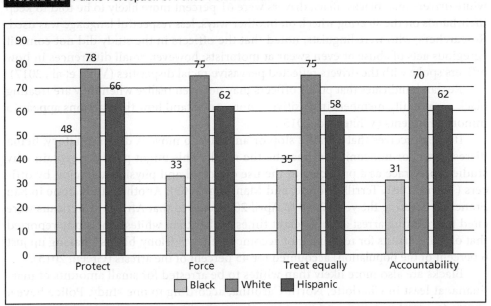

Source: Based on Pew Research Center public opinion report. (Morin and Stepler, 2016)

swearing by police officers (Weitzer, 1999), and that middle-class African Americans express more negative attitudes than do lower-class African Americans (Weitzer, 1999). Age, income, sex, and education; living in metropolitan areas; and experiences with police all have been shown as influencing attitudes toward police; however, race remains a key variable even after controlling for other factors, arguably because blacks report having more negative interactions with police, are more likely to be exposed to negative media portrayals of police misconduct, and are more likely to live in high-crime areas where police employ a more combative style (Reisig and Parks, 2000; Weitzer and Tuch, 2004). Perceptions of police vary quite a bit between black populations in different cities (Sharp and Johnson, 2009).

The videos one sees on YouTube show terrible examples of police officers who are rude and abusive to the citizenry, but academic studies using observers indicate that residents (both black and white) are initially disrespectful to police *three times* as often as police are initially disrespectful to residents (15 percent compared to 5 percent). Factors associated with being disrespectful include heightened emotion, number of bystanders, presence of intoxicants, being mentally impaired, and being in a disadvantaged neighborhood (Engel et al., 2011; Mastrofski, Reisig, and McCluskey, 2002; Reisig et al., 2004).This research also showed that blacks were less likely than whites to experience initial police disrespect (Mastrofski, Reisig, and McCluskey, 2002). A more recent study, however, showed the opposite. In a study of the body cam video transcripts of 981 stops conducted by 245 Oakland officers in April 2014, researchers found that police were more likely to call white drivers "sir," or "ma'am," or to address them by a courtesy title and their last name. Black drivers were more likely to be addressed by their first name, or "bro," "dude," or "bud." Disparities remained even after controlling for race of the officer, the location and the outcome of the stop, and the severity of the infraction. Researchers also found that officers were 57 percent more likely to offer an apology, to thank, or otherwise speak in what is considered a respectful way to white drivers than blacks. Black drivers were 61 percent more likely to be told to keep their hands on the steering wheel, or, in other ways, less respectful language was used. Researchers, who were linguists, noted that the officers in the study did not commit egregious acts of abuse or even swear at motorists; however, small differences in how officers spoke with the drivers reflected pervasive racial disparities (Voigt et al., 2017).

Research indicates that police officers may not even realize when they are treating black community members insensitively, nor understand how their actions appear to minority residents (Whitehead, 2015).

If one perceives that a traffic stop or an order to move is discriminatory, being disrespectful or noncompliant may be the result. This might partially explain why studies show race as a predictor in the use of verbal and physical coercion by officers (Terrill, 2001; Terrill, Paoline, and Manning, 2003). Another study done in San Francisco covering the years 2010 to April 2015 showed that African Americans were cited for resisting arrest at a rate eight times higher than whites. The study reported that of 9,633 arrests for resisting, not accompanied by a felony, blacks (making up just 6 percent of the population) accounted for 45 percent of the arrests (Green, 2015).

Blacks are also more likely than whites to be arrested for small amounts of marijuana, at least in Charlotte, North Carolina, according to one study. Police have a choice to arrest or ticket, and in an investigation of two years of data, it was found that blacks were arrested 28 percent of the time compared to 10 percent of whites, leading to over 700 arrests of blacks compared to less than 100 arrests of whites. Police argue that it may have been because blacks were more likely to be suspected dealers (Harrison, 2016).

It is also important to consider the effect of neighborhoods on how officers interact with those they encounter. Research shows that police employ a more guarded, forceful, and formal approach in high-crime neighborhoods (De Angelis and Wolf, 2016). Unfortunately, blacks are more likely to live in such neighborhoods and, thus, they are more likely to be treated as suspicious by police officers who are trained to respond to environmental cues to notice criminal activity and to stay safe.

African Americans are not the only minorities who are subject to differential enforcement patterns. Perhaps some of the most egregious cases of discriminatory law enforcement occur on this nation's southern borders (Crank, 2003; Huspek, Martinez, and Jiminez, 2001; Romero, 2006). Huspek, Martinez, and Jiminez (2001) argued that border agents act this way because they are encouraged by the "rhetoric of fear" and tacit acceptance of any means necessary to reduce or discourage illegal immigration. Former Sheriff Arpaio in Maricopa County (Phoenix) was sued by the Department of Justice over his practices regarding the treatment of Hispanics in his jurisdiction. Investigators found that Hispanic drivers were four to nine times more likely to be stopped, and one-fifth of the traffic stops appeared to be unconstitutional. There was a general culture of bias against Hispanics, including the use of excessive force against Latinos, a reduction of policing services to the Latino community, and a gender and/ or national origin bias by failing to adequately investigate sex crimes. The judicial ruling ordered cameras in every deputy's car, increased data collection and reporting, a community advisory board, and a court-appointed monitor to ensure the agency is taking steps to prevent discrimination. In 2015, Arpaio was back in court facing civil contempt charges for violating the order after news reports emerged exposing at least one deputy who was arrested for "shaking down" illegal immigrants (Billeaud,

2015; Parvini, 2015). He settled that court case, but in 2017, was convicted of criminal contempt for the same defiance of the federal court order. His defense was that he didn't understand it (Cassidy, 2017).

Some argue that disparate treatment of Hispanics has not gained the same attention among advocates as has allegations of discriminating against blacks because of the history and culture of Hispanics. They form a disperse group of different national origins, they have no national figureheads, and a large number are in this country illegally, and that tends to silence those who fear deportation (Rojas and Schmidt, 2016).

Racial Profiling

Racial profiling occurs when a police officer makes a stop based entirely on race or ethnicity. Generally racial profiling refers to traffic stops based on race, leading to the use of the term "Driving While Black." A "pretext stop" refers to the practice of police officers to use some minor traffic offense to stop the individual, specifically to look for other evidence of wrongdoing, usually by a consent search. The Supreme Court has upheld the legality of such stops in *Whren v. U.S.,* 517 U.S. 806, 1996. In general, minorities are targeted because of a belief that they are more likely to be criminal.

racial profiling
Basing a decision solely on the race/ethnicity of the other party (i.e., to stop and question or to conduct a traffic stop).

Racial profiling began when federal agents developed a profile of drug smugglers to assist border patrol and custom agents in airports. The list of indicators included travel patterns and behavior as well as demographic indices, such as race. The concept was expanded to highway drivers by state patrol officers who were attempting to stem the flow of drugs up through the interstates in Florida, Georgia, Texas, and other southern states (Crank, 2003; Harris, 2004). Observers contend that what eventually happened is that the behavioral and other indices of profiling were abandoned, so that decisions to target suspected drug-involved individuals were reduced purely to race. Racial profiling became known as the practice of officers stopping blacks for minor traffic violations, for example, failing to use a turn signal, to search the car for drugs.

Studies on racial profiling show that minorities may be stopped in numbers far greater than their proportion of the population would indicate however, the methodology of early racial profiling studies was problematic (Engel, Calnon, and Bernard, 2002; Smith and Alpert, 2002). Comparing stops to simply the percentage of population is not very accurate because it does not consider the percentage of nonwhite drivers, the percentage of nonwhite drivers who engage in traffic offenses, or the percentage of minorities in the geographic area that is being targeted by heavier patrols.

A Bureau of Justice Statistics study, utilizing an addendum to the National Crime Victimization survey, showed that more black drivers than white or Hispanic (13 percent versus 10 percent) were pulled over for traffic stops, but, interestingly, no difference existed for "street stops" (individuals stopped while walking). Blacks were less likely to believe that police acted appropriately in the stops. White drivers were searched and ticketed at a lower rate than black drivers (Langton and Durose, 2013). A recent study utilizing data from 132 different agencies in 16 states for a total of over 55 million traffic stops found dramatic racial differences in some jurisdictions. For instance, in one jurisdiction, blacks were seven times more likely to have their car searched than whites in a traffic stop. An important finding of this study was the disparity among jurisdictions—some showed more racial disparity than others and these patterns tended to be consistent over the years. Hispanics were also more likely to have their autos searched; in one jurisdiction, they were eight times more likely to be searched than whites. Researchers speculated one reason for the disparity might have been saturation patrols in minority neighborhoods (Baumgartner, Christiani, Epp, Roach, and Shoub, 2017; Hart, 2017).

In another study, researchers differentiated "traffic stops" and "investigatory stops," a distinction made between police stops that occur because the driver commits a clear violation and those where the officer is using the stop for investigatory purposes. The first stop is short and results in a ticket; the second kind of stop is longer and always includes a request for a consent search. There is little racial difference in those stopped for the first type of search, but there is in the second type. In the study, 60 percent of all stops for whites were for traffic safety, versus 35 percent for blacks; however, 52 percent of all stops for blacks (versus 34 percent for whites) were for such minor reasons that the stop was coded as investigatory. In these types of searches, individuals are stopped for driving too slowly, broken lights, failure to signal, and other pretexts to initiate a search for drugs (Epp, Maynard-Moody, and Haider-Markel, 2014). The investigatory stop is proactive policing for crime (mostly drug) control. It is a cost/benefit question as to whether the benefit gained is worth the cost in the antipathy it generates among those who are stopped.

A *New York Times* study of stops of tens of thousands of traffic stops and arrests in North Carolina found racial differences: black motorists had their cars searched twice as often as whites, but contraband was found more often proportionally when whites were searched. Use of force was more common when the person stopped was black. Four times as many blacks as whites were arrested on a sole charge of resisting or obstructing an officer (LaFraniere and Lehren, 2015).

Studies are becoming more sophisticated. For instance, recognizing that in certain times of the day, the lack of light makes it difficult to identify the race/ethnicity of the driver, the so-called veil of darkness test looks at stops during those hours of the day compared to daylight hours to determine if there are differences in the percentages of whites and blacks stopped. These studies show clear racial differences. One troubling finding has been that, while many states have instituted detailed reporting practices to record drivers' race and ethnicity for traffic stops, the disparity in stops has not changed much in some jurisdictions since the early 2000s (LaFraniere and Lehren, 2015).

In the news stories of racial profiling, there are egregious cases where black citizens have been treated extremely badly by police officers. Now that cellphone videos exist, it has made it easier for whites to understand why many blacks fear and distrust police. These cases are rare; however, even in cases where the police officer is polite, the perception of feeling discriminated against may affect the driver's attitude and sometimes results in needless violence. Many of the shootings of black men in recent years have started with a traffic stop for a minor violation. Observers note that police officers could stop almost any driver because of the pervasiveness and complexity of traffic laws. Whether the officer does stop a driver, then, becomes, not just a legal decision, but an ethical one which we will analyze in the Ethical Dilemma box.

Another type of police stop is a "Terry stop" or investigatory detention. In *Terry v. Ohio*, 392 U.S. 1, 1968, the Supreme Court allowed officers to hold someone for a "reasonable" length of time when they encountered the person on the street and had a reasonable suspicion that there had been or was going to be a crime committed. The officer was also allowed to pat down or "frisk" the person for weapons to ensure the officer's safety. This has led to a widespread practice of stopping individuals, generally

ETHICAL DILEMMA

Should you stop a late model car driven by two young black men when you see them make a right turn without signaling? The neighborhood is known for drug deals and you suspect that if you stop and search the car, you will find evidence of drug use.

Law

What does the law say about racial profiling? In cases such as *United States v. Martinez-Fuerte,* 425 U.S. 931, 1976, the U.S. Supreme Court has basically legitimized the use of race as a criterion in profiles (although lower courts are not in agreement when race seems to be the sole or primary reason for the stop). Further, pretext stops (where police stop a driver because of some minor traffic violation, but the real reason is to investigate suspected criminal activity) have been accepted by the Court in *Whren v. United States,* 517 U.S. 806, 1996, in effect allowing the police to use their discretion to enforce minor laws as a tool to implement race-based stops. Generally, the law allows the use of race as one element in the decision to stop, but does not allow it to be used as the sole element in the decision to stop or for profiling purposes. Some jurisdictions require officers to fill out cards that provide information on the traffic stops they make, noting the driver's race, but no state prohibits a traffic stop even if the primary purpose is investigatory.

Policy

Police policies have undergone dramatic change in the last 20 years regarding racial profiling. Many departments have instituted data collection procedures and training to sensitize officers to the possibility that their discretion was being used in a racial or ethnic discriminatory manner.

Ethics

Do ethical rationales help us determine whether racial profiling, if legal, is ethical? A utilitarian argument for racial profiling would be that the "end" of drug interdiction justifies the "means" of harassing and inconveniencing a group believed to be disproportionately responsible. However, it appears that the end is not well served. The "hit rate" for finding drugs is lower for African Americans than it is for other racial groups. Harris (2004) proposes the idea that when officers use race in decision making, they become less effective, not more effective, because they do not concentrate on what is important for investigation— behavior, not demographics.

An ethical formalist system would probably not support profile searches for drugs because this approach is treating those individuals as a means, and it is probably contrary to the universalism principle unless everyone would agree that they should be stopped in the same manner. Because most of us would object to numerous stops every week by police who have no reason to be suspicious other than the color of our skin, it violates the first part of the categorical imperative. The ethics of care would not endorse a racial profiling policy because it would not be meeting the needs of all concerned and would place some people's needs above others; however, there might be an argument when the threat is specific and extreme and the inconvenience minor.

young black males, in high crime neighborhoods or in housing developments because of the suspicion that they were involved in drug sales. While police view this as a reasonable approach to crime control, those stopped multiple times a week as they go about their business do not.

At the height of the stop-and-frisk practice in 2011, NYPD officers stopped 685,724 individuals under some type of investigatory detention. Civil liberties advocates complained bitterly that the stops were discriminatory since minorities were more likely to be stopped than whites without legal justification. This conclusion was reached because the officers' stop cards that were supposed to detail the reasonable suspicion for the stop were often boilerplate, with no specific legal reason for the stop. The stops were also unproductive since very seldom did the stop lead to the recovery of a weapon or an arrest. Only about 12 percent of stops led to arrests or citations (Rosenfeld and Fornango, 2017). Further, it harmed the relationship between the

NYPD and the minority community. Empirical support that the increase in investigatory stops led to declining crime rates has been weak, other than "hot spot" research that shows crime drops temporarily when police blanket a neighborhood (Ferrandino, 2016); although, at least one empirical study did find a negative statistical relationship between crimes and number of stops in precinct areas (more stops led to less crime reports) (Rosenfeld and Fornango, 2017). The problem is the relationship between police practice, crime reports, and actual crimes is extremely complicated. What police do may decrease crime or it may simply decrease (or increase) the public's willingness to report crime.

Because of a judicial order, the election of Bill DeBlassio, and the return of Bill Bratton as police commissioner, the stop-and-frisk practices of NYPD took a dramatic turn. Stops dropped 93 percent from 2011 to 2014 declining to 33,631 (Ferrandino, 2016). A report by the federal monitor of NYPD, released in May 2017, indicated that, in 2015, there were only 22,563 stops, and the stops were much more likely to lead to arrests than in prior years. His statistical analysis of stops between 2013 and 2015 showed that racial disparity in stops decreased, but didn't disappear. This study examined number of stops per census districts similar in crime and determined that there were still differences in the numbers of stops of blacks and Hispanics as compared to whites, but the disparity was much less (Baker, 2017). Despite dire warnings that such a dramatic reduction would lead to increased crime, New York City is not one of the cities that has experienced dramatic spikes in homicide or violent crime in recent years. There is a real question, then, whether frequent stops based on suspicion, provide enough efficacy to overcome the equity concerns of those stopped.

The experience of New York should be instructional for other cities who are also facing scrutiny over stop-and-frisk practices. Milwaukee, for instance, has been sued by the ACLU for what is alleged to be a pattern of discriminatory stops. In supporting documents, it was shown that from 2007 to 2015, the number of arrests declined from 37,217 to 23,059, but the number of investigatory stops increased 228 percent from 14,258 to 46,830. What is as interesting, however, is the number of traffic stops increased 186 percent from 52,339 to 149,604, lending apparent support for critics who argue that police have increasingly been used as revenue producers for cities and local jurisdictions (Barton and Luthern, 2017).

Evidence indicates that racial profiling (either through traffic stops or investigatory stops) doesn't occur necessarily because officers are racist. It is an entrenched part of policing because there is a suspicion of black men held by white and black police officers, combined with the pressure to conduct investigatory stops to obtain drugs and other contraband. This pattern of enforcement may lead to a script of resistance and "disrespect" on the part of those stopped, which, in turn, incites some officers to ratchet up the force used so that a simple stop ends up in a resisting arrest charge, or, worse—the use of lethal force (Bouie, 2014, 2015). In the In the News Box, the killings of black men all began with a simple traffic stop.

Police Shootings of Blacks

The killings of Alton Sterling, Philando Castile, Laquan MacDonald, and Walter Scott reinforce the perception that black men are unfairly and needlessly killed by police officers. Statistics do indicate black men are disproportionately the victims of police shootings. In a *Washington Post* analysis of shootings, blacks were shot at 2.5 times

📑 IN THE NEWS | *Police Shootings*

Newspaper reports in the last several years have provided detailed descriptions of examples of police shootings that should never have happened. Black males are often the victims of mistaken perceptions of threat or they are shot when running away. For instance, in one case, Darrius Stewart was in the back seat of a friend's car in Memphis when a police officer stopped them for a missing headlight. Stewart had two out-of-state warrants and when he ran, the officer shot him. Walter Scott, shot by former police officer Michael Slager, was originally stopped for a minor traffic violation. Philando Castile was also stopped for a minor traffic violation before he was shot by a police officer when the officer was told by Castile that he had a concealed weapon and the officer believed he was reaching for it. Samuel DuBose was shot in the head after being stopped near the University of Cincinnati for a missing car tag. In these and other cases, a broken headlight, expired tag, or nonsignaling resulted in death.

Source: Lowery, 2015.

the rate of whites (Kindy, Lowery, Rich, and Tate, 2016). Of course, shootings are not randomly distributed across the population. The explanation that blacks are shot more often because they are disproportionately involved in violent crime or that they are disproportionately more likely to assault police officers (both true to some extent) explains this disproportional reality only partially (Bowes, 2015). From what we know, police shootings are more likely to occur in certain areas of the city, and these areas are more likely to be minority neighborhoods; thus, it may be that both whites and blacks are equally likely to be the targets of police shootings if they lived in the same high crime areas.

It is possible that police officers are more likely to perceive blacks as a greater threat, even controlling for other elements of the situation. Evidence for this lies only in anecdotal data from open-carry states, where white men seem to be able to approach officers carrying visible weapons without raising the officers' alarm compared to incidents where minority children are shot for having toy guns (Tamir Rice, Andy Lopez), and black men are shot merely for holding a gun that is merchandise in a store (John Crawford III) (Jonsson, 2014; Wines, 2014).

Laboratory findings are mixed. Some research shows that police officers participating in a shoot/don't shoot scenario were *slower* to shoot when the suspect was black than when the suspect was white. These results indicate that police officers are aware of and compensate for bias, although it is possible that the findings are an artifact of the research itself (James, Vila, and Daratha, 2014). The implicit bias studies conducted at the Kirwan Institute for the Study of Race and Ethnicity at Ohio State University have been accumulating research findings for years showing how implicit bias affects perceptions of and probably actions toward members of minority groups. Even if police officers can control cognitive biases in a laboratory setting, findings also show that cognitive control is impeded by fatigue, fear, and high arousal, thus their actions may be different on the street (Correll, Hudson, Guillermo, and Ma, 2014).

One recent study utilized: (1) the NYPD's records of 5 million stop-and-frisk events, (2) the Police–Public Contact Survey, a nationally representative sample of civilians, (3) event summaries from all incidents in which an officer discharges his weapon at civilians including both hits and misses from three large cities in Texas (Austin, Dallas, and Houston), six large Florida counties, and Los Angeles County, and

(4) a random sample of police–civilian interactions from the Houston police department from arrest codes in which lethal force is more likely to be justified. The study found that the race of the suspect *did not* influence the likelihood of fatal shootings by police. However, blacks and Hispanics were 50 percent more likely than whites to be the targets of all other uses of force. The study has been criticized because much of the primary data used comes from police officer reports, with the assumption that the accuracy of the reports would favor the report writer. Since the data also provided an observed differential use of force in less-than-lethal situations, the assumption that the findings do not accurately represent reality is less persuasive (Fryer, 2016).

To understand whether there is racial bias in officers' decisions to shoot, it is important to have all the facts. Unfortunately, we do not have accurate national statistics. Police departments are not required to report shootings to any central database. It is very important to have a base number (of all shootings) before we can understand the factors that affect the decision to shoot. It would be even more beneficial to have data regarding all the situations where an officer was legally allowed to shoot and did not. Unfortunately, that type of data will never be available; that is why researchers use shoot–don't shoot scenarios in a laboratory setting. The media stories of black men shot by police in the last several years do illustrate a problem of race relations we cannot ignore, but it is also important to remember that these media stories are a distorted reality because we do not know of all the other shootings (of black, Hispanic, and white men and women) that have taken place. More importantly, we have no way of knowing anything about the many unknown situations where officers had a legal authority to shoot and chose not to. It is not a good comparison to simply look at percentage of population figures when evaluating whether there is a racial component to police officer decisions to shoot because the individuals involved do not occur randomly across the population. Most police killings involve individuals who are engaged in criminal or at least suspicious activity. In about 80 percent of all police shootings, the suspect is armed (Kindy, 2015; Philly.com, 2014). The most negative reports in the media describe truly horrible situations, such as the Walter Scott shooting, but these tragic incidences should not be conflated to represent all police shootings, because they are not representative.

The decision to shoot is often made in a split second, sometimes in the heat of a struggle, or in the presence of uncontrolled fear. Officers should never feel so afraid of being punished for using their weapon that they do not make the correct decision to protect themselves or others; neither should they ignore the very real possibility that implicit bias makes them see black males differently . . . even 14 year olds who have a toy gun, or compliant young men who are simply reaching into the car for their license.

Discretion and the Use of Force

Police have an uncontested right to use force when necessary to apprehend and/or subdue any suspect of a crime. They have a right to use lethal force only if they believe that the suspect poses a threat to the officer or others (*Tennessee v. Garner*, 471 U.S. 1105, 1985). When their use of force exceeds that which is reasonably necessary to accomplish their lawful purpose, it is defined as excessive force and is unethical and illegal (*Graham v. Connor*, 490 U.S. 386, 1989). Under the Supreme Court holding from this case, officers have the right to use "reasonable" force in any interaction with the public, as determined by the facts and circumstances. They are not obligated to use the least possible force. They can use any level of force that would be used by a reasonable officer in the same situation.

In this section, we will first discuss the absence of an accurate national databank on police-caused fatalities or any national source of use-of-force statistics. Next, a review of research identifying factors involved in the use of force (of the target, situation, and officer) will be offered. A special section on Tasers focuses on the use of that device. Finally, current approaches to reduce the number of police shootings will be reviewed.

Probably the most well-known use-of-force incident in this country was that by law enforcement officers against Rodney King, revealed by the amateur video and widely disseminated. This can still be seen on YouTube even though the event occurred in 1991. In the Rodney King incident, an initial act of passing a police vehicle and leading officers in a chase led to the involvement of 12 police cars, one helicopter, and up to 27 officers. The incident resulted in King being struck at least 56 times, with 11 skull fractures, a broken cheekbone, a fractured eye socket, a broken ankle, missing teeth, kidney damage, external burns, and permanent brain damage (Kappeler, Sluder, and Alpert, 1994).

The King incident is an example of lawful force or excessive force, depending on one's perception. In the video, King clearly continued to try to rise and the officers continued to use their conducted energy devices (CEDs), kick, and hit him with their batons. Some argue that the officers continued to hit him because he continued to resist; others argue that he continued to resist because he was disoriented and was trying to escape the injuries being inflicted upon him. LAPD policy interpreted reasonable force as proportional to the level of resistance; however, that leaves a large area of discretion for the individual officer. It is for this reason, that use of force is a legal issue, a policy and training issue, and, also, an issue of ethics.

What We Know and Don't Know

As stated before, the events in Ferguson, North Charleston, Chicago, and Baltimore brought a great deal of public scrutiny to police use of deadly force. Many were surprised to find that there is no good national statistic as to how many people are killed by police each year, and certainly we have no way to know how many people are shot each year by police and do not die. Nor is there any national database of other nonlethal uses of force.

The supplemental homicide reports provided by the FBI include a category of justifiable homicide (a legal killing almost always performed by a law enforcement officer). However, it has been known for quite some time that the number reported is a woeful undercount of the true number of homicides because police departments are not obligated to provide statistics (Hickman, Piquero, and Garner, 2008). Klinger (2012) compared internal reports from the Los Angeles Police Department to FBI numbers and found that the 184 homicides by police in the FBI report was 46 percent lower than the 340 uncovered in internal reports.

The FBI reports show that the number of individuals killed by police has been increasing even while the crime rate has declined. According to official reports, officer-involved killings averaged in the 400s in the last decade or so (reported in Schmidt, 2015). This compares to averages in the 200s in the 1960s–1970s and an average of 350 in the 1980s to early 2000s. Independent estimates of the number of recent killings based on other sources put the average number per year at double the official number and closer to 1,000 (Wines and Cohen, 2015). This disparity in numbers is troubling and it does make any longitudinal comparisons impossible because the explanation for the increasing numbers reflected in the FBI report may be simply that more incidents are being formally reported (Johnson, 2014).

In 1994, the Violent Crime Control and Law Enforcement Act was passed requiring the attorney general to acquire data about the use of excessive force by law enforcement officers and publish yearly reports. The annual reports required by Congress in the 1994 law were never produced (Doyle, 2014b). Estimates of the use of force come from other sources, such as the Police–Public Contact Survey and single city studies (Hickman, Piquero, and Garner, 2008).

It is also important to note that these are raw numbers, not rates per 1,000. Obviously, the population of the country is greater in recent years than in past decades; therefore, one cannot compare across time logically without constructing a rate that takes the population base into consideration. Even if rates are computed, it doesn't tell us much because we don't know if there are more people with guns. Recall that most of those killed by police are armed. In some studies, it has been found that at least 80 percent of individuals killed had weapons (reported in Kindy, 2015; Philly.com, 2014). If there are more guns in society, there will be more incidents where officers feel threatened. It is also important to note that officers strongly object to criticism that the shooting is unjustified if the subject was unarmed, because if the assailant physically attacks the officer, he may wrestle the officer's gun away and use it against the officer. Thus, any physical altercation could turn deadly because of the presence of the officer's firearm. It is possible that officers are increasingly facing suspects who physically attack them. In short, we don't really know whether shootings are an increasing problem or not.

There are major efforts underway to obtain better statistics. Some states have pursued legislation to require police departments to report shooting data to a central source. Several other organizations, such as the American Bar Association, have announced they are constructing databanks of shootings.

Factors in the Use of Force

The most important thing to know is that use of force seems to be present in a very small percentage of the total encounters between police and citizens and *excessive* force (force not justified by law or policy) occurs in less than 1 percent of interactions with the public. Second, research indicates that a small percentage of officers seem to be responsible for a disproportionate percentage of the force incidents. Finally, some studies do find an association between force and race or socioeconomic status, but other factors, such as demeanor, seem to be even more influential.

A Bureau of Justice Statistics (BJS) study reported that force was used in about 1.6 percent of all police–citizen interactions (Ducrose, Langan, and Smith, 2007). However, use of force seems to vary depending on the city. Garner, Maxwell, and Heraux (2002) found in their study that use of force ranged from 12.7 percent of encounters in one city to 22.9 percent of encounters in another city. In addition, a national survey of law enforcement agencies found that the rate of use-of-force events varied by region, with the highest in the South (90 incidents per 100,000), followed by the Northeast (72), the Midwest (68), and the West (50) (Terrill, 2005). It is also important to note that the figures above are describing use of force, not excessive force. Excessive force is estimated to occur in a miniscule portion of total encounters with the public—estimated at one-third of 1 percent (Micucci and Gomme, 2005).

Characteristics of the target that seem to be correlated with use of force include race, sex (male), disrespectful demeanor, emotionality, mental illness, intoxication, presence or perception of a weapon, the suspect's violent criminal record (knowledge of), suspect's use of force, gang membership, and socioeconomic status.

Situational characteristics correlated with the use of force include the number of citizens present (positive association), the number of police officers present (positive association), and whether the encounter involved a car or foot pursuit.

Characteristics of the officers involved in use of force include sex (male), age (younger), and ethnicity (being Hispanic). Psychological traits of the officer have been identified as well, including lack of empathy, antisocial and paranoid tendencies, inability to learn from experience, a tendency not to take responsibility for actions, and cynicism. Officers who use force have also been found to have a stronger identification with the police subculture. Another factor in the tendency to use force was being involved in a traumatic event or prior injury (thus, use of force would be a type of posttraumatic stress behavior; Alpert and Dunham, 2004; Alpert and MacDonald, 2001; Garner, Maxwell, and Heraux, 2002; Terrill and Mastrofsky, 2002; Terrill, Paoline, and Manning, 2003).

It should be emphasized that these studies and the factors identified are associated with the use of force, not necessarily *excessive* force. Even though force is rare in terms of the percentage of times used of the total number of interactions between police and citizens, that does not mean it is not a problem. In past research, surveys of officers indicated that up to a quarter of officers have at least "sometimes" used more force than necessary (Weisburd and Greenspan, 2000). Even one video of excessive force can poison the relationship between a police department and its citizenry.

Use of Tasers (CEDs)

The Taser is one type of conducted energy device (CED), but the word *Taser* has come to be used in common language to refer to any CED. The devices use electrical stimuli to interfere with the body's nervous system, impairing the muscular control of the target. It has been introduced with the hope that using it as an alternative to lethal force could save lives.

Generally, research indicates that CEDs seem to be associated with a decrease in the number of deaths of suspects, a decrease in the number of injuries to suspects, and a decrease in the number of injuries to officers (Dart, 2004; National Institute of Justice, 2008; White and Ready, 2009; Williams, 2010, 2013). Supporters allege that CEDs are safe in most cases and are potentially dangerous only when there is some underlying medical condition. One study found that death was more likely in cases where the target was under the influence of drugs or mentally ill and when the device was used more than once (White and Ready, 2009); another study found evidence that high risk groups (drug intoxicated or those experiencing excited delirium) were vulnerable (Williams, 2013).

The International Association of Chiefs of Police recommends that a CED not be used on juveniles, the elderly, or pregnant women, and should not be used repeatedly or by multiple officers. Other police groups promote guidelines that prohibit the use of Tasers when a subject is merely verbally noncompliant, is handcuffed, or is intoxicated or has a clear medical condition. There are no consistent national policies, however, and some agencies ignore some or all the proposed guidelines. CEDs have been used on "schoolchildren," the "mentally disturbed or intoxicated," the extremely obese who can't comply with officers' orders, and individuals who are verbally combative with police (Amnesty International, 2007). There are no good numbers indicating how many people have died because of CED use because medical examiners simply do not know the contributing factor of the electrical charge in any fatality as compared to drug intoxication, a heart condition, or some other medical condition. It has also been noted that Taser International has sued medical examiners who have listed the CED as a cause of death and have aggressively funded research that shows no association between CED use and death (Laughland, Lartey, and McCarthy, 2015). The potential for injuries from the CED is possibly underestimated, certainly by those who sell it, such as Taser International (Laughland, Lartey, and McCarthy, 2015; Montemayor, 2016; Terrill and Paoline, 2011).

In December 2009, the Ninth Circuit Court of Appeals ruled that a police officer could be held liable when a CED is used on a person who poses no immediate threat (*Bryan v. McPherson*, 590 F.3d 767, 2009). There have been hundreds of federal lawsuits against municipalities for alleged abuses (Cook, 2014; O'Brien, 2013; Plohetski and Dexheimer, 2012).

CED use, like use of force in general, varies dramatically from city to city. It was reported that in North Charleston (where Walter Scott was shot in the back by ex-officer Michael Slager in the spring of 2015) Tasers were employed 825 times from 2010 to 2014. In Tyler, Texas, a city about the same size but with 150 fewer officers, Tasers were used only 65 times. North Charleston has faced several lawsuits from Taser use, including incidents involving Slager (Binder, Fernandez, and Mueller, 2015).

Departmental policies play a role in CED use, with those departments having flexible or vague policies also being the ones with more use of CEDs by officers. Like any use of force, CEDs can play an important role in law enforcement and are certainly a preferred alternative to lethal force; however, it is possible that they should be moved up the continuum of force in training to equate to close-to-lethal force options.

Responses to Uses of Force

It is inevitable that police officers will need to use some level of force in response to noncompliant and resisting suspects. In almost all cases, their actions are supported by the law and policy. Cases where officers' uses of force meet the definition of a crime are extremely rare. In most cases of lethal and nonlethal uses of force, officers are not indicted or charged (and in most cases, rightfully so). A major report from South Carolina showed that officers fired at 209 suspects in the last five years, killing 79, but only 3 were accused of misconduct, and no officer has ever been convicted of any crime (LeBlanc, 2015). An investigation by a newspaper in New York City found that at least 179 people were killed by on-duty NYPD officers (and 43 by off-duty officers) over the past 15 years, and just three of the deaths led to an indictment in state court (but 10 of the off-duty killings led to convictions) (Marzulli and Gregorian, 2014). In a *Washington Post* analysis of police shootings, despite the thousands of fatal shootings by police since 2005, only 54 officers were charged, and most were cleared or acquitted in the cases that have been resolved (Fisher, Higham, and Hawkins, 2015).

The reason officers who are charged are usually acquitted is that juries must decide beyond a reasonable doubt that the officer was *not* in fear of his life in order to find him guilty of any crime. If the officer testifies that he or she was in fear of imminent death or grievous injury, it is difficult for the prosecutor to disprove that fear unless other proof exists that there clearly was no cause for such fear.

One would expect that most officers shoot only in those situations where they are legally justified, therefore, there should be few, if any, prosecutions of officers for their use of force. However, some argue that prosecutors are unwilling to pursue charges against officers because of the close working arrangements between prosecutors and police officers and/or that police cannot conduct such investigations fairly and objectively. Juries are also unlikely to believe that officers would use illegal force. Recently, officers have been more likely to be charged or indicted for shootings or other uses of force that result in serious injury; for instance, 18 were charged in 2015 with murder or manslaughter compared to an average of 5 in the years before (Friedersdorf, 2015; Simpson, 2015; Wing, 2015).

Civil suits are more likely to be successful than criminal prosecutions. The reason is that the level of proof necessary to show legal liability is lower. Also, suits are often settled by cities before even reaching trial. Supporters of police argue that cases are inappropriately settled since the officer did nothing wrong. No good case analysis exists to explore this question, especially since such settlements often have gag orders attached to them prohibiting either side from disclosing any information. The amount of money paid by taxpayers to settle these suits is staggering. For instance, according to one estimate, over $1 billion has been paid out in the last five years, with the yearly total increasing annually (Wing, 2015).

Officers may not be criminally charged, but might still face discipline for violating policy. The reason is that although an officer may have been compelled to utilize lethal or nonlethal force given the resistance or threat presented by the suspect, the officer may have created the situation by not attempting to deescalate or may have violated policy by, perhaps, not waiting for back-up before engaging. These officers may be disciplined or even fired.

Recently, the Department of Justice has become more aggressive in investigating and identifying problematic use-of-force patterns in several cities. More than 20 cities have been the target of DOJ attention. A federal investigation typically ends with either a judicially approved **consent decree** or joint memorandums of agreement that detail a range of changes the department must complete. One recent DOJ investigation and report targeted Baltimore. Review of all uses of deadly force between 2010 and 2016 and a sample of nondeadly uses of force led to a conclusion that there was a pattern of the use of excessive force. DOJ investigators pointed to deficiencies in BPD's policies, training, and oversight of officers' force incidents. The report indicated that officers unnecessarily escalated encounters and frequently resorted to physical force in response to noncompliance, even in cases of no imminent threat to the officer or others. Another finding was that due to a lack of training and improper tactics, individuals with mental health issues were often dealt with using physical force. BPD officers were also criticized for using force on restrained individuals and those fleeing who were not suspected of violent crimes (USDOJ, 2016). An investigation and review of Philadelphia shootings resulted in findings that indicated that officers did not receive consistent basic or in-service training on firearm use, received little or no deescalation training, did not experience reality-based training, and the shooting after-review

consent decree
A legal agreement between the Justice Department and a police department whereby the police department agrees to perform specified activities and submit to monitoring to ensure that the department meets the terms of the agreement to avoid a lawsuit.

QUOTE & **QUERY**

In a democratic society, people have a say in how they are policed, and people are saying that they are not satisfied with how things are going.

(Sean Whent, the police chief in Oakland, Calif.)

Source: Apuzzo, 2015.

 Do people have the power to "have a say" in how they are policed?

process focused only on policy to the exclusion of officer decision-making or tactics (Fachner and Carter, 2015).

Seattle, Los Angeles, New Orleans, Phoenix, Ferguson, Baltimore, and Chicago have all been investigated by the Department of Justice. In these investigations, use of force is one of the elements of concern, with findings often including: failure to implement a use-of-force policy, failure to train, failure to monitor, failure to adequately investigate, and/or failure to discipline. Generally, such investigations point to the culture of force, lack of training, lack of clear, coherent use-of-force policies, and lack of discipline as contributing to systemic problems. We will discuss consent decrees in more detail in the next chapter.

Recently, a small set of law enforcement officials have called for new approaches in training and a renewed emphasis on how to defuse situations to avoid the use of force. It has been reported that 58 hours of training is given to recruits in the use of firearms and 49 hours in defensive tactics, but only 8 hours in deescalation techniques (Apuzzo, 2015). The Police Executive Research Forum (PERF), comprised of former law enforcement officers, seeks to increase the training emphasis on deescalation and presented a set of guidelines or principles that included

- prohibiting firing into a moving car;
- using deescalation strategies before resorting to force;
- abandoning the so-called 21 feet rule that advised shooting a suspect with a knife if he came within 21 feet because of the perceived likelihood that the officer could be fatally injured; and
- administering first aid immediately, even taking the shooting target to the hospital immediately without waiting for an ambulance (Baker, 2016).

PERF evidently borrowed many of the proposals from existing practices in departments around the country. The group noted that in 1972, New York City police officers shot 994 people; however, they changed the rules regarding force and in 2014, only 79 were shot by NYPD officers. Despite acceptance from some city police chiefs and sheriffs, there was also strong resistance. The Fraternal Order of Police and the International Association of Chiefs of Police issued a joint statement denouncing the proposed principles, arguing that they were out-of-touch with the officers on the street. Critics pointed to Supreme Court cases that allowed police to shoot into moving vehicles (*Mullenix v. Luna*, 136 S. Ct. 305, 2015; *Plumhoff v. Rickard*, 134 S. Ct. 2012, 2014). They argue that the negative narrative of policing is perception, not reality, and that hard rules for use-of-force leave officers in untenable situations (Jackman, 2016).

QUOTE & **QUERY**

"What a ridiculous piece of claptrap!"

(the vice president of the Association for Los Angeles Deputy Sheriffs referring to one of the principles promoted by PERF).

Source: Jackman, 2016.

? Do you think police should adopt the principles set out in the following document: http://www.policeforum.org /assets/30%20guiding%20principles.pdf.

Another factor in use of force patterns is whether policies are enforced and officers are disciplined. News reports of incidents paint a troubling picture across the country of officers who have multiple uses-of-force complaints and receive little if any punishment. One has only to track the cases documented in videos on Youtube.com or the Cato Institute's website documenting police misconduct to see that some departments "wink" at excessive force by a few individual officers. One report indicated that out of 10,000 abuse complaints in Chicago between 2002 and 2014, only 19 resulted in any discipline (Kristian, 2014).

Some evidence indicates that police departments can change their level of use of force by changing policies. The District of Columbia, for instance, after being put under a court order with a monitor, went from 32 police shootings (with 12 deaths) in 1998 to only 17 in 2001 with 3 deaths (C. Murphy, 2002). Alpert and MacDonald (2001) found that agencies that required supervisors to fill out use-of-force forms had lower levels of use of force than did agencies that allowed officers to fill out their own forms. Baltimore police cut their use of Tasers nearly in half in 2016 when commanders put new limits on when officers can fire the stun guns, officials said (Donovan, 2017).

Whether it be lethal force, a Taser, or physical blows, officers have been given the discretion to employ force that, if performed by citizens, would be illegal. We expect them to use such power wisely, and they have a legal duty to do so—that is, they must make reasonable decisions based on the facts and circumstances of each case. Officers are trained in the law and departmental policies, but individual discretion determines reasonableness. Further, as we have discussed, sometimes what officers have a legal right to do may not be wise or ethical, given other alternatives. There are those "lawful but awful" cases where the use of force was ruled legal, but it was either a grievous mistake on the part of the officer in his or her perception of danger or the situation was created by the officer's actions, thus the use of force might have been avoided. Police officers do not have a choice—they must carry a gun and they must be prepared to use it. In some situations, young, inexperienced, or psychologically unprepared officers shoot in situations where there is no reasonable perception of threat. They have ended up in jail or lost their career. In very few cases, officers may have a predilection to use force, even deadly force, and have not been controlled by their department. Why many other police officers react so defensively to criticism of these cases, perhaps, is because, even in these situations, the officer does not have a goal to go out and kill someone; they are doing their job which is sometimes a very dangerous job and one that most of us do not want. In the same way that doctors sometimes through negligence, oversight, or simple mistake, kill their patients; officers do too. In the same way that doctors are rarely charged with criminal negligence because the bar is set very high for criminal culpability, but often pay civil damages, officers do too. One last point to be made is that most officers are devastated when they use lethal force. This trauma is exacerbated when mistakes are made, as the following Walking the Walk box shows.

WALKING THE WALK

In 2016, a Prince George's County police officer was killed in a firefight near a police station, mistaken for the suspect because he was in plainclothes and off duty. The bullet that killed him came from a fellow officer. The tragedy doesn't happen frequently, but it does happen. Between 1987 and 2014, FBI data shows that 79 police officers were killed by another officer, most from "accidental shootings" that resulted from "crossfires, mistaken identities, firearm mishaps."

Gary Sommers is one of the few individuals who know it happens because he also shot and killed his partner and best friend 27 years ago on a drug raid. Sommers was inconsolable until another officer who had also accidentally killed another cop came to his aid and helped him through

(continued)

the torment. Sommers, since that time, has helped other officers across the country who have found themselves in the same horrible circumstances.

Some officers quit, some never recover from the guilt. A few, like Sommers, help others even though it brings back the feelings and regret that accompanied their own mistake. He had been on the force 11 years and his best friend and partner was Mark Murphy. In 1988, in a raid against heavily armed drug dealers, Murphy was bending down to prepare a hydraulic jack to crack the door and Sommers held a gun ready to shoot if the dealers began shooting. In a fateful moment, a suspect burst out of the door, Sommers, thinking he was armed, shot and Murphy, at the same instant, stood up to tackle the suspect. Sommers shot and killed Murphy.

Sommers was at the hospital and attended Murphy's funeral. He considered suicide. He talked to John Gott,

another officer who had killed a fellow officer. He received a letter from President George H.W. Bush, who knew Murphy through a security detail Murphy had worked for him. President Bush, in his letter, recounted a military mission where two of his crewman had died and explained how he didn't feel he should have survived. The letter counseled patience, explaining that time did heal. Murphy's family was forgiving, but his actions devastated Sommers and affected his family.

Sommers never did another drug raid but he didn't commit suicide and he didn't quit the force. His choice was to overcome his guilt. He became a firearms instructor and began to reach out to other officers who experienced the same guilt. He just talks to them about his friendship with Murphy, about the support that is there from the community, and how he survived.

Source: McCoy, 2016.

▌Discretion and Criminal Investigations

How officers use discretion in their interactions with minority members and decisions to use force are the hot button topics of our time; however, discretion is an issue pervasive in all policing. In this last section, we will focus on issues related to what will be called proactive investigations and reactive investigations.

Proactive Investigations

In proactive police investigations, police officers initiate investigations rather than simply respond to crimes. Drug distribution networks, pornography rings, and fences of stolen property all tend to be investigated using methods that involve undercover work and informants. In this type of undercover operation, deception is recognized as an integral part of police work.

According to one author, "Deception is considered by police—and courts as well—to be as natural to detecting as pouncing is to a cat" (Skolnick, 1982: 40). Offenses involving drugs, vice, and stolen property are covert activities that are not easily detected. Klockars (1984) described types of police deception, including *placebos* (lies in the best interest of those being lied to), and *blue lies* (used to control the person or to make the job easier in situations where force could be used). Barker and Carter (1991, 1994) described *accepted lies* (used during undercover investigations and sting operations), *tolerated lies* ("necessary evils," such as lying about selective enforcement), and *deviant lies* (used in the courtroom to make a case or to cover up wrongdoing). As discussed in Chapter 5, these lies, sometimes called "testilying," can be extremely detrimental to the police officer's credibility and his or her department. If an officer has a reputation for "*deviant lies*," his or her value as a witness is extremely diminished. The In the News box discusses the use of "Brady lists" by prosecutors. These are lists of officers that prosecutors prefer not to or outright refuse to use as witnesses—most often because the officer's integrity has been compromised.

💬 IN THE NEWS | *Brady Lists*

The term "Brady list" refers to *Brady v. Maryland,* 373 U.S. 83, 1963, a case that resulted in the requirement of prosecutors to disclose potentially exculpatory information to the defense. Recent cases have made clear that officer witnesses' potential credibility problems must be disclosed to the defense who will challenge their credibility if they testify. News stories from California, Florida, and other jurisdictions indicate that prosecutors compile so-called "Brady lists" to make sure not only to provide the information to the defense but also to avoid those officers as witnesses. Police unions vigorously oppose such lists, arguing that they are sometimes incorrect and they damage the officer's career. Officers who damage their credibility by lying in court or on official documents (such as affidavits in support of search warrants), or even disciplined for lying to superiors in internal investigations, damage their effectiveness as police officers. If a police officer is not able to testify, or a defense attorney can question his or her credibility, his or her value as an officer is sorely compromised.

Sources: Christensen, 2012; Gutierrez and Minugh, 2013; Leonard, 2013.

Police operations that provide opportunities for crime change the police role from one of discovering who has committed a crime to one of discovering who might commit a crime if given a chance. For instance:

- Police officer decoys dress as drunks and pretend to pass out on sidewalks with money sticking out of their pockets.
- Undercover officers, posing as criminals, entice doctors to prescribe unneeded medications that are controlled substances, such as Percocet and Oxycontin.
- Police undertake various stings in which they set up fencing operations to buy stolen goods.

Sometimes, certain individuals are targeted in undercover operations. Arguably, the selection should be based on reasonable suspicion. However, Sherman (1985b) reported that "tips" are notoriously inaccurate as a reason to focus on a certain person. The charge of biased target selection is easy to make; for instance, politicians may complain they have been targeted when they are caught in stings. Recently, another complaint has been that the person is targeted, not for what they did, but, rather, what they own, because of asset forfeiture.

Asset Forfeiture

Some critics allege that, because of **asset forfeiture** laws, police target individuals based more on what assets they can seize rather than other variables (Balko, 2011a). Asset forfeiture enabling laws were passed in the 1980s. Congress amended the Comprehensive Drug Abuse Prevention and Control Act to allow federal agencies to keep the cash and property they seized if the property was a product of or used in a criminal enterprise. Federal enabling laws were soon copied by state governments to allow state and local law enforcement to confiscate and keep property under state laws. Criminal forfeiture laws require a criminal conviction, but civil forfeiture laws, which are used in over 80 percent of the cases at the federal level, do not require a criminal conviction (Ingraham, 2016b). It is reported that 80 percent of property forfeitures now are not even associated with arrests (Worrall and Kovandzic, 2008). The legal action is

asset forfeiture A legal tool used to confiscate property and money associated with organized criminal activity.

brought against the property itself. Because it is a civil action, in most states, no criminal conviction is required to confiscate the property, the level of proof is only preponderance, and the property owner must hire his or her own attorney to challenge the confiscation.

The use of and amount seized in forfeiture actions have grown exponentially. In 1986, for instance, the Department of Justice's forfeiture fund was a mere $93.7 million, but by 2014, it had exploded to $4.5 <u>billion</u>! (Wisnieski, 2016). One report indicates that the DEA has confiscated $28 billion in the last 10 years (Wilber, 2017). The total forfeiture amounts in the states are unknown because many states do not keep sufficient records or refuse to share the information. According to the Institute for Justice, a libertarian-leaning legal rights organization that has published highly critical reports of asset forfeiture, net proceeds from civil forfeitures across 14 states more than doubled between 2002 and 2013, jumping from around $100 million to $250 million (Institute for Justice, 2017; Rodd, 2017). Ohio, for instance, confiscated $26 million worth of property between 2010 and 2012; most cases involved less than $15,000 (Rodd, 2017).

The forfeiture actions can be of cash, but the law also allows the confiscation of vehicles, houses, and other property. The Institute of Justice reports that the median value of forfeited property ranged from about $450 in Minnesota to $2,050 in Utah (Institute for Justice, 2017; Rodd, 2017). Other reports indicate even smaller average confiscations of around $200 (Ingraham, 2016b). Critics allege that most of those targeted are poor and cannot afford to defend themselves.

There are troubling examples of innocent people caught up in forfeiture actions. One such case involved two men who were driving to Las Vegas to gamble. They were carrying $16,000 in cash when they were stopped on a traffic stop. Police discovered the cash in a consent search and seized it with the suspicion that it was money for or from a drug deal. There was no evidence to charge the men, but the money was held and the prosecutor initiated a civil forfeiture case (remember that the level of proof is much lower in civil cases). The men eventually got their money back, but it took two years and they had to hire an attorney (Rodd, 2017). Law enforcement agents seized $11,000 from a college student at an airport because his suitcase smelled like marijuana. He wasn't charged but he lost his money (Ingraham, 2016b). In another case, the IRS confiscated the entire bank account of a convenience store owner because he was depositing small amounts of cash frequently, raising their suspicions. He eventually won, but it took years and he had to pay an attorney to get his own money back (Ingraham, 2016b).

State laws vary in when property can be seized and how much the law enforcement agency gets to keep of seized property. For instance, in eight states, the local agency does not get to keep any seized property—it goes into a state general fund. In 25 states, the agency gets to keep 100 percent of the property. The remaining states allocate a percentage to be kept by the agency with the rest going into a general fund (Ingraham, 2016b).

A way around state law, however, is a federal program called "equitable sharing." In this program, if a local agency and federal agency work together to seize the property, the local agency gets to keep up to 80 percent. This circumvents state law. Missouri, for example, has a strict forfeiture law that requires a criminal conviction and forfeitures go into a general fund. Law enforcement agencies do not keep what they seize. Missouri forfeitures between 2000 and 2013 equaled only about $1.5 million; however,

Missouri law enforcement agencies received $126 million from the federal government through the equitable sharing program (Rodd, 2017).

Researchers who have looked at this issue have not found that there are more forfeiture actions in those jurisdictions that can keep all the proceeds versus those who must turn the money or properties over to the state general fund. However, they did find that there were more "adoptive forfeitures" in restrictive states, where local law enforcement handed over arrests to federal law enforcement who then shared the proceeds with the local law enforcement agency under the equitable sharing program (Worrall and Kovandzic, 2008).

In 2015, the equitable sharing program was revised and restricted (O'Harrow, 2015). Former Attorney General Eric Holder issued new rules limiting the federal program. The new rules barred local law enforcement from using federal law to seize property without warrants or criminal charges, although exceptions included the confiscation of illegal firearms, ammunition, explosives, and property associated with child pornography. Local law enforcement agencies and sheriffs' departments strongly objected to the limitations since, it was reported, 20 percent or more of their budget, depended on forfeited funds (O'Harrow, Horwitz, and Rich, 2015).

In December of 2016, the Department of Justice announced they had suspended the program (Wisnieski, 2016); however, in March 2017 it was begun again with the announcement that the reason it had been suspended was only budgetary and accumulated funds now allowed them to begin sending money back to local departments (Ingraham, 2016a). On the federal level, the FAIR Act was introduced in Congress in 2016 with bipartisan support. The Act would have increased the burden of proof required in federal cases and direct the Department of Justice to deposit forfeited assets in the Treasury Department's general fund, rather than to law enforcement accounts. The bill did not pass and is now considered dead given the current administration's support for asset forfeiture actions (Ingraham, 2016a). Attorney General Jeff Sessions has expressed strong support for asset forfeiture and equitable sharing, so it is unlikely that any restrictions will be made to it.

Asset forfeiture has increasingly become the target of scrutiny by legal groups, the news media, and governmental bodies. Opponents come from opposite ends of the political spectrum, including conservative organizations such as the American Legislative Exchange Council, and the Charles Koch Institute, libertarian groups, such as the Institute for Justice, and liberal advocacy groups, such as Common Cause and the American Civil Liberties Union. A series of newspaper exposes (e.g., *Washington Post, Orlando Sentinel*) and private reports (e.g., two editions of *Policing for Profit* by the Institute for Justice) on forfeiture patterns show clear cases of abuse. Individuals have lost their home or car because a family member was involved in drugs and travelers have lost money they were carrying for purchases or to give to relatives (O'Harrow, Horwitz, and Rich, 2015; Wilber, 2017; Williams, Holcomb, Kovandzic, and Bullock, 2010). Even the Inspector General of the DEA has issued a critical report after examining 100 cases of seizure. Less than half of the cases resulted in any further investigation or charges, creating the perception, according to the report, that the agency was more interested in the seizure than in advancing crime control (Wilber, 2017).

Law enforcement officials have pushed back against their critics, arguing that asset forfeiture is an effective way to dismantle and weaken drug organizations. They also contend that it is an appropriate method to recover property when criminal prosecution may not be feasible, for example, the case of Kenneth Lay, the former CEO of

Enron who died before he could be charged. Civil forfeiture allowed some of his assets to be confiscated and used to compensate victims (Ingraham, 2016b). They also argue, more problematically, that asset forfeiture monies are necessary additions to the budget allocated to them (Wilber, 2017). How forfeiture funds can be used varies from state to state, but in many cases, it is used to supplement overtime budgets and even hire officers. Critics contend that if law enforcement agencies depend on forfeiture profits for their operating budget, this creates a dangerous motivation for criminal enforcement.

Many states have passed or are considering laws that will tighten forfeiture laws, making it more difficult for law enforcement officials to confiscate and keep property. For instance, in 2017, Republican Gov. John Kasich of Ohio signed a measure barring forfeiture under $15,000 without a criminal conviction (Rodd, 2017). The requirement of a criminal conviction is a game changer since most confiscations cases are not accompanied by a criminal conviction; in fact, many times the individual isn't even charged with a criminal offense if they sign over their property or don't contest the confiscation. Other states have changed the level of proof from preponderance to "clear and convincing" that the property was involved in or a product of a crime (Rodd, 2017).

In Missouri, a bill has been proposed that would curb the use of the equitable sharing program by limiting the ability to seize property to that over $100,000. Ohio has already passed a similar law. California's law sets a lower threshold of $40,000 (Rodd, 2017). Bills introduced in Colorado, Illinois, Indiana, North Dakota, and Wisconsin also aim to establish limitations on equitable sharing, state civil forfeitures, or both (Rodd, 2017). In recent years, over 50 bills have been proposed in 22 states to limit forfeiture, but many did not pass (Balcerzak, 2015).

The concern over asset forfeiture is that when there is a profit motive for law enforcement, there is the temptation to make that the prime directive rather than crime control. There is certainly cause for concern when groups from every side of the political spectrum find cause to criticize the program. In the In the News box on the next page, one example of how out-of-control schemes for forfeiture can occur is presented.

The Use of Informants

informants
Civilians who are used to obtain information about criminal activity and/or participate in it so evidence can be obtained for an arrest.

Informants are individuals who are not police officers but assist police by providing information about criminal activity, acting as buyers in drug sales, or otherwise setting up a criminal act so that police may gather evidence against the target. Informants perform such services for a reward: for money, to get charges dropped or reduced, or—in some documented cases—for drugs supplied by an officer. They may inform on former associates to get back at them for real or perceived wrongs or they may cooperate with police to get rid of criminal rivals. They may also cooperate because they are being coerced by police to do so, by threats of arrest or arrests of their loved ones. Little academic attention has been directed to the use of informants except for Miller (2011) who documents the strange role of the informant in that he or she is viewed as essential to law enforcement even while being detested since law enforcement shares the same antipathy toward snitching as their criminal targets.

Informants often have been or are probably engaged in criminal activities themselves (Heath, 2013; Lord, 2014). In some instances, the police handlers protect the informant from prosecution (Scheingold, 1984). In one case that is reputed to be

💬 IN THE NEWS

A Miami Herald news' story describes how Bal Harbour, a small Florida town, partnered with Glades County Sheriff's Department, 100 miles away, to form the "Tri-county Task Force" with the objective of creating a sting operation. Agents from the two law enforcement agencies posed as money launderers who advertised their capabilities to drug cartel members. The goal was to participate in the equitable sharing program whereby they would feed information to the DEA and then receive the lion's share of the confiscated drug money and property. The Glade County Sheriff deputized two retired police officers living in New York to work the deals there. The police chief of Bal Harbour had the confidential informants to make the deals happen.

They were quite successful and traveled to Las Vegas, New York City, and even San Juan to get drug money from criminals, carrying it back to Florida to launder through local banks and businesses. One pickup in San Juan was $499,860; most were in the hundreds of thousands. They averaged two deals a week. Eventually, the total take was more than $55.6 million from drug cartels, although there may have been much more. The undercover officers evidently traveled first class, staying at luxury hotels, with generous travel budgets to keep up their facade. The police laundered the money and kept at least $1.7 million for themselves as broker fees. They returned the rest to the criminal groups. When the scheme ended, they had made no arrests or major drug seizures, although federal agents had made arrests, and Bal Harbour received money through the equitable sharing program.

The task force's end arrived when the federal Inspector General's office sent investigators to audit how Bal Harbour Police Department was using asset forfeiture funds. The resulting investigation led to the resignation of the police chief and the eventual disbanding of the task force when it could not produce any authorization from the state attorney general's office for their activities. After the Task Force was ended, auditors could not track where the money went; they found $28 million had been deposited but was not in the records kept by the detectives. Records showed officers withdrew cash totaling $1.3 million from the undercover bank accounts, but there are no records to show where the money was spent.

The Tri-County Task Force worked with the DEA, but was not monitored by state prosecutors. The former chief said the activities of the task force led to over 200 federal arrests, but the DEA could not confirm any arrest or drug seizure numbers.

Records show that task force tips to the DEA led to nearly $30 million seized in 2010 and 2011; but during that same period, it laundered $50 million. There is no clear conclusion on how much money went through the task force although it could be over $80 million. The FBI began an investigation but closed it. Several of the law enforcement officers involved have retired, although some are still on the force.

Source: Sallah and Bernstein, 2015.

the basis for the 2006 movie *The Departed*, it came to light that an FBI agent, John Connelly, protected two mob informers, James "Whitey" Bulger and Stephen Flemmi, even after they had committed murders (Anderson, 2010; Lush, 2007).

The federal witness protection program has provided new identities for some witnesses after they have accumulated bad debts or otherwise victimized an unwary public. The rationale for informant protection is that greater benefit is derived from using them to catch other criminals than their punishment would bring. This also extends to overlooking any minor crime they engage in during the time they provide information or afterward if that is part of the deal (Marx, 1985a). This is clearly a utilitarian rationale and, as with all utilitarian justifications, it only makes sense if the math is correct; that is, whether greater benefits are indeed created. One of the problems in using informants is that it presents temptations for police officers to slide into unethical acts because of their relationships with informants (Hermann, 2009).

Because rewards are contingent upon delivering some evidence of crime to law enforcement; informants have an incentive to lie and there are several cases where many people ended up in jail or prison because an informant lied to obtain payment (Curry, 2002; Rezendes, 2014; Powell, 2014). One news report indicated that Denver paid informants $213,987 between 2009 and 2014 (Steffen and Osher, 2015).

Another concern in the use of informants is the danger posed if they are discovered. Informants are often recruited by threatening them with prosecution (Lord, 2014). Thompson (2015) described many cases where informants and witnesses to a crime in the District of Columbia were killed. The dangers of being an informant against dangerous offenders should be clear, but, often informants are not given the protection that undercover officers would receive.

Strict protocols for the use of informants would prevent the use of unreliable informants as well as guard against the temptation to manufacture informants. Fitzgerald (2009) offers a standard practice template in the use of informants, including identifying and documenting the informant, strict accounting of funds, having two officers present in interactions with informants, monitoring any buys, obtaining a written statement, and other procedures to ensure chain of custody. The Commission on Accreditation for Law Enforcement Agencies (CALEA) has also developed such standards. There is also a manual from the U.S. Attorney General's office on how informants should be legally and ethically used, including how to properly register them (Hermann, 2009). Some officers openly admit that they could not do their job without informants. There is conflicting information regarding the value of informants and whether they are essential (Dunningham and Norris, 1999). South (2001) summarizes the ethical issues with using informants as follows:

- Getting too close and/or engaging in love affairs with informants
- Overestimating the veracity of the information
- Being a pawn of the informant who is taking advantage of the system for money or other reasons
- Creating crimes by letting the informant entrap people who would not otherwise have committed the crime
- Engaging in unethical or illegal behaviors for the informant, such as providing drugs
- Letting the informant invade one's personal life
- Using coercion and intimidation to get the informant to cooperate.

The Use of Undercover Officers

Undercover officers may pretend to be drug dealers, prostitutes, johns, crime bosses, friends, and—perhaps—lovers to collect evidence of crime. They must observe or even participate in illegal activities to protect their cover. Undercover work is said to be a difficult role for individual officers, who may play the part so well that they lose their previous identity (Marx, 1985b). There may be a disturbing belief system among undercover officers that laws don't apply to them or that they are exempt from the law because of their assignment. It has been found that undercover officers possess high levels of neuroticism and low levels of impulse control, and that there are adverse psychological effects from the experience of being undercover (Mieczkowski, 2002). Stress from undercover work depends on the length of the operation and how personally the officer becomes involved with his or her targets.

There is damage to all when personal relationships are used deceptively; in fact, some argue that an intimate relationship may take precedence over a concern for social well-being generally (Schoeman, 1985). This comes from an ethics of care position. In this ethical system, the relationship of two people is more important than rights, duties, or laws. There is no forfeiture of rights in the ethics of care position; thus, one can't say that the suspect deserves to be deceived.

Another issue concerning undercover operations is entrapment. **Entrapment** occurs when an otherwise innocent person commits an illegal act because of police encouragement or enticement. Currently, the Supreme Court looks at the defendant's background, character, and predisposition toward crime (a subjective test) rather than the objective test that evaluated whether police actions provided essential elements to the crime (*United States v. Russell*, 411 U.S. 423, 1973). A similar defense is "outrageous government conduct;" that is an argument that the government agents' actions were fundamentally unfair so as to violate basic due process.

Recently, critics argued that undercover police officers "created crime" by suggesting robberies of drug dealers to residents of poor neighborhoods in Baltimore in 2013, netting 17 convictions. Because the targets had prior records, the subjective test resulted in a finding that they were predisposed to crime and no case was lost to an entrapment defense (Duncan, 2013). These so-called stashhouse stings utilize informants who go to bars or use other contacts and ask individuals to participate in robbing a drug location with the promise of millions in return. Federal cases by ATF officers, based on these "stashhouse stings," were thrown out by a judge in Los Angeles for "outrageous government conduct." The judge described the government's actions as "trawling" for crooks in seedy neighborhoods without any level of suspicion. Of concern to the judge evidently was that 9 of 10 of those convicted in the stings were black or Hispanic. The government strongly objected to the characterization of the stings as racially motivated and argued that targets generally come to their attention through others; however, in 2015, the U.S. Attorney quietly dropped the most serious charges against 27 of the defendants in the Chicago series of stings (Eckholm, 2014, 2015a). In 2016, a report of the Department of Justice investigation of the cases was released, despite the government's attempt to seal it. The report indicated there was a statistical certainty that the stings were racially biased, with a finding that there was only a 0.1 percent chance that agents could have selected so many minorities by chance (Heath, 2016a).

Wisnieski (2015) points out that the legal justification for these stings comes from *U.S. v. Black*, No.11-10036 (9th Circuit 2013), in which the court set an extremely high bar to prove outrageous government conduct. The case has been cited by judges since then to affirm convictions even if they condemn, in their holding, the actions of the government. Generally, undercover actions are analyzed under utilitarian ethics. Marx (1985a) proposed a set of questions to ask before engaging in any undercover operation that are consistent with utilitarianism:

- How serious is the crime being investigated?
- How clear is the definition of the crime—that is, would the target know that what he or she is doing is clearly illegal?

QUOTE & QUERY

Sometimes you develop these relationships with these traffickers. . . You know, they're stone psychopathic killers, but they have great personalities. So, it's very difficult when you have to arrest them and put them in prison for a number of years. . . It is a moral dilemma, because, again sometimes these guys become your family.

(Michael Vigil, retired undercover agent)
Source: Martin, 2015.

How would you resolve the moral dilemma?

entrapment When an otherwise innocent person commits an illegal act because of the police encouragement or enticement.

- Are there any alternatives to deceptive practices?
- Is the undercover operation consistent with the spirit as well as the letter of the law?
- Is it public knowledge that the police may engage in such practices, and is the decision to do so a result of democratic decision making?
- Is the goal prosecution, as opposed to general intelligence gathering or harassment?
- Is there a likelihood that the crime would occur regardless of the government's involvement?
- Are there reasonable grounds to suspect the target?
- Will the practice prevent a serious crime from occurring?

Thus, utilitarianism may justify undercover operations or condemn them depending on the utility derived and the harm done to all parties involved. Act utilitarianism would probably support deceptive practices, but rule utilitarianism might not, because the actions, although beneficial under certain circumstances, might in the long run undermine and threaten our system of law. Under act utilitarianism, one would measure the harm of the criminal activity against the methods used to control it. Deceptive practices, then, might be justified in the case of drug offenses but not for business misdeeds, or for finding a murderer but not for trapping a prostitute, and so on.

The difficulty of this line of reasoning, of course, is to agree on a standard of seriousness. I might decide that drugs are serious enough to justify otherwise unethical practices, but you might not. Pornography and prostitution may be serious enough to some to justify unethical practices, but to others only murder or violent crime would justify the practices. Religious ethics would probably condemn many kinds of police actions because of the deceptions involved. Ethical formalism would probably also condemn undercover operations where innocent people are deceived because the actions could not be justified under the categorical imperative. Recall that, under ethical formalism, you cannot use people as a means to an end; therefore, if innocent people would be used, it would violate the categorical imperative. Egoism might or might not justify such actions, depending on the officer involved and what his or her maximum gain and loss were determined to be.

Many people see nothing wrong—certainly nothing illegal—in using any methods necessary to catch criminals. But we are concerned with methods in use before individuals are found guilty. Can an innocent person, such as you, be entrapped into crime? Perhaps not, but are we comfortable in a society where the person who offers you drugs or sex or a cheap way to hook into cable television turns out to be an undercover police officer? Are we content to assume that our telephone may be tapped or our best friend could be reporting our conversations to someone else? When we encounter police behavior in these areas, the practices have been used to catch a person who, we know after the fact, had engaged in wrongdoing, so we believe that police officers are justified in the deception and invasion of privacy. What protectors of due process and critics of police investigation practices help us to remember is that those practices, if not curbed, may be used just as easily on the innocent as on the guilty.

These investigative techniques are unlikely to be eliminated. Perhaps they should not be, as they are effective in catching many people who should be punished. Even if one has doubts about the ethics of these practices, it is entirely possible that there is no other way to accomplish the goal of crime control.

Reactive Investigations·

In reactive investigations, a crime has already occurred and the police sift through clues to determine the perpetrator. When police and other investigators develop an early prejudice concerning who they believe is the guilty party, they look at evidence less objectively and are tempted to engage in noble-cause corruption to convict. This can take the form of ignoring witnesses or evidence or even manufacturing evidence to shore up a case against an individual.

Rossmo (2008) brings together descriptions of several investigations that failed because of the human tendency to ignore evidence that does·not fit preconceived notions. In these cases, the true criminal was not discovered and others were suspected, and sometimes charged and convicted, because police officers did not follow proper protocol in the collection and interpretation of evidence. Protocol is necessary to avoid errors in judgment when a criminal investigator who "knows" someone is guilty happens to be wrong. Good investigators do not let their assumptions influence their investigations, because assumptions jeopardize effectiveness. Unfortunately, Rossmo's examples show that proper investigative methods are sometimes discarded when police officers think they know who committed the crime.

This tendency to slant the evidence is not limited to police investigators. FBI lab examiners have compromised cases by completing shoddy work and misrepresenting their findings. In effect, they were not objective scientists, but rather, coconspirators with police. This led to overstating their findings on the witness stand and covering up tests that were done improperly. In the late 1990s, Frederick Whitehurst, a chemist in the FBI lab, exposed shoddy lab procedures eventually leading to widescale investigations and congressional hearings. He was suspended and ultimately won a whistleblower lawsuit. Since leaving the FBI, Whitehurst earned a law degree and is now the executive director of an independent organization called the Forensic Justice Project, which collects and disseminates information about controversial forensic science (Serrano and Ostrow, 2000).

Crime labs across the country have been implicated in either shoddy practices or actively slanting evidence to convict the defendant. "Drylabbing" is a term for making up scientific results without running any tests. Such scandals have forced prosecutors' offices to reexamine hundreds, if not thousands, of cases across the country to determine if wrongful convictions have occurred (Axtman, 2003; Gass, 2015a; Hays, 2005; Reimer, 2015). This problem seems to be more pronounced when labs are part of the law enforcement organization rather than independent from law enforcement.

The problem is that once investigators decide who the guilty party is, they may ignore evidence that doesn't fit with their idea of who did it and how it was done. It is human nature to complete the puzzle—to see things that conform to one's way of looking at the world. Good police work doesn't close the door to contrary evidence, but human nature does. Utilitarian ends-oriented thinkers may be more likely to ignore contrary evidence or overstate existing evidence if they believe they have the guilty party. Ethical formalism, however, emphasizes duties, not consequences, so those whose ethical values lean toward ethical formalism may be less likely to slide into the types of behavior that have put these forensic professionals under scrutiny.

Interrogation

Interrogating a person one believes to be guilty of a crime is probably an extremely frustrating experience. How do you get someone to confess? In past eras, the infamous "third degree" (beating) or threats of force were used to get a confession, but the use of physical force to obtain a conviction has been illegal for quite some time (*Brown v. Mississippi*, 297 U.S. 278, 1936). Legal proscriptions against beatings and torture are based on the belief that torture renders a confession unreliable. Tortured victims might confess to stop their suffering; thus, the court would not get truthful information. Many would argue that whatever information is gained from an individual who is physically coerced into confessing or giving information is not worth the sacrifice of moral standards even if the information is truthful. Human rights treaties condemn such practices, regardless of the reason for the interrogation.

Recently, we have come to find out how illegal interrogations have led to wrongful convictions. Extremely coercive interrogations have occurred in Chicago (recall from an earlier chapter the John Burge scandal) and Brooklyn with prosecutors reexamining hundreds of cases where a conviction was obtained based on the investigation and/or interrogation by Detective Louis Scarcella. The discovery of his problematic methods occurred after several men were exonerated and released from prison (Saul, 2014).

In many cases, those who give false confessions are mentally handicapped or are juveniles, like Anthony Caravella, who was a mentally challenged 15 year old when he gave a false confession after being interviewed by police officers as a witness to a crime (Elinson, 2013; McMahon, 2013). The infamous case of the Central Park 5 (who falsely confessed to rape and assault) involved teenagers (Getlin, 2002; Tanner, 2002). Burge's and Scarcella's tactics are aberrations today, but officers do use persuasion and deception. The classic father confessor approach (a sympathetic paternal figure for the defendant to confide to) or "good cop/bad cop" (a nice guy and a seemingly brutal, threatening officer) are ways to induce confessions and/or obtain information without using force (Kamisar, LeFave, and Israel, 1980). Evidence indicates that deception and skill work more effectively than physical abuse in getting suspects to confess. Skolnick and Leo (1992) have presented a typology of deceptive interrogation techniques. The following is a summary of their descriptions of these practices:

- Calling the questioning an interview rather than an interrogation by questioning in a noncustodial setting and telling the suspect that he [or she] is free to leave, thus eliminating the need for *Miranda* warnings
- Presenting *Miranda* warnings in a way designed to negate their effect, by mumbling or by using a tone suggesting that the offender had better not exercise the rights delineated or that they are unnecessary
- Misrepresenting the nature or seriousness of the offense—for instance, by not telling the suspect that the victim has died
- Using manipulative appeals to conscience through role playing or other means
- Misrepresenting the moral seriousness of the offense—for instance, by pretending that the rape victim "deserved" to be raped—to get a confession
- Using promises of lesser sentences or nonprosecution beyond the power of the police to offer
- Misrepresenting identity by pretending to be lawyers or priests
- Using fabricated evidence such as polygraph results or fingerprint findings that don't really exist

⬛ 📱 IN THE NEWS │ *Questioning the Reid Method*

In 2017, a major police consulting firm, Wicklander-Zulawski & Associates, that trains local and federal officers in interrogation techniques, announced that they were no longer using the Reid method because of the risk of false confessions. The Reid Method, taught since 1984, licensed by John E. Reid & Associates, utilizes confrontation and deception to obtain confessions.

A representative of that company argued that their method has been upheld in court, does not utilize confrontation unless there is evidence of guilt, and the consulting company had not been using new material and updates. The main issue seemed to be, however, that the use of trickery and deception was so powerful that it made the suspect feel that truth was not an option.

Source: Hager, 2017.

The trouble is that these interrogative techniques can be so effective they result in false confessions. While the Supreme Court has ruled that physical coercion used to obtain a confession is unconstitutional, there is no such proscription against deception (see, for instance, *Frazier v. Cupp*, 394 U.S. 731, 1969). In fact, 92 percent of police said they have lied about evidence to induce a confession (Forrest and Woody, 2010). It is unlikely that police officers are aware of laboratory findings that show that ordinary people will falsely confess to acts they did not do when faced with fake evidence by experimenters. Other elements that lead to false confessions are isolation, fatigue, and individual tendencies to be obedient to authority (Forrest and Woody, 2010; Kassin, 2015). The danger of lying about evidence that doesn't really exist is that it can overcome the will of even the innocent. Recently, the use of some interrogation tactics has been reevaluated as described in the In the News box.

Challenges to convictions based on confessions obtained when police interrogators deceive the defendant are based on voluntariness—and the test used by lower courts at this point seems to be whether police deception would induce an innocent person to plead guilty. An example of such a case occurred in 1989 when 17-year-old Marty Tankleff confessed to killing his parents. Even though there was no physical evidence to link him to the crime, interrogators told the teenager that hairs found on his mother pointed to him, that they had obtained a spot of blood from his shoulder that was matched to his mother, and that his father had emerged from a coma long enough to tell them that Marty had attacked them. All of this was untrue, but it convinced the teen to confess. He served 19 years in prison before having the conviction dismissed and charges vacated (Kassin et al., 2010).

Courts may also employ a "shock the conscience" standard. If what the officers do seems to be too egregious, any evidence obtained will be excluded (*Moran v. Burbine*, 474 U.S. 412, 1986). Of course, this raises the question as to what shocks one's conscience. In practice, the lower courts have interpreted the Supreme Court's reluctance to place any restrictions on deception during interrogation as a green light to allow most forms of deception (Magid, 2001). Some state courts, however, have ruled as inadmissible confessions obtained by creating and using faked physical evidence, such as fake lab reports or fingerprint analysis results (*Florida v. Cayward*, 522 So. 2d. 971, 1989; Kassin et al., 2010), as opposed to merely lying about the presence of such reports. In one case, police used what they called "an investigative prop," which was a faked crime lab DNA report. The interrogators had been told by lab examiners that the DNA of the suspect matched the sample from the crime scene, but they didn't have the report, therefore, they faked one to use in the interrogation. The prosecutor who was present during this interrogation was so troubled by the actions of the officers that he notified his superiors and the district attorney's office notified the defense attorney. There was no confession, therefore, no legal ramifications. In this state, an appellate court had ruled that confessions obtained with manufactured evidence were inadmissible (Plohetski, 2012). Courts may draw the line at this type of deception for two reasons. First, some argue that there is too great a possibility that such evidence may somehow find its way into the courtroom, which would be perpetrating a fraud upon the court; and, second, the use of manufactured evidence has a much greater possibility of inducing a false confession from a person who knows they did not do the crime, but assumes they cannot convince a jury if there is a positive DNA match, so they confess to get a plea deal.

Trainum (2008) notes how he never would have believed that an innocent person would confess to a crime they didn't commit until he reviewed a videotaped interrogation that he had conducted on a female suspect accused of murder. After a long interrogation, the woman confessed to the crime, even describing how she dumped the body. There was some evidence to tie her to it as well, including an ATM video of a person who resembled her using the victim's ATM card and a handwriting analyst who said it was her signature. However, she had an alibi and officers found she was telling the truth about being somewhere else when the crime occurred. Trainum writes how he reviewed the interrogation videotape and realized that he had unconsciously fed her information about the crime.

Some researchers estimate that about five percent of confessions are false (Kassin et al., 2010). Such confessions are one of the leading causes of false convictions (along with faulty eyewitness identification and mishandling of evidence). Research indicates that suspects don't always understand their *Miranda* rights, and juveniles are especially prone to psychological manipulation. There are attempts to reduce false confessions by requiring corroborating evidence before the confession can be used in court, and several jurisdictions now require confessions (at least of serious crimes) to be videotaped (Kassin et al., 2010). Alaska, Minnesota, Illinois, Washington, D.C., Maine, New Mexico, Wisconsin, and North Carolina now require videotapes of interrogations of serious crimes. There is no evidence that it has resulted in reduced numbers of confessions (Alpert and Noble, 2009). However, Forrest and Woody (2010) point out that when expert testimony is used to educate the jury about the dangers of manufactured evidence and the fact of false confessions, convictions go down.

It is certainly much easier to justify deception than physical coercion and intimidation during an interrogation. The justification is the same: deception is an effective and perhaps necessary means to get needed information from a resisting subject. Deontological ethics would focus on the duty of the officer. Because an officer has a duty to follow the law, any form of deception that has been ruled illegal would not be ethically justified. Do the actions conform to the categorical imperative? If the officer had a brother or mother who was accused of a crime, or was accused themselves, would they believe their actions justified? If not, then they cannot be supported by ethical formalism.

Under utilitarianism, there may not be any utility in such actions because they may result in false confessions. Keith Longtin was held by Prince George County, Maryland, police detectives for 38 hours after his wife was raped and stabbed to death.

He alleges that during this time, police officers accompanied him to the bathroom, would not let him call an attorney, and continually questioned him (employing different teams of interrogators). Finally, they said that he told them what happened, but he remembers it as them telling him what happened to his wife and asking him to speculate about how the murder occurred. A sex crimes investigator noticed the similarity between the attack and other rapes in the area, and after the rape suspect was arrested, a DNA test proved that this man killed Longtin's wife. Longtin was freed after eight months in jail, and all charges were dropped; however, if it had not been for the other investigator's actions, Longtin's confession would have most probably led to a conviction. Longtin's case and four other homicide confessions that were thrown out because other evidence proved they were false confessions led to a federal monitor for this law enforcement agency (Witt, 2001).

It is important to note that police officers do not intend for innocent people to go to prison; what occurs can be considered noble-cause corruption in that the officers believe the defendant to be guilty and utilize otherwise unethical means to obtain a confession. The trouble is that sometimes they are so effective they make innocent people falsely confess. The rationale is purely utilitarian, but the actual utility of the actions is miscalculated.

Conclusion

In this chapter, we explored some of the ways that police use of authority, power, persuasion, and force have created ethical dilemmas and sparked controversy. It seems that every few decades we enter into a period of intense scrutiny of law enforcement: The 1960s Civil Rights era led to increased diversity; the Rodney King incident led to better use-of-force policies, as well as public opinion shifting against racial profiling and discriminatory enforcement. The Ferguson and Baltimore protests have led to scrutiny and reform efforts. The Trump administration and the appointment of Attorney General Sessions have signaled a return to unquestioned support for policing. It would be better, however, if support for policing and police officers and legitimate scrutiny or demand for the highest levels of professionalism was not a forced choice. Constant vigilance may be (as they say) the price of freedom.

Chapter Review

1. **Evaluate evidence that law enforcement officers perform their role in a discriminatory manner.**

    Minorities express less satisfaction with police than do whites and report they experience more disrespect. Studies show that minorities experience racial profiling for so-called investigatory or pretext traffic stops, and they are more likely to be searched. Stop-and-frisk practices tend to focus on minorities as well, although the fact that blacks and Hispanics live in high-crime neighborhoods contributes to the disparity in rates.

2. **Present information concerning the prevalence of and factors associated with the use of force by police officers.**

   The use of force seems to be present in less than two percent of all encounters with the public; however, it takes place more often in certain cities and during certain types of encounters. It is also true that some officers seem to be involved in uses of force more often than others. Correlates of uses of force have been identified including sex of officer and target (male), age of officer and target (20s–30s), presence of alcohol and/or mental illness, noncompliance, and officer personality traits.

3. **Enumerate predictors associated with the use of excessive force.**

   There seems to be evidence that excessive force occurs in certain types of calls (pursuits) and with certain groups (minorities). Female officers are less likely to use excessive force; however, any correlations should be viewed with caution since the sample size is so small. The legal standard for what is appropriate force is reasonableness.

4. **Present the ethical issues involved in proactive investigations.**

   Ethical issues concern how the targets of undercover investigations are chosen, whether informants are reliable, whether informants are protected from sanctions for their own criminal behavior, whether such operations create crime or entrap individuals, and whether undercover operations violate the privacy rights of individuals who are deceived.

5. **Present the ethical issues involved in reactive investigations.**

   Ethical issues concern the tendency of police investigators to not remain objective in their interpretation and collection of evidence if they believe they know a suspect is guilty. Also, the use of physical coercion during interrogation is clearly illegal, but deception is not and is perhaps just as powerful. There is a possibility that such tactics may lead to false confessions.

Study Questions

1. Do blacks receive discriminatory police services? What is the evidence?
2. What factors are associated with the use of force?
3. Describe Barker and Carter's typology of lies.
4. List the questions posed by Marx that police should use before engaging in undercover operations.
5. What are some of the methods of interrogation according to Skolnick and Leo?

Writing/Discussion Exercises

1. Write an essay on (or discuss) whether you think it is ever right for a police officer to stop someone based on race or ethnicity. Do you think that it is ethical for police to enforce immigration laws by asking whether suspects, witnesses, and/or victims are legal residents?

2. Write an essay on (or discuss) appropriate tools in interrogation. For this essay, you should review important court cases and research typical police practices. Should interrogations be videotaped? Should attorneys always be present? Should juveniles ever be interrogated without their parents? Should deception be used? If so, what kinds?

3. Write an essay on (or discuss) the best explanation for excessive force. If you could be a change agent in a police department, describe the changes or procedures you would institute that you believe would reduce the incidence of excessive force.

Key Terms

asset forfeiture	entrapment	racial profiling
consent decree	informants	

ETHICAL DILEMMAS

Situation 1

You are a rookie on traffic patrol. You watch as a young black man drives past you in a new silver Porsche. You estimate the car's value at around $50,000, yet the neighborhood you are patrolling in is characterized by low-income housing, cheap apartments, and tiny houses on the lowest end of the housing spectrum. You follow him and observe that he forgets to signal when he changes lanes. Ordinarily you wouldn't waste your time on something so minor. What would you do?

Situation 2

You are a homicide investigator and are interrogating someone you believe picked up a 9 year old in a shopping mall, and then molested and murdered the girl. He is a registered sex offender, was in the area, and although he doesn't have any violence in his record, you believe he must have done it because there is no other suspect who had the means, opportunity, and motive. You have some circumstantial evidence (he was seen in a video following the child) but very little good physical evidence. You really need a confession to make the case. You want to send this guy away for a long time. After several hours of getting nowhere, you have a colleague come in with a file folder and pretend that the medical examiner had obtained fingerprints on the body that matched the suspect's. You tell him that he lost his chance to confess to a lesser crime because now he is facing the death penalty. He says that he will confess to whatever you want him to if the death penalty is taken off the table. Do you tell him what you did? Do you tell the prosecutor?

Situation 3

You are a federal agent and have been investigating a major drug ring for a long time. One of your informants is highly placed within this ring and has been providing you with good information. You could "turn" him because he faces a murder charge: there is probable cause that he shot and killed a coworker during an argument about five years ago, before he became involved in the drug ring. You have been holding the murder charge over his head to get him to cooperate and have been able, with the help of the U.S. District Attorney's office, to keep the local prosecutor from filing charges and arresting him. The local prosecutor is upset because the family wants some resolution in the case. You believe that the information he can provide you will result in charges of major drug sales and racketeering against several of the top smugglers, putting a dent in the drug trade for your region. At the same time, you understand that you are constantly risking the possibility that he may escape prosecution by leaving the country and that you are blocking the justice that the family of the murdered victim deserves. What would you do?

Situation 4

You are a rookie police officer who responds to a call for officer assistance. Arriving at the scene, you see a ring of officers surrounding a suspect who is down on his knees. You don't know what happened before you arrived, but you see a sergeant use a Taser on the suspect, and you see two or three officers step in and take turns hitting the suspect with their nightsticks about the head and shoulders. This goes on for several minutes as you stand in the back of the circle. No one says anything that would indicate that this is not appropriate behavior. What would you do? What would you do later when asked to testify that you observed the suspect make "threatening" gestures to the officers involved?

Situation 5

You are a male suspect in a murder case. You were drunk the night of the homicide and did meet and dance with the victim, a young college girl. You admit that you had a lot to drink, but are 99 percent sure that you didn't see her except in the bar. The trouble is that you drank way too much and passed out in someone's apartment close to the bar rather than drive home. The girl was found in an apartment in the same complex. Police are telling you that they have forensic evidence that ties you to the murder. They say that they have her blood on your clothes and that it is your DNA in the sperm found in her body. They have been interrogating you now for several hours, and you are beginning to doubt your memory. You are also told that if you plead guilty, you would probably get voluntary manslaughter and might get probation, but if you insist on your innocence, you will be charged with first-degree murder and face the death penalty. What would you do?

(Obviously, this situation shifts our focus from the criminal justice professional's dilemma. If you decided earlier that the police tactic of lying about forensic evidence is ethical, this hypothetical illustrates what might happen when innocent suspects are lied to—assuming you are innocent!)

Police Corruption and Responses

7

Former officer Michael Slager was charged with the killing of Walter Scott in North Charleston, South Carolina. After a mistrial in state proceedings, he pleaded guilty to federal charges in May 2017.

Getty Images News/Getty Images

Learning Objectives

1. Provide examples of two types of police misconduct: economic corruption and abuse of authority.

2. Describe individual explanations of corruption and potential solutions.

3. Explain organizational explanations of corruption and potential solutions.

4. Describe societal explanations of corruption and potential solutions.

Frank Serpico is arguably the most famous police officer in the United States, even though he hasn't worked in law enforcement since 1972. As an NYPD detective, his whistleblowing led to the Knapp Commission. Serpico was shot in what was suspected of being a setup by fellow officers, although no one was ever charged. The name Serpico continues to elicit two different reactions. For some, it represents the epitome of an honest and brave man who stood against corruption at great risk to self. For others, it represents a "rat," a man who turned his back on his friends, and, for some officers, to be called a "Serpico" is a serious insult. Why we still talk about Frank Serpico is that his story includes all the elements of the problem of police corruption. From what we know, the problem is often "vertical" in that supervisors and administrators are either involved, have been involved, or, more often, actively try to cover up or ignore the corruption. Second, the problem is known to other officers, and even if only a few are involved, the "blue curtain" shields them. Finally, whistleblowers that expose the corruption are considered traitors and, sometimes, retaliation occurs as the In the News box and Walking the Walk box describe.

IN THE NEWS | *Whistleblower in Oregon*

An internal affairs supervisor was concerned that Portland police were not sharing information about officers who had credibility issues with prosecutors for so-called Brady lists (named after *Brady v. Maryland*, 373 U.S. 83, 1963) which requires prosecutors to share exculpatory information with defense attorneys). He alerted the prosecutor to five officers who had credibility issues, including being accused of sexual harassment, misrepresentation, and lying to internal affairs. In all cases, the officers' supervisors had recommended sustaining the allegations but the chief overturned those recommendations. In response to his calling attention to the problem, he was investigated, and eventually, transferred and passed over for promotion by two former chiefs. He was finally promoted under a current chief. "I took my hits for that," he said.

Source: Bernstein, 2017.

WALKING THE WALK

In the movie *Training Day*, a new recruit is "schooled" in the methods of a veteran, decorated cop that included brutalizing suspects, planting drugs, and generally committing crimes to catch the criminals. In a real-life version of *Training Day*, Keith Batt earned a criminal justice degree at California State University at Sacramento and fulfilled his life's dream by being hired by the Oakland Police Department. He graduated at the top of his recruit class and became an Oakland police officer in 1999.

Batt was assigned to Clarence Mabanag as his field training officer. Almost from the first day, Batt says, he was told to falsify offense reports and to use force on suspects. Batt did as he was told for two and a half weeks, including hitting a suspect and lying on an offense report, because he knew that he would be retaliated against if he did not. Then he decided that he could not continue to be a police officer if it meant violating the law he was sworn to uphold. He quit the Oakland force and turned in his FTO and the other officers to internal affairs.

Mabanag and other officers, including Matt Hornung, Jude Siapno, and Frank (Choker) Vazquez, were known as the "Riders." According to testimony, they patrolled their western poverty-stricken district of Oakland with an iron fist and used excessive force, planted drugs, and intimidated witnesses as the means to keep the peace. Partly as a result of Keith Batt's report, all four officers were fired and charged with a range of offenses, including obstruction of justice, conspiracy to obstruct justice, filing false police reports, assault and battery, kidnapping, and false imprisonment. Not everyone applauded Keith Batt's decision to testify against them. According to one fellow officer at the time, "These guys are awesome cops, they never did anything to anybody who was innocent, just pukes, criminals, see? They just got a little too intense and went over the line." Even residents had mixed feelings, with some arguing that it took a tough cop to police a tough street. As one resident said, "The only thing the bad people understand is force." During the ensuing scandal, Oakland paid out $11 million to settle civil suits from 119 victims of police officers (including the Riders) and ended up under a court-ordered federal consent decree. Hornung, Mabanag, and Siapno were prosecuted between 2000 and 2005, but the juries either acquitted them or were deadlocked. Vazquez is a fugitive of justice, believed to be in Mexico. Batt has been honored as a courageous whistleblower who stood up to the "blue curtain of secrecy," but also has been vilified as a liar who feared a negative evaluation. He became a respected police officer in Pleasanton, California, and received an award for "ethical courage." But Clarence Mabanag is also a police officer in a different department in southern California, which hired him after the deadlocked jury verdict. In February 2009, in response to their appeal, an independent arbitrator ruled that the city was justified in dismissing Mabanag and Siapno.

Sources: Bay City News, 2007; Institute for Law Enforcement Administration, 2008; Lee, 2004; Zamora, Lee, and van Derbeke, 2003.

There is no doubt that most police officers are honest and strive to be ethical in all they do; however, examples of corruption and graft in law enforcement agencies are not difficult to find. In this chapter, we provide a more detailed discussion of misconduct. For our purposes, we divide misconduct into two broad categories: economic corruption and abuse of authority. Economic corruption can be defined as the use of one's position to obtain improper financial benefit. Abuse of authority is when the power and authority of the office is misused. First we discuss prevalence, then we provide examples. Finally, individual explanations for corruption are presented, followed by organizational and societal explanations. This same order is followed when discussing responses and potential solutions.

A long list of commissions and task forces have investigated police corruption, including the Chicago Police Committee (in 1931), the Knapp Commission (New York City in 1972–1973), the Kolts Commission (Los Angeles County in 1992), the Mollen Commission (New York City in 1993), the Philadelphia Police Study Task Force (in 1987), the Christopher Commission (Los Angeles in 1996), the New Orleans Mayor's Advisory Committee (in 1993), and the St. Clair Commission (Boston in 1992). Bayley and Perito (2011) analyzed 32 different commissions that investigated police corruption; 13 were in the United States. Space prohibits any description of corruption in other countries, but the same scandals occur worldwide. Transparency International charts perceptions of corruption and New Zealand and Scandinavian countries always rank highest. The United States is ranked below Canada and Great Britain and has a ranking of 20 of all countries in the latest report. At the bottom of the current rankings were countries such as Uzbekistan, Afghanistan, Myanmar, North Korea, and Somalia (Transparency International, 2014; 2017).

Even though there is a large body of literature on police corruption, few studies have been able to measure its extent and prevalence. An obvious barrier to discovery is getting police officers to admit to wrongdoing. One early study reported that, by officers' own accounts, 39 percent of their number engaged in illegal uses of force, 22 percent perjured themselves, 31 percent had sex on duty, 8 percent drank on duty, and 39 percent slept on duty (Barker and Carter, 1994). In a sample of narcotics officers, Stevens (1999) reported that 63 percent said they had very often heard of narcotics officers using more force than necessary to make an arrest, 26 percent had often heard of other officers personally consuming and/or selling drugs, and 82 percent had very often heard of other narcotics officers violating the civil rights of suspects. These numbers must be interpreted carefully in that they do not mean that large numbers of officers were corrupt, only that a fairly large number of officers were aware of at least one officer's misconduct. Fyfe and Kane (2006; also see Kane and White, 2009) studied police officers in New York City who were terminated for cause and found that only 2 percent of officers in the 22 years under study (1975–1996) were terminated for misconduct. This study's findings must also be interpreted with caution since the number of officers who come to the attention of supervisors and are officially sanctioned by termination is probably quite a bit lower than the numbers who commit corrupt acts. Further, officers are sometimes terminated for rule breaking that does not fit into any category of corruption.

Before one can begin to research prevalence, it would be necessary to have some shared understanding of a definition of corruption. There are many definitions and typologies in the literature. Fyfe and Kane (2006: 37–38), for instance, reviewed the literature, and then identified a long list of types of misconduct:

- Profit-motivated crimes (all offenses with the goal of profit except those that are drug-related)
- Off-duty crimes against persons (all assaultive, non-profit-related crimes off-duty)
- Off-duty public-order crimes (not including drugs, and most commonly DWI [driving while intoxicated] and disorderly conduct)
- Drugs (all crimes related to possession, sale, conspiracy, and failing departmental drug tests)
- On-duty abuse (use of excessive force, psychological abuse, or discrimination)
- Obstruction of justice (conspiracy, perjury, official misconduct, and all other offenses with the goal of obstructing justice)
- Administrative/failure to perform (violating one or more departmental rules, policies, and procedures)
- Conduct-related probationary failures (simple failure to meet expectations)

In the discussion to follow, we will offer a much simpler typology of simply economic corruption and abuse of authority.

Economic Corruption

Corruption has been described as "acting on opportunities, created by one's authority, for personal gain at the expense of the public one is authorized to serve" (Cohen, 1986: 23). *Baksheesh*, a euphemism for graft, is endemic in many developing countries where officials, including law enforcement officers, expect *baksheesh* before doing the job they are supposed to do; alternatively, they extort money in exchange for not doing their job. "It's just the way it is" is the explanation for why such corruption exists. Obviously, the problem is not systemic in this country; however, one can find many examples of police officers using their position to acquire unfair benefits.

In 1973, the Knapp Commission used the terms *grass eaters* and *meat eaters*: accepting bribes, gratuities, and unsolicited protection money was the extent of the corruption engaged in by grass eaters, who were passive in their deviant practices. Meat eaters participated in shakedowns, "shopped" at burglary scenes, and engaged in more active deviant practices. The Mollen Commission, which investigated New York City Police Department corruption 20 years later (1993), concluded that meat eaters were engaged in a qualitatively different kind of corruption in more recent times. Beyond just cooperating with criminals, the corrupt cops were active criminals themselves, selling drugs, robbing drug dealers, and operating burglary rings. The In the News box on the next page illustrates that it is not only New York that has this problem.

Economic corruption includes gratuities (when they conflict with law and policy), kickbacks (e.g., from towing companies), overtime schemes, misuse/appropriation of departmental property, payoffs (payment for shifts, promotions, or other benefits), ticket "fixing," bribery/extortion (shakedowns of storeowners or protection money to drug dealers), and theft from burglary scenes or from drug raids. The more serious acts in this list are also crimes. An important distinction should be made between

IN THE NEWS | *"Meat Eaters" in the News*

News accounts in 2017 described how a rogue team of East Cleveland police officers committed perjury and planted evidence. They also stole from and robbed drug dealers, manufacturing evidence to justify raids and turning in only some of the money seized. They were secretly recorded "shaking down" a dealer who was working with the FBI for $3,000. Three of the former officers are in prison. Dozens of people have had their convictions overturned or charges dropped because of the actions of the officers.

In Santa Ana, California, a police officer was fired (but got his job back in an arbitration hearing) after a secret video went viral on YouTube.com that showed the officer and several other officers during a 2015 raid of Sky High Holistic, a marijuana dispensary. The video showed the officers smashing security cameras; however, they didn't see the hidden camera. The hidden camera recorded the officers eating marijuana edibles from the shop and taking other products. One officer was charged with vandalism and petty theft, and he was fired but the city's personnel board reduced his punishment to a seven-week suspension and a transfer from the special enforcement team to the patrol division. Other officers involved in the raid were also fired and are appealing to the city's personnel board.

In Houston, an officer who had been applauded as an "officer of the year" was caught on video illegally selling assault rifles and sensitive information to undercover informants who posed as drug dealers. Allegedly he has been secretly working for a drug cartel since 2006, providing them with firearms, bulletproof vests, luxury vehicles, police scanners, and database access. His nephew was a member of the cartel and provided evidence against him.

Sources: Emett, 2016; Gerda, 2017; Schuppe, 2017.

---

crimes and ethical transgressions. It is an insult to law enforcement officers when certain actions, such as stealing from a burglary scene or taking money from a drug dealer to guard a shipment of drugs, are discussed as if they were ethical dilemmas in the same category as whether to avoid responding to a minor traffic accident or whether an officer should call in sick so he can go fishing. Stealing from a burglary scene and conspiring to protect drug dealers are crimes. The officers who engage in such acts are criminals who are quite distinct from officers who commit ethical lapses akin to other workers.

Gratuities

Gratuities are items of value received by an individual because of his or her role or position rather than because of a personal relationship with the giver. The widespread practices of free coffee in convenience stores, half-price or free meals in restaurants, and half-price dry cleaning are examples of gratuities. Frequently, businesspeople offer gratuities as a token of sincere appreciation for the police officers' work. Although the formal code of ethics prohibits accepting gratuities, many officers believe there is nothing wrong with them, seeing gratuities as small rewards for the difficulties they endure in police work.

gratuities Items of value received by an individual because of his or her role or position rather than because of a personal relationship with the giver.

Justifications for gratuities include the idea that some businesses need (and should pay for) extra protection; that they are no different than the perks of other occupations; that they compensate for poor pay; and that they cement community relations, for example, when the officer stays and drinks coffee with the storeowner (Kania, 1988; Prenzler, 1995).

Research indicates that people do not support gratuities, but do not think they are very serious either, especially when the items were infrequent, food, or inexpensive

(Lord and Bjerregaard, 2003; Prenzler, 1995). Critics of gratuities argue that they "erode public confidence in law enforcement and undermine our quest for professionalism" (Stefanic, 1981: 63). Cohen (1986) believes that gratuities violate the social contract because citizens give up their liberty to exploit only to be exploited. Critics (Coleman, 2004a, 2004b; Ruiz and Bono, 2004) argue against gratuities for the following reasons:

- Police are professionals, and professionals don't take gratuities.
- Gratuities are incipient corruptors because people expect different treatment in return.
- Gratuities are an abuse of authority and create a sense of entitlement.
- Gratuities add up to substantial amounts of money and can constitute as high as 30 percent of an officer's income.
- Gratuities can be the beginning of more serious forms of corruption.
- Gratuities are contrary to democratic ideals because they are a type of fee-for-service for public functions that are already paid for through taxes, such as police protection.
- Gratuities create a public perception that police are corrupt.

Kania (1988, 2004) argues that only when either or both the giver and taker (officer) have impure intent are gratuities wrong. For instance, it would be an unethical exchange if the intent of the giver was to give in exchange for some future service, not as reward for past services rendered. In Kania's scheme, ethical exchanges are only when true rewards or gifts with no expectation of future acts are offered and received with no expectations.

Where should one draw the line between harmless rewards and inappropriate gifts? Is a discount on a meal okay, but not a free meal? Is a meal okay, but not any other item, such as groceries or tires or car stereos? Do the store or restaurant owners expect anything for their money, such as more frequent patrols or overlooking sales of alcohol to underage juveniles? Should they expect different treatment from officers than the treatment given to those who do not offer gratuities? Suppose that an officer is told by a convenience store owner that she can help herself to anything in the store—free coffee, candy, cigarettes, chips, magazines, and the like. In the same conversation, the store owner asks the officer for her personal cellphone number "in case something happens and I need to get in contact with you." Is this a gift, or is it an exchange? Should the officer accept the free merchandise?

Many merchants give free or discount food to officers because they like to have police around, especially late at night. The question then becomes the one asked frequently by citizens: Why are two or three police cars always at a certain restaurant? Police argue that they deserve to take their breaks wherever they want within their patrol area. If it happens that they choose the same place, that shouldn't be a concern of the public. However, an impression of unequal protection occurs when officers make a habit of eating at certain restaurants or congregating at certain convenience stores. Free meals or even coffee may influence the pattern of police patrol and, thus, may be wrong because some citizens are not receiving equal protection.

"The blue discount suit," according to Ruiz and Bono (2004), was a term that indicated how officers felt about gratuities, explaining how officers expected merchants to extend free merchandise with the saying, "If you got no pop, you got no cop." Officers

ETHICAL DILEMMA

You are a police officer who, after eating at a new restaurant, is told that the meal is "on the house." You did not go to that restaurant knowing the owner gave free meals to police officers. Should you accept the offer?

Law

While bribery laws punish taking or receiving something of value in return for a specific act of omission or commission related to one's office, conflict-of-interest laws punish merely taking something of value prohibited by the law when one holds a public office, with no necessity to show that a specific vote or decision was directly influenced by receipt of the valued items or services. Conflict-of-interest laws recognize the reality that public official's discretion is compromised after receiving things of value from stakeholders, even if there is no way to prove a direct connection. In *Skilling v. U.S.* 130 S. Ct. 2896, 2010, the Supreme Court invalidated a federal "honest services" law as being unconstitutionally vague. The law (18 U.S.C. Sec. 1346) made it a crime to deprive someone of honest services. The federal prosecutor did not have to prove a specific bribe or kickback, but only that there was some loss of honest services from the suspect to their clients or fiduciaries (because of private dealing or conflict of interest). Even if state conflict-of-interest laws could withstand a similar legal challenge, such laws would probably not apply to a free meal anyway because the value is too low to assume any influence.

Policy

Many departments have policies against gratuities while others specify some nominal value of goods that may be received. Gratuity policies are often the most ignored of all policies and considered to be hypocritical by the rank and file since the administration often solicits goods from the same type of vendors that might offer gratuities to individual officers. Policies that are not enforced and prevalently ignored are problematic in the organization.

Ethics

Professional ethics discourages gifts or gratuities when the profession involves discretionary judgments about a clientele (i.e., judges, professors, appraisers, and inspectors). Whether gifts are unethical relates to whether one's occupation or profession involves judgments that affect the gift givers. The police obviously have discretionary authority and make judgments that affect store owners and other gift givers. This may explain why some think it is wrong for police to accept gifts or favors. It also explains why so many other people do not see anything wrong with some types of gratuities, for police officers in most situations are not making decisions that affect the giver and, instead, are simply providing a service, such as responding to a burglary or disturbance call.

Ethical formalism would indicate that we must be comfortable with a universal law allowing all businesses to give all police officers certain favors or gratuities, such as free meals, free merchandise, or special consideration. However, such a blanket endorsement of this behavior would probably not be desirable. The second principle of ethical formalism indicates that each should treat every other with respect as an individual and not as a means to an end. In this regard, we would have to condemn gratuities in cases where the giver or receiver had improper motives according to Kania's typology. This also explains why some gifts seem acceptable. When something is given freely and accepted without strings, there is no "using" of others; therefore, it might be considered an innocent, honorable act by both parties.

If utilitarian ethics were used, one would have to weigh the relative good or utility of the interaction. On one hand, harmless gratuities may create good feelings in the community toward the officers and among the officers toward the community (Kania's "cementing the bonds" argument). On the other hand, gratuities often lead to perceptions of unfairness by shopkeepers who feel they are being taken advantage of, or those who feel they are not receiving the appropriate police protection because they don't give gratuities, by police who think they deserve rewards and don't get them, and so on. Thus, the overall negative results of gratuities, even "harmless" ones, might lead a utilitarian to conclude that gratuities are unethical.

The ethics of virtue would be concerned with the individual qualities or virtues of the officer. A virtuous officer could take free coffee and not let it affect his or her judgment. However, if the officer does not possess virtues, such as honesty, integrity, and fairness, even free coffee may lead to special treatment. Further, nonvirtuous officers would seek out gifts and gratuities and abuse their authority by pursuing them.

bring up the seeming hypocrisy of a departmental prohibition against individual officers accepting gratuities, yet at the same time there may be an administrative policy of actively soliciting and receiving donations from merchants for departmental events, such as pastries, coffee, or more expensive catering items.

MacIntyre and Prenzler (1999) found that most officers would not write a ticket to someone who had given them gratuities. Another study found that gratuities influenced police patrol coverage (DeLeon-Granados and Wells, 1998). More research is needed to see if these findings would be replicated.

Graft

Graft exploitation of one's role for illegal financial benefit, e.g., bribes or protection money

Graft is the exploitation of one's role by accepting bribes or protection money. Graft also occurs when officers receive kickbacks from tow truck drivers, defense attorneys, or bail bond companies for recommending them. In Klockars, Ivkovic, and Haberfeld's (2004) international comparison of officers' views regarding hypotheticals drawn to illustrate various forms of corruption, officers in the United States rated bribery as the second most serious offense. Only theft from a crime scene was rated as more serious.

Examples of graft involve a range of seriousness from "cheating a little" on overtime to sophisticated schemes that utilize police powers for private gain. For instance, a former Savannah-Chatham police chief was convicted for running interference for a gambling operation for 10 years, earning payoffs to protect it (Skutch, 2014). Other schemes in the news involved officers getting kickbacks for calling certain tow-truck companies and receiving money and goods for illegally using police computers to run background investigations (CNN.com, 2011; Guilfoil, 2010; Saltzman, 2010).

Abuse of Authority

Abuse of authority involves officers' misuse of the power and authority inherent in their positions. The most serious abuse of authority is when officers use their legal power to use force against individuals without just cause as described in the In the News box.

Barker and Carter (1994) and Fyfe and Kane (2006) discuss police abuse of authority that can be summarized as follows:

- Physical abuse—excessive force, physical harassment, and retaliatory brutality
- Psychological abuse—disrespect, harassment, ridicule, excessive stops, intimidation, and deception in interrogation
- Legal abuse—unlawful searches or seizures, manufacturing evidence, perjury, planting evidence, and hiding exculpatory evidence

Professional Courtesy and Ticket Fixing

One practice not included in the typologies above is called "professional courtesy," which refers to the practice of not ticketing an officer who is stopped for speeding or for other driving violations. Obviously, officers do not ticket everyone they stop. They often give warnings instead, and that is a legitimate use of their discretion. Whether to ticket or give a warning should depend on objective criteria, such as the seriousness

IN THE NEWS | *Abuse of Authority?*

Two cases in New York involve potential abuses of power. In the first case, two NYPD police detectives were charged with felony and misdemeanor assault, and perjury because of beating Karim Baker, 26, a uniformed postal worker in October of 2016. Baker said he had been harassed since 2014, when he gave street directions to the man who ambushed and killed NYPD officers Wenjian Liu and Rafael Ramos before killing himself. He said he has been stopped approximately 20 times over 10 months. The detectives stopped their car and approached him sitting in his car after he had finished his shift. They asked to see identification and told him he was parked too close to a fire hydrant. Mr. Baker tried to call 911, but the officers began hitting him and dragged him from the vehicle. He was charged with resisting arrest, disorderly conduct, and criminal possession of a controlled substance. Mr. Baker sustained spinal fractures and a knee injury. A grand jury indicted the officers after they watched the surveillance video from a business across the street from the arrest that contradicted the detectives' account. The vehicle was more than 15 feet

from the hydrant and Baker did not resist the detectives before he was beaten. The detectives opted for a bench trial without a jury and were acquitted in 2017. Baker has filed a $100 million lawsuit against the city.

In another case, a cellphone recording shows that a mail carrier was almost hit by a car driven by plainclothes officers as he was delivering a package. He yelled at the car and the car backed up and the officers jumped out and challenged Gray. After some words were exchanged, Gray was handcuffed and placed in an unmarked car without a seatbelt. The officers left Gray's postal vehicle unattended and double-parked. Then the officers rear-ended a vehicle on the way to the precinct and Gray was injured in the impact. Gray spent four hours at the station and then was issued a summons for disorderly conduct. Ironically, Gray's wife is a police officer. A lieutenant who was the highest ranking officer of the four was placed on administrative duty in April of 2016. The Postal Service's office of inspector general is investigating whether any federal laws were violated.

Sources: Bellafante, 2016; Carrega, Parascandola, and Greene, 2017; Southall 2016a, 2016b.

of the violation. If the officer would let another person go with a warning in the same situation, there is no ethical issue in giving a warning to a fellow officer. However, if *every other person* would have received a ticket, but the officer did not issue one *only because* the motorist was a fellow officer, that is a violation of the code of ethics ("enforce the law . . . without fear or favor"). It is a violation of deontological universalism as well as utilitarianism. Under deontological ethics, it is the officer's duty to enforce the law against everyone, including officers. Under utilitarianism, the fact that the speeding officer can cause an accident means that the utility for society is greater if the ticket is issued, for it might make the officer slow down, and by doing that, accidents can be avoided.

Justifications for not ticketing other officers are diverse and creative. For instance, some honest justifications are purely egoistic: "If I do it for him, he will do it for me one day." Other justifications are under the guise of utilitarianism: "It's best for all of us not to get tickets, and the public isn't hurt because we're trained to drive faster." One troubling aspect of professional courtesy for traffic offenses is that the practice tends to bleed over into other forms of misconduct. Officers who are stopped for driving while intoxicated are sometimes driven home rather than arrested, but this application of discretion is less likely to be afforded to any other citizen. In some cases of domestic violence, victims of police officer husbands or boyfriends describe how the responding officers do nothing or take their complaints more lightly than they would if the alleged perpetrator was not a police officer.

The idea that officers are above the law is insidious. Officers who believe that they should not have to follow the same laws they enforce against others may be more prone to other forms of abuse of authority as well. It should also be noted that many officers think that they are held to a *higher* standard of behavior than the public. Officers point out that a domestic violence, DUI, or any other arrest may cost them their job. The argument against this position is that other jobs also are at risk if one receives a DUI (bus drivers, train conductors, pilots), and, perhaps, one who has taken an oath to uphold the law, but engages in unlawful behavior should not have the job.

One step more serious than not ticketing an officer (or anyone) solely for preferential reasons is "fixing" a ticket that has already been written. The reason is that such acts could be considered and charged as "tampering with official documents." A major ticket-fixing scandal in New York City involved a widespread practice in one precinct of "fixing" tickets for friends and family. A former lieutenant was fired and convicted of obstruction for tipping the officers to the investigation. The Bronx district attorney's office estimated that ticket-fixing cost the city more than $1 million in ticket revenue (Hu, 2014).

On-Duty Use of Drugs and Alcohol

Carter (1999) discussed the extent of on-duty drug use, citing previous research that found up to 20 percent of officers in one city used marijuana and other drugs while on duty. That seems to be a high figure; in other surveys, about 8 percent of employees reported drug use and only 3 percent of all workers in a "protective services" category reported drug use. In a more recent survey, protective service employees were the least likely to report any drug use (Mieczkowski, 2002). The sources are not exactly comparable and all are dated, but we have no current information about prevalence.

Certain circumstances are present in law enforcement that, perhaps, create more opportunities for drug use. Elements of police work (especially undercover work) that can lead to drug use include exposure to a criminal element, relative freedom from supervision, and uncontrolled availability of contraband. Drug use by officers creates the potential for even more serious misbehavior, such as stealing evidence, being blackmailed to perform other unethical or illegal actions, and being tempted to steal from drug users instead of arresting them. This, of course, is in addition to the obvious problem of compromising one's decision-making abilities by being under the influence of any drug while on duty.

In a study of drug use, it was found that officers used drugs to relieve stress and for social reasons. No predictors emerged as to which officers were more likely to be drug users. The study results also noted other crimes that were associated with drug use, including giving drugs to others, providing confidential information to suppliers and theft (Gorta, 2008).

The use of drug tests during the hiring process is longstanding, but periodic and/or random drug testing of employed officers is a more recent policy. Generally, courts have upheld the right of law enforcement agencies to employ drug testing, applying the balancing test between a compelling governmental interest and individual privacy rights. Officers have some due process rights, however, and they must be notified of the policies and procedures involved in the agency's drug testing, have access to the findings, and have available some sort of appeal process before sanctions are taken (Mieczkowski, 2002). In Fyfe and Kane's (2006) study of police officers terminated for cause in New York City, the most common reason for termination was a failed drug test.

Alcohol use is more socially acceptable than drug use, and it has also been cited as a problem. In one survey, it was found that about 8 percent of those in protective services occupations (which include police officers) reported heavy alcohol use. This compared to 12 percent of construction workers and 4 percent of sales workers (Mieczkowski, 2002). Barker and Carter (1994) indicated that 8 percent of officers reported drinking alcohol on duty. The problem of drinking on duty does not involve the vulnerability to blackmail that drug use does, but there are obvious problems, and officers who are aware of another's on-duty intoxication are faced with an ethical dilemma of whether to take official action. Officers may choose to informally isolate themselves from drinking officers by refusing to partner with them or avoid working calls with them.

Sexual Misconduct

It is a sad reality that a few police officers use their position of authority to extort sex from female citizens (there doesn't seem to be the parallel situation of female police officers extorting sex from male victims). Egregious cases in the United States include rapes by officers on duty, and by jailers in police lockups, and a few instances where the sexual misconduct of police officers was widespread and protected by departmental supervisors (McGurrin and Kappeler, 2002). The Cato Institute sponsors the National Police Misconduct Reporting Project, which acts as a clearinghouse for misconduct reports across the nation. It was reported that 9.3 percent of all civilian complaints on police involved sexual misconduct, the second most common form of misconduct after excessive use of force (Packman, 2011).

📱 IN THE NEWS | *Police Predators*

In Pasco, Washington, former officer Richard Aguirre had relationships with underage girls and used other officers' names to access a law enforcement database to look up the addresses of women and young girls, and the boyfriends of his former lovers; none of the searches had anything to do with any official investigation. In 2014, he was arrested for sexually assaulting a woman in his home. When he was forced to submit a sample of DNA, it matched a 1986 murder of a sex worker near Spokane.

In San Diego, Christopher Hayes was fired and received a felony conviction for forcing women to perform sex acts. Also in San Diego, former officer Anthony Arevalos was convicted in 2011 of extorting sex acts from women and is serving eight years in prison.

In other cases, a Texas officer told a motorist she could drive off without a ticket if she let him lick her feet or take her underwear; a Charlotte-Mecklenburg, N.C. officer went to prison for pressuring a half-dozen women for sex during traffic stops; a school resource officer in Atlanta molested a 12-year-old developmentally disabled girl as he drove her around town after school one day and was sentenced to 20 years in prison; a New Mexico officer was sentenced to 9 years in prison for assaulting a high school intern; a Georgia deputy was sentenced to 25 years in prison after he falsely accused and arrested a bar waitress, who spoke little English, and took her to his apartment where he raped and beat her.

Finally, Daniel Holtzclaw, a former Oklahoma City officer, forced at least 12 black women to perform oral sex during traffic stops and raped others in their homes. In a highly publicized trial he was found guilty and sentenced to over 200 years in prison. His case is on appeal.

Source: Davis, 2014; King, 2015; KUSA, 2016; Spina, 2015.

Stinson, Brewer, and Mathna (2015) analyzed 771 sex-related arrest cases from 2005 to 2008 of 555 sworn officers at 449 nonfederal law enforcement agencies in 44 states. Less than 1 percent of the offending officers were female; most were patrol officers. The modal time in service was one to five years. On-duty and off-duty offenses were about equally divided. A majority (70 percent) of the victims were minors (under 18). Most of the cases involving a child victim occurred when the officer was off duty and most of the cases involving an adult victim occurred when the officer was on duty. Forcible fondling was the most serious offense charged in most cases, followed by forcible rape, statutory rape, and forcible sodomy. This study and others like it show that sexual misconduct of officers is not a negligible problem and involves more serious crimes and victimization than previously believed.

Kraska and Kappeler (1995) looked at a sample of 124 cases of police sexual misconduct and proposed a continuum of sexual invasion that ranged from some type of invasion of privacy to sexual assault. This range of behavior includes: viewing a victim's photos or videos for prurient purposes; field or custodial strip searches; illegal detentions; services for sex; and sexual assault. Sapp's (1994) inventory of sexual misconduct includes: nonsexual contacts that are sexually motivated (nonvalid traffic stops); voyeurism; inappropriate contact with crime victims; and sexual demands of suspects or offenders.

Prostitutes, homeless, and minority women are populations that are extremely vulnerable to sexual extortion by police officers, because people tend not to believe them. But women who have been subject to intimidation and outright assault come from all social classes. Officers argue that, if sex occurred, it was consensual. The problem is that when officers acting in their official capacity meet women (as victims, witnesses, defendants, or suspects), the power differential makes consent extremely problematic. When a rapist is a police officer, victims feel completely powerless. Michael Ragusa, a former officer, is serving a 10-year sentence for sexually assaulting three women. One of his victims moved out of the county, unable to shake her fear every time she saw a man in uniform (Merchant and Sedensky, 2015). There is a troubling pattern whereby police officers accused of serious sexual misconduct have charges dropped or downgraded and then move and obtain law enforcement positions in other jurisdictions. (McGurrin and Kappeler, 2002; Merchant and Sedensky, 2015).

Sexual harassment of fellow officers is also a problem. About three-quarters of female officers report being sexually harassed (Kraska and Kappeler, 1995; Maher, 2010). It may be that the culture of policing is particularly conducive to sexual harassment. It has been described as a "macho" or "locker room" culture even though women have been integrated into patrol since the early 1970s. Female officers today do not encounter the virulent harassment and hostility that was present in the 1970s when patrol forces were first integrated, but some remnants of that culture remain. For instance, female officers who pretend to be prostitutes are targeted for sexual innuendos, jokes, and other forms of comments about their body and dress, with mixed findings as to whether this rises to sexual harassment (Dodge, Starr-Gimeno, and Williams, 2005; Maguire and Nolan, 2011; Nolan, 2001).

Criminal Cops

The extremely serious side of misconduct is usually associated with the drug trade and involves officers who cross over into being more criminal than cop. There have been scandals of criminal cops in every decade. In the 1980s, the "Miami River Rats" committed armed robberies of drug deals, and at least one homicide (Dorschner, 1989; see also Rothlein, 1999). The "Buddy Boys" in New York operated almost openly in a precinct rife with lesser forms of corruption. Ultimately, 13 officers in a precinct of only a little over 200 were indicted for crimes ranging from drug use to drug sales and armed robbery (Kappeler, Sluder, and Alpert, 1984/1994).

In the 1990s, Michael Dowd testified to the Mollen Commission that he and other officers accepted money for protecting illegal drug operations, used drugs and alcohol while on duty, robbed crime victims and drug dealers of money and drugs, and even robbed corpses of their valuables (Kappeler, Sluder, and Alpert, 1994). The Rampart scandal that exploded in the late 1990s, involving a rogue anti-gang task force, tarnished the reputation of LAPD for years afterward. Other scandals occurred in Indianapolis (Murray, 2009), New Orleans, Boston, and Philadelphia (Graham and Gormisky, 2010); and it continues with scandals currently unfolding in several cities across the country. These officers are a minuscule portion of the more than a million law enforcement professionals, but their actions damage the credibility of all.

Costs of Corruption

We have examined a range of corruption, from the arguably trivial (gratuities) to criminal acts that include murder. The costs to communities are considerable. First, there is the cost of lost prosecutions. Literally thousands of cases across the country have had to be dismissed because prosecutors could not trust that the evidence provided by police officers was legitimate or the officer had lost credibility as a witness in all cases because of his or her wrongdoing.

Although civil lawsuits or civil rights lawsuits against errant officers are notoriously difficult to win, many cities and police departments have faced large judgments or agreed to large settlements. By one analysis, the settlement money paid out by the 10 American cities with the largest police forces increased by 48 percent from 2010 to 2014, to nearly $250 million annually (Gass, 2015b). These lawsuits are most often claims of police brutality, traffic accident claims, or wrongful death suits due to police shootings. In some instances, the numbers represent settlements for old cases, and some cities have shown recent declines in the amounts paid out; however, no one disputes that these money judgments have, for the most part, increased (Gass, 2015b). Thus, ironically, residents who are the victim of police misconduct also end up paying for it through taxes.

There are two ways that cities become responsible: first, if the plaintiff can show a pattern and practice, for example, lack of training, that led to the actions of the officer; or, second and most common, cities routinely indemnify an officer against lawsuit judgments. What this means is that the officer is sued individually, but if he or she loses, the city will pay the judgment. Cleveland has been reported as coming up with a way around their fiscal responsibility, however, in that they refuse to indemnify the officer but city attorneys help the officer file bankruptcy. In those cases, even if the plaintiff wins, no party is responsible for the settlement (Balko, 2016).

There is no way to know the total amount of money taxpayers pay across the nation in any given year because of police misconduct. Some specific localities do not even keep tallies of how much is spent in judgments or in settling lawsuits, but news reports call attention to the costs of misconduct. The amounts below are not consistent in what they cover, for example, while some count only misconduct settlements, others may count settlements involving auto collisions; however, they give an idea of how expensive police misconduct can be for cities:

Baltimore—$6.4 million settlement for the Freddy Gray case; from 2011 to 2014, $5.7 million;

Boston—more than $36 million to resolve 2,000 legal claims and lawsuits against the police department between 2005 and 2015 (mostly brutality and wrongful death claims);

Chicago—nearly $5.4 million just to settle three cases of misconduct in 2012–2013; more than a half-*billion* dollars to resolve police brutality cases between 2004 and 2014;

Cleveland—$8 million between 2003 and 2013 on claims related to police misconduct;

Los Angeles—about $101 million between 2002 and 2011;

Minneapolis—$14 million in payments in the previous seven years; in 95 payouts between 2006 and 2012, only eight led to officers being disciplined;

New York City—in fiscal year 2013, $138 million; in fiscal year 2014, $217 million; the Eric Garner case alone was $5.9 million; $348 million to settle misconduct cases between 2006 and 2011 (Dardick, 2013; Gass, 2015b; Hennelly, 2015; McKinney, 2015; Wallack, Ransom, and Anderson, 2015).

It is estimated that Philadelphia pays out about $10 million a year because of police abuse and misconduct. Between 2011 and 2015, officials settled more than 200 cases alleging that the cops used excessive force, and about 120 cases were settled on claims that police falsely arrested someone. In 2015, 184 lawsuits against police were filed. The claims are settled with funds from a city indemnity fund for legal settlements. City officials argue the 150 or so cases settled every year are not necessarily indicative of an officer's wrongdoing. Each year, the police commissioner receives a report describing patterns with recommendations for policy changes. An independent researcher, however, found that there was little effort to analyze information from lawsuits to reduce civil liability. This differs from Los Angeles, a city that requires the police department to describe corrective action for any claim paid over $20,000 (Allyn, 2015; Denvir, 2015).

Despite the costs to the city of such lawsuits, there is no evidence to indicate that they are a deterrent to errant police officers. In fact, one study showed that there is no follow-up generally with the police officers involved. The lawsuit doesn't appear in the officers' personnel records, nor does anyone keep track of patterns or problem officers (Milligan, 2015). Only recently in New York has an automated system been implemented that tracks lawsuits and feeds information back to the police department for discipline or training purposes (Lewis and Veltman, 2015). In some cities, investigations for lawsuits proceed out of the city's legal department and the police department isn't even involved. A troubling practice was exposed in Baltimore where, when the city settles with an individual in one of these cases, there is usually a gag order imposed on the plaintiff that means that they cannot talk about what happened to them or they will lose their settlement money. This impedes the public's ability to know how widespread police misconduct is or whether an individual officer has a history of misconduct. There is no easily available source to find out how many cities utilize this practice (Craven, 2015).

Police officials sometimes don't even know when the city settles because it is a decision made by city officials outside the police department. Police officers believe that city lawyers are too quick to settle "nuisance" claims, where the officer is not at fault; however, when such cases do go to trial, there is the risk of a much larger judgment (Schwartz, 2010). The important point to note though is that civil lawsuits seem to be independent from the department's own discipline system and, rarely, is there the mechanism to take note of when officers become the target of lawsuits multiple times.

Explanations of Deviance

Explanations of corruption can be categorized into individual, organizational, and societal, based on the identified factors. These factors then provide an avenue for how to reduce misconduct. It is important to note at the outset that there is rarely only one factor or group of factors responsible for corruption scandals. Generally, a constellation of factors is present.

Individual Explanations

The most common explanation of police officer corruption is the **rotten-apple argument**—that the officer alone is deviant and that it was simply a mistake to hire him or her. This argument has been extended to describe *rotten bushels*—groups of officers banding together to commit deviant acts. The point of this argument is that nothing is wrong with the barrel, that deviance is individual, not endemic.

rotten-apple argument The proposition that the officer alone is deviant and that it was simply a mistake to hire him or her.

Sherman (1982) explained that deviant officers go through what he called a "moral career" as they pass through various stages of rationalization to more serious misdeeds in a graduated and systematic way. Once an individual gets past the first "moral crisis," it becomes less difficult to rationalize new and more unethical behaviors. While it seems to be true that corrupt officers who come to the attention of authorities engage in a range of minor misconduct to serious behavior, there is no good evidence to indicate that something like taking gratuities inevitably leads to more serious forms of misconduct. Many police officers have clear personal guidelines on what is acceptable and not acceptable.

Police routinely deal with the seamier side of society—not only drug addicts and muggers but also middle-class people who are involved in dishonesty and corruption. The constant displays of lying, hiding, cheating, and theft create cynicism, and this, in turn, may develop into a vulnerability to temptation because officers may redefine corrupt acts as acceptable behaviors. Following are some rationales that police might easily use to justify unethical behavior (Murphy and Moran, 1981: 93):

- The public thinks every cop is a crook, so why try to be honest?
- The money is out there; if I don't take it, someone else will.
- I'm only taking what's rightfully mine; if the city paid me a decent wage, I wouldn't have to get it on my own.
- I can use it because it's for a good cause—my son needs an operation, or dental work, or tuition for medical school, or a new bicycle.

Greene, Piquero, Hickman, and Lawton (2004) found that 15 characteristics were significantly related to receiving departmental discipline in the Philadelphia Police

Department, including being younger, being previously rejected for hire, experiencing military discipline, scoring low on some sections of academy training, and receiving academy discipline. Officers having six or more of these risk factors were 2.5 times more likely to receive departmental discipline (2004: iv). The research found that 22 factors were significantly related to receiving a citizen complaint of physical abuse, including being younger, receiving military discipline, having one's driver's license suspended, having ever been placed under arrest, and having had one or more deceptive polygraph results. Greene, et al. (2004) found that higher levels of cynicism predicted disciplinary actions, shootings, and other misconduct. They also found that officers who worked in districts with lower ethics scores were more likely to be involved in shootings, but no other relationships were found. Note that this study did not collect the data in a way that would allow them to match the actions and attitudes of individual officers; instead they had to aggregate ethics scores by district level.

Fyfe and Kane (2006; also see Kane and White, 2009) identified correlates related to termination in their study of NYPD. College-educated officers were less likely to be terminated. They found that women were more likely than male officers to be terminated during their probation, although male officers were more likely to be terminated for brutality and bribery. Black officers were also more likely to be terminated. Other groups more likely to be terminated during probation included those under 22, those who had prior negative employment histories, dishonorable discharges, and/or did poorly in the academy. Also at high risk were those with prior citizen complaints, prior criminal history, and a history of a public-order offense. Nonindividual factors included being assigned to posts with low supervision and high citizen contact. These findings must be viewed with caution, however, as they are only from one department, they utilize only official reports of misconduct, and they do not control for other variables. Manning (2009) criticized Kane and White's (2009) study because it combined misconducts like administrative rule-breaking with much more serious deviance such as lawbreaking.

Criminological theories have been used to explain misconduct. Hickman, et al. (2001) found that officers with lower self-control were more likely to report fellow officers engaged in misconduct. These researchers assumed that asking respondents to estimate other officers' misconduct could be used as a proxy for self-misconduct (this assumption may be problematic). Researchers have also concluded that social learning theory is supported; in other words, officers learn deviance from each other (Chappell and Piquero, 2004). Pogarsky and Piquero (2004) found that the threat of extra-legal and legal sanctions did potentially deter misconduct and that the trait of impulsivity tended to reduce the effect of such threats.

Harris (2010a, 2010b) adds to this discussion by offering a life-course perspective to officer misconduct. He used citizen complaints as a measure of misconduct, acknowledging that this is a somewhat problematic measure. He found that being female, having a higher education, and not being a minority are related to lower levels of receiving citizen complaints. Other findings were that officers tend to receive citizen complaints early in their career and there is a desistance over the course of the career; however, most officers in his sample had fewer than three complaints over their entire career. There was a group of officers who received a higher level of citizen complaints, and the number did not decline as dramatically as all other officers after the sixth year. This small group of officers (5 percent) received 20 percent of all complaints. One explanation is that those officers with disproportionately high complaint numbers are more likely to make arrests and a high number of arrests leads to complaints, but Harris found that productivity (arrest) measures were not related to the number of citizen complaints. He also found that internally generated complaints were more likely to be substantiated in formal disciplinary proceedings (Harris, 2012).

One emerging individual explanation for some types of police misconduct is post-traumatic stress disorder (PTSD). Researchers have found that about 14 percent of military veterans may experience some symptoms of PTSD and other research indicates that between 3 and 17 percent of police officers experience these symptoms as well. As noted in an earlier chapter, many police officers are military veterans, so there is the potential that a military veteran may already have PTSD when he or she experiences trauma in policing. Other research indicates that 7–35 percent of all police officers display some PTSD symptoms, or what is called subclinical PTSD. Symptoms include hypervigilance, trouble sleeping, anger control issues, and flashbacks. Factors involved in developing PTSD symptoms include the following:

- Witnessing the death of a law enforcement officer or viewing the body at the scene, especially when the victim was a friend or partner
- Accidentally killing or wounding a bystander, especially if the victim is a child
- Failing to stop a perpetrator from injuring or killing someone
- Killing or wounding a child or teenager, even if the life of the officer was threatened by the person injured or killed
- Viewing the body of a child victim, particularly if the officer has children (especially if the officer's child is the same age and sex as the victim)
- Interacting with grieving family members or friends of homicide victims
- Feeling caught in a violent riot, especially if the officer cannot use deadly force to defend himself or herself for fear of hurting children in the mob
- Viewing particularly bloody or gruesome scenes
- Observing an event involving violence or murder, but not being able to intervene
- Being undercover and constantly "on guard" because of the likelihood of being hurt, killed, or discovered
- Being threatened by suspects who have been indicted, are being tried, or are incarcerated (Hamidi and Koga, 2014)

Research also shows that PTSD symptoms are correlated with family violence and alcohol abuse (Hamidi and Koga, 2014). More research is needed to determine if officers who engage in drinking on duty, excessive force, and other forms of misconduct may also display PTSD symptoms.

Organizational Explanations

Various elements of the organization can breed misconduct. Recall from Chapter 4 that organizational factors that affect ethical behavior include small work-group influences. Isolated work groups develop their own micro-climate that can be one that does not conform to organizational ethics. Other organizational elements include perverse incentives and a culture that does not emphasize integrity.

Small Work Groups

Small work groups are exemplified by special units and narcotics task forces. There seems to be a pattern in news stories of these small work groups developing a micro-culture of unethical behavior. The most famous example of this is the Ramparts scandal in Los Angeles, but other examples across the country exist as well and scandals continue to emerge every year. In Philadelphia, patterns of misconduct (theft from drug dealers, sales of drugs, and falsifying evidence) in narcotics squads date back to the early 1980s, including the "One Squad" scandal, the "Five Squad" scandal, an unnamed scandal in the early 1990s involving five narcotics officers, and another scandal in 2000 with officers accused of using false information to get search warrants, planting evidence and committing perjury, and stealing drugs, cash, and valuables from drug dealers (Slobodzian, 2009).

Most recently, a newspaper series spurred an internal investigation of a Philadelphia narcotics squad who were accused by Latino bodega owners of raiding their stores, turning off the security cameras, and then (allegedly) stealing money and goods from the stores. The squad was also accused of planting drugs, falsifying warrant affidavits, and stealing from drug dealers, and one of them was accused of sexual assault by several women. Ultimately, the only officer punished was the one who agreed to work with investigators and prosecutors. The others either were not tried, or they were acquitted when they went to trial. Juries evidently did not believe the witnesses against the officers, many of whom had criminal records, despite (or perhaps because of) their vivid descriptions of being dangled over balconies, threatened with the seizure of their homes, held in hotel rooms for days, or beaten as the officers kept score on who could inflict the most debilitating injuries.

The officers won back their jobs along with back pay for the years they were off the force in an arbitration hearing; however, because the district attorney continued to refuse to use the officers as witnesses, all have been reassigned to positions outside of narcotics. Two were promoted by city officials against the police commissioner's recommendation. Five of the acquitted officers have filed a defamation lawsuit against the district attorney, mayor and police commissioner. Their attorney argued they were a highly successful narcotics squad and the decision to refuse their cases and charge them defamed their reputation. The attorney argued that the campaign against them was a turf war over forfeited drug money (Fazlollah and Whelan, 2015; Roebuck, 2015).

Despite the acquittals, the city has settled 21 of the estimated 135 civil rights cases stemming from the officers' actions. Also, a judge has overturned 158 convictions based on the officers' testimony. It is estimated that over 500 cases have been vacated since the officers' indictments in 2014 (Faziollah, Slobodzian, and Steele, 2012; Slobodzian and Fazlollah, 2015).

Perverse Incentives

As noted in Chapter 4, organizational incentives may encourage unethical behavior. When there is pressure to achieve a goal without a corresponding message that ethical means are just as important, organizational actors are tempted to take shortcuts. The best example of how good practices can result in bad outcomes is the Compstat program, a computerized crime-counting method that emphasizes accountability of middle managers. William Bratton is credited with beginning the program in New York

City. He also brought it with him to Los Angeles in 2002 when he took over as police chief of Los Angeles.

Back in New York, the program continued but became the center of a scandal when it was alleged that some precincts were routinely downgrading crime reports, even calling victims to encourage or coerce them to withdraw the report or change the facts. Adrian Schoolcraft, an officer in the 81st precinct, first reported the practice to the Quality Assurance division of the NYPD with examples of victims whose crimes were misrecorded, but nothing was done. Then he went to the media. He also had secretly recorded tapes of roll calls where supervisors urged the officers to make arrests, regardless of whether there was probable cause, and employ a very aggressive style of policing in one housing project, telling officers to make the arrest and think of a reason later. After the news broke, Schoolcraft was retaliated against and even, at one point, under the orders of high-level police supervisors, was forcibly taken to a mental ward in a Queens hospital, supposedly because he left work early the day before and was not answering his phone. It took him six days to obtain his release. Schoolcraft was suspended from the NYPD and now lives in upstate New York. He filed a $50 million lawsuit against the NYPD, the city, and the hospital. In 2015, the suit against the city and police department was settled for $600,000 exclusive of back pay and benefits (S. Brown, 2015; Goodman, 2015). In 2012, a report by the NYPD Quality Assurance Division supported Schoolcraft's claims (Parascandola, 2012). Academic research also supported the allegations that midlevel managers felt great pressure and crime reports were routinely downgraded in NYPD (Eterno, Verma, and Silverman, 2014). More recently, there has been at least one news report of 19 officers being charged with downgrading crime reports, identified by the NYPD's own quality assurance program after an anonymous tip (Baker, 2015a).

Arguably, Compstat can be an effective tool for improving the accountability of middle managers and ultimately improve police services for the community, or it can create pressure for "making the numbers" that causes police to downgrade serious crime reports and increase stops and arrests. An interesting new twist on Compstat is using the same principle to track procedural justice. In a recent news article, an innovative way to measure how residents feel about NYPD will use technology that accesses cellphones, requests the reader to go to the survey, and geocodes the location. Responses cover how they feel about the NYPD and satisfaction scores will be evaluated based on districts, evidently in a similar way that crime statistics was used in Compstat. Some express concern about privacy even though the NYPD won't have individual phone numbers and individuals will be volunteering to fill out the survey (Baker, 2017a).

Organizational Culture

Both the formal culture and the informal culture may generate deviance. Crank and Caldero's (2000, 2005) "noble-cause" explanation of some types of deviance (described more fully in Chapter 5) is an organizational explanation of corruption although it focuses on the subculture of policing.

Gilmartin and Harris (1998) also have discussed why some officers become compromised and argue that it is because the law enforcement organization does not adequately train them to understand and respond to the ethical dilemmas they will face. They coined the term *continuum of compromise* to illustrate what happens to the officer. The first element is a "perceived sense of victimization," that refers to what happens when officers enter the profession with naïve ideas about what the job will be like. Citizen disrespect, bureaucratic barriers, and the justice system's realities sometimes make officers cynical, with a feeling that no one cares and that they are needlessly exposed to danger. Cynicism leads to distrust of the administration and the citizenry. At that point, the officer is alienated and more prone to corruption. Gilmartin and Harris also talk about the officers' sense of entitlement and how that can lead to corruption. There is a sense that the rules don't apply to them because they are different from the citizenry they police. This leads to the "blue curtain of secrecy," discussed more fully in Chapter 5, when officers believe it is more ethical to cover up for other cops than it is to tell the truth.

Crank (1998: 187) and others have noted that there is a pervasive sense among rank-and-file police that administrators are not to be trusted: "Officers protect each other, not only against the public, but against police administrators frequently seen to be capricious and out of touch." The classic work in this regard is Reuss-Ianni's (1983) study of a New York City precinct in the late 1970s. She described the "two cultures" of policing—street cops and management cops. She observed that law enforcement managers were classic bureaucrats who made decisions based on modern management principles. This contrasted with the street-cop subculture, which still had remnants of quasi-familial relationships in which "loyalties and commitments took precedence over the rule book" (1983: 4). The result of this conflict between the two value systems was alienation of the street cop. Despite the gulf between management and line staff, most agree that employee behavior is influenced directly by the behavior of superiors. One might note that most large-scale police corruption that has been exposed has implicated very high-level officials. Alternatively, police departments that have remained relatively free of corruption have administrators who practice ethical behavior on a day-to-day basis.

Research reveals that close supervision, especially by midlevel managers such as sergeants, reduces the use of force and incidents of misconduct by officers (Walker, 2007). Huberts, Kaptein, and Lasthuizen (2007) obtained measures of corruption (or what they called integrity violations) by asking officers to report what they knew was happening. The independent variable was leadership style. Findings indicated that role modeling was significant in limiting unethical conduct of an interpersonal nature (sexual harassment, discrimination, and bullying), while strictness in supervision seemed to be more important in controlling the misuse of resources, fraud, and other forms of financial corruption. A third component of leadership was described as openness and referred to leaders encouraging subordinates to talk to them about ethical dilemmas. This was associated with fewer violations in several areas, especially in favoritism and discrimination. Interestingly, this study of more than 6,000 police officers found that strictness had no effect on reducing the gratuitous use of violence, but that role modeling and openness did.

As discussed in previous chapters, the concept of organizational justice has been advanced by the pioneering work of Tom Tyler (1990) who distinguished procedural justice (whether people feel the process is fair) and outcome justice (whether they think the decision is fair). There has been a growing body of literature that explores how these concepts affect citizenry and employees (for instance, Tyler and Huo, 2002; Tyler and Wakslak, 2004). De Angelis and Kupchik (2007) found that officers' satisfaction with the discipline system was more influenced by procedural justice elements (perceptions of fairness in the process) than outcome. Wolfe and Piquero (2011) found that police officers' beliefs about organizational justice were associated with the likelihood of ethical misconduct. Those who believed their organization was fair were less likely to engage in the code of silence or believe in noble-cause corruption. Perceptions of organizational justice have been associated with feelings of self-legitimacy and identification with the organization, less cynicism, and favorable perceptions of community policing (Nix and Wolfe, 2015). Further, researchers found lower levels of police misconduct among those who more strongly agreed that the organization was just (Reynolds, 2015). All research indicates that to ensure ethical employees, the organization must treat workers ethically. The police organization is no different from other organizations in this regard.

Societal Explanations

Murphy and Caplan (1989) argue that lax community standards over certain types of behavior (gambling, prostitution) and lack of support from prosecutors and the courts (or corruption at that stage of the system) lead to police corruption. Police hear mixed messages from the public regarding certain types of crime. They are asked to enforce laws against gambling, pornography, and prostitution, but not too stringently. They are expected not only to enforce laws against drunk driving but also to be tolerant of individuals who aren't really "criminal." They are expected to uphold laws regarding assault unless it is a family or interpersonal dispute that the disputants want to settle privately. In other words, we want the police to enforce the law unless they enforce it against us. Also, rationalizations used by some police when they take bribes or protection money from prostitutes or drug dealers are made easier by the public's tolerant stance toward certain areas of vice; for example, to accept protection money from a prostitute may be rationalized by the relative lack of concern that the public shows for this type of law breaking.

We also ask the police to take care of social problems, such as the homeless, even if they must step outside the law to do so. Extra-legal means are acceptable if they are not used against us. Citizens who want police to move the transients out of a park or get the crack dealers off the corner aren't concerned with the fact that the police might not have the legal authority to do so. If a little "informal" justice is needed to accomplish the task, that is fine with some people, if it is used against those we don't like.

When we accept and encourage such extra-legal power in some situations, we shouldn't be surprised when it is used in other situations as well. The police role as enforcer in a pluralistic society is problematic. The justification for police power is that police represent the public: "The police officer can only validly use coercive force when he or she in fact represents the body politic" (Malloy, 1982: 12). But if the police do not represent all groups, their authority is oppressive. Police take their cue from the community they serve. If they serve a community that emphasizes crime control over individual rights or other public service, we will see the results of that message in the way laws are enforced. The point is that, to a large degree, the community creates the police department by what it demands and what it is willing to overlook.

Reducing Police Corruption

Comprehensive lists of suggestions to reduce police misconduct and corruption have been proposed (Carter, 1999; Malloy, 1982; Metz, 1990; Prenzler and Ransley, 2002; Wood, 1997). Some date back decades but that doesn't mean they have been implemented. Such lists include the following:

- Increase the salary of police
- Eliminate unenforceable laws
- Establish civilian review boards
- Improve training in ethics (including specific training for supervisors)
- Set realistic goals and objectives for the department
- Provide ethical leadership
- Perform audits (of resources and funds paid to informants)
- Have financial disclosure rules
- Provide a written code of ethics
- Provide a whistleblowing procedure that ensures fair treatment
- Improve internal affairs units
- Rotate staff in some positions
- Have better evidence handling procedures
- Employ early warning systems
- Use video cameras in patrol cars
- Use covert high technology surveillance
- Employ targeted and randomized integrity testing
- Conduct surveys of police and the public
- Decriminalize vice crimes

Note that most of these suggestions target administrative changes rather than identifying the individual officer as the problem. In more recent years, body cameras, requiring police to carry their own insurance, docking pensions for misconduct, and other suggestions have been offered to reduce the costs of misconduct. In the next sections, we take a closer look at some of these means to reduce corruption and improve the ethical climate of police agencies.

"Rotten Apple" Responses

"Rotten apple" approaches to reducing misconduct focus on the individual officer. There is an assumption that, if an officer or officers are found to be deviant, the wrong person was hired or there needs to be better training, or better monitoring/discipline.

Improving Screening

Background checks, interviews, credit checks, polygraphs, drug tests, and other screening tools are used to eliminate inappropriate individuals from the pool of potential hires. The extent of screening varies from department to department, but generally has become more sophisticated, especially in the use of psychological testing and interviews. Sanders (2008) argues that the process is more "weeding out" than selecting in those candidates best suited to policing and points out that it is hard to develop tools to identify traits that are associated with successful police performance when, in fact, there is no consensus on what makes a good police officer. Most research on the effectiveness of screening tools utilizes academy test scores or firings as the measure of good (or failed) performance.

The most common pre-employment screening tool that is used by law enforcement agencies is the Minnesota Multiphasic Personality Inventory (MMPI or its subsequent versions) (Arrigo and Claussen, 2003; Dantzker and McCoy, 2006). The Inwald Personality Inventory (IPI) was developed to measure personality characteristics and behavioral patterns specific to fitness for law enforcement. Researchers have found that the IPI more accurately identifies individuals who are unsuccessful in law enforcement (terminated) (cited in Arrigo and Claussen, 2003). The so-called Big Five (extroversion, neuroticism, agreeableness, conscientiousness, and openness) have been the target of enough studies to indicate that they are reliable measures of personality and, of those, conscientiousness seems to be the most relevant to job performance; however, there has been very little research done to determine if the trait accurately measures police performance success (Arrigo and Claussen, 2003; Claussen-Rogers and Arrigo, 2005; Sanders, 2008).

Education and Training

Education has been promoted as a necessary element to improve the ethics of policing and research does show that educated officers were less likely to be terminated from NYPD (Fyfe and Kane, 2006). However, many of the unethical officers described in this book have been college graduates.

Ethics training in the academy, and in in-service courses, is common and is recommended for all police departments today. Reuss-Ianni (1983) described how, after the Knapp Commission uncovered wide-ranging corruption in the New York Police Department, ethical awareness workshops were begun. Unfortunately, they have not stopped the periodic corruption scandals that have occurred since that time.

The International Association of Chiefs of Police (2008) found that about 80 percent of responding agencies said they committed resources to ethics instruction, although most courses simply employed lectures and were four hours or less. The major recommendations of the IACP based on this study were to provide job-specific training on ethics and to differentiate training for recruits, in-service, and management, as well as other units. Another recommendation was that ethics training begin with recruits and be an integral part of the departments' structure and policies. The IACP also recommended enhancing content and using appropriate learning styles. A final recommendation was that departments concentrate more on ethics training for field-training officers (IACP, 2008).

Recall from Chapter 4 that New Orleans and Springfield, Massachusetts are piloting "Ethical Policing is Courageous" (EPIC). This unique and innovative training takes the approach that officers should help other officers stay out of

QUOTE & QUERY

Would you stop your partner from getting shot if you could? Why wouldn't you stop your partner from being fired if you could?

(An instructor in the EPIC training program)
Source: Robertson, 2016a.

? Is the EPIC training a viable response to the "blue curtain of secrecy"?

trouble and that intervening when another officer is about to commit misconduct is not "snitching" but, rather, may save a career (Robertson, 2016a).

Various models of ethics training exist but there is not enough data to understand the most effective approaches. Moran (2005) described several models of police ethics training, including a view of ethics as a "shield" to protect officers from trouble, as a programmed element in the officer's training "hardwire," as a mission or crusade, or as a "command from on high," along with the sanctions for disobeying. Conti and Nolan (2005) found that ethics training typically is structured in such a way to encourage conformity to the "traditional image and identity of police officers."

Integrity Testing

integrity testing
"Sting" operations to test whether police officers will make honest choices.

Integrity testing occurs when a police officer is placed in a position where he or she might be tempted to break a rule or a law and monitored to see what he or she will do. New York City has used integrity testing since the late 1970s, after the Knapp Commission exposed widespread corruption. Field associates were recruited straight from academies to investigate suspected officers (Reuss-Ianni, 1983: 80). Integrity testing is like undercover work in that unsuspecting officers are tempted with an opportunity to commit an illegal or corrupt act, such as keeping a found wallet or being offered a bribe (Marx, 1991).

Most police officers have highly negative attitudes about integrity testing. Spokesmen argue that "testing raises serious issues regarding privacy, deception, entrapment, provocation, and the legal rights of individuals" (Prenzler and Ronken, 2001a: 323–324). There is a widespread belief that such testing is unfair, overly intrusive, wasteful of resources, and detrimental to morale. One study of opinions of police managers found that the majority agreed that targeted integrity testing had a place in the investigation of wrongdoing, but that random testing was ill-advised (Prenzler, 2006).

Early Warning or Audit Systems

Research indicates that a small percentage of officers often accounts for a disproportionate number of abuse or corruption complaints (Barker, 2002; Walker and Alpert, 2002). Early warning systems look at number of complaints, use-of-force reports, use-of-weapon reports, reprimands, or other indicators to identify officers. Intervention may include more supervision, additional training, counseling, reassignment, transfer, referral to an employee assistance program, fitness for duty evaluation, and/or dismissal (Walker and Alpert, 2002). These programs have been endorsed by the National Institute of Justice and have been incorporated into several consent decrees between cities and federal courts to avert civil rights litigation.

Walker (2007) reports that early warning systems vary in the elements they count and where they set the threshold of concern. The systems also have various objectives: some departments use them to flag officers who need discipline, but other departments see them as part of employee assistance programs. Supervisors are alerted when an officer's behavior changes, with the objective to identify and respond to stress. Consider that the rate of suicide among Chicago Police officers is 60 percent higher than other police departments across the United States; in the past decade, 13 officers have been killed in the line of duty but twice that many committed suicide (Grimm, 2017). If these officers could be identified earlier, perhaps their suicides could have been prevented. A study using 13 years of Charlotte-Mecklenburg data showed that the best predictor of police misbehavior was past behavior, but another significant predictor was when the officer was involved in numerous high stress calls such as domestic violence and suicide calls (Lee, 2016). This indicates that early intervention systems might be able to identify officers who are in distress emotionally and intervening early could, perhaps, avert tragedies.

One cannot simply count the number of incidents or complaints, because the officer's shift and duty, length of service, types of calls responded to, and other factors affect the number of complaints (Walker and Alpert, 2002; Walker, Alpert, and Kenney, 2000). Also, some researchers have found that simply counting use-of-force reports does not capture problematic officers without further identifying those who exceed the ratio of reasonable force in response to the resistance of the subject. To only count uses of force falsely tags some officers as problematic (Bazley, Mieczkowski, and Lersch, 2009). Hassell and Archbold (2009) argued that using citizen complaints as a proxy for bad officers is problematic because, in their study, citizen complaints were associated with officer productivity, but not with any individual characteristics. Recall, however, that Harris (2005) did not find an association between productivity and the number of complaints.

These programs are only as effective as the elements that go into the triggering system and the interventions that occur after the identification of a problem. Many departments have such systems in name only and there is little or no use of the information, or there are crucial missing elements to the triggers, such as disciplinary proceedings. The DOJ report of Baltimore, for instance, noted that the early warning system was not operational in any effective way because some disciplinary records were excluded. In other cities, no one ever looked at the data generated by the system. In many of the DOJ consent decrees, there is an agreement that the department will improve, revive, or institute an early warning system (Kelly, 2016).

Body Cameras

Police departments have increasingly purchased and equipped their officers with body cameras. The Obama administration allocated $263 million for a three-year program to expand training for local police departments, including $75 million that would purchase 50,000 cameras through a matching program (Wilson, 2015). The Brennan Center (2016) shows the wide variety in policies and implementation levels of the tool across the nation.

Video has been an incredibly powerful tool to support allegations of brutality and abuse of authority. Officers now are beginning to use cameras too. They are increasingly supportive of body cameras as studies establish that citizens' behavior improves when they know they are being filmed and camera footage helps officers defend themselves against false charges of misconduct. However, there are critics. Some argue that misbehaving police officers could simply turn off the camera when they wanted to, although procedures in place create disincentives for officers to do so. A more unresolvable criticism is that the cost of the cameras and storing the unimaginable amount of video that would be collected make widespread use unfeasible. A related issue is how to make video available for freedom of information requests. Some footage would be restricted when it is part of an ongoing investigation, but the cost involved of storing, indexing, and retrieving footage is prohibitive. Another major criticism is the invasion of privacy such cameras may create. Should officers ask for permission before filming in private homes? Should officers be able to turn off the cameras as they talk to citizens who may turn into confidential informants? Should cameras be turned off when victims or intoxicated individuals are unclothed? Rules regarding whether and when police officers should turn off the cameras is being worked out in those jurisdictions that have purchased or are making plans to purchase them.

Preliminary studies of body cameras are promising. In San Diego, an internal report showed that in 2015, citizen complaints decreased by 40 percent, use of "personal body" force by officers was reduced by 46.5 percent, and use of pepper spray was reduced by 30.5 percent (Perry, 2015). A later report in 2017 continued to show reductions in citizen complaint and uses of high-level force. Interestingly, overall use of force by officers had risen 14 percent since 2013, but high-level use of force, such as physical take-downs or employing Tasers, chemical agents or weapons was down 16.4 percent. One explanation offered was that officers were writing reports of force more accurately than in years past because video helped them remember what happened on calls (Garrick, 2017).

Rialto, California was the site of the first well-known, controlled study. Complaints against officers fell by 88 percent and use of force by 60 percent (Farrar, 2013). More recently, a British study of 2,000 British and American officers and 1.4 million working hours were studied over a year showed a 93 percent decline in citizen complaints when body cameras were implemented (Kirka, 2016). Cameras protect both citizens and police officers; that is perhaps why the initial resistance of police to the use of cameras has faded.

Public Databases of "Bad" Cops and the National Decertification Index

Many people simply do not trust police departments to root out individuals who should not have the power and authority inherent in the position. One response in recent years has for individuals or groups to construct databases of wrongful actions. The Cato Institute's National Police Misconduct Reports present daily updates of news items drawn from media across the country. One can scroll through the reports and find reported misconduct for any given day or month since the reports began several years ago. The "worst case" of officer misconduct is highlighted every month (see: www.policemisconduct.net). This is a privately funded attempt by a libertarian-leaning organization to provide the public with information that cannot be obtained through any public source; however, there is little analysis, it is simply a presentation of unedited news items.

Professor Philip Stinson has also been collecting misconduct reports through the media in a similar way, but entering them into a database for study. His database allows one to examine the thousands of misconduct instances to explore patterns of officer characteristics, victim characteristics, and regional characteristics (Stinson, Brewer, and Mathna, 2015; Stinson, Todak, and Dodge, 2013). In a 2016 DOJ-funded study, Stinson and his colleagues looked at officers arrested between 2005 and 2011. The researchers compiled 6,724 cases, or about 960 cases per year, involving about 792 officers. The most common crimes were simple assault, drunken driving, and aggravated assault, but substantial arrests occurred for sex crimes. Of concluded cases, about 72 percent of officers were convicted. More than 40 percent of the crimes were committed on duty, and nearly 95 percent of the officers charged were men. Of those cases where outcomes are known, only 54 percent of the officers were fired. Roughly two-thirds of all the arrests were made by an agency that didn't employ the officer (Stinson, Liederback, Lab, and Brewer, 2016).

The New York Legal Aid Society, the largest organization of public defenders in the country with over 650 lawyers, has also been developing a "cop accountability" database. Over 3,000 officers and their reputed misconduct have been entered thus far. The project was created to help defense attorneys question the credibility of police officers in court. The American Civil Liberties Union has also begun a database project by filing open records requests in seven selected cities requesting all discipline and citizen complaint information about officers who have been the subject of alleged police brutality (Neyfakh, 2015).

A public interest group has created a similar database for Illinois (Better Government Association, 2015). The Invisible Institute, a civic organization of journalists, has created a police misconduct database after winning a lawsuit to gain access to the discipline records of the Chicago Police Department. The Citizen Data Project is accessible and interactive (go to https://cpdb.co/data/L21wjD/citizens-police-data-project) and includes misconduct records and news reports. Information has shown that officers with many misconduct complaints are training new recruits, that complaints filed by white residents were more likely to be upheld than those filed by black citizens, and that the early intervention program is ineffectual. One can now see that Jason Van Dyke, the officer who shot Laquan McDonald in November of 2015 as he was walking away, had 19 citizen complaints and two misconduct lawsuits against him (Gourarie, 2016).

Such efforts are designed to bring light to the subject of police misconduct. One of the reasons that private groups have created these data bases is that, in many states, disciplinary records are not open to public scrutiny. This ethical issue is discussed on the next page.

Ironically, even police departments may not have information about an officer's prior misconduct. The National Decertification Index (NDI, see: www.iadlest.org/projects/ndi20.aspx), was begun in 2005, and is maintained by the International Association of Directors of Law Enforcement Standards and Training (IADLEST), funded by the membership fees of individual members. The index includes about 20,000 officers who have lost their license, but it is not complete (Childress, 2016). The index receives reports from only 39 states. Reporting is voluntary and, therefore, no assumption should be made as to the completeness or accuracy of the records. Georgia, for instance, decertifies many more officers than other states with weaker standards, but does not share their list with the NDI. There is no consistency in decertification across states anyway. While in some states, police departments are obligated to report misconduct that is serious enough to disqualify an individual from being a police officer and the state commission then will investigate and possibly decertify the officer; in other states, the state commission has no authority to decertify, or only felony criminal convictions are sufficient for a state commission to decertify. Six states do not decertify officers for misconduct at all: California, Hawaii, Massachusetts, New Jersey, New

QUOTE & **QUERY**

Compiling a list of police officers who are alleged to be "bad" based upon newspapers stories, quick-buck lawsuits, and baseless complaints—many of which are lodged in revenge by criminals seeking to punish an arresting officer—does nothing more than soil the reputation of the men and women who do the difficult and dangerous job of keeping this city and its citizens safe.

(Pat Lynch, head of the NYPD police officers' union.)
Source: Reported in Neyfakh, 2015.

? Does this quote convince you that databases of misconduct are a bad idea?

ETHICAL ISSUE

Should Disciplinary Records Be Secret and Exempt from Public Records Requests?

In the national discussions that followed the events of Ferguson and Baltimore, many people were surprised to discover that some states kept police disciplinary records secret. In 23 states and the District of Columbia police disciplinary records are confidential; 15 states allow some limited access; and only 12 states allow discipline records to be accessed with open records requests. Interestingly, conservative states like Florida and Texas have the most lenient laws on access, while "blue" states like California and New York have the strongest secrecy laws, probably because law enforcement unions are more powerful. Texas, Kentucky, and Utah, for instance, allow access to records where the officer was found guilty of the alleged offense.

New York offers some of the strongest protections to officers. A 1976 state law requires such information to be kept secret to the extent that it is difficult to even find names of officers involved in shootings. The law was passed to shield disciplinary records from defense lawyers, who would use the information in court to attack the credibility of officers (ironically this is exactly the purpose of Brady rules that require prosecutors to share such information). According to New York's civil rights code, section 50-a, incident reports involving police, disciplinary records, evaluations, and personnel records are secret, not subject to open records requests, and may not even be cited in court without judicial approval. Over time, the protection was extended to correctional officers and firefighters. The protection is so complete that even the civilian review board has had trouble accessing information to investigate cases, leading to the creation of a new inspector general position with subpoena power. Several open-government groups have sued to overturn this civil service law, but as of 2017, they have lost in several lawsuits and the protections remain in place.

California has similar protections. In *Copley Press, Inc. v. Superior Court of San Diego County*, S128603, 2006, the state supreme court interpreted civil service laws to protect from public disclosure any public documents regarding police discipline involving actions taken under color of authority. An attempt to pass legislation to overturn the effect of the holding and open discipline records to the public was met with strong resistance from police unions who appeared *en masse* during the legislative hearing on the

issue and were successful in scuttling the proposed change despite polling that indicated 80 percent of the public was in favor of the legislation. When the Los Angeles County Sheriff's department put together a list of 300 officers who have had issues that subject them to Brady disclosure, the police union sued to prevent the list from being shared with prosecutors (who are legally bound to disclose to defense attorneys when they know impeachable information about prosecution witnesses). Prosecutors have compiled their own list from news accounts that name officers and their own personal experience with officers, but these lists have also been criticized by law enforcement groups.

If discipline records and punishments are not public, there is little accountability. Chicago Police Department was forced to release discipline data from 2011 to 2015 after a lawsuit by the Invisible Institute, an organization of journalists created to pursue transparency and public access. The history revealed, for instance, that Jerome Finnigan had 68 citizen complaints against him for which he had never been disciplined, including accusations of excessive force and illegal searches. In 2011, Finnigan admitted to robbing criminal suspects and ordering a hit on a fellow police officer he suspected of turning him in. In fact, there evidently was no discipline in 99 percent of the more than 28,000 misconduct complaints against Chicago police officers (Gourarie, 2016).

Not only are discipline records secret in many states, there are also many cities where contracts with the police union demand the destruction of disciplinary records and citizen complaints after some stated period in many states. Union officials argue that this is so one act cannot derail an officer's career and reduces the impact of unsubstantiated allegations. Critics contend this practice prohibits the ability of citizens from accessing information to show that an officer has a history of misconduct.

Supporters of such secrecy argue that police do not give up their right of privacy by being employed as a police officer, that they would be subject to harassment and potentially threatening public actions if their identities and disciplinary proceedings were revealed, and that the media or public have free access to speak with witnesses or complainants in instances of alleged misconduct and other avenues of investigation. Critics of secrecy argue that police officers are public servants, and, as such, the public has a right to know when an officer has a pattern of misconduct. Observers note that when black men are killed by police officers, inevitably any criminal record of the person shot will be disclosed to the press; however, in those states where disciplinary records are secret, the officer may have a troublesome record of misconduct, but that information is legally sealed.

Efforts are underway in many states, for example, California, New York, and Maryland, to urge the state legislature to change laws in the interest of transparency, accountability, and public trust, but there is strong resistance on the part of police unions who are a powerfully political lobby group.

Law

As stated above, whether there is disclosure or not in each state depends, first, on enabling legislation and, then, on the court's interpretation of such laws. States can have different legal rights recognized until or unless there is a Supreme Court decision that has legal authority over all 50 states.

Policy

In those states where disciplinary investigations and records are secret, police departments can tightly control that information. The officer may have a legal action against the department if they do not. Departments can release aggregate numbers (how many officers have been disciplined), but if they released information protected by civil service laws, they could be sued. Thus, policy follows law.

Ethics

Utilitarian ethics would weigh up the costs and benefits of disclosure versus secrecy for the officers involved, the department, and the community. Negative effects of such secrecy are that errant police officers are protected. Even if they are fired from one department they can go on to be hired by others and this evidently happens quite frequently. When a person has been victimized by a police officer, they are prevented from finding out that the officer has a record of similar actions. When communities want to understand what kind of police force they have, they are restricted from important information; including which officers have a history of wrongdoing and whether officers who commit misconduct are appropriately punished. Benefits from the

secrecy are mostly for the individual officer and department. Individual officers and their families can be targeted. When Darren Wilson's name (the officer who shot Michael Brown in Ferguson, Missouri) was revealed, he and his family were subjected to such a barrage of death threats that they were placed in hiding for their own safety. When the disciplinary records of Officer Danny Pantaleo (the officer who administered the hold that was believed to be responsible for Eric Garner's death) were illegally leaked to the press, he received threats. Often, disciplinary proceedings are conducted over technical rule violations, not actions that victimize the public in any way, yet those proceedings would also be exposed to the officer's detriment. Disciplinary proceedings often result in finding the officer was innocent of the alleged wrongdoing, but that finding would probably be less prominently reported than the allegations, leading to unfairness in shaping public perceptions.

Ethics of care would attempt to meet the needs of both parties in arriving at a resolution; therefore, the safety of officers and residents would be paramount. The community's need to know is probably dependent on how well the discipline system deters officers' transgressions. Remember that the ethics of care is not concerned with rights but, instead, focuses on needs. So, there is a need to deter or get rid of problem officers, but if the department does that effectively, there is less or no need to know how and when they do it or who is a problem officer. Ironically, however, without such information being public, it is impossible to know if problem officers are being dealt with appropriately.

Is such secrecy consistent with ethical formalism? It would be if someone could be in favor of the policy regardless of who they were in the situation (officer, other officers, chief, journalist, victim of police brutality, or citizen). This is the first element of the categorical imperative.

As with many other policy decisions, attempting to determine an ethical policy depends on facts that we often do not have. For instance, there is no study available that examines the 27 states with open disclosure to determine if it has led to officers being victimized. There is no real evidence on either side to support the position, thus the language of the argument is of "rights" rather than the utilitarian's emphasis on utility.

Sources: Feuer, 2017b; Greenhut, 2015; Joseph, 2016; Kaplan, 2015; Lau, 2017; Lewis, Landen, and Veltman, 2015; Maddaus, 2016; O'Connell, 2016; Shackford, 2017; Williams, 2015c; Wilson, 2015.

York, and Rhode Island. Twenty states only decertify because of criminal convictions. The lack of consistency in laws, policies, and procedures make any comparison across states of rates of decertification very difficult (Associated Press, 2015b; Atherley and Hickman, 2013; Merchant, 2016). An Associated Press (2015) inquiry collected and analyzed decertification records nationwide from 2009 to 2014. Of the nearly 9,000 cases in which officers were decertified, about 1,000 officers lost their licenses for sexual assault or sex crimes such as possessing child pornography and misconduct that ranged from propositioning citizens to consensual but prohibited on-duty intercourse.

One of the problems of no national decertification consistency is that officers who have engaged in misconduct or even criminal behavior may simply move on and get another law enforcement job. Many have resigned in lieu of discipline so they wouldn't end up on the registry anyway. Even officers who have committed sexual misconduct have been known to move to another location and then commit sexual assault. These "gypsy cops" may move several times and there seems to be a practice of not alerting the new department to problematic officers, or the departments hire these officers anyway because the officers do not require the expensive basic academy training that new recruits need. Unions tend to obstruct state efforts to improve reporting and decertification standards and argue that officers who are fired from one department shouldn't be "blacklisted" (Childress, 2016; Fisher, 2016; Merchant and Sedensky, 2015; Williams, 2016b). Perhaps there should be some national standards as to when an officer should lose his license—being fired for lack of punctuality wouldn't be cause, but a sustained finding of illegal use of force would be grounds to never work as an officer again.

In the DOJ consent decree for Ferguson, Missouri, one of the mandates was for the police department to check all new lateral hires against the NDI (Merchant, 2016). Several states are considering changes to laws concerning decertification (Childress, 2016). Wisconsin, for instance, now requires police departments to notify the state Justice Department of officers who are fired or resigned during an internal investigation and will make the data available to agencies who can compare officers' names to those registered. The state agency cannot dictate who sheriffs or police chiefs choose to hire, but they will now be aware of past trouble, such as one deputy who resigned after he was charged with raping a coworker and promptly got a new job in another agency, or an officer who was fired for soliciting sexual favors from drivers in traffic stops who also found a new job because his personnel file was sealed (Anderson, 2017). One target of change should be confidentiality agreements whereby an officer agrees to resign in return for a confidentiality agreement on the part of his agency promising not to disclose his misconduct other agencies. Critics argue these agreements are against the public interest.

"Rotten Barrel" Responses

Organizational explanations address elements of the police organization, including such things as improving investigation and disciplinary procedures.

Internal Affairs Model, Civil Service, and Arbitration

In one sense, the **internal affairs model** is also a rotten-apple approach to reducing corruption, since the model provides the mechanism whereby the department investigates and punishes the miscreant officer. One could also, however, see the internal affairs model as a rotten barrel approach in that if a department's internal affairs

internal affairs model A review procedure in which police investigators receive and investigate complaints and resolve the investigations internally.

department was widely seen as toothless, then the message to individual officers would be that the department did not care about wrongdoing. Unfortunately, internal affairs units are perceived as ineffective (by the public) and biased (by police officers). It is also the case that civil service protections in many cities mandate that if an officer is disciplined, he or she can request the case go to arbitration, which often results in reducing the level of punishment set by the police chief (Stephens, 2011).

There is no research that evaluates the actual effectiveness of internal affair models (Walker, 2007), only many news reports of citizen dissatisfaction and tallies of the number of complaints versus the number of complaints founded or the number that result in any form of discipline. Part of the problem with the internal discipline model is that citizens may be discouraged from reporting misconduct of police to other police; especially if the process is complicated or intimidating. Both the San Antonio police department and many police departments in Nebraska have been criticized for the way the citizen complaint processes were handled. In San Antonio, an investigation indicated that the police departments discouraged civilians from filing complaints, argued with them, and accused them of lying. In the Nebraska review, the threat of being prosecuted for perjury on the complaint form itself was not uncommon, and critics argue that this statement intimidates people, as does the requirement that they must talk to an internal affairs investigator. Website instructions were often absent or confusing and anonymous complaints were not accepted (Skelton, 2014; Texas Civil Rights Project, 2011). National standards for civilian complaint processes encourage police departments to accept anonymous complaints since many people are too intimidated to complain openly.

There are consistent findings that a small number of officers in any department receive disproportionally large number of complaints, but, few complaints are sustained and, in some departments, they receive little or no discipline even if the complaints are sustained. In the Invisible Institute's analysis of Chicago's discipline records, it was found that white complainants accounted for 20 percent of all complaints, but 60 percent of complaints that resulted in discipline. About 30 percent of all complaints were of officers who had more than 10 complaints. These officers represented only 10 percent of the force (Kaplan, 2015).

Ironically, officers don't seem to trust the internal discipline mechanisms any more than citizens do. While citizens feel that complaints are ignored and officers are protected, officers feel that some of their peers get special treatment and the purpose of such systems is purely "gotcha" rather than a constructive process of improving performance (Stephens, 2011). Recall the horrible events in California in 2013 when Christopher Dorner issued his "manifesto" and shot the daughter of police captain Randal Quan and her fiancé. Dorner also killed two law enforcement officers. Ultimately, the unprecedented manhunt for him ended in a mountain cabin where he shot himself. Dorner most probably suffered from mental issues that spurred him to such extreme measures, but the trigger for his actions was reported to be a perceived unfair discipline hearing that resulted in his termination. He was terminated for lying after he reported that his FTO kicked a mentally ill man in the face. He believed he was terminated for going against the blue curtain of secrecy. During the massive manhunt and amid public questions as to whether the charges Dorner made against the unfairness of the disciplinary procedures had any degree of truth, LAPD Chief Beck promised that Dorner's case would be reopened and an investigation would take place. Several months later, a report was released written by a special assistant to the chief that concluded that his firing was justified. Findings indicated that Dorner had experienced problems beginning in the academy that made his success as a police officer unlikely. The report concluded he used the complaint process for his own agenda; he complained about his FTO 13 days after the event immediately after he was told he would be given an unsatisfactory rating; and, that the kick could not be substantiated due to the mental illness of the individual and the lack of witness reports (Leonard, Rabin, and Blankstein, 2013; Orlov, 2013). The importance of Dorner's case is not that he was or was not telling the truth about his FTO's use of excessive force or the fairness of the discipline process; it was the fact that the possible truth of this serial killer's "manifesto" resonated with the public and, evidently, some officers as well who spoke anonymously about their suspicions that his description of favoritism and racism in the department had some elements of truth.

Even when internal affairs and police department administrators decide to punish an officer with a suspension or termination, arbitrators often reverse the punishment. Studies have shown that arbitrators routinely "split the difference" and reduce the punishment assessed by the chief, sometimes requiring the errant officer to be rehired (Iris, 1998, 2002; Stephens, 2011). The explanation some give as to why this pattern exists, even for what seem to be egregious acts of misconduct, is that arbitrators must be selected with the agreement of both parties and those who routinely upheld the chief's punishments would not be approved by the officer or union. Another explanation (from the arbitrators and union representatives who support the process) is that departments often have such poorly written or nonexistent policies that it would not be fair to punish officers without adequate due process (Horn, 2009).

Stephens (2011) presents several suggestions for improving the internal discipline process, including discipline matrixes (similar to sentencing guidelines) that spell out in advance what the range of punishment might be for types of misconduct. This would tend to reduce the feelings of officers that there is unfairness in the process. Another improvement would be to tie education and training to the discipline process so that the focus shifts from punishment to improving performance. Mediation between the citizen complainant and officer might be a better solution than punishment. Peer review has not been used but is an intriguing possibility for reducing the perception of unfairness in the process.

Some departments have enlarged the mission of internal affairs to become anticorruption units. These units, especially in other countries, now undertake a mission of not only investigation and punishment but also deterrence and prevention. Such units may undertake integrity testing, promote awareness, improve selection and screening procedures, develop performance standards, and in other ways "police" the police to minimize corruption (Moran, 2005). This may represent the future of internal anticorruption models.

civilian review/ complaint board
An outside agency or board that includes citizens and monitors and/or investigates misconduct complaints against police.

Civilian Review/Complaint Boards

Civilian review/complaint boards have been in existence since the mid-1960s in some cities, despite continued resistance from some police officer groups. In the 1980s, there were only 13 civilian oversight agencies in America. Today, there are more than 200 (Wogan, 2017, citing Walker). They exist in a dizzying array of configurations, either along with or instead of outside inspector general offices, ombudsmen, or police monitor offices. The civilian review model has a board of civilian (or civilian and police) members who monitor and review internal investigations and discipline of officers. Kansas City created one in 1970 and Berkeley's Civilian Review Board began in 1973 (Attard, 2010). Walker (2001) reviewed the range of civilian review models, but did not find that any one model seemed to be better than any other. Researchers argue that it is difficult to measure the success of such bodies because increased complaints may mean that there is greater trust in the process, not necessarily an increase in misconduct (Prenzler and Ronken, 2001b; Worrall, 2002). The National Association for Civilian Oversight of Law Enforcement has published reports highlighting the various models of civilian oversight. For example, complaint-and-review-based models tend to be less expensive because they rely on citizen volunteers, but they also may lack resources, expertise, and independence. A recent review of various models highlighted the strengths and weaknesses of the investigation model (this model conducts investigations after receiving complaints), the review model (this model reviews the quality of investigations done internally and makes recommendations), and the auditor/monitor (the panel includes a separate auditor or inspector general office with full-time staff). The conclusion was that no one model is best and that the best approach is to tailor the model to the specific needs of the community (De Angelis, Rosenthal and Buchner, 2017).

The board may also respond to appeals and act in an advisory role for systemic change. Some civilian boards have powers of subpoena while others do not (Ferdik, Rojek, and Alpert, 2015; Prenzler and Ronken, 2001b). Prenzler and Ronken (2001b) reported that external review models have about the same substantiation rate as do internal affairs models—about 10 percent of all complaints filed. The major criticism of such models is that they are not truly independent, for police still conduct the investigations. Prenzler (2000) argues that the "capture" theory is operative in civilian review models. This occurs when the regulatory or investigative body is "co-opted" by the investigated agency through informal relationships; in police civilian review boards, it is often the case that they recommend even lighter punishment than recommendations generated internally.

Even if civilian review agencies find an officer responsible for misconduct, they usually have no independent power to punish and simply refer the case back to the police department for discipline. For instance, it was reported that, in Minneapolis, from October 2012 through March 2015, 962 complaints with a total of 919 separate allegations were submitted—392 were dismissed, 216 were submitted to supervisors for coaching, 33 were submitted for mediation and another 202 were given to investigators for at least a preliminary investigation. Only 36 allegations were found to have merit, only one officer was disciplined based on a community member's complaint. Dissatisfaction has led to suggestions the board (the Minneapolis Office of Police Conduct Review) be disbanded. A spokesperson argued that many of the cases involved law enforcement officers outside the Minneapolis Police Department, many of the cases were still open, and there was nothing wrong with sending a case back to a supervisor for coaching instead of discipline since the goal was to change behavior, not simply inflict discipline (Norfleet, 2015).

New York City's civilian review board was established in 1992. Complaints are investigated by the board and then referred to the police department for formal disciplinary action. In 2009, about 40 percent of these cases were declined (Hauser, 2009). In 2012, an agreement was reached with the NYPD whereby lawyers for the board were given the power to undertake the disciplinary hearings of officers accused of misconduct, although the administrative judges will still be police employees and the police commissioner will still have the ultimate authority over decisions. There has been a widespread perception that the board was a "toothless tiger" since, from 2002 to 2010, of the 2,078 officers the board recommended be terminated, police decision makers terminated only 151 officers (Baker, 2012).

One problem with civilian review boards is that, as noted above, in some states all disciplinary records are considered outside the scope of public records and exempt from open records requests. In states like California and New York, even the civilian review board has difficulty accessing disciplinary records. Critics object that this is highly inconsistent with transparency and democratic policing.

Civilian review boards are often an element in a police reform campaign initiated by a DOJ investigation. In Seattle, for instance, even though there had been a civilian auditor (Office of Professional Accountability, OPA), a DOJ–SPD settlement order mandated the creation of a Community Police Commission (CPC). This was not a civilian review board that examined police complaints, but a body with a larger mandate that had input into a range of issues, including a revision of the use-of-force policy (Walker, 2015). The OPA was not seen as independent from the police department and lacked credibility and recent changes have addressed those perceptions by removing the office from police headquarters and having complainants interact with civilians.

Most civilian review boards have only the power to recommend discipline, but in Oakland, city residents voted to grant the civilian body the power to discipline and even fire the police chief. Oakland Police Department has had a long history of trouble; for instance, recall the "Riders" scandal described in the Walking the Walk box earlier in the chapter. The police department has been under federal oversight since 2003. More recently, several officers have been caught up in a sex scandal involving a teen prostitute who was the daughter of a dispatcher. One officer evidently involved committed suicide. Critics of placing that amount of power in a civilian body argue that it also removes the responsibility for bad officers from the chief and leadership of the department (Wogan, 2017).

Creating or strengthening a civilian review/complaint board is often on the list of mandated changes in consent decrees. There is strong support for allowing residents some access and input into how a police department "polices" its officers. The exact make-up and power of such a body is quite different, however, from city to city.

Changing the Culture

If the police culture influences the level of police misconduct, it is important to change it. Harris (2005) discusses the difficulty of changing an entrenched negative police culture, but offers examples of how it can be done. He argues that in successful change efforts, the department has reconceptualized its mission, developed measurements of what matters most, improved recruiting, changed training to emphasize human rights at least as much as crime fighting, and changed the incentive and reward structure to encourage service-oriented policing as much as crime control. He argues that change occurs as generations of new police officers take over.

As mentioned in Chapter 5, current efforts to shift the culture away from a military model with an emphasis on force (warrior model) to one more protective of civil rights (guardian model) are under way (Rahr and Rice, 2015). In an evaluation of the Washington State Training Commission's shift to a guardian philosophy, a team of researchers developed an instrument to measure attitudinal and knowledge shifts. The recruit class was statistically different from a comparison group in several scales, including one measuring support for CIT training, but not the two designed to measure guardian concepts (empathy and respect) (Helfgott et al., 2015).

Changing the culture in a police department requires addressing elements of the subculture, for example, the blue curtain of secrecy. It also requires examining whether organizational justice is perceived by officers. As discussed earlier, evidence indicates that officers who do not feel the department is fair will create a stronger subculture in defense. Any department that wants to change its culture should look first to create a vision and mission, with everyone participating in the creation of departmental aspirations. Then, every policy and informal practice should be evaluated as to whether it is consistent or inconsistent with that mission. An important element of culture is what leaders say, and more importantly, what they do.

Ethical Leadership

As discussed in Chapter 4, improving leadership is an essential element in improving the ethical climate of any organization. Research shows that supervisors shape the attitude of line officers toward wrongdoing. When misconduct is punished, it is perceived as more serious; if it is treated lightly, the opposite occurs (Lee, Lim, Moore, and Kim, 2011). Even if leaders are not directly involved in corruption, encouraging or participating in the harassment and ostracism directed at those who expose wrongdoers supports an organizational culture that punishes whistleblowers. In some departments, there is a perception that favored cliques are not punished for behaviors for which others would receive punishment. This climate destroys the trust in police leadership that is essential to ensure good communication from the rank and file.

The practice of administrators to cover up wrongdoing is arguably an even more insidious problem than individual officer misconduct. In Los Angeles, Detective Russell Poole, a robbery-homicide detective, uncovered the activities of the anti-gang task force in the Ramparts Division, but his investigation was shut down by his superiors, who also retaliated against him for not agreeing to participate in suppressing evidence of the misconduct. A year later, the Ramparts scandal exploded anyway. Evidence indicated that between 1995 and 1998 the officers lied, planted evidence, beat suspects, and shot unarmed suspects. Officers also evidently held parties to celebrate shootings, gave out plaques when one killed a gang member, and spread ketchup at a crime scene to imitate blood. Hundreds of cases had to be reviewed by the staff in the prosecutor's office to evaluate whether there was a possibility of manufactured evidence. Some evidence indicates at least 99 people were framed by Ramparts officers. The city had to use $100 million from tobacco settlements to cover anticipated lawsuits. Eleven officers were fired, and 40 convictions were overturned (Deutsch, 2001; Glover and Lait, 2000; Golab, 2000; Jablon, 2000; Lait and Glover, 2000; Sterngold, 2000). The LAPD came under a federal court monitor because of the scandal, although it has since been released from the consent decree.

After Hurricane Katrina in 2005, 17-year-old James Brissette and 40-year-old Ronald Madison, both unarmed, were killed by police officers, who also seriously wounded four others on the Danziger Bridge. The group were crossing the bridge in search of food and the officers opened fire. A cover-up included planting a gun, fabricating witnesses, and falsifying reports. Some supervisors were involved in the cover-up. Eventually, five former police officers were convicted in 2011, but the convictions were set aside because of prosecutorial misconduct. In 2016, the officers pled guilty to reduced charges and dramatically reduced sentences (Kunzelman and McGill, 2016; Robertson, 2016b). Other cases during the flood were also eventually revealed. In one case, Henry Glover was mistakenly shot and then police officers burned the body to prevent investigation and beat members of the Glover family to keep them quiet. Those officers were acquitted, but the city has settled several cases with the families of the victims for $13.3 million (Robertson, 2016c).

Attempts to cover up scandals are usually unsuccessful and, arguably, only make the situation worse when the corruption is inevitably exposed. To combat police corruption, it seems clear that the key is to have leadership that is not afraid to expose the "skeletons in the closet" and deal with problems openly without attempting to hide them from the public.

Societal Responses

It is difficult to conceive of how society can affect police corruption; however, it is possible that this is the most important part of the discussion. As noted repeatedly within these chapters, recently we have seen a new era of scrutiny regarding what is occurring in American policing. Communities can promote clear expectations regarding what type of policing they are willing to accept, through legal means, and federal intervention if necessary. There is a saying that a community gets the government they deserve, and it may also be said that a community gets the policing they demand.

Consent Decrees

Civil rights cases against police officers are rare. In one newspaper investigation using nearly 3 million caseload records, it was found that U.S. Attorneys declined 96 percent of civil rights cases against officers between 2005 and 2015. The rate of declination for other cases was about 23 percent. Prosecutors must be able to show that police officers had a clear intent to violate constitutional rights. In many police shootings, for instance, the officer may have violated policy, but that is a long way from proving they willfully violated the person's constitutional rights. Even if their actions were reckless or negligent, that is not sufficient for guilt under a civil rights prosecution (Bowling and Conte, 2016).

However, another avenue that involves more systemic change is the use of "pattern and practice investigations" by the Department of Justice Civil Rights Division. Because of the Rodney King incident, Congress in 1994 passed the Violent Control and Law Enforcement Act (42 U.S.C. Sec. 14141), which authorizes the Department of Justice to investigate and bring a lawsuit for "equitable remedies" against police departments that are found to have a "pattern or practice" of unconstitutional actions. In the last two decades, there have been 67 DOJ investigations; about 25 have resulted in consent decrees with cities such as Seattle, Miami, Pittsburgh, Washington, D.C.,

Detroit, Oakland, and Los Angeles. Recently, Ferguson, Baltimore, and Chicago were the subject of a federal investigation due to recent events. The Obama administration opened roughly 24 investigations, with 14 ending in consent decrees (Gurman, 2017b; Kelly, Childress, and Rich, 2015).

Consent decrees are mandated reforms, approved by a federal judge, with a court-appointed monitor to oversee progress. The order includes changes in policies or procedures; it may require hiring more officers and/or increasing training for officers. The most common targets for change involve policies concerning use of force, citizen complaint procedures, in-car video use, racial profiling, data collection, early warning systems, and expanded training (e.g., CIT, deescalation, and implicit bias).

The major complaint that police and city officials have against DOJ investigations that end in consent decrees is that they are extremely expensive. Ross and Parker (2009) reported that the Los Angeles Police Department spent $30–$40 million annually for the 12 years they were under monitoring. Sometimes, monitoring drags on for years as the city struggles to meet the reform goals. Seattle's annual budget for police training increased from $5 million to $13.6 million because of the 2012 consent decree (Jones, Niquette, and Nash, 2016). In New Orleans, the mandated changes and court monitor cost the city an estimated $55 million (Gurman, 2017b). The reforms demanded in Ferguson, Missouri, are estimated to be as high as $10 million over a three-year period (Jones, Niquette, and Nash, 2016).

Police chiefs argue that monitoring has become a "cottage industry" with monitors' pay sometimes running into millions of dollars with no incentive to end the supervision (Goode, 2013). Other costs include damage to the department's reputation, and a reduction in morale and potentially the loss of good officers (Ross and Parker, 2009). Newark and Ferguson both initially refused to enter into an agreement but then relented when DOJ officials threatened a lawsuit; however, beginning in 2015, the DOJ lost more than one case when it sued for compliance with its recommendations.

More recently, this adversarial and expensive process has been supplanted by what is called collaborative reform. This approach is utilized when a city or police department asks the DOJ to investigate and is willing to undergo reform. It circumvents the courts. Instead DOJ offers technical assistance and subject matter experts to help a police department target and improve areas of concern (Goode, 2015). The first collaborative reform initiative occurred in 2011 in Las Vegas. San Francisco was the tenth city to enter a collaborative reform agreement with DOJ in 2016. Investigators interview residents, community leaders, police officers, and other stakeholders; they also analyze use-of-force, staffing, and other data. Then, instead of court-ordered reform agreements, DOJ pays for experts to come and help the department meet stated goals. In Las Vegas, the police department completed 72 of 80 recommended reforms and officer-involved shootings dropped by nearly 40 percent. Because of its voluntary nature, collaborative reform engenders less resistance (Mendoza, 2016). Collaborative reform efforts have taken place in Philadelphia; St. Louis County in Missouri; and Spokane, Washington.

Recently, there have been several attempts to evaluate whether the consent decree process has been successful in generating long-lasting reform. Detroit entered into a federal consent agreement in 2003 in response to allegations of excessive force by officers, mistreatment of witnesses, and unconstitutional conditions of confinement.

Despite intervening scandals, monitoring finally ended in 2016. City officials have claimed that police reform has reduced police misconduct lawsuits from 105 in 2012 to 40 in 2016. The city paid out $4.9 million in 2016, down from $7.3 million in 2015. The millions saved from fewer lawsuits arguably makes the cost of reform efforts reasonable. Reforms included the implementation of an early warning system, a Compliance Accountability Unit, staffed by civilian auditors, and 40 hours of training each year (Hunter, 2017). The agreement cost Detroit more than $50 million, including $15 million for court-appointed monitoring teams (Gurman, 2017b).

The Justice Department's investigation of Seattle in 2010 led to a consent decree in 2012 that addressed training, procedures, and record-keeping. A large focus of the reform was to implement CIT training, since there are so many calls that involve individuals in mental health crisis. Recent data indicates that with roughly 10,000 calls a year involving behavioral crisis, officers used force just 2 percent of the time. City officials call the intervention an unequivocal success (Gurman, 2017b).

Pittsburgh was the site of the first federal consent decree 21 years ago. Many of the issues that were targeted in the 1997 consent decree still are headline issues today: poor training, racial bias, and use of force. Pittsburgh changed its strip search policy, began documenting traffic stops, instituted "cultural diversity" training, and tracked civilian complaints. In 2002, the federal court released Pittsburgh and the department was considered a model of progressive policing. Unfortunately, observers conclude that the changes "did not stick" and Pittsburgh once again is experiencing the same problems as other cities that have been recently targets of investigation (Stolberg, 2017).

In a *Washington Post/Frontline* investigation, community members, police officials, and officers were interviewed about the effects of consent decrees in their city. Most agreed that the reforms have led to modernized policies, new equipment, and better training. However, use-of-force reports increased in five of the ten departments examined during and after the consent decree. None of the departments could complete reforms by deadlines. Officer morale was reported to decline during the decree monitoring period. Reforms are not necessarily sustained after monitoring ends (Kelly, Childress, and Rich, 2015).

One academic analysis examined the relationship between consent decrees and civil rights litigation in 23 targeted jurisdictions. Researchers found that consent decrees were associated with modest reductions in the risk of civil rights filings (Powell, Meitl, and Worrall, 2017). Critics note, however, that it is difficult to separate out the effects of the consent decree intervention from the public scrutiny and activist activity that brings the city to the attention of the DOJ in the first place. Further, the number of Section 1983 complaints are one proxy, perhaps, for police misconduct, but it is only one measure and does not capture at all any positive change in police departments that result from consent decrees. Some argue that forced change is unlikely to lead to lasting police reform, thus the more recent collaborative reform model may have more measurable results in improving police–citizen relations (Harmon, 2017).

Walker (2017), in a review of several single-city evaluations, concluded that, for the most part, consent decrees were successful in reforming police departments to reduce use-of-force abuses, increase training and accountability, and address citizen concerns. He noted that virtually all consent decrees had these elements: improving use-of-force policies, better reporting of use-of-force with supervisor oversight, an early intervention system, and improving the accessibility of the citizen complaint process.

It seems clear that the number of DOJ investigations and consent decrees will decline under the Trump administration (Mark, 2017; Dewan and Oppel, 2017; Gurman, 2017a). Both President Trump and Attorney General Sessions have indicated they do not approve of federal intervention in local police affairs. They have expressed concerns that federal intervention lowers morale and results in "de-policing" whereby police officers do not proactively patrol for fear of being involved in a misconduct situation (Gurman, 2017a). Police unions have complained bitterly about federal investigations. Interestingly, in the two most recent DOJ investigations, officials in Chicago and Baltimore objected when it appeared that the DOJ planned to withdraw its reform demands (Stolberg, 2017).

Other Societal Responses

In response to the Black Lives Matter movement and other protests, President Barack Obama created the Task Force on Policing in the 21st Century composed of a mix of academics and police professionals (President's Task Force, 2015). They held hearings across the country and heard from stakeholders from all sides. The report detailed a comprehensive list of needed changes in policing (See: https://cops.usdoj.gov/pdf /taskforce/TaskForce_FinalReport.pdf). The changes proposed included: training to deescalate violence, implicit bias, and CIT training, further study on the use of body cameras, replacing the "war" culture with "guardian" principles, and improving the employee assistance programs to help officers deal with stress. The Panel's report was met with hostility by many police groups who perceived the process as "anti-police," however, it is important to note that the 21st Century Panel on Policing included police leaders as well as members of the public, aided by experts. The report makes it clear that police officers' discretion must be guided by a strong understanding of their purpose and an ethical code.

In Maryland, a task force recently issued 22 separate recommendations for legislation or policy changes, including: increasing the time allowed before victims of police brutality must file complaints, reducing the right of a police officer to not give a statement for 10 days after a shooting to five days, creating a unified complaint system for tracking problem officers, providing special whistleblower protections to police officers who expose wrongdoing, and allowing the public to watch police disciplinary boards. The police union objected to all the recommendations, but several of the reforms were passed (E. Cox, 2016; Wiggins, Hicks and Nirappil, 2016).

The Vera Institute of Justice, in a study of legislation during 2015–2016, found 79 changes in the laws of 34 states that concerned policing. This compares to fewer than 20 changes in the previous three years. The types of changes included: policing practices around use of force, racial profiling and body-worn cameras; enhanced protections for public recordings of police; new requirements for maintaining and reporting data on police operations; and, improving accountability in instances of police use-of-force and misconduct cases, especially those incidents that result in death (Vera Institute of Justice, 2017).

All of us act as external stakeholders to police practices. There is a correction effect that occurs when the public becomes aware of problems. One thing that is not helpful is to paint all police as evil or brutal or any other adjective. It is certainly not the case that, just because there are issues in Chicago or Baltimore, every community has a police force with problems. Indeed, the vast number of police departments in this country have good relationships with their communities. Even in the departments that have had scandals, the numbers indicate that corruption lies with an extremely small number of officers. The blue curtain of secrecy (refusing to expose peers' misconduct) is more pervasive; however, even that is beginning to change and most substantiated discipline cases are when fellow officers report misconduct.

All too often, society is not concerned when uses of excessive force are directed to the "criminal element" in society and the general feeling is that "those types" of people deserve it. The problem is once policing jumps the track of legality, there is no longer any control on the power and coercive force police officers use. Extra-legal "street justice" may be used on a drug dealer or serial rapist, but it might also be used against a law-abiding neighbor who uses his or her cellphone to record an arrest. Further, the heavy-handed policing that targets so-called quality-of-life issues, referring to minor ordinances such as sign placement and prohibitions on roller-skating on sidewalks, but does so solely through arrests and citations rather than efforts to improve the community leads to excessive monitoring and, some would say, harassment in certain neighborhoods. The emphasis on arrests and stops, rather than public satisfaction with police, leads to negative community perceptions, distrust, and lack of cooperation when police need to investigate serious crimes. It also provides more opportunity for police officers to stray into unethical uses of their power.

It is also important to truly understand what police officers face on the street and not succumb to knee-jerk responses that if police shoot someone, it must be a bad shooting; or if citizen complaints are not founded, there must have been collusion to protect the officer. The fact is that a miniscule number of police *ever* use their guns and when they do, most do so reflexively and suffer psychological trauma afterward. No one defends the horrible cases in the news like the killing of Walter Scott, but let us not forget there are 12,000–17,000 agencies (evidently no one really knows given the range of numbers in various sources) with about 750,000 officers.

Before we end the chapter, it is important to revisit the reason why we should revere and respect all police officers who voluntarily enter a profession where they offer their lives to save others. The In the News box illustrates this high calling and the nobility of those who serve. The concern we have over the few who abuse their position should never eclipse the honor and heroism of the majority.

IN THE NEWS | *To Protect and Serve*

Sarah Geren was driving home at 2:45 a.m. in 2016 near Tampa when she saw the headlights of a car heading straight toward her on the expressway. She said she flashed her lights on and off, trying to warn the wrong-way driver and pulled over to the right as far as she could, but the headlights kept coming. Then Deputy John Robert Kotfila Jr. passed her and placed his car between her and the oncoming vehicle, deciding in a split second to act as a shield to protect her. The collision was devastating. The 30-year-old deputy was taken to Tampa General Hospital where he died from his injuries. Deputy Kotfila's paternal and maternal grandfathers, father, uncle, and brother were also law enforcement officers. Geren said, "I was a random person on a random road at a random time. He saved me."

Source: Morelli, 2016.

Conclusion

In this chapter, we reviewed a wide range of corruption, categorized into economic corruption and abuse of authority. Explanations of law enforcement deviance can be categorized into individual, organizational, and societal explanations. We also examined a wide range of suggestions for combating police corruption, categorized into these same levels, for example, individual (education and training), organizational (civilian review), and societal (legislative changes).

Chapter Review

1. **Provide examples of two types of police misconduct: economic corruption and abuse of authority.**

   Economic corruption includes any activity wherein a police officer uses his or her position to acquire economic benefit illegally or against policy. Gratuities and graft (bribery, kickbacks, and "pads") are examples of economic corruption. Abuse of authority includes physical or psychological abuse of the citizenry or violations of policy and/or law in the performance of one's duties (e.g., excessive force, ignoring evidence, and coercive interrogation).

2. **Describe individual explanations of corruption and potential solutions.**

   Individual explanations target the individual officer, such as identifying personality characteristics. Suggestions to reduce corruption include improved screening and psychological testing, training, integrity testing, early warning systems, the use of body cameras, and databases of misconduct.

3. **Explain organizational explanations of corruption and potential solutions.**

   Organizational explanations look at factors that encourage or support misconduct, such as the police subculture or an ineffective discipline system. Proposed responses include improving internal affairs units, civilian review boards, changing the culture, and improving the leadership.

4. **Describe societal explanations of corruption and potential solutions.**

   Societal explanations focus on what messages society sends to their police department that might encourage lawlessness. Proposed solutions include revising legislation and external stakeholder scrutiny, such as the President's Task Force on 21st Century Policing.

Study Questions

1. What countries score high in integrity according to Transparency International?
2. Describe several types of economic corruption and abuse of authority corruption.
3. What are the arguments for and against the acceptance of gratuities?
4. List and describe the three categories of explanations for police deviance and an example of each category.
5. Describe the benefits and disadvantages of body cameras.

Writing/Discussion Exercises

1. Write an essay on (or discuss) gratuities. Provide a persuasive argument as to whether gratuities should be acceptable. If you are arguing that they are ethical and should be acceptable, discuss what limits, if any, should be placed upon them.

2. Write an essay on (or discuss) the potential disciplinary sanctions that should be taken against officers who commit legal, policy, and/or ethical transgressions. What is the rationale for the administration of punishment? Which acts warrant more severe sanctions? What should be done with an officer who has a drinking or drug problem? Taking a bribe? Stealing from a crime scene? Hitting a handcuffed suspect? Having checks bounce? Being disrespectful to a member of a minority group? Sexually harassing a coworker?

3. Write an essay on (or discuss) the best methods to reduce noble-cause corruption among officers. Are they the same methods as those that should be used to reduce egoistic corruption for pecuniary gain? Explain why or why not. Also explain why you think the selected methods would work.

Key Terms

civilian review/complaint boards
graft
gratuities

integrity testing
internal affairs model
rotten-apple argument

ETHICAL DILEMMAS

Situation 1
You are a rookie police officer on your first patrol. The older, experienced officer tells you that the restaurant on the corner likes to have you guys around, so it gives free meals. Your partner orders steak, potatoes, and all the trimmings. What are you going to do? What if it were just coffee at a convenience store? What if the owner refused to take your money at the cash register?

Situation 2
There is an officer in your division known as a "rat" because he testified against his partner in a criminal trial and a civil suit. The partner evidently hit a handcuffed suspect in the head several times in anger, and the man sustained brain injuries and is now a paraplegic. Although none of the officers you know supports the excessive use of force, they are also appalled that this officer did not back up his partner's testimony that the suspect continued to struggle, to justify his use of force. After all, punishing the officer wasn't going to make the victim any better. Now no one will ride with this guy, and no one responds to his calls for backup. There have been incidents such as a dead rat being placed in his locker, and the extra uniform in his locker was set on fire.

One day you are parking your car and see your buddies in the employee parking lot moving away from his car; they admit they just slashed his tires. Each officer is being called into the captain's office to state whether he or she knows anything about this latest incident. Your turn is coming. What are you going to do?

Situation 3

Officers in your squad are a great bunch but there are a couple who have a habit of telling racist jokes. You have ignored them up to this point because you don't want to stand out and no one else seems to care, but they joke in front of citizens and you are afraid someone is going to file a complaint. One night you and your partner are eating dinner with these two and they start joking about the African American waitress, using derogatory language. They are loud and you are afraid that she or others in the diner are going to hear them. What should you do? What do you think will happen if you speak up?

Situation 4

You are a police officer testifying in a drug case. You have already testified that you engaged in a buy-bust operation, and the defendant was identified by an undercover officer as the one who sold him a small quantity of drugs. You testified that you chased the suspect down an alley and apprehended him. Immediately before you caught up with him, he threw down several glassine envelopes filled with what turned out to be cocaine. The prosecutor finished his direct examination, and now the defense attorney has begun cross-examining you. He asked if you had the suspect in your sight the entire time between when you identified him as the one who sold to the undercover officer and when you put the handcuffs on him. Your arrest report didn't mention it, but for a couple of seconds you slipped as you went around the corner of the alley and fell. During that short time, the suspect had proceeded a considerable distance down the alley.

You do not think there was anyone else around, and you are as sure as you possibly can be that it was your suspect who dropped the bags, but you know that if you testify to this incident truthfully, the defense attorney might be able to argue successfully that the bags were not dropped by the suspect and get him acquitted of the much more serious charge of possession with intent to distribute. What should you do?

Situation 5

You (a female police officer) have been working in a small-town police department for about six months. A fellow police officer persists in making comments about how pretty you are, how you don't look like a police officer, how you shouldn't be dealing with the "garbage" out on the streets, and so on. He has asked you out more than a dozen times even though you have told him every time that you are not interested and that you want him to stop asking you out and to stop making comments. Although he hasn't made any derogatory or offensive comments, his constant attention is beginning to make you not want to go to work. You have a romantic partner, and you are not interested in your fellow officer. You have mentioned it to your FTO, who is a sort of father figure, but he likes the guy and tells you to ignore him. You want to file a sexual harassment charge against him but hesitate because, although you do feel harassed, you don't feel especially threatened; further, you know that you would encounter negative reactions from the other officers in the department. What should you do?

Law and Legal Professionals

8

Eric Thayer/Getty Images

Former director of the FBI, James Comey, testified in front of Congress. He has become a very public figure because of choices he has made and his firing by President Trump.

M ichael Morton went to work in the early morning hours of 1986 never realizing that his life, as he knew it, was over. He had left his wife sleeping. When he arrived home, he found crime tape, police officers, and crime-scene investigators. That morning a neighbor had found his three-year-old son wandering the street covered in blood. His wife had been bludgeoned to death. Morton was charged and convicted, the only evidence being a note he left taped to the bathroom mirror that rebuked her for not having sex with him the night before. For 24 years he was incarcerated in Texas prisons fighting his conviction. Finally, in 2011, a Williamson County judge ordered him to be immediately released because DNA evidence proved that he was innocent and another man guilty of his wife's death.

Later, it was learned that Ken Anderson, the prosecutor during the original trial (who went on to become a judge), did not provide the defense with evidence of a bloody bandana

Learning Objectives

1. Describe the justifications for law, including protections against harm to others, offensive conduct, harm to self, and harm to societal morals.

2. Explain the role of law in society and the paradigms that have developed to understand how law is formed and enforced.

3. Compare the idea of our criminal law system as an adversarial system to other descriptions of how the courtroom works and the relationships between the legal professionals.

4. Discuss the controversy concerning the role of advocate as legal agent or moral agent.

5. Describe the history and source of legal ethics for attorneys and judges. Explain the types of ethical rules that exist and compare them to the subculture of winning.

found near the home or the statement of Morton's son, who reportedly told his grandmother that a "monster" hurt his mommy and that his daddy was not at home. For six years, the district attorney, John Bradley, who had been an assistant district attorney at Morton's original trial, fought the requested DNA testing of the bandana. When it was finally tested, the blood on the bandana turned out to be Christine Morton's and DNA found on it was matched to another man. Even then, Bradley fought against a new trial for Morton. The Innocence Project of New York assisted Morton in his defense along with Houston attorney John Raley, who contributed thousands of hours *pro bono* to the case. When a prosecutor in neighboring Travis County and the Innocence team members noticed similarities between the murder of Christine Morton and an unsolved murder that took place two years after the Morton murder, they had the unknown DNA compared and it matched. Further, the murders were eerily similar in that household objects were piled on the bodies. Mark Alan Norwood has since been convicted of both murders and received a life sentence.

Ken Anderson, the county's district attorney for 16 years and district judge for 10 years, was investigated in a unique "court of inquiry" and, ultimately, pleaded guilty to contempt for withholding evidence and received a 10-day jail sentence and forfeited his law license. Critics argued that it was a light punishment for being instrumental in a man's wrongful imprisonment for 25 years, especially since he did not have to forfeit his judicial pension (Colloff, 2013; Lindell, 2012).

The Michael Morton case is only one case of many where innocent people have been exonerated, usually based on DNA. The National Registry of Exonerations, a project of the University of Michigan Law School, University of California Irvine Newkirk Center for Science & Society, and the Michigan State University College of Law, currently lists 2,025 exonerations that they have documented since 1989 (see: https://www.law.umich.edu/special/exoneration/Pages/about.aspx). The Innocence Project (see: www.innocenceproject.org), lawyers in a loosely affiliated group that use DNA to help exonerate individuals, have successfully achieved the release of 349 individuals as of summer 2017. It seems every week the media presents a new case of an individual who spent decades in prison for a crime he or she did not commit. The most common factor in these wrongful convictions is mistaken eyewitness testimony, but the unethical acts of police and prosecutors also often play a role.

Just as Ferguson, Missouri, and Baltimore, Maryland, have triggered a national conversation about police, so, too, have highly publicized exonerations like Michael Morton's, triggered a national consciousness that the justice system sometimes creates injustice. Also, just as with law enforcement, the focus has targeted the actions of prosecutors, judges, and defense attorneys, since it is they who are instrumental in making sure the system works. In other ways besides wrongful convictions, individuals in the system dramatically affect individuals' lives. In the In the News box, for instance, it is unclear why an unknown number of prosecutors, defense attorneys, and judges did not recognize, as the months and years went by, that there was something wrong with the system when a teenager languished in jail without due process, even after attempting suicide.

In this chapter and the next two chapters, we will discuss the ethics of legal professionals. These three chapters are set up in a similar way as the three chapters on law enforcement. In this first chapter, we will examine some basic issues concerning the role of the law in society in the same way that we explored the history of policing. We also present the formal and informal ethical codes that guide legal professionals'

🖳 IN THE NEWS | *Kalief Browder*

We would like to think that the criminal justice system provides due process and works the way it should. Unfortunately, that is not always the case. Kalief Browder was only 16 years old when he was arrested and charged with second-degree robbery. He was remanded without bail after being indicted because he had been on probation at the time of the charges. He spent three years in Rikers Island jail waiting for a trial. Because the Bronx courts are so overcrowded, every time the prosecutor asked for a week's continuance, the delay would turn to six weeks. There is a speedy trial guarantee, but if the prosecutor says they are ready for trial, scheduling delays are not counted. Once, after two years had elapsed, a judge offered to let him go with time served if he would plead guilty to two misdemeanors, but he refused because he wasn't guilty. Finally, in 2013 after appearing in court over 37 times without any conviction, the judge told him that the prosecutor's office was not able to proceed to trial because the man who had claimed Browder had taken his backpack (creating the alleged crime of robbery) had moved away. In Rikers Island, housed with 600 other boys 16–18 years old, he had experienced physical and emotional abuse and spent the equivalent of two years in solitary confinement. While at Rikers, he attempted suicide at least six times. After his release, he attempted to begin his life again. He had missed his high school graduation, and all his friends had moved on and began their lives. He began attending a community college and maintained a 3.5 GPA, but struggled with depression and paranoia. He attempted suicide six months after his release. The story generated a great deal of interest in Browder's case, and he met celebrities and an anonymous donor paid for his community college tuition. Still, he struggled. In June 2015, his name was again in the news when he committed suicide by hanging himself. His attorney said that he never overcame the jail experience. The publicity has made many ask: how many more Kalief Browders are there in our nation's jails?

Sources: Ford, 2015; Gonnerman, 2013, 2015.

actions, just as we did in Chapter 5 where the law enforcement code and subculture was discussed. In Chapter 9, we will examine the discretion of legal professionals and how such discretion creates ethical dilemmas, a similar approach to the discussion in Chapter 6. Finally, in Chapter 10, we will examine cases of misconduct and corruption and responses to them, just as we did in Chapter 7 for law enforcement professionals.

▌ The Role of Law

laws Formal, written rules of society.

Our **laws** serve as the written embodiment of society's ethics and morals. Laws are said to be declarative as well as active; they declare correct behavior and serve as a tool for enforcement. While **natural law** refers to the belief that some law is inherent in the natural world and can be discovered by reason, **positivist law** refers to those laws written and enforced by society. This type of law is of human construction and, therefore, fallible (Mackie, 1977).

natural law The idea that principles of morals and rights are inherent in nature and not human-made; such laws are discovered by reason but exist apart from humankind.

We can trace the history of law back to very early codes, such as the Code of Hammurabi (ca. 2000 bce), which mixed secular and religious proscriptions of behavior. These codes also standardized punishments and atonements for wrongdoing. Early codes of law did not differentiate between what we now distinguish as public wrongs (criminal law) and private wrongs (torts). Criminal law is more closely associated with enforcing the moral standards of society, yet it is by no means comprehensive in its coverage of behavior.

positivist law Human-made law.

Laws, in the form of statutes and ordinances, tell us how to drive, how to operate our business, and what we can and cannot do in public and even in private. They are the formal, written rules of society. Yet, they are not comprehensive in defining moral behavior. There is a law against hitting one's mother (assault), but (in many states) no law against financially abandoning her, yet both are considered morally wrong. We have laws against bad behavior, such as burglarizing a house or embezzling from our employer, but we have few laws prescribing good behavior, such as helping a victim or contributing to a charity. The exception to this consists of **Good Samaritan laws**, which are common in Europe. These laws make it a crime to pass by an accident scene or witness a crime without rendering assistance. Some states do have laws called Good Samaritan laws, but they are civil and protect medical professionals who stop at an accident scene and administer aid to the victims from being sued. These laws provide some level of immunity to those who stop and render aid, but they do not require helping as the Good Samaritan laws in Europe do.

> **Good Samaritan laws** European legislation that prohibits passing by an accident scene or witnessing a crime without rendering assistance; can also refer to laws that provide protection from civil suits for individuals who stop and render aid.

Law controls behavior by providing sanctions but also, perhaps even more important, by teaching people which behaviors are acceptable and which behaviors are not. Thus, academics argue whether, for instance, *Brown v. Board of Education*, 347 U.S. 483, 1954, came after a shift in people's values and attitudes toward segregation or the legal holding that ruled segregation was illegal was the change agent in transforming values and attitudes. Probably both statements are true. There is a dynamic between the law and public opinion, and the power of law is most noticeable "at the margins" where it heralds social change or, to the contrary, acts as a resistant force to evolving belief systems. Laws at the margin are those where strong opposing positions exist (e.g., abortion, same-sex marriage, drug laws, and gun-control laws). Law is the final word, but it is also dynamic, shifting to reflect changing belief systems.

Just as important as a tool of behavior control and change, the law provides a blanket of protection for individuals against the awesome power of the state. We cherish our Constitution and the Bill of Rights because we understand that in those countries that do not have our legal traditions, citizens have no protection against tyranny and oppression. We know that our bedrock of rights set down by our founding fathers ensures, to some extent, that even if government officials wanted to do us harm or treat us in a way that offends the concept of due process, they could not do so without violating the law. Thus, the law is our social contract. It dictates limits on our own behavior, but also provides protection against governmental violations. Legal professionals are supposed to ensure that this contract is enforced, even though cases such as the Michael Morton case, which opened this chapter, show that sometimes this does not happen. Before we focus on legal professionals, however, it is necessary to take a step back and examine law itself.

Justifications for Law

The major justification for corrective (criminal) law is prevention of harm. Under the **social contract theory**, law is a contract; everyone gives up some liberties and, in return, is protected from others who have their liberties restricted as well. Thomas Hobbes' (1588–1679) claim that self-preservation (the law of the jungle) is paramount, and John Locke's (1632–1704) view that property is a natural right created the foundation for the social contract theory. According to this theory, members of society were originally engaged in a "war of all against all." According to Hobbes (1651), everyone has chosen to "lay down this right to all things; and be contented with so much liberty against other men, as he would allow other men against himself." Hobbes said that to avoid this war of all against all, people needed to be assured that people will not harm one another and that they will keep their agreements. But how much liberty should be restricted, and what behaviors should be prohibited? Rough formulas or guidelines indicate that the law should interfere as little as possible with natural liberties and should step in only when the liberty in question injures or impinges on the interests of another. The justifications for law most often cited are preventing harm to others, preventing offensive behavior, preventing harm to self, and protecting societal morals. Each of these will be discussed next.

Preventing Harm to Others

John Stuart Mill (1806–1873) proposed the "harm principle," which basically is the idea that every individual should have the utmost freedom over their own actions unless they harm others. In this view, the law would restrict only those actions that can or do cause harm to others, such as assault, attempted murder, or theft. Most of our criminal laws are created to punish individual harms. The least controversial are those which we have inherited from the common law; however, legislators continue to add new laws all the time, supposedly to prevent harm.

Preventing Offensive Behavior

There are some actions that do not exactly harm others, but give rise to disgust or offense. Such actions as public lewdness, disturbing public behavior, noise, or other actions that infringe on the quality of life of others can be the subject of laws, and individuals who flaunt such laws may be fined or punished in some way. These laws are sometimes controversial because there is an argument that no law should restrict an individual's behavior if it only creates inconvenience or disgust, and does not damage others' interests. For instance, many cities control the population of homeless people and beggars by a variety of laws because their presence and their actions upset and frighten tourists and downtown workers. Some of these laws, such as vagrancy laws, have been overturned by the Supreme Court for unduly infringing on personal liberties (*Papachristou v. Jacksonville*, 405 U.S. 157, 1972), but others have been upheld, such as "no camping" ordinances to dissuade the homeless from congregating in a downtown area.

Ethical justifications for laws preventing offense (but not harm) are more problematic than laws preventing harm. One may prefer to not see homeless and have laws that prohibit people from begging, but under ethics of care, criminalizing poverty would not be acceptable, nor would no-camping laws that punish behavior that is not harmful, only offensive.

Preventing Harm to Self (Legal Paternalism)

legal paternalism
Refers to laws that protect individuals from hurting themselves.

Many laws can be described as examples of **legal paternalism**—laws in which the state tries to protect people from their own behavior. Examples include seat belt laws, motorcycle helmet laws, speed limits, drug laws, licensing laws, alcohol consumption

💬 IN THE NEWS | *Criminalizing Homelessness*

A California government group examined laws that affected the homeless and found 500 anti-homeless laws in 58 California cities. Laws included prohibitions against: "(1) standing, sitting, and resting in public places; (2) sleeping, camping, and lodging in public places, including in vehicles; (3) begging and panhandling; and (4) food sharing." The last law was like one in Florida which was used against Arnold Abbott, 90,

in Fort Lauderdale; he was repeatedly cited for feeding the homeless.

California's law against vagrants, passed to stop the tide of migration from the Great Plains Dust Bowl catastrophe in the 1930s, was struck down as unconstitutional in 1941. Over half of the current laws have been passed since 1990 in response to an increase of homeless people in the 1980s.

Source: Allgov.com, 2015.

and sale laws, smoking prohibitions, and laws limiting certain types of sexual behavior. The strict libertarian view would hold that the government has no business interfering in a person's decisions about these behaviors if they don't negatively affect others. The opposing view is that if a person is a member of society (and everyone is), he or she has a value to that society, and society is therefore compelled to protect the person with or without his or her cooperation.

It may also be true that there are no harmful or potentially harmful behaviors to oneself that do not also hurt others, however indirectly, so society is protecting others when it controls everyone. Speeding drivers may crash into someone else, drug addicts may commit crimes to support their habit, gamblers may neglect their families and cause expense to the state, and so on. Some believe that government can justify paternalism only with certain restrictions. These rules try to create a balance between an individual's liberty and government control (Thompson, 1980):

- The decision-making ability of the person may be somehow impaired by lack of knowledge or competency (e.g., tobacco and alcohol prohibitions for minors).
- The restriction should be as limited as possible (e.g., DUI laws state a legal limit that is when someone is likely impaired by alcohol or drugs).
- The laws should seek only to prevent a serious and irreversible error.

Paternalistic laws can be supported by an ethics of care. Remember that in this framework, morality is viewed as integral to a system of relationships. The individual has ties to society and to every other member of society. Rights are less important in this framework; therefore, to ask whether society has a *right* to intervene or an individual has a *right* to a liberty is not relevant to the discussion. Current debates regarding laws that attempt to influence people's lifestyle choices (such as smoking and eating) illustrate this debate. A large segment of the public become outraged whenever legislation is proposed that is perceived to control private decisions of eating, drinking, smoking, or other activities of adults or their children. Many also believe that government has a moral and legal duty to provide healthcare. Expensive healthcare is made necessary, to some extent because of people's lifestyle choices; therefore, if government takes a larger role in providing healthcare, should it also have a larger say in lifestyle, for example, banning or taxing soda?

Preventing Harm to Societal Morals (Legal Moralism)

legal moralism
A justification for law that allows for protection and enforcement of societal morals.

The law also acts as the moral agent of society, some say in areas where there is no moral agreement. This rationale is called **legal moralism**. Some sexual behaviors, gambling, drug use, pornography, and even suicide and euthanasia are defined as wrong and are prohibited. The laws against these behaviors may be based on principles of harm or paternalism, but they also exist to reinforce society's definitions of moral behavior. For example, consensual sexual behavior between adults arguably harms no one, yet the Georgia state law prohibiting sodomy was upheld by the U.S. Supreme Court in *Bowers v. Hardwick,* 478 U.S. 186, 1986, although later effectively overturned in *Lawrence v. Texas,* 539 U.S. 558, 2003. More recently, there continues to be debate about same-sex marriage even though the Supreme Court has issued a decision, as described in the In the News box, that establishes the right of same-sex couples to have their marriages legally recognized. The underlying justification that both sides employ is legal moralism.

Pornography (at least that involving consenting adults) that is defined as obscene is prohibited, arguably because of moral standards, not harmful effect. Under the legal moralism rationale, obscenity is prohibited simply because it is wrong. The issue has become even more complicated with the increasing use of the Internet and the ease with which individuals may obtain pornographic materials from anywhere in the world. Privacy rights conflict with the government's right to enforce morality.

It should also be noted that whether an action is moral or immoral is a different question than whether there should be laws and governmental sanctions regarding the behavior. In some cases, individuals may agree that an action is immoral, but at the same time may not believe that the government should have any power to restrict an individual's choice. We do not have a legal system that completely overlaps our moral code, and some would argue that it would be impossible in a society as heterogeneous as ours for this to occur.

Drug laws can be justified under preventing harm to others, preventing harm to self, or legal moralism. Public opinion has shifted in this area as well and now a slim majority of Americans favor legalizing marijuana. While only 34 percent of those polled by the Gallup organization supported legalization in 2004, 60 percent supported legalization in 2016 (Swift, 2017). In 2017, 26 states and the District of Columbia have legalized medical uses of marijuana and 7 states and the District of Columbia have legalized small amounts of marijuana for personal use: Alaska, California, Colorado,

IN THE NEWS | Same-Sex Marriage

This country has seen a sea change toward same-sex marriage with public opinion shifting to support and state laws following. As of April 2015, 30 states had legalized same-sex marriage, either by statute or case law. The Supreme Court, in *United States v. Windsor,* 570 U.S. __, 2013, heard a challenge to the federal Defense of Marriage Act and held §3 of the Act (that defined marriage as solely between a man and a woman) a violation of the Fourteenth Amendment. Then, in January 2015, the Court consolidated cases from four different states to consider the legality of bans on same-sex marriage. On June 26, 2015, in *Obergefell v. Hodges,* 576 U.S. ____, 2015, the Supreme Court held that the right to marry is a protected liberty interest and all states must license and recognize same-sex marriages.

Source: CNN.com, 2015.

Maine, Massachusetts, Nevada, and Washington. Research is ongoing to determine whether legalization has led to an increase of crime or other negative effects. Colorado and Washington were the first to decriminalize and there are mixed findings. Some law enforcement groups report that the number of DUI-marijuana arrests has increased, but there is some question as to whether a comparison can be made since testing for marijuana didn't take place before legalization, and it is impossible to establish whether impairment is caused by cannabis (since many arrests include alcohol intoxication as well and marijuana can stay in the bloodstream long after impairment would occur). There have also been reports that overdoses have increased, for example, children who eat cannabis-infused candy or "drug-tourists" who do not understand the potency of the product. A review of available findings from the libertarian Cato Institute concluded that there has been little significant positive or negative effect of marijuana legalization. Crime has not increased substantially, use patterns for marijuana, cocaine, and alcohol show no pattern associated with marijuana legalization, teen use has not substantially increased, and traffic fatalities show no increases association with legalization. On the positive side, Colorado now collects close to $150 million in tax revenues each year (Dills, Goffard, and Miron, 2016). It is important to note that research continues and it may be the case that future studies show that marijuana decriminalization does have harmful effects. As with all research, it is important that researchers are objective.

The changes in drug laws and same-sex marriage laws show that public views on issues of morality shift. Laws against adultery used to be very common and are nonexistent today. Other crimes that existed in the 1700s are no longer crimes today (e.g., blasphemy and being a "common scold"). Some propose that only those actions that violate some universal standard of morality, as opposed to merely a conventional standard, should be criminalized. This "limited legal moralism" would prevent the situation of some groups forcing their moral code on others. Of course, this begs the question of what behaviors would meet this universal standard. Even child pornographers argue that their behavior is unfairly condemned by a conventional, rather than a universal, morality. The vast profits that are made by producing and distributing child pornography indicate that many people buy such products. Does this mean that it is simply a matter of choice and not some universal moral sense that should influence whether children being used as objects of sexual gratification be a criminal act?

The types of laws justified by moralism have also been called the "gray" area of crime in that the wrongness of such actions are not black and white, and there is disagreement that some actions (e.g., prostitution, gambling, and drug use) are wrong at all. It is not surprising that law enforcement professionals often engage in ethically and legally questionable behavior in these "gray" areas. Police will ignore prostitution, for instance, until the public complains, and police may routinely let petty drug offenders go rather than take the trouble to arrest. Prosecutors may let gamblers go with a warning if no publicity is attached to the arrest. Decision makers in criminal justice use discretion in this way partly because these behaviors are not universally condemned. Consider, for instance, the argument that organized crime grew tremendously during Prohibition and that an unknown number of law enforcement officers, prosecutors, and judges accepted bribes or were involved in protection rackets. Some argue that the same scenario has occurred because of the so-called war on drugs. Recall that many of the misconduct examples presented in the last chapter involved drugs. The rationalization of authorities who are inclined to accept protection money or bribes is that offenders are engaged in providing a commodity that the public desires. Also, one might note that it is somewhat hypocritical enforcing laws against gambling in states where there is a state lottery.

Paradigms of Law

Our understanding of the law's function in society is informed by more fundamental views of the world around us, called paradigms. Basically, paradigms are models of how ideas relate to one another, forming a conceptual model of the world around us. A paradigm helps us organize the vast array of knowledge that we absorb every day. We see the world and interpret facts in a way that is influenced by our paradigms—for example, if we have a paradigm that government is corrupt, everything we read and hear will be unconsciously scanned for facts that fit our paradigm, and inconsistent or contrary facts will be ignored and/or forgotten. If our paradigm is that the system is racist, then news stories and statistics that support that notion will be remembered better than information that is not consistent; contrarily, if our paradigm is that the system is fair, the same would apply in reverse. Paradigms aren't bad or good; they are simply a function of how the human mind works. Our paradigms can shift, of course, when we are confronted with overwhelming facts that come from trusted sources or personal experiences that are contrary to our paradigm.

The three paradigms that might affect our view of the law, whether we are legal professionals, legislators, or citizens are the consensus paradigm, the conflict paradigm, and the pluralist paradigm.

Consensus Paradigm

consensus paradigm The idea that most people have similar beliefs, values, and goals and that societal laws reflect the majority view.

The **consensus paradigm** views society as a community consisting of like-minded individuals who agree on goals important for ultimate survival. In the consensus paradigm, law serves as a tool of unification. Émile Durkheim (1858–1917) viewed criminal law as a manifestation of consensual norms; we define an action as criminal because most of the populace holds the opinion that it is wrong (Durkheim, 1969).

Law contributes to the collective conscience by showing us who is deviant. The consensus view would point to evidence that people agree on, for the most part, what behaviors are wrong and the relative seriousness of different types of wrongful behavior. Criminology, except for critical or radical criminology, holds a consensus paradigm in that theory construction generally does not question the law itself. In the consensus paradigm:

- *Law is representative.* It is a compilation of the dos and don'ts that we all agree on.
- *Law reinforces social cohesion.* It emphasizes our "we-ness" by illustrating deviance.
- *Law is value-neutral.* It resolves conflicts in an objective and neutral manner.

Conflict Paradigm

conflict paradigm The idea that groups in society have fundamental differences and that those in power control societal elements, including law.

The **conflict paradigm** views society as being made up of competing and conflicting interests. According to this view, governance is based on power; if some win, others lose, and those who hold power in society promote self-interest, not a greater good.

This perspective sees law as a tool of power holders to maintain and control the status quo: those who control major social institutions determine how crime is defined (Quinney, 1974; Reasons, 1973; Sheley, 1985).

Those holding a conflict paradigm would point to laws against only certain types of gambling as evidence that the ruling class punishes the activities of other classes more severely than their own activities (e.g., numbers running is always illegal, yet some states have legalized horseracing, dog racing, and/or casinos). The Quote and Query box illustrates that the belief that law is used by the powerful against those without power is longstanding.

It is true that the definition of what is criminal often excludes corporate behavior, even though it may be just as harmful to the public as street crime. The *regulation* of business, instead of the *criminalization* of harmful business practices, arises, arguably, from the ability of those in powerful positions to redefine their activities to their own advantage. The obvious example to support this view of law is that not a single banking or investment company executive has been prosecuted for activities related to the catastrophic 2007–2008 collapse of the U.S. economic system and resulting recession that forced millions out of work and/or out of their homes. Fraudulent mortgage practices went on, banks dealt in improper and risky derivative trading, and CEOs continued to receive large bonuses, telling shareholders the companies were profitable, even while they were falling into bankruptcy. The Troubled Asset Relief Agency distributed billions (provided by taxpayers) to banks that were deemed "too big to fail." The loss and damage done to the country was immeasurable, yet the lack of punishment led some pundits to say that the bankers at the top were "too big to jail." At this point, the statute of limitations has run out for the types of financial fraud that might have been charged.

The Safety and Health Administration, the Food and Drug Administration, the Federal Aviation Administration, and other similar governmental agencies are charged with the task of enforcing regulations governing business activities in their respective areas; however, regulatory sanctions are not as stigmatizing or painful as criminal convictions. Critics also argue that the relationships between the watchdog agencies and those they watch are frequently incestuous: heads of business are often named to watchdog agencies, and employees of these agencies may move to the business sector they previously regulated. The Deepwater Horizon oil spill in the Gulf of Mexico was the worst in history; some allege that it occurred because the federal agency employees responsible for overseeing deep sea drilling and monitoring safety procedures accepted expensive trips and engaged in personal relationships with oil executives (CNN.com, 2010).

Generally, in the conflict paradigm:

- *Law is repressive*. It oppresses the poor and powerless by differential definitions and/or enforcement.
- *Law is a tool of the powerful*. Those who write the laws do so in a way to promote their economic and political interests.
- *Law is not value-neutral*. It is biased and bent toward the interests of the powerful.

QUOTE & QUERY

Laws are just like spiders' webs, they will hold the weak and delicate who might be caught in their meshes, but will be torn to pieces by the rich and powerful.

Anacharsis, 600 BCE

The more mandates and laws which are enacted, the more there will be thieves and robbers.

Lao-Tze, 600 BCE

What do these statements mean? Is it true that laws are manipulated by the powerful and oppress the weak?

Pluralist Paradigm

pluralist paradigm
The concept that there are many groups in society and that they form allegiances and coalitions in a dynamic exchange of power.

The **pluralist paradigm** shares the perception that society is made up of competing interests; however, pluralism describes more than two basic interest groups and recognizes that the power balance may shift when interest groups form or coalitions emerge. These power shifts occur as part of the dynamics of societal change.

Pluralism views law as influenced by interest groups that are in flux. Some interests may be at odds with other interests, or certainly the interpretation of them may be. For instance, conservation of natural resources is a basic interest necessary to the survival of society, but it may be interpreted by lumber companies as allowing them to harvest trees in national forests if they replant; alternatively, interpreted by conservation groups as mandating more wilderness areas. According to the pluralist paradigm, laws are written by the group whose voice is more powerful at any given time.

The definition of crime may change, depending on which interest groups have the power to define criminal behavior and what is currently perceived to be in the best interests of the most powerful groups. For example, for many years, Federal Sentencing Guidelines mandated punishment for crack cocaine in a way that was 100 times harsher (based on quantity) than powder cocaine, even though they were chemically the same substance. Conflict theory would have explained such a discrepancy by noting that poor people use crack and rich people use powder cocaine; however, it cannot explain why the 100:1 ratio has been addressed with judicial efforts to reduce the disparity, and why, in the summer of 2010, Congress passed legislation reducing the disparity between the two types of cocaine to about 18 to 1. A pluralist paradigm would point to the growing public sentiment that the sentencing guidelines were unfair. Diverse groups such as the ACLU, Families Against Mandatory Minimums, and other interest groups do have power to affect law when they join together and garner a certain level of public support. Recently, politicians as diverse as Rand Paul and Bernie Sanders have advocated eliminating or reducing draconian federal drug sentences. This political shift supports the pluralist view that law is dynamic and changes reflect shifting coalitions and public sentiment, as does the shift back again now that the Trump administration is in place. Attorney General Sessions has indicated he is in favor of returning to full prosecution and maximum sentences.

Another example where interest groups' power seems to shift back and forth is immigration law. There is little argument that resources to protect the border could be enhanced to prevent further illegal entries. There also seems to be little argument that there are about 11 million people in this country that have overstayed visas or slipped into the country without proper authorization. While some maintain that all those here without proper authorization should be deported, the opposite position is that there should be amnesty for everyone. An intermediate position was taken by the Obama administration. For instance, the Development, Relief, and Education for Alien Minors Act (DREAM Act) promised citizenship to those who were brought into this country at a young age by their parents if they obtained a college degree or entered the military. The Obama administration also prioritized for deportation only those who committed serious crimes. The Trump administration, in contrast, has attempted to get Congressional funding for a border wall, has begun deportation hearings against some "Dreamers," and has retracted the instruction to immigration authorities to focus only on serious criminals. These recent political shifts show that law is interpreted and enforced in different ways. Legal professionals, then, become not mere robots who enforce all laws, all the time, but, rather, interpreters of law who apply it dynamically, influenced by shifting economic, social, and personal factors. In the Walking the Walk box for this chapter, former FBI director James Comey's commitment to the law has made him a national figure; some believe he is an example of one who lives by his ethics, others believe him to be corrupted by politics.

WALKING THE WALK

One of the hallmarks of our democracy is the separation of law and politics. Unlike other countries, we do not have a history of politicians utilizing the criminal law system to pursue their opponents either before or after an election. Losers in political contests are not jailed on flimsy charges. The justice system is not used as a personal tool of those in power. This long tradition depends on the independence and integrity of those in charge of investigative and legal agencies.

Before 2016, James Comey, formerly a U.S. attorney in Manhattan and a deputy attorney general before being appointed as FBI director, has always been known for his independence and integrity. A well-known incident cemented his reputation. During the Bush administration in 2004, Mr. Comey, as deputy attorney general, was acting AG and refused to sign a reauthorization of National Security Agency surveillance programs that he believed were legally flawed. When he heard that White House aides were attempting to get AG Ashcroft's signature while he was sick and under pain medication in a hospital, Comey rushed over and reportedly stood in the door of the room refusing to let the aides inside.

He was widely respected by both Republicans and Democrats, and even though a registered Republican, President Obama asked him to be the director of the FBI based on that reputation. As FBI director, Comey was known as someone who was apolitical and who did what he believed was right, regardless of the political implications. He was also known as someone who would stand up to his boss, the attorney general, and, was perhaps somewhat egotistical and self-righteous. It has been reported that, in speeches he would reference the dark days of J. Edgar Hoover's FBI and maintain that it was vitally important that the law enforcement agency must never have any taint of political motive or extralegal influence.

The Clinton–Trump presidential race forever changed Comey's reputation—some say because he changed the election. Both sides of the aisle used to respect him; in 2016, both Republicans and Democrats found reason to distrust his motives and question his integrity. Whatever one might say of Comey's decision making, we can probably agree that his intent was to do the right thing.

Several incidents in the presidential race placed Comey squarely in the spotlight. First, in July of 2016, without input or approval from Attorney General Lynch, he gave a press conference and stated the investigation into whether Hillary Clinton had violated any laws using a private server was over and no charges would be filed. To prove criminal culpability, they needed evidence that she knowingly set up the server to mishandle classified information and, although the private server was a spectacularly bad decision, there was no smoking gun that proved intent. He also, however, took the opportunity to severely criticize her decision to use a private server to the point where listeners believed charges would be filed until the very end of his speech. Now both sides were angry—Clinton supporters for the scolding and Trump supporters for not filing criminal charges.

Then, due to still murky motives, on October 28, 2016, less than two weeks before the election, he sent a letter to Congress announcing that the investigation was reopened because of many e-mails found on Anthony Weiner's laptop that came from or were sent to his wife, Huma Abedin, Clinton's top aide. Evidently, the decision to publicize the reopening of the investigation was not made lightly and Comey met with agents and lawyers for days before he made the decision to go public. One factor in his decision was supposedly a hacked e-mail from a Democratic party official that purportedly said that the investigation would be squashed by Attorney General Lynch; however, FBI officials believed that the e-mail was forged. Another factor was the ill-fated meeting between former President Clinton and Attorney General Loretta Lynch at an airport. Comey reportedly believed that if Hillary Clinton won the election, the Justice Department would be under suspicion that it

(continued)

had subverted the investigation into her alleged mishandling of classified documents. Attorney General Lynch and her deputy Sally Yates did not agree with the decision to go public, but did not expressly forbid Comey, knowing that if they did, it would appear to be political.

It turned out that the review, which was expected to take months, took much less time because they reviewed only e-mails sent from or to Mrs. Clinton. Only about 3,000 of those were potentially work-related. A dozen or so e-mail chains contained classified information, but nothing that wasn't already known to the FBI. Mere days before the election, Comey wrote to Congress that "we have not changed our conclusions [that there should be no criminal charges]."

FBI policies are clear that they do not announce investigations until they are over, nor make public statements close to elections. The announcement of reopening the investigation violated both policies. Reportedly, his reasoning was that because he told Congress the investigation was over, he had to tell Congress when it was reopened. He also reportedly said that he couldn't let politics influence the decision one way or the other.

What was not known until after the election was that the FBI was also investigating whether individuals in the Trump campaign had colluded with Russia to influence the election. Even under direct questioning by Congress in the fall he refused to confirm or deny that an investigation was occurring. It wasn't until March 2017 that Mr. Comey confirmed the Russia investigation. Thus, Democrats felt Comey had put his finger on the scale by keeping one investigation secret while publicly announcing the second. It should be noted that President Obama's administration and some members of Congress knew about the Russian investigation as well. The reason to keep it quiet was evidently because publicizing it would look like an intentional attempt at influence and might delegitimize the election in the eyes of the pubic. Comey reportedly even wanted to write an op-ed to alert the public to the danger of Russian interference (not specifically through the Trump campaign), but was not given permission to do so.

It was an ironic twist to a career where decisions had always been made to reinforce the reality and appearance of independence. For instance, it was reported that Comey wouldn't play basketball with President Obama because it would give the appearance that the two were closer than they should be given their roles. He reportedly told FBI employees that they could not consider the effects of their decisions, only whether their actions were consistent with facts and law. Critics are more skeptical and assume that he was more worried about his and the FBI's reputation if Clinton was elected and the second investigation found something damning in the e-mails. Legal ethicists agree that Comey was in a unique position, but his first mistake was criticizing Mrs. Clinton in his first announcement rather than simply announcing the investigation was closed. Then he compounded that mistake by making the second announcement regardless of his reasoning for doing so.

Since the election, Comey testified that there was no evidence to support President Trump's claims that former President Obama wiretapped him. He reportedly was deeply uncomfortable when invited to have dinner with the president and asked the president's staff to go through official channels when inquiring about investigations. In May 2017, he was fired by President Trump, but that has not ended the saga. He is scheduled to testify about the investigations and about President Trump's alleged attempts to persuade him to end the investigation focused on Michael Flynn. To his great dismay, however, his ethics and integrity are no longer unassailable.

Source: Apuzzo, Schmidt, Goldman, and Lichtblau, 2017; Schmidt, 2017; Shane and LaFraniere, 2016.

First, Let's Kill All the Lawyers

Public perceptions of lawyers indicate that the public has little confidence in their ability to live up to ideals of equity, fairness, and justice. In 2016, respondents in a Gallup Poll rated their level of trust in the integrity of attorneys. Only about 18 percent indicated that attorneys possessed "high" or "very" high standards of honesty and ethics. In contrast, 47 percent of individuals rated police officers as having high or very high standards. Several professions were rated lower than lawyers, such as business executives, stock brokers, and HMO managers. Professions that scored the lowest were used car salesman (only 9 percent) and members of Congress (only 8 percent rated this group as having high or very high standards of honesty and ethics) (Gallup Poll, 2017b).

In the 1980s, the law scandal was the savings and loan fiasco, in which the greed and corruption of those in the banking industry were ably assisted by the industry's attorneys, and the taxpayers picked up the bill for the bankrupt institutions and outstanding loans. The scandal of the 1990s was the Bill Clinton–Monica Lewinsky investigation, with opinions mixed as to which set of lawyers was more embarrassing—those who could coach President Clinton that oral sex wasn't technically "sexual relations" or the special prosecutor, Kenneth Starr, and his assistants, who spent millions of dollars in an investigation of semen stains and the definition of sex. The new century brought us the debacle of WorldCom and Enron, and, again, lawyers played a central role, along with business executives and accountants.

After 9/11 and the War on Terror, White House counsel parsed the definition of torture in secret memoranda. Then the national economy went into free fall due to Wall Street, again aided ably by their highly paid attorneys. For many, it seemed a virtual replay of the savings and loan scandal of the 1980s, and many wondered how it could have happened again. For every CEO and bank official who skirted the finer points of law and ethics, there was an attorney by his or her side.

Limiting our focus to only those attorneys in the criminal justice system, it seems every day there is another news story of a person who has been exonerated by Innocence Project attorneys, reportedly because of egregious errors and/or unethical behaviors on the part of prosecutors, defense attorneys, and judges. On the other hand, it is also attorneys who help the wrongfully convicted regain their freedom, attorneys who prosecute white-collar villains, and attorneys who defend the Constitution. The Quote and Query box puts the problem in a humorous light.

Perhaps the best explanation for the longstanding distrust of lawyers is that they typically represent trouble. People don't require a lawyer unless they believe that a wrong has been done to them or that they need to be defended. In fact, let us not forget the full context of the quote, "The first thing we do, let's kill all the lawyers," widely used as a stab at attorneys. In Shakespeare's *Henry VI, Part 2*, the scene involves a despot who, before making a grab for power, argues that the first thing he must do is kill all the lawyers, for it is lawyers who are the guardians of law. However, the reason the existing power holders in the play were vulnerable to an overthrow in the first place was that they were using the law to oppress the powerless. The law can be either a tool of oppression or a sword of justice, with lawyers and judges as the ones who wield its power.

> ## QUOTE & **QUERY**
>
> Lawyers are upset. They have discovered what they believe to be an alarming new trend: People don't like them. . . We wish to reassure lawyers. This wave of anti-lawyer feeling is nothing new. People have always hated you.
> *Source: Roth and Roth, 1989: i.*
>
> **?** This passage is humorous, but the underlying problem is not. Why do people have such low opinions of lawyers?

Law and the Legal Professional

Historically, a large percentage of elected officials have been lawyers, and 25 of 45 presidents have been lawyers. Our nation's leaders and historical heroes have just as likely been lawyers (Abraham Lincoln, for example) as military generals, and our nation's consciousness is permeated with the belief in law and legal vindication. However, it seems that the percentage of attorneys in Congress is declining. In the 1800s, lawyers made up about 80 percent of Congress; but by 2016, they comprised less than 40 percent (Swenson, 2016).

The perception of the lawyer as an amoral "hired gun" is in sharp contrast to the ideal of the lawyer as an officer of the court, sworn to uphold the ideals of justice declared sacrosanct under our system of law. The public tends to agree with a stereotype of lawyers as amoral, motivated by money, and with no conscience or concern for morality. From ancient times, the ethics of those associated with the legal process has been suspect. Plato and Aristotle condemned advocates because of their ability to make the truth appear false and the guilty appear innocent. This early distrust continued throughout history. Early colonial lawyers were distrusted and even punished for practicing law. For many years, lawyers could not charge a fee for their services because the mercenary aspect of the profession was condemned (Papke, 1986). Gradually, lawyers and the profession itself were accepted, but suspicion and controversy continued over fees and qualifications. Partly to counteract public antipathy, lawyers formed their own organization, the American Bar Association (ABA), in 1878. Shortly afterward, this professional organization established the first ethical guidelines for lawyers; these became the Model Code of Professional Responsibility, discussed later in this chapter.

Apparently, even lawyers don't think much of their profession. A *National Law Journal* study found that over 50 percent of lawyers described their colleagues as "obnoxious" (reported in Kreiger, 2009: 882). In one study of 6,200 attorneys across four states, lawyers with the highest incomes weren't as happy as lawyers working in public service jobs for substantially lower pay. Least happy were general practice, family law, and private criminal defense attorneys (Weiss, 2014). In a 2006 poll, about 55 percent of attorneys were satisfied with their career, and only 44 percent of all lawyers would recommend it as a career (S. Ward, 2007).

The ideal of the justice system is that two advocates of equal ability will engage in a pursuit of truth, guided by a neutral judge. The truth is supposed to emerge from the contest. Actual practices in our justice system may be quite different. Does the "best" opponent always win? If a powerful and rich defendant can hire the best criminal lawyer in the country, complete with several assistants and investigators, the prosecutor (who is typically overworked and understaffed) may be overwhelmed. Of course, this is the exception. More commonly a defendant must rely on an overworked and probably inexperienced public defender or an attorney who can make criminal law profitable only by high caseloads and quick turnover.

Indigent Defense

In *Gideon v. Wainwright*, 372 U.S. 335, 1963, the Supreme Court held that the Sixth Amendment guarantees that indigent (poor) criminal defendants receive legal representation. It is estimated that in recent years, about 80 percent of all criminal defendants utilize publicly funded attorneys because of indigency. Jurisdictions use either public defender offices or court-appointed attorneys (private attorneys who receive individual cases from the court and maintain their own private practice), or a combination of the two. About 22 states administer and fund at the state level; 18 rely primarily on county funding; the remaining states have some hybrid system (Mariano, 2015).

The system of indigent defense in this country is extremely underfunded (Breitenbach, 2016; Lefstein, 2011; Pfaff, 2016). In one study of how states spent their Byrne Justice Assistant Grant funds from the Department of Justice, it was found that in fiscal year 2009, $20.8 million went toward prosecution, and only $3.1 million went to public defense. A total of $1.2 billion was allocated for all programs, meaning that the public defense allocation amounted to roughly one-quarter of 1 percent (Mariano, 2015). It is reported that real spending on indigent defense has fallen by 2 percent, even while the number of felony cases has risen by approximately 40 percent (Pfaff, 2016).

Some states even charge for public defenders. South Dakota evidently charges defendants $92 per hour for the public defender, even though they are eligible only if found to be indigent. Their failure to pay these charges and other court costs often lands them back in jail, where it costs the state $94 a night to house them. South Dakota has announced that it will suspend the driver's licenses of people who cannot pay. As of July 2016, 31,638 people owed the state more than $16 million in judicial system fines and restitution (Breitenbach, 2016).

Several private and public advocacy groups (e.g., Sixth Amendment Center, Brennan Center, The Constitution Project, the Gideon at 50 Project, the American Bar Association, and the National Association of Criminal Defense Attorneys) have brought attention to the fact that indigent legal aid is so overburdened that representation likely falls below Constitutional requirements. Studies show that standards for defense indicate caseloads should be no more than 150 felonies per year, but in some jurisdictions, public defenders carry at least twice that number (Lefstein, 2011; Mariano, 2015). The problem of indigent defense exists in immigration law as well. A study by Cardozo Law School's Immigration Justice Clinic found that 33 percent of cases in deportation hearings received inadequate legal assistance (Markowitz, 2011).

Research, unfortunately, supports the proposition that those who can afford private retained attorneys receive "better" representation as measured by conviction and length of sentence (Cohen, 2011; Martinez and Pollock, 2008). It appears that court-appointed attorneys may be the worst option, with at least one study showing they cost more than public defenders, took longer to resolve cases, and obtained worse results for clients, including sentences that were, on average, eight months longer (Liptak, 2007). Eldred (2013) reports that cognitive biases operate to make public defenders unaware that they provide a lower level of representation than indigent clients deserve. The argument is that with such high caseloads, attorneys are incapable of investigating, conducting legal research, and doing the proper amount of preparation for each case, then psychological mechanisms reduce the stress that would be created if the attorney believed the defendant was not receiving an adequate defense. To counter that admission and resulting stress, attorneys evidently experience confirmation bias, motivated reasoning, and overconfidence bias. Confirmation bias results in the brain remembering information that fits with preconceived ideas, therefore if a public defender remembers only the pieces of evidence that lead to a belief that the defendant is guilty, it becomes easier to agree to a plea agreement. Motivated reasoning occurs when defense attorneys are forced to "triage" cases (ignoring some or giving them the least possible amount of time to save time and energy for the "winnable" ones). There is an unconscious pressure to find reasons that it is acceptable to do so (e.g., "most defendants are guilty anyway"). Finally, there is a tendency of all of us to inflate our abilities and competence. Some argue that it is ethically acceptable to triage cases because plea agreements may be favorable to defendants (Carroll, 2015), which is true, but it also is the case that many defendants become victims to an assembly line of justice with mere minutes spent with a defense attorney.

Observers also note that public defenders do not ordinarily complain about excessive caseloads because they do not want to antagonize their politician funders.

Court-appointed attorneys have an even greater motivation to keep quiet since, if they complain that they must take too many appointments to competently defend the clients to make it financially feasible, they would probably be told that other attorneys would be happy to take such appointments (Carroll, 2015).

Researchers have argued that funding public defenders adequately would cost money initially, but might reduce mass incarceration. Pfaff (2016) found that the primary source of prison growth in the 1990s and 2000s was the increased filing of felony charges that in the past would have been misdemeanor charges or no charges at all. He argues that a robust defense might keep individuals out of prison that probably shouldn't be there.

The "Criminalization of Poverty"

The Department of Justice investigation of Ferguson, Missouri's police department did not find racial discrimination in the police force, but it did find that the city's revenue was largely based on funds from petty arrests and fines, mostly from people who were already poor and most of these people were African American. There is an emerging discussion in this country about the "criminalization of poverty."

It seems that after the recession in 2008, large and small municipalities began to utilize the criminal justice system as a revenue stream. Police officers write tickets and arrest, even for minor misdemeanors, prosecutors enforce them, judges assess fines and court costs, and court personnel become debt collectors in an increasingly

IN THE NEWS | *Indigent Defense in Missouri and Louisiana*

The ACLU of Missouri and the MacArthur Justice Center has filed a class action lawsuit claiming Missouri has failed to meet its constitutional obligation to fund its public defenders. Supporting documents argue that the state should spend an additional $20 million per year and hire more than 300 additional lawyers to meet basic constitutionally adequate representation to indigent defendants. State public defenders have been pleading for years for more resources. Lack of representation has led to people being jailed because of the lack of time or resources to defend them adequately. When a Missouri Supreme Court in 2012 approved a rule permitting public defenders to decline appointments if they have overloaded caseloads for three consecutive months, the legislature passed a new law that barred the defenders' ability to refuse cases despite caseloads that made adequate representation possible. In the St. Louis County office, it is estimated that attorneys are over their capacity by 265 percent. One public defender in 2014 was assigned nearly 400 juvenile cases, prompting a Department of Justice

investigation. Since state legislators are working with a $500 million shortfall, it is unlikely that new funding will be directed in indigent defense unless a judicial order forces the state to comply.

In Louisiana, the Southern Poverty Law Center, the Lawyers' Committee for Civil Rights Under Law, and two law firms have sued the state on behalf of 13 criminal defendants, and are seeking class action status to cover all the indigent defendants accused of noncapital crimes in Louisiana, alleging that lack of funding is denying effective counsel to the poor. The lawsuit describes several defendants who have been jailed for months without ever seeing a public defender, or have seen their attorney for extremely short periods of time even though they are going to trial. Supporting documents show that the median level of funding is $238 for each case. Judges routinely appoint civil attorneys without any criminal law experience to represent people on waiting lists.

Similar lawsuits are being litigated in Florida, Michigan, Missouri, Utah, Idaho, and New York.

Sources: Bott, 2017; Santana, 2017.

mercenary approach that bears little resemblance to justice or crime control. If poor people can't pay fines, they incur even heavier financial penalties for nonpayment, which then lead to jail sentences where, in some locales, they are charged for medical care and necessities that leave them with even more debt (Mador, 2014). Even when people serve time—either in jail or in prison—they may be released with thousands of dollars owed, as well as fees for probation or parole supervision. This debt begins the cycle anew.

The Vera Institute's Manhattan Bail Project study in 1962 found that those released on personal recognizance were just as likely to return for trial as those released on bail. These findings led to The Bail Reform Act of 1966 that eliminated financial bond for most federal defendants, and to jurisdictions around the country adopting personal recognizance programs that allowed low-risk individuals to be released prior to their case being adjudicated. Personal bonds save money for taxpayers by reducing jail populations and help those charged by allowing them to continue to work and pay bills before resolving their court case. Perhaps because of the massive building boom in prisons and jails that occurred in the 1990s, these no-bond releases fell out of favor and the number of people jailed instead of released on recognizance increased. The Department of Justice estimates that local jail populations grew by 19.8 percent between 2000 and 2014 and pretrial detainees accounted for 95 percent of that growth. In mid-2014, the DOJ says 60 percent of those held in local jails were pretrial detainees—with daily costs ranging from $80 to $190 per day (Laird, 2016).

Today, advocates are once again pushing jurisdictions to consider pretrial release for low-risk individuals (Shafroth and Schwartzol, 2017). Opponents, including the American Bail Coalition, argue that pretrial release runs the risk of individuals not showing up for court dates and the use of risk assessment instruments is expensive. Opponents of pretrial release point to research that finds those who are bailed out have higher appearance rates than those who are released on personal bonds (Laird, 2016). However, more recent studies show no significant difference (Carmichael, Naufal, Wood, Caspers, and Marchbanks, 2017). The methodology for such studies is challenging because it is difficult to control for factors that might also affect the risk of absconding (Laird, 2016). The key to making effective release decisions is having accurate risk assessment tools. The Arnold Foundation has funded a risk assessment called the Public Safety Assessment (PSA) that was developed from 1.5 million court cases from 300 U.S. jurisdictions. It has nine questions that can be answered from criminal records and does not require an interview. About 29 jurisdictions were using the PSA or working on implementing it as of late 2015 (Laird, 2016). States like Kentucky, New York, New Jersey, and Maryland have already begun to reduce the practice of using bail and increased their personal recognizance releases. In other states, there have been lawsuits by public interest lawyers against sheriffs, district attorneys, and county officials for assessing bail with no regard for people's ability to pay. Interestingly, in some locales sheriffs and prosecutors are on the side of those advocating pretrial release rather than bail (Hardy, 2017; Laird, 2016).

It appears that some jurisdictions have decided to charge even people who have charges dropped. In Ramsey County, Minnesota, even when someone is arrested and then is released with charges dropped, they are charged a "booking fee." Also, the money that might have been in their pocket at the time is returned to the individual on a debit card, but that card has an array of fees so that only a portion of the person's money can be retrieved (Liptak, 2016).

🗨 IN THE NEWS | *Challenging Bail*

In Harris County, Texas, when a federal lawsuit was filed alleging that bail practices punished poor people by keeping them locked up despite their low risk of absconding, the sheriff, a judge, and the district attorney testified against themselves. Sheriff Ed Gonzalez testified that most of the people in his jail were poor and disproportionately black or Hispanic, agreeing that it was not a rational system. In San Francisco, the city attorney and state attorney general refused to defend themselves against a similar lawsuit.

Advocates are zeroing in on petty offenders with misdemeanor charges who do not pose a risk to the public, face minor punishments, and cannot pay even modest $500 or less bail amounts. It was reported that if defendants such as these had been released on their own recognizance, Harris County, Texas could have saved

$20 million over six years. Instead, hearing examiners are imposing $5,000 bonds on homeless people who were arrested for sleeping under an overpass.

Even though Texas law requires consideration of the ability to pay, the reality seems to be that bail is set based on a schedule of the crime and criminal history of the offender. At a bond hearing, the examiner can raise or lower the bond or issue a personal bond instead, but the defendant does not typically have an attorney to advocate for him. The county had already begun making changes even before the lawsuit, providing public defenders at bond hearings, and developing a guideline whereby examiners should utilize personal bonds for 12 low-level misdemeanors. A risk assessment instrument was also being considered for adoption. County attorneys argue that the lawsuit threatens these innovations.

Source: Hardy, 2017.

Across the country it appears that municipalities and counties are inventing new ways of raising revenue from individuals enmeshed in the criminal justice system. In Colorado, five towns raised more than 30 percent of revenue from traffic tickets and fines. Also, in Colorado, several individuals sued to have the money they paid for court costs, fines, and restitution returned after they were acquitted of crimes. Lower courts decided that individuals could petition the state's exoneration board to have the funds returned. The Supreme Court of the United States, in *Nelson v. Colorado*, No. 15-1256, April 19, 2017, ruled that this practice was a violation of due process and held that keeping money that was based on an invalidated conviction was a violation of the U.S. Constitution. This case provides a strong precedent for those lawsuits against booking fees and other costs assessed against individuals who are later not charged or acquitted.

An extremely pervasive issue across the country seems to be poor people being jailed for nonpayment of court costs and fines. The problem with this is that it is unconstitutional to have what is, in effect, debtor's prisons/jails. The Supreme Court, in *Tate v. Short*, 401 U.S. 395, 1971 and *Bearden v. Georgia*, 461 U.S. 660, 1983, ruled that individuals cannot be jailed for not paying fines or court costs unless there is a determination that there is an ability to pay and the nonpayment was willful. Yet in one journalist's investigation, some lower-level court judges in Texas were ignorant of the illegality of imposing days in jail for fee amounts that indigents could not pay. Some magistrates had no idea that they were supposed to hold indigency hearings to determine if the individual had the means to pay despite it being spelled out in an instruction manual for judges. In at least nine courts, there was no documentation that any poverty hearings were ever held, clearly it was an unlikely proposition that everyone in that jurisdiction had the ability to pay. In El Paso, fines for traffic and other low-level offenses brought in more than $11 million each year, about 4 percent of the city's total revenue (Taggart, 2015).

In several news articles and studies, examples are given of individuals who receive a traffic fine of several hundred dollars and, because of late charges and surcharges, end up owing more than the original fine several years later. In some cases, they are sent to jail which removes the fine, but they still owe the court fees and surcharges. States can suspend drivers' licenses for nonpayment of court fines and that makes it impossible to keep or find a job (Laird, 2016; Taggart, 2015).

In March of 2016, officials at the Justice Department wrote a letter to courts in all 50 states warning them that jailing individuals for nonpayment could run afoul of the law (Hsu, 2016). Lawsuits around the country are challenging bail practices and the practice of jailing for nonpayment of court fines and fees (Shapiro, 2015). Jennings, Missouri, a town near Ferguson, agreed to pay $4.7 million to an estimated 2,000 mostly poor, black residents in a settlement of a class action lawsuit. The recipients had been jailed for unpaid court fines and charges, many of them for minor offenses such as traffic tickets. Plaintiff attorneys reported to the press that there were 90 surrounding cities that had the same practices that must be changed either by legislation or by lawsuits. It has been reported that some jurisdictions receive more revenue from traffic court fees and fines than from sales or property taxes (Hsu, 2016).

Things are beginning to change. In 2015, California instituted an amnesty program for drivers with lesser infractions, allowing them to pay 50 or 80 percent of what they owe, depending on their income. The program was instituted because of civil rights advocates objecting to spiraling costs for traffic violators due to increased fines and draconian late charges. Traffic fines have increased to fill the budget cuts brought on by the recession; for instance, the fine for running a red light was $103 20 years ago, but $490 today with add-on fees. If a person doesn't pay, the costs can jump to over $800 (Harbison, 2015). After the DOJ investigation of Ferguson, Missouri, there were major changes in how the city utilized fines to bolster the budget. The courts in St. Louis County collectively took in $53 million in fines and fees in the year that ended June 2014, but that amount dropped to just $29 million in the year ending June 2016. There was a 42 percent decrease of traffic cases. In Ferguson, traffic cases dropped by 85 percent. The jail is almost empty because people are being released on their own recognizance without having to post bail. In Ferguson, only $579,000 was raised through the municipal court in 2016 compared to over $2 million two years ago. Neighboring Missouri towns have had similar dramatic declines in the amount of money brought in by their municipal courts (Kohler, 2017).

The National Task Force on Fines, Fees, and Bail Practices has now released guidelines to help judges determine when they should assess fines and when they should not. Recall that some judges did not know that they could not jail people who did not pay their fines unless they had the ability to pay and chose not to. Judges could not tell individuals to get their relatives to pay their court costs and fines or they would be jailed. Judges evidently did not have any guidelines in some locales for determining who was too poor to pay. A "bench card"—a clear set of instructions—has been developed and distributed to state judges across the country. The two-page set of guidelines provides standards to determine who falls below the poverty line, and how to come up with alternative sanctions, like reducing a fine, extending the time to pay it, or requiring community service. The chief justice of the Supreme Court of Ohio and other judges, attorneys, and advocates from around the country served on the Task Force (Shapiro, 2017).

The dangerous reality is that when fees from offenders are necessary to fund city services and the various criminal justice components, there is no incentive to reduce crime, rather the system benefits by creating criminals to perpetuate a revenue stream (Robertson, 2015).

Courtroom Workgroups

Blumberg (1969) and Scheingold (1984) refer to the practice of criminal law as a *confidence game* because the prosecutor and the defense attorney conspire to appear as something they are not—adversaries in a do-or-die situation. What is more commonly the case is that the prosecutor and the defense attorney will still be working together when the client is gone. Attorneys may display adversarial performances in the courtroom, but the "show" lasts only if the jury is in the room, and sometimes not even then. Defense attorneys, prosecutors, and judges work together every day and often socialize together; they may even be married to each other. Many defense attorneys are ex-prosecutors. In some respects, this is helpful to their clients because the defense attorneys know how the prosecutor's office works and what a reasonable plea offer would be. But one must also assume that the prosecutorial experience of these attorneys has shaped their perceptions of clients and what would be considered fair punishment.

bureaucratic justice The approach in which each case is treated as one of many; the actors merely follow the rules and walk through the steps, and the goal is efficiency.

Another perspective describes our courts as administering **bureaucratic justice**. Each case is only one of many for the professionals who work in the system, and the actors merely follow the rules and walk through the steps. The goal of the system—namely, bureaucratic efficiency—becomes more important than the original goal of justice. Also, because each case is part of a workload, decision making takes on more complications. For instance, a defense lawyer may be less inclined to fight hard for a "loser" client if the lawyer wants a favor for another client later in the week. The prosecutor may decide not to charge a guilty person to get him or her to testify against someone else. In this sense, each case is not tried and judged separately, but is linked to other cases and processed as part of a workload.

The bureaucratic system of justice involves procedures and policies that, although not intentionally discriminatory, may contribute to a perception of unfairness. For instance, a major element in bureaucratic justice is the presumption of guilt, whereas the ideal of our justice system is a presumption of innocence. District attorneys, judges, and even defense attorneys approach each case presuming guilt and place a priority on achieving the most expeditious resolution of the case. This is the basic rationale behind plea bargaining, whether it is recognized or not: the defendant is presumed to be guilty, and the negotiation is to achieve a guilty plea while bargaining for the best possible sentence. The lowest possible sentence is the goal of the defense, whereas the highest possible sentence is the goal of the prosecutor. Plea bargaining is consistent with the bureaucratic justice system because it is the most efficient way of getting maximum punishment with minimum work.

wedding-cake illustration The model of justice in which the largest portion of criminal cases forms the bottom layers of the cake and the few "serious" cases form the top layer; the bottom-layer cases get minimal due process.

One other perception of the criminal justice system is that of Samuel Walker's (1985/2005) **wedding-cake illustration**, based on a model proposed by Lawrence Friedman and Robert Percival. In this scheme, the largest portion of criminal cases forms the bottom layers of the cake and the few "serious" cases form the top layer. The top layer is represented most dramatically by cases such as the murder trials of O. J. Simpson and Casey Anthony, or the criminal trial of Bernard Madoff. In these highly publicized cases, defense attorneys are extremely skilled (and highly paid). They employ trial consultants, investigators, and public relations specialists. Prosecutors match these resources. However, the bottom of the cake is represented by the tens of thousands of cases that are processed every year in which defendants may meet with an attorney only once or twice for a few minutes immediately before agreeing to a plea arrangement.

Because the public is exposed only to the top of the wedding cake, people develop a highly distorted perception of the system. The U.S. public may be disgusted with the multitude of evidentiary rules and the Byzantine process of the trial itself. However, these concerns are valid for only a very small portion of criminal cases. In most cases, there is no trial at all and the process is an assembly line. What happens to individuals is largely determined by the courtroom work group (composed of all the actors in the court process, including defense attorneys, prosecutors, and judges).

The courtroom work group shares definitions of seriousness and operates as a unit to keep the dynamics of the courtroom static despite changes that are forced upon it. Changes in the justice system that have occurred over time, such as the exclusionary rule and determinate sentencing, have had surprisingly little impact on court outcomes because of a shared perception of serious crime and appropriate punishment. Most crime is considered trivial, and the processing of these cases involves little energy or attention from system actors (Walker, 1985/2005).

Dershowitz's view of the criminal justice system, as displayed in the Quote and Query box, is obviously (as Dershowitz admits) an exaggeration, but he does touch on some aspects of the system that many people agree with, such as a widespread perception of guilt and a general view that case processing is routine for everyone except the individual at risk of conviction. The major ethical problem with this view (if it does represent reality) is that innocence, truth, and due process are perceived as inconvenient and expendable.

QUOTE & QUERY

Alan Dershowitz, a well-known defense attorney and law professor, presents the "rules" of the courtroom:

Rule I: Almost all criminal defendants are, in fact, guilty.

Rule II: All criminal defense lawyers, prosecutors, and judges understand and believe Rule I.

Rule III: It is easier to convict guilty defendants by violating the Constitution than by complying with it, and in some cases it is impossible to convict guilty defendants without violating the Constitution.

Rule IV: Almost all police lie about whether they violated the Constitution in order to convict guilty defendants.

Rule V: All prosecutors, judges, and defense attorneys are aware of Rule IV.

Rule VI: Many prosecutors implicitly encourage police to lie about whether they violated the Constitution in order to convict guilty defendants.

Rule VII: All judges are aware of Rule VI.

Rule VIII: Most trial judges pretend to believe police officers whom they know are lying.

Rule IX: All appellate judges are aware of Rule VIII, yet many pretend to believe the trial judges who pretend to believe the lying police officers.

Rule X: Most judges disbelieve defendants about whether their constitutional rights have been violated, even if they are telling the truth.

Rule XI: Most judges and prosecutors would not knowingly convict a defendant whom they believe to be innocent of the crime charged (or a closely related crime).

Rule XII: Rule XI does not apply to members of organized crime, drug dealers, career criminals, or potential informers.

Rule XIII: Nobody really wants justice.

Source: Dershowitz, 1982: xxi.

 Do you believe this is more accurate than the idealized vision of the adversarial system of justice?

Legal Agent or Moral Agent?

Many lawyers believe that loyalty to the client is paramount to their duties as a professional. This loyalty surpasses and eclipses individual and private decision making, and the special relationship said to exist between lawyer and client justifies decisions that otherwise might be deemed morally unacceptable. Others argue that an attorney must never abandon his or her own moral compass and if the client desires some action that the attorney would not countenance, ethics demand that he or she convince the client not to do so or withdraw. Historians indicate that this dilemma has been problematic for lawyers since the first ethics codes were written. In writings in the 1800s, lawyers were admonished not to "plate sin with gold," (defend a wrong action by finding a legal justification for it), but others wrote that "a lawyer is not accountable for the moral character of the cause he prosecutes, but only for the manner in which he conducts it" (reported in Ariens, 2008: 364, 367).

The conundrum of what to do when a client wants you to commit some act contrary to good conscience occurs in both civil and criminal law. The following are the types of positions described and defended:

- *Legal agent.* One position is that the attorney is no more than the legal agent of the client. The lawyer is neither immoral nor moral, but merely a legal tool. This position is represented by the statement, "I am a lawyer, first and foremost."

- *Special relationship.* A more moderate position is that the loyalty to the client presents a special relationship between client and lawyer, like that between mother and child or with a trusted friend. This protected relationship justifies fewer actions than the legal agent relationship. The lawyer is expected to dissuade the client from taking unethical or immoral actions, but loyalty would preclude absolutely going against the client's wishes.

- *Moral agent.* The third position is that the lawyer is a moral agent who must adhere to his or her own moral code. The client's interests come first only if they do not conflict with the lawyer's morality and ethical code. If there is a conflict, the lawyer follows his or her conscience.

Shaffer and Cochran (2007) offer a slightly different typology, describing the *godfather* (promotes clients' interests above all others), the *hired gun* (does whatever the client wants), the *guru* (controls the client with his own moral compass as guide), and the *friend* (engages the client in moral dialogue and tries to convince the client of a proper course of action and refuses only after the client insists). The hired gun and guru are like the legal agent and moral agent roles described earlier.

Some critics of the legal agent approach reject perspectives that discount the lawyer's responsibility as an individual to make his or her own moral decisions. In this view, lawyers should be the legal *and* moral agents of their clients rather than merely legal agents (Postema, 1986). This position is represented by the statement, "I am a person first, a lawyer second." The argument is that one cannot be virtuous when pursuing a client's evil objectives (Cohen, 1991).

Cohen (1991: 135–136) suggests some principles for attorneys to follow to be considered moral:

- Treat others as ends in themselves and not as mere means to winning cases.
- Treat clients and other professional relations who are relatively similar in a similar fashion.
- Do not deliberately engage in behavior that is apt to deceive the court as to the truth.
- Be willing, if necessary, to make reasonable personal sacrifices—of time, money, popularity, and so on—for what you justifiably believe to be a morally good cause.

- Do not give money to, or accept money from, clients for wrongful purposes or in wrongful amounts.
- Avoid harming others in the process of representing your client.
- Be loyal to your clients, and do not betray their confidences.
- Make your own moral decisions to the best of your ability, and act consistently upon them.

The rationale for these principles seems to be an amalgamation of ethical formalism, utilitarianism, and ethics of care in that a lawyer should be concerned when the other side may be victimized or harmed by the actions of one's client (Cohen, 2002; Vogelstein, 2003). Some of the principles may seem impossible to uphold and may be subject to bitter criticism, especially on the part of practicing civil attorneys. For instance, how does one avoid harming the other side in a civil dispute when compromise is impossible and one side will be a winner and the other the loser?

The legal agent position is that it is impossible and unethical to substitute one's own moral code for one's clients (Memory and Rose, 2002). This position would point to rules already in place to prevent unscrupulous acts, for example, the Model Rules of Professional Conduct. Arguably, decisions regarding justice and morality are so subjective that it is unnecessary and unwise to substitute a lawyer's morals for the client's (Memory and Rose, 2002). The only thing that would be accomplished would be the loss of clients' trust in lawyers.

In general, Cohen (1991) and Memory and Rose (2002) seem to agree that the Model Rules should prevent the most egregious misconduct of lawyers. Their disagreement comes from the value they place on rules versus individual responsibility for more ambiguous moral judgments. In the legal profession, the noble cause is winning a case (at all costs). In a culture that supports "ends" thinking (winning) over "means," rules are no more likely to control misconduct by lawyers than they do some police officers.

Research indicates that the position taken by attorneys depends partially on whom they represent. On the one hand, public defenders take a more authoritarian role and seem to support the attorney as a "guru" or moral agent who tells the client what to do; attorneys for corporations, on the other hand, are apt to follow a more client-centered, legal agent approach (Mather, 2003).

It should be noted that the Model Rules do show glimmers of the moral agent idea. For instance, Model Rule 2.1 states that "a lawyer may refer not only to law but to other considerations such as moral, economic, social, and political factors" in making decisions. This indicates that the rules do encourage attorneys to look to the ethical systems to resolve problems. Again, though, the rules are not much help when the client and the attorney strongly disagree over what is the right thing to do.

QUOTE & QUERY

About half the practice of a decent lawyer consists in telling would-be clients that they are damned fools and should stop.

Source: Reported in Glendon, 1994: 76.

You're an attorney. It's your duty to lie, conceal and distort everything, and slander everybody.

Source: Giradeaux, 1949: Act Two.

? Which of these statements represents a legal agent statement? Which represents a moral agent statement?

Ethics for Legal Professionals

Formal ethical standards for lawyers and judges were originally promulgated by the American Bar Association in the *Model Code of Professional Responsibility*. The original canons, adapted from the Alabama Bar Association Code of 1887, were adopted by the ABA in 1908 and have been revised frequently since then. In 1983, the ABA switched its endorsement of the Model Code as the general guide for ethical behavior to the *Model Rules of Professional Conduct*. The Model Rules continue to be revised periodically, responding to changing sensibilities and emerging issues. Today's Model Rules cover many aspects of the lawyer's profession, including areas such as client–lawyer relationships, the lawyer as counselor, the lawyer as advocate, transactions with others, public service, and maintaining the integrity of the profession (ABA, 2015a).

The rules require that attorneys zealously protect and pursue a client's interest within the boundaries of the rules while maintaining a professional and civil demeanor toward everyone involved in the legal process. Critics charge that the rules have replaced earlier ethical codes that expressed ethical norms based on a moral tradition with regulatory, some might say, picayune prohibitions (Ariens, 2008). Others argue that by placing pure client interest ahead of a transcendent professional ethos, lawyers have lost the meaning and value that used to be associated with the practice of law, and this lack of professional purpose undercuts public confidence and is the cause of a "cycle of cynicism" (Kreiger, 2009).

Section 1 of the rules is titled "Client–Lawyer Relationship." This section offers rules that require the attorney maintain a level of competence in his or her field and not take cases that are beyond his or her expertise. Rules in this section also govern the relative power between the attorney and the client—in other words, who should make decisions regarding the legal strategy to pursue the client's interest. The rules mandate that attorneys, once they take a case, practice due diligence, communicate with their client, and assess appropriate fees. One rule demands attorneys maintain confidentiality regarding information obtained in their representation of a client. We will discuss client confidentiality more fully in Chapter 9. There are also rules that guide the attorney when there are conflicts of interest, such as the attorney should not have two clients who have competing interests or take on clients whose interests may conflict with the attorney's interests. These protections extend to former clients as well.

Section 2 offers rules concerning the lawyer's role as counselor, and Section 3 covers those situations where the attorney is pursuing the client's interest as an advocate. The Model Rules require that the attorney only pursue legitimate claims (Rule 3.1), and not engage in needless delays (Rule 3.2). Further, the attorney has an ethical obligation of "Candor Toward the Tribunal" (Rule 3.3), which means, for instance, that when presenting a legal argument, the attorney must present opposing case law as well. There are additional rules that cover fairness, decorum, trial publicity, and when the lawyer is a witness.

The Model Rules have been written for all attorneys and, thus, most of them are not directly relevant to criminal defense or prosecutors. However, Rule 3.8, "Special Responsibilities of a Prosecutor," is directed to the prosecutor. Two provisions were added to the rule which put an affirmative duty on the prosecutor to do something when there is reason to believe a wrongful conviction has occurred (Mulhausen, 2010; Saltzburg, 2008):

(g) When a prosecutor knows of new, credible, and material evidence creating a reasonable likelihood that a convicted defendant did not commit an offense of which the defendant was convicted, the prosecutor shall: (1) promptly disclose that evidence to an appropriate court or authority, and (2) if the conviction was obtained in the prosecutor's jurisdiction, (a) promptly disclose that evidence to the defendant unless a court authorizes delay, and (b) undertake further investigation, or make reasonable efforts to cause an investigation, to determine whether the defendant was convicted of an offense that the defendant did not commit.

(h) When a prosecutor knows of clear and convincing evidence establishing that a defendant in the prosecutor's jurisdiction was convicted of an offense that the defendant did not commit, the prosecutor shall seek to remedy the conviction.

These provisions were in response to the growing number of cases where innocent people have been released from prison after being exonerated. New York was the first state to revise its state ethics rules to assign these duties to prosecutors. The ABA adopted the rule in 2008, but few states have done so. Only state bar rules have the force of law and most states have not adopted this rule.

In other instances, prosecutors get exemptions from rules other attorneys must follow. For instance, Model Rule 3.4(b) states that "[a] lawyer shall not . . . offer an inducement to a witness"; however, prosecutors pay informants and reduce sentences in return for testimony. Model Rule 4.2 states that a lawyer shouldn't communicate with an opposing party unless his or her lawyer is present, yet defendants are often contacted by investigators working for the prosecutor, at least during the investigatory stage of the prosecution. Finally, ethics rules prohibit attorneys from using deceit yet prosecutors routinely are involved at the stage of investigation where detectives utilize deceit in interrogations and have even participated. A few state ethics rules expressly allow all lawyers to utilize investigatory deceit, but this is highly controversial (Joy and McMunigal, 2016).

Another section of the Model Rules is titled "Transactions with Persons Other than Clients." In this section, rules require the lawyer to maintain truthfulness in statements to others, and not communicate with opposing parties except through their attorneys. Other rules cover practices concerning unrepresented persons and the rights of third persons. In a section that covers how law firms should operate, there are many rules concerning the relationships between attorneys in firms, between firms, and with other non-lawyer associates. One rule, for instance, bars attorneys from using "runners;" these non-attorneys find cases by following up on accidents or finding victims of torts or defective merchandise and then refer them to the attorney.

The section on public service mandates that lawyers provide some *pro bono* (free) legal service, and otherwise contribute to the legal community and society in general. It also cautions against acting against clients' interests in one's activities in public service. Another section covers how the attorney may advertise and communicate with prospective clients. There are also rules about how to advertise specialties or being board certified. Section 8 is titled "Maintaining the Integrity of the Profession" and covers bar admission and discipline. Rule 8.2 is directed specifically to "Judicial and Legal Officials." Rule 8.3 dictates that attorneys have an ethical obligation to report professional misconduct. Rule 8.4 more specifically details misconduct, and the final rule covers the authority to enact discipline (Martyn, Fox, and Wendel, 2008).

In addition to the Model Rules, there is also the American Law Institute's Restatement of the Law Governing Lawyers (Martyn, Fox, and Wendel, 2008). Developed in 2000, the Restatement provides guidelines and commentary covering most of the same issues that the Model Rules cover. Some of the sections of the Restatement are the following:

- Admission to Practice Law
- A Lawyer's Duty of Supervision
- A Lawyer's Duties to a Prospective Client
- Client–Lawyer Contracts

- Duty of Care to a Client
- A Lawyer's Duty to Safeguard Confidential Client Information
- Using or Disclosing Information to Prevent Death or Serious Bodily Harm
- Client Crime or Fraud
- Falsifying or Destroying Evidence

The Restatement has eight chapters and 135 different sections. Note that the ABA and American Legal Institute (ALI) promulgate these ethical codes, but state bar associations must adopt them to have any effect. It is the state bar associations (and the federal bar) that have the power to discipline attorneys, the most serious punishment being disbarment. Finally, it should be noted that the Model Rules and the Restatement cover the practice of law generally; thus, most of the commentary and elements relate to civil practice. Because our discussion focuses exclusively on criminal defense attorneys, prosecutors, and criminal court judges, we will be referring to the *ABA Criminal Justice Standards*, as developed by the American Bar Association in 1991–1992 and recently revised (ABA, 2015b). These standards offer guidelines and commentary directed specifically to the practice of criminal law. Ethical issues in criminal law may involve courtroom behavior, perjury, conflicts of interest, use of the media, investigation efforts, use of immunity, discovery and the sharing of evidence, relationships with opposing attorneys, and plea bargaining.

Standards relating to ethical obligations of defense attorneys appear in Chapter 4, "The Defense Function" and cover a multitude of issues, such as these:

- Function of defense counsel
- Punctuality
- Public statements
- Duty to the administration of justice
- Access and the lawyer–client relationship
- Duty to investigate
- Control and direction of litigation
- Plea bargaining
- Trial conduct
- Appeal

Chapter 3 of the *ABA Criminal Justice Standards* covers the prosecution function. There are also *National Prosecution Standards* promulgated by the National District Attorneys Association. Recall that Model Rule 3.8, described in preceding paragraphs, also covers the duties of a prosecutor. Ethical guidelines for prosecutors make special note of the unique role of the prosecutor as a representative of the court system and the state. Some of the sections of the *ABA Standards for Prosecutors* cover:

- Working with police and other law enforcement agents
- Working with victims, potential witnesses, and targets
- Contact with the public
- The decision to initiate or to continue an investigation
- Selecting investigative techniques

- Use of undercover law enforcement agents and undercover operations
- Use of the investigative powers of the grand jury
- The prosecutor's role in addressing suspected law enforcement misconduct
- The prosecutor's role in addressing suspected judicial misconduct
- Illegally obtained evidence
- Responding to political pressure

These standards for legal professionals in the criminal justice system are much more specific than the Law Enforcement Code of Ethics. Instead of being aspirational, the standards are specific guidelines for behavior.

Ethical Guidelines for Judges

To help guide judges in their duties, the *Model Code of Judicial Conduct* was developed by the ABA (see: https://www.americanbar.org/groups/professional_responsibility /publications/model_code_of_judicial_conduct.html). The latest revision was in 2010. This code identifies the ethical considerations unique to judges. It is organized into four canons, which are overriding principles of ethical behavior, and under each canon there are more specific rules. The four canons of the code are as follows (ABA, 2017):

1. A judge shall uphold and promote the independence, integrity, and impartiality of the judiciary, and shall avoid impropriety and the appearance of impropriety.
2. A judge shall perform the duties of judicial office impartially, competently, and diligently.
3. A judge shall conduct the judge's personal and extra judicial activities to minimize the risk of conflict with the obligations of judicial office.
4. A judge or candidate for judicial office shall not engage in political or campaign activity that is inconsistent with the independence, integrity, or impartiality of the judiciary.

The primary theme of judicial ethics is impartiality. We must be confident that the judge's objectivity isn't marred by any type of bias. Judges should not let their personal prejudices influence their decisions. To avoid this possibility, the ABA's code specifies that each judge should try to avoid all appearance of bias as well as actual bias. To this end, the rules prohibit a judge from engaging in speeches or activities that indicate bias. Such ethical rules, however, cannot impinge on the right of free speech. In *Minnesota v. White,* 536 U.S. 765, 2002, the Supreme Court held that Minnesota's rule prohibiting judges from making speeches violated the First Amendment.

We expect judges, like police officers and prosecutors, to conform to higher standards of behavior than the rest of us. Therefore, any hint of scandal in their private lives also calls into question their professional ethics. Judges must be careful to avoid financial involvements that may threaten their objectivity. Of course, the elephant in the living room is that many judges are elected, thus there is a perception that those who contribute to the election campaigns receive special treatment. Almost 90 percent of voters and even 80 percent of judges believe that campaign contributions of interest groups are used to try and shape judicial opinions and 76 percent of voters and 46 percent of judges believe that contributions have at least some influence on judges' decisions (Shepherd, 2013: 1).

For state court positions, eight states use partisan elections, 14 states use nonpartisan elections, 19 states use some form of appointment or legislative selection, and in 9 states there is a mix of elections and appointments between the different levels of judgeships (National Center for State Courts, 2017).

When judges are elected, they must solicit campaign contributions. There has been recent attention to the vast sums that have flowed to judicial campaigns in recent years. Campaign financing has dramatically increased, from $83.3 million in 1990–1999 to $206.9 million in 2000–2009 (an average of $23 million per year) (Shepherd, 2013: 1). In 2011–2012, it increased to $33.7 million (Bannon, Velasco, Casey, and Reagan, 2013). Much of the money spent is "dark money," contributed by political action committees (PACs) that are not required to disclose donors. The money is used most often for "issue ads" that attack opponents. Donors may, and probably are, individuals and/or companies who have had or will have cases in front of the judges. In *Citizens United v. FEC*, 558 U.S. 310, 2010, the Supreme Court infamously held that corporations were people, or at least had the same rights as people; specifically, a First Amendment right to spend as much money as they wanted. States, since that holding, have been prohibited from limiting corporate spending on elections.

One might expect that judges who receive large campaign contributions from individuals or corporations would recuse themselves when these corporations have cases before the judge, but this does not always happen. Brent Benjamin ran for the West Virginia Supreme Court funded by $3 million from Massey Energy, a coal company. The amount far exceeded the total of all other contributions in his campaign. When an appeal of a case came before the court involving the company, he did not recuse himself, and he, along with the majority, overturned a $50 million judgment against the company. In an appeal to the U.S. Supreme Court concerning the refusal of the judge to recuse himself, the Court held that the facts of the case violated a proportionality standard to be used to determine when a single contribution to a campaign might give rise to a conflict of interest. The Supreme Court sent the case back to the West Virginia courts for rehearing and, with only one original judge sitting, the West Virginia court ruled 4 to 1 again in favor of the coal company, *Caperton v. Massey*, 129 S. Ct. 2252, 2009, which some people took to mean that the coal company was faultless and some people took to mean that the coal company had exerted financial pressure on those judges also. The Massey Coal Company was in the news again in the spring of 2010 when 29 miners died in an explosion, and a subsequent investigation showed hundreds of violations, and a pattern of ignoring safety regulations and cover-ups. A settlement agreement was reached where the new owners of the mine agreed to pay $210 million to compensate survivors and family members of the dead, institute safety measures, and pay outstanding fines (Reuters, 2011; Yost, 2010). More recently, Don Blankenship, the former CEO, was indicted by a federal grand jury in West Virginia for many charges related to lying to federal investigators, ignoring safety violations, and conspiring to cover up conditions from federal inspectors (Sullivan, 2014). In 2016, Blankenship was convicted of conspiracy to violate federal mine safety standards and sentenced to a year in prison, a year of supervised release, and a fine of $250,000. He is appealing that decision (Blinder, 2016).

There is a relationship between contributions and judicial decisions. The more campaign contributions from business justices receive, the more likely the judge decides in favor of business litigants. The relationship holds only for partisan and nonpartisan election systems, not retention election systems (Shepherd, 2013). This study examined civil business-related judicial decision making not criminal law; however, the same concerns would apply. Corporations are sometimes the subject of criminal investigations, and business executives sometimes find themselves the target of criminal investigation and prosecution. Even in local races, bias is introduced when local attorneys are the largest donors to judicial campaigns. The question as to whether judges are influenced by campaign contributions seems to have been answered, the only remaining question is to what extent in each case.

Culture and Ethics

The Model Code of Professional Responsibility dictated that lawyers should be "temperate and dignified" and "refrain from all illegal and morally reprehensible conduct." The Model Rules require that "a lawyer's conduct should conform to the requirements of the law, both in professional service to clients and in the lawyer's business and personal affairs." These prescriptions are like those found in the Law Enforcement Code of Ethics, and like law enforcement, it is the case that the real world of lawyers does not always conform to the vaunted ideals of the Model Rules.

The major subcultural pressure found in many law offices, including prosecutors' offices, that sometimes conflict with formal ethics, is the culture of winning. Patrick Fitzgerald (2009), a well-known and highly respected former U.S. attorney, in an essay concerning ethics in the prosecutor's office, identified office culture as an important component to ensure that prosecutors acted ethically. He also identified a "good" office as one that hires not just smart people, but individuals who express values conducive to public service and integrity. Too often, prosecutors feel the pressure of getting convictions rather than pursuing justice.

The other major theme in the legal subculture is the pervasive sense that all defendants are guilty and this attitude leads to cynicism and unethical behaviors on the part of both prosecutors and defense attorneys. Defense attorneys are the most important actors in preventing miscarriages of justice, yet there is pressure to cooperate with the "system" of moving individuals through rapidly and efficiently (discussed above as the bureaucratic justice system). The defense attorney may also believe in the guilt of the accused, so personal belief systems may also encourage shortcuts and less than zealous defense.

Conclusion

In this chapter, we have explored the role and justification for law, and how our paradigms affect how we see law function in society. While some view law as enforcing the will of the majority, others see law as a tool of oppression by those in power. The justification for law is primarily prevention of harm, including paternalistic laws that seek to protect individuals from themselves, and laws that enforce society's morals. The attorney and judge are the human embodiments of the law. They create the reality of how law operates. Two major issues today that shape how our legal system impacts individuals is the underfunding of indigent defense, and the related problem of how the entire system discriminates against the poor by using bail instead of personal bonds, charging high nonpayment fees and court charges, and jailing individuals for nonpayment. Rules defining ethical conduct for legal professionals come from their state bar, but the ABA has promulgated Model Rules that most state bar associations either adopt completely or adapt. Like our discussion concerning law enforcement professionals' noble-cause corruption, we note that there is a sub-culture of winning that competes with, and sometimes eclipses, the ethical standards that attorneys learn in law school. Also, the justice system has a pervasive culture that induces cynicism in those who are a part of it, with an attendant belief system that all defendants are guilty.

Chapter Review

1. **Understand the justifications for law, including protections against harm to others, offensive conduct, harm to self, and harm to societal morals.**

   The primary justification for law is the social contract—we each give up the right to do whatever we want in return for protection. John Stuart Mill advocated the "harm principle," which justified laws only when they prevented harm (i.e., assault and murder). Other justifications include preventing offensive conduct (i.e., lewd behavior and public disturbance). Another justification is to prevent harm to self. Legal paternalism refers to laws in which the state tries to protect people from their own behavior (i.e., seat belt laws and motorcycle helmet laws). Finally, laws prevent harm to societal morals (legal moralism), but these laws are often controversial because we don't all agree on right and wrong behaviors (i.e., pornography and gambling).

2. **Explain the role of law in society and the paradigms that have developed to understand how law is formed and enforced.**

   Basically, paradigms are models of how ideas relate to one another, forming a conceptual model of the world around us. In the consensus paradigm, law enforces the will of the majority, and most people agree on what should be illegal. In the conflict paradigm, law is a tool of the power holders to control the powerless. In the pluralist paradigm, law is dynamic and changeable depending on coalitions of various interest groups.

3. **Compare the idea of our criminal law system as an adversarial system to other descriptions of how the courtroom works and the relationships between the legal professionals.**

   The ideal of the justice system is that two advocates of equal ability will engage in a pursuit of truth, guided by a neutral judge. The truth is supposed to emerge from the contest. The system has also been described as a "confidence game" where the prosecutor and the defense attorney conspire to appear as adversaries when, in fact, they will still be working together when the client is gone. Another view is that of bureaucratic justice, where the goal is efficiency, not truth or justice. One other view is that of a wedding-cake model, in which a few celebrated cases receive the most attention and resources, a middle group of cases receive a moderate amount of resources, but the vast majority of cases are processed through the system with minimal energy and minimal due process.

4. **Present the controversy concerning the role of advocate as legal agent or moral agent.**

   The legal agent is a position where the attorney is no more than the legal tool of the client and does his or her bidding if it is not illegal. The moral agent approach is that the lawyer must adhere to his or her own moral code. The client's interests come first only if they do not conflict with the lawyer's morality and ethical code. A third position is that of a "special relationship" where the attorney attempts to convince the client to do what is right, but the position is not clear on what the course of action would be if the client refuses.

5. **Describe the history and source of legal ethics for attorneys and judges. Explain the types of ethical rules that exist and compare them to the subculture of winning.**

   The ABA's Model Rules of Professional Conduct provide the ethical code for attorneys, although each state must adopt them to have effect. The ABA's Model Code of Judicial Conduct provides ethical standards for judges. Once adopted by a state bar, ethical rules have the force of law in each state, and lawyers may face a range of sanctions up to disbarment for violating the rules. There is a subculture in the law that promotes putting the client's interests ahead of everything, and winning is valued over all else. Another subcultural theme in criminal law is that all defendants are guilty.

Study Questions

1. List some laws justified by legal paternalism. Provide the rationale for such laws, as well as opposing arguments. Discuss some types of laws that are justified by legal moralism. What are the major arguments for and against such laws?

2. Discuss how pluralism differs from the conflict paradigm and provide examples to support the view.

3. Describe in detail the evidence for and against the bureaucratic justice model of the system.

4. Describe the additions to Rule 3.8 for prosecutors and why they were adopted.

5. Provide some examples of the types of issues covered in Chapter 3 (for prosecutors) and Chapter 4 (for defense attorneys) of the *ABA Criminal Justice Standards*.

Writing/Discussion Exercises

1. Write an essay on (or discuss) how the conflict and consensus paradigms would interpret the following: decriminalization of marijuana for medical purposes, stem cell research, passage of hate-crime legislation, prohibiting the use of race in admissions procedures in universities and in competitions for state scholarships, and laws prohibiting racial profiling in police stops.

2. Write an essay on (or discuss) the legitimate functions of law in society. Do you agree with laws that prohibit gambling? Drinking while driving? Underage drinking? Prostitution? Liquor violations? Drugs? Helmet laws for bicycles or motorcycles? Leash laws? Seat belts? Smoking in public places? Can you think of any

paternalistic laws not mentioned above? Analyze pornography, gambling, homosexuality, and drug use under the ethical systems discussed in Chapter 2. What other laws have limited Americans' (or certain groups') freedoms? Can they be justified under any ethical rationale?

3. Write an essay on (or discuss) whether or not the justice system is simply a bureaucratic assembly line that does not promote justice as much as it simply ensures its own survival, with an emphasis on production. What should be the professional goals of the various actors in the system (judges, prosecutors, defense attorneys)?

Key Terms

bureaucratic justice
conflict paradigm
consensus paradigm
Good Samaritan laws

laws
legal moralism
legal paternalism
natural law

pluralist paradigm
positivist law
social contract theory
wedding-cake illustration

ETHICAL DILEMMAS

Situation 1
You ride a motorcycle, and you think it is much more enjoyable to ride without a helmet. You also believe that your vision and hearing are better without a helmet. Your state has just passed a helmet law, and you have already received two warnings. What will you do? What if your child were riding on the motorcycle? Do you think your position would be any different if you had any previous accidents and had been hurt?

Situation 2
You are a legislator who believes absolutely and strongly that abortion is a sin. You have polled your constituents and are surprised to find that the majority do not believe that the government should legislate the private decision of a woman to have an abortion. Should you vote your conscience or the will of your constituents?

Situation 3
You are a district attorney prosecuting a burglary case. The defendant is willing to plead guilty in return for a sentence of probation, and you believe that this is a fair punishment because your evidence may not support a conviction. However, the victims are upset and want to see the offender receive prison time. They insist that you try the case. What should you do?

Situation 4
You are a prosecutor with the unwelcome task of prosecuting a 12 year old for a particularly brutal assault. You personally believe that the child basically went along with his older brother in the assault, and you think that he should have been left in the juvenile system. However, the juvenile court judge waived him to the adult system, and the media and the victim's family are demanding that he be tried as an adult. You have to decide whether to try him for attempted murder, assault, or some lesser crime. You could deny the waiver and send the case back to juvenile court. What will you do? How do you determine your duty? Is it to the victims, to society, or to your own conscience?

Situation 5

You are a judge who believes that individuals should be allowed to choose when to die. You personally had to watch both your parents die long and agonizing deaths because your state does not have a right-to-die statute. Before you is a doctor who is being prosecuted for giving a lethal dose of morphine to a patient dying of terminal cancer. The family of the patient did not want the prosecution, most of the public is not in favor of the prosecution, but the prosecutor believes that if there is a law in place, it should be enforced. The doctor has opted for a bench trial. What would you do?

Discretion and Dilemmas in the Legal Profession

9

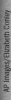

Harris County District Attorney Kim Ogg is known as one of several progressive prosecutors around the country who advocate for bail reform and de-emphasize prosecution and punishment for minor marijuana offenses.

Learning Objectives

1. Describe the ethical issues faced by defense attorneys.

2. Describe the ethical issues faced by prosecutors.

3. Describe some of the areas of forensic science that have been challenged by opponents.

4. Describe the ethical issues faced by judges.

5. Describe how federal sentencing guidelines have changed due to Supreme Court decisions.

ameron Todd Willingham was executed by the state of Texas on February 17, 2004. Many people believe he was innocent of killing his three little girls by arson in Corsicana, Texas, in 1991. His original trial was tainted, arguably, by the tunnel vision of police and fire investigators who believed that he was guilty. Fire investigators made conclusions about the fire that were not supported by the fire science at the time. For example, the testimony that pour marks were found indicating an accelerant was used was not consistent with the knowledge that hot fires had flashovers that resembled pour marks. Dr. Frederick Hurst, a fire science specialist, was instrumental in freeing Ernest Willis, who had also been on death row in Texas for a fire that killed his children because of incorrect conclusions by fire investigators at the time of his trial. Hurst also wrote a scathing report about the incorrect conclusions in the Willingham investigation. Unlike Willis, Willingham was executed (Mills, 2005).

In 2005, Texas established a commission to investigate cases where forensic science was used in criminal prosecutions. One of the first cases reviewed by the Texas Forensic Science Commission was the Willingham

258

case. In the summer of 2010, the group issued a preliminary finding that the state deputy fire marshal and assistant fire chief based their testimony on flawed science, but they also found that the men were not negligent or guilty of misconduct in any way (Lindell, 2009; Lindell and Embrey, 2009; Turner, 2010). The final report had nothing to say about Willingham's guilt or innocence, just that flawed science was used as evidence. A district court judge ruled that Willingham was innocent, but was admonished for exceeding his authority for doing so.

In Chapter 6, we described ethical dilemmas for police officers as inevitable because of the discretion inherent in the role. The same is true of legal professionals. If we accept that discretion is an operating reality in the justice system, we must ask in what ways legal professionals use this discretion. If individual value systems replace absolute rules or laws, the resulting decisions may be ethical or unethical. For instance, a judge may base a decision on hypertechnical rules, on basic fairness, or on prejudicial beliefs. There are many other situations where one's biases and prejudices may not be so easily identified. Judges' rulings on evidentiary matters are supposed to be based on rules of evidence, but sometimes there is room for interpretation and individual discretion. While most judges use this discretion appropriately and make decisions in a best effort to conform to the spirit of the evidentiary rule, other judges use arbitrary or unfair criteria, such as personal dislike of an attorney, disagreement with a rule, or a desire for one side or the other to win the case.

Although the roles and duties of a defense attorney, prosecutor, and judge are very different, what they do have in common is a great deal of discretion. As the Willingham case illustrates, it is entirely possible that the actions of the defense attorneys, prosecutors, and judges in a criminal case can set in motion events that can take the life of an innocent man.

Ethical Issues for Defense Attorneys

Due process, including notice, neutral fact finders, cross-examination, and presentation of evidence and witnesses, is supposed to minimize mistakes in judicial proceedings that might result in the deprivation of life, liberty, or property. The defense attorney is there during the important steps of the process to ensure that these rights are protected. For instance, defense attorneys present during interrogation can make sure no coercion is used, at lineups they make sure the identification is fair and unbiased, and during trial they ensure adequate cross-examination and presentation of evidence.

Many defense attorneys in private practice started out as prosecutors. This sometimes causes problems when they have trouble making the transition from "good guy battling evil" to the subtler role of defender of due process. If the attorney cannot make the transition from prosecution to defense and feel comfortable in the role, it is difficult to offer a zealous defense (R. Cohen, 2001). Some argue that the system tends to operate under a presumption of guilt. Indeed, defense attorneys are often in the position of defending clients they know are guilty. The rationale for defending a guilty person is that everyone deserves due process before a finding of guilt and punishment. If defense attorneys are doing their job, we can be more confident that justice has been served. If they are not doing their job, we have no system of justice, and none of us is safe from wrongful prosecution and the awesome power of the state to investigate, prosecute,

QUOTE & **QUERY**

"I decided that Mr. Tucker deserved to die, and I would not do anything to prevent his execution."

This statement was made by defense attorney David Smith of Greensboro, North Carolina, who accepted a capital appeal case and then admitted that he "sabotaged" the appeal of his client because he believed the man deserved execution. The attorney went through a moral crisis afterward and confessed to the state bar what he did.

Source: Rimer, 2000.

? Would you be able to defend a clearly guilty defendant? Why or why not?

and punish. In the Quote and Query box, one lawyer decided that justice demanded that he subvert the role of the defense attorney. What is the attorney's responsibility to the client when he or she knows the client is guilty of a horrible crime?

Responsibility to the Client

[A defense attorney's duty is] to serve as the accused's counselor and advocate with courage and devotion (Standard 4-1.2[b]).

The *ABA Criminal Justice Standards*, 4th edition (ABA, 2015b), will be used to highlight selected ethical issues for defense attorneys and prosecutors. In the first standard we will discuss, defense attorneys are exhorted to serve as counselor and advocate; however, they are always in the position of balancing the rights of the individual client against their overall effectiveness for all their clients. Extreme attempts to protect the rights of one person will reduce the defense attorney's ability to advocate effectively for other clients. Furthermore, defense attorneys must balance the needs and problems of the client against their ethical responsibilities to the system and the profession.

A lawyer is supposed to provide legal assistance to clients without regard for personal preference or interest. Once he or she takes a case, a lawyer is not allowed to withdraw except

- if the legal action is for harassment or malicious purposes;
- if continued employment will result in violation of a disciplinary rule;
- if discharged by a client; or
- if a mental or physical condition renders effective counsel impossible.

In other cases, a judge *may* grant permission to withdraw when the client insists on illegal or unethical actions, is uncooperative and does not follow the attorney's advice, or otherwise makes effective counsel difficult. In general, judges are loath to

▌📱 IN THE NEWS | *The Duty to Defend*

The American Civil Liberties Union (ACLU) is typically associated with liberal causes, however, the Oregon chapter encountered a strong backlash from supporters in May of 2017 because of their decision to defend an alt-right group against the Portland mayor's request to have their permit cancelled. There was concern that, in light of the tragic murder of two good Samaritans who were killed defending a woman in a hijab and her friend by a Neo-Nazi sympathizer, the risk of violence was too high.

The ACLU has a long history of defending free speech. Recall the infamous Skokie, Illinois incident in 1978 discussed in Chapter 2. The Ku Klux Klan planned to march in an area of town filled with Holocaust survivors. When the town attempted to stop them, the ACLU defended them and lost many donors because of it. In this recent decision, once again individuals have vowed to withdraw their financial support. The legal principle, however, is clear—if free speech exists, it must exist for everyone.

Source: Westneat, 2017b.

allow a defendant to proceed with a *pro se* defense (defending oneself) because of the risk that the conviction will be overturned on appeal. Nor are judges likely to allow withdrawal if it will delay ongoing proceedings. Legal ethics mandate that people with unpopular causes and individuals who are obviously guilty still deserve counsel and that it is the ethical duty of an attorney to provide such counsel.

Specialty Courts

With the rise of specialty courts (e.g., drug courts), defense attorneys, prosecutors, and judges take on quite different roles from the more typical adversary approach in regular criminal courts. There is an emphasis placed on the actors as a team, and the judge plays a much more active role, interacting with the defendant and monitoring progress. In these courts, the defense attorney appears almost redundant since the court's goal is to do what is best for the client/defendant.

In fact, Meekins (2007) argues that defense attorneys face sensitive and serious ethical challenges in such courts because they should not forget that their primary responsibility is to the client, just as in a criminal trial, even if it means objecting to and arguing against treatment options. There is a tendency for defense attorneys in such courts to persuade clients to accept treatment, even in post-adjudicative systems, where the client must plead guilty in order to obtain treatment. Once the client is in the program, the defense attorney faces issues involving communication with clients and confidentiality, because of the monitoring that such courts undertake while the client is in treatment and under supervision. Even though drug courts are set up to promote the best interest of the client, the defense attorney's role as advocate should not be sacrificed, and the individual lawyer should not forget his or her role in the desire for such courts to be successful.

Conflicts of Interest

> *Defense counsel should not permit their professional judgment . . . be adversely affected by loyalties or obligations to other . . . clients . . . or other interests or relationships (Standard 4-1.7[b]).*

This standard, along with Model Rules 1.7, 1.8, 1.10, and 1.11, covers conflicts of interest. Attorneys are supposed to avoid any conflicts of interest when defending clients. The attorney must not represent two clients who have opposing interests—for instance, codefendants in a criminal case—for one often will testify against the other. The attorney would find it impossible in such a situation to represent everyone fairly. Disciplinary rules even prohibit two lawyers in a single firm from representing clients with conflicting interests.

Although attorneys may not ethically accept clients with conflicting interests, there is no guidance on the more abstract problem that all criminal clients in a caseload have conflicting interests if their cases are looked upon as part of a workload rather than considered separately. Many defense attorneys make a living by taking cases from people with very modest means or taking court-appointed cases with the fee set by the court. The defense attorney then becomes a "fast-food lawyer," depending on volume and speed to make a profit. However, quality may get sacrificed along the way.

plea bargain
Exchange of a guilty plea for a reduced charge or sentence.

Most of the cases in the criminal justice system are settled by a **plea bargain**, an exchange of a guilty plea for a reduced charge or sentence. The defense attorney's goal in plea bargaining is to get the best possible deal for the client—probation or the shortest prison sentence that the prosecutor is willing to give for a guilty plea. The defense attorney is aware that he or she cannot aggressively push every case without endangering an ongoing relationship with the prosecutor. A courtroom appearance may be an isolated event for the client, but for the defense attorney and prosecutor it is an ongoing, weekly ritual; only the names of the defendants change. Because of the nature of the continuing relationship, the defense attorney must weigh each case against the continuing relationship with the prosecutor.

Another conflict of interest may arise if the attorney desires to represent the client's interests in selling literary or media rights. Standard 4-3.6 specifically forbids entering into such an agreement before the case is complete. The temptations are obvious: if the attorney hopes to acquire financial rewards from a share of profits, his or her professional judgment on how best to defend the client may be clouded. It is debatable whether putting off signing such an agreement until the case is complete removes the possibility of unethical decisions. The potential for biased judgments is obvious. For instance, if an attorney has a client who has committed a particularly spectacular crime, there is the potential for celebrity status only if the case comes to trial, so a plea bargain—even if it is in the best interest of the client—may be considered less carefully by the attorney. Today, it seems as if criminal cases have become the new soap operas with 24-hour news coverage and endless analysis (e.g., consider the Casey Anthony, Jodi Arias, or Steven Avery cases). In these cases, there is a tornado of media coverage and lawyers may be influenced by the celebrity that comes with being in the center of the storm. For instance, in 2016, the attorney for Jody Arias faced ethics charges for publishing a book while her case was still under appeal, but so did the prosecutor! Both wrote books about the case after Arias' conviction, but before appeals were final (Kiefer, 2016).

Zealous Defense

Defense counsel should act zealously within the bounds of the law and . . .may not, execute any directive of the client which violates the law . . .(Standard 4-1.2[d]).

Few would challenge the idea that all people deserve to have their due process rights protected. However, what many people find unsettling is the zeal with which some defense attorneys approach the courtroom contest. How diligent should the defense be in protecting the defendant's rights? A conflict may arise between providing an effective defense and maintaining professional ethics and individual morality. Lawyers should represent clients zealously within the bounds of the law, but the law is sometimes vague and difficult to determine.

Ethical standards and rules forbid some actions. The lawyer may not

- engage in motions or actions to intentionally and maliciously harm others;
- knowingly advance unwarranted claims or defenses;
- conceal or fail to disclose that which he or she is required by law to reveal;
- knowingly use perjured testimony or false evidence;
- knowingly make a false statement of law or fact;

- participate in the creation or preservation of evidence when he or she knows or it is obvious that the evidence is false;
- counsel the client in conduct that is illegal; and
- engage in other illegal conduct.

The attorney is also expected to maintain a professional and courteous relationship with the opposing attorneys, litigants, and witnesses and to refrain from disparaging statements or badgering conduct. The defense attorney must not intimidate or otherwise influence the jury or trier of fact or use the media for these same purposes.

Despite these ethical rules, practices such as withholding evidence, manufacturing evidence, witness badgering, and defamation of victims' characters are sometimes used as tactics in the defense arsenal. For instance, the practice of bringing out the sexual history of rape victims is done purely to paint her as a victim who deserved or asked for her rape. Even though rape-shield laws prohibit exposés of sexual history solely to discredit the reputation of the victim–witness, attorneys still attempt to bring in such evidence. Destroying the credibility of honest witnesses is considered good advocacy. For instance, if a witness accurately testifies to what he or she saw, a good attorney may still cast doubt in the jurors' minds by bringing out evidence of the use of eyeglasses, mistakes of judgment, and other facts that tend to obfuscate and undercut the credibility of the witness. Attorneys will do this even when they know that the witness is telling the truth. An ethical defense may include questioning the credibility of all prosecution witnesses; it is the zealousness by which it is done that defines the actions as ethical or unethical.

Most ethical conflicts arise over subtle questions of how far one should go to provide a zealous defense. It is sometimes difficult to determine when a defense attorney's treatment of a witness is badgering as opposed to energetic cross-examination, or when exploring a witness's background is character assassination as opposed to a careful examination of credibility. Some attorneys focus attacks on opposing counsel. For example, female attorneys have reported that opposing male attorneys attempt to infantilize, patronize, or sexualize them in front of the judge and jury, as a tactic to destroy their credibility. Whispering during opposing counsel's opening or closing, rolling one's eyes in response to a statement or question, or making other verbal or physical gestures indicating disbelief, amusement, or disdain are part of the arsenal of the trial attorney. They are considered by some to be fair and within the rules of the "game."

Jury Consultants

Attorneys often contend that a trial has already been won or lost once they have selected the jury. Whether this is true, attorneys are increasingly using psychologists and other experts to help them choose which members of a jury panel would make good jurors. A good juror for a defense attorney (or prosecutor) is not someone who is unbiased and fair, but rather, someone who is predisposed to be sympathetic to that attorney's case. Jury experts, through a combination of nonverbal and verbal clues, identify those jury panel members who are predisposed to believe the case presented by the attorney. Some allege that jury consultants can help to stack juries with the least sophisticated or most educated group, or any other type of group desired by the attorney.

Some lawyers survey a large sample of the population in the community where the case is to be tried to discover what certain demographic groups think about issues relevant to the case, so these findings can be used when the jury is selected. Another method uses a **shadow jury**—a panel of people selected by the defense attorney to represent the actual jury. This shadow jury sits through the trial and provides feedback to the attorney on the evidence being presented during the trial. This allows the attorney to adjust his or her trial tactics in response.

> **shadow jury**
> A panel of people selected by the defense attorney to represent the actual jury; sits through the trial and provides feedback to the attorney on the evidence presented during the trial.

Attorneys have always used intuition and less sophisticated means to decide which jury members to exclude, but the more modern tactics are questioned by some as too contrary to the basic idea that a trial is supposed to start with an unbiased jury (Smith and Meyer, 1987). Consultants also provide services such as

- preparing witnesses;
- assisting with mock trials;
- developing desirable juror profiles;
- conducting phone surveys on public attitudes about a case;
- analyzing shadow juries; and
- giving advice on effective posture, clothing choice, and tone of voice.

Can our ethical systems help determine what actions are ethically justified in defending a client zealously? Utilitarianism and egoism would probably allow a wider range of actions, depending on the interests or rewards represented by the case. Ethical formalism and religion might restrict the actions of a defense attorney to those allowed by a strict interpretation of the Model Rules. Ethics of care seems inconsistent with the advocacy role of the defense attorney since his or her role is to pursue the best interests of the client, which may come at the expense of others. Ethics of care is consistent with specialty courts and restorative justice programs where everyone's needs are considered.

Confidentiality

> *[Defense counsel has] a duty of confidentiality regarding information relevant to the client's representation . . . (Standard 4-1.3[a]).*

> **attorney–client privilege** The legal rule by which an attorney cannot disclose confidential information regarding his or her client except in a very few specified circumstances.

The **attorney–client privilege** refers to the inability of authorities to compel an attorney (through subpoena or threat of contempt) to disclose confidential information regarding his or her client. The ethical duty of confidentiality prohibits an attorney from disclosing to any person, or using for one's own gain, information about one's client obtained through the attorney–client relationship. Any attorney who breaches confidentiality may face disbarment.

Confidentiality is inherent in the fiduciary relationship between the client and the attorney, but more important is that the client must be able to expect and receive the full and complete assistance of his or her lawyer. If a client feels compelled to withhold negative and incriminatory information, he or she will not be able to receive the best defense; thus, the lawyer must be perceived as a completely confidential agent of the client. Parallels to the attorney–client relationship are relationships between husband and wife and between priest and penitent. In these cases, the relationship creates a legal entity that approximates a single interest rather than two interests, so a break in confidentiality would violate the Fifth Amendment protection against self-incrimination (Schoeman, 1982).

According to Model Rule 1.6, the only situations wherein a lawyer can ethically reveal confidences of a client are these:

- When the client consents
- When disclosure is required by law or court order
- When one needs to defend oneself or employees against an accusation of wrongful conduct
- To prevent reasonably certain death or substantial bodily harm
- To prevent the client from committing a crime or fraud that is reasonably certain to result in substantial injury to the financial interests or property of another and the lawyer's services have been used to accomplish that end
- To prevent, mitigate, or rectify substantial injury to the financial interest or property of another that is reasonably certain to result or has resulted from the client's commission of a crime or fraud when the lawyer's services have been used

One of the most debated portions has been the part of this rule that specifies what type of crime justifies divulging the confidences of a client. The Model Code (used before the Model Rules) allowed disclosure to prevent *any* crime. An earlier version of the Model Rules dictated that an attorney could ethically violate a client's confidence only to prevent a future crime involving imminent death or grievous bodily harm. Many state bar associations refused to adopt the restrictive rule or enlarged it to include any crime. The current version *requires* disclosure of financial crimes if there is substantial injury, but it also *allows* disclosure to mitigate or rectify a financial crime. The Enron and WorldCom situations, in which CEOs defrauded shareholders while their accountants and lawyers remained quiet, no doubt influenced the committee that updated this rule (Ariens, 2009).

Neither the restrictive rule nor the inclusive rule regarding disclosing a client's future crime applied to the Garrow incident (described in the Walking the Walk box), so the lawyers felt ethically bound to withhold the location of two bodies from the family of the victims. Do the ethical systems support keeping the client's confidences in a situation such as the one faced by Frank Armani when defending Robert Garrow?

It should be noted that the rule of confidentiality does not apply to physical evidence. Anything that is discoverable in the possession of a client is equally discoverable if in the possession of an attorney. Therefore, an attorney must hand over files or other incriminating evidence subject to a valid search warrant, motion, or subpoena. If the attorney is merely told where physical items may be found, he or she is not obliged to tell the authorities where they are. For instance, if a client tells an attorney that a murder weapon is in a certain location, the attorney cannot divulge that information to authorities. However, if the client drops a murder weapon in the attorney's lap, the lawyer runs the risk of being charged with a felony if it is hidden or withheld from the police. If the attorney is told where a murder weapon is and goes to check, that information is still protected; however, if the attorney takes the weapon back to his or her office or moves it in any way, then the attorney may be subjected to felony charges of obstruction of justice or evidence tampering. Belge was charged in the Garrow case because he moved the body of the victim when he went to check the location that Garrow described, although he was never convicted.

The confidentiality rule seems to be justified by utilitarianism because society benefits in the long run from the presence of attorney–client confidence. Therefore, this confidence should be sacrificed only when it endangers a life, which would be a greater loss than the benefit of client–attorney trust. Religious ethics might condemn the attorney's actions because withholding information—for instance, the location of the bodies in the Garrow case described in the Walking the Walk box—was a form of deception. In the Roman Catholic religion, however, a similar ethical dilemma might arise if someone were to confess to a priest. In that case, the priest could not betray that confession no matter what the circumstances.

WALKING THE WALK

Frank Armani may be one of the most revered, and hated, lawyers in the past century. In 1973, Armani was asked to represent Robert Garrow, accused of murder and attempted murder. Garrow, who had already served eight years in prison for rape, was identified as the man who tied up four college students and brutally stabbed one to death, although luckily the other three got away. Because of the similarity of the attacks, Garrow was also suspected of being responsible for another murder of a young man. The man's companion was missing, and authorities were desperate to either find her alive or find her body. One other young woman was also missing, and Garrow was suspected of being responsible for her disappearance as well.

Armani took the case because he had previously represented Garrow on a minor charge. Armani brought in Francis Belge, a criminal defense attorney. During their questioning of Garrow, he confessed to the murders of the two missing women and told the lawyers where the bodies were hidden. The two lawyers confirmed that the bodies were where Garrow said they were, and they even took pictures. In one location, the girl's head was 10 feet away from her torso, and Belge moved the head closer to the body before he took the picture. In the other case, the body was in an abandoned mine shaft, and the lawyers lowered each other down to take pictures.

The lawyers believed that attorney–client confidentiality prevented them from revealing the location of the bodies or even that Garrow had confessed to being involved. They did, however, imply to the district attorney that Garrow might reveal the location in a plea agreement. They were trying to get the prosecutor to agree to an insanity plea with commitment to a mental hospital. The prosecutor refused the deal, and before the case could come to trial for the first murder, the two girls' bodies were found. Garrow was the prime suspect.

In the small town where the trial was held, the two attorneys were shunned, vilified, and threatened. Both missing girls' families had pleaded with the attorneys to tell them if their daughters were alive or dead, and the families had no doubt that the attorneys knew more than they would reveal. Their suspicions became clear because after Garrow was convicted, Armani and Belge admitted in a press interview that they had known about the bodies all along.

The enraged prosecutor charged Belge with the crime of "failure to give a proper burial" and threatened both with obstruction of justice. The criminal charges were dropped, as were the state ethics charges, but both attorneys endured threats and the virtual loss of their law practices. One newspaper editorial at the time called Armani "a malignant cancer on the society that fostered him" and "less than useless to the human race." Belge left the practice of law entirely, and Armani was forced to build up his practice again after most of his clients left him. His marriage almost failed, and he flirted with alcoholism and suffered two heart attacks during the long ordeal.

When asked why he kept the murderer's secrets, Armani explained that civil rights are for the worst of us because, only then, are they there for the best of us. Eventually he was recognized for his ethical courage, but many still disagree on his stand that the client's confidentiality rights are more important than "common decency." One thing that no one can dispute, however, is that he paid a high price for his ethical principles.

Sources: Hansen, 2007: 28–29; Zitrin and Langford, 1999.

Under ethical formalism, the lawyer's actions must be such that we would be willing for all others to engage in similar behavior under like circumstances. Could one will that it become universal law for attorneys to keep such information secret? What if you were the parents in the Garrow case who did not know the whereabouts of their daughter, or even if she was alive or dead? It is hard to imagine that you would be willing to agree with this universal law. If you were the criminal, however, you would not want a lawyer to betray confidences that would hurt your case. If you were a lawyer, you would want a rule encouraging a client to be truthful so you would be able to provide an adequate defense. Ethical formalism is also concerned with duty; it is obvious that the duty of an attorney is always to protect the interests of his or her client. However, there are also larger duties of every attorney to protect the integrity of the justice system.

The ethics of care would be concerned with the needs of both the client and the parents in the Garrow case. This ethical system might support a resolution in a less absolutist fashion than the other rationales. For instance, when discussing the Garrow case in a college classroom, many students immediately decide that they would call in the location of the bodies anonymously, thereby relieving the parents' anxiety and protecting, to some extent, the confidential communication. One could make the same type of phone call in the case of the wrongfully convicted, if an attorney had evidence that could help the person prove his or her innocence. However, this compromise is unsupported by an absolute view of confidentiality because it endangers the client, but it does protect the relationship of the attorney and the client and still meets the needs of others concerned.

While the attorney–client privilege is sacrosanct, some argue that there should be some exceptions when keeping quiet harms third parties. It is quite troubling, for instance, to ponder how many people are in prison for crimes they did not commit and somewhere an attorney for the real criminal knows, but cannot do anything about it.

Duty Regarding Perjury

Defense counsel should not knowingly offer false evidence . . . (Standard 4-7.6[b])

A defense attorney's ethics may also be compromised when a client insists on taking the stand to commit perjury. Model Rule 3.3 specifically forbids the lawyer from allowing perjury to take place; if it happens before the attorney realizes the intent of the client, the defense must not use or refer to the perjured testimony (Freedman, 1986; Kleinig, 1986). The quandary is that if the attorney shows his or her disbelief or discredits the client, this behavior violates the ethical mandate of a zealous defense, and to inform the court of the perjury violates the ethical rule of confidentiality.

Pellicotti (1990) explains that an attorney should first try to dissuade the client from committing perjury. If the client persists in plans to lie, the attorney then has an ethical duty to withdraw from the case, and there is some authority that the attorney should disclose the client's plan to the court. Withdrawal is problematic because it will usually jeopardize a case, and disclosure is even more problematic because, arguably, it will affect the judgment of the hearing judge. The Supreme Court has weighed in on the dilemma by holding, in *Nix v. Whiteside*, 475 U.S. 157, 1986, that it does not violate the defendant's Sixth Amendment right to counsel for the attorney to refuse to allow the defendant to commit perjury.

Pellicotti (1990) describes the *passive* role and the *active* role of an attorney with a client who commits perjury. In the passive role, the attorney asks no questions during direct examination that would elicit untruthful answers and may make a statement that the client is taking the stand against the advice of an attorney. The attorney does not refer to perjured testimony during summation or any arguments. The active role allows for the attorney to disclose to the court the fact of the perjured testimony. There is no great weight of authority to commend either approach, leaving attorneys with a difficult ethical dilemma. The best defense of some attorneys is not to know about the lie in the first place.

If the attorney is not sure that the client would be committing perjury, there is no legal duty to disclose. The weight of authority indicates that the attorney with doubts should proceed with the testimony; any disclosure of such doubts is improper and unethical. Thus, some attorneys tell a client, "Before you say anything, I need to tell you that I cannot participate in perjury, and if I know for a fact that you plan to lie, I cannot put you on the stand," or they ask the client, "What do I need to know that is damaging to this case?" rather than ask if the client is guilty of the crime. Further, many attorneys argue that all defendants lie about everything and they can't be believed anyway. If this is true, some attorneys may conclude that since they don't know with certainty that the defendant is lying, they can allow the defendant to say anything they want on the stand.

The ethical issues for defense attorneys revolve around being an advocate for the client, while at the same time, performing as an officer of the court. Zealous defense within the bounds of the law is the primary duty of a defense attorney.

Ethical Issues for Prosecutors

Prosecutors do not serve an individual client; rather, their client is the system or society itself, and their mission is justice. On the other hand, prosecutors want to win and so they are influenced by this desire. The Quote and Query box provides some advice from Patrick Fitzgerald, an extremely well-respected former U.S. Attorney for the northern district of Illinois.

As the second line of decision makers in the system, prosecutors have extremely broad powers of discretion. The prosecutor acts like a strainer; he or she collects some cases for formal prosecution while eliminating a great many others. Prosecuting every case is impossible. Resources are limited, and sometimes evidence is weak, making it unlikely to win a conviction. Early diversion of such cases saves taxpayers money and saves individuals trouble and expense.

QUOTE & **QUERY**

There are a couple of golden rules that I have picked up over the years . . . .
First, never say anything to a witness that you would not want to see on the front page of the *New York Times* . . . .
The second rule . . . is to never do anything if you would not feel comfortable explaining to a Second Circuit judge why you did it.
Source: Patrick Fitzgerald, U.S. Attorney, 2009.

? Is this similar to the front page test described in Chapter 2?

Use of Discretion

A prosecutor should seek or file criminal charges only if the prosecutor reasonably believes that the charges are supported by probable cause, . . . and . . . [are] in the interests of justice (Standard 3-4.3[a]).

The prosecutor must seek justice, not merely a conviction. Toward this end, prosecutors must share evidence, exercise restraint in the use of their power, represent the public interest, and give the accused the benefit of reasonable doubt. Disciplinary rules are more specific. They forbid the prosecutor from pursuing charges when there is no probable cause. Standard 3-4.4 presents a list of acceptable factors prosecutors can use to decide whether and what to charge. They include the following:

- The strength of the case
- The prosecutor's doubt that the accused is in fact guilty
- The extent or absence of harm caused by the offense
- The impact of prosecution or nonprosecution on the public welfare
- The background and characteristics of the offender, including any voluntary restitution or efforts at rehabilitation
- Whether the authorized or likely punishment or collateral consequences are disproportionate in relation to the particular offense or the offender
- The views and motives of the victim or complainant
- Any improper conduct by law enforcement
- Unwarranted disparate treatment of similarly situated persons
- Potential collateral impact on third parties, including witnesses or victims; cooperation of the offender in the apprehension or conviction of others
- The possible influence of any cultural, ethnic, socioeconomic, or other improper biases
- Changes in law or policy
- The fair and efficient distribution of limited prosecutorial resources
- The likelihood of prosecution by another jurisdiction
- Whether the public's interests in the matter might be appropriately vindicated by available civil, regulatory, administrative, or private remedies

Despite these ideals of prosecutorial duty, an unstated influence over prosecutorial discretion is that prosecutors want to and must win to be considered successful. A decision to prosecute is influenced by the factors above, but also political and public pressures, a "gut" feeling of guilt or innocence, prison overcrowding, and career factors. The prosecutorial role is to seek justice, but justice doesn't mean the same thing to everyone and certainly does not mean prosecuting everyone fully. Whether to charge is one of the most important decisions of the criminal justice process. The decision should be fair, neutral, and accomplished with due process, but this is an ideal that is sometimes supplanted by other considerations.

In recent years critics have observed that there are over 4,000 federal criminal laws and innumerable other laws that are embedded in regulatory law, many of which do not have any *mens rea* requirements. When so many acts (e.g., interstate transport of hyacinths or trafficking in unlicensed dentures) could conceivably lead to prison terms, some argue there is too much power vested in prosecutors (Grissom, 2010).

Prosecutors don't usually use their charging power for intimidation or harassment, but other factors may be involved in the decision to charge. For instance, a prosecutor might pursue some types of crimes, such as child abuse or drugs, more intensely than others. How sure should a prosecutor be that a suspect is guilty before prosecuting? Can a prosecutor threaten to prosecute the spouse or child of a defendant as pressure to get them

QUOTE & QUERY

But while he may strike hard blows, he is not at liberty to strike foul ones. It is as much his duty to refrain from improper methods calculated to produce a wrongful conviction as it is to use every legitimate means to bring about a just one.

Source: Justice Sutherland in Berger v. United States, *295 U.S. 78, 88, 1935.*

? What would be the best way to prevent prosecutors from using improper methods that lead to wrongful convictions?

to agree to a plea bargain? Can a prosecutor ethically prosecute one individual of a crime, obtain a conviction, and then prosecute another individual for the same crime? It has been known to happen (Zacharias and Green, 2009). The Quote and Query box refers to the prosecutor's unique role in the criminal justice system.

Other considerations that affect the decision to charge include pressure from law enforcement—for instance, to offer a lesser charge in return for testimony or information that could lead to further convictions. There is also the pressure of public opinion. Prosecutors might pursue cases that they otherwise would have dropped if there is a great deal of public interest in the case. The victim also affects the decision to prosecute. Some victims (the very young or old, those with criminal records, those of dubious reputations) don't make good witnesses; therefore, prosecutors are less likely to prosecute. Jurors may not believe victims with mental impairments and the prosecutor may have a harder time getting a conviction. Sexual assault cases are notoriously hard to prosecute when they involve acquaintances in "date-rape" situations. The In the News box describes one incident whereby the pattern of a prosecutor's decision not to charge caught the attention of the Department of Justice.

Prosecutors in state capitals often have "public integrity" units that prosecute wrongdoing on the part of public officials. Some prosecutors might file charges against political opponents at election time, but other prosecutors might be falsely accused of such political considerations when they do charge politicians with public-integrity violations. Inevitably, federal prosecutions of politicians are labeled as "political witch-hunts" even if the Department of Justice has an equal number of investigations against members of the opposite party.

A special case of discretion and charging is the decision to pursue a capital homicide conviction. Prosecutors have the power to decide whether to seek the death penalty or a prison term. Clearly, the decision to seek the death penalty is not made uniformly across jurisdictions. One of the biggest considerations is cost. Because capital trials are

IN THE NEWS | *Justice Denied?*

In 2012, the Department of Justice initiated an unprecedented investigation in Missoula, Montana, after a scandal, widely reported in the news media, described the lack of prosecution of sexual assaults involving athletes at the University of Montana. Several female students alleged they were drugged and gang raped by male students and the Missoula County Attorney's office did not pursue any charges. The women described how they received little support from the university, the police, or the prosecutor's office and were told that the cases couldn't go forward because rape was hard to prove. The Department of Justice began the investigation as a possible civil rights violation (gender discrimination). The county prosecutor filed suit against the Department of Justice arguing that they had no jurisdiction over his office, but in 2014, a settlement was reached whereby a range of reforms would ensue and the Montana Attorney General would review any sexual assault case if charges were not filed. The suit against the DOJ was dropped although the county prosecutor insisted that there was no jurisdiction.

Source: Haake, 2014.

extremely expensive, counties that have bigger budgets are more likely to seek the death penalty; they have the resources and staff to handle the cases (Hall, 2002).

Various studies have attempted to describe prosecutors' decision making; one cites office policy as an important influence (Jacoby, Mellon, and Smith, 1980). Some office policies emphasize legal sufficiency where cases are not pursued unless there is a strong chance of conviction. Other policies may have other priorities, such as rehabilitation. Budget cuts may influence office policy to focus only on serious cases and plead out all others. In one study of two counties, it was found that prosecutors' decisions were guided by two basic questions: "Can I prove the case?" and "Should I prove the case?" At first, the objective strength of evidence was the determining factor for prosecutors. Later, the seriousness of the offense, the defendant's criminal history, characteristics of the defendant and victim, and contextual factors became increasingly influential. Often, contextual constraints, for example, rules, resources, and relationships, became more important than evaluations of the strength of the evidence, the seriousness of the offense, and the defendant's criminal history (Frederick and Stemen, 2012).

Another study looked at the prosecutor as operating in an exchange system. The relationship between the prosecutor and the police was described as one of give and take. Prosecutors balance police needs or wishes against their own vulnerability. The prosecutor makes personal judgments about which police officers can be trusted. Exchange also takes place between the prosecutor's office and the courts. When the jails become overcrowded, prosecutors recommend deferred adjudication and probation; when dockets back up, prosecutors drop charges. Finally, exchange takes place between defense attorneys and prosecutors, especially because many defense attorneys have previously served as prosecutors and may be personally familiar with the procedures and even personalities in the prosecutor's office (Cole, 1970).

On the one hand, discretion is considered essential to the prosecutorial function of promoting individualized justice and softening the impersonal effects of the law. On the other hand, the presence of discretion is the reason that the legal system is considered unfair and biased toward certain groups of people or individuals. Even though we would not want to eliminate prosecutorial discretion, it could be guided by regulations or internal guidelines.

Cassidy (2006) argues that the ethics of virtue can help determine ethical decisions for prosecutors because neither Model Rule 3.8 nor the Standards gives prosecutors much guidance. He argues that if prosecutors display the virtues of courage, honesty, justice, and fairness, they would make the right decisions when faced with dilemmas. Admitting that the virtues of courage, honesty, and prudence are only slightly more abstract than the concept of justice, Cassidy urges prosecutors' offices to seek employees who already exhibit a virtuous character. Qualifications for hiring should include evidence that the individual is honest and sensitive to others. Further, those working in a prosecutor's office should be rewarded for virtuous behavior over and above simply winning cases.

Duty to Disclose

A prosecutor should make timely disclosure to the defense of information . . . that tends to negate the guilt of the accused, . . . (Standard 3.5.4[a–c]).

The obligation to disclose exculpatory evidence was established in *Brady v. Maryland,* 373 U.S. 83, 1963, *Giglio v. United States,* 405 U.S. 150, 1972, *United States v. Agurs,*

427 U.S. 97, 1976, and *United States v. Bagley*, 473 U.S. 667, 1985. Evidence that is material (likely to change the outcome of the trial) must be disclosed. "*Brady* motions" are standard pretrial motions requesting all exculpatory evidence held by the prosecutor. There can be a *Brady* violation/error even if the prosecutor truly did not know or remember the evidence existed if the evidence might have changed the course of the trial. It is unintentional error when the prosecutor should have disclosed something, mistakenly believing it was not material or not knowing it existed, and intentional misconduct when the prosecutor hid or suppressed exculpatory evidence that would weaken his or her case. In either case, if an appellate court finds a *Brady* violation, the conviction can be overturned. Whether any discipline occurs in the cases of intentional misconduct is another question.

The ABA's Standing Committee on Ethics and Professional Responsibility has concluded that a prosecutor's ethical duty to share exculpatory information exceeds even the requirements of the *Brady* holding. Prosecutors have a duty to disclose even if they don't believe it is exculpatory. Some offices have "open file" policies wherein defense attorneys can have any information about evidence or witnesses that prosecutors have. *Brady* violations are one of the most frequent forms of prosecutorial misconduct and will be discussed in Chapter 10.

Conflicts of Interest

> . . . the prosecutor's professional judgment or obligations [should not] be affected by the prosecutor's . . . other interests or relationships. (Standard 3.1-7[f]).

About 15 percent of chief prosecutors are part time compared to about half in the early 1990s (Perry, 2011). Obviously, this poses the possibility of a conflict of interest. It may happen that a part-time prosecutor has a private practice, and there may be situations where the duty to a private client runs counter to the duty of the prosecutor to the public. In some cases, a client may become a defendant, necessitating the prosecutor to hire a special prosecutor. Even when there are no direct conflicts of interest, the pressure of time inevitably poses a conflict. The division of time between the private practice, where income is generated by the number of cases and hours billed, and prosecuting cases, where income is fixed no matter how many hours are spent, may result in a less energetic prosecutorial function than one might wish. Joy (2016) discusses the problematic situation of individuals serving as prosecutors, defense attorneys, and judges all during the same time, even if not, obviously, in the same case. Lower level judges are often part time and he describes some individuals who serve as part-time judges as well as part-time prosecutors in other courts while at the same time maintaining a criminal defense practice. This mixing of the roles must create unique and problematic ethical issues for these individuals.

It is well known that the prosecutor's job is a good steppingstone to politics, and many use it as such. In these situations, one must wonder whether cases are taken based on merit or on their ability to place the prosecutor in the public eye and help his or her career. Rudy Giuliani, Kamala Harris, Chris Christie, Bob McDonnell, Ed Rendell, and many other politicians began as prosecutors. Did they make decisions as prosecutors with an eye to their future aspirations? Would it be unethical if they did?

Populous counties have many assistant district attorneys (ADAs), perhaps hundreds, and only the district attorney is elected. Many ADAs work in the prosecutor's office for several years and then move into the private sector. The reason has largely to do with money. ADAs earn a median salary of about $63,000, and after 10–20 years of experience the median salary is about $100,000 (Payscale, 2017). This compares to starting salaries in some litigation firms of $200,000 (although many attorneys with their own practice make much less than prosecutors). The question then becomes: does the career plan to enter private practice as a litigator affect their prosecutorial decision to take a case to trial or affect their trial tactics?

One potential conflict of interest that has been in the news recently is when law enforcement officers are accused of wrongdoing. Because so few law enforcement officers face charges for shootings or alleged abuses of force, the argument is that the local prosecutor's office is unable to use their discretion fairly in making the decision to bring charges because they work with the police officers every day and depend on them to gather evidence and provide witness testimony. Thus, just as critics maintain that police departments can't police themselves, a similar criticism is made that prosecutors can't be trusted to charge police officers since it conflicts with their working relationships. This has led to recent calls for special prosecutors or attorneys from the attorneys general offices in each state to deal with cases involving police officers. Prosecutors generally discount such claims by pointing to successful cases of prosecution and larger offices have entire divisions that target public officials (including police officers).

Asset Forfeiture

The financial resources that can be seized with minimal due process in asset forfeiture may also pose a type of conflict of interest for prosecutors. Although police are most often associated with asset forfeiture, they must depend on the prosecutor to take the legal steps of seizing property. As discussed in Chapter 6, the origins of civil forfeiture were in the Comprehensive Drug Abuse and Control Act of 1970, the Organized Crime Control Act of 1970, and similar state laws. These laws created legal mechanisms for the federal and/or state government to seize assets associated with illegal activities. There are several problematic issues with civil asset forfeiture. The exclusionary rule does not apply to civil forfeiture proceedings, so some allege that police are now pursuing assets instead of criminals, because they do not have to worry about evidence being suppressed. Also, in a civil forfeiture proceeding, the defendant does not have a right to legal aid; and, in fact, may not even be present when a judge signs the order to seize their house or car or cash. Perhaps one of the most troubling aspects of civil forfeiture is that third parties are often those most hurt by the loss. For example, the spouse or parents of a suspected drug dealer may lose their home. The owner does not have to be involved in criminal activity; the property just must be associated with it. There is no requirement for any seriousness level of criminality either so a house can be seized for one $20 drug deal. Home seizures in Philadelphia received a great deal of press coverage several years ago when minor drug sales by adult children resulted in mothers and grandmothers losing their homes. A Pennsylvania appellate court ruled that the seizures were a violation of due process unless prosecutors could prove that the homeowner was substantially involved in the illegal activity (Mondics, 2014).

Asset forfeiture has created strange bedfellows with conservative/libertarian groups like Right on Crime (http://rightoncrime.com/tag/civil-asset-forfeiture/)

joining academic legal groups like the Brennan Center (www.brennancenter.org
/analysis/anyone-not-cop-favor-%E2%80%9Ccivil-forfeiture%E2%80%9D-laws)
and civil liberties groups like the ACLU (www.aclu.org/issues/criminal-law-reform/
reforming-police-practices/asset-forfeiture-abuse) in their criticism. There is something fundamentally wrong, critics say, in government agents (prosecutors and police)
receiving profits from the use of their powers because there is too great a temptation to
have money influence the decision making.

Plea Bargaining

*The prosecutor should not set unreasonably short deadlines, . . . A prosecutor should
not knowingly make false statements of fact or law. . . . the prosecutor should disclose
to the defense . . . information currently known to the prosecutor that tends to negate
guilt, mitigates the offense or is likely to reduce punishment. (Standard 3-5.6 [a–f]).*

As discussed earlier, there are serious ethical concerns over the practice of plea bargaining. In jurisdictions that have determinate sentencing, plea bargaining has become
"charge bargaining" instead of sentence bargaining. Most conclude that plea bargaining, even if not exactly in keeping with due process, is certainly efficient and probably inevitable. If the goals of the system are crime control or bureaucratic efficiency,
plea bargaining makes sense. If the goals of the system are the protection of individual
rights and the protection of due process, plea bargaining is much harder to justify.
Arguments given in defense of plea bargaining include the heavy caseloads, limited
resources, legislative over-criminalization, individualized justice, and legal problems
of cases (legal errors that would result in mistrials or dropped charges if the client
didn't plead) (Knudten, 1978; Mariano, 2015). Plea bargaining continues to be prevalent across the United States; felony defendants are 20 times more likely to plead than
go to trial (Hashimoto, 2008: 950). Guidelines providing a range of years for certain
types of charges would help individual prosecutors maintain some level of consistency
in a particular jurisdiction, yet no one knows how many offices have such guidelines
or manuals in place.

Even if the practice of plea bargaining can be justified as an ethical way to reduce
the number of cases going to trial, there are practices that prosecutors sometimes use
within plea bargaining that are ethically questionable and the ABA's updated Standards
have warned against them. Specifically, prosecutors are not supposed to overcharge—
that is, charge at a higher degree of severity or press more charges than could possibly
be sustained by evidence—so they can bargain down. Prosecutors should not mislead
defense attorneys by inflating the amount of evidence or the kind of evidence they
have before or during the plea process. Also, prosecutors should not engage in false
promises, fraud, misrepresentation of conditions, deals without benefit of counsel,
package deals, or threats during plea bargaining yet these tactics have been known to
happen (Gershman, 1991; McKelway, 2013; Sapien and Hernandez, 2013). Critics contend that prosecutors hold all the cards in plea bargaining.

Another discussion is whether the prosecution should have to share exculpatory
evidence (facts that support innocence) with the defense before or during plea bargaining. Recall that in *Brady v. Maryland*, 373 U.S. 83, 1963, the Supreme Court held
that the prosecution must share any exculpatory information with the defense that is
material to the case (which means if it would affect the outcome of the trial) when they

ETHICAL ISSUE

Should Prosecutors Plea Bargain?

The practice of exchanging a reduced charge or a reduced sentence for a guilty plea is widespread. Although some disagree with the practice and say it leads to innocent people pleading guilty and a reduction in the integrity of the system, most argue that the system couldn't work without the practice and, in fact 95 percent of cases are resolved without a trial. Also, proponents argue that it is ethical to give the offender something in exchange for not putting the state to the expense of a trial.

Law

U.S. Supreme Court opinions have legitimated the use of plea bargaining. They have held that prosecutors and judges must abide by the agreements made and that defendants cannot turn around and claim afterward that the exchange was unfair. The Supreme Court has also allowed prosecutors to threaten harsher sentences if the defendant does not plead (*Bordenkircher v. Hayes*, 434 U.S. 357, 1978) and held that plea bargaining is a "critical stage" and that ineffective counsel, if proven, could invalidate a plea agreement (*Padilla v. Kentucky*, 559 U.S. 356, 2010). The Supreme Court also held that not conveying a plea offer to the defendant was ineffective counsel and when the defendant was convicted at trial, reinstatement of the original plea offer was the appropriate remedy (*Missouri v. Frye*, 566 U.S. 134 2012).

Policy

Different prosecutors' offices handle plea bargaining differently. Some have guidelines, and others leave it to the prosecutor's discretion. In general, there are informal office policies so that some offices give more generous offers than other jurisdictions do. Plea bargaining is something that is covered in the training of new prosecutors.

Ethics

Prosecutors' ethical issues with plea bargaining revolve around what is the "right" amount of punishment to offer. Defense attorneys' ethical issues include the extent to which they will try to convince individuals to plead if they swear they are innocent. Judges have ethical issues as well, in that they do not have to accept a plea in a case where they do not believe evidence is sufficient to uphold the verdict.

As stated before, plea bargaining is justified by utilitarianism. It is efficient and benefits both the defendant and the state. There is a calculus to be made depending on how many innocent people plead guilty to get out of jail; if it is any appreciable number, the negative utility of punishing innocents may outweigh the benefits of an efficient sentence resolution. It may also be justified by the ethics of care if a prosecutor is seeking to meet the needs of all parties concerned (e.g., victim, offender, and peripheral individuals) by coming up with a unique plea agreement. It is possible that the prosecutor can, through plea bargaining, moderate an unfair application of sentencing statutes by, for instance, reducing the charge to achieve a shorter sentence if an offender agrees to drug treatment.

---

ask for it, but it is unclear whether such a requirement applies pre-plea or only before trial. A West Virginia Supreme Court ruling determined that it was a violation of the rights of a criminal defendant to withhold material exculpatory evidence during plea negotiations. In this case, the court allowed a man to retract his guilty plea after he was convicted and sentenced of rape and robbery because the prosecutor withheld DNA test results that excluded him as the rapist. He maintained that he was 19 years old and coerced to plead guilty by the prosecutor and his public defender, but if he had known about the DNA results, he would have never pleaded guilty (Eckholm, 2015b).

Note that the *ABA Criminal Justice Standards* do dictate an affirmative duty to share exculpatory information with the defense during plea bargaining, but legal observers predict that the Supreme Court would not apply *Brady* to pre-plea negotiations because the legal rationale is fairness of trial, not voluntariness of plea. In fact, U.S. attorneys and some state prosecutors routinely require the defendant to waive *Brady* rights as part of a plea arrangement. Obviously knowing about any exculpatory information is important to make the decision to plead guilty or not. Prosecutors resist the interpretation of *Brady* that requires them to provide the defense with exculpatory evidence before a plea because they lose bargaining power. Proponents of pre-plea discovery argue that it violates due process to allow a defendant to think there is no exculpatory evidence when, in fact, there is (Hashimoto, 2008).

Criticism of plea bargaining extends to the federal level as well. In 2013, federal prosecutors went after the 26-year-old co-creator of Reddit and RSS and charged him with 13 felony fraud counts, which could have meant 35 years in prison. The prosecutors were accused of overcharging and heavily criticized in the news when the computer whiz committed suicide (McKelway, 2013). Critics allege that prosecutors have become accustomed to "piling on" every conceivable charge to coerce defendants to plead guilty. Because of federal mandatory minimum laws and enhancements, federal prosecutors have immense power to persuade defendants. For instance, a defendant may be threatened with a sentence of life without parole if he or she insists on a trial and loses. This is the so-called trial penalty. Judges have publicly criticized the prosecutors' actions and argued that not even the prosecutors believe in the justness of such sentences. One judge wrote that the prosecutor's action "coerces guilty pleas and produces sentences so excessively severe they take your breath away" (quoted in McKelway, 2013). In one study, it was found that federal prosecutors used a prior-convictions sentence multiplier in 24 percent of plea bargained sentences, but used the sentencing enhancer in 72 percent of trial convictions. It is not surprising then, that only 3 percent of cases go to trial (McKelway, 2013). Defense attorneys state that they must advise their clients to plead because the potential cost of extremely long sentences is too high even in cases of weak evidence or potential innocence.

Another study found that there was a huge disparity in the use of prior-felony or gun enhancement sentences on the part of prosecutors leading to some individuals serving decades longer than others for no reason other than which prosecutor had the case (Sapien and Hernandez, 2013).

Media Relations

The prosecutor should not make . . . a public statement that . . . will have a substantial likelihood of materially prejudicing a criminal proceeding. . . . (Standard 3-1.10 [c]).

The prosecutor has an important relationship with the press. The media can be enemy or friend, depending on how charismatic or forthcoming the prosecutor is in interviews. Sometimes, cases are said to be "tried in the media," with the defense attorney and the prosecutor staging verbal sparring matches for public consumption. Prosecutors may react to cases and judges' decisions in the media, criticizing the decision or the sentence and, in the process, denigrating the dignity of the system. More often, the defense attempts to sway the press to a sympathetic view of the offense, which is easier to accomplish during prosecutorial silence.

In many celebrated criminal cases, the prosecutor and defense utilized the media to promote their version of events. The Sam Sheppard case (supposedly the case that spurred the idea for *The Fugitive* television series and movie) was the first one to illustrate the power of the media and related misconduct by the prosecution, such as discussing evidence with reporters that could not be admitted at trial. The media storm was actively encouraged by the prosecutor and ultimately led to the Supreme Court ruling that due process had been violated (*Sheppard v. Maxwell*, 384 U.S. 333, 1966).

ABA Model Rule 3.6(b) is a prohibition against out-of-court statements that a reasonable person should expect would have a substantial likelihood of materially prejudicing a proceeding. Defense attorneys might be expected to make statements to exonerate their client and disparage the state's case, but prosecutors' statements have a greater ring of authority. The rule specifies that no statements should be given involving topics such as the character, credibility, reputation, or criminal record of a party, suspect, or witness, the identity of a witness, expected testimony, test results, physical evidence, or any inadmissible evidence, and other topics that may influence public opinion about the case.

The case of the Duke University lacrosse players accused of rape resulted in the prosecutor (Mike Nifong) being disbarred. In this high-profile 2007 case, a stripper alleged that she was raped by members of the lacrosse team after she was hired to perform at a party for them. Very early in the case, the district attorney made several public statements indicating that the athletes were guilty, and they weren't going to get away with the crime just because they were white and rich and the alleged victim was black and poor. No doubt the fact that the district attorney was in a hotly contested election had something to do with his decision to make such public statements so early in the case.

As the investigation progressed, the victim's story changed in substantive ways about who raped her and when it took place. Furthermore, no physical evidence substantiated her story. Despite this, the district attorney continued to make comments to the media that the players were guilty. Later, the alibi of one defendant was substantiated by an ATM camera showing that he was somewhere else when the rape was supposed to have taken place. Still Nifong did not drop the charges and instructed a lab technician to drop a sentence from his report indicating that the semen found on the alleged victim contained the DNA of several unknown males, but not the accused men's.

Eventually, the state attorney general sent in a special prosecutor to handle the case, and this prosecutor promptly dropped the charges against the accused college athletes. Nifong was publicly sanctioned and was disbarred from the practice of law. The case is a good example of why public expressions of guilt are strictly prohibited: The prosecutor gets locked into a position that is difficult to back out of if exculpatory evidence emerges. After Nifong had committed himself to the conclusion that the college men were guilty, he found himself under intense pressure to pursue the case, even in the face of contradictory evidence (Jeffrey, 2007).

Expert Witnesses

> *A prosecutor . . . should not seek to dictate the formation of the expert's opinion on the subject (Standard 3-3.5[d]).*

The use of expert witnesses has risen in recent years. Psychiatrists often testify as to the mental competency or legal insanity of an accused. Criminologists and other social scientists may be asked to testify on topics such as victimization in prison, statistical evidence of sentencing discrimination, the effectiveness of predictive instruments for prison riots and other disturbances, risk assessment for individual offenders, mental health services in prison, patterns of criminality, battered-woman syndrome, and so on (Anderson and Winfree, 1987). A whole range of experts in the field of criminalistics also have emerged as important players in criminal prosecutions.

Expert testimony is allowed as evidence in trials when it is based on sound scientific method. The Supreme Court has defined a standard as to when scientific evidence can be admitted in a trial. Specifically, the so-called *Daubert* standard includes the idea that the judge is gatekeeper to make the determination of relevance and reliability. The judge must find it more likely than not that the expert's methods are reliable and reliably applied to the facts at hand. The expert can only testify as to scientific knowledge if it can be demonstrated that the testimony is the product of sound "scientific methodology" that may include hypothesis testing using empirical methods. Other factors include whether the expert's findings have been subjected to peer review and publication, the known or potential error rate, and whether there are standards and controls concerning the research that have been followed (*Daubert v. Merrell Dow Pharmaceuticals*, 509 U.S. 579, 1993).

When experts are honest in their presentation as to the limitations and potential bias of the material, no ethical issues arise. However, expert witnesses may testify falsely claiming a level of accuracy, or make testimony appear factual when some questions are not clearly answerable. Because of the **halo effect**—essentially, when a person with expertise or status in one area is given deference in all areas—an expert witness may endow a statement or conclusion with more legitimacy than it warrants.

Some expert witnesses always appear on either the defense side or the prosecution side and doing so should create questions about their credibility. For instance, a doctor who was often used by prosecutors in one jurisdiction during capital sentencing hearings became known as "Dr. Death" because he always determined that the defendant posed a future risk to society—one of the necessary elements for the death penalty. Although this doctor was well known by reputation to prosecutors and defense attorneys alike, juries could not be expected to know of his predilection for finding future risk and would take his testimony at face value unless the defense attorney brought out this information during cross-examination (Raeder, 2007).

The use of expert witnesses can present ethical problems when the witness is used in a dishonest fashion. Obviously, to pay an expert for his or her time is not unethical, but to shop for experts until finding one who benefits the case is unethical, for the credibility of the witness is suspect. Another difficulty arises when the prosecutor obtains an expert who develops a conclusion or a set of findings that would help the defense. Ethical rules do not prohibit an attorney in a civil matter or criminal defense attorneys from merely disregarding the information; however, prosecutors operate under a special set of ethics because their goal is justice, not pure advocacy. Any exculpatory information should be shared with the defense; this obviously includes test results and may also include expert witness findings (Giannelli and McMunigal, 2007).

halo effect The phenomenon in which a person with expertise or status in one area is given deference in all areas.

CSI and the Courts

For many years, forensic experts have testified regarding factual issues of evidence ranging from ballistics to blood spatter. Television shows such as *CSI* contributed to the mystique of the crime-scene investigator as a scientific Sherlock Holmes who uses physics, chemistry, and biology to catch criminals. However, the reality is that some of this "expert" testimony has been called "*junk science*" (McRoberts and Mills, 2004; McRoberts, Mills, and Possley, 2004). Also, lab examiners who work for police laboratories may exhibit a heavy prosecution bias that colors their analysis and testimony.

As mentioned in Chapter 6, labs all over the country have been investigated and even shut down for shoddy practices or biased analyses. Scandals have occurred with labs in Houston, Cleveland, Chicago, Omaha, Oklahoma City, Washington, D.C., Boston, Indianapolis, and San Francisco; and state crime labs in Virginia, Maryland, California, Illinois, Maryland, North Carolina, Oklahoma, West Virginia, Mississippi, and New York. Even the vaunted FBI lab has been the center of scandal in their faulty ballistics testing and misleading testimony in hair analysis, among other issues (Balko, 2011b; Giannelli, 2012; Murphy, 2012; Trager, 2014).

While each locale had unique circumstances, there have also been patterns of problems. Shoddy practices and/or incompetent lab examiners have been found in several investigations. Labs have been found to practice poor procedures that allow contamination, use inadequate equipment, and have poorly trained or unqualified lab technicians (in some cases not even meeting minimal standards of knowledge). In a New York investigation, an examiner had been working for 15 years with no training and didn't even know how to use the microscope he supposedly used to conduct trace evidence and hair analysis. He evidently made up reports using a "cheat sheet" left by a former supervisor. This examiner committed suicide, but before his death, implicated many others in the lab and accused supervisors of countenancing widespread malfeasance and report-fudging to aid prosecution efforts (Balko, 2009).

In 2012, a Massachusetts forensic chemist admitted she had falsified thousands of drug tests. She was arrested and later admitted to mixing up evidence samples, fabricating results, and lying about having a master's degree in chemistry from the University of Massachusetts. Over 1,000 requests for new trials were filed and around 500 defendants were released. Evidently this analyst, Annie Dookhan, manufactured test results to impress her superiors with her productivity. She was convicted and sentenced to three to five years in prison but was released early on parole in 2016.

Another Massachusetts forensic chemist, Sonja Farak, was also arrested for tampering and theft because she used drug evidence to satisfy her own drug habit (Trager, 2014). She reportedly smoked or swallowed every type of drug the lab had for the eight years before she was caught, beginning with the lab's methamphetamine supply they used as a comparison standard. She pleaded guilty and did not go to trial. Her thefts were discovered in 2013, but prosecutors did not notify defense attorneys that the testimony against their clients was tainted until a defense attorney obtained a court order demanding the release of the investigation (Jackman, 2017) Thefts of portions of drug samples and replacing the stolen drugs with other substances has occurred in other labs as well (Trager, 2014). Once this occurs, literally thousands of criminal cases are compromised (Tobin and Spiegleman, 2013). Cases around the country (e.g., in South

Carolina, Florida, and Texas) where analysts' training, competence, or honesty are questioned have become a pattern (Trager, 2014).

Another pattern of wrongdoing is when lab examiners are clearly slanted toward the prosecution in their work and overstate their findings to the jury, or even manufacture test results ("drylabbing") that benefit the prosecution. Another tactic used is to suppress any test results or findings that are exculpatory (e.g., DNA that doesn't match) (Axtman, 2003; KTRK, 2009; Liptak, 2003; Possley, Mills, and McRoberts, 2004; Tobin and Spiegleman, 2013; Trager, 2014). Critics argue that forensic examiners are too closely aligned with law enforcement and want to get the results that support the theory of the case. Carefully controlled studies have shown that forensic specialists have reversed their opinion on the same evidence when the "right" suspect was switched (Tobin and Spiegleman, 2013). In another study, forensic psychologists evaluated the risk of hypothetical subjects and were told in some cases that they were hired by the prosecution and in others they were hired by the defense. Those who were supposedly hired by the prosecution had significantly higher risk scores, indicating what the researchers called "an allegiance effect" (Murrie, Boccaccini, Guarnera, and Rufino, 2013). The psychological bias inherent in the matching procedure (in hair, fingerprints, and other evidence) when one knows the suspect's sample is extremely problematic even for examiners who attempt be objective in their examination (Tobin and Spiegleman, 2013).

What happens in these scandals is that thousands of cases must be reviewed, some retried, and some individuals have been exonerated. In some cases, millions of dollars in settlements for those falsely incarcerated have been paid by taxpayers. For instance, the Virginia State Crime Lab, upon review of many cases, excluded 76 felons as the source of biological evidence in their supposed crimes. A review of the results by the Urban Institute found that there were 37 potential wrongful convictions. Some of the defendants had died; some had already served their prison terms, but an unknown number could have still been in prison (Green, 2010).

Another issue has been that when the labs or individual lab examiners have been identified as biased or incompetent, neither defense attorneys nor their convicted and imprisoned clients are notified. The FBI was strongly criticized for abandoning the lead composition analysis but making very weak efforts to locate any individuals who had been wrongfully convicted based on their testimony. The same pattern occurred when problems arose with hair analysis testimony.

criminalistics
The profession involved in the application of science to recognize, identify, and evaluate physical evidence in court proceedings.

Even when mismanagement, shoddy practices, and untrained staff aren't the issue, many areas of the science of **criminalistics** seem to be more art than science. Criminalists have been defined as professionals who are involved in the "scientific discipline directed to the recognition, identification, individualization, and evaluation of physical evidence by the application of the natural sciences to law-science matters" (Lindquist, 1994: 59). Questions have been raised about the reliability of virtually all areas of criminalistics.

• *Hair analysis.* A Justice Department study of 240 crime labs found hair-comparison error rates ranging from 28 to 68 percent. Hair-comparison testimony is so suspect that it is outlawed in Michigan and Illinois (Hall, 2002). Basically, hair analysis is simply an analyst visually inspecting two samples under a microscope and determining if they are "consistent." When the analyst has a pro-prosecution bias and knows that they are looking at the suspect's hair sample, the potential for misidentification is obvious. There is no such thing as "matching" samples when there is only visual inspection; however, testimony is often inflated and misrepresented to the jury as if the analyst scientifically concluded that the two hair samples came from the same source (Fisher, 2008).

In 2013, the FBI agreed to review more than 2,000 criminal cases in which the FBI conducted microscopic hair analysis of crime-scene evidence and analysts testified about their findings to determine if the jury might have been misled. The investigation was prompted by the exoneration of three men in three different cases—Kirk Odom, Santae Tribble, and Donald Gates—by DNA testing in which FBI hair examiners had told juries that the defendants' hair matched hair at the crime scenes, based on microscopic hair analysis. In fact, subsequent DNA testing found that none of the hair samples matched the defendants and that one was from a dog. The probability of accuracy in the matches was wildly overstated.

The FBI admitted that hair analysis was a problem years ago and, since the 1970s, had taken the position that hair analysis could not lead to a positive identification match; however, examiners regularly testified to the near certainty of matches. In fact, an Inspector General's report brought attention to the problem of the examiners' testimony in 1999 (Hsu, 2014). Only in 2013 was the first systematic review of FBI examiners' testimony begun to determine how widespread the problem was. There were over 2,500 cases identified in which hair analysis might have been offered. Only 342 have been reviewed thus far. Of these, 268 cases included hair analysis testimony; 35 of these cases led to an execution. Of these cases, 95 percent of the time the testimony overstated the science and 26 of the 28 examiners overstated the matches (Hsu, 2015).

- *Arson investigation.* Arson "science" started when arson investigators used their experience with thousands of fires, confessions of suspects, and crude experiments to identify burn patterns and accelerants. "Facts" such as "fires started with accelerants burn hotter" have been disproved. So-called pour patterns that have been used as proof of arson have now been associated with a natural phenomenon called "flashover," which occurs when smoke and gas in a room build to a point where the entire room explodes in flames, consuming everything. The flashover effect also calls into question the traditional belief that if the floor showed burning, it was arson, because it was believed that heat rises so the floor shouldn't show burning unless an accelerant is used (Fisher, 2008; Possley, Mills, and McRoberts, 2004).

In the Cameron Todd Willingham case that opened this chapter, the Innocence Project commissioned a panel to study some of the arson "facts" that were presented in the trial, and the study proved that many were not supported. For instance, glass cracking in a spidery fashion may not be because the fire was started with an accelerant; it is just as likely to be caused by water sprayed by firefighters. There also was no way to prove that the fire had multiple origins. However, fire investigators may still testify in court based on science that is called by some "a hodgepodge of old wives' tales" (Tanner, 2006).

- *Ballistics testing.* The FBI lab examiners testified in thousands of cases about lead composition analysis to tie suspects to the bullet retrieved at the crime scene. The theory was that the chemical composition of bullets in a single production batch was more similar than bullets from other batches. Bullets owned by the suspect are compared to the crime-scene bullet, and the expert testifies as to their similarity.

Independent scientific tests by the National Research Council indicated a large margin of error; chemical compositions between batches are more similar than believed, and the chemical composition within a batch can vary quite a bit depending on several factors. These findings indicated that ballistics experts from the FBI lab and other labs had testified in a way that greatly overstated the importance of the chemical matches (Piller, 2003; Piller and Mejia, 2003). Although the FBI stopped comparative bullet lead analysis in 2004 in response to these findings, FBI lab experts testified in cases that had already been analyzed through 2005. Also, the FBI was criticized for not releasing a list of cases in which lab examiners testimony was based on the faulty science. Several individuals had their murder convictions thrown out when appellate judges decided that the ballistics testimony materially affected the outcome of the trial (Post, 2005; Solomon, 2007; Tobin and Spiegleman, 2013).

Another type of ballistics testing is matching the marks on a bullet and a gun to determine if the bullet was used in that gun. Despite what the television shows portray, this matching has not proven to be very accurate in scientific tests. Ironically, because it has been admitted for so long in criminal cases, judges cite precedent to argue why they must allow it, even though experts in the field know the technique is highly inaccurate (Tobin and Spiegleman, 2013).

- *DNA testing.* The use of DNA evidence has risen dramatically in recent years. Based on the scientific principle that no two individuals possess the same DNA (deoxyribonucleic acid), a DNA "fingerprint" is analyzed from organic matter such as semen, blood, hair, or skin. Whereas a blood test can identify an individual only as being a member of a group (e.g., all those with blood type A positive), DNA testing can determine, with a small margin of error, whether two samples come from the same individual. This has been described as the greatest breakthrough in scientific evidence since fingerprinting, but there are problems with its use. Careless laboratory procedures render results useless, and there are no enforced guidelines or criteria for forensic laboratories conducting DNA tests.

  Labs often have only a small amount of organic matter to extract DNA. They use a procedure whereby the incomplete DNA strand is replicated using computer simulation models. This procedure allows a DNA analysis of the tiniest speck of blood or skin, but critics argue that it opens a door to a margin of error that is unacceptable. Without vigorous investigation and examination of lab results from the opposing counsel, incorrect DNA test results or poorly interpreted results may be entered as evidence and used to determine guilt or innocence.

  A different problem has emerged when DNA testing is done and the results help the defense by excluding the defendant from possible suspects. In these cases, prosecutors have an ethical duty to provide test results to the defense; however, there are cases where this is not done.

- *Fingerprint analysis.* Most citizens assume that fingerprint analysis is infallible, that all criminals' fingerprints are accessible through computer matching technology, and that fingerprint technicians can retrieve fingerprints from almost any surface and can use partials to make a match. Unfortunately, the reality is far from what is seen on television. There have been attempts to undertake a comprehensive analysis of how much of a partial print is necessary to have a reliable match—an objective that is resisted by professional fingerprint examiners. Most fingerprints are partials and smudged. Some studies show that about a quarter of matches are false positives.

In 2006, the federal government settled a suit for $2 million after three FBI fingerprint examiners mistakenly identified the fingerprint related to a terrorist bombing in Madrid, Spain, as belonging to an Oregon lawyer and he was detained even though he had an alibi. European fingerprint analysts discovered the error (Associated Press, 2004). Standards do not exist for determining how many points of comparison are necessary to declare a match (Mills and McRoberts, 2004). Problems with fingerprint analysis have found their way into the courtroom and there is a movement among defense attorneys to challenge fingerprint evidence under the *Daubert* standard (arguing that it has not been developed using scientific methods). This defense has been unsuccessful; however, if defense attorneys do succeed in excluding fingerprint evidence, it would be a ground-shifting event in criminalistics and criminal law (Fisher 2008; Garrett and Neufield, 2009).

- *Bite mark comparison.* There is no accurate way to measure the reliability of bite mark comparisons, yet forensic dentists have given testimony that resulted in convictions of several innocent defendants, and several individuals exonerated through DNA evidence were convicted largely on evidence of bite mark identification. Evidently, the experts sometimes can't even agree if an injury is a bite mark at all. One study indicated that identifications were flawed in two-thirds of the cases. Even their own organization cautions that analysts should not use the term "match," because the technique is not exacting enough, but many do. Contrary to popular belief, a bite mark is not just like a fingerprint. Teeth change over time, and the condition of the skin or other substance holding the bite mark changes the indentation patterns of teeth (McRoberts and Mills, 2004). So-called experts have confused juries by confabulating dentition and bite marks since there is general agreement that identity can be established within reasonable parameters of error by comparing dental records to a full set of teeth (i.e., comparing dental records to a corpse). However, bite marks only typically involve the front teeth, and there is no evidence to indicate that bite marks are similar every time; furthermore, there are no standards to guide agreement that there is a match. Critics argue that bite mark testimony does not meet the *Daubert* standard (evidence must be from a reliable scientific methodology), but courts let the evidence in because it is presented as merely identification, not science (Beecher-Monas, 2009). The Texas Forensic Science Commission has recommended a total ban on bite mark evidence because of the lack of scientific proof to support it, with the statement that at least two dozen men convicted or charged with murder or rape based on bite marks have been exonerated nationwide since 2000 (Associated Press, 2016).

- *Scent identification.* A Texas deputy, Keith Pikett, now retired from the Fort Bend County Sheriff's Department, became semi-famous and in demand along with his dogs for finding and identifying criminals through "scent lineups." The dogs evidently could identify criminals through scents left at the scene or on property.

In one case, the dogs led the police from the crime scene to the home of the alleged offender, even though the house was miles away. Critics contend that Pikett gave the dogs unconscious clues to tag the suspect, and, in other cases, there was no way the dogs could do what Pikett says they did. The state's appellate court threw out the murder conviction of Richard Winfrey who was convicted of murdering his neighbor and sentenced to 75 years based almost entirely on the scent identification evidence. All other evidence at the crime scene—DNA, fingerprints, a bloody footprint, and 73 hairs—belonged to some unknown person. The judge ruled that the scent identification evidence could not be used in court unless corroborated by other evidence (Lindell, 2010a, 2010c). There have been other wrongful convictions based on scent evidence as well (e.g., William Dillon). While dogs can be useful tools in criminal investigations, it is important to establish their skill and the credibility of the training and handler before allowing such testimony.

- *Other forensic evidence.* Other types of evidence have been introduced at trials and been subject to criticism, including handwriting analysis, boot or shoe print identification, and fiber identification.

In 2009, the National Academy of Sciences issued a 225-page report on forensics and crime labs across the country. It was a highly critical report, incorporating the descriptions of many cases of innocent people convicted because of faulty scientific evidence. The authors concluded that crime labs lacked certification and standards, and that many forensic disciplines, including most of those described above, were not grounded in classic scientific methods; DNA analysis was the exception. Much of the problem is that pattern recognition (e.g., fingerprints, bite marks, tool marks, and handwriting) have no agreed upon scientific standard for when to conclude a match. The report called on Congress to establish a national institute of forensic science to accredit crime labs and require that analysts be certified. In 2013, the National Forensic Science Commission was established with eventually 32 external stakeholders who made recommendations to the Department of Justice. Attorney General Sessions disbanded the panel in 2017 with a statement that forensic science improvements would be pursued internally.

Zealous Prosecution

The duty of the prosecutor is to seek justice, not merely to convict (Standard 3-1.2[b]).

Just as the defense attorney is at times overly zealous in defense of clients, prosecutors may be overly ambitious to attain a conviction. The prosecutor, in preparing a case, is putting together a puzzle, and each fact or bit of evidence is a piece of that puzzle. Evidence that doesn't fit the puzzle is sometimes conveniently ignored. The problem is that this type of evidence may be exculpatory, and the prosecutor has a duty to provide it to the defense.

Both defense attorneys and prosecutors sometimes engage in tactics such as using witnesses with less than credible reasons for testifying, preparing witnesses (both in appearance and testimony), and "shopping" for experts. Witnesses are not supposed to be paid, but their expenses can be reimbursed, and often this is incentive enough for some people to say what they think the prosecutor wants to hear. A tool in the prosecutor's arsenal that the defense attorney does not have is that prosecutors can make deals to reduce charges in return for favorable testimony.

Jailhouse Informants

The use of jailhouse informants is a particularly problematic issue. Jailhouse informants usually testify that a defendant confessed to them or said something that was incriminating. Often the "pay" for such testimony is a reduction in charges, but it could be reduced sentencing or being sent to a specific prison, or any other thing of value to the informant. It could even be money. Jailhouse informants' credibility should always be questioned and false testimony is one of the most frequent factors identified in wrongful convictions (Kirchmeier, Greenwald, Reynolds, and Sussman, 2009). Raeder (2007) points out that jailhouse informants not only respond to solicitations from police and prosecutors, sometimes they are entrepreneurs who are used multiple times in many prosecutions. She argues for ethical standards whereby prosecutors should use such informants only when they can point to specific factors that support the truthfulness of the testimony.

Research shows that even though jailhouse informant testimony is highly questionable, it is very effective. Respondents in one research study who decided whether to convict or acquit in hypothetical cases were given transcripts that either included a jailhouse informant's testimony that the defendant confessed or did not. Those who read the confession were much more likely to convict, and whether the informant received money or even a shortened sentence did not affect their greater likelihood of convicting if they were given the jailhouse house informant's testimony. More troubling was that respondents were just as likely to convict even if they were told the informant had testified in previous cases and even when expert testimony was added that called into question the credibility of informants (Neuschatz et al., 2012). If true, this means that prosecutors have an immense power to shift the course of a trial with the use of jailhouse informants and to blithely say that the jury can adequately assess the credibility of the person is highly debatable.

Many of the cases where an innocent person eventually is exonerated involve jailhouse informants. In these cases, the more common misconduct of prosecutors is a *Brady* violation, where they do not reveal to the defense attorney that there has been a deal made with the informant or any negative history of the informant that would affect his or her credibility. In some cases, however, the prosecutor has also allowed the informant to lie on the stand about receiving a deal for his testimony.

For instance, in 2015, Joseph Sledge was released from prison 37 years after being wrongfully convicted of murder. Evidence (hair that was believed to be the murderer's) that had been reported as lost was found years after it had been requested by the defense for DNA testing. A three-judge panel appointed by the North Carolina Supreme Court heard the DNA evidence as well as a recantation from the jailhouse informant who testified that he had lied at the trial in return for leniency on his own drug case. He testified he had been coached by the prosecutor as to what to say on the stand (Drew, 2015).

Generally, jailhouse informants rarely come forward unless there is an explicit or implicit reward. Observers point out that if the defense offered anything of value to witnesses for favorable testimony it would be considered felony bribery, but prosecutors routinely cut deals with co-crime partners, other suspects, and jailhouse informants. To have years cut off a prison sentence or to have charges reduced is every bit as valuable as cash, so why isn't it considered bribery? In *Giglio v. United States,* 405 U.S. 150, 1972, the Supreme Court said that the prosecutor had a duty to disclose any deals made with informants or any other information that would implicate the credibility of a witness. Garrett and Neufeld (2011) reported that in one locale, prosecutors did not offer deals until *after* the informant testified, allowing him to truthfully answer "no" when the defense asked if he had received anything for his testimony. Prosecutors knew that if they didn't come through with a deal afterward the jail grapevine would ensure the flow of jailhouse informants would stop so the process worked for everyone except the defendant. Raeder (2007) points out that, after a major scandal involving prosecutors and jail officials working in concert to put jailhouse informants in the cells of defendants, Los Angeles had instituted a policy that dramatically restricted the use of jailhouse informants with no deterioration of its conviction rate. Illinois has passed legislation concerning the use of such testimony in capital cases, and Canada has instituted stringent guidelines for the use of jailhouse informants (Garrett and Neufeld, 2011). A new Texas law (House Bill 34), that will become effective September 1, 2017, requires prosecutors to keep thorough records of all jailhouse informants they use, including the benefits they received. This information must be disclosed to defense lawyers, who may use it in court to challenge the informant's reliability or honesty. The Act is a measure designed to reduce wrongful convictions and also requires law enforcement to record interrogations in most cases.

📱 IN THE NEWS | *Jailhouse Informant Scandal*

In Spring 2015 Superior Court judge Thomas Goethals issued an order disqualifying the entire Orange County District Attorney's Office (all 250 prosecutors) from continuing to prosecute a major death penalty case. He did so after a pattern of misconduct was revealed where sheriffs' deputies placed informants in cells with suspects to obtain confessions or incriminating information and prosecutors misled the court about the practice and did not disclose exculpatory information obtained from the jailhouse informant. It was also reported that two informants with extensive criminal records had received more than $150,000 from law enforcement agencies for obtaining information from jailed suspects awaiting trials.

The case that spurred the scandal was the murder prosecution of Scott Dekraai, who pleaded guilty to killing his ex-wife and seven other people in 2011. In the Dekraai case, a public defender discovered that a jailhouse informant who had testified had done the same thing in another case. Further investigation revealed how widespread the practice was and led to years of courtroom wrangling as defense attorneys sought the jail records that tracked the informants and jail staff blocked

the efforts. In recent hearings, deputies have pleaded their Fifth Amendment rights to remain silent. In 2017, the penalty phase for Dekraai is still going on.

The Orange County District Attorney's Office has responded by criticizing the defense attorney, the judge and the media as blowing out of proportion a few *Brady* mistakes. The adamantly deny they have committed Constitutional violations relative to *Massiah v. United States*, 377 U.S. 201, 1964. In that case, the Supreme Court held that if a jailhouse informant was an agent of the government (doing the government's bidding and asking questions of the defendant), then there was a Sixth Amendment violation because it was an interrogation without an attorney present.

In 2016, District Attorney Rackauckas created a special panel of retired judges and law professors to examine the practices in his office, and the panel's findings indicated that the prosecutor's office suffered from a lack of leadership that lead to a culture of winning at all costs. Rackauckas disputed the findings, but agreed to appoint a special ethics officer for the office and call in the Department of Justice for an investigation.

Source: Hamilton and Queally, 2016; Lithwick, 2015b.

ETHICAL DILEMMA

You are a prosecutor who is preparing a case against a defendant accused of a brutal rape and murder of a young child. The suspect lived in the same neighborhood as the child and is a registered sex offender. He says he didn't do it, of course, but has no alibi for the time in question, and you know in your gut that he did the crime. Unfortunately, you have no scientific evidence that incriminates him. You do have one witness who thinks she saw his car close to the playground where the child was taken, and you can prove he didn't show up for work the afternoon of the abduction. You are hoping that someone in the playground will be able to make a positive ID. One day you receive a call from the detective on the case. He tells you that there is a man in the jail cell with the defendant who says that the defendant confessed to him. The informant is willing to testify to it, but he wants a reduction in his own sentence. You meet with the man, who is a drug offender, and sure enough, he says that the defendant "spilled his guts" and told him that he took the little girl and killed her when she wouldn't stop screaming. You feel you've got the conviction sewn up. You proceed to trial. The second morning of the trial, you find out that your star witness had made a similar deal in his last drug case in a different jurisdiction and received probation for a substantial amount of meth. Since the trial has begun, double jeopardy applies. Do you reveal the information to the defense? Do you put him on the stand and let the jury decide whether to believe him or not?

Law

There are some laws restricting the use of jailhouse informants, for example, requiring corroborating testimony or requiring a lie detector test. (To see a collection of such laws, go to http://www.snitching.org/p/legislation.html). The Model Rules, which have the force of law when adopted by a state bar, dictate that prosecutors cannot put false information on the stand, but if you were the prosecutor, would you tell yourself that you don't "know" the informant is lying and, therefore, you are not violating the rule? On the other hand, the Model Rules and *Brady* motions do indicate that the information about the prior case be given to the defense since it could be considered exculpatory as it calls into question the credibility of the witness. The 2014 Michael Morton Act in Texas mandates that all prosecutors in the state maintain an "open file" policy meaning defense attorneys should have access to everything prosecutors have unless there is some reason it should be secret. As mentioned above, the *Massiah* case clearly prohibits prosecutors from directing jailhouse informants to ask questions to get confessions.

Policy

In 2005, Los Angeles created an office policy that discouraged the use of jailhouse informants. Most jurisdictions do not, although they may have an office policy of not taking a case to trial that hinges on such testimony. All offices have policies that dictate responding to *Brady* motions, but some offices also have an "open file" policy that allows the defense to have access to any information the prosecutor has except the identity of confidential informants or other information that needs to be kept secret. It is possible that some offices will begin to have policies regarding jailhouse informants since so many of those exonerated have been convicted partially on the testimony of these witnesses.

Ethics

Utilitarian ethics tolerate actions that lead to a good end, but, in this case, there is not much evidence to indicate that the defendant is guilty so it is questionable that conviction is even a good end. Therefore, any "bad means" (such as keeping the information from the defense) may result in a bad end as well. The more difficult ethical issue is whether to continue with the trial at all. Juries are loath to let a murdering sex offender go free and are likely to believe that if someone is prosecuted, they are more than likely guilty. Therefore, even if you provide the information to the defense, it is possible that they will be unable to undercut the credibility of the informant and the defendant will be found guilty. Utilitarian ethics may support such an action if it results in the greatest benefit for the majority. Ethical formalism may not if one interprets a prosecutor's duty as pursuing justice, since a case dependent on a witness who is probably lying is contrary to due process. This explains why jurisdictions are moving away from using jailhouse informant testimony unless it can be corroborated.

Ethical Issues for Judges

Perhaps the best-known symbol of justice is the judge in a black robe. Judges are expected to be impartial, knowledgeable, and authoritative. They guide the prosecutor, defense attorney, and all the other actors in the trial process from beginning to end, helping to maintain the integrity of the proceeding. This is the ideal, but judges are human, with human failings. As mentioned in the last chapter, the potential for bias is exacerbated because judges are elected. Judicial elections are increasingly funded with huge amounts of money. Special interest groups called political action committees (PACs) fund television commercials that are supposedly issue-oriented but thinly veiled attack ads on opponents. The attention to judicial races is largely due to the impact of decisions on civil matters, but the politicization of the bench has affected criminal law also. Judicial decision making seems to have become increasingly political. Judges are the arbitrators of law; when they become merely tools of the politically powerful, then "the rule of law" is threatened.

Conflict of Interest

> *A judge shall uphold and promote the independence, integrity, and impartiality of the judiciary, and shall avoid impropriety and the appearance of impropriety. (Canon 1, Model Code of Judicial Conduct)*

One of the most commonly heard criticisms of judges is that they are not objective. If a judge has some interest in the case—financial, social, or emotional—then their decision making is questioned. The most newsworthy example of this was when President Trump (during the presidential campaign) complained that the federal judge, Gonzalo Curiel, hearing the case regarding Trump University was biased against him because the judge was Mexican. He called for an investigation of the judge. The case was eventually settled.

A more typical allegation is that judges are favorably disposed toward businesses who contribute campaign funds. A study by the Center for Public Integrity examined three years of financial disclosure reports filed by federal appellate judges and found 24 cases where they ruled on cases in which they owned stock in a company that was one of the parties in the case. In all cases, the judges ruled in favor of the companies. In one case, the appellate judge owned $100,000 worth of stock in a company he ruled in favor of in a civil case. Judges typically argue that they are unaware of the companies in their portfolio but when they own individual stocks (rather than mutual funds), that ignorance is not as persuasive (O'Brien, Weir, and Young, 2014).

In the 2007 Model Code of Judicial Conduct, one of the most debated areas was how judges should comport themselves in terms of public speaking and political engagement. The ideal, of course, is that judges should not have any preconceived ideas of who is right or wrong in any controversy they will rule on, but the reality is that judges do not live in a vacuum and, of course, have opinions, values, and beliefs regarding the issues of our times. The rules have been changed to accommodate First Amendment challenges that were upheld in *Minnesota v. White,* 536 U.S. 765, 2002 (McKoski, 2008). Now judges are freer to do speaking engagements and appear at advocacy functions, but there are still ethical issues when a judge indicates a clear bias in a current issue that may come before him or her.

Even the Supreme Court is not immune to charges of conflicts of interest. The late Justice Scalia was criticized for several decisions in which he participated after having made public comments indicating his opinions regarding the legal issue. Justice Thomas has been criticized for not recusing himself in cases where his wife has been associated with the parties involved; for instance, in *Bush v. Gore,* 531 U.S. 98, 2000, she was working with a group collecting resumes for the future Bush administration; in *NFIB v. Sebelius,* 567 U.S. ___, 2012, a case challenging the Constitutionality of the Affordable Care Act, she was the head of a group fighting against the healthcare legislation. In neither case did he recuse himself. Justice Kagan had to recuse herself from 21 of the first 58 cases during her first term because she was formerly the solicitor general and was associated with the government in several cases where the United States was a party. More recently, Justice Ginsburg may have compromised herself in 2016 when she made several disparaging remarks about candidate Trump, joking that she would move to New Zealand if he won the election. Now that the Trump administration's travel ban will end up being considered by the Supreme Court in October 2017, she could be challenged as biased. There is a website (FixtheCourt.com) devoted to improving the transparency and ethics of the Supreme Court since; technically, they are not bound by the Code of Judicial Conduct or any other ethics code.

McKeown (2011) notes that, in some cases, recusal motions are frivolous or border on harassment. Recusal is necessary when a judge has a financial interest in the case, but also when disability, bias, or relationship to the parties might influence the judgment or give the appearance of impropriety. Note that under federal rules, judges must recuse themselves even if there is no bias but a reasonable observer might question the impartiality of the judge. Judges make that determination themselves when a party files a recusal motion. It is also the case that they can ethically only recuse themselves for just cause, not because of any other reason (such as the case is a political minefield and they don't want to be associated with it).

Use of Discretion

A judge shall uphold and apply the law, and shall perform all duties of judicial office fairly and impartially. (Rule 2.2., Model Code of Judicial Conduct)

As we have learned in several previous chapters, discretion refers to the authority to make a choice between two or more actions. Judges have discretion in appointing guardian *ad litem* or indigent cases to attorneys. The practice of awarding indigent cases to one's friends or for reasons other than qualifications may not only be unethical but also may have serious consequences for the defendant. In 2000, the Texas Bar Association (2000) reported that some lawyers who received appointments had been disciplined by the state bar and there was no system for monitoring the quality of the representation. In 2006, a major newspaper ran a series of articles highly critical of the system of appointing lawyers for capital habeas corpus appeals for death row inmates. The investigation found that some lawyers turned in ridiculously short appeals that did not cover even the most obvious points and/or were poorly written and then billed the state for large sums of money (Lindell, 2006a, 2006b, 2006c). Stung by the widespread criticism, the Texas Court of Criminal Appeals has since revised the appointment system for capital cases, putting in place procedures to ensure qualified attorneys are appointed. When habeas corpus appellate attorneys are competent, they may literally save the lives of innocent men and women; thus, whom the judge appoints is an extremely important decision.

Interpretation of Law and Rules

Judges are like the umpire in an athletic contest; they apply the rules and interpret them. Although rules of law are established in Rules of Criminal Procedure and case law, there is still a great deal of discretion in the interpretation of a rule—what is reasonable, what is probative, what is prejudicial, and so on. A judge assesses the legality of evidence and makes rulings on the various objections raised by both the prosecutors and the defense attorneys. A judge also writes the extremely important instructions to the jury. These are crucial because they set up the legal questions and definitions of the case.

One of the clearest examples of judicial discretion is in the application of the exclusionary rule, which basically states that when the evidence has been obtained illegally, it must be excluded from use at trial. The exclusionary rule has generated a storm of controversy because it can result in a guilty party avoiding punishment because of an error committed by the police. The basis for the exclusionary rule is the right to due process. The ideals of justice reject a conviction based on tainted evidence even if obtained against a guilty party. A more practical argument for the exclusionary rule is that if we want police officers to behave in a legal manner, we must have heavy sanctions against illegalities. Arguably, if convictions are lost because of illegal collection of evidence, police will reform their behavior. Actual practice provides little support for this argument. Cases lost on appeal are so far removed from the day-to-day decision making of the police that they have little effect on police behavior. In the succeeding years since the cases that recognized the rule, such as *Mapp v. Ohio,* 367 U.S. 643, 1961, several exceptions to the exclusionary rule have been recognized. Judges can now rule that the illegally obtained evidence be allowed because of public safety (*New York v. Quarles*, 467 U.S. 649, 1984), good faith (*U.S. v. Leon*, 468 U.S. 897, 1984), or inevitable discovery exceptions (*Nix v. Williams* 467 U.S. 431, 1984). In another case, the Supreme Court held the exclusionary rule didn't apply to evidence obtained in a stop and search case even though it was based on an invalid warrant (*Herring v. United States*, 555 U.S. 135, 2009).

In addition to applying the exclusionary rule, the judge is called upon to decide various questions of evidence and procedure throughout a trial. Of course, the judge is guided by the law and legal precedent, but in most cases each decision involves a substantial element of subjectivity. For instance, a defendant may file a pretrial petition for a change of venue. This means that the defendant is arguing that public notoriety and a biased jury pool would make it impossible to have a fair trial in the location where the charges were filed. It is up to the judge, however, to decide if that indeed is true or whether, despite pretrial publicity, the defendant will be assured of a fair trial. If judges are biased either toward or against the prosecution or defense, they have the power to make it difficult for the other side through their pattern of rulings on objections and evidence admitted. Even a personal dislike of either lawyer may be picked up by jury members, and it does affect their attitude toward that side's case.

Despite the belief that simply applying the rules will lead to the right conclusion or decision, the reality is that judges and justices are simply human, and biases can influence their decision making. The suspicion that some appellate court judges decide where they want to end up and make up the argument to get there is one that is hard to deny after a careful reading of some case decisions. At other times, appellate decision making seems to reflect a complete absence of "equity" thinking (basic fairness) in place of a hypertechnical application of rules. Petitions that are denied because a deadline was missed or appeals denied because they were not drawn up in the correct fashion despite obvious substantive legitimacy are examples of this application of discretion. One example of this "form over fairness" occurred in 2009 in Texas. Sharon Keller, the Chief Justice of the Court of Criminal Appeals refused to accept a death penalty appeal because it was after 5 p.m. The man was executed. This hypertechnical application of rules was considered so wrong that 19 attorneys filed an ethics complaint against Keller (Lindell, 2007, 2010b). Several years later, she punished one of the attorneys involved for a late filing by prohibiting him from bringing any cases to the court for 12 months, despite him being the attorney at record for a dozen death penalty cases. Because other attorneys had not been so severely punished, it had the appearance of retaliation (Lithwick, 2015a).

Another example of hypertechnical rules versus justice is the case of Johnny Conner, who was convicted of murder committed during an attempted robbery. His trial attorney neglected to bring forward evidence in which the witnesses described the robber as "sprinting" away from the scene, but Conner had nerve damage in his leg and could only limp. The appellate attorney brought up the issue on appeal, but he neglected to attach any medical evidence, so the appellate judges refused to consider it as new evidence. The attorney general of Texas later argued that, *regardless of the factuality of the evidence*, it should not be allowed in the federal appeal because it was not admitted in the state appeal (Lindell, 2006c). Johnny Connor was executed in August 2007 and critics noted that there was a real possibility that a devotion to the rules resulted in the execution of an innocent man.

Judges may simply apply black and white rules, or they may attempt to enact the "spirit of justice." In June 2010, the majority of the Supreme Court decided that basic fairness and the spirit of justice should be more important than rules. An inmate missed the deadline for an appeal because his attorney did not communicate with him for years despite the inmate's numerous and increasingly frantic written pleas to file the appeal. He even provided the attorney with the information necessary to file it. He also asked the Florida court to replace the attorney, but they refused, and when he filed a *pro se* brief five weeks late, they rejected it. The federal circuit court decided that the circumstances were not "extraordinary"; therefore, the missed deadline must result in rejecting the appeal regardless of its merit. The Supreme Court disagreed, arguing that due process is more important than what Justice Breyer described as "the evils of archaic rigidity" (*Holland v. Florida*, 560 U.S. 631, 2010). At least in this case, basic fairness overcame hypertechnical rules.

One commentator notes that, today, federal judges are so constrained by the restrictions on using habeas corpus to remedy federal rights violations, that it is almost impossible to hear these cases. In *Curiel v. Miller*, 830 F.3d 864, 2016, a federal judge remarked that decades ago, state criminal defendants could use the federal courts and a habeas corpus petition

QUOTE & QUERY

This Court has never held that the Constitution forbids the execution of a convicted defendant who has had a full and fair trial but is later able to convince a habeas court that he is "actually" innocent. Quite to the contrary, we have repeatedly left that question unresolved, while expressing considerable doubt that any claim based on alleged "actual innocence" is constitutionally cognizable.

Source: Justice Scalia, dissenting in In Re Troy Davis, 557 U. S. 952, 967, 2009.

? Was Justice Scalia saying that there is no Constitutional right for those actually innocent to be heard by the courts, and, so long as the trial was fair, it was acceptable to execute innocent individuals?

to challenge incorrect state court interpretations of the U.S. Constitution. Narrowing of the use of *habeas corpus* occurred through court decisions by the Supreme Court and the Anti-Terrorism and Effective Death Penalty Act of 1996. Now, a federal court cannot overturn a state court decision unless it is clearly contrary to a Supreme Court opinion clearly established at the time. Because the Supreme Court only hears about 80 cases a year, it may be that the issue will never reach the Supreme Court, but even if it does and the Supreme Court decides contrary to the state court interpretation, the state decision would not be overturned because the federal decision came after the state decision (O'Neill, 2017).

Sentencing

Another area of judicial discretion is in sentencing. Judges have an awesome responsibility in sentencing offenders and yet receive little training to guide their discretion. It is also true that judges' decisions are scrutinized by public watchdog groups and appellate-level courts.

Evidence indicates that judges' decisions must be based at least partially on personal standards, for no consistency seems to appear between the decisions of individual judges in the same community. Hofer, Blackwell, and Ruback (1999) point out that most of the disparity in sentencing in the federal system before the advent of the sentencing guidelines occurred because of different patterns exhibited by individual judges. They cited studies that found, for instance, that judges' sentences were influenced by whether they had been prosecutors and by their religion. One interesting study, however, indicated that we shouldn't be too quick to assume how judges might rule. For instance, it was found that white and black judges in Louisiana gave about 14 percent longer sentences to juvenile offenders of their own race and were 5 percent more likely to sentence to jail rather than probation members of their own race (Guo, 2016).

The other extreme is when judges have *no* discretion in sentencing. **Federal sentencing guidelines** were written by Congress requiring the judge to impose a specific sentence unless there was a proven mitigating or aggravating factor in the case. The sentencing guidelines did reduce disparity among federal judges (Hofer, Blackwell, and Ruback, 1999); however, the guidelines received a great deal of criticism because of the extremely long sentences applied to drug crimes. Racial bias was alleged in that the sentence for crack cocaine crimes was 100 times longer than sentences for powder cocaine crimes, even though these two drugs are chemically the same. The argument supporting this disparity was that crack cocaine was more associated with other crimes and more addictive; however, there was a widespread belief that the disparity was simply racist. African Americans are much more likely to be convicted of crack crimes, and white Americans are more likely to be convicted for powder cocaine (Hofer, Blackwell, and Ruback, 1999).

Some federal judges, such as J. Lawrence Irving in 1991 and others, were so appalled by the length of drug sentences as required by the sentencing guidelines that they refused to sentence offenders. Some even quit, refusing to impose the mandated sentences, which they considered to be ridiculously long and overly punitive in certain cases (Tonry, 2005). Congress continued to ignore the pleas to make the sentences more equitable, but, in a series of cases, the U.S. Supreme Court basically invalidated the mandatory nature of federal sentencing guidelines. First, they ruled that the defendant's Sixth Amendment rights were violated if the judges used elements

federal sentencing guidelines
Mandated sentences created by Congress for use by judges when imposing sentence (recent Supreme Court decisions have overturned the mandatory nature of the guidelines).

⌨ IN THE NEWS | *Judicial Sentencing*

A Santa Clara County judge was heavily criticized when he sentenced former Stanford swimmer 20-year-old Brock Turner to only six months in jail and probation for sexually assaulting an unconscious woman. He served only half that sentence before release. The case received national publicity for the two good Samaritans who stopped Turner from further assaulting the woman, for the impassioned witness statement the woman posted on social media that went viral, and, because Judge Aaron Persky's sentencing, while within the parameters of law, seemed too lenient. Turner could have faced 15 years in prison and the prosecutor had recommended a six-year prison term. Critics contend that because Turner was white,

an athlete, and came from the middle class, he was accorded favored treatment. Complaints were filed but the judge was cleared of misconduct by the California Commission on Judicial Performance. The body reported that it did not find clear and convincing evidence of bias, abuse of authority, or other basis to conclude that Judge Persky engaged in judicial misconduct warranting discipline. Critics vowed to have the judge removed from the bench in a recall election.

California lawmakers then passed legislation that expanded the definition of rape and increased penalties for offenders who assault unconscious victims. Turner's sentence would not be possible under the new law.

Source: Rocha, 2016.

to increase the sentence without first proving such elements in a court of law (*United States v. Booker*, 543 U.S. 220, 2005). Then they ruled that judges could adjust the sentences downward if it was reasonable to do so (*Kimbrough v. United States*, 552 U.S. 85, 2007). Finally, they extended that ruling to all federal cases, not just drug cases (*Gall v. United States*, 552 U.S. 38, 2007). The standard to be used to evaluate any legal error in sentencing is an abuse of discretion test rather than if the sentence was required because of extraordinary circumstances (Barnes, 2007). Finally, in August 2010, President Obama signed into law legislation that reduced the disparity to 18:1 from 100:1. The new law also eliminated the five-year mandatory minimum sentence for crimes involving five grams of cocaine or more. Attorney General Sessions has indicated his support for mandatory minimum sentences and his belief that reducing the sentences of drug dealers is not in the public interest so it is likely that there will be more changes to come.

If judges stay within statutory limits, their discretion is generally unquestioned when they make sentencing decisions. In 2016, however, one judge did receive a national backlash against one sentence as the In the News box below describes.

Conclusion

In this chapter, we examined how the discretion of defense attorneys, prosecutors, and judges leads to ethical dilemmas. There are crucial differences in the duties and ethical responsibilities of defense attorneys and prosecutors. The prosecutor's goal is justice, which should imply an objective pursuit of the truth; however, we know that sometimes the only goal seems to be winning. Judges have their own unique ethical dilemmas, and their discretion can be understood in the two areas of court rulings and sentencing.

Chapter Review

1. **Describe the ethical issues faced by defense attorneys.**

   Defense attorneys have ethical issues that arise in the areas of responsibility to the client (they must defend clients even if they believe they are guilty and whether or not the client can pay once appointed), conflicts of interest (balancing an individual client against overall effectiveness as an attorney with a caseload of many), zealous defense (determining the limits of what should be done to defend clients), and confidentiality (keeping clients' confidences even if it harms third parties).

2. **Describe the ethical issues faced by prosecutors.**

   The prosecutor must seek justice, not merely a conviction. Ethical issues may arise in the areas of: use of discretion (determining whom to charge), conflicts of interest (and how they affect decision making), plea bargaining (specifically, whether to overcharge and/or hide exculpatory evidence), media relations (and how much to reveal about the case), expert witnesses (including the halo effect, discovery, and the use of forensic evidence), and zealous prosecution (what is acceptable in zealous prosecution).

3. **Describe some of the areas of forensic science that have been challenged by opponents.**

   Only DNA evidence has not received a barrage of criticism regarding the lack of scientific method involved in analysis. Hair analysis, arson investigation, ballistics, fingerprint analysis, bite mark identification, and scent identification have been criticized.

4. **Describe the ethical issues faced by judges.**

   Ethical issues for judges occur in the areas of how to interpret the law or rules (letting biases affect their judgments) and sentencing. While judges can use their discretion to sentence, they should be guided by reasonableness, not any personal or public bias.

5. **Describe how federal sentencing guidelines have changed due to Supreme Court decisions.**

   Sentencing guidelines were widely criticized as racially biased in that crack cocaine earned a punishment 100 times more serious than powder cocaine. Federal judges were hamstrung by the mandatory nature of the sentencing guidelines and could not sentence a drug offender to a shorter term of imprisonment. In *Booker v. U.S.*, the Supreme Court held that the mandatory nature of the guidelines was a violation of due process. The guidelines are now advisory.

Study Questions

1. Explain the confidentiality rules of defense attorneys, and some situations where they may be able to disclose confidential information.

2. Compare the potential conflicts of interest of defense attorneys and those of prosecutors.

3. List and describe the functions of jury consultants and why they are criticized.

4. Describe the different factors that are acceptable and unacceptable for prosecutors to consider when making the decision to charge or what to charge.

5. List the types of information that can be disclosed to the media and the information that should not be revealed to the media by prosecutors.

Writing/Discussion Exercises

1. Write an essay on (or discuss) the proper role of defense attorneys regarding their clients. Should attorneys pursue the wishes of their clients even if they think it is not in the clients' best interest? What if it would hurt a third party (but not be illegal)? Do you think that attorneys should maintain confidentiality if their clients are involved in ongoing criminal activity that is not inherently dangerous?

2. Write an essay on (or discuss) what your decision would be if you were on a disciplinary committee evaluating the following case: a prosecutor was working with police in a standoff between a triple murderer and police. When the murderer demanded to talk to a public defender, the police did not want to have a public defender get involved, so the prosecutor pretended to be one. He spoke with the suspect on the telephone and lied about his name and being a public defender. The man then surrendered to police. The prosecutor was sanctioned by the state bar for misrepresentation and was put on probation and required to take 20 hours of continuing legal education in ethics, pass the Multistate Professional Responsibility Examination, and be supervised by another attorney. In your essay, describe what you think should have occurred and why.

3. Write an essay on (or discuss) the legality/ethics of the following actions of a prosecutor:

    *   Announcing a suspect of a drive-by shooting to the media so the offender was in danger from rival gang members, and then offering protective custody only if the man would plead guilty.

    *   Authorizing the arrest of a 10-year-old boy who confessed to a crime, even though there was no serious possibility that he was guilty, to pressure a relative to confess.

    *   Authorizing the arrest of one brother for drugs, even though the prosecutor knew the charge would be thrown out (but the young man would lose a scholarship to college), to have leverage so that he would give evidence against his brother.

Key Terms

attorney–client privilege	federal sentencing guidelines	plea bargain
criminalistics	halo effect	shadow jury

ETHICAL DILEMMAS

Situation 1

Your first big case is a multiple murder. As defense attorney for Sy Kopath, you have come to the realization that he really did break into a couple's home and torture and kill them while robbing them of jewelry and other valuables. He has even confessed to you that he did it. However, you are also aware that the police did not read him his *Miranda* warning and that he was coerced into giving a confession without your presence. What should you do? Would your answer be different if you believed that he was innocent or didn't know for sure?

Situation 2

You are completing an internship at a defense attorney's office during your senior year in college. After graduation, you plan to enter law school and pursue a career as an attorney, although you have not yet decided what type of law to practice. Your duties as an intern are to assist the private practitioner you work for in a variety of tasks, including interviewing clients and witnesses, organizing case files, running errands, and photocopying. A case that you are helping with involves a defendant charged with armed robbery. One day while you are at the office alone, the defendant comes in and gives you a package for the attorney. In it you find a gun. You believe, but do not know for a fact, that the gun is the one used in the armed robbery. When the attorney returns, he instructs you to return the package to the defendant. What should you do? What should the attorney do?

Situation 3

You are an attorney and are aware of a colleague who could be considered grossly incompetent. He drinks and often appears in court intoxicated. He ignores his cases and does not file appropriate motions before deadlines expire. Any person who is unlucky enough to have him as a court-appointed attorney usually ends up with a conviction and a heavy sentence because he does not seem to care what happens to his clients and rarely advises going to trial. When he does take a case to trial, he is unprepared and unprofessional in the courtroom. You hear many complaints from defendants about his demeanor, competence, and ethics. Everyone—defense attorneys, prosecutors, and judges alike—knows this person and his failings, yet nothing is done. Should you do something? If so, what?

Situation 4

You are a prosecutor in a jurisdiction that does not use the grand jury system. An elderly man has administered a lethal dose of sleeping tablets to his wife, who was suffering from Alzheimer's disease. He calmly turned himself in to the police department, and the case is on the front page of the paper. It is entirely up to you whether to charge him with murder. What would you do? What criteria did you use to arrive at your decision?

Situation 5

You are a deputy prosecutor and must decide whether to charge a defendant with possession and sale of a controlled substance. You know you have a good case because the guy sold drugs to students at the local junior high school, and many of the kids are willing to testify. The police are pressuring you to make a deal because the defendant has promised to inform on other dealers in the area if you don't prosecute. What should you do?

Ethical Misconduct in the Courts and Responses 10

AP Images/Paul Moseley

The wrongfully convicted, like John Nolley, serve decades in prison for crimes they did not commit, sometimes because of unethical actions taken by justice professionals.

Learning Objectives

1. Detail the types of misconduct that have been associated with defense attorneys, prosecutors, and judges.

2. Explain the reasons why such misconduct occurs.

3. Describe some factors in wrongful convictions.

4. Discuss some proposals to improve the justice system and reduce ethical misconduct.

5. Describe the concepts associated with judicial activism or constructionism and how this issue relates to ethical misconduct.

Reading the cases described on the Innocence Project's website or on the Exoneration Registry is difficult because it is truly disheartening to become aware of the blatant racism, laziness, tunnel vision, and/or ambition that leads criminal justice actors to commit actions that contribute to innocent people being incarcerated for decades. A few of the thousands of cases illustrate the pattern:

James Curtis Giles—Giles was exonerated of a gang rape after spending 10 years in prison and 14 years as a registered sex offender. There was no physical evidence linking him to rape and he had an alibi. Police investigators ignored the real perpetrator, a man also named James Giles, who was a crime partner of the other defendant, lived closer to the victim, and matched her description of the attacker (Garay, 2007).

Clarence Brandley—Convicted of rape and murder, Brandley was reportedly told that he was going to hang for the crime because he was black. Caucasian pubic hairs found on the victim were lost, witnesses were coerced, and defense attorneys were not told of witnesses whose statements pointed to another perpetrator.

297

At one point, he was nine days away from being executed. Even after a judge ruled that there was enough evidence to show innocence, it took another two years for him to be released (Davies, 1991; Radelet, Bedau, and Putnam, 1992).

Jeffrey Deskovic—Convicted of the murder of 15-year-old Angela Correa, Deskovic was a 16-year-old classmate. He was interrogated and given a polygraph exam without his parents or an attorney present. Deskovic's mental health was suspect even before the onerous interrogation, and he was hospitalized as suicidal afterward. No physical evidence linked him to the murder, and seminal fluid found in the victim was never compared to sex offender DNA databases. After spending decades in prison, the DNA was finally compared and matched to another man, already serving time for another rape/murder (Snyder, McQuillan, Murphy, and Joselson, 2007).

Kevin Fox—Kevin Fox was convicted of the murder of his own 3-year-old girl. Her body was found about a mile away from his home. Despite searchers finding shoes with the true killer's name, a police report of a burglary next door to the Fox home the night she disappeared, and a police officer who had talked to the killer after relatives had reported him as being extremely agitated the day after the child's body was found, police focused on Fox and set out to prove him guilty. He was subjected to a long interrogation without food or water, and was offered involuntary manslaughter and release on bond if he would plead guilty. He confessed, but immediately retracted. Despite his confession being inconsistent with the medical examiner's report of injuries, he was charged with first-degree murder. The prosecutor pursued the death penalty and made public statements that the child had been sexually abused during her lifetime, although there was no proof ever produced and her pediatrician said that was categorically false. When the DNA from the body was analyzed, it came back to an unknown profile. Charges against Fox were dropped but community members still believed he was guilty. Years later the case was reopened and the true killer was identified (Dardick, 2010).

While ethical misconduct on the part of legal professionals is not always the reason innocent people end up in prison, unfortunately in many cases it is.

Ethical Misconduct

In the sections to follow, it is true that more attention is given to the misconduct of prosecutors and judges than defense attorneys. This is not to say that defense attorneys are more ethical than the other two groups; however, except for public defenders, defense attorneys are not public servants as are the other two groups of legal professionals. It is a legitimate argument that prosecutors and judges have higher duties than defense attorneys because they represent the body politic. They are the public servants referred to in Chapter 4 who have immense powers of discretion but also are held to higher standards of behavior in their public and private life.

Defense Attorney Misconduct

The major complaint about defense attorneys is that they do not communicate regularly with clients. Complaints received by bar associations generally involve clients who believe that they are not getting what they paid for, in that attorneys don't return their calls, don't keep them informed about what is being done on their case, and don't seem to be putting any effort in the case after they have been paid. This is true for civil attorneys as well; however, criminal defendants are helpless since they may be in jail.

Some attorneys meet with their client only before hearings or other court appearances. Perhaps most neglect occurs because of large caseloads. Many attorneys operate under a crisis management approach whereby the to-do list every week can only accommodate those tasks that are at deadline or after a deadline has passed. The consequence is that some cases do not get the attention they should—witnesses are not contacted, legal research is not conducted, and exculpatory evidence is not asked for.

Ineffective Counsel

One of the most often cited reasons for false convictions (in addition to eyewitness testimony) is ineffective assistance of counsel. The legal standard for what constitutes ineffective counsel is set quite high—so high that in the case of Calvin Burdine, whose lawyer slept through parts of his trial, the state appellate court said that if a lawyer wasn't sleeping during a *crucial* part of the trial, it wasn't ineffective counsel. After the defense attorneys appealed in federal court, the 5th Circuit decided that due process required that Burdine deserved a new trial (*Cockrell v. Burdine*, 262 F.3d 336, 2002). Other behaviors reported of lawyers in capital and other cases include the following (Schehr and Sears, 2005):

- Attorneys' use of heroin and cocaine during trial
- Attorneys letting the defendant wear the same clothes described by the victim
- Attorneys admitting that they didn't know the law or facts of the case
- Attorneys not being able to name a single death penalty case holding
- Attorneys drinking heavily each day of the trial and being arrested for a 0.27 blood alcohol level

Cases identified by the Innocence Project or by the Exoneration Registry include many examples of criminal defense attorneys not bringing forward alibi evidence or other exculpatory evidence. Cases also include those where defense attorneys did not challenge the testimony of jailhouse informants, or, in other ways, provided such a poor defense that convictions occurred, even with little or no evidence against innocent defendants.

There are also cases where the attorney has crossed the line from zealous defense to breaking the law. In a few cases, defense attorneys go to extreme lengths to change the course of testimony, such as bribing witnesses or judges, allowing their client to intimidate a witness, or instructing their client to destroy physical evidence or to manufacture an alibi and then commit perjury. In San Antonio, a local attorney pled guilty to bribing a local judge for lenient sentences and other favors for his clients. In return, he paid for repairs on the judge's car. The judge did not run for reelection and eventually also pled guilty (Perez, 2015). Most misconduct by defense attorneys probably falls into the realm of negligence, not criminal behavior, as was the case in the In the News box.

IN THE NEWS | *Criminal Defense*

A Baltimore defense attorney was arrested and arraigned on charges of obstruction of justice and witness intimidation in May 2017. He and his investigator were allegedly recorded as telling a rape victim's husband that she risked deportation if she came to court to testify against their client. They also offered her $3,000.00 to not appear to testify. Then they suggested that her husband just find their client and beat him up. Their client was charged with second-degree rape, third- and fourth-degree sex offenses, and second-degree assault.

Source: Fenton, 2017.

Prosecutorial Misconduct

It is important to recall that the duty of prosecutors is to seek justice, not convictions. Even so, prosecutors want to win, and there are few checks or monitors on their behavior (Elliott and Weiser, 2004). When prosecutors forget that their mission is to protect due process, not merely win the case, misconduct can occur. The types of misconduct range from minor lapses of ethical rules to commission of criminal acts. The In the News box describes an extreme case of alleged criminal conduct.

Most prosecutorial misconduct involves unethical or illegal means to obtain convictions, not pecuniary graft. There is no source that has an accurate accounting of the number of cases marred by prosecutorial misconduct in any jurisdiction. Various investigations have uncovered hundreds of instances where prosecutors either commit unethical acts or break the law. Prosecutorial misconduct includes concealing exculpatory evidence (both testimonial and physical), misleading the jurors as to the meaning of evidence, suppressing expert witness reports when they were exculpatory, and even withholding evidence that pointed to the culpability of their witness as the real killer instead of the person they were prosecuting (Armstrong and Possley, 2002; Kirchmeier, Greenwald, Reynolds, and Sussman, 2009). The Veritas Initiative reviewed more than 4,000 state and federal rulings between 1997 and 2009 in California and identified 707 cases where courts found prosecutorial misconduct. These cases are an undercounting of what probably occurs because they came from appeals. In 159 cases, appellate courts set aside the verdict or declared a mistrial. Only 10 prosecutors received any form of disciplinary action from the state bar (Ridolfi and Possley, 2010). An updated study found 102 more cases in 2010 where 130 instances

---

▐💬 IN THE NEWS | *Criminal Prosecution*

Seth Williams is Philadelphia's top prosecutor, heading an office of 300 prosecutors. In 2016, he was indicted on federal charges of bribery and obstruction. He was elected to the office in 2010 and, until his career burst into a flame of scandal, he had won accolades for innovations in the prosecutor's office. Charging documents indicate he asked for thousands of dollars in bribes from individuals who faced legal charges. A 29-count indictment describes some of the exchanges. In return for intervening in one case, he accepted foreign trips, a used Jaguar convertible, and other gifts including a $205 Louis Vuitton necktie and a Burberry watch. He is also accused of stealing from his own mother, taking $20,000 of Social Security and pension income intended to pay for her nursing home. Despite a salary of over $175,000 a year, Williams was known for complaining about not having enough money to pay for his lifestyle. He had already

been assessed a large fine by the Philadelphia Board of Ethics for failure to report more than $175,000 in gifts he had accepted, including a new roof, luxury vacations, Eagles sidelines passes, and use of a defense attorney's home in Florida. The federal investigation evidently uncovered e-mails where he asked for a vacation trip and admonished the man to give him at least a week when he wanted his help in criminal matters.

He did not resign even when his trial started in June 2017; however, two weeks into the trial he abruptly sent a resignation letter to the mayor and pleaded guilty. The plea agreement with the federal prosecutor had him pleading guilty to one count in return for dropping all other charges. Williams faces up to five years in prison, $250,000 in restitution, a $62,000 fine that has already been assessed by the election board for mishandling campaign funds, and the loss of his pension.

Sources: Roebuck and Brennan, 2017; Roebuck, Gambacorta, and Brennan, 2017; Roebuck, 2017.

of prosecutors' misconduct were identified. In 26 of the cases, judges set aside convictions or sentences, declared a mistrial, or barred evidence specifically because of the misconduct. These studies identified 107 prosecutors who committed more than one case of misconduct, and a few were cited for misconduct four, five, and six times (Martinez, 2011).

The Innocence Project (working with the Veritas Initiative) conducted similar studies in New York, Texas, Arizona, and Pennsylvania. Researchers searched through Westlaw database and reviewed trial and appeals court decisions addressing allegations of prosecutor misconduct between the years 2004 and 2008, and searched through state bar disciplinary records. New York had 151 findings of prosecutor misconduct and 3 prosecutors were disciplined. In Texas, there were 91 findings of prosecutor misconduct and only 1 prosecutor disciplined. In Arizona, 20 incidents of prosecutor misconduct were found and 3 prosecutors disciplined. Pennsylvania had 46 findings of prosecutor misconduct with 2 prosecutors disciplined.

The California District Attorneys Association (CDAA) and the Texas District & County Attorneys Association (TDCAA) published reports strongly critical of the methodology of the research into prosecutorial misconduct. These organizations reanalyzed the cases used in the California and Texas studies. Their findings indicate that prosecutorial misconduct is extremely rare and that prior studies incorrectly and unfairly conflated unintentional error with misconduct (CDAA, 2012; TDCAA, 2012).

Cox reexamined a sample of the California cases and all the Texas cases as a validity check against the Veritas and district attorney associations' findings, finding that the district attorney's analysis undercounted cases of misconduct by misclassifying them as error (T. Cox, 2016). She found the types of prosecutorial misconduct or errors most commonly noted included improper comments during closing arguments, eliciting improper testimony from a witness, and prejudicial statements made to the jury. *Brady* violations accounted for very few of the instance of misconduct (less than 6 percent). Only 20 percent of misconduct findings resulted in a conviction or sentence being overturned. Significant themes included the lack of consistent language used by judges to identify misconduct and error, the lack of judicial concern over whether the prosecutor had the intent to commit misconduct or simply made a mistake, the role that lack of prosecutor training and experience plays in the occurrence misconduct, and the lack of agreement between appellate cases and prosecutors themselves regarding the prevalence of *Brady* violations. She concluded that appellate decisions are not suitable sources of data for identifying and policing prosecutor misconduct because judges are often unclear regarding their findings of misconduct or error, or may not reach a decision regarding misconduct at all. Furthermore, harmless error analysis is used; therefore, the intent of the prosecutor is less important than the strength of the state's case against a defendant in determining the consequences of misconduct. She also noted that the prosecutor culture may also contribute to the amount of misconduct and error that occurs and, although prosecutors considered *Brady* violations to be the most common types of misconduct, they appeared in less than 10 percent of the appellate case decisions in the study.

Kirchmeier et al. (2009) discuss four types of prosecutorial misconduct: withholding exculpatory evidence, misusing pretrial publicity, using false evidence in court, and using peremptory challenges to exclude jurors despite *Batson v. Kentucky*,

476 U.S. 79, 1986, which prohibited race discrimination in jury selection. When a prosecutor violates the *Batson* ruling and uses peremptory challenges in a racially discriminatory manner, there should be some sanction; however, the prosecutor must show only that he or she had some other reason for exclusion, and the legal standard is whether there is any explanation for the exclusion, even if implausible (*Purkett v. Elem*, 514 U.S. 765, 1995). Statistics from the Equal Justice Initiative, a legal advocacy group, indicate that black jurors are dismissed at a blatantly disproportionate rate compared to white jurors. In some jurisdictions, blacks were removed three times as often as whites and, in another jurisdiction, 80 percent of blacks were struck from capital cases by prosecutors (*New York Times*, 2010). There is really no way to know if a prosecutor uses a peremptory challenge because of the race of the potential juror, but in some cases, there are suspicious indications such as codes for racial appearance on the prosecutor's notes. Some other types of misconduct are discussed next.

Improper Conduct, Improper Relationships

There are some examples in the news where it appears the prosecutors involved did not take their duty as public servants seriously. For instance, the Two-Ton Contest in Illinois has been written about by several authors. It occurred when prosecutors participated in a contest to see who could convict 4,000 pounds of flesh. In the attempt to win, they vied to handle cases of the most overweight defendants and, one assumes, let their prosecutorial judgment be affected by the size of the defendant (Medwed, 2009). In other instances, such as the one described in the In the News box, a prosecutor and police detective together subvert justice.

IN THE NEWS | *Prosecutorial Misconduct*

Michael Vecchione was a top prosecutor in Brooklyn before his and a disgraced former police investigator's actions led to an investigation of over 70 cases that might have resulted in wrongful convictions. Both men retired, leaving the office to reexamine scores of cases they worked on. One of the cases identified was Jabbar Collins who served 15 years in prison before he was released and settled his lawsuit against the city for $10 million. A court released him because of evidence that Assistant District Attorney Vecchione coerced false testimony. A federal judge called Assistant District Attorney Vecchione's conduct "horrific" and said that he was "disturbed" and "puzzled" that the District Attorney did not punish him. A prosecution witness who has recanted said Vecchione threatened to hit him with a coffee table and make him stay in jail unless he testified for the prosecution. Vecchione was also accused of *Brady* violations, intimidating a second witness with jail, and promising a third witness that his probation violation would be cleared. There was also testimony that law enforcement officials from the Brooklyn District Attorney's Office held witnesses in hotel rooms against their will and without legal justification, and prosecutors used forged, falsely "sworn" applications to obtain warrants to arrest and detain individuals who were merely prospective witnesses. The police investigator, Louis Scarcella, has been implicated in over 70 cases where there is evidence that innocent people have been convicted because of coerced confessions, intimidated witnesses, and/or perjured testimony. In at least five Scarcella cases, the individuals have been exonerated. Most of them date back to the 1980s and 1990s and observers note that the patterns do not point to simply one rogue detective, but, rather, the collusion of prosecutors and detectives to move cases through the system.

Sources: Clifford, 2014; Marzulli, 2015; Robles, 2013a, 2013b; Saul, 2014.

Suborning Perjury and Jailhouse Informants

Model Rule 3.3(a) forbids an attorney from knowingly allowing false evidence to be admitted; some argue that "knowingly" is too strict a standard because prosecutors have argued that they did not "know" that the evidence was false and that an objective negligence standard should be used instead (Zacharias and Green, 2009). Like a defense attorney's quandary when a witness commits perjury, a prosecutor must also take steps to avoid allowing false testimony to stand. The prosecutor's role is the easier one because there are no conflicting duties to protect a client; therefore, when a prosecution witness perjures himself or herself, the prosecutor has an affirmative duty to bring it to the attention of the court.

Recall from Chapters 5 and 7 that the prevalence of "testilying" by police officers is unknown, but many believe that it is widespread. Researchers, observers, and especially defense attorneys believe that testilying would not occur as much if not for the active or passive acceptance of the practice by prosecutors (L. Cunningham, 1999; S. Cunningham, 2016). In 1999, in the small Texas town of Tulia, many black defendants were convicted based on the perjured testimony of one police investigator. The prosecutor knew that the police officer on the stand had lied about his past, yet he did not disclose that information and allowed the perjury to stand. It was also revealed that the investigator lied about the defendants as well. After the intervention of the ACLU and, eventually, the governor of Texas commuting the sentences, the dozens of people convicted were finally released. The prosecutor was sanctioned by the Texas bar and almost lost his law license. Many believe he should have, considering his role in the convictions (Herbert, 2002, 2003).

Recall from Chapter 9 that the use of jailhouse informants has become increasingly subject to scrutiny as their role in wrongful convictions becomes apparent. Prosecutors who use jailhouse informants today are on notice that research shows there is a high probability that their testimony is false. Jailhouse informants have been implicated in many wrongful convictions.

Misconduct Involving Expert Witnesses

Misconduct also occurs when prosecutors intentionally use scientific evidence that they know to be false. There are proven instances where prosecutors put on the stand so-called experts that they knew were unqualified and/or their expertise was without merit (Gershman, 2003). Prosecutors may bolster a witness's credentials or allow him or her to make gratuitous and unsupported claims on the witness stand, such as to state "unequivocally" that the fingerprint, hair, or lip print was the defendant's.

Giannelli and McMunigal (2007) and Fisher (2008) describe a long list of expert witnesses who became well known for their pro-prosecution bias and outlandish testimony in bite marks and other areas. So-called experts include Louise Robbins (who testified in one notorious case that a boot mark matched the defendant's even though no other forensic examiner agreed) and Michael West (who supposedly invented a way to use light to identify bite marks on murder victims and always seemed to find a match to the suspect). Joyce Gilchrist, a forensic chemist from Oklahoma, was implicated in several exonerations for her hair analysis testimony in which she overstated the accuracy of the procedure and/or simply lied (Fisher, 2008; Raeder, 2007). Fred Zain evidently systematically lied, altered lab reports, and suppressed test results

QUOTE & **QUERY**

There are disturbing indications that a non-trivial number of prosecutors—and sometimes entire prosecutorial offices—engage in misconduct that seriously undermines the fairness of criminal trials. The misconduct ranges from misleading the jury, to outright lying in court and tacitly acquiescing or actively participating in the presentation of false evidence by police.

Judge Alex Kozinski, 9th Circuit Court of Appeals—the judge who barred the entire office of prosecutors from Orange County, California, from appearing in his court.

Source: Ferner, 2016.

 Do you think the judge should have barred the entire office of prosecutors because of unethical behavior?

favorable to the defense (Possley, Mills, and McRoberts, 2004). These experts continued to be used by prosecutors even after appellate courts had excoriated their testimony and they were widely criticized by peers (Fisher, 2008).

Prosecutors have had experts suppress information that was favorable to the defense and not put it in their report or not conduct tests that might be helpful to the defense. Sometimes expert reports are provided to the defense but delay is used to undercut the ability of the defense to use the information. In other cases, experts are asked not to write a report at all if their findings do not help the prosecution, or prosecutors have the report filed as inconclusive so that they do not have to provide it to the defense (Giannelli and McMunigal, 2007). In their closing arguments, prosecutors may overstate the expert's testimony so "is consistent with" becomes "matched" (Gershman, 2003: 36). In some egregious cases, prosecutors have simply lied about physical evidence, such as stating that the red substance on a victim's underpants was blood when, in fact, it was paint (Gershman, 2003; *Miller v. Pate*, 386 U.S. 1, 1967). The quote in Quote and Query indicates that at least some judges notice prosecutorial misconduct.

Brady Violations

The most common charge leveled against prosecutors, failure to disclose evidence, stems from a duty to reveal exculpatory evidence to the defense. In Chapter 9, the obligation to disclose exculpatory evidence established in *Brady v. Maryland* 373 U.S. 83, 1963 was discussed. Prosecutor Charles Sebesta was disbarred from the practice of law in the state of Texas for *Brady* violations and other misconduct during the Anthony Graves' trial. The 1992 murder of six family members, include four children, traumatized a town. Police quickly arrested Robert Carter, the father of one of the children. He named Anthony Graves as the person who helped him commit the murders, although he later recanted. Anthony Graves was convicted despite having an alibi and no evidence that he even knew the people killed. The prosecutor used Carter's testimony, and the testimony of five inmates and jailers who swore they heard Graves confess, even though it was later discovered they had committed perjury. Graves' case was reopened when a journalism class found evidence that Sebesta never shared Carter's recantation with Graves' attorneys. Evidently Sebesta obtained an indictment against Carter's wife and told Carter he would prosecute her if Carter did not testify against Graves. After Graves' trial, the charges against Carter's wife were dropped. The prosecutor who was brought in to retry the case found it highly unlikely that charges would be dropped against anyone who had participated in a multiple homicide. After she began evaluating the evidence, she came to realize that Graves was innocent and took steps to secure his release. After Graves' exoneraton, in June 2015, a three-person panel of the Texas State Bar Association voted to strip Sebesta of his law license (Colloff, 2011).

Prosecutors who engage in acts such as those described in the In the News box not only risk losing the immediate case, but also lose their credibility and undercut the trust and faith we place in the justice system.

IN THE NEWS | *Federal Prosecutor Misconduct*

Ted Stevens was a senator from Alaska before his death in an airplane crash. A federal judge threw out his federal conviction for conflict of interest and bribery in 2009 after an FBI agent that had been an investigator on the case reported that prosecutors tried to hide a witness and did not share transcripts where Bill Allen, their star witness, made contradictory statements. Justice Department prosecutors used pending charges of sexual misconduct with underage girls as leverage for Allen's testimony, a fact not shared with defense attorneys.

In another case involving federal prosecutors, Dr. Ali Shaygan was acquitted of 141 counts of illegal prescriptions of painkillers and federal prosecutors were admonished by a federal justice who suspected them of witness tampering and secretly taping conversations with Shaygan's lawyers. U.S. District Court judge Alan Gold accused the federal prosecutors of knowingly and repeatedly violating ethical guidelines and acting in bad faith.

In New Orleans, the convictions of Robert Faulcon Jr., Kenneth Bowen, Robert Gisevius Jr., Anthony Villavaso II, and Arthur "Archie" Kaufman, the officers who had been convicted of homicide and a cover-up in the Danziger Bridge incident after Hurricane Katrina, were overturned. Federal Judge Kurt D. Engelhardt ruled that "grotesque prosecutorial misconduct" on the part of federal prosecutors left him no choice but order new trials for all the men. The prosecutors, he argued, had created a prejudicial atmosphere by anonymously posting comments before and during the trial at Nola.com, the website of the *New Orleans Times-Picayune*.

Sources: Hagan, 2012; Johnson, 2009; Linderman, 2013; Perksy, 2009 .

Judicial Misconduct

Public exposés of judicial misconduct are rare. Operation Greylord, in Chicago, took place in the 1980s. Because of an FBI investigation, 92 people were indicted, including 17 judges, 48 lawyers, 10 deputy sheriffs, 8 police officers, 8 court officials, and a member of the Illinois legislature, and 31 attorneys and 8 judges were convicted of bribery. Judges accepted bribes to "fix" cases—to rule in favor of the attorney offering the bribe. Not unlike law enforcement's "blue curtain of secrecy," not one attorney came forward to expose this system of corruption, even though what was occurring was well known (Weber, 1987).

In the infamous "kids for cash" scandal in Pennsylvania, former judges Michael Conahan and Mark Ciavarella in Lucerne County were prosecuted for almost literally "selling" youthful offenders to a private correctional facility. They were charged with racketeering, money laundering, fraud, bribery, and federal tax violations for accepting millions of dollars in return for sending juveniles who appeared before them to a private correctional facility. Conahan had earlier shut down the county-run youth corrections center, so they would have to send the kids to the private facility. The judges conducted hearings without appointing lawyers for the juveniles and then sent them to the private facility for minor offenses. The scandal led to overturning hundreds of juvenile convictions and releasing many of the juvenile offenders sent to the facility. No one can explain why the scheme had not been exposed years before or why prosecutors, probation officers, or defense attorneys never questioned what was happening. But red flags were raised. A newspaper had done an exposé on harsh juvenile sentencing in 2004, and a defense attorney had filed a complaint with the state judicial disciplinary board in 2006, but the board failed to act until after the two judges had been indicted by the federal grand jury. The investigation began after another judge in the jurisdiction went to the FBI with his suspicions. Conahan pleaded guilty to a racketeering conspiracy charge and was sentenced to 17 years in prison. Ciavarella went to trial, was convicted of racketeering, was sentenced to 28 years in prison, and must pay $965,000 in restitution.

Biased Decisions

Most judges strive to fulfill their role with integrity and honesty, taking care to protect the appearance and reality of justice. Judicial canons require judges to avoid even the appearance of bias or impropriety. In Chapter 9, the rule against conflict of interests was discussed. Misconduct is alleged when judges do not recuse themselves and/or act in ways that give preferential treatment to individuals or groups.

There is a prohibition on attorneys and judges discussing a case outside the presence of the other attorney, this is called *ex parte* communication and is prohibited because it gives one side preference over the other. Because of working conditions, this is much more likely between prosecutors and judges than with defense attorneys. This rule applies to casual conversations as well as more formal interchanges or offerings of information. *Ex parte* communications create the perception (if not the reality) of bias and if a judge favors one side or the other, due process is imperiled; for instance, one Houston judge was investigated for sending text messages during the trial to the prosecutor suggesting a line of questioning to help bolster the prosecution's case. There were allegations that it was not the first time she had done so (Horswell, 2013).

In Chapter 9, we discussed the expectation that judges maintain an unbiased position toward any issue that might come before him or her. In some cases, judges have been asked to recuse themselves because they have indicated to news media that they already had opinions on a case before it was concluded. In 2006, the late Justice Scalia, in a public speech, opined that giving full due-process rights to detainees in Guantanamo was "crazy" and made remarks referring to his son, who was serving in Iraq at the time. Several groups demanded that he recuse himself from the case of *Hamdan v. Rumsfeld,* 548 U.S. 557, 2006, because the case was about what, if any, due-process rights in American courts the detainees deserved. Justice Scalia did not recuse himself, and Hamdan did win his case, with the Supreme Court holding that detainees deserved some due process and that the military commissions that were created at the time were not sufficient. Scalia was in the dissent, however, so arguably one might conclude that he had already made up his mind before the case was decided (Lane, 2006).

Other Misconduct

Swisher (2009) lists and discusses various forms of judicial misconduct, including

- failing to inform defendants of their rights,
- coercing guilty pleas,
- exceeding sentencing authority,
- exceeding bail authority,
- denying full and fair hearings or trials,
- abusing the criminal contempt power,
- ignoring probable cause requirements,

IN THE NEWS | Judicial Misconduct

Judge Joseph Boeckmann in Arkansas resigned before a disciplinary committee could fully investigate allegations from dozens of people that he had propositioned male defendants for nude photographs and sexual favors in return for leniency. Male defendants described how they were given community service and then asked to take off their shirts, and let the judge take photos of them bending over "to prove they had performed community service." Sometimes he touched their buttocks. Some men agreed to let him take nude photos and some said they agreed to be spanked by the judge. The head of the Arkansas Judicial Discipline and Disability Commission called it "if not the worst, among the worst cases of judicial misconduct" in state history. Gossip and allegations had existed for 30 years about the judge. Only recently, however, did several victims file a lawsuit and submit charges to the Judicial Discipline board. The judge denied all charges but resigned. An investigation uncovered over 4,000 pictures of nude or semi-nude men on the judge's computer; and records that showed defendants who had their charges dropped despite being repeat offenders. Some of them listed the judge as their employer or listed as their residence houses owned by the judge. Possibly at least 35 potential victims have or will come forward. The Judicial Commission's investigation ended with the judge's resignation but there might be a criminal investigation underway.

In another case, former Nashville Judge Casey Moreland was charged with five felony counts and arrested in March 2016. Allegations are that he offered leniency to at least two women in exchange for sex. There are also allegations that he attempted to get one of the women to recant her allegations against him, and when she refused, he developed a scheme to frame her by planting drugs in her car and then having her arrested. He also was alleged to have interfered in a traffic stop of his girlfriend by telling the police officer to not give her a ticket. He could face a maximum of 80 years in prison and a fine of $1.25 million.

Former Pennsylvania Supreme Court Justice Seamus P. McCaffery resigned in 2014 before an ethics investigation would have probably stripped him of his pension. McCaffery was accused of exchanging 234 e-mails containing pornographic materials, interfering in civil courts in cases involving individuals who paid referral fees or contributed to his campaign, and fixing a traffic ticket for his wife.

Federal District Court Judge Mark E. Fuller of the Middle District of Alabama was arrested and charged with battery in early August 2014 for beating his wife. Other allegations against the judge were that he had also beat his first wife, had an affair with his current wife who was his court bailiff at the time, refused to recuse himself from cases where the federal government was a party even though he received millions in federal money in his private business, and orchestrated the arrest and conviction of the former governor, refusing to recuse himself from that case even though there had been enmity between the two. He refused to step down until June of 2015 when the U.S. Judicial Conference, recommended impeachment. Fuller resigned to keep his federal pension.

Sources: Barchenger and Boucher, 2016; Blinder and Robertson, 2014; Friedman, 2015; Lauer, 2016; McCoy and Purcell, 2014.

- denying defendants' rights, and
- penalizing defendants for exercising their rights.

Other forms of unethical behavior are less blatant. Judges have a duty to conclude judicial processing with reasonable punctuality. However, there are widespread delays in processing, partly because of the lack of energy with which some judges pursue their dockets. In the same jurisdiction, and with a balanced assignment of cases, one judge may have only a couple dozen pending cases and another judge may have literally hundreds. Some judges routinely allow numerous continuances, set trial dates far into the future, start the docket call at 10:00 a.m., conclude the day's work at 3:00 p.m., and in other ways take a desultory approach to swift justice.

Pimentel (2009) notes that while egregious cases of judicial misconduct appear in the news (i.e., sexual misconduct or bribery), the more prevalent forms of misconduct may only be known to the attorneys who practice before the judge (i.e., favoritism, racial or gender bias, and arbitrary decision making). However, it is extremely rare for attorneys to file complaints against judges. In fact, Pimentel notes one case in which an attorney reported that his client bribed a judge, and, as a result, the attorney was disciplined by the bar association for revealing client confidences. Nothing happened to the judge.

We must be careful not to paint with too broad a brush. Only a few judges are involved in the most egregious examples of unethical behavior, such as taking bribes or trampling the due-process rights of defendants, just as only a small percentage of police officers, defense attorneys, and prosecutors commit extreme behaviors. Most judges are ethical and take great care to live up to the obligations of their role. However, as with the other criminal justice professionals, sometimes there are systemic biases and subtle ways in which the principles of justice and due process are subverted.

Factors in Wrongful Conviction

Recall from Chapters 3 and 8 that wrongful convictions are increasingly appearing in the news. The factors that seem to be correlated with wrongful convictions clearly indicate that legal professionals must take responsibility for reducing the possibility of such gross miscarriages of justice. It should be recognized that while sometimes prosecutors are implicated as pivotal in a wrongful conviction (e.g., Ken Anderson in the Michael Morton case), in other cases, prosecutors have been pivotal in helping to free someone.

When wrongful convictions were compared with cases where a factually innocent defendant was indicted but the prosecution was dropped or didn't result in a conviction, researchers found that these factors influenced the likelihood of a wrongful conviction: state punitiveness, a weak case, error during forensic testimony, age and prior criminal history of the defendant, honest mistaken identity by an eyewitness, and poor representation by a defense attorney (Gould et al., 2014; see also, Gould, Carrano, Leo, and Young, 2012). Other factors (perjury by informants, police and prosecutorial misconduct, false confessions, "junk science," ineffective assistance of counsel) have been discussed previously.

Mistaken Eyewitness Testimony

Mistaken eyewitness testimony is the most frequently identified factor in wrongful convictions. We know more today about the vagaries of eyewitness memory today than we have in previous years. Research shows that memory is not as accurate as some people (including jurors) believe. Mistaken eyewitness testimony may not involve any wrongdoing on the part of police or prosecutors; however, in some cases, improper police or prosecutor behavior influenced witnesses to identify the wrong person. For instance, police officers may repeatedly ask victims if they were sure that the suspect was not the person, or using "show-ups" that present only one person to the witness instead of a lineup. Research shows that people are woefully poor witnesses and, more dangerous, are convinced they are right about the identification by the time of trial.

The Supreme Court rejected an argument that judicial review of eyewitness testimony was necessary even given the research that showed how faulty it was (*Perry v. New Hampshire*, 132 S. Ct. 716, 2012). This leaves it to prosecutors' offices to make sure such testimony is credible. Suggestions include using sequential identification (since witnesses feel pressure to pick one person from a regular lineup even if told none of the people may be the suspect), and double-blind identifications where the law enforcement official does not know which person is the suspect (to avoid giving conscious or unconscious cues) (Wise and Safer, 2012). These science-based techniques to improve accuracy are only helpful if prosecutors and law enforcement investigators are motivated to use them.

False Confessions

False confessions are another important factor in wrongful convictions. Chapter 6 covered how police behavior can induce a person to confess by coercive and/or deceptive interrogations, but prosecutors are also complicit in participating in or using false confessions. False confessions are so powerful that juries have convicted individuals even when there is exculpatory DNA evidence introduced at trial. Prosecutors explain away the DNA by saying in rape cases that the victim may have had consensual sex with someone else before the rape by the defendant, and, in murder cases, that explanations exist for the presence of unknown persons, for example, someone came along after the murder and had sex with the corpse was used as an explanation in one case! Garrett (2011), in his review of wrongful convictions, identified 40 cases of false confessions; over half were given by juveniles or mentally challenged suspects.

Eddie Lowery spent 10 years in prison for a rape he didn't commit. His confession included elements of the crime that only the perpetrator would have known. He confessed because police told him he failed a lie detector test and he believed that they wouldn't let up until he confessed. How did his confession include details of the crime scene? Because they coached him, said Lowery, correcting him on every element of his confession until he got it right. Lowery received $7.5 million in a suit against the police department in Riley County, Kansas (Garrett, 2011).

The "Norfolk Four" were four sailors who were convicted of rape and murder in 1997. They allege that they falsely confessed to the crime because of the coercive interrogation tactics of a police investigator. He told them that if they didn't confess, they would die. There was no other evidence to link them to the crime. Before they were brought to trial, another man, who knew the victim, confessed, admitting he did it alone, and his DNA was found at the crime scene, yet the prosecutors continued with their case against the Norfolk Four. One of the Norfolk Four served eight years before being released, but the other three were still in prison until being pardoned by Virginia's governor in August 2009. The pardon was conditional and the men were released on parole, but had to register as sex offenders. In 2017, they finally received a full pardon by the current governor who referred to additional evidence of innocence. For instance, Robert Glenn Ford, the police detective who interrogated them, was later found guilty of extortion and lying to the FBI and sentenced to 12-and-a-half years in prison (Boghani, 2017).

Racial Bias

Garrett's (2011) study of 250 exonerees found that 70 percent were minorities. Whereas some of the cases probably involve pure and extreme racial prejudice, a prevalent factor in false convictions is a subtler form of racism. Many in the criminal justice system tend to prejudge the guilt of the accused, especially if they are black men. There is a pervasive stereotypical belief that all defendants are guilty, and a disproportionate number of defendants are black. This thought pattern shapes and distorts decision making on the part of prosecutors who may sift and use evidence in a way that will support these predetermined beliefs. Also noted is a higher rate of error in cross-racial identification, stereotyping, and lack of resources among minority defendants (Schehr and Sears, 2005).

Confirmatory Bias

Confirmatory bias is when someone ignores evidence that is contrary to what they believe. Confirmatory bias may lead to wrongful convictions because prosecutors ignore evidence that tends to refute their theory of the case. It might even lead to the noble-cause corruption discussed in Chapter 5. Just as police may commit misconduct when they think they have the guilty party, so, too, may prosecutors bend and even break the rules when they are sure the defendant is guilty. For instance, some prosecutors may not disclose evidence to the defense because they perceive that as possibly endangering their ability to get a murderer off the street. Alternatively, these individuals may be affected by confirmatory bias in that they truly cannot see the exculpatory nature of the evidence because they believe so strongly that the defendant is guilty.

▌ Explanations for Misconduct

The ideal, or vision, of our justice system is that it is fair, unbiased, and, through the application of due process, arrives at the truth before finding guilt and assessing punishment. The reality is that the law is administered by humans with human failings and that errors and misconduct result in innocent people being convicted, incarcerated, and sometimes executed. In this section, prosecutors get a disproportionate amount of attention because they are public servants and owe special duties to the public.

Prosecutors have similar powers of discretion as police officers, and they seem to also have a subculture that creates pressure to cut corners to gain a conviction. In the Quote and Query, a prosecutor explains how the mission of justice becomes subverted.

QUOTE & **QUERY**

. . . In 1984, I was 33 years old. I was arrogant, judgmental, narcissistic and very full of myself. I was not as interested in justice as I was in winning. To borrow a phrase from Al Pacino in the movie And Justice for All, *"Winning became everything." . . . After the death verdict in the Ford trial, I went out with others and celebrated with a few rounds of drinks. That's sick. I had been entrusted with the duty to seek the death of a fellow human being, a very solemn task that certainly did not warrant any "celebration."*

Marty Stroud, a New Orleans prosecutor in the Glenn Ford wrongful conviction case. Ford served 30 years before being exonerated. The quote is from Stroud's letter to the newspaper apologizing for what happened. Read his letter here: www.shreveporttimes.com/story/opinion /readers/2015/03/20/lead-prosecutor-offers -apology-in-the-case-of-exonerated-death-row -inmate-glenn-ford/25049063.

? Is it wrong for prosecutors to celebrate convictions?

Explanations of Prosecutor Misconduct

In response to a question about why prosecutors commit the various forms of misconduct described earlier, one commentator explained succinctly, "Because they can." The office of the prosecutor is one of the least scrutinized in the criminal justice system and has not experienced the intense analysis directed to law enforcement or the courts. Hidden from public view are the decisions as to whom to prosecute and what charges to file. Furthermore, when wrongdoing is exposed, there is little chance of serious sanctions.

Prosecutors are immune from Section 1983 liability for their decision to prosecute or actions taken in preparation for or during trial (*Imbler v. Pachtman*, 424 U.S. 409, 1976). The Supreme Court has also ruled that prosecutors cannot be subject to civil suits against them, even in cases of egregious rule breaking, if it concerns their adversarial function or prosecutorial decisions (*Connick v. Thompson*, 563 U.S. 51, 2011). Prosecutors have limited immunity for actions taken during the investigative phase of a case and for administrative activities. Thus, lying for a warrant, coercing confessions, or making false statements to the press could expose them to liability, but rarely does (Kirchmeier et al., 2009; Zacharias and Green, 2009). Prosecutors have limited immunity when giving legal advice to police officers (T. Cox, 2016; Cox, Cunningham and Pollock, 2017).

When Mike Nifong was sued by the lacrosse players for statements made to the press and other misconduct, the city refused to indemnify him and he declared bankruptcy. Thomas Lee Goldstein was more successful in obtaining damages. He was wrongfully convicted in Los Angeles County partially due to the prosecutor's misconduct. In this case, the prosecutor used a jailhouse informant who testified that Goldstein confessed, but the informant lied on the stand that he had never been an informant in the past. In fact, he had and had received money for previous testimony in another case. The prosecutor allowed the perjury to stand. Goldstein had his case overturned and was exonerated and sued on a theory of misconduct during the administrative functions of the prosecutor role. A lower court barred his suit holding that the prosecutor's actions fell under his immunity protections and he appealed that decision; however, he ended up settling with the city for $7.95 million (Cathcart, 2010; Zacharias and Green, 2009).

At this point, the Supreme Court has shown no inclination to take away prosecutors' immunity. In *Pottawattamie County v. McGhee and Harrington, 556 U.S. 1198, 2009*, the parties settled before the Supreme Court reached an opinion. However, during oral arguments, the justices seemed concerned that reducing the immunity of prosecutors would make them more hesitant to aggressively prosecute crime and subject them to frivolous lawsuits. The case involved two men who were wrongfully convicted when they were teens and served almost 30 years in prison because a prosecutor helped assemble and present false testimony against them and hid evidence that implicated the relative of a city official. They settled for $12 million with the county before the Supreme Court made any decision whether the immunity of prosecutors extends to the acts of preparing false testimony to be used in court. In another case, the Supreme Court reaffirmed prosecutorial immunity even when the prosecutor violated *Brady* rules by not disclosing exculpatory information about a jailhouse informant to the defense (*Van De Kamp v. Goldstein*, 555 U.S. 335, 2009).

In 2011, John Thompson's favorable verdict by a federal trial court awarding him $14 million for prosecutorial misconduct by the New Orleans prosecutors' office was overturned by the Supreme Court. Thompson was convicted of robbery and murder when New Orleans prosecutors withheld exculpatory test results of blood found at the crime scene that was not his. He spent 18 years in prison for a crime he did not commit. After he was exonerated, he filed a Section 1983 suit against the district attorney's office, arguing there was deliberate indifference in allowing prosecutors to violate *Brady* rules (to turn over exculpatory evidence to the defense). The Supreme Court ruled 5–4 that District Attorney Harry Connick, Sr. could not be held liable for a single *Brady* violation (*Connick v. Thompson*, 131 S. Ct. 1350, 2011). In *Truvia v. Connick,*

No. 14-708, 5th Cir., 2014, several individuals who had been exonerated sued District Attorney Connick again. There was ample evidence that withholding exculpatory evidence occurred in many cases in the Orleans Parish District Attorney and there was a lack of training. Twelve additional exonerations since 1990 were detailed. The Fifth Circuit Court of Appeals, however, held that there was not sufficient evidence to prove that the Orleans Parish District Attorney's office had a custom or policy of withholding exculpatory evidence and the Supreme Court denied certiorari.

Raeder (2007) argues that one of the reasons for prosecutorial misconduct is that the Model Rules and Standards do not cover many of the activities described as misconduct, or they refer to them obliquely with no clear guidance. Furthermore, there are few complaints against prosecutors, except in high-profile cases. Gershman (1991) writes that prosecutors misbehave because it works and they can get away with it. Because misconduct is scrutinized only when the defense attorney makes an objection and then files an appeal (and even then the appellate court may rule that it was a harmless error), there is a great deal of incentive to use improper tactics in the courtroom. The simple fact is that most prosecutors who commit wrongdoing are not disbarred or punished in any way and, in fact, some go on to be judges and politicians (Armstrong and Possley, 2002).

In a review of nine years of cases in New York City by Propublica, a liberal civil rights advocacy group, only one prosecutor was found to have been seriously punished for cases that were later overturned because of prosecutorial misconduct, such as *Brady* violations, coaching witnesses, hiding witnesses, or lying to the judge. Their review of cases found that even serial offenders received raises and commendations and apparently experienced no consequences for misconduct, even in cases where appellate judges rebuked the prosecutor. If there are grievances against prosecutors investigated by the state bar's disciplinary committee, such proceedings are usually done in secret with no public access to their findings (Sapien and Hernandez, 2013).

In the discussion of wrongful convictions earlier, confirmatory bias was described as related to noble-cause corruption in that once there is a determination that the defendant is guilty (by police and prosecutors), this perception may lead to misconduct to make sure a conviction is obtained. Grometstein (2007) also applies the concept of noble-cause corruption to prosecutors, arguing that they adopt a utilitarian ethic of using bad means to get a conviction, like police officers. Aronson and McMurtrie (2007), in their discussion of prosecutorial misconduct, identify the issue as "tunnel vision," arguing that prosecutors work under a bias that defendants are guilty; therefore, they ignore exculpatory evidence. Like the problems this causes with police investigators, these authors discuss several psychological processes that contribute to misconduct:

- The presence of confirmatory bias (human tendency to seek to confirm rather than disconfirm)
- Selective information processing (only recognizing evidence to fit one's theory)
- Belief perseverance (believing one's original theory of the case despite evidence to the contrary)
- Avoidance of cognitive dissonance (adjusting beliefs to maintain existing self- perceptions)

Acker and Redlich (2011) also describe tunnel vision, expectancy theory, and confirmation bias as reasons for false convictions. Medwed (2009) discusses the prosecutor's "conviction psychology" and noted the fact that prosecutors work closely with police officers and victims and their families, and the emotional connections make it difficult to maintain professional objectivity in cases. Grometstein (2007) emphasizes the relationship between the prosecutor and the victim, arguing that the prosecutor spends even more time with the victim than do police officers, leading to pressure to convict.

Cummings (2010) used Bandura's moral disengagement theory to explain intentional prosecutorial misconduct, concentrating on three types most relevant to prosecutors:

- Reconstructing conduct as morally justified
- Obscuring personal agency
- Blaming or dehumanizing defendants

The first type refers to "noble-cause corruption," prosecutors (like police) feel they are on the side of the righteous, and so what they do can be justified. The second relates to office policies that have "batting averages" and pressure to convict that make it difficult for a prosecutor to express anything other than a strong conviction orientation. The final idea is, again, like police in that the culture of some prosecutors' offices includes an orientation toward defendants that dehumanizes them by using "scum," "slime," and similar words. In one study, it was found that there were 34 different words—all negative—that were used to refer to defendants (Cummings, 2010).

Explanations for Misconduct of Judges

The immunity of judges insulates them from the effects of their decisions, although their decisions are public and can create storms of controversy. Their case holdings can be scrutinized and their courtroom behavior may be grounds for an appeal. Even so, it is difficult for attorneys to challenge judges' actions or testify against them in disciplinary proceedings (Swisher, 2009). Thus, some judges evidently believe they are invulnerable and use the office as a personal throne. In the Pennsylvania case where two judges received kickbacks for sending kids to a private prison, employees and lawyers explained that anyone who criticized the judges, even slightly, found themselves facing retaliation. Judges have immense power and, as the saying goes, "power corrupts." Attorneys tend to keep their head down and their opinions to themselves even when judges are clearly in the wrong. State judicial commissions rarely sanction judges, and voters tend to be oblivious to the reputation of judges, often voting along strict party lines, thus "bad" judges keep getting reelected.

Responding to Misconduct

Voters have some control over who become a prosecutor and judge, but once in office, most stay in the good graces of a voting public unless there is a major scandal or an energetic competitor. A range of potential responses to prosecutorial misconduct have been offered or implemented. Many of these have weaknesses that prevent their effectiveness. It should be noted also that prosecutors' associations believe that major changes in responses are unnecessary because they argue that prosecutorial

IN THE NEWS | Misconduct or Crime?

Governor Jerry Brown of California signed a new law in 2016 that will make it a felony for prosecutors to tamper with evidence or hide exculpatory material from the defense. Previously these acts were misdemeanors. They could be punished by 16 months, two or three years in prison, depending on the severity of the violation. The CDAA initially had opposed the bill but switched to a neutral position. The law was written in response to the jailhouse informant scandal involving the prosecutor's office in Orange County discussed in the last chapter. Some described the law as "disincentivizing" prosecutorial misconduct.

Sources: Ferner, 2016; Goffard, 2016.

misconduct is extremely rare. The In the News box describes how legislators in California are responding to prosecutorial misconduct.

Professional and Judicial Sanctions

To enforce rules of ethics, the American Bar Association (ABA) has a standing committee on ethical responsibility to offer formal and informal opinions when charges of impropriety have been made. Also, each state bar association has the power to sanction offending attorneys by private or public censure or to recommend a court suspend their privilege to practice law. Thus, the rules enforced by the state bar have essentially the power of law behind them. The bar associations also have the power to grant entry into the profession because one must belong to the bar association of a state to practice law there. Bar associations judge competence by testing the applicant's knowledge, and they also judge moral worthiness by background checks of individuals. The purpose of these restrictive admission procedures is to protect the public image of the legal profession by rejecting unscrupulous or dishonest individuals or those unfit to practice for other reasons. However, many believe that if bar associations were serious about protecting the profession, they would also continue to monitor the behavior and moral standing of current members with the same care they seem to take in the initial decision regarding entry.

Disciplinary committees investigate a practicing attorney only when a complaint is lodged against him or her. The investigative bodies have been described as decentralized, informal, and secret. They do little for dissatisfied clients because most client complaints involve incompetence and/or lack of attention and these charges are vague and ill-defined (Marks, Raymond, and Cathcart, 1986). Many bar disciplinary committees are hopelessly understaffed and overburdened with complaints. Complaints may take years to investigate, and in the meantime, if prospective clients call, they will be told only that the attorney is in good standing and has no substantiated complaints. A study of attorney discipline by an organization for legal reform reported that only 3 percent of investigations by state disciplinary committees result in public sanctions and only 1 percent end in disbarment (*San Antonio Express News*, 2002). A more recent study looked at a small sample of complaints submitted to the Florida bar association and found that variables that were associated with cases being sent forward for further review included being a solo practitioner, and the complainant being a legal professional; and the only factor that was significantly associated with a sustained finding and discipline imposed was being a solo practitioner (Piquero et al., 2016).

While individuals with complaints against their lawyers in the civil arena receive little satisfaction, criminal defendants are arguably even less likely to have anyone care or rectify incompetence or unethical behavior on the part of their attorney. One of the most common complaints against attorneys is that they allow deadlines to pass or miss court dates. Criminal defense attorneys could face civil suits for their incompetence or poor work performance, sanctions from their bar association, and even be cited by courts for contempt, but such events are rare. Recall from Chapter 8 that 80 percent of criminal defendants resort to publicly funded attorneys (either public defenders or court-appointed) and these systems are woefully underfunded. Thus, it is possible that the poor legal representation received by many is due to overworked and under-resourced attorneys.

It seems that prosecutors may be even less likely to be the target of bar discipline committees than criminal defense attorneys. Such information is hard to access because disciplinary proceedings may be secret, but the numbers of prosecutors investigated, much less sanctioned, seem to be very small, maybe as low as 2 percent of all complaints filed result in discipline (Sullivan and Possley, 2016).

Zacharias and Green (2009) proposed that Model Rule 1.1 requiring all attorneys to display a level of competency could be used against prosecutors who use evidence that they should know is false or withhold evidence from the prosecution. The advantage of using the competency rule rather than the rule prohibiting the use of false testimony is that the "knowing" standard is difficult to meet (the prosecutor must "know" the evidence is false), but competency would be an easier standard to meet. For example, prosecutors who use jailhouse informants that are extremely questionable or otherwise engage in acts that they should know have the potential to result in innocent people being convicted could be disciplined without having to prove they knew they were changing the course of the trial.

Misconduct in the courtroom is sometimes orally sanctioned by trial judges, but prosecutors are rarely directly mentioned in appellate holdings even when case decisions are overturned. Many times, when there is clear misconduct, the court rules it is harmless error and does not even overturn the conviction. Recently, some states, through legislation, have created more stringent responses to prosecutorial misconduct and will require overturning cases even if there is no way to prove that such misconduct affected the outcome of the case (T. Cox, 2016; Kirchmeier et al., 2009; Sullivan and Possley, 2016).

Rethinking Prosecutorial Immunity

Some have argued that the evidence of prosecutorial misconduct supports rethinking prosecutorial immunity, and perhaps employing criminal sanctions against prosecutors (Raeder, 2007). For instance, the Texas Judiciary and Civil Jurisprudence Committee has considered a bill that would establish liability for prosecutors in cases of extreme misconduct, giving them only qualified immunity (like police officers), rather than absolute immunity. Supreme Court Justice John Paul Stevens has also spoken out on removing the judge-made absolute immunity enjoyed by prosecutors, arguing that Congress never intended prosecutors to be immune from Section 1983 liability. Change would have to come from state legislatures and Congress (for the federal system) and then the new legislation would no doubt be challenged by prosecutors.

Better Training, Better Supervision

There is some argument that prosecutors do not get sufficient training on *Brady* obligations that then lead to some of the *Brady* violations that appear in wrongful convictions. Prosecutors' associations advocate enhanced training on *Brady* obligations to reduce violations. Some argue that requiring prosecutors to work with Innocence Commissions to counteract the psychology of conviction at all costs would be helpful. It has also been suggested that prosecutors' offices should have ethics officers and sanction employees who cross over the line. There should also be clear and public policies in each prosecutor's office concerning the use of jailhouse informants and turning over exculpatory material (Kirchmeier et al., 2009; TDCAA, 2012).

Scheck (2010), one of the founders of the Innocence Project, explains that the criminal justice process could learn from quality assurance programs in medicine. He proposes that many of the mistakes of prosecutors are due to being overworked and careless. In other words, it isn't that they intend to suppress evidence from the defense, it is that they forget to disclose it; similarly, other mistakes occur because of a lack of quality control in the process. The medical establishment underwent a fundamental improvement in the quality of care when checklists were begun in operating rooms. Error rates plunged to near zero in the same hospitals that had been experiencing unacceptably high rates. Scheck says this same approach should be used in prosecutors' offices to uncover *Brady* material and make sure it gets to the defense. Other procedures should be an internal discipline review system that would undertake a systematic review of mistakes made and identify the prosecutors involved. Responses would depend on the reason for the mistake. If prosecutors erred because of overwork, then resources should be allocated to reduce those errors; if a prosecutor was ignorant of his or her duties under the law, then training was necessary. However, if the prosecutor intentionally violated the law or ethical obligation, then discipline was necessary.

Conviction Integrity Units

While the number of Innocence Project affiliates is growing and the groups have been successful in identifying cases and prevailing in court, they can't be the only solution to the problem of false convictions. Craig Watkins, former district attorney of Dallas County, instituted the first conviction integrity unit in his office in 2007. The unit reviews DNA cases that have been identified by the Innocence Project of Texas and all cases where DNA evidence has identified unknown suspects in addition to the defendant. By 2014, the office had freed 33 people, was investigating 30 cases, and had a backlog of 200 cases (Barber, 2014). Watkins lost a reelection campaign in 2014, ironically because of ethical scandals (including possible misuse of asset forfeiture funds) and political missteps, but his Republican successor promised to continue the work of the unit.

By 2014, over a dozen cities or counties had similar units, including San Francisco, Chicago, San Jose, Brooklyn, Detroit, Denver, Philadelphia, and Cleveland. By 2017, the Registry of Exonerations reports that there are 29 such units in the 2,300 prosecutors' offices across the country. These units have been responsible for exonerating 225 individuals up to 2016 (National Registry of Exonerations, 2017). Recall from Chapter 8 that the ABA added two sections to Rule 3.8 for prosecutors that concerned their ethical duty to investigate and remedy when there is a chance that an innocent person has been convicted. Even though most states have not adopted those changes, these units pursue the spirit of the rule changes.

Sometimes a similar body is formed at the state level. The North Carolina Innocence Inquiry Commission was created in 2007 by N.C.G.S. §§ 15A-1461 through 15A-1470. The commission has the power to order a formal inquiry by a three-judge panel appointed by the Chief Justice of the North Carolina Supreme Court. Since 2007, the commission received 2,035 cases and 1,985 had been reviewed and closed by March 2017. Ten people have been exonerated. The remaining cases are under review (North Carolina Innocence Commission, 2017).

Mandatory DNA Testing

As mentioned earlier, DNA has been the vehicle by which many innocent prisoners have obtained their release from prison. Even after many years, a small amount of pre-served DNA evidence could exclude someone or help to identify the real perpetra-tor of a crime. Some states have mandated DNA testing of old cases when the inmate requests it. Still other offices, however, actively oppose retesting of DNA. In *District Attorney v. Osborne*, 557 U.S. 52, 2009, the Supreme Court, in a 5–4 decision led by the conservative majority, ruled that defendants had no constitutional right to DNA evidence, even if it was still held by the state and even if they were willing to pay for its testing. In this case, the prisoner argued that the testing done in his trial matched him only to 1 in 6 black men and more advanced tests available today could determine more accurately that he was not the rapist. Alaska argued that such a right would jeop-ardize the finality of case decisions when the trial was otherwise fair. One wonders, however, how a trial could be thought of as fair if an innocent person was convicted. One also wonders why the Supreme Court would not consider access to such evidence a part of due process. Contrary to this decision, many states are taking steps to make mandatory the preservation of biological evidence in criminal cases and creating a state right to postconviction DNA testing, even though such testing is prohibitively expensive and evidence must be kept in conditions sufficient to allow for later testing.

Private Crime Labs and Enhanced Due-Process Procedures

Because of the pro-prosecution bias that is said to exist in state or local police crime labs, there have been calls for private labs to test evidence. More than half of all labs in the country report directly to a law enforcement organization. Sometimes the bias is direct, but more often it is subtle and examiners may not even be aware of how they slant findings to the prosecution (cognitive bias). While there is an argument that pri-vate labs would not be subject to the same cognitive bias as employees of law enforce-ment agencies, a contrary argument is that examiners would still feel pressure because their continued contract would be the incentive to produce favorable results. A hybrid suggestion is that most testing would continue at state crime labs but periodically evi-dence would be sent to private labs for verification. Private labs could also be sued more easily than governmental entities, giving them the incentive to follow proper procedures (Balko, 2011b).

The research on eyewitness identification errors has led to procedural sugges-tions that can increase the accuracy of identifications (e.g., sequential photo arrays and double-blind examiners). While the Supreme Court does not seem to be interested in mandating such procedures as essential to due process, there is no reason why states or even local prosecutors' offices shouldn't. The more safeguards there are in eyewitness identification, the less chance there is of an innocent person being convicted.

Procedures can also ensure that obtaining confessions occurs in a manner designed to minimize the potential for false confessions. While the legal standard is whether coercion was present and the bar is set very high, some suggestions to deal with false confessions have emerged. One suggestion is to videotape all interrogations (not just the confession) (Garrett, 2011). More generally, suggestions include the requirement that all confessions have corroborating evidence, that lawyers be required to be present, and that stricter exclusionary rule applications be applied when there is evidence of coercion. As mentioned previously some locales have either eliminated or dramatically constrained the use of jailhouse informants because of the high probability that they are lying to gain some benefit.

There is new attention to and interest in addressing the weaknesses of the justice system to reduce the number of wrongfully convicted. It is important to note, however, that the new rules, sanctions, and guidelines that address jailhouse informants, confessions, eyewitness identifications, and other factors that have been identified as contributing to wrongful convictions will be effective only if there are ethical legal professionals who are committed to ensuring that there truly is justice for all.

Unfortunately, there is little reason for the prosecutor who sees injustice occur to come forward. In *Garcetti v. Ceballos,* 547 U.S. 410, 2006, the Supreme Court ruled against a prosecutor who was retaliated against for trying to rectify what he saw as a violation of due process. In this case, Richard Ceballos was an attorney for the Los Angeles County District Attorney's office. He submitted a memorandum to his superiors detailing his findings that a search warrant obtained by law enforcement officers had serious flaws and recommended the case be dismissed. Instead, his supervisor continued the prosecution. Ceballos, against orders, provided the defense with a copy of his memorandum and was called as a defense witness. He was subsequently passed over for promotions and sanctioned in other ways, and filed a Section 1983 claim arguing that his First Amendment rights were violated. The Supreme Court, in a 5–4 decision, held that the First Amendment did not apply to public servants during their public duties. Sadly, this decision may act as a barrier to public officials who attempt to challenge what they believe to be miscarriages of justice. However, the Court revised this ruling in *Lane v. Franks,* 573 U.S. 13, 2014, holding that the First Amendment does protect public employees who provide truthful sworn testimony, under a subpoena, in a hearing that is outside of ordinary job duties, even if the testimony addresses information learned at work. Writing the opinion, Justice Sotomayor claimed that the act of testifying in court "sets it apart from speech made purely in the capacity of an employee" (p. 9). Moreover, she wrote, "It would be antithetical to our jurisprudence to conclude that the very kind of speech necessary to prosecute corruption by public officials—speech by public employees regarding information learned through their employment—may never form the basis for a First Amendment retaliation claim. Such a rule would place public employees who witness corruption in an impossible position, torn between the obligation to testify truthfully and the desire to avoid retaliation and keep their jobs" (p. 11).

In fact, some argue that it is the attorneys and other professionals who work in the courtroom that are responsible for prosecutorial misconduct if they don't report it. Defense attorneys, clerks, judges, and others all have the duty to report any action that threatens the integrity of the court. Sullivan and Possley (2016) in a wide-ranging discussion of prosecutorial misconduct and how to address it argue that the way to reduce misconduct includes these five approaches:

1. instituting an open-file pretrial discovery requirement on prosecutors (similar to the Morton Act in Texas) that could even substitute for the *Brady* rule;

2. abandoning the harmless error test for reversing convictions; even if there is sufficient evidence of guilt, serious prosecutorial misconduct should be met with reversal;

3. identifying errant prosecutors by name in trial and appellate opinions;

4. stripping prosecutors of full immunity and giving them qualified immunity instead as protection from civil damages for misconduct; and

5. authorizing the Department of Justice's Office of Inspector General to handle investigations of alleged misconduct by federal prosecutors.

Ethical misconduct by prosecutors is expensive and threatens the very legitimacy of our legal system. When prosecutors have been found to have engaged in a *Brady* violation, put a questionable jailhouse informant on the stand, or winked at police perjury, anyone convicted can argue that the same misconduct occurred in his case. As more of these cases come to light, more suspicion is cast on all prosecutors whenever there are allegations of misconduct. Conviction integrity units are expensive to operate and take needed resources away from prosecuting current criminals. Unfortunately, guilty perpetrators may go free when police and prosecutors don't do their job legally and ethically. In one case where prosecutorial misconduct led to a conviction being overturned, Troy Bennett pleaded guilty to a lesser charge, was released, and then confessed to the murder he was originally charged with, effectively getting a free pass because of prosecutorial misconduct (Sapien and Hernandez, 2013). The problem is that when there is no confidence in justice system actors, then every case needs to be relitigated. The cost to the system of misconduct is incalculable. Thus, any utilitarian arguments prosecutors who are inclined to commit misconduct may make are weak and unpersuasive considering the costs at stake.

It is important to remember that legions of police, lab examiners, prosecutors, and judges engage in the honorable profession of pursuing justice for victims of crimes without committing any of the acts described in these chapters. Just as suspects should not be deprived of due process and be the victims of "noble-cause" corruption because of a belief that they are guilty, neither should prosecutors (or police officers) be presumed guilty because they are charged with misconduct. Just because there is an allegation in an appeal that prosecutors engaged in misconduct, does not make it so. Individuals on the side of defending the wrongfully convicted may be subject to confirmation bias as well and have their own ethical blinders on regarding what is legal and ethical when they believe that they are advocating for an innocent person in prison. It is also important to remember that in many of the cases where someone has been exonerated, the original conviction took place in the 1980s when large cities were struggling with incredibly large caseloads related to drugs and crime. The crime rate is, in some categories, far less than half of what it was in the 1980s; prosecutors' offices today have more resources to devote to each case and some also have the desire to reevaluate old cases to make sure they were prosecuted correctly. Our Walking the Walk box describes one prosecutor who believed it was his duty to do so.

WALKING THE WALK

Kenneth Thompson was Brooklyn's District Attorney for a short three years. By all accounts, his life, while short, was well-lived and he represented the very best of professional advocacy. Thompson won the election from his predecessor, Charles Hynes, who left under a cloud of scandal. Mr. Thompson became Brooklyn's first black district attorney. His mother was one of the first female police officers in New York City. He was a federal prosecutor before starting his own firm specializing in civil rights.

After he took office, he expanded the conviction integrity unit to ten lawyers from two, and added three detective investigators. He also added a review panel of lawyers and a law professor consultant. The conviction integrity unit has been instrumental in releasing Jeffrey Deskovic and over 20 others. Thompson also established a policy to avoid prosecuting most low-level marijuana arrests. He instituted an amnesty program called "Begin Again" that allowed people to expunge old warrants. The idea was that years of zero-tolerance policing led to tens of thousands of low-level offense warrants; Brooklyn alone had over 250,000 open warrants, some dating back to the 1970s. If people showed up, waited in line, and filled out some paperwork, and, assuming they didn't have serious charges, they could leave with a clean record. At the first event in June of 2016, 1,000 people showed up and Thompson worked the lines himself to increase trust. Many people evidently thought it was a trap and they would be arrested.

It's difficult to balance the rights of all groups and he was criticized for prosecuting New York City police officer Peter Liang who accidentally killed a resident in a housing project stairwell; but also criticized by the other side for recommending probation for the officer. Others might see his position as balancing justice and mercy. He was arguably just getting started on criminal justice reform when he was diagnosed with cancer. He died in October 2016 at the age of 50. According to the Editorial Board of the New York Times, "His intimacy with the perspectives of both law enforcement and minority communities made him unusually well positioned to balance a respect for the justice system even as he fought to fix it from the inside." His legacy continued as those who ran for the office after his death vowed to continue his work and the changes he had put in place.

Sources: Baker, 2015b; Editorial Board, 2016; Feuer, 2017a.

Judicial Independence and the Constitution

Before we leave this set of chapters on legal professionals, it is helpful to revisit some basic perspectives of law and how one's perspective or paradigm colors how we view judicial decisions or applications of the law. One view of law is that it is neutral and objective and that formal and absolute rules of law are used in decision making. However, the reality is that lawmakers, law enforcers, and lawgivers are invested with a great deal of discretion in making and interpreting the law. Professionals in law enforcement, the courts, and corrections use their discretion wisely and ethically, or, alternatively, they may use their discretion unethically. Far from being absolute or objective, the law is a dynamic, ever-changing symbol of political will. In this text, we address the ethical issues in the *implementation*, rather than the *creation*, of law. As you learned in political science or government classes, the creation of law is political. Laws are written by federal and state representatives who supposedly enact the public will. One might think that once a law is created, its implementation would be straightforward, but it should be clear by now that this is not the case. An appellate court can change over time and be influenced by political shifts in power. Far from being static, the implementation of law reflects political realities, in direct contrast to the ideal of judicial independence that is the cornerstone of our system of government.

If the judiciary is not independent of political powers, this calls into question the very existence of the checks and balances upon which this country's government is constructed. For instance, many Democrats suspected that the political composition of the Supreme Court had a great deal to do with its decision in the case challenging the Florida vote after the Bush–Gore presidential election in 2000. Whether the allegations are true, it should be obvious that the strength of the justice system rests on the independence of its judiciary.

The system of federal prosecutors and the federal law enforcement agencies, which include the Federal Bureau of Investigation (FBI) as well as many others, is also supposed to be removed from political influence. If we do not trust that a true separation of powers exists, then we have no trust in our government. The reason why there was such a political uproar over the firings of eight federal prosecutors on a so-called "hit list" in 2007 by the Bush administration was because they were evidently fired for not carrying out the wishes of the administration. While it is true that there is usually a widespread replacement of U.S. attorneys at the beginning of a new administration, it is quite another thing when U.S. attorneys are targeted for not doing the administration's bidding in terms of what prosecutions they pursue (Carr and Herman, 2007; Johanek, 2008). The reason why the Obama administration's IRS scandal stuck a deep chord in individuals on both sides was because of the allegations that governmental power was used against enemies. Now, questions exist about the Trump administration's attempts to influence the justice system (through firings of at least one U.S. attorney as described in the In the News Box) or attempts to influence federal law enforcement (by firing James Comey). It is probably very tempting as a sitting president to use the

⬛📱 IN THE NEWS | *Separation of Powers*

No one contests the right of a new president to request the resignations of U.S. Attorneys. It is a right that is exercised routinely by most elected presidents. What is not acceptable, however, is any hint of influence from a sitting president or any employee on the prosecutor's discretion to investigate, charge, or prosecute individuals. Therefore, President Bush's firing of U.S. attorneys mid-term received a scathing critique by the Justice Department because it had more than a hint of political influence over prosecution. After President Trump's inauguration, he asked for the resignation of Preet Bharara, the U.S. attorney in Manhattan. Bharara was extremely well known and widely respected as a fierce prosecutor. He prosecuted insider trading and hedge fund fraud cases, a case against J.P. Morgan bank, the Times Square bomb plotter Faisal Shahzad, and Al Qaeda terrorist Khalid Al-Fawwaz for the bombings of U.S. embassies in Kenya and Tanzania. He was not afraid to go after the politically well-connected, such as a former aide to New York Governor Andrew Cuomo. The reason several news stories focused on the firing was because President Trump had earlier asked Bharara to stay. The other reason was that, according to Bharara, there was a series of troubling phone calls from President-elect Trump, and then President Trump to Bharara. While he took the first two calls before the election, Bharara chose not to return a call from President Trump after he became president and contacted President Trump's chief of staff, suggesting that the president should be counseled about contacting a United States attorney directly. He believed that, especially considering his jurisdiction, it was not wise to have private conversations. The next day Mr. Bharara saw that he was on a list of 48 attorneys who were asked to tender their resignations. Since he had been called to a personal meeting and asked to stay on, he believed it was a mistake. It wasn't and he was fired.

Sources: Bright, 2017.

great resources available to protect friends and punish enemies. However, the greatest strength of our system of government is the separation of powers.

If the justice system, including prosecutors and judges, is a pawn or an agent of political power, due process is a sham and the very essence of democracy is threatened. The importance of due process is that even criminals and enemies of the state are given due-process rights that protect them from errors in the deprivation of life, liberty, and property. If due process is reserved only for those who are not enemies of the state, all are threatened because anyone may become an enemy. If for some reason state power would become despotic, it would be likely to label as enemies anyone favoring open government and democracy. What this illustrates is that the law (and the nature of its protections) is more important than the state and, indeed, is even more important than threats to the state. Those who are more influenced by political allegiance than allegiance to due process and civil liberties create a weak link in the mantle of protection against despotic state power.

The U.S. Supreme Court, as the ultimate authority of law in this country, decides constitutionality, and these interpretations are far from neutral, despite the myth of objective decision making. This is the reason that the selection of Supreme Court justices (as well as all federal judges) is such a hard-fought political contest. Ideological positions do make a difference, and no one is fooled that a black robe removes bias. The confirmations of John Roberts as Chief Justice (during the Bush administration) and Sonia Sotomayor and Elena Kagan (during the Obama administration) illustrate this. When Justice Scalia died in 2016, President Obama nominated Merrick Garland to replace him. Senate Republicans refused to even hold a confirmation hearing for Garland spurring bitter criticism from Democrats. Then when President Trump nominated Neil Gorsuch, Democrats vowed to filibuster against his nomination. Republicans employed the "nuclear option," meaning that Gorsuch was confirmed on a simple majority. Neither side opposed the two men on academic or judicial qualifications. Both, by all accounts, were well qualified. The fight is about political ideology and the intent to place on the bench those who will make decisions in conformance with one's ideology. What is interesting is that so-called liberal justices have been appointed by Republican presidents: Justices John Paul Stevens (appointed by Gerald Ford), David Souter (appointed by George H.W. Bush), and Sandra Day O'Connor (appointed by Ronald Reagan) were not considered activist or liberal when they were appointed but moved in that direction compared to the justices who have been appointed since then (Greenhouse, 2007). Today, some say Justice Kennedy is the most important man in America because he is often the swing vote that shifts the decision from four to five or five to four. Justices Roberts, Alito, and Thomas typically return conservative decisions (e.g., pro-business and anti-criminal defendant), and Justice Gorsuch is expected to vote with this group. Justices Ginsburg, Kagan, Sotomayor, and Breyer return liberal verdicts (although this is a generalization). The fate of the most important social questions in this country being at the discretion of one individual should be deeply concerning to Americans.

Judicial Activism

strict constructionists
The view that an individual has no rights unless these rights are specified in the Constitution or have been created by some other legal source.

Our law derives from the Constitution. Two basic philosophies regarding how to apply constitutional principles are at work in the legal arena. The first group might be called **strict constructionists** because they argue that the Constitution should be implemented as written, and if any changes are to take place in rights, responsibilities, or liberties, the changes should take place through the political system (Congress).

The extreme view of this position is that if a right isn't in the Constitution, it doesn't exist. So, for instance, the right to be free from state interference in the decision to abort one's fetus does not exist in the Constitution; therefore, it doesn't exist and cannot be created except through the actions of duly elected representatives. Strict constructionists argue that just because something *should* be a right doesn't mean that one can decide the framers meant for it to be a right. Judges should not create law.

Interpretationists (or activists) have a looser reading of the Constitution and read into it rights that the framers might have recognized or that should be recognized because of "evolving standards." They argue that the Constitution is meant to be a living document and that the language of the framers was intentionally written as to accommodate interpretation based on changing times and circumstances. Concepts such as due process, for instance, from the Fifth and Fourteenth Amendments, are flexible so they can be used to address new questions and new concerns. Interpretationists place less emphasis on precedent, minimize procedural obstacles (such as standing, ripeness, and federalism), and offer less deference to other political decision makers (e.g., they use the strict scrutiny test rather than the rational relationship test when evaluating governmental actions). The debate as to whether the Constitution should be strictly construed or liberally interpreted is an old one, as the Quote and Query box indicates.

> **interpretationists**
> An approach to the Constitution that uses a looser reading of the document and read into it rights that the framers might have recognized or that should be recognized as a result of "evolving standards."

Critics of judicial activism point out that just because judicial activists have been promoters of civil liberties and socially progressive causes, such as integration and free speech, there is no absolute necessity that activism would always champion such individual rights. Activism could, for instance, be just as likely to recognize greater rights of the state to restrict individual liberties (Wolfe, 1991), or invalidate congressional acts by an interpretation of the Constitution that favored restricting laws obtained through the democratic process (some say this is the case with the *Citizens United v. Federal Elections Commission*, 558 U.S. 50, 2010, a decision that invalidated a law putting limits on corporate campaign spending).

Proponents of activism argue that the federal government itself has not been content to stay within the boundaries of its enumerated powers as specified in the Constitution, and that proliferation of the federal government's reach into all areas of criminal and civil law through the expansive interpretation of the Commerce Clause requires greater judicial checks. Furthermore, there are limits to judicial power, including impeachment, confirmation, congressional definition of appellate powers, and the power to override a Supreme Court opinion through a constitutional amendment (Wolfe, 1991).

When the Court was in its most activist phase during the Warren Court (1953–1969), it delivered broad opinions that have had dramatic effects on the political and legal landscape. The Warren Court was called activist or liberal because it recognized a whole range of civil liberties and due-process rights for groups that had been historically

---

QUOTE & **QUERY**

When we are dealing with words that also are a constituent act, like the Constitution of the United States, we must realize that they have called into life a being the development of which could not have been foreseen completely by the most gifted of its begetters.

Sources: Oliver Wendell Holmes Jr., Supreme Court Justice, 1902–1932, as quoted in Wolfe, 1991: 36.

? Does this quote by Holmes indicate he was a strict constructionist or an interpretationist?

disenfranchised. The source of such rights was found in an expansive reading of the Constitution and based on the idea of "fundamental liberties"—those freedoms and protections that the framers would have recognized if they had been asked. Central to this view is the idea of **natural rights**. Recall that the natural law ethical system holds that there are natural laws of ethics that humans may or may not discover. Several of the authors of the Bill of Rights were natural law theorists; thus, taken out of the context of their time, they would probably recognize that humans have the following rights:

natural rights
The concept that one has certain rights just by virtue of being born, and these rights are not created by humans, although they can be ignored.

- To be free
- To be treated equal to other groups
- To be able to make decisions about personal matters without governmental interference
- To be free from torture and punishments that degrade the human spirit
- To have some protections against state power

In addition, there may be recognition that humans also have rights:

- To basic survival needs
- To avail themselves of opportunities to better themselves

The first set of rights leads to less government; the second set leads to more government. That is why the political terms *conservative* and *liberal* are not strictly comparable to "strict constructionist" and "interpretationist" and why there is such confusion when these terms are being used to describe judicial and political appointees and elected officials. "Liberals" argue that if the Warren Court hadn't interpreted the Constitution to recognize civil rights, blacks would still be eating at separate lunch counters. Constructionists argue that if interpretationists had their way, the courts would be involved in every decision from birth to death.

The Supreme Court's constructionist justices: John Roberts, Samuel Alito, Clarence Thomas, and Antonin Scalia have been instrumental in restricting the coverage of the *Miranda* warnings, upholding federal antiabortion laws, cutting free-speech rights of public school students, strictly enforcing procedural requirements for bringing and appealing cases, limiting the ability to use racially conscious measures to achieve or preserve integration, invalidating public corruption laws and campaign finance laws, and generally supporting law enforcement powers, with some exceptions. On the other hand, the Supreme Court has also recognized unconstitutionality in capital punishment and life without parole for juveniles and ruled against the government's secret program to store electronic communication data of all Americans. Recent case decisions have recognized religious liberty rights for Muslims to grow beards in prison (*Holt v. Hobbs*, 574 U.S. ___, 135 Sup. Ct. 853, 2015), the requirement to obtain a warrant before searching a cellphone (*Riley v. California*, 573 U.S. ___, 134 Sup. Ct. 2473, 2014), and the rejection of the so-called provocation rule that removed immunity from police if they created the situation where they felt in danger of their lives (*Los Angeles County v. Mendez*, No. 16-369, U.S. Supreme Court, May 30, 2017).

Judges' political leanings shouldn't influence these decisions, but it is hard to argue that there is no correlation. One thing is clear: a judge is human and carries baggage of personal, political, and social bias. The importance of the foregoing discussion is to illustrate the law is not an equation that comes out with the right answer to every problem. Because there is room to interpret, individual ethics becomes extremely important. Prosecutors' and judges' ethics should lead them to use their discretion in ways that promote justice. We all, however, must be involved in a continuing, serious discussion about what justice means. For instance, should federal prosecutors "lighten up" on heavy charging of drug offenders or should they enforce the law to its full extent? Should asset forfeiture be restricted and curtailed or is it a legitimate punishment if one is involved, even peripherally, in crime? Should jailhouse informants be banned or should they be used when there is other evidence that points to guilt? Should we eliminate plea bargaining or does it resolve cases quickly helping both the defendant and the system? These are within the individual discretion of system actors, but they take their cues from what the public seems to want. The focus on wrongful convictions and police misconduct during the Obama administration has given way in the Trump administration to calls for returns to full prosecution, mandatory minimums and reducing the Department of Justice's demands for police reform. The adage that we get the government we deserve once again seems relevant as system actors shift and respond to political winds and public sentiment.

Conclusion

One might expect that the public's respect and trust for legal professionals, as guardians of the justice system, would be high, but that is not the case. Part of the reason is the ability to take either side in a controversy. We should not forget, however, that attorneys and judges protect the bedrock of our structure of laws.

In criminal justice, it is crucial that legal professionals remember and believe in the basic tenets of due process and be ever vigilant against the influence of prejudice or bias in the application of law toward the pursuit of justice. Unfortunately, there are cases where defense attorneys, prosecutors, and judges do not uphold the ethical standards of their profession and instead engage in various forms of misconduct. Although the types of misconduct vary depending on one's role in the system, each can be explained by individual enrichment (money, status, or time), or by ends/means thinking due to confirmatory bias (like noble-cause corruption for police officers).

There is a need to improve the ethics of the system, as evidenced by the Innocence Project's exonerations of hundreds of people who ended up in prison because of the failings of the system and system actors. Just as important is to make sure the same "rush to judgment" isn't directed to system actors when allegations of misconduct arise. Despite those who advocate strict constructionism, applying the law can never be truly objective or formulistic. Every decision is made through a reasoned and, one hopes, ethical interpretation of the law rather than by a robotic response. If the law is a living entity, legal professionals are its life's blood.

Chapter Review

1. **Detail the types of misconduct that have been associated with defense attorneys, prosecutors, and judges.**

   Misconduct by defense attorneys includes ignoring cases, incompetence, and going over the line when defending clients, including presenting false evidence. The types of prosecutorial misconduct include withholding exculpatory evidence, misusing pretrial publicity, using peremptory challenges to exclude jurors, and using false evidence in court. Misconduct by judges includes allowing bias (including bribery) to influence their decision making and acting arbitrarily and otherwise abusing their power.

2. **Explain the reasons why such misconduct occurs.**

    Misconduct occurs because the disciplinary functions carried out by the state bar associations rarely result in serious sanctions. Prosecutors experience very little oversight and seldom suffer from sanctions when violating the ethical rules in their zeal to obtain a conviction. Courts often rule such misconduct as harmless error. Judges are feared by employees and lawyers who hesitate to file complaints against them. Also, prosecutors, like police, may be prone to confirmatory bias or what we have called noble-cause corruption in prior chapters.

3. **Describe some factors in wrongful convictions.**

    The most commonly noted factor in wrongful convictions seems to be an error in eyewitness identification. Other factors include *Brady* violations, coerced interrogations that lead to false confessions, jailhouse informants, poor representation by defense attorneys, police and prosecutorial misconduct, false confessions, and faulty or perjured forensic testimony.

4. **Discuss some proposals to improve the justice system and reduce ethical misconduct.**

    Suggestions to improve the system have been to institute official Innocence Projects or conviction integrity units. Suggestions also include more training and ethics officers. Also, some have suggested reevaluating prosecutorial immunity and using civil and criminal sanctions against prosecutors who create and use false evidence and engage in other forms of misconduct to obtain convictions. Other proposals more specifically to reduce the possibility of wrongful convictions include using videotape confessions, restricting the use of jailhouse informants, and using sequential and double-blind identifications to avoid improper influence over witnesses.

5. **Understand the concepts associated with judicial activism or constructionism and how this issue relates to ethical misconduct.**

    An activist judge is one who believes such concepts as due-process and liberty rights are evolving and the founding fathers did not mean for the rights enumerated in the Constitution to remain static throughout time. Constructionists argue that legislators should make law, not judges. One's opinion regarding this—and one's values, opinions, and biases in general—affect decision making, so judges' opinions on cases can be predicted ahead of time in many cases. This calls into question judicial neutrality and reminds us that, in the end, our system of laws is a system of people who enforce the law, and thus it is only as good or bad as the people in the system.

Study Questions

1. What is the legal test to determine an attorney is so incompetent as to violate the Constitutional right of counsel?

2. What are the types of ethical violations that have been associated with prosecutors?

3. Discuss the explanations for prosecutorial misconduct.
4. What factors have been identified as contributing to false convictions?
5. What is the evidence to indicate a pervasive pattern of racial bias in the system?

Writing/Discussion Exercises

1. Using ethical and moral criteria, write an essay on (or discuss) courtroom practices: the use of videotaped testimony, allowing television cameras into the courtroom and jury room, victim statements during sentencing, preventive detention, neighborhood justice centers, the use of a waiver to adult court for violent juvenile offenders, and any others that have been in the news recently.

2. After watching a movie that presents a legal dilemma (e.g., *Presumed Innocent, 12 Angry Men, Philadelphia,* or *Michael Clayton*), write an essay on (or discuss) the ethical dilemmas of the characters. Use one or more of the ethical frameworks provided in Chapter 2.

3. Write an essay on (or discuss) judicial activism. Present the arguments on both sides of the question as to whether judges should interpret or simply apply the Constitution. Provide more current examples (the current Supreme Court docket) and predict how justices will decide. If one can predict the decisions of the justices on the Supreme Court, where does that leave the idea that no case is prejudged?

Key Terms

interpretationists	natural rights	strict constructionists

ETHICAL DILEMMAS

Situation 1
You are a defense attorney who is defending a man against a charge of burglary. He tells you that he was drunk on the night in question and doesn't remember what he did. He asks you to put him on the stand, and when you do, he responds to your questions by stating unequivocally that he was home watching a television show, describing the show and plotline. You understand that you cannot participate in perjury, but to call attention to his inconsistent stories would violate other rules, such as confidentiality and zealous defense. What do you do?

Situation 2
You are a member of a jury. The jury is hearing a child molestation case in which the defendant is accused of a series of molestations in his neighborhood. You have been advised by the judge not to discuss the case with anyone outside the courtroom, and especially not with anyone on either side of the case. Going down in the elevator after the fourth day of the trial, you happen to ride with the prosecutor in the case. He tells you that the man has a previous arrest for child molestation, but that it has not been allowed in by the judge, as being too prejudicial for the jury. You were fairly sure that the guy was guilty before, but now you definitely believe he is guilty. You also know that if you tell the judge what you have heard, it will probably result in a mistrial. What would you do? What should happen to the prosecutor?

Situation 3

You are a court administrator and really like Judge Sonyer, your boss. He is pleasant, punctual, and hardworking. One day, you hear him talking to the prosecutor in chambers. He is talking about the defendant in a trial that is about to start, and you hear him say that "the son-of-a-bitch is as guilty as sin." You happen to be in law school and know that, first, the prosecutor and judge should not be talking about the case without the presence of the defense attorney, and, second, the judge has expressed a preexisting bias. The judge's statement is even more problematic because this is a bench trial and he is the sole determiner of guilt or innocence. What would you do?

Situation 4

You are a federal judge and are about to start a federal racketeering trial that is quite complicated. Prosecutors allege that certain lobbyists funneled money into political campaigns by "washing" it through individual employees of a couple of large corporations. Still, the evidence seems equivocal—at least what you've seen so far. You get a call from one of your state's U.S. senators (who is not implicated in the case, although members of his party are), and the conversation is innocuous and pleasant enough until the senator brings up the case and jocularly pressures you to agree with him that it is a "tempest in a teapot." Then he mentions that a higher, appellate-level judgeship will be opening soon and that he is sure you would like his support on it. The message is not subtle. What would you do?

Situation 5

You are a defense attorney who sees a judge in your jurisdiction having dinner with a prosecutor. Both are married to other people. You happen to have a case in front of this judge and the prosecutor is your opponent. You consider that you could request the judge recuse himself from the case, but this may create animosity, and if he refuses, it could be detrimental to your client. Alternatively, you could keep quiet and use the information on appeal, but this may mean your client spends years in prison. Finally, you could do nothing and hope that the judge is not biased toward the prosecution in his rulings. What would you do?

The Ethics of Punishment and Corrections

11

AP Images/Eric Risberg

Death row, like this one at San Quentin prison in California, holds individuals who are given the most severe punishment available – death.

Learning Objectives

1. Provide the definitions of punishment and treatment and explain their rationales.

2. Describe how the ethical frameworks justify punishment.

3. Describe ethical rationales for and against capital punishment.

4. Identify major themes from the ethical codes for correctional officers, treatment professionals, and probation and parole officers.

5. Explain how occupational subcultures affect adherence to professional ethics codes.

The field of corrections, which will be the topic in this next set of three chapters, encompasses county and state jails, prisons, community corrections, including probation and parole, and various correctional programs. Correctional professionals, like law enforcement and legal professionals, have a great deal of discretion and power over the lives of offenders.

As you may know, the United States has about 2.1 million people in jails and prisons. We incarcerate many more people per capita than other western, industrialized countries. At a rate of about 700 per 100,000, the United States incarcerates about seven times more people than Norway (72), France (98), or Canada (118) and a little less than five times more people than the United Kingdom (147) (Wagner and Walsh, 2016).

The reason our imprisonment rate is so much higher is not because of higher crime, but, because of our inclination to punish with incarceration rather than any other sentencing alternative (Raphael and Stoll, 2008). A careful analysis of sentencing patterns by Pfaff (2011) shows that the dramatic increase in

329

incarceration rates that began in the 1980s was largely due to the decision of prosecutors to seek prison terms for convicted individuals, and, to a lesser extent, increased sentence length and changes in parole release and revocation.

Further, we were roughly comparable to other countries in our punishment practices until the 1980s, at which time the incarceration rates increased dramatically every year. Recently, the rate and numbers in prison have plateaued, and many states, have even showed decreases in the number incarcerated (Kaeble and Glaze, 2016; Pollock, 2016). The number incarcerated in jail or prison decreased by 2.3 percent from 2014 and was its lowest level since 2004 (Kaeble and Glaze, 2016). Some states have created double-digit declines since 1999, including New Jersey, New York, Rhode Island, and California. Interestingly, states' decrease or increase in the number of people imprisoned does not seem to show any correlation with whether the state's crime rate has increased or decreased (Pew Research Center, 2016).

While the incarceration rate per 100,000 is 466 for white men, it is 1,130 for Hispanic men and an amazing 2,791 for black men. Women are incarcerated at a much lower rate: 51 per 100,000 white women are incarcerated, compared to 65 for Hispanic women and 113 per 100,000 for black women (Bureau of Justice Statistics, 2015). At year-end 2015 an estimated 6,741,400 persons were supervised by U.S. adult correctional systems (prison, jail, probation, or parole). This is a decrease of about 115,600 persons from year-end 2014 and represents almost 3 percent of the total adult population. The interested reader can go to the Bureau of Justice Statistics (https://bjs.gov/) to see how imprisonment patterns have changed over the years.

It is important to emphasize that the imprisonment patterns we see are a function of individual discretion on the part of sentencing judges, legislators who pass mandatory minimum laws, and prosecutors who choose how to charge and what sentences to recommend. We see this clearly by looking at the pattern of increases in sentence length over the last several decades and how they vary dramatically by state. In Florida, the average time served rose by 166 percent, while in New York, sentence length increased only 2 percent (Goode, 2012).

Did the incredible rise in incarceration cause crime rates to fall? The consensus seems to be that incarceration practices were partially responsible for the dramatic decline in crime that began in the early 1990s, but, quickly reached a point of diminishing returns as incarceration rates kept increasing as crime decreased. One estimate is increased incarceration accounted for approximately 6 percent of the reduction in property crime in the 1990s but less than 1/100th of the decline of property crime in the 2000s, and had no effect on violent crime rates (Roeder, Eisen, and Bowling, 2015). A National Academy of Sciences commission that reviewed all studies on the relationship between incarceration and crime concluded that changes in punishment policies were the main and proximate drivers of the growth in incarceration. Prosecutors and judges became harsher in their charging and sentencing. However, over the four decades of steadily increasing incarceration rates, the rate of violent crime rose, then fell, rose again, then declined (Travis, Western, and Redburn, 2014).

Beginning in the last several years, many groups have advocated rethinking the use of prison and sentencing policies like mandatory minimums. The Coalition for Public Safety (www.coalitionforpublicsafety.org) is funded by the MacArthur Foundation as well as the conservative Koch brothers, political power brokers that generally contribute to the most conservative politicians. The Coalition states their mission is to "reform our criminal justice system to make it more just, more fair, and more effective." On their website, they advocate fair sentencing, fair and appropriate use of incarceration at both the federal and state level, and "fair chances" (addressing collateral consequences of a criminal conviction). The interesting thing about this advocacy is that it is bipartisan and both conservative and liberal advocates share the same message that our mass incarceration practices must be reexamined considering social science and common sense. While not all groups agree on all items, some of the proposals or changes that have received attention are briefly summarized below:

- Reducing zero tolerance policies in schools that led to suspensions for very minor acts of misbehavior.

- Addressing the "school-to-prison pipeline" that has transformed school discipline into the entry into the criminal justice system using municipal tickets.

- Reevaluating the direct filing laws that allowed juveniles to be charged as adults (also the waiver procedures that accomplish the same thing) leading to juveniles being incarcerated in correctional facilities for adults.

- Considering raising the age at which juveniles must be dealt with through the juvenile court system considering recent research indicating juveniles' decision-making ability is not fully developed.

- Rolling back mandatory minimum laws at both the federal and state level (these laws restrict the discretion of judges to sentence in some crime categories).

- Moving marijuana out of the Schedule 1 drug category, which is for drugs that have a high risk of addiction and no legitimate medical value.

- Decriminalizing possession of small amounts of marijuana to a "ticketable" offense or decriminalizing small amounts for personal use.

- Reviving or increasing the scope of pretrial release programs to reduce the number of people in jail simply because they can't afford bail.

- Evaluating the system of fines and fees that have created new "debtors" prisons for offenders who have crushing debt they can't pay solely because of criminal justice-related fines and fees.

- Specialty courts, such as drug courts, veteran's courts, and courts for the mentally ill, which divert individuals from the system at the "front end."

- Reestablishment of parole and good time in those states that had abolished one or both means to reduce sentences for good behavior.

- Evaluation of the use of solitary confinement given findings of the pervasiveness in which it is used and the deleterious effects it has on the human psyche.

- Reentry initiatives that assist offenders who are released to the community with job placement and other programs designed to reduce recidivism.

- "Ban the box" initiatives that question the legitimacy of using prior arrest as a categorical disqualifier for some jobs and programs that reward employers with tax incentives for hiring ex-offenders.

- Addressing collateral consequences of a criminal conviction, such as drug offenders being denied federal Pell grants or federal housing and, in some states, lifetime bans on voting.

- Improvement of indigent defense so that offenders can be diverted from the system (when appropriate) sooner, rather than later, in the process.

The impetus for the change is both pragmatic (corrections costs have skyrocketed to consume ever-increasing portions of budgets) and moral (conservative rationales especially speak to the power of redemption and urge policies that support reformation). With the election of President Trump, the movement for reform and revision of sentencing policies has halted, at least on the federal level. Legislation written to eliminate or revise mandatory minimum sentences for drug offenders has no chance of being voted on and there doesn't seem to be any support for some of the other criminal justice reforms in this administration (George, 2017). There is still a great deal of activity at the state level however. Thirty states have limited sentence length and expanded alternatives to incarceration despite some opposition from district attorneys' and sheriffs' organizations (Oppel, 2017).

Two famous quotes resonate in any discussion of ethics in corrections. The first is from Dante's *Divine Comedy*: "*Abandon all hope, ye who enter here.*" This inscription at the portal to hell, often scrawled as graffiti in prisons, unfortunately encapsulates what some prisons mean to those who are sent there. Fyodor Dostoyevsky was reputed to have provided the second quote: "*The degree of civilization in a society can be judged by entering its prisons,*" which cautions that the best of us still have certain duties of respect and care toward the worst of us.

Once someone has been found guilty of a criminal offense, the type of punishment must be determined. Punishments range from a suspended sentence to death. Sometimes punishment includes treatment, at least in name. Offenders may be required to participate in treatment programs or self-help groups such as Alcoholics Anonymous. They may be required to get their GED or obtain some type of job training. In addition to formal, legal punishments, there are informal, extra-legal punishments that should not exist, but unfortunately do exist. Those with a criminal record may never be able to recapture a derailed career or find a decent job again. Inmates are raped and beaten by other inmates and sometimes even by correctional officers. Their personal property is destroyed. Some get sick or injured and receive inadequate medical treatment. Prisoner advocates maintain that these events should never be part of the formal punishment of prison, but others strongly believe that the prisoner "shouldn't do the crime if he (or she) can't do the time." Prisoners form an unsympathetic "victim" group perhaps explaining why public support for reform is usually lukewarm at best.

According to one author (Leiser, 1986: 198), five elements are essential to the definition of **punishment**:

punishment
Unpleasantness or pain administered by one in lawful authority in response to another's transgression of law or rules.

1. There are at least two persons—one who inflicts the punishment and one who is punished.

2. The person who inflicts the punishment causes a certain harm to the person who is being punished.

3. The person who inflicts the punishment has been authorized, under a system of rules or laws, to harm the person who is punished in this particular way.

4. The person who is being punished has been judged by a representative of that authority to have done what he or she is forbidden to do or failed to do what he or she is required to do by some relevant rule or law.

5. The harm that is inflicted upon the person who is being punished is specifically for the act or omission mentioned in condition four.

We also need to define **treatment**. According to correctional terminology, treatment may be anything used to induce behavioral change. The goal is to eliminate dysfunctional or deviant behavior and to encourage productive and normal behavior patterns. In prison, treatment includes diagnosis, classification, therapy, education, religious activity, vocational training, and self-help groups.

This chapter and the next two follow the format we have established in the previous sections on law enforcement and legal professionals. In this chapter, we will first explore relevant issues, such as the various rationales for punishment, with special attention to capital punishment, present the formal codes of ethics for correctional professionals and describe occupational subcultures that sometimes conflict with the formal code of ethics. In Chapter 12, we will discuss some ethical dilemmas for correctional professionals that arise because of the discretion inherent in these roles. In Chapter 13, we will review past and current instances of misconduct by correctional professionals, explanations proposed for such behavior, and suggestions for improving the ethical climate in corrections.

> **treatment**
> Anything used to induce behavioral change with the goal of eliminating dysfunctional or deviant behavior and encouraging productive and normal behavior patterns.

Rationales for Punishment and Corrections

The rationale for punishment and corrections comes from the social contract. In the same way that the social contract forms the basis for police power, it also provides a rationale for further control in the form of punishment and corrections. Recall that according to the social contract theory, we avoid social chaos by giving the state the power to control us. In this way, we protect ourselves from being victimized by others by giving up our liberty to aggress against others. If we do step outside the bounds of this agreement, the state has the right to control and punish us for our transgressions. Concurrently, the state is limited in the amount of control it can exert over individuals. To be consistent with the social contract, the state should exert its power only to accomplish the purpose of protection; any further interventions in civil liberties are unwarranted.

Corrections pursues a mixture of goals, including retribution, reform, incapacitation, deterrence, and rehabilitation. The longstanding argument between proponents of punishment and proponents of treatment reveals a system without a clear mandate or rationale for action. Can treatment and punishment occur at the same time? Some argue that because punishment has the goal of inflicting pain on an individual, it is fundamentally incompatible with the goal of treatment (Garland, 1990). Others argue that there is no reason that positive change cannot occur in a correctional setting.

One of the most problematic issues in justifying punishment is that what we do to offenders change over time (and place). If what we consider appropriate punishment changes, how can any specific punishment be just under universalism or natural law theory? In other words, in earlier centuries we might have executed a pickpocket. Was that just, or is it just today to put that person on probation? Is it just to incarcerate 19-year-olds who have sex with 16-year-olds today when in times past (or, perhaps, in future times) they would not be imprisoned at all? Prisoners in different prisons have vastly different sentences. How can the worst prison be fair if it is chance whether a prisoner ends up there or in a prison with better living conditions? Finally, at various times, courts have invalidated laws or punishments, but not made their ruling retroactive; in that case, people who are already in prison stay there. Consider the states that

IN THE NEWS | *Fair Punishment?*

In 2010, the Fair Sentencing Act was passed to reduce the disparity between federal sentencing rules for crack and powder cocaine, reducing the disparity from 100:1 to 18:1. The bill did not apply retroactively, thus, thousands in federal prisons were incarcerated only because they were sentenced before 2010 and would have received much shorter sentences if sentenced under the new law. To address this inequity, a clemency initiative was created whereby federal prisoners sentenced under the old laws could apply for clemency (length of sentence is reduced, criminal conviction remains). Stringent requirements were put in place, including the following:

- Their original sentence was longer than current mandatory sentences for the same offense.
- They are nonviolent, low-level offenders without "significant ties to large-scale criminal organizations, gangs, or cartels."

- They have served at least 10 years of their sentence.
- They do not have a "significant criminal history."
- They have demonstrated good conduct in prison.
- They have no history of violence before or during their current imprisonment.

A working group called Clemency Project 2014 was formed to provide inmates with pro-bono (free) attorneys to help them with their clemency application. Over 30,000 inmates applied. President Obama began approving clemency to offenders in December 2014 and by the end of his term had issued clemency/commutation orders for 1,927 people. It is estimated that 98 percent of them were the drug offenders under the program. The clemency program closed because President Trump indicated he would not be granting any clemency or commutations to inmates who met the criteria.

Sources: Reilly, 2016; Smart, 2017.

have legalized marijuana—if individuals are in prison for possession because they were sentenced before the decriminalization occurred, can that be just? How can that be logical or fair if the punishment no longer exists? The In the News box describes one attempt to make punishment more equitable for some people after changes in sentencing laws reduced the amount of punishment for drug offenders.

An important question to ask is: "Whom are we punishing?" Studies show that only a small minority of individuals who commit crimes end up in prison; furthermore, we may assume that those individuals are not representative of the larger population. Those in our jails and prisons are there not only because they committed crimes, but also because they are poor, members of a minority group, or powerless. Certain types of criminals, for example, white-collar offenders and corporate criminals, tend to avoid the more punitive sanctions of the corrections system. Despite attempts to reduce disparity, sometimes there doesn't seem to be any logic or consistency in the amount of punishment for offenders.

Long ago, criminals were viewed as sinners with no ability to change their behavior, so punishment and incapacitation were the only logical ways to respond to crime. Jeremy Bentham (1748–1832) and Cesare Beccaria (1738–1794) viewed the criminal as rational and as having free will and, therefore, saw the threat of punishment as a deterrent. Neoclassicists such as Adolphe Quetelet (1796–1874) and André-Michel Guerry (1802–1866) recognized that insane persons and juveniles could not be held entirely responsible for their actions and, therefore, believed that they should not be punished. In the 1800s, the positivist school looked for differences between criminals and noncriminals. The search for differences eventually, in the 1960s and 1970s, led to the short-lived rehabilitative era and the **treatment ethic**—the idea that all criminal acts were symptoms of an underlying pathology. The treatment programs created in the last hundred years or so operate under the assumption that we can do something to offenders to reduce their criminal activity. That "something" may involve

- treating a psychological problem, such as a sociopathic or paranoid personality;
- addressing physiological problems, such as alcoholism or addiction; and
- responding to social problems, such as chronic unemployment, with vocational training and job placement.

Obviously, the perception of the criminal influences the rationale for correction and punishment. The two major justifications for punishment and treatment are **retribution** and **prevention**. The retributive rationale postulates that punishment is a sufficient goal, whereas the prevention approach views punishment as a means of prevention rather than an end.

Retribution

The retributive rationale for punishment is consistent with the social contract theory. Simply stated, the retributive rationale is that the individual offender must be punished because he or she deserves it (Mackie, 1982). Retribution may support punishment, but also limits it: only those who commit crimes should be punished, and only to the extent equal to the wrong.

What is an appropriate amount of punishment? This is a difficult question even for the retributivist. The difference between a year in prison and two years in prison is measurable only by the number of days on the calendar, not by how it is experienced by different people. Should this be considered during sentencing? Punishment of any kind affects individuals differently. For instance, a whipping may be worse than death for someone with a low tolerance for pain, better than prison for someone with a great need for freedom, and perhaps even pleasurable for someone who enjoys physical pain. Prison may be experienced as an inconvenience for some, and such a traumatic experience for others that it may induce suicide. Our current system of justice seldom recognizes these individual vulnerabilities or sensitivities to various punishments.

The rehabilitative era of the 1960s and early 1970s promoted sentencing based on a prevention rationale that supported the idea that individuals should be incarcerated until they were rehabilitated. That gave way to a retribution-based "just deserts" or justice model in the late 1970s and 1980s. Basically, the **justice model** reverted back to a retributive idea that individuals are rational and that, even though free will may not exist perfectly, the concept must serve as a basis for the criminal law. Punishment is to be used for retribution, not deterrence, treatment, or any other purpose. This led to "truth in sentencing" laws that restricted early releases, parole, and indeterminate sentences based on whether the inmate had changed (Fogel, 1975).

The **just deserts model**, appearing about the same time as the justice model, was also retributive and based punishment on "commensurate deserts" (von Hirsch, 1976, 1985; von Hirsch and Maher, 1992). According to von Hirsch, the leading proponent of the just deserts model, crimes should be weighed in seriousness based on their recidivism potential. Offenders who commit similar crimes should be punished equally, but the rank ordering of crimes should be determined by recidivistic potential.

treatment ethic
The idea that all criminal acts are symptoms of an underlying pathology.

retribution
A rationale for punishment that states that punishment is an end in itself and should be balanced to the harm caused.

prevention
A rationale for punishment that views it as a means rather than an end and embraces any method that can deter crime, painful or not (includes deterrence, rehabilitation, and incapacitation).

justice model
David Fogel's conceptualization that the punishment of an individual should be limited by the seriousness of the crime, although treatment could be offered.

just deserts model
Von Hirsch's conceptualization that the punishment of the individual should be purely retributive and balanced to the seriousness of the crime.

Garland (1990) offered a different view, proposing that the emphasis of society should be on socializing and educating citizens. The punishment that was still necessary for those who broke the law should be viewed as morally expressive and retributive. Feeney (2005) continues this idea that sentencing should be purely retributive, and be "morally significant" in that it expresses condemnation of the behavior. Both writers were like the earlier just deserts theorists in that they believed punishment should be retributive rather than serve the goals of deterrence.

The 1990s and up through today has been described as the era of **penal harm**; this refers to the idea that the system intentionally or uncaringly inflicts pain on offenders during their imprisonment. There is very little attempt to rehabilitate and no attempt to minimize punishment or its harmful effects (Clear, 1996; Cullen, 1995). As noted earlier, the United States stands apart from most countries in the number of citizens incarcerated. If asked to describe the reasons for punishment, most people would probably propose either the retributive, just deserts rationale (because they deserve it), or a deterrence argument (so they don't do it again).

penal harm
The idea that the system intentionally inflicts pain on offenders during their imprisonment or punishment, because merely depriving them of liberty is not considered sufficiently painful.

Prevention Rationale

Three common justifications or rationales for punishment can all be subsumed under a general heading of "prevention." Prevention assumes that something should be done to the offender to prevent future criminal activity. There are three possible methods of prevention: deterrence, incapacitation, and treatment. Each of these is based on certain assumptions that must be considered in addition to the relevant moral questions. For instance, it is a factual question as to whether people can be deterred from crime, but it is a moral question as to what we should do to an individual to ensure deterrence.

Deterrence

There are two types of **deterrence**. Specific deterrence is what is done to offenders to prevent them from deciding to commit another offense. General deterrence is what is done to an offender to prevent others from deciding to engage in wrongful behavior. The first teaches through punishment; the second teaches by example.

Our right to deter an individual offender is rooted in the same rationale used to support retribution. By membership in society, individuals submit themselves to society's controls. If we think that someone's actions are damaging, we will try various means to persuade him or her to cease that activity. The implicit assumption of a deterrence philosophy is that in the absence of controls, society would revert to a jungle-like, dangerous "war of all against all"; we need the police and official punishments to keep us in line. Under this rationale, the true nature of humankind is perceived to be predatory and held in check only by external controls. The Quote and Query box enumerates the key points of view in this justification for punishment.

The rationale behind specific deterrence depends on the effectiveness of punishment in deterring future bad acts by the individual being punished. The rationale supporting general deterrence is somewhat problematic. If we know that a term of

deterrence
Specific deterrence is what is done to offenders to prevent them from deciding to commit another offense. General deterrence is what is done to an offender to prevent others from deciding to engage in wrongful behavior.

QUOTE & **QUERY**

1. Those who violate others' rights deserve punishment.
2. However, there is a countervailing moral obligation not to deliberately add to the amount of human suffering, and punishment creates suffering.
3. Deterrence results in preventing more misery than it creates, thereby justifying punishment.

Source: Adapted from von Hirsch, 1976: 54.

? Is this utilitarian thinking or ethical formalism? Explain your answer.

imprisonment will not deter an offender but can deter others, can it still be justified? Under general deterrence, the offender is used as a tool to teach a lesson to the rest of us. The sociologist Emile Durkheim (1857–1917) believed that the value of criminals is in establishing the parameters of acceptable behavior. Their punishment helps the rest of us define what is "good."

If one's goal is purely general deterrence, there does not necessarily have to be an original crime. Consider a futuristic society wherein the evening news routinely shows or describes the punishments received by a variety of criminals. The crime—or the punishment, for that matter—does not have to be real to be effective. If punishing innocent people for crimes they *might* do were just as effective as punishing criminal offenders, this action might satisfy the ends of deterrence, but would obviously not be acceptable under any system of ethics—except perhaps act utilitarianism.

Incapacitation

Another rationale is to prevent further crime through **incapacitation**. Strictly speaking, incapacitation does not fit the classical definition of punishment, for the purpose is not to inflict pain but only to hold an offender until there is no risk of further crime. The major issue concerning incapacitation is prediction. Two possible mistakes are releasing an offender who then commits further crimes and not releasing an offender who would not commit further crimes.

Carrying the goal of incapacitation to its logical conclusion, one would not have to commit a crime at all to be declared potentially dangerous and subject to incapacitation. We now incarcerate career criminals for life—not for their last offense, but for what they might do if released. These "habitual-felon laws" were justified by the prediction that these criminals will continue to commit crimes, yet studies indicated that prediction instruments were little better than chance in correctly predicting who would recidivate (Auerhahn, 1999). Prediction today has become incredibly more sophisticated with algorithms that predict risk—for decisions regarding bail, pre-release, probation, supervision level, and release from prison. There are grave legal and ethical issues in using any predictive devices to sentence an offender, or even to increase supervision level or make decisions about parole if the prediction instruments use factors such as unemployment and zip code to predict. The tools may be racially discriminatory—not in their intent, but in their implementation since some factors will be correlated with race. This issue becomes even more problematic because the algorithms in risk instruments are often purchased from private vendors, considered proprietary, and, therefore, not subject to scrutiny from outsiders (Ritter, 2013; Starr, 2014; Tashea, 2017).

There are also ethical issues in how we incapacitate sex offenders. Sex offender registries are now mandatory for many offenders and they are available to the public. While states vary in the extent of the restrictions on sex offenders, typically there are housing restrictions, GPS monitoring (and requirements to pay for it), onerous filing requirements (in some states, sex offenders must be on the registry for the rest of their life no matter how young they are or how serious the crime), and work restrictions. Critics are now beginning to question whether the incapacitation tools have gone too far. One problematic issue in some states is that sex offenders (of all types from statutory rape to pornography) are combined with all offenders against children in one

incapacitation
Holding an offender to prevent further crime (incapacitation is not punishment since any pain is unintended).

registry. This is misleading even though typically the crime descriptions are accessible through the registry as well. The most typical criticisms of sex offender registries are that

- juveniles should be given special consideration since they may be more amenable to change,
- some offenders (such as those convicted of statutory rape when there is a small gap in age between the partners and the sex was consensual) shouldn't be on the registry at all, and
- the registries have been known to trigger vigilantism and some sex offenders have been killed by citizens.

Critics also note that the recidivism of sex offenders is no different from other offenders and, in some studies, is a bit lower. Because a sex offender is often a family member of the victim, the harsh sanctions directed to these offenders may lead the victim and family to hide the abuse. They do not want the offender punished so severely and/or they do not want the public shame of having a registered sex offender for the public to see (Pollock, 2013a; Vitiello, 2008).

Another incapacitative tool that is being used against sex offenders is civil commitment. The Supreme Court has declared that there are no due process or Eighth Amendment violations in civilly committing a sex offender after his punishment term has expired if there is some due process before the decision is made (*Kansas v. Hendricks*, 521 U.S. 346, 1997; *U.S. v. Comstock*, 560 U.S. 126, 2010). This means that a sex offender may serve his sentence, and then be civilly committed for an undetermined period, if certain statutory requirements are met.

three-strikes laws
Sentencing legislation that imposes extremely long sentences for repeat offenders—in this case, after three prior felonies.

Three-strikes laws are defended under an incapacitative rationale because it is argued that repeat offenders are more likely to commit future crimes, so they should be held for long periods of time. More than half of all states now have some type of three-strikes or habitual-felon laws.

California's three-strikes law has received the most attention nationally. A lesser known two-strikes provision was also part of the law that provided for a 25-year sentence to those with two felony convictions. California's law was different from most states in that it included almost all felonies while other states limited the three-strikes provision to violent felonies. Critics argued that for both practical and ethical reasons, the California three-strikes sentence was bad policy. It incarcerated past the crime-prone age years, and it incarcerated nonviolent offenders for 25 years or life. There were also wildly disparate rates of three-strike sentences across the state. Some prosecutors frequently utilized three strikes for nonviolent offenders; others never did (King and Mauer, 2001; Leonard, 2009; Zimring, Hawkins, and Kamin, 2001). Another troubling aspect of three-strikes laws was that African Americans tended to be disproportionately affected (Cole, 1999).

The U.S. Supreme Court ruled in 2003 that California's three-strikes law was not grossly disproportionate and deferred to the state's authority in setting punishments (*Ewing v. California*, 538 U.S. 11, 2003; *Lockyer v. Andrade*, 538 U.S. 63, 2003). Various attempts to reduce the law's harshness were unsuccessful until 2012 when Proposition 36, a voter-initiated ballot, changed California's three-strikes law. Now, only certain violent felonies are eligible for the application of three strikes. A provision also allowed those in prison with life sentences to petition to have their sentence revised.

Treatment

If we can find justification for the right to punish, can we also find justification for treatment? Treatment is a very different approach from the moral rejection implicit in retributive punishment. Treatment implies acceptance rather than rejection, support rather than hatred. However, the control over the individual is just as great as with punishment; some people would say it is even greater.

What is treatment? We sometimes consider anything experienced after the point of sentencing to be treatment, including education, prison discipline, and religious services. A court was obliged to define treatment in *Knecht v. Gillman*, 488 F.2d 1136, 1973, when inmates challenged the state's right to use apomorphine, a drug that induces extreme nausea and a feeling of imminent death, as a form of aversive conditioning. In its holding, the court stated that calling something "treatment" did not remove it from Eighth Amendment scrutiny. In other words, merely labeling some infliction of pain as treatment would not necessarily render it immune from legal challenge as cruel and unusual punishment. Generally, courts have further defined treatment as that which constitutes accepted and standard practice and which could reasonably result in a "cure."

The Supreme Court has never recognized a legal right for prisoners to receive rehabilitative treatment (although there is a Constitutional right to medical and dental treatment) unless the sentencing law expresses a purpose of treatment, such as extended punishment for sex offenders. In so-called totality-of-circumstances cases where a court decides that prison conditions constitute cruel and unusual punishment, lack of rehabilitative programming is listed as one of several issues, including violence levels and sanitation, but the absence of programming has never been sufficient, by itself, for a ruling. The ethical issue is that despite no legal duty to do so, does a state owe an inmate some type of programming to improve themselves while they are incarcerated?

The Supreme Court has also not accepted the principle that prisoners should be free from treatment if the state chooses to impose it. The Court held, in *Washington v. Harper*, 494 U.S. 210, 1990, that an inmate's right to refuse antipsychotic medication did not outweigh the state's need to administer it if there was a showing that the inmate posed a security risk. Recall from *Knecht v. Gillman* that inmates do have a right to refuse aversive conditioning treatment if the pain and discomfort imposed was considered akin to punishment, therefore falling under the scrutiny of the Eighth Amendment.

There is no Supreme Court case that tells us whether the involuntary use of medroxyprogesterone acetate (MPA), which is sold under the brand name of Depo-Provera, or other drugs or hormones to induce "chemical castration" in sex offenders would be a violation of the 8th or 14th Amendments. Some states mandate its use when an offender has committed multiple crimes; some when the victim is under a certain age. In some states, the treatment is voluntary (Tullio, 2009). Is there an ethical issue in forcing inmates to take drugs, including those that induce chemical castration?

According to some experts, treatment can be effective only if it is voluntary; others disagree. It is true that much of the treatment that inmates and other correctional clients participate in is either implicitly or directly coerced. Providing treatment for those who want it is one thing; requiring those who are resistant to participate in psychotherapy, group therapy, or religious activities is quite another. Although a retributivist rationale would not support treatment, it is obviously consistent with a prevention rationale, if the results show success in reducing recidivism.

The evaluation literature on rehabilitative treatment programs could fill a room. We now have more than 50 years of evaluations, as well as dozens of meta-analyses and exhaustive reviews of the literature on rehabilitation. It is simply not true that "nothing works," as was widely believed through the 1980s and 1990s (for review, see Pollock, 2016). However, what works is more complicated than one program for all offenders. One interesting finding that comes from evaluation research is that, evidently, sometimes a program works because of the staff characteristics, not the modality of the program. Thus, we can see again that the individual ethics and performance of public servants (treatment professionals in corrections) have a great deal to do with how well the system (in this case, treatment) works.

Ethical Frameworks for Corrections

The retributive and prevention (including deterrence, incapacitation, and treatment) rationales for punishment are well established and can be found in corrections textbooks. The ethical systems that were introduced in Chapter 2 are discussed less commonly in corrections texts, but they form the underlying philosophical rationales.

Utilitarianism

The principle of utilitarianism is often used to support the prevention rationale of punishment: deterrence, incapacitation, and treatment. According to utilitarianism, punishing or treating the criminal offender benefits society and this benefit outweighs the negative effect on the individual offender. It is a teleological argument because the morality of the punishment is determined by the consequences derived—reduced crime. Jeremy Bentham was the major proponent of the utilitarian theory of punishment and established basic guidelines for its use.

Bentham believed that punishment works when it is applied rationally to rational people, but is not acceptable when the person did not make a rational decision to commit the crime, such as when the law forbidding the action was passed after the act occurred, the law was unknown, the person was acting under compulsion, or the person was an infant, insane, or intoxicated (Bentham, 1843; also see Beccaria, 1764/1977). The utility of the punishment would be lost in these cases; therefore, punishment could not be justified (Borchert and Stewart, 1986). Bentham's basic formula for punishment provides that the utility of punishment to society (by deterring crime) outweighs the negative of the punishment itself (it is negative because it is painful). Utilitarian theory also supports treatment and incapacitation if these can be shown to benefit society. If, for instance, treatment and punishment were to have equal amounts of utility for society, treatment would be the more ethical choice because it has a less negative effect on the individual. Likewise, if incapacitation and punishment would be equally effective in protecting and providing utility to society, the choice with the least negative effects would be the ethical one.

Some argue that the harms inherent in imprisonment in either jail or prison are so extreme that they must be counterbalanced by rehabilitative programs to result in a greater good (Kleinig, 2001b). It is certainly true that, for minor offenders, the harm caused by incarceration far exceeds the harm they caused to a victim or society. It is also problematic when drug users (as opposed to dealers) are incarcerated because the harm caused to others by their actions may be less than the harms that they may endure in this nation's jails and prisons, such as beatings by other inmates, economic exploitation, rape, and gratuitous abuse by correctional officers.

Ethical Formalism

While utilitarianism supports prevention goals, ethical formalism clearly supports a retributive view of punishment. It is deontological because it is not concerned with the consequences of the punishment or treatment, only its inherent morality. It would support the idea that a criminal is owed punishment because to do otherwise would not be according him or her equal respect as a human. However, the punishment should not be used for any other end but retribution. Treatment is not supported by ethical formalism because it can be viewed as violative of the second element in the categorical imperative (do not treat others as a means). Involuntary treatment may be seen as using the offender as a means to protect society. The Quote and Query box presents Immanuel Kant's views.

Several arguments support this retributive rationale. First, Mackie (1982) discusses the universal aspects of punishment: the urge to react in a hostile manner to harm is an element inherent in human nature; therefore, one might say that punishment is a natural law. Another supporting argument is found in the principle of forfeiture, which postulates that when one intrudes on an innocent person's rights, one forfeits a proportional amount of one's own rights. By restraining or hurting a victim in some way, the aggressor forfeits his or her own liberty; in other words, he or she forfeits the right to be free from punishment (Bedau, 1982). The major point to remember about ethical formalism as an ethical rationale for punishment is that it does not need to result in any good end, such as deterrence. The offender should receive punishment because he deserves it, not because it will result in something useful for him or society.

> ### QUOTE & **QUERY**
>
> Juridical punishment . . . can be inflicted on a criminal, never just as instrumental to the achievement of some other good for the criminal himself or for the civil society, but only because he has committed a crime; for a man may never be used just as a means to the end of another person. . . Penal law is a categorical imperative, and woe to him who crawls through the serpentine maze of utilitarian theory in order to find an excuse, in some advantage to someone, for releasing the criminal from punishment or any degree of it, in line with the pharisaical proverb "it is better that one man die than that a whole people perish"; for if justice perishes, there is no more value in man living on the earth. . .
>
> *Source: Immanuel Kant, The Science of Right, 1790.*

 Do you understand what Kant was trying to say? Rephrase the passage to make it more simple and current.

Ethics of Care

The ethics of care would probably not support punishment unless it was essential to help the offender become a better person or help the victim become whole. This ethical system defines good as that which meets everyone's needs—victims and offenders alike. Several authors have discussed the ethics of care in relation to the justice and corrections system. For instance, Heidensohn (1986) and Daly (1989) discuss differences in the perception of justice from a care perspective versus a retributive perspective—as female and male perceptions, respectively. The female care perspective emphasizes needs, motives, and relationships, while the male retributive perspective emphasizes rights, responsibilities, and punishments.

The corrections system, ideally, is supported by a caring ethic because it considers offender needs. Community corrections, especially, emphasize the relationship of the offender to the community. From this perspective, one should help the offender to become a better person because that is what a caring and committed relationship would entail. Retributive punishment and deterrence are not consistent with the ethics of care. However, some say that retribution and a care ethic are not, nor should they be considered, in opposition to each other. Restorative justice, which is discussed in more detail in Chapter 13, might be considered the merger of the two in that this approach views the offender as responsible for the wrong committed, but the responsibility is satisfied by reparation to the victim rather than by punishment and pain.

Rawlsian Ethics

John Rawls presents an alternative to utilitarianism and retributivism. Rawls's defense of punishment starts with Kant's proposition that no one should be treated as a means, and with the idea that each should have an "equal right to the most extensive basic liberty compatible with a similar liberty to others." According to Rawls, a loss of rights should take place only when it is consistent with the best interests of the least advantaged. Rules regarding punishment would be as follows (cited in Hickey and Scharf, 1980: 169):

1. We must punish only to the extent that the loss of liberty would be agreeable were one not to know whether one were to be the criminal, the victim, or a member of the general public (the veil of ignorance).

2. The loss of liberty must be justified as the minimum loss consistent with maintenance of the same liberty among others.

Furthermore, when the advantage shifts—when the offender instead of the victim or society becomes the one with the least advantage—punishment must cease. This theory leaves a lot of unanswered questions. For instance, if victims were chosen carefully (e.g., only those who would not suffer financially or emotionally) and the criminal was from an impoverished background, the criminal would still be at a disadvantage and, thus, not morally accountable for his or her actions. This rationale for punishment promotes the idea that the criminal act creates an imbalance between offender and victim, and that punishment should be concerned with regaining that balance. The utilitarian thread in this proposition is that by having this check-and-balance system in determining punishment, all of society benefits.

▌ Punishments

We have discarded many punishments that were acceptable in earlier times, such as flogging, hanging, banishment, branding, cutting off limbs, drawing and quartering, and pillories and stocks. Although we still believe that society has the right to punish, what we do in the name of punishment has changed substantially. As a society, we became gradually uncomfortable with inflicting physically painful punishments on offenders, and as these punishments were discarded, imprisonment was used as the substitute. However, we still employ capital punishment, at least in some states.

Inside prison, we have only relatively recently abandoned physical punishments as a method of control (at least formally), but that is not to say that prisons are not injurious. In addition to the illegal corporal punishments that are inflicted by officers and fellow inmates, prison is painful because it consists of banishment and condemnation; it means separation from loved ones and involves the total loss of freedom. More subtly, it is an assault on one's self-esteem and prevents the individual from almost all forms of self-definition, such as father, mother, professional, and so on. About the only self-definition left is as a prison "tough guy" (or woman)—a stance that destroys the spirit and reduces the individual to a baser form of humanity. Super max prisons, which will be discussed separately, are, arguably, even more painful and injurious.

The Eighth Amendment protects everyone from **cruel and unusual punishment**. Although what is "cruel and unusual" is vague, several tests have been used to define the terms, such as the following, discussed in *Furman v. Georgia* 408 U.S. 238, 1972:

- *Unusual* (by frequency). Punishments that are rarely, if ever, used thus become unusual if used against one individual or a group. They become arbitrary punishments because the decision to use them is so infrequent.

- *Evolving standards of decency*. Civilization is evolving, and punishments considered acceptable in the past century are no longer acceptable in this century.

- *Shock the conscience*. A yardstick for all punishment is to test it against the public conscience. If people are naturally repelled by the punishment, it must be cruel and unusual by definition.

- *Excessive or disproportionate*. Any punishment that is excessive to its purpose or disproportionately administered is considered wrong.

- *Unnecessary*. There must be a purpose of punishment; generally, it is to deter crime. Thus, we should administer only the amount necessary to do so.

These tests have eliminated the use of the whip and the branding iron, yet some say that corporal punishment, at least the less drastic kinds such as whipping, is less harmful than a long prison sentence. After all, a whipping takes perhaps days or weeks to get over, but a prison sentence may last years and affect all future earnings.

Although probation is considered a "slap on the wrist" as a punishment, some conditions (rules) attached to a probation have been criticized as cruel. So-called shaming conditions include DWI offenders having special license plates that indicate to other drivers that the driver has been convicted of DWI; probation officers putting up signs in the yard or nailing them to the door of convicted sex offenders' homes, warning people that a sex offender lives there; announcing to a church congregation one's criminal conviction and asking for forgiveness; and taking out an advertisement in the town newspaper for the same purpose. These types of shaming punishments hark back to the days of the stocks and pillory, when punishment was arguably effective more because of the community scorn received than the physical pain involved. Whitman (1998) argued that the use of such penalties is contrary to a sense of dignity and creates an "ugly complicity" between the state and the community by setting the scene for "lynch justice."

Braithwaite (2000), and others, distinguish between **stigmatizing shaming** and **reintegrative shaming**. The first is a rejection of the individual and has negative effects; the second is only a rejection of the person's behavior and creates a healthier relationship between the individual and his or her community.

cruel and unusual punishment
Punishment proscribed by the Eighth Amendment.

stigmatizing shaming
The effect of punishment whereby the offender feels cast aside and abandoned by the community.

reintegrative shaming
Braithwaite's idea that certain types of punishment can lead to a reduction of recidivism if they do not involve banishment and they induce healthy shame in the individual.

ETHICAL DILEMMA

You are a judge about to sentence an offender for his third DWI. He will receive a mandatory time in jail, but then he will be on probation, supervised by your court. The other district judges in your jurisdiction have begun to utilize unusual probation conditions, such as requiring the offender to go to church, put a sign on their house indicating their crime, and so on. You are urged by the prosecutor to require this DWI offender to have a special sign made for his car that indicates he is a DWI offender; this would be in addition to the ignition-lock device that will be attached to his car that prevents ignition if the driver has over the legal limit of alcohol in his or her blood.

Law

There is a question as to whether such punishments violate the Eighth Amendment. Most would argue they are not cruel and unusual, certainly not compared to a prison sentence. On the other hand, some state laws typically demand that probation conditions have a "rehabilitative function." In that case, there would have to be proof shown that these shaming punishments assisted rehabilitative goals. The other legal challenge would be a Fourteenth Amendment challenge by the offender's family who are also impacted by the punishments with no due process. For instance, a family member might drive the car with the DWI sign and be wrongly stigmatized by it. In general, judges have imposed these punishments without much serious challenge, partly because they come with probation rather than a prison sentence.

Policy

As stated in an earlier chapter, judges are not subject to any office policy. They are fiercely independent and tend to sentence and run their court in very individualistic ways. However, they are influenced by public opinion and so if there is a strong pressure to utilize some form of sentencing; if they want to be reelected, their decisions are obviously affected.

Ethics

We could also examine these conditions considering the ethical systems discussed earlier. One issue, as noted, is the effect that shaming conditions have on family members of offenders and whether these conditions constitute a type of extra-legal punishment for them without any due-process procedures of trial and conviction. Punishments such as house signs and other public disclosures subject family members to stigma along with the offender, and, because they haven't broken any law, it would be a violation of ethical formalism (because they are being used as a means). Generally, utilitarianism would support such punishments only if it could be shown to result in a greater good. There is little research that shows they deter, but, then again, there is no evidence to indicate that they result in worse recidivism numbers than more traditional forms of punishment such as prison. The ethics of care would be concerned for all involved, so, once again, how these punishments affect family members would be an issue. In conclusion, the ethics of inflicting a punishment such as a sign on a car that the person has been convicted of DWI probably is less ethically questionable when no one else would be using the car, when the person is a multiple offender, and other methods of deterrence have been attempted first.

Sex offender registries are also a type of stigmatizing and shaming punishment, and, in some cases, lead to fatal results. Many offenders have been harassed and threatened, the house of one was set on fire, and garbage was thrown all over the lawn of another. A sex offender in New Hampshire was stabbed, and, in 2006, a man in Maine evidently targeted sex offenders and killed two before killing himself (Fahrenthold, 2006). A similar case occurred in Port Angeles, Washington, where two offenders on the registry were killed (Associated Press, 2012a).

Supermax prisons, with 24-hour isolation and few or no programs of self-improvement, have also been considered cruel and unusual (Pollock, 2013a). There are allegations that supermax prisons were designed for the worst of the worst prisoners who were so violent that the inhumane conditions were necessary for safety, but that states are now using them for troublemakers who are not especially dangerous (See, e.g., *Wilkinson v. Austin* et al., 545 U.S. 209, 2005). Others contend that mentally ill offenders who cannot control their behavior are sent to supermax prisons, and become even more ill because of the isolation and lack of medical services (Haney, 2008).

Haney (2008) describes the supermax as having an "ideological toxicity," an "ecology of cruelty," and a "dynamic of desperation." He explains that the ideology of the supermax is toxic in that it is purely punishment with no redeeming elements of rehabilitation or hope. It is the "penal harm" ideology magnified. "Ecology of cruelty" refers to the architecture and policies of supermaxes that are structured to employ more and more punishment to the inmates inside. Because there are no available rewards to encourage positive behavior, the cycle of punishment spirals to horrible levels that become normal to those working within the institution. Haney describes the "dynamics of desperation" as the inevitable tension that exists between the correctional officers and guarded and the tendency for relationships between them to escalate into cruelty. Inmates react in seemingly irrational violence and/or unruliness because of the powerlessness of their environment, and officers react with greater and greater force, going through a cycle where each side's hatred of the other is reinforced. In this sense, Haney argues, the prison affects not only the inmates but also the correctional officers, who become desensitized to its violence and become cruel enforcers because the environment reinforces the notion that the inmates do not deserve to be treated as human. Officers are faced with moral crises when their behavior is normalized to a level of cruelty that would seem abnormal to anyone not inured to the environment of a supermax.

There are also those who believe that the supermax violates the 1994 UN Convention against Torture and Other Cruel, Inhuman or Degrading Treatment or Punishment. Generally, courts have not found the conditions of the supermax prison to constitute cruel and unusual punishment, except for the mentally ill. The In the News box describes a federal lawsuit regarding this issue.

IN THE NEWS | *ADX—"A Clean Version of Hell"*

ADX Florence is a "supermax" federal prison housing Ted Kaczynski (Unabomber), Terry Nichols (the Oklahoma City bomber), Eric Rudolph (the Atlanta Olympics bomber), and Zacarias Moussaoui (an Al Qaeda member that would have been part of the 9/11 attack if he hadn't been arrested). It houses organized crime figures, domestic terrorists, and serial killers, but it also houses those who rack up infractions at other prisons. Inmates spent 23 hours a day alone in their cells. In a lawsuit against the Bureau of Prisons (BOP), several years ago, the legal team met inmates who swallowed razor blades, were shackled to their beds for days and weeks at a time, ate their own fingers or feces, and, in other ways, clearly demonstrated mental problems so severe that they should have been in a psychiatric facility. Instead, they were at a supermax where, when one inmate came back from the hospital after slashing his neck in a suicide attempt, was told to mop up his blood. Their stories seemed to indicate that the prison itself may have caused at least some of their mental issues. The BOP surprisingly agreed to settle the lawsuit submitting to a list of 27 demands that required, among other things, diagnoses and a treatment plan for the mentally ill inmates. There was no financial settlement as part of the deal. The men are still in prison, but have been transferred to other prisons and are now on medication.

Source: Binelli, 2015.

Capital Punishment

What sets capital punishment apart from all other punishments is its quality of irrevocability. This type of punishment leaves no way to correct a mistake. For this reason, some believe that no mortal should have the power to inflict capital punishment because there is no way to guarantee that mistakes won't be made. The growing number of innocent men and women who came perilously close to being executed, as described in Chapter 10, indicates that we have an imperfect system.

Public support for capital punishment has swung up and down. Public opinion polls reveal that public support for the death penalty declined gradually through the 1960s, reaching a low of 44 percent in 1966, but then increased in the next 30 years. In the late 1990s, 75–80 percent supported the death penalty. By 2008, only 63 percent of Americans supported capital punishment (Harris Poll, 2008). In 2016, 60 percent of Americans favored capital punishment for murderers according to the Gallup poll. The Pew Research Center presented even lower numbers, with only 56 percent of the public favoring capital punishment (Pew Research Center, 2015). The number of executions has declined substantially from a high of 98 executions in the year 1999 to 20 in 2016 (Death Penalty Information Center, 2017).

Retentionists (who believe that we should continue to utilize capital punishment) and abolitionists (who believe that we should not execute anyone) both use utilitarianism, ethical formalism, and religion as moral justifications. Retentionists argue that capital punishment is just because it deters others from committing murder and it deters the individual who is executed. This is a utilitarian argument. They also argue that capital punishment is just because murder deserves a proportional punishment. This argument is more consistent with ethical formalism. Finally, they argue that the Bible dictates an "eye for an eye." This is, of course, a (Judeo-Christian) religious justification for capital punishment.

Abolitionists argue that capital punishment has never been shown to be effective in deterring others from committing murder; therefore, the evil of capital punishment far outweighs any potential benefits for society because there is no proof that it deters. This is a utilitarian argument. Abolitionists might also utilize the categorical imperative under ethical formalism to argue that deterrence is using the individual as a means to an end. Finally, abolitionists would point to the religious command to "turn the other cheek," an argument against any Christian justification for capital punishment.

The reason why utilitarianism can be used to justify or oppose capital punishment is that the research on deterrence is mixed. Those who have summarized the evidence marshaled on both sides of the deterrence question found little support for the proposition that executions are useful deterrents, although there are contrary findings by other researchers. The National Academy of Sciences reported that the science of death penalty deterrence research was not reliable, accurate, or valid enough to make policy decisions upon (Kronenwerter, 1993; Land, Teske, and Zheng, 2009; Walker, 1985: 79). However, despite the lack of research for general deterrence, many are still convinced that it does deter, at least the individual offender (although technically executing the offender does not result in deterrence but incapacitation). Ethical formalism supports capital punishment; however, the imperfect nature of the system is problematic. Recall that under the categorical imperative, you should act in a way that you can will it to be a universal law. In this case, knowing that innocent people may be sentenced to death, could you agree that murderers should be executed if you did not know whether you were the victim, the murderer, the judge, or an innocent person mistakenly convicted!

Religion, also, can be and has been used to support *and* condemn capital punishment. As with other issues, Christians have pointed to various verses in the Bible to justify their position. Kania (1999), for instance, presents a comprehensive religious justification for capital punishment, along with a social contract justification.

Should all murderers be subject to capital punishment, or are some murders less heinous than others? Should we allow defenses of age, mental state, or reason? If we do apply capital punishment differentially, doesn't this open the door to bias and misuse? Evidence indicates that capital punishment has been used arbitrarily and discriminatorily in this country. One study, cited by the Supreme Court, indicated that minorities are more likely to be executed when their victims are white; in Georgia, black offenders charged with killing a white person were 4.3 times more likely to be sentenced to death than those charged with killing a black person. Yet the Supreme Court stated that this evidence of statistically disproportional administration was not enough to invalidate the death penalty because it did not prove that there was discrimination in the immediate case (*McClesky v. Kemp*, 481 U.S. 279, 1987).

Because our justice system is based on rationality, executions of persons with mental illness and mental retardation have been vehemently criticized. The Supreme Court has ruled that executing the mentally ill is cruel and unusual (*Ford v. Wainwright*, 411 U.S. 399, 1986; Miller and Radelet, 1993), as is executing the mentally challenged (*Atkins v. Virginia*, 536 U.S. 304, 2002). Further cases have evaluated how serious mental retardation must be to serve as a bar to capital punishment and the means to test levels of intelligence to determine whether execution is Constitutionally permissible (*Hall v. Florida*, 572 U.S. __, 2014; *Moore v. Texas*, 581 U. S. __, 2017).

It has also been ruled that it is a violation of the Eighth Amendment to execute for any other crime than murder (*Kennedy v. Louisiana*, 554 U.S. 407, 2008). Other legal challenges to capital punishment have targeted whether jurors must be unanimous, the selection of jurors, whether judges can overrule juries, and the means and methods of execution (e.g., *Baze v. Rees*, 553 U.S. 35, 2008). These are all legal questions, but moral ones too. The morality of capital punishment is still very much a topic of debate, and it elicits strong feelings on the part of many people. The quote illustrates a decision by a Supreme Court Justice to withdraw support for the use of capital punishment.

The Supreme Court has also ruled that it is cruel and unusual to execute individuals who were under 18 at the time of their crime. The Court considered research that shows juveniles have less control over their impulses than adults and are more amenable to change, therefore, they are not the most heinous of murderers (Dejarnette, 2015; *Roper v. Simmons*, 543 U.S. 551, 2005). This research has also led to some states considering revising their juvenile justice system described in the In the News box.

QUOTE & **QUERY**

From this day forward, I no longer shall tinker with the machinery of death. For more than 20 years I have endeavored . . . to develop . . . rules that would lend more than the mere appearance of fairness to the death penalty endeavor. . . Rather than continue to coddle the court's delusion that the desired level of fairness has been achieved . . . I feel . . . obligated simply to concede that the death penalty experiment has failed. It is virtually self-evident to me now that no combination of procedural rules or substantive regulations ever can save the death penalty from its inherent constitutional deficiencies . . . Perhaps one day this court will develop procedural rules or verbal formulas that actually will provide consistency, fairness, and reliability in a capital-sentencing scheme. I am not optimistic that such a day will come. I am more optimistic, though, that this court eventually will conclude that the effort to eliminate arbitrariness while preserving fairness "in the infliction of [death] is so plainly doomed to failure that it and the death penalty must be abandoned altogether." . . . I may not live to see that day, but I have faith that eventually it will arrive....

Source: Justice Harry Blackmun in a dissenting opinion in Callins v. Collins *510 U.S. 1141, 1994.*

? Do you agree with Justice Blackmun? Why or why not?

IN THE NEWS | *Punishing Juveniles*

A new law in New York will raise the age of criminal responsibility from 16 to 18 by 2019. In some states, 17 year olds are automatically prosecuted as adults. At this point, at least seven states have raised the age of criminal responsibility to 18, and several more are considering new legislation to raise the age for prosecution in adult criminal court. A few states (Connecticut and Vermont) have considered raising the age of criminal responsibility to 21. These changes are because of growing evidence that juveniles think differently than adults, or more accurately, don't think before they act at all. There is other research to show that youth who are prosecuted and punished in juvenile court are less likely to recidivate than those who go through the adult system. Statistics from states that brought more juvenile offenders into the juvenile justice system years ago seem to support the notion that spending a bit more on juvenile offenders in the juvenile system reduces recidivism and costs years later.

Source: Wiltz, 2017.

Should Punishment be Profitable?

In Chapter 8, the "criminalization of poverty" was described as the increasing practice of generating general revenue funds by onerous fees and late charges attached to minor offenses. Low-risk individuals who can't pay bail stay in jail, while those who can pay are released. Individuals who receive traffic tickets or are found guilty of fine-only offenses end up owing thousands of dollars, because of late charges they can't pay and, sometimes, end up in jail even though it is unconstitutional to jail people solely based on their inability to pay debts.

Pretrial diversion programs were quite popular in the late 1970s but fell out of favor with the ramping up of the drug war and imprisonment binge in the 1980s. Today, the programs seem to be coming back and allow individuals the chance to avoid adjudication and a criminal conviction if they complete requirements and stay out of trouble. However, what is different about today's programs is that they typically cost money and if the accused is not able to pay, they do not get to participate. A pretrial diversion program in New York City, for instance, involves 12 weeks of classes, 24 hours of community service, and a clean record. If the accused completes these requirements, the charges will be dismissed and arrest expunged. This diversion program can cost over $1,000, and programs may cost up to $5,000 in other areas. If a person completes the classes and community services, but still owes any amount of money, their case will be sent back to court for prosecution. In most jurisdictions, defendants are required to enter a guilty plea to be eligible for diversion, so, in effect, there is no prosecution if they fail on diversion, they are automatically convicted of the original offense. This makes the program attractive to prosecutors with weak cases. In many jurisdictions, prosecutors have the discretion to refer defendants to the diversion programs and, also, benefit financially from the program's fees—either because it is run in-house, or because a private contractor pays fees back to the jurisdiction. Some jurisdictions, like Cook County (Chicago) do not charge a fee to offenders in their diversion program, but others charge a fee even to apply to have program staff determine eligibility. In a review of the programs across the country, there seemed to be no consistency in fees, what crimes were eligible for diversion, requirements, or the length of programs. In a few instances, prosecutors have used the diversion fee account as their own personal bank account, one paying himself more than $300,000 from it. In other instances, the programs appear to have inched over from discretionary diversion into outright bribery where defendants pay inflated amounts for diversion and to have their charges dismissed (Dewan and Lehren, 2016). In other jurisdictions, the diversion program is run by a private company and their profit motive acts as an incentive to keep participants if they can pay. If they can't, they may be sent to jail regardless of their risk to the community or lack of further criminal activity. For-profit companies are sometimes awarded contracts because they promise bigger kickbacks, called administrative fees, to the county (Romney, 2017).

This practice of squeezing revenue out of the offender population and their families continues even after correctional sentencing. It is important to note that the fees associated with probation supervision, electronic monitoring, mandatory drug treatment, jail and prison medical care, phone calls, and other goods or services to prisoners only began in earnest in the 1980s, simultaneously with the incredible increase in incarceration rates across the country. Cash-strapped states and municipalities began seeking to recoup some of the costs of their expensive correctional policy choices by making offenders pay for their punishment. Making offenders pay was congruent with the harsh, penal harm philosophy, and popular with voters. However, these practices increase the gulf between the haves (who easily pay for treatment alternatives to imprisonment) and the have-nots (who are being incarcerated sometimes solely because they don't have enough money to pay their fees and court costs).

Many jurisdictions now charge those in jail a daily fee, like the fees gaolers charged in the 1700s and 1800s. Jail inmates are charged $20–$60 a day—whether they are serving time or being held before adjudication. If they can't pay, the debt follows them after release. Just as in the 1700s, those who have money can buy comfort. Some inmates of Los Angeles County Jail can pay up to $175 a day to be housed in suburban jails. They may get such perks as iPods, flat-screen television, computer, private cells, and work release programs in these pay-to-stay jails. Some even allow inmates to order in food! At least 26 small cities around Los Angeles have these programs where they will take Los Angeles prisoners—for a price. While most offenders have been convicted of DUI, even inmates who committed serious crimes such as child abuse, rape, and possession of child pornography have served their time in jails that are cleaner, safer, more comfortable, and come with many more perks than a normal jail experience. Some of these city jails take offenders from out-of-state (Santo, Kim, and Flagg, 2017). California isn't alone in allowing celebrities and the very rich to experience a very different jail experience from normal inmates. Journalists describe many examples of the rich and famous receiving special treatment (Clarke, 2010; Santo, Kim and Flagg, 2017).

Probation used to be touted as a cost-saving alternative to prison. When probation supervision fees were introduced in the 1980s, probation became an even bigger attraction for states struggling to meet the costs of a construction boom of prisons; however, probation supervision fees are one of the biggest barriers to success for probationers who often struggle to find a job and pay for housing and food. This issue is exacerbated when a state or county contracts out probation services to a private company who adds a profit margin onto the costs of supervision and is even less likely to accommodate individuals who cannot pay. Some of these programs are being sued by civil rights advocates who argue it is a Constitutional violation to threaten to revoke probation and jail probationers merely because of an inability to pay. In *Bearden v. Georgia*, 461 U.S. 660, 1963, the Supreme Court said as much (Dewan, 2015).

It is not clear which state began charging inmates for medical care, however, it appears that today, most do. Only eight states do not have medical co-pays for prisoners. States charge inmates from a couple dollars to $8 to see a doctor. Texas charges a flat $100 yearly fee for health services and, if not paid out of inmate account funds, the debt follows the inmate after release. While a $5 co-pay does not seem like much, many inmates have no financial resources in prison and, if they do work, they usually make less than 50 cents an hour. One doctor's visit could cost a month's wages (Sawyer, 2017). Proponents explain that it deters prisoners from needlessly taking up medical staff members' time. Critics argue that this practice is dangerous because inmates who are sick are likely not to get treated because they can't or won't pay the fee and end up getting sicker, which will eventually cost the state more for expensive medical treatment, or they are contagious and infect many more inmates than if their medical need had been met immediately. In the closed environment of the prison, any contagious illness has the potential to turn into an epidemic (Sawyer, 2017).

Generating a revenue stream from offenders seems to be going on all over the country by states and local entities in pretrial, probation, jail, and prison settings. The reason it is morally questionable is that the offender population is, by and large, poor, so charging for correctional services or release options increases the differential sentencing between those who can pay and those who can't. In many cases, poverty, and not the seriousness of the crime, is inextricably linked to how long someone is enmeshed with the criminal justice system. Further, there is something inequitable about punishing someone by depriving them of liberty and, also, charging them for it. What is even more insidious, however, is when a whole profit industry is based on imprisonment.

Despite critics, the industry of private prisons is big business bringing in over $3 billion per year (Cohen, 2015). Inserting a profit motive into the state's power to imprison is fraught with ethical and legal issues. There have been instances of rigged bidding (where politicians and decision makers are rewarded for sending contracts to certain firms), contract performance problems (when private companies don't provide the services they promised), and issues with poorly trained or overworked staff

---

▌ 🖥 IN THE NEWS │ *Prison Savings?*

In 2016, news reports indicated that the Michigan Department of Corrections set up a 30-person unit of monitors to oversee the contracts with food, medical treatment, and other service providers after a scandal over the former prison food contractor. The scandal with the food vendor included food shortages, maggots in the kitchen, smuggling of drugs and other contraband, and workers engaging in sex acts with inmates. The Michigan Department of Corrections spent about $250 million in 2015 on about 185 service contracts, including about 70 substance abuse contracts, more than a dozen sex offender related contracts and about a dozen prisoner reentry contracts with community service agencies. One report indicated that the Department spent about $2.1 million to monitor just the food contract between December 2013 and August 2015. Critics of privatization point out that, typically, evaluations of privatization show cost savings from administrative costs, but don't include, or underestimate, the cost of monitoring contracts.

Source: Egan, 2016.

(leading to violence and escapes). Some believe that punishment and profit are never compatible and that linking the two has led to a variety of historical abuses (such as the contract labor system in the South) and current scandals.

In 2015, 8 percent of the total number of state and federal prisoners were held in privately operated facilities that were under the jurisdiction of 29 states and the BOP. The number of prisoners held in private facilities in 2015 (126,300) decreased 4 percent (5,500 prisoners) from year-end 2014 (Carson and Anderson, 2016). CoreCivic (formerly Corrections Corporation of America) and the GEO Group (formerly Wackenhut Corrections Corporation) are the largest players in the private prison industry, holding a little more than half of all private prison beds (more than 60,000 beds in the United States alone). Both companies structure themselves as realty trusts with operational portions of the enterprise separated into different companies to reduce tax liabilities (Stroud, 2013). In addition to the "big two," more than a dozen smaller companies across the nation are competing for the private prison bids put out by the states.

For decades, there have been news stories of and lawsuits based on sexual abuses, escapes, and violence in private prisons; but, to be fair, such events occur in state-run facilities as well. In some states, corruption scandals have occurred whereby politicians were paid to send contracts to private companies (Etter, 2015). In other states, private prison contracts have been rescinded in the wake of lawsuits proving the prisons were run poorly, treatment was nonexistent, and violence was at unacceptably high levels (Mitchell, 2014). One recent journalistic investigation into a private prison detailed the personnel issues that can arise when private companies pay bare minimum wage for a stressful and difficult job (Bauer, 2016).

Proponents argue that private corrections can save the state money. Private corporations are said to be more efficient; they can build faster with less cost and less red tape, and they have economies of scale (they can obtain savings because of their size). States and local governments are bound by a myriad of bidding and siting restrictions, unlike private corporations. While some studies have concluded that private prisons

IN THE NEWS | *Corruption in Corrections*

In 2017, news reports detailed the prosecution and conviction of Chris Epps, the corrections commissioner of Mississippi. He was sentenced to almost 20 years in prison for accepting at least $1.4 million in bribes and kickbacks in return for more than $800 million in contracts to private providers. He rose through the ranks from prison guard to become the longest serving corrections commissioner in Mississippi's history. At the height of his power, he was the president of the American Correctional Association and the Association of State Correctional Administrators. He also had several homes and luxury cars, mainly because of Cecil McCrory, who was owner of a private corrections company. Between 2007 and when Epps was indicted in 2014, McCrory paid tens of thousands of dollars to Epps in cash plus he paid off the mortgages of both of Epps' homes. In return, Epps steered contracts to McCrory's corrections company or another private company who paid McCrory. One such deal was described whereby Epps personally urged MTC, a Utah-based private prison company that received the contract to run all the private prisons in the state, to hire McCrory and, when he was hired, they split the fee. After he was indicted, Epps provided information about McCrory and several other people, including state legislators, who were also implicated in the corruption.

Sources: Fausset, 2014; Gates, 2017.

produce results equal to those of state institutions for less cost, others find that they are not cost-effective (Lundahl, 2007; Pollock, 2013a; Selman and Leighton, 2010). The problem is that many of the evaluations of private prisons are funded by private prison companies or libertarian groups that advocate private enterprise taking over government functions; thus, the objectivity of the evaluators is questionable (Bourge, 2002). At least one academic evaluator who has published articles showing private prisons are more cost-effective has owned $500,000 worth of stock in a private prison company, thus raising concern about his objectivity (Geis, Mobley, and Shichor, 1999). Common sense would dictate that private prison companies would have a difficult time squeezing profit for shareholders without cutting costs. While the CEOs of CCA and GEO make $2–$3 million in salary each year, correctional officers earn, on average, $10,000 less than their state-employed counterparts (Selman and Leighton, 2010: 137). The In the News box describes how greed can ruin the careers of individuals in private and public correctional agencies.

Reports are published with titles that clearly indicate the conclusions, such as "*Too Good to Be True: Private Prisons in America*" (2012, by the Sentencing Project), and "*Unholy Alliance: How the Private Prison Industry Is Corrupting Our Democracy and Promoting Mass Incarceration*" (2011, by PICO National Network and Public Campaign). What these reports describe is a very troubling association between private prison companies that financially benefit from increased rates of incarceration and legislators who write laws that affect incarceration levels. Private prison companies send large sums of money to legislators' campaign funds and/or party coffers, and lobbyists for private prisons work with legislators to write laws that result in a greater likelihood of incarceration for illegal immigrants and mandatory minimum sentences that result in more incarceration for drug offenders. It is reported that private prison companies have given more than $10 million to candidates since 1989 and have spent nearly $25 million on lobbying efforts. Conservative politicians and political action committees (PACs) are the largest beneficiaries. For instance, the Republican Party of Florida PAC received nearly $2.5 million from GEO and CCA between 1989 and 2014 (Cohen, 2015).

Many would argue that what is good for this business is bad for the country. Private prison companies stand in direct conflict with (and opposition to) the trend to decriminalize, deinstitutionalize, and deconstruct this nation's prison–industrial complex. There was no coincidence that the stock market value of these companies dropped precipitously when the Obama administration announced that the federal government would be phasing out its contracts with private prison providers, nor was it coincidental that when Attorney General Sessions publicly stated that the order was void and federal contracts with private prison companies would probably increase because of incarcerating immigration violators, the stock price jumped up 43 percent (Carroll, 2017).

Leighton (2014) describes "perverse incentives" where private prisons require contracts with governmental entities that guarantee occupancy rates of 90–95 percent. Thus, if they enter a 20-year contract with a private prison company, they must provide those numbers of inmates or pay anyway. There is no incentive under this system to reduce prison populations. He argues that privatization does have a role in corrections, but only if there is a shift in incentives to reward rehabilitative success and prevention rather than warehousing.

Private prison companies have also moved into housing immigration detainees. In past years, private prison company representatives were criticized for being involved in writing legislation regarding mandatory minimum sentencing. There is a troubling repetition of the practice of the lobbyists and CEOs of private corrections companies becoming involved in legislation, only this time as it concerns immigration, with the suspicion that, once again, what is good for the company (increasing numbers of illegal immigrants housed in massive detention centers) is not necessarily good for the country. More people are sent to federal prison for immigration offenses than for violent crime, weapons, and property offenses combined (Wilder and Mosqueda, 2014). This trend to criminalize and incarcerate immigration violators, ramped up during the Obama administration, has accelerated under the Trump administration.

Small towns that depend on detention facilities and prisons for jobs will see an increase in jobs and tax revenue with President Trump's immigration enforcement policies. In January 2017, ICE incarcerated about 40,000 people a day in immigration detention centers; however, President Trump issued a memo to Homeland Security officials calling for that number to double to 80,000, and, in the budget he sent to Congress, he called for enough funding for an additional 17,000 immigrants to be detained each day (Verdugo, 2017).

In Eloy, Arizona, for instance, which has four private detainment facilities, CoreCivic is now the biggest employer and taxpayer. Townspeople can't help but see the growing numbers of immigrant detainees as a good thing despite reports from Human Rights Watch (HRW) and Community Initiatives for Visiting Immigrants in Confinement (CIVIC) that there is an unusually high number of deaths and suicides in the facilities. Jobs are hard to come by and working at the prison is the best job in town. Like the old company towns of bygone days, CoreCivic engenders a fierce loyalty and defensiveness (Carroll, 2017).

A very troublesome element of privately run detainee centers and prisons is that they have been ruled exempt from open-records laws, which apply to public agencies, including departments of corrections. Shielding the inner workings of these companies is justified as protecting "trade secrets." The ACLU and other groups have difficulty gaining access and investigating private detainment facilities, but allege that shocking mistreatment and lack of medical care exists resulting in an unusually high number of deaths and riots for what should be a low-security population (ACLU, 2011; Wilder, 2013; Wilder and Mosqueda, 2014). Another legal issue is that prisoners don't have the same legal protections evidently as those housed in state facilities. In *Minneci v. Pollard*, 132 S. Ct. 617, 2012, the Supreme Court decided that prisoners in a private prison could not utilize federal courts to allege constitutional violations since prison employees were private employees. The Justices argued that there were state tort remedies available, but opponents argued this creates an equal protection issue between prisoners housed in private prisons compared to prisoners in state or federally run prisons. Federal and state legislators have the power to restrict the use of or put rules in place to monitor the activities of private corrections companies, but whether they will do so while accepting campaign donations is an interesting question and one that will play out differently depending on each state.

Formal Ethics for Correctional Professionals

The American Correctional Association's (ACA) Code of Ethics outlines formal ethics for correctional officers and other correctional personnel. This code has many similarities to the Law Enforcement Code of Ethics presented in Chapter 5. For instance, integrity, respect for and protection of individual rights, and service to the public are emphasized in both codes, as are the importance and sanctity of the law. Also, the prohibition against exploiting professional authority for personal gain is stressed in both codes.

The ACA code indicates that members should exhibit honesty, respect for the dignity and individuality of human beings, and a commitment to professional and compassionate service. The following principles are identified:

- Protect legal rights
- Show concern for the welfare of individuals
- Promote mutual respect with colleagues and criticize only when warranted
- Respect and cooperate with all disciplines in the system
- Provide public information as consistent with law and privacy rights
- Protect public safety
- Refrain from using one's position to secure personal privileges or advantage or let these impair objectivity
- Avoid conflicts of interest
- Refrain from accepting gifts or services that appear improper
- Differentiate one's personal views from professional duties
- Report any corrupt or unethical behaviors
- Refrain from discriminating because of race, gender, creed, national origin, religious affiliation, age, disability, or other prohibited categories
- Preserve the integrity of private information; abide by civil service rules
- Promote a safe, healthy, and harassment-free workplace (the ACA Code is available on the ACA website under the "About Us" link. http://www.aca.org.asp).

In an interesting discussion of implementing an ethics program for correctional officers, Barrier et al. (1999) described how officers presented elements of what they thought were important in an ethics code:

- Acting professionally
- Showing respect for inmates and workers
- Maintaining honesty and integrity
- Being consistent
- Acting impartially
- Being assertive but not aggressive
- Confronting bad behavior but reinforcing good behavior
- Standardizing rule enforcement
- Respecting others
- Practicing the Golden Rule
- Encouraging teamwork
- Using professional language
- Not abusing sick leave
- Telling inmates the truth
- Admitting mistakes.

The American Jail Association has a similar code of ethics for jail officers. The preamble states that the jail officer should avoid questionable behavior that will bring disrepute to the agency. The code mandates that officers keep the institution secure, work with everyone fairly, maintain a positive demeanor, report what should be reported, manage inmates even-handedly without becoming personally involved, take advantage of training opportunities, communicate with individuals outside the agency in a way that does not bring discredit, contribute to a positive environment, and support professional activities (American Jail Association, available at www.aaja.org/ethics.aspx).

Formal ethical guidelines for probation and parole officers are provided by the ACA Code of Ethics, and possibly by their own state ethics codes. Federal probation officers subscribe to the Federal Probation and Pretrial Officers Association's ethical code. The formal ethics of the profession is summarized by the ideal of service—to the community and to the offender. As with other codes, the federal probation officer is exhorted to

- maintain "decorum" in one's private life,
- avoid granting or receiving favors or benefits that are connected to the position,
- uphold the law with dignity,
- strive for objectivity in performance of duties,
- "appreciate the inherent worth of the individual,"
- cooperate with fellow workers and related agencies,
- improve professional standards,
- recognize the office as "a symbol of public faith" (Federal Probation and Pretrial Officers Association, available at www.fppoa.org/code-of-ethics).

Ethical codes exist for other correctional professionals as well. Treatment professionals typically belong to a professional organization, and this organization will have a code of ethics, such as the National Association of Social Workers Code of Ethics or, for psychiatrists, the Principles of Medical Ethics with Annotations Especially Applicable to Psychiatry. Mental health counselors adhere to the code of ethics of the American Mental Health Counselors Association, and psychologists follow the Ethical Principles of Psychologists and Code of Conduct. There are also organizations or separate divisions of professional organizations specifically for correctional workers in that profession, such as the Criminal Justice Section of the American Psychological Association. Finally, the American Correctional Health Services Association and the American Association for Correctional and Forensic Psychology also have their own ethical codes to guide their members. The American Association for Correctional and Forensic Psychology's code includes the following sections: Offender's Right to Dignity and Respect, Avoid or Minimize Harm, Maintain and Advocate for Competent Mental Health Services and Rights, and Social Responsibility. The Ethical Principles of Psychologists promote five aspirational principles: beneficence (do no harm), fidelity and responsibility (create relationships of trust), integrity (honesty and truthfulness in science and practice), justice (fairness), and respect for rights and dignity (protect privacy and self-determination) (cited and described in Bonner and Vandecreek, 2006).

The American Correctional Health Services Association is an affiliate of the American Correctional Association and has developed a code of ethics for health care providers in correctional facilities, including medical care workers as well as mental health professionals. In developing this code, they surveyed their members and consensus emerged as to the leading principles that should guide professionals in providing healthcare in corrections: respect for human dignity, beneficence, trustworthiness, autonomy, prevention of harm, and promotion of a safe environment. The code includes "should" statements such as "Respect the law," "Recognize a responsibility to seek changes in those requirements that are contrary to the best interest of the patient," and "Honor custody functions but not participate in such activities as escorting inmates, forced transfers, security supervision, strip searches, or witnessing use of force" (described in Bonner and Vandecreek, 2006). These codes, in general or specific language, attempt to provide guidance to members who strive for ethical performance of their duties.

Occupational Subcultures in Corrections

Another similarity between the corrections field and law enforcement is that there seems to be an occupational culture that is, in some ways, contrary to the ethical codes. Although the ethical codes clearly call for fair and objective treatment, integrity, and high standards of performance, the actual practices found in some agencies and institutions may be quite different.

The Correctional Officer Subculture

The correctional officer subculture has not been described as extensively as the police subculture, but some elements are similar. First, the inmate may be considered the enemy, along with superiors and society in general. Moreover, the acceptance of the use of force, the preference toward redefining job roles to meet only minimum requirements, and the willingness to use deceit to cover up wrongdoing seem to have support in both subcultures (Crouch, 1986; Grossi and Berg, 1991; R. Johnson, 2002).

In an excellent study of the officers' world, Kauffman (1988: 85–112) notes the following norms of the correctional officer subculture:

- *Always go to the aid of another officer.* Like law enforcement, the necessity of interdependence ensures that this is a strong and pervasive norm in the correctional officer subculture.

- *Don't lug drugs.* This prohibition is to ensure the safety of other officers, as is the even stronger prohibition against bringing in weapons for inmates. The following norm against "ratting" on a fellow officer may exclude informing on an officer who is a known offender of this lugging norm.

- *Don't rat.* In ways like the law enforcement subcultural code and, ironically, the inmate code, correctional officers also hate those who inform on their peers.

- *Never make a fellow officer look bad in front of inmates.* This applies regardless of what the officer did, for it jeopardizes the officer's effectiveness and undercuts the appearance of officer solidarity.

- *Always support an officer in a dispute with an inmate.* Similarly to the previous provision, this prescribes behavior. Not only should one not criticize a fellow officer, but one should support him or her against any inmate.

- *Always support officer sanctions against inmates.* This is a specific version of the previous provision, which includes the use of illegal physical force as well as legal sanctions.

- *Don't be a white hat.* This prohibition is directed at any behavior, attitude, or expressed opinion that could be interpreted as sympathetic toward inmates. Kauffman also notes that this prohibition is often violated and does not have the strong subcultural sanctions that accompany some of the other norms.

- *Maintain officer solidarity against all outside groups.* This norm reinforces officer solidarity by making any other group, including the media, administration, or the public, the out-group.

- *Show positive concern for fellow officers.* Two examples are (1) never leave another officer a problem, which means don't leave unfinished business at the end of your shift for the next officer to handle, and (2) help your fellow officers with problems outside the institution, which means lending money to injured or sick officers or helping in other ways.

If a correctional officer violates the subcultural code, the sanctions are felt perhaps even more acutely than by police officers, because one must work closely with other correctional officers all day long. Whereas police officers cite the importance of being able to trust other officers as backups in violent situations, one could make the argument that correctional officers have to trust each other more completely, more implicitly, and more frequently, given that violence in some institutions is pervasive and unprovoked, and that the correctional officer carries no weapon. An officer described to Kauffman (1988: 207) the result of violating peer trust:

> *If an incident went down, there was no one to cover my back. That's a very important lesson to learn. You need your back covered and my back wasn't covered there at all. And at one point I was in fear of being set up by guards. I was put in dangerous situations purposely. That really happened to me.*

Fear of violating the code of silence is one reason that officers do not report wrongdoing. Loyalty is another reason. Correctional officers feel a strong esprit de corps like the previously discussed loyalty among police. This positive loyalty also results in covering for other officers and not testifying or reporting offenses. McCarthy (1991) discusses how theft, trafficking in contraband, embezzlement, and misuse of authority went unreported by other correctional officers because of loyalty and subcultural prohibitions against "ratting."

A pattern of complicity also prevents reporting. New officers cannot possibly follow all the many rules and regulations that exist in a prison and still adequately deal with inmates on a day-to-day basis. Before long they find themselves involved in activity that could result in disciplinary action. Because others are usually aware of this activity and do not inform supervisors, an implicit conspiracy of silence develops so no one is turned in for anything because each of the others who might witness this wrongdoing has engaged in behavior that could also be sanctioned (Lombardo, 1981: 79).

In the years-long scandal at Rikers Island in New York referred to in the In the News box, correctional officers who used brutal retaliation against inmates were rarely punished and a conspiracy of silence ensued. One incident was documented

▣ IN THE NEWS | *Rikers*

In 2010, a correctional officer was sentenced to six years for his role in the death of a juvenile inmate at Rikers. An investigation revealed that a rogue group of officers used beatings and extortion by inmate "enforcers" to keep order in a facility where young offenders, aged 16–18, were housed. Other correctional officers entered guilty pleas and received sentences of two years.

Since that case, Rikers has been the target of a major investigatory series of reports by the *New York Times*, and investigation by federal prosecutors into the treatment of juvenile offenders that resulted, in the summer of 2014, in a blistering 79-page report documenting pervasive abuse and cover-ups in the juvenile lock-up. The report detailed a "culture of violence" and "code of silence" of correctional officers. In June of 2015, a settlement agreement was announced in a class action lawsuit that mandated a court-appointed monitor for the jail, a substantial increase in the number of cameras, body cameras worn by some correctional officers, use-of-force training, beefed up security to prevent contraband from coming in to the

facility, and improved accountability measures for correctional officers who used inappropriate force. Changes over the last several years have included a reduction in the number of uses of force, improved programming for juveniles, the elimination of solitary for juveniles, improved mental health screening, hiring new officers, and improved training, but problems at Rikers continues.

Joseph Ponte, brought in as commissioner to spur the reforms, resigned in the wake of an investigation into the misuse of state vehicles and his absence from New York for 35 work days—evidently he spent those days at his former home in Maine. He was credited with many of the reforms that were undertaken and supported by the governor, but he was also criticized for not upholding a role model of integrity at the top of the organization. The latest report from the court monitor detailed increasing violence by and against correctional officers and a broken disciplinary system that excuses uses of force by officers. Recent news stories paint a troubling picture that the problems of Rikers aren't going to go away anytime soon.

Sources: Weiser, Schwirtz, and Winerip, 2014; Schwirtz and Winerip, 2015a, 2015b; Weiser, 2015; Rashbaum and Schwirtz, 2017; Schwirtz and Rashbaum, 2017.

where two inmates in segregation threw urine or some liquid on correctional officers and they were forcibly extracted from their cells, strapped to gurneys, taken to the medical clinic (because there were no cameras there) and repeatedly beaten in the head and body to the point that blood sprayed on the walls and the medical staff pleaded with the correctional officers to stop (Winerip and Schwirtz, 2014a). In the investigative reports of Rikers, many instances were detailed where correctional officers and their supervisors would lie on incident reports to justify uses of force. Staff and inmates were intimidated into silence (Winerip and Schwirtz, 2014a, 2014b).

The correctional officer code, and informal sanctions against whistleblowers, varies from institution to institution, depending on permeability, the administration, the level of violence from inmates, architecture, and the demographic profile of officers. Distrust of outsiders, dissatisfaction, and alienation are elements of both the police subculture and the correctional officer subculture. In both professions, individuals must work with sometimes unpleasant people who make it clear that the practitioner is not liked or appreciated. Further, there is public antipathy (either real or perceived) toward the profession, which increases the social distance between criminal justice professionals and all others outside the profession. The working hours, the nature of the job, and the unwillingness to talk about the job to others outside the profession intensify the isolation that workers feel.

WALKING THE WALK

Tom Murton found his career dramatically altered when he was hired by the Arkansas Department of Correction as its director of corrections. He had been instrumental in setting up the prison system for the state of Alaska in the late 1950s and was teaching at Southern Illinois University when he was hired by Governor Winthrop Rockefeller, who wanted to modernize the Arkansas prison system. Upon arriving in 1967 to head the Tucker prison farms, he discovered abuses and inhumane conditions, described later in several writings by Murton and immortalized in the movie *Brubaker*. The U.S. Supreme Court case of *Holt v. Sarver*, 442 F.2d 304 (8th Cir. 1971), also documented the abuses, which included subjecting prisoners to electric shocks, staff taking food meant for prisoners and feeding them a disgusting gruel, forcing inmates into a metal box for long periods of time as a punishment, allowing prisoners to guard and

inflict brutal discipline on other prisoners, and other inhumane treatments. Murton began to address these issues and received information that more than 200 inmates had disappeared and were listed as escapees. Acting on the information of one informant, he dug up (on the grounds of the prison) two bodies that had injuries exactly as the inmate had described. One had been decapitated, and one had a crushed skull. Even though one of the bodies was eventually positively identified as a missing inmate, opposing testimony at the legislative hearing called in response to his investigation proposed that the bodies were from an old church cemetery. Instead of pursuing the matter further and digging up more bodies or testing them in any way for age and other identifying marks, state officials fired Murton and threatened him with prosecution as a grave robber if he didn't leave the state. He never worked in corrections again.

Sources: Murton, 1976; Murton and Hayams, 1969.

It should also be pointed out that some researchers believe that some of the values embedded in the correctional officer subculture may not be shared by most officers—a concept referred to as **pluralistic ignorance**. This refers to the idea that a few outspoken and visible members do not reflect the silent majority's views. In a prison, this may mean that a few officers endorse and publicize subcultural values, whereas most officers, who are silent, privately believe in different values (R. Johnson, 2002/2006). Kauffman (1988: 179) found this to be true in attitudes toward the use of force (where the silent majority did not endorse it to the extent of the verbal minority) and toward the value of treatment (which was silently supported). In the Walking the Walk box, one correctional administrator went against the pattern of cover-ups in a state system, and his actions eventually cost him his career.

> **pluralistic ignorance**
> The prevalent misperception of the popularity of a belief among a group because of the influence of a vocal minority.

Treatment Professionals

While there may be subcultural elements from correctional officers that migrate to those who work in treatment roles in correctional facilities, there doesn't seem to be much research documenting it. Thus, we can only assume that when treatment professionals such as psychologists and counselors work in a prison or other correctional facility, they are not a part of the correctional officer subculture, but they may have a different, albeit weaker subculture of their own. Similarly, correctional medical care professionals may be influenced in greater or lesser ways by the "penal harm" atmosphere that pervades some correctional institutions where inmates are seen as not deserving of the care associated with medical services outside the prison. Ethical issues exist for treatment professionals that are different from those of correctional officers, and these will be described in the next chapter.

The Probation/Parole Officer Subculture

The subculture of probation and parole officers has never been documented as extensively as that of police and correctional officers. Because of differences between these professions, the subculture of the former is not as pervasive or strong as that of the latter. Probation and parole officers do not feel as isolated as police or correctional officers do. They experience no stigmatization, they have normal working hours, they do not wear a depersonalizing uniform, and they have a less obviously coercive relationship with their clients. These factors reduce the need for a subculture. Still, one can probably identify some norms that might be found in any probation or parole office:

- *Cynicism.* They have a norm of cynicism toward clients. The subculture promotes the idea that clients are inept, deviant, and irredeemable. Probation and parole professionals who express positive attitudes toward clients' capacity for change are seen as naïve and guileless.

- *Lethargy.* There may be in some offices a pervasive subcultural norm of lethargy or minimal work output. This norm is supported by the view that officers are underpaid and overworked.

- *Individualism.* A norm of individualism can be identified. Although parole and probation officers may seek opinions from other professionals in the office, there is an unspoken rule that each runs his or her own caseload. To offer unsolicited opinions about decisions another person makes regarding his or her client violates this norm of autonomy.

Even though there does not seem to be the "blue curtain of secrecy" to the same extent as is found in policing, there no doubt is a norm against informing on colleagues for unethical or illegal behaviors. This relates somewhat to the norm of individualism, but is also part of the pervasive occupational subculture against informing on colleagues. Probation and parole officers may see and hear unethical behaviors and not feel comfortable coming forward with such information. If they work in an office where the norm against exposing such wrongdoing is strong, they may indeed suffer sanctions like those of police and correctional officers for exposing others' wrongdoing.

Some offices develop norms that accept unethical practices and lethargy. Once this occurs, it becomes a difficult pattern to change. If it is already present, a single officer will have a hard time not falling into the pattern. If all officers feel overwhelmed by their caseloads and their relative lack of power to do anything about failure, the result may be that they throw up their hands and adopt a "who cares?" attitude. If the supervisor does not exhibit a commitment to the goal of the organization, does not encourage workers, treats certain officers with favoritism, or seems more concerned with his or her personal career than with the needs of the office, there is an inevitable deterioration of morale. If the organization does not encourage and support good workers, it is no wonder that what develops is an informal subculture that encourages minimum effort and treats organizational goals with sarcasm and cynicism.

Conclusion

In this chapter, we have looked at the justifications for punishment (retribution and prevention) and some of the ethical rationales for punishment (e.g., utilitarianism, ethical formalism, and ethics of care). What we do to offenders is influenced by our views on things such as free will and determinism, the capacity for individual change, and the basic nature of humankind. The limits of punishment have been subject to the laws and mores of each historical era. Today, our punishments primarily consist of imprisonment or some form of restricted liberty, such as probation or parole. There are current conversations over the legality and morality of stigmatizing shaming punishments and supermax prisons. The death penalty continues to be used; however, the controversy surrounding it continues as well. The privatization of corrections and squeezing profits from offenders pose troubling ethical issues.

Formal ethics for those who work in corrections come from their professional organizations, such as the American Correctional Association. Common to all the codes are adherence to the law, respect for persons, and maintaining objectivity and professional standards of competence. Like police officers, there are elements in occupational subcultures that sometimes conflict with and subvert formal ethics.

Chapter Review

1. **Provide the definitions of punishment and treatment and explain their rationales.**

   According to Leiser, punishment is defined as follows: there are at least two persons—one who inflicts the punishment and one who is punished; a certain harm is inflicted; the punisher has been authorized, under a system of rules or laws; the punished has been judged by a representative of that authority by some relevant rule or law; and the harm that is inflicted upon the person who is being punished is specifically for the act or omission relevant to such law. The definition of treatment is that which may create behavioral change. The rationale for punishment and treatment comes from the social contract. Further, specific rationales for punishment include retribution and prevention (deterrence, incapacitation, and treatment).

2. **Describe how the ethical frameworks justify punishment.**

   Utilitarianism is often used to support the three prevention rationales of punishment: deterrence, incapacitation, and treatment. According to utilitarianism, punishing or treating the criminal offender benefits society, and this benefit outweighs the negative effect on the individual offender. Ethical formalism clearly supports a retributive view of punishment. It is deontological because it is concerned not with the consequences of the punishment or treatment, only its inherent morality. The ethics of care would probably not support punishment unless it was essential to help the offender become a better person.

3. **Describe ethical rationales for and against capital punishment.**

   Retentionists argue that capital punishment is just because it deters others from committing murder and it deters the individual who is executed. This is a utilitarian argument. They also argue that capital punishment is just because murder deserves a proportional punishment. This argument is more consistent with ethical formalism. Finally, they argue that the Bible dictates an "eye for an eye." This is, of course, a (Judeo-Christian) religious justification for capital punishment. Abolitionists argue that capital punishment has never been shown to be effective in deterring others from committing murder; therefore, the evil of capital punishment far outweighs any potential benefits for society because there is no proof that it deters. This is a utilitarian argument. Abolitionists might also argue that capital punishment violates the categorical imperative. Finally, abolitionists would point to the religious command to "turn the other cheek" an argument against any religious (Christian) justification for capital punishment.

4. **Identify major themes from the ethical codes for correctional officers, treatment professionals, and probation and parole officers.**

   Codes come from professional organizations such as the American Psychological Association, or more specific organizations for correctional personnel such as the ACA. Elements of codes for correctional officers, treatment personnel, and those who work in community corrections all seem to include the following elements: integrity, respect for and protection of individual rights and autonomy, service to the public, sanctity of the law, and prohibitions against exploiting professional authority for personal gain.

5. **Explain how occupational subcultures affect adherence to professional ethics codes.**

   Subcultural elements are, in some ways, like those of law enforcement—the inmate is the "enemy" along with superiors and the public, acceptance of the use of force, the preference toward redefining job roles to meet only minimum requirements, and the willingness to use deceit to cover up wrongdoing for fellow officers. Treatment and probation/parole subcultures are not strong, probably because they do not share the same characteristics of the job as law enforcement and correctional officers. Generally, the major issue of these subcultures seems to be an attitude toward the client/offender that is pessimistic and cynical, with a belief that offenders are not deserving of the respect according to nonoffenders.

Study Questions

1. Define punishment using the elements provided by Leiser.

2. What are the three different objectives or approaches to prevention? Explain some issues with each.

3. How would Bentham defend punishment? Contrast that position with Kant's position.

4. What are the criticisms of the supermax prison? Compare the elements of the supermax to the Supreme Court's definition of cruel and unusual punishment.

5. What are the arguments for and against private prisons?

Writing/Discussion Exercises

1. Write an essay on (or discuss) the "pains" of different types of punishment for different people, including yourself. Would you rather spend a year in prison or receive a severe whipping? Would you rather spend a year in prison or receive five years of probation with stringent restrictions? Would you rather spend a year in prison or pay a $30,000 fine?

2. Write an essay on (or discuss) your views on the justification for punishment. If you knew for certain that prison did not deter, would you still be in favor of its use? Why? If we could predict future criminals, would you be willing to incapacitate them before they commit a crime in order to protect society? Explain.

3. Write an essay on (or discuss) your views on the use of capital punishment and the reasons for your position. Now take the opposite side, and give the reasons for this view.

Key Terms

cruel and unusual punishment	penal harm	stigmatizing
	pluralistic ignorance	shaming
deterrence	prevention	three-strikes laws
incapacitation	punishment	treatment
just deserts model	reintegrative shaming	treatment ethic
justice model	retribution	

ETHICAL DILEMMAS

Situation 1
A legislator has proposed a sweeping new crime and punishment bill with the following provisions for punishment. Decide each issue as if you were being asked to vote on it:

*   Mandatory life term with no parole for any crime involving a weapon
*   Corporal punishment (using an electrical apparatus that inflicts a shock) for all personal violent crimes
*   Mandatory five-year prison sentences for those convicted of DWI
*   Public executions
*   Abolition of probation, to be replaced with fines and prison sentences for those who are not able to pay or are unwilling to do so.

Situation 2
Another legislator has suggested an alternative plan with the following provisions. Vote on these:

*   Decriminalization of marijuana
*   Mandated treatment programs for all offenders who were intoxicated by alcohol or other drugs at the time of the crime
*   Restructuring the sentencing statutes to make no sentence longer than five years, except homicide, attempted homicide, robbery, and rape

- Implementation of a restitution program for all victims whereby offenders stay in the community, work, and pay back the victims for the losses and/or injuries they received.

Situation 3

Your state allows relatives of homicide victims to witness the execution of the perpetrator. Your brother was killed in a robbery, and the murderer is about to be executed. You receive a letter advising you of the execution date and your right to be present. Would you go? Would you volunteer to be the executioner?

Situation 4

Your house has been burglarized. Your community has a new sentencing program, and the program's directors have asked you to participate along with the offender who burglarized your house. As you understand it, this means that you would be sitting down with representatives from the police department and court system and the offender and his family. The group would discuss and come to an agreement on the appropriate punishment for the crime. Would you do it? Why or why not?

Situation 5

You are a legislator who is the chairman of a committee that is making decisions about whether to build a new prison or contract with a private prison provider. You are visited by a lobbyist for one of the companies that is being considered and he explains that the company is sponsoring a "fact finding" trip to Scandinavia and other parts of Europe to tour several prisons and meet with correctional officials. He invites you and your spouse to go with the group. You would stay in very nice hotels and have social and entertainment events as well as the official activities—everything would be paid for by the company. He explains that because it is a fact-finding or educational trip for you, it does not violate your state's laws or ethics code. Would you go?

Discretion and Dilemmas in Corrections

12

This prison in Chino, California is like many across the country where correctional officers must supervise inmates in a way that does not violate the law or their ethical codes.

Lucy Nicholson/Reuters

Learning Objectives

1. Describe the role conflict of correctional officers.

2. List and describe some ethical issues for correctional officers.

3. Compare the challenges that face jail officers as compared to correctional officers in prisons.

4. Explain the role conflict of treatment professionals and provide examples.

5. List and describe the ethical issues of probation and parole officers.

John Edwards was abandoned by his parents and raised by a foster mother, but was on the streets at a young age. He turned to male prostitution and acquired HIV. His horrible childhood doesn't excuse the fact that he killed his ex-wife and another person. Edwards was convicted of the murders and incarcerated in a Florida penitentiary where, in a scuffle, he bit a correctional officer in the face. He reportedly laughed and told the officer, "Now you have it, too." That decision led to his transfer to Charlotte Penitentiary where a group of correctional officers called "The Family" used beatings and force to instill fear in the inmates. When Edwards was brought into the prison, the two transfer officers and the receiving officers kicked and punched him in the head and abdomen, slammed him into the wall, and beat him until he couldn't stand up. When he was on the floor, they continued to kick him. The beatings continued through several shift changes; each new set of officers administered their own punishment for his assault on a fellow correctional officer. At one point, officers threw his food on the floor and made him get on all fours to eat it and then kicked him in the head when he did.

365

On the third day, Edwards used his identification badge and his teeth to hack open a vein in his arm. He was found lying in a pool of blood, and officers kicked him again before they dragged him to the infirmary. The nurses were told to write a report that the injuries they saw were present when he was received at the prison. They bandaged his wound, but did not stitch the open vein, then took him to a close-custody room and put him in four-point restraints (where wrists and ankles are restrained on the four corners of a cot). Edwards lay there naked and bleeding. The captain who had participated in and supervised his beatings came in again and beat him and kicked him in the genitals as he lay there. Finally, Edwards bled to death. The autopsy report indicated gross medical negligence (York, 2012).

Gary York, a former investigator for the Florida State Inspector General's office, describes the case and subsequent trial of those involved. The information about what happened came from two correctional officers who confessed and two who witnessed the abuse. Eventually, 10 people were arrested. Two captains, three sergeants, six officers, and three nurses lost their jobs. Of those arrested, three told the truth, pleaded guilty, and were sentenced to probation and community service. The seven who denied everything went to trial and were acquitted. It was reported that several jurors went out and celebrated with the officers and their families after the verdict. Jurors told reporters that they couldn't convict the officers because, after all, Edwards was a murderer (York, 2012).

Edwards death is not an isolated case. It is an unfortunate reality that inmates sometimes die in prison, and in a few cases, the death is caused by the actions of correctional officers and is entirely preventable. Some of these inmates are unsympathetic victims, and juries, like the jury in the Edwards case, do not hold officers accountable because of the despicable character of the victim, ignoring the despicable nature of the actions that led to the death.

Correctional professionals are exposed to the worst members of our society. They risk being punched, bitten, and spit upon; being showered with urine or feces; and being subjected to a constant barrage of profanity and aggressive commands, demands, and criticisms by some inmates. Many inmates are psychotic or have mental problems so severe that one cannot turn one's back on them for fear of being attacked. Other inmates have, for many reasons, developed into the most hardened, violent, manipulative, unremittingly unpleasant individuals to deal with that can be imagined. Correctional officers work with these individuals daily and all are changed because of working in the prison. Friedrich Nietzsche said, "Whoever fights monsters should see to it that in the process he does not become a monster. And if you gaze long enough into an abyss, the abyss will gaze back into you."

The descriptions of what occurs in this nation's prisons certainly give credence to that thought. There are correctional officers who have become more criminal than the criminals they supervise, and many others who pretend not to see. Inmate violence against correctional officers spurs officer violence against inmates which, in turn, creates the probability of more violence as inmates and correctional officers alike sink into a spiral of retaliation. This does not describe all prisons or jails, but it does describe some. Like our discussion of law enforcement, most correctional officers in jails and prisons do their jobs to the best of their ability and within the bounds of the law, but there are a small percentage who take it upon themselves to be judge, jury, and, in some cases, executioners of inmates.

Institutional correctional personnel can be divided into two groups: (1) correctional officers and their supervisors and (2) treatment professionals, a group that includes educators, counselors, psychologists, and all others connected with programming and services. These groups have different jobs and different ethical issues. There are also community correctional professionals, including probation and parole officers and staff in work release and halfway houses. All correctional professionals share the two goals of protecting society and assisting in the reform of the criminal offender.

Throughout this text, discretion has been shown as pivotal in each phase of the criminal justice system. In corrections, discretion is involved when a correctional officer chooses whether to write a disciplinary ticket or merely delivers a verbal reprimand; this is like the discretion that police have in traffic stops. Discretion is also involved when the disciplinary committee decides to punish an inmate for an infraction. The punishment can be as serious as increasing the length of a sentence through loss of good time or as minor as a temporary loss of privileges. This type of discretion is like the discretion of the prosecutor and judge in a criminal trial. Officers make daily decisions regarding granting inmates' passes, providing supplies, and even answering questions. Probation and parole officers have discretion in when to file a violation report or what to recommend if a client violates one or more conditions of their supervision. Halfway house personnel issue disciplinary infractions and have the authority to make recommendations whether a resident should be returned to a prison or granted early release.

As always, when the power of discretion is present, the potential for abuse is also present. Sometimes, correctional professionals have the *power* to do things that they don't have the *legal authority* to do. That is, some officers can deny an inmate a pass to go to the doctor even though, according to the prison rules, the inmate has a right to go; officers on a night shift can turn off the water to an isolated tier so that inmates can't flush their toilets or get water to drink, even though there is no security reason for the action. When officers exceed their authority, inmates' only recourse is to write a grievance. Professional ethics, as provided in a code of ethics, should guide officers and other staff members in their use of discretion and power, but, as with law enforcement and legal professionals, adhering to a code of ethics is influenced by the occupational subculture and institutional values. There are also examples where correctional officers become as criminal as the inmates they are supposed to be supervising, either because they abuse their power to administer illegal punishment, or because of the temptation of money that can be earned for smuggling in contraband.

Correctional Officers

Correctional officers (COs) are like police officers in that their uniform represents the authority of the institution quite apart from any personal power of the person wearing it. Some COs are uncomfortable with this authority and do not know how to handle it. Other COs revel in it and misperceive the bounds of authority given to them as a representative of the state. The following statement is a perceptive observation of how some COs misuse the authority they have:

> *[Some officers] don't understand what authority is and what bounds you have within that authority.... I think everyone interprets it to meet their own image of themself. "I'm a corrections officer! [slams table] You sit here! [slam] You sit there!" rather than, "I'm a person who has limited authority. So, you know, I'm sorry, gentlemen, but you can't sit there. You are going to have to sit over there. That's just the rules," and explaining or something like that the reason why. (Kauffman, 1988: 50)*

This observer obviously recognizes that the uniform bestows the authority of rational and reasonable control, not unbridled domination. The power of the CO is limited. It is impossible to depend on the authority of the uniform to get tasks accomplished, and one must find personal resources—respect and authority stemming from one's personal reputation—to gain cooperation from inmates. In fact, a common refrain of correctional officers is that they only control the institution because the inmates let them. While not entirely true since they do have controls and sanctions at their disposal, the idea of one correctional officer amidst 200 inmates (a typical ratio in a housing unit) does tend to support the idea that the keepers rule only with the tacit consent of the kept.

Some officers who perceive themselves as powerless in relation to the administration, the courts, and society in general may react to this perceived powerlessness by misusing their little bit of power over inmates. They may abuse their position by humiliating or disrespecting those in their control. It also may be the case, as some argue, that CO brutality stems from a fear of being victimized. The old saying "a strong offense is the best defense" describes this explanation of officer brutality.

Like police officers, correctional officers have a range of coercive control over inmates, from loss of liberty to lethal force, if necessary. This power may be misused. Blatant examples are an officer who beats an inmate or coerces sex from an inmate. The possibility for these abuses of power exists because of the powerlessness of the offender relative to the officer. Inmates have even less power against officer abuses than do citizens on the street against police officers' abuses of power. Inmates' powerlessness is exacerbated by public antipathy and disinterest. Sensitivity to ethical issues in corrections involves recognition and respect for the inherent powers and concurrent responsibilities of the profession.

Not surprisingly, COs and inmates tend to agree on a description of a good officer as one who treats all inmates fairly with no favoritism but who does not always follow rules to the letter. Discretion is used judicially; when a good officer decides to bypass rules, all involved tend to agree that it is the right decision. A good officer is not quick to use force, or afraid of force if it becomes necessary. A good officer treats inmates in a professional manner and gives them the respect they deserve as human beings. A good officer treats inmates in the way anyone would like to be treated. If an inmate abuses the officer, that inmate will be punished, but through formal, not informal, channels. In some cases, the officer will go far outside regular duties to aid an inmate who is sincerely in need; however, he or she can detect game playing and cannot be manipulated. These traits—consistency, fairness, and flexibility—are confirmed as valuable by research (Johnson, 2002).

correctional officer
The term that replaced the old label of *guard*, indicating a new role.

During the rehabilitative era of the 1970s, professional security staff in corrections exchanged the old label of *guard* for a new one—**correctional officer**. Crouch (1980, 1986) examined how changing goals (from custody to rehabilitation) in the 1970s and 1980s created role conflict and ambiguity for the correctional officer. Also in the 1970s, federal courts recognized an expanding number of prisoner rights, including the rights to exercise religious beliefs, obtain medical care, and enjoy some due process before being punished for prison infractions. The disruption in the "old way" of doing things created real chaos, and the 1970s and 1980s brought danger, loss of control, and stress for officers. In addition to increasing prisoner rights, the advent of unionization, professionalism, and bureaucratization changed the correctional officer's world (Crouch, 1980, 1986; Pollock, 2013a; Johnson, 2002; Silberman, 1995).

The prisoners' rights era of the 1970s was short-lived and gave way to the "due deference" era of today, where courts are more apt to defer to prison officials. Now, when responding to prisoner challenges, prison officials only must prove a "rational relationship" between prison policies or procedures and the correctional goal of safety and security (Pollock, 2013a). The Prison Litigation Reform Act (PLRA) of 1996 drastically curtailed the ability of inmates to file lawsuits and made it nearly impossible for federal courts to order consent decrees or order injunctive relief. It also limited attorney's fees.

Today, correctional officers probably think that inmates have too many rights. However, the courts' retreat into due deference has arguably led to the current era of penal harm. Periodically, abuse scandals bring federal lawsuits and court monitors into some state systems, but across the country, prisons are largely out-of-sight and out-of-mind for most people. When legal rights are limited, professional ethics must step into the breach to guide what is appropriate treatment of those in custody.

A New Era of Corrections?

Brown v. Plata, 563 U.S. 493, 2011, with its 5–4 decision, indicated no strong consensus on the part of the justices; however, the court decision did indicate that there are limits to the due deference position. In this case, the Supreme Court ordered the state of California to release prisoners if they could not provide a constitutionally mandated level of medical care. This case continued a challenge from an earlier case *Madrid v. Gomez*, 889 F. Supp 1146 (N.D. Cal. 1995). The state and lower federal courts had been in contention for years as to whether the state was obligated to improve medical care for prisoners and, if so, by how much. When the state balked at the lower federal court order to allocate huge new sums of money to improve care or release prisoners, the case went before the Supreme Court and their affirmation of the lower court's order surprised everyone.

The record indicated that the abysmal level of medical care in California prisons led directly to the death of at least 34 prisoners. The alleged deficiencies included the following:

- Inadequate medical screening of incoming prisoners
- Delays in or failure to provide access to medical care, including specialist care
- Untimely responses to medical emergencies
- The interference of custodial staff with the provision of medical care
- The failure to recruit and retain sufficient numbers of competent medical staff
- Disorganized and incomplete medical records
- A "lack of quality control procedures, including lack of physician peer review, quality assurance, and death reviews"
- A lack of protocols to deal with chronic illnesses, including diabetes, heart disease, hepatitis, and HIV
- The failure of the administrative grievance system to provide timely or adequate responses to complaints concerning medical care

The state's response to the case decision was AB 109 and AB 117, signed into law on October 1, 2011, otherwise known as the Realignment Act, which shifted a large responsibility of corrections for nonviolent offenders to the counties. In November 2012, Proposition 30 was passed, creating permanent funding for counties to take greater responsibility for offenders. California, which had been operating its prisons at 200–300 percent over capacity, was committed to reducing its prison population to 155 percent of capacity by 2012, which it did, and to 140 percent of capacity by 2016 (Simon, 2014). From a high of 173,000 inmates in 2006, the prison population declined to 128,000 inmates in 2015 and has declined even further to less than 135 percent of capacity in 2016.

The language of the Supreme Court in the *Plata* decision focused on human rights and it appeared that the justices were literally shocked and appalled at the inhumane conditions that were tolerated in the California prisons. While California clearly leads the country in the multiyear effort to reduce prison populations, some have argued that the policy to shift the responsibility of dealing with offenders to the county level carries its own problems. Also, as we will discuss in this chapter and the next, merely reducing the number of inmates does not necessarily change a culture that supports a level of neglect and/or abuse that rises to cruel and unusual punishment. California is not alone in these issues. There are recurring scandals across the country that indicate unethical and unprofessional treatment of inmates occurs as predictably as the changing seasons.

Relationships with Inmates

One would assume that the general relationship between officers and inmates is one of hatred. That is not necessarily the case. As Martin (1993), a prisoner writer, points out the posturing and vocalization from either side come from a small number, with most inmates and officers living in an uneasy state of truce, hoping that no one goes over the line on either side. The Quote and Query box points out the extremes in relationships between convicts and correctional officers.

Most correctional officers and inmates prefer to live in peace and understand that they must treat each other with some modicum of respect to get along. Even though prisoners have been known to come to the aid of officers in physical confrontations, in general, inmates support their fellow inmates, and correctional officers support their fellow correctional officers, regardless of how little support the individual deserves. Thus, a brutal correctional officer may be protected by his fellows, and a racist correctional officer will not be informally or formally sanctioned. Likewise, an assaultive inmate will not be kept in check by his peer group unless his actions are perceived to hurt their interests.

reciprocity
Sykes's term denoting the situation in which officers become indebted to inmates and return favors.

An officer's ethics and professionalism are seriously threatened when relationships with inmates become personal. Gresham Sykes (1980) discussed the issue of **reciprocity** in supervision: Officers become dependent on inmates for task completion and smooth management of the housing unit; in return, COs may overlook inmate infractions and allow some favoritism to enter their supervision style. An example of a type of reciprocal relationship that may lead to unethical actions is that between an officer and an informant. Several authors have described how rewarding informants sometimes creates tension and trouble in a prison environment even though management often depends on the information (Hassine, 1996; Marquart and Roebuck, 1986).

COs involvement with inmates can occur because of daily contact combined with shared feelings of victimization by the administration. Officers may start to think they have more in common with inmates than with the administration, especially now that officers are more likely to come from urban areas, come from minority groups, and be more demographically like the inmates they supervise. This is especially true for jails. This shared identity, in addition to treatment by administration that seems arbitrary and unfair, may create bonds with inmates that interfere with professional duties. Identification and friendship may lead to unethical conduct, such as ignoring infractions or doing illegal favors for an inmate. The favors may seem innocuous at first—a shared cigarette or cold soda, but then escalate to the point that the officer can be blackmailed (McCarthy, 1991; York, 2012, 2013).

The subcultural norms against sympathizing with or becoming too friendly with inmates may be a tool to prevent officers from becoming personally involved with inmates and compromising their professional integrity. An officer who is too close to inmates is seen by other officers as untrustworthy. The officer subculture minimizes this possibility with a view of inmates as animalistic and not worthy of human sympathy. Some correctional officers then treat inmates accordingly. In fact, how they are treated by COs is sometimes described by inmates as more painful than any physical deprivations. Kauffman (1988) also notes, however, that inmates themselves make it difficult for COs to continue to hold sympathetic or friendly views because of the inmates' negative behaviors.

Just as officers may act in unethical ways when they like an inmate, they also may abuse their authority with inmates they do not like. These extra-legal harassments and punishments may include "forgetting" to send an inmate to an appointment, making an inmate stay in "keeplock" longer than necessary, or pretending not to hear someone locked in a cell asking for toilet paper or other necessary items (Kauffman, 1988; Lombardo, 1981/1989). Because prisoners are in a position of need, having to ask for things as simple as permission to go to the bathroom, officers have the power to make inmates feel even more dependent than necessary and humiliated because of their dependency. The relative powerlessness of officers in relation to their superiors, the administration, and society in general creates a situation where some take advantage of their only power—that over the inmate. The gulf between the status of the guards and guarded is the theme of the Quote and Query box.

For officers, the potential of injury or being taken hostage is never far from their mind, and may affect to a certain extent their supervision of inmates, for it is potentially dangerous to be personally disliked. Also, on a day-to-day basis, some inmates are friendly, some are funny, and some are good conversationalists. This strange combination of familiarity and fear results in a pervasive feeling of distrust. Officers insist that "you can be friendly with inmates, but you can never trust them." Mature officers learn to live with this basic inconsistency and can differentiate situations in which rules must be followed from those in which rules can be relaxed. Younger and less perceptive officers either take on a defensive attitude of extreme distrust or are manipulated by inmates because they are not able to tell the difference between good will and gaming.

QUOTE & QUERY

Some convicts hate all prison guards. They perceive them as the physical manifestation of their own misery and misfortune. The uniform becomes the man, and they no longer see an individual behind it.... Many guards react in kind. The hatred is returned with the full force of authority. These two factions become the real movers and shakers in the prison world. They aren't a majority in either camp, but the strength of their hatred makes its presence known to all.

Source: Martin, 1993: 94–95.

? How would one reduce the level of hate between these small numbers of prisoners toward correctional officers and correctional officers toward prisoners?

QUOTE & **QUERY**

I never shake hands with an inmate. . . They neither are nor ought to be viewed as equals.
Source: George Beto, administrator of Texas prison system, 1962–1972, quoted in Dilulio, 1987: 177.

[T]he sergeant had succeeded in making me feel even more isolated from the world that existed outside the prison walls. I was no longer so proud to be an American. I was just a convict without rights.
Source: Victor Hassine, inmate, 1996: 52.

Because legitimate power is so unevenly distributed between the keepers and the kept, left to its own inertia abuses of that power will inevitably creep into any prison without diligent and sensitive oversight.
Source: Patrick McManus, state correctional official, reported in Martin, 1993: 333.

? Should the attitude of correctional professionals be that inmates are not worthy of a handshake, or does that isolation from the "community of man" create the potential for abuse?

Sexual Relationships and Sexual Abuse in Prison

Sexual relationships are another type of unethical relationship between correctional officers or staff members and inmates. One of the results of the gender integration of corrections that occurred in the 1980s has been the rise of sexual misconduct and sexual abuse, which is mostly heterosexual, but can also be same-sex as well.

Until the mid-1800s, female prisoners were housed together with men in jails, with predictable results. Women were raped and sexually exploited, and they sold themselves for food and other goods. Various scandals and exposés of prostitution rings led to women's reform groups pressuring legislatures to build separate institutions for women in the late 1800s and early 1900s. These women's prisons were staffed by female matrons. This pattern of single-sex facilities with female staff continued until the 1980s, when female correctional officers challenged the hiring patterns of state prison systems that barred them from working in institutions for men. They were successful in achieving the right to work in men's prisons. Through the 1980s into the 2000s, the number of female correctional officers working in prisons for men rapidly increased, but so did the number of male correctional officers working in prisons for women because "legally" equal protection worked in both directions. Sexual abuse and sexual misconduct complaints have risen with the increased number of men in women's prisons (in some state systems male officers comprise over 50 percent of the total force in the women's prison) and, also, the number of women in prisons and jails for men.

The idea of prison rape is pervasive in our culture and is even the source of (poor) jokes in popular culture. The problem of prison rape was largely believed to be male inmate-on-inmate violence. Added to this problem, however, was a growing realization through the 1990s into the 2000s that female inmates were being sexually coerced and/or physically assaulted by male correctional officers. The Prison Rape Elimination Act (PREA), passed by Congress in 2003, mandated that every state keep a record of prison rapes and allocated money to study the problem and develop solutions. This source of data provided surprising findings: first, there was a great deal of sexual victimization occurring between female inmates (although not violent physical assault), and, second, there was a surprising amount of sexual interaction (not necessarily coerced) between male inmates and female officers.

The latest PREA prisoner survey data available is for 2011. This prisoner survey defines "nonconsensual sex acts" as oral, anal, or vaginal penetration, masturbation, and other sexual acts. "Abusive sexual contacts" is defined as unwanted contact involving touching of buttocks, thigh, penis, breasts, or vagina in a sexual way. "Sexual victimization" includes both categories. More women than men in prison reported any type of sexual victimization by other inmates (6.9 percent compared to 1.7 percent). About equal numbers of women and men in prison reported staff sexual misconduct of any type (2.3 percent of women compared to 2.4 percent of men). This survey also was administered in jails. About 3.6 percent of female jail inmates reported any type of sexual victimization by other inmates (compared to 1.4 percent of males); and 1.4 percent of female jail inmates reported sexual misconduct by guards (compared to 1.9 percent of males). Survey results indicated that the most vulnerable inmates were those who reported having mental health issues, were committed for sex offenses, and were homosexual or bisexual (these results are from the combined pool of male and female inmates). It's important to realize that these national averages mask quite extreme differences between facilities. One of the important findings of the study was that sexual assault (rape) was rare, but more inmates experience other forms of sexual victimization involving unwanted touching and sexual harassment (Rantala, Rexroat, and Beck, 2014). The Bureau of Justice Statistics has also led a survey of former prisoners and 9.6 reported some form of sexual victimization while in prison. Again, victimization was roughly divided between inmate and staff member perpetrators (Beck and Johnson, 2012). Juvenile institutions have also been surveyed and over 10 percent of juvenile inmates reported ever being sexually victimized by staff members (Beck, Guerino, and Harrison, 2010). As described in the In the News box, transgender and homosexual inmates are more likely to be sexually victimized as well as inmates incarcerated for

IN THE NEWS | *Vulnerable Inmates*

An especially vulnerable group to prison rape are transgender inmates who have feminine characteristics, but, because their sex-change is not complete, are housed in prisons for men. These inmates report rape and other forms of sexual victimization as well as a lack of protection by correctional authorities who don't seem to care and correctional officers who actively torment the individuals. Two transgender inmates describe what their life was like in prison in news stories and chronicle a horrifying series of physical violence. "Passion," in a Texas prison, explains that she realized she was transgender in prison although prison officials do not recognize her as such because she did not begin the transition process. Through her years in prison, she was coerced into sexual relationships with gang members for protection. When she refused sexual advances she has been choked, raped, and physically assaulted. Prison officials refused to put her in protective custody even after she reported attacks. She has been in 3 of the 10 prisons categorized as "high risk" for sexual assault by the PREA reports. Because of her reporting the attacks and filing grievances to try and get protective custody, she was attacked by gang members and slashed in the face requiring 36 stitches. She has been suicidal. After 10 years of requesting protective custody, she was finally transferred there 10 days after a *New York Times* reporter asked to interview her.

Ashley Diamond lived as a transgender woman since adolescence and had been taking hormones for 17 years, but when she went to a Georgia prison intake center in 2012, she had to strip alongside male inmates. At 33, it was her first time in prison, and her sentence was for burglary, but she was sent to a maximum-security prison. She was raped seven times by other inmates, called a "he-she thing" by correctional officers, and punished with solitary confinement for "pretending to be a woman." She tried to castrate herself and attempted suicide.

She filed a federal lawsuit and in March of 2015 the Justice Department intervened on her behalf. The lawsuit asks the court to direct prison officials to provide her hormone therapy, to allow her to express her female identity through "grooming, pronoun use and dress," and to provide her safer housing. The Justice Department declared hormone therapy to be necessary medical care, and ruled that the prison must treat "gender dysphoria" like any other health condition and provide "individual assessment and care." She and her lawyers allege that prison authorities are retaliating against her for the lawsuit and there is a real concern that she will not survive her prison sentence.

Source: Sontag, 2015a, 2015b.

sexual crimes. Another vulnerable group are those with mental health issues (Beck, Berzofsky, Caspar, and Krebs, 2013; Owen et al., 2008). While contact between male inmates and female correctional officers is more likely to be consensual, there are instances in women's prisons where male COs have committed violent rapes of female prisoners, and many more instances where they used threats and intimidation to coerce women to engage in sex (Henriques, 2001; Owen et al., 2008; Pollock, 2014).

Periodically, news stories report instances where female inmates have been coerced to have sex with prison or jail correctional officers who threaten to plant drugs on them or write them up for disciplinary infractions if they do not submit (Coherty, Levine and Thomas, 2014; Owen et al., 2008; Plog, 2014; Stein, 2015). A Justice Department investigation of the Julia Tutwiler prison in Alabama found rampant sexual abuse with officers allegedly forcing women to engage in sex acts just to obtain basic sanitary supplies. Male officers openly watched women shower or use the toilet, staff helped organize a "strip show," prisoners received a constant barrage of sexually offensive language, and prisoners who reported improper conduct were punished, according to investigation findings. Allegedly, at least one-third of the 99 officers at Tutwiler had sex with prisoners (United States Department of Justice, 2014). The federal investigators accused the highest level of administrators of knowing about the abuse and doing nothing about it: "Officials have been on notice for over 18 years of the risks to women prisoners and, for over 18 years, have chosen to ignore them" (Acting Assistant Attorney General Jocelyn Samuels, quoted in Coherty, 2014). The Department of Justice and Alabama entered into an agreement that included a federal monitor at the prison and a wide range of changes in the prison, including identifying vulnerable inmates, and better investigation and punishment for sexual misconduct by correctional officers (Stein, 2015).

Although in most prisons and jails only a few correctional officers sexually victimize female inmates, more allow it to happen by setting the tone of the prison. Staying silent while other officers sexualize prisoners by ribald comments, allowing officers to demean and belittle inmates, and participating in conversations where women are referred to by their body parts allow the true predators to victimize. A prison culture that disparages and demeans inmates gives the green light to brutal individuals who wear a uniform. This situation is like the earlier discussion about rogue police officers who come to believe drug offenders and others are fair game for victimization because they don't deserve the same rights as the rest of us.

It should be noted that female inmates may also be victimized by female officers and male inmates are victimized by male officers. In one case in south Texas, a male prison nurse used drugs to extort sex from male inmates. When an inmate reported the nurse, prison investigators had the inmate wear a wire and his offer of drugs for oral sex was caught on tape (Santo, 2015). The In the News box describes another alleged case of same-sex abuse.

Female officers also engage in sexual relationships with inmates. In fact, the most recent PREA survey reported 79 percent of all instances of staff sexual misconduct were female officers having sex with male inmates (Beck and Johnson, 2012). This statistic is misleading of course because 93 percent of state prison inmates are male and most sexual interactions of male inmates are with female correctional officers or staff members. For example, the New York prison escape of 2015 was aided by Joyce Mitchell, a civilian prison employee, who admitted smuggling in tools and having a sexual relationship with one of the inmates. In a Baltimore jail scandal in 2014, 13

📱 IN THE NEWS | *Sexual Abuse*

A federal appeals court judge ruled that "any malicious sexual contact" by a correctional officer could be a constitutional violation. In the case, two former male inmates filed a lawsuit against a New York correctional officer and his superiors. The complaint alleged that the officer maliciously and gratuitously touched their genitals, including in one case, grabbing the inmate's penis during a frisk, and asking "What's that?" The lawsuit presented information that indicated over 20 inmates had filed complaints about this officer for sexual harassment and touching that went beyond searches for security purposes. Inmates were warned they would go to solitary confinement if they resisted him as he touched them. A lower court, applying a 1997 court ruling, said that because the touching occurred through clothing, and did not cause physical harm, there was no constitutionally protected injury, but the appellate court said that norms had changed, sexual abuse of prisoners would not be tolerated, and any contact with genitalia that does not have a legitimate correctional purpose, and/or is done with the intent of sexual satisfaction or to humiliate the inmate violates the Eighth Amendment.

Source: Clifford, 2015.

female correctional officers were indicted for smuggling in contraband to the state-run jail. Many of these female correctional officers were in sexual relationships with the inmates; in fact, the ringleader, a Black Guerilla gang leader, impregnated four different correctional officers (Toobin, 2014). This case is described in the In the News box.

Some correctional officers go down a "slippery slope" of developing a personal relationship with an inmate by talking about their private life, then sharing pictures, then perhaps talking with the inmate's family outside of the prison. In some cases, the inmate "grooms" the officer to be a "mule" (carrying in illegal contraband) by developing the sexual relationship; in these cases, it is the officer who ends up being coerced and manipulated instead of the other way around.

In both women's and men's prisons, inmate altercations sometimes occur because they are fighting over the affections of an officer, who knowingly or unknowingly has encouraged the inmates' beliefs that they are a love interest. In a few instances, female officers engage in sexual relationships with more than one inmate (York, 2012, 2013); more often, female officers think they are in a committed love relationship. Male officers seem to be more likely to engage in serial or multiple relationships with inmates or engage in sexual activity without a relationship at all; it is merely a financial exchange or coerced sex. The motivations are different in these two circumstances, but the ethics of the activity are not—they are a violation of policy and law.

Beginning in the mid-1990s, many states began to change or add new laws to make even consensual sexual relationships with inmates illegal. Part of the reason for the law was the difficulty of prosecuting correctional officers whose defense was that the inmate was willing. Even if the inmate was willing to testify against the guard, jurors were not likely to believe an inmate over a guard. In 1990, just 18 states had laws expressly prohibiting sexual abuse of inmates, but by 2006, such laws existed in all 50 states. It is a felony in all states but Iowa and Maryland where it is a misdemeanor; however, prosecutions are rare (Santo, 2015). In many cases, staff members are "walked off" the unit and fired; in some cases, they are merely transferred to another prison (Dial and Worley, 2008; Marquart, Barnhill, and Balshaw-Biddle, 2001; Worley and Worley, 2011; York, 2012, 2013).

IN THE NEWS | Sex, Drugs, and Smuggling

A smuggling scheme in the Baltimore City Detention Center (BCDC), a state-run jail, ended in indictments and sentences for 25 people, including 13 guards. Federal investigators uncovered widespread smuggling of cellphones and other contraband for prison gang members from the Black Guerrilla Family (BGF) back in 2009. The correctional officers were all women and many were engaged in sexual relationships with the inmates. Over a dozen cellphones were also confiscated; the phones were evidently used to manage criminal activities on the outside. Inmates paid for the drugs and other contraband by texting 14-digit numbers to load money onto Green Dot MoneyPak cards belonging to BGF members. Gang leaders, in turn, used the Green Dot cards to pay their suppliers and buy cars, jewelry, and other goods. It is reported in some sources that the ringleader bragged about making $15,000 a month by the smuggling operation.

The ringleader was Tavon White, a BGF gang leader. He was in the jail awaiting trial for attempted murder. He had a sexual relationship with an unknown number of female correctional officers, but at least four of them had given birth to babies by him. Another inmate had relationships with at least five female guards. Martin evidently bought diamond rings and luxury cars for the women with income earned by their smuggling. Two of the correctional officers had his name tattooed on their body—one on her neck and the other on her wrist. In addition to smuggling in prescription pills, cellphones, and other contraband, correctional officers tipped off BGF members about law enforcement "shakedowns," stood lookout while the correctional officers had sex with inmates, and facilitated BGF assaults in the prison.

The longevity of the operation as well as its pervasiveness calls into question the management of the facility. Fourteen high-ranking administrators were transferred or retired after the indictments were announced. Correctional officers could smuggle in contraband in their underwear because searches were cursory. They evidently carried in cellphones for inmates to use even though cellphones were prohibited. It was reported that 75 percent of the 650 correctional officers in the facility were women (BCDC houses 2,000–2,300 inmates). Many of the female correctional officers were very young, one started working when she was 18. It is possible that some were recruited by the gangs even before being hired. According to papers in the legal cases against the gang members, documents were found in one Maryland prison that detailed how new BGF recruits were taught to target female COs with low self-esteem, insecurities, and certain physical attributes because they would be easily manipulated.

All involved were indicted in 2013 on charges of drug conspiracy, extortion, money laundering, and/or racketeering. The defendants faced a maximum 20-year imprisonment if convicted. Many involved pled guilty and were sentenced in 2014. After announcing the sentences, Maryland officials vowed changes, including improved background checks for correctional officers, more polygraph tests once the correctional officers were hired, the recruitment of 100 male correctional officers, repair of surveillance cameras, new search protocols, and weekly reviews to determine if any detainee has been held longer than 18 months. The facility was closed completely in 2015 and inmates were sent to other jails in the Baltimore area.

Sources: CBSDC.com, 2015; Fenton, 2010; Gray, 2014; Toobin, 2014.

Use of Force

"tune-ups"
"Lessons" taught to inmates by Texas prison guards that involved verbal humiliation, profanity, shoves, kicks, and head and body slaps.

The use of force is a legal and sometimes necessary element of correctional supervision. Most observers say that the serious abuse that occurred in the past such as **"tune-ups"** in the Texas prisons that involved "verbal humiliation, profanity, shoves, kicks, and head and body slaps," "ass-whipping," and using blackjacks and batons to inflict injury, or the **"Tucker telephone,"** an electrical device that was attached to the genitals of inmates to deliver severe shocks as a form of torture in an Arkansas prison farm do not take place today (Crouch and Marquart, 1989: 78; Murton, 1976)

There is no doubt that prisons were more brutal in past decades. One Texas prison warden described hanging inmates on cell bars so their feet did not touch the floor and leaving them overnight, or making them stand on a 2 by 4 or a barrel for hours; if they fell off, the time would start again (Glenn, 2001: 25–26). This same warden described a situation in which an inmate tried to escape, was shot, and then was hung on the front gate, bleeding, for the field hoe squads to see as they came back from the fields. This was described by Glenn as an "effective . . . object lesson" rather than brutality (2001: 44). Glenn also described a prison captain who played a "game" with inmates whom he believed weren't working hard enough on the hoe squad. The captain had them tied and stripped, and then lowered his pants and threatened to sodomize them (2001: 69). These practices reflect a lawless prison culture that does not exist today.

Ironically, as violence by officers decreased in the late 1970s and 1980s, it opened the door to the violence of inmate gangs and cliques. Inmates in the 1980s had less to fear from correctional officers but more to fear from one another as racial gangs and other powerful cliques or individuals solidified their control over prison black markets (Crouch, 1986). There was a time in the 1970s and 1980s when officers described some prisons as "out of control." There were prisons where correctional officers were afraid to walk into living units, and inmates literally controlled some parts of the prison (Carroll, 1998; Taylor, 1993).

Today, prisons are not as violent, but illegal uses of force do still exist (Prendergast, 2003; York, 2012, 2013). In *Hudson v. McMillian*, 503 U.S. 1, 1992, the U.S. Supreme Court held that injuries need not be serious to constitute a constitutional violation, if the injury was purely gratuitous (unnecessary). As with the use of force in law enforcement, policy definitions of *necessary force* are vague. This may mean that the resort to violence is absolutely the last alternative available, or it may mean that force is used when it is the most convenient way to get something accomplished.

Beatings of inmates who attack other correctional officers are utilitarian; they serve as warnings to all inmates that they will receive similar treatment if they attack COs. Officers might also defend the action on retributive grounds because the inmate would probably not be punished for the attack through legal channels. However, these retaliations always represent the most brutal and inhumane aspects of incarceration and damage the integrity of all correctional professionals. In addition, by allowing such activity to go unpunished, citizens are complicit in a system that withdraws basic human sympathy and civil liberties from some individuals (inmates).

The problem with not punishing officers who beat inmates as retaliation for injuring officers is some COs take it as a green light to beat inmates who talk back or who don't give them the proper respect, and, maybe, some COs feel it is also acceptable to beat inmates who are black or Hispanic or mentally ill. In fact, the *New York Times* investigation of Rikers Island jail found that of 129 cases of inmates injured so badly by officers that they required outside medical care, three-quarters had mental health issues (Winerip and Schwirtz, 2014b). The In the News box describes violence in another state.

Tucker telephone
An electrical device attached to the genitals of inmates that delivered severe shocks as a form of torture; formerly used at an Arkansas prison farm.

Maintaining Morality in Prison

Correctional officers report that they experience a great deal of stress and stress-related illnesses, such as hypertension, are common among officers, as well as social problems such as alcoholism and divorce. Some reports indicate that these problems

IN THE NEWS | Prison Violence

Eight North Carolina inmates filed lawsuits alleging that officers in a solitary confinement block routinely beat inmates in hallways that did not have surveillance cameras. In one prison, the "boom boom" room was so-named because of the lack of surveillance cameras. Inmates allege they were taken there to be beaten. All but one of the eight inmates won settlements from the state. One prisoner described how he was handcuffed from behind and then three officers beat him, fracturing his pelvic, left arm, and facial bones. The beating put him in a wheelchair, unable to walk, for a year. Uses of force have risen sharply over the past decade. According to the state's own records, uses of force by prison staff increased more than 60 percent from 2006 to 2016—years when the prison population remained at roughly the same level. The news article describing the pattern of assaults explained that some correctional officers fueled a culture of violence and corruption. Since 2012, more than 25 state correctional officers have been fired for inappropriate uses of force. Others were not fired even though the state settled inmates' claims rather than defend the abuse in lawsuits. In many other cases, inmates and/or their families complain to legal advocates, but state representatives argue there is no evidence of abuse. They also state that they are providing improved training to help correctional officers deal with tense situations without the use of force.

Source: Alexander, 2017a, 2017b.

exist in higher numbers with correctional officers than with police officers. Correctional officers feel criticized and even scorned by many, so it is little wonder that they adapt to their role by sometimes unethical and egoistic patterns of behavior. Yet it is important to understand the consequences of such a position. Kauffman (1988: 222) talked to officers who reported that they had lost their morality in the prison:

> *These officers experienced anguish at the change that was wrought in them by the prison environment: Initially, many attempted to avoid engaging in behavior injurious to inmates. . . . . As their involvement in the prison world grew and their ability to abstain from morally questionable actions within the prison declined, they attempted to neutralize their own feelings of guilt by regarding prisons as separate moral realms with their own distinct set of moral standards or by viewing inmates as individuals outside the protection of moral laws. When such efforts failed, they shut their minds to what others were doing and to what they were doing themselves.*

Without a strong moral and ethical code, correctional officers may find themselves drifting into relativistic egoism: behavior that benefits the individual is acceptable, despite long-term effects or inconsistencies with their duty and their personal value system. The result is a feeling of disillusionment and anomie, and the side effects can be serious dissatisfaction and depression. To maintain a sense of morality in an inherently coercive environment is no easy task, yet a strong personal ethical code is probably the best defense against being changed by the negative environment of the prison.

Jail Officers

Little has been written about jail officers, who may be sheriff's deputies completing their assignment at the jail before they can be "promoted" to street patrol. Sometimes, jail officers are street deputies who are transferred back to the jail as punishment. In other situations, jail officers are not deputies and have a separate title and lower pay scale. Generally, the skills associated with managing jail inmates are discounted when compared to street patrol or investigation. They shouldn't be, and some might argue that it is a much more difficult job to be a jail officer than either a sheriff's deputy on the street or a correctional officer of a prison.

Jail officers deal with more visitation (with a concomitant potential for smuggling). They deal with highly stressed individuals who are just coming in from the street or on their way to prison, and, because of the transitory nature of the population, jail officers may not know much about the inmates. Jail inmates include juveniles, violent criminals, misdemeanants, mentally ill, and mentally challenged. Offenders may come into jail intoxicated, have undiagnosed epilepsy or other diseases, suffer overdoses, or be suicidal. Jail officers deal with individuals who are experiencing despair and anxiety over the legal issues and must be constantly alert to the possibility of suicide. Some jail officers, especially in urban areas, may live in the same communities as the jail inmates and their families. All this combines to create many management challenges.

There is a need for greater professionalization of jail officers. The position should not merely be a dreaded rite-of-passage assignment, a punishment, or a steppingstone to deputy status, because the body of knowledge required to perform the job well is different from that which a street deputy needs. Recently there has been an attempt to professionalize the image of jail officers, starting again with a code of ethics (discussed in the last chapter).

The constant activity and chaotic environment of a jail often create unique ethical dilemmas. Many jail inmates, especially those with mental illness, cannot or will not follow rules. Prisoners and correctional officers alike do not tolerate their irrational behavior very well. Jail officers tend to deal with all troublesome behavior as a discipline issue. Is throwing feces a behavioral problem or an indication of mental illness? Sometimes it is both. When the person is placed in isolation (as in segregation), the situation may bring on hallucinations, anxiety attacks, and distorted thinking (Turner, 2007). Mentally ill inmates are more likely to be charged with rule violations, including physical or verbal assaults on staff members, and more likely to be injured, yet jail officers are not trained to be mental health specialists.

Unfortunately, in jails one can find the same type of unethical behavior that one finds with police and prison officers. Jail officers can be uncaring and insensitive to human needs. A few officers use their position to bolster their own ego by abusing their power over inmates. More are probably negligent in that they simply do not care and necessary duties go undone. Then again, other jail officers may be described as human service officers, who seek to enrich their job by taking on more of a counseling role with inmates. Once again, most professionals in corrections, as in law enforcement and the courts, simply try to do their job to the best of their ability every day.

IN THE NEWS | *Denver Jail*

The report on the Denver jail issued by an outside review group in May 2015 was the culmination of a long scandal over problems of excessive force in the Denver jail, including the case of Jamal Hunter. The city settled that case for $3.25 million admitting that Hunter was beaten, almost suffocated, and held down while his genitals were scalded with boiling water by a group of inmates with the complicity of a jail guard. Another incident was the death of a

(continued)

IN THE NEWS | *Denver Jail (Continued)*

homeless "preacher," Marvin Booker, who was allegedly choked to death after being tased in a scuffle with jail correctional officers. Jail inmates won numerous claims of excessive force totaling millions of dollars; sometimes the incidents took place in full view of security cameras.

A group of task forces created in the spring of 2014 issued 40 recommendations to improve the jail, including automatic notifications of excessive force complaints, an independent monitor, a review of the Taser policy, creating a corporal position and adding more sergeant positions, Crisis Intervention Team Training (CIT), shorter work shifts, and a revised break policy. Also, an outside review team issued a scathing description of management and resources with 14 key findings and 277 recommendations for change. Some of the findings show that basic management practices were not followed; for example, there was no method for counting inmates who were at court or at the hospital, and correctional officers were not trained in how to monitor for contraband or other problems in the pods. Even the consultants found heroin,

homemade hooch, and inappropriate photographs in the jail pods. There was no identification of gang affiliation for cell assignments. There was no staffing plan. The use-of-force investigations did not meet minimum standards of thoroughness and objectivity. Employees were not searched when they came into the jail. Deputies did not know policies and the policy handbook was out of date. Supervisory staff had difficulty taking corrective action against deputies because of the employee grievance procedures in place. The report also noted that the culture of the jail needed to change; deputies had very little training in deescalation tactics. It was also noted that deputy training was largely for patrol officers on the street, and they did not receive a skillset specific to the problems of supervising inmates in a jail.

Since 2015, the jail has appointed a new sheriff. A new community advisory board has been appointed. Other reforms have addressed some of the problems, but observers note that the jail is dangerously overcrowded and understaffed, and leadership issues continue.

Sources: Cotton, 2014; Murray, 2014; Phillips, 2015, 2017.

ETHICAL DILEMMA

An inmate asks you to mail a letter for him because he's on daylock with no privileges. He tells you that you can open the envelope and look at it to make sure it is okay; it is only a birthday card for his daughter. If it doesn't get in the mail today, she will not get it in time. He is a good inmate, never gives you any trouble, and has helped you out a few times with more troublesome inmates. You believe that there is nothing wrong with the card, and you think the guy got a bad deal with the discipline anyway because he was only out of place and that usually gets only a warning, not daylock. You also know that if you do the favor for him, he will continue to be a help to you on the tier, and if you don't, he'll probably hold it against you. What should you do?

Law

Some acts committed by correctional officers are crimes. Obviously, smuggling drugs is a crime and an officer who

smuggled would probably end up with a prison sentence himself. Taking items out of the prison is against the rules and could be considered bribery if the officer received money or anything of value for transporting the contraband. In this case, while taking the letter out is obviously against the rules, since the officer is not receiving anything of value from the inmate to do so, there may be no law involved.

Policy

Policies against taking letters out of the institution for inmates exist because such activities bypass censorship and intelligence-gathering procedures. While in this case it could be that it is only an innocent birthday card, it could also be a code for something else that gang intelligence officers would flag. It could also be a situation where the inmate was under a judicial order to not contact his daughter. Another consideration is that the inmate may be

(continued)

ETHICAL DILEMMA *(Continued)*

testing the officer to see if he may be willing to do more serious acts in the future. If he does take the letter out against the rules, the inmate has gained a little control over him because he can report the officer and get him in trouble. Next time, he may ask the officer to do something a little more serious and, then the next time, something more serious, so that the officer becomes entirely controlled by the inmate. Policies exist for a reason, even if they may not make sense in one case.

Ethics

An egoistic rationalization would be that a favor done for the inmate may result in benefit to the officer because the inmate owes him; however, as noted earlier, it may backfire because the officer will also "owe" the inmate for him to keep quiet about the rule violation. A utilitarian rationale would weigh up the costs and benefits to all concerned, but, as usual with utilitarian reasoning, there is no way to know all the possible ramifications of the act ahead of time, or even what the true nature of the act is (innocent card or something else). An ethical formalist would abide by the duties of the role, which, in this case, is to obey the policy about not carrying out letters. Ethics of care reasoning would attempt to solve the problem so the officer may take the card and talk to his sergeant or lieutenant to see if an exception to the suspension of mail privileges could be granted. This way would meet the needs of the inmate, protect the officer from any negative effect of breaking the rule, and protect the institution since the superior officers would presume to know more about the circumstances of the inmate and whether the card was innocent or not.

Treatment Staff

The unique issues facing correctional treatment professionals derive from their dual goals of treating the individual and being an employee (or contractor) of the state with a corresponding duty to maintain safety and security (whether in an institution or community setting).

Other ethical issues that correctional treatment personnel may be faced with are like those experienced in a more general way by all treatment professionals, so available sources dealing with ethics in the helping professions would also be applicable to those who work in the corrections field (see, for instance, Braswell, Miller, and Cabana, 2006; Corey, Corey, and Callanan, 1988).

The ethical issues for treatment professionals have grown as the number of inmates in both prisons and jails with serious mental health problems has grown. It is estimated that there are 10 times as many mentally ill in prison as in psychiatric facilities (Treatment Advocacy Center, 2014: 3). Mentally ill prisoners, who comprise at least 10 percent of the population of prisons and jails, and some estimates put it at much higher, present enormous problems for both correctional officers and treatment staff.

The professional goal of all treatment specialists is to help the client, but sometimes helping the client is at odds with the safety and security of the institution. For instance, prison psychologists may be privy to information or confessions that they feel bound to hold in confidence, even though this may jeopardize the security of the prison. Assessing risk also involves mixed loyalties. Any treatment necessarily involves risk. How much risk one is willing to take depends on whether the public should be protected at all costs, in which case few people would ever be released, or whether one thinks the public must risk possible victimization to give offenders a chance to prove themselves.

Providing therapy in prison is rife with professional ethical dilemmas. For instance, therapists must provide a safe place to talk, but offenders have committed horrible crimes and it is difficult to balance one's reaction to immorality with professional neutrality. Another issue is how much to allow the client/inmate to dwell on the negative elements of the prison environment that are real and important to them, but ultimately not relevant to the reasons why they are incarcerated. Transference is another problem, inmates have had little experience dealing with anyone who presents a caring approach and, so, it is potentially a problem when the inmate begins to believe the relationship is something other than therapist and client (Bryan, 2016).

A basic issue is whether to provide treatment to people who do not want it. One of the elements of codes of ethics for treatment professionals is that one should respect the autonomy of individuals, and this generally is interpreted to mean no forced treatment. In corrections, however, treatment professionals are often involved in what may be considered coerced treatment. Psychiatrists and psychologists must reconcile their professional ethics in two fields—corrections and psychiatry—and at times this is hard to do. Psychiatrists in corrections, for instance, believe at times that they are being used for social control rather than treatment (Tanay, 1982). Disruptive inmates, although needing treatment, pose security risks to prison officials, so intervention, especially the use of antipsychotic drugs and barbiturates, often takes the form of control rather than treatment.

The practice of using antipsychotic drugs is especially problematic for treatment professionals. Although the Supreme Court determined in *Washington v. Harper*, 494 U.S. 210, 1990, that the administration of such drugs to unwilling inmates is not unconstitutional, the practice must be scrutinized and held to due-process protections to uphold professional ethical standards. Some observers have alleged that inmates are being maintained on high dosages of drugs during their prison stay. Once released, they may go through withdrawal and have no assistance from community mental health facilities (Martin, 1993). On the other hand, not providing antipsychotic medication puts the individual in a downward spiral of psychosis exacerbated by the stress of the prison itself (Treatment Advocacy Center, 2014).

Psychologists in correctional settings have two ethical codes to follow: the American Psychological Association's Ethical Principles of Psychologists and Code of Conduct and the code for the American Association for Correctional and Forensic Psychologists. Some principles of the *Ethical Principles of Psychologists* seem especially relevant to corrections. For instance, in Standard 3.11, psychologists who are providing services through other organizations are instructed to provide information beforehand to clients about

- the nature and objectives of the services,
- the intended recipients,
- which of the individuals are clients,
- the relationship the psychologist will have with each person and the organization,
- the probable uses of services provided and information obtained and who will have access to the information, and
- the limits of confidentiality.

This obviously affects institutional psychologists, who must make clear to inmates their responsibility to custody concerns.

Other principles also reflect the reality of correctional placements. For instance, in Standard 3.10, psychologists are mandated to obtain informed consent for treatment; however, the ethical code recognizes that some activities without consent may be mandated by law or governmental regulation. The standard does state that when treatment is court-ordered, the individual must be informed of the nature of the anticipated services and any limits of confidentiality.

Haag (2006) describes some ethical dilemmas of prison psychologists in Canada, which apply to the United States as well. In his discussion, he mentions the following issues:

- *Confidentiality*. The inability to keep prisoners' secrets.
- *Protection of psychological records*. Whether or not psychologists should create "shadow files" that are not subject to view by other staff.
- *Informed consent*. Whether consent is possible from a coerced population.
- *Assessment*. What the psychologist's role is when assessment is used for correctional purposes?
- *Corroboration*. The importance of not accepting everything the inmate says, as the inmate may be engaged in "impression management."
- *Refusal of services*. Whether psychologists should honor an inmate's refusal of psychological services.
- *Nondiscrimination*. Treating all inmates equally regardless of group membership or individual characteristics.
- *Competence*. The importance of being aware of the boundaries of one's competence.
- *Knowledge of legal structure*. Being aware of the rights of the parties involved.
- *Accuracy and honesty*. Making clear the limits of predictive validity of psychological assessments.
- *Misuses of psychological information*. Refusing to allow file information to be misused to damage an inmate's interests.
- *Multiple relationships*. Avoiding dual roles (such as assessment and treatment), which is problematic and creates confusion for the client.

As in the legal profession, confidentiality is an issue for psychologists. The ethical principles (Standard 4.01) address this issue. Psychologists have a primary obligation and take reasonable precautions to protect confidential information obtained through or stored in any medium, recognizing that the extent and limits of confidentiality may be regulated by law or established by institutional rules or professional or scientific relationships. Treatment professionals in corrections must inform their clients, whether they are prison inmates or on some form of supervised release in the community, of the extent or limitations of the confidentiality. It may be that there is no confidentiality at all when the counselor, psychologist, or other professional is employed by the court. In any environment, psychologists and counselors must be aware of the *Tarasoff* rule (*Tarasoff v. Regents of the University of California*, 17 Cal. 3d 425, 1975) from a case that held a psychologist liable for not warning a victim of imminent harm from one of his clients. Treatment professionals do have legal duties to third persons if they have cause to reasonably believe that one of their clients is going to harm that person.

Treatment and security concerns clash in many instances. The treatment professional must choose between two value systems. To emphasize security concerns puts the psychiatrist or counselor in a role of a custodian with professional training used only to better control inmate behavior. To emphasize treatment concerns puts the professional in an antagonistic role vis-à-vis the security staff, and he or she may be in situations where these concerns directly conflict.

In an online resource for community treatment staff, some ethical principles were presented with discussion. These included the following:

- *Do no harm.* The discussion brought up the point that the best thing to do in some cases is no intervention at all since the harm done in bringing an individual into the criminal justice system outweighs the benefit to society or the individual. Focus on a person's deficiencies may only exacerbate them when more supportive interventions might provide more utility. This is a utilitarian concept.

- *Respect people as ends.* The discussion concerned treating people as having intrinsic value and not just considering them numbers or diagnoses. Also, included was the idea of allowing the participants some role in determining what they need and respecting legal rights. These concepts are consistent with ethical formalism.

- *Do what is best for everyone under the circumstances.* This discussion counsels that everyone can't be helped all the time, but the treatment professionals just do the best they can to help everyone, although there was also a warning that sometimes what is best is not clear. This is consistent with the ethics of care position.

- *Don't abuse or exploit participants.* This discussion self-evidently proscribes unethical actions against participants. It is consistent with all ethical systems.

- *Don't intervene unless competent.* This discussion concerns not operating outside one's field of expertise and keeping up with professional training as an obligation. It is consistent with all ethical systems.

- *Actively strive to improve the program and community.* The discussion brings up the point that it is not clear how far one's ethical obligations carry when there are problems in the community that go well beyond one's job description. There are no easy answers to this question. It is consistent with all ethical systems, but most congruent with ethics of care.

- *Maintain confidentiality of clients.* The discussion presents the various complexities of this simple principle in that sometimes the treatment professional has other competing responsibilities, such as to funders or legal actors. This principle is consistent with all ethical systems, except for those circumstances when it does not result in the greatest amount of utility for all, in which case it would be inconsistent with utilitarianism.

- *Disclosure is important.* The discussion described different types of disclosure, such as what types of information must be shared, including how long the program would last, the cost (if any), and so on. It is important to be transparent and provide information to the clients in order that their consent is knowing and voluntary. This is consistent with all ethical systems.

- *Be concerned with conflicts of interest.* The discussion included personal, financial, political, and professional conflicts. For instance, conflicts that compromise professional judgments include having a relative in the treatment program, having a relationship with a client, having one's job or income depend on judgments rendered, engaging in a business relationship with a client, and so on. This principle is consistent with all ethical systems (Community Tool Box, 2012).

Faith-based treatment programs, such as the Prison Fellowship Ministries, a Washington, D.C., group created by former Watergate figure Charles "Chuck" Colson, can be found in many prisons. The program is Christ-centered, biblically rooted, and values-based, and it emphasizes family and community. Inmates volunteer for the program (see: www.prisonfellowship.org). Having such programs in prison raise several issues. Some argue that the programs violate the separation of church and state and are an unconstitutional violation of freedom of religion. If a Christian program offers hope for early release or other advantages, Muslims or those following other religions may participate only if they also compromise their faith. Administrators of such programs must take care not to intrude upon the religious freedom of inmates and not use the benefits of the program to coerce religious conformity.

Probably the most prevalent issue for treatment professionals is how to maintain one's commitment to a helping profession while being in an environment that does not value the goals and mission of treatment. This dichotomy of treatment versus punishment creates a myriad of ethical issues for treatment professionals. The Walking the Walk box describes the ethical dilemma of one such professional.

WALKING THE WALK

Dr. Eric Reininga was a psychologist employed by the California Department of Corrections and Rehabilitation (CDCR) until he was fired in 2015. He alleges in a federal lawsuit against his former bosses that he was fired for coming forward about wrongdoing when no one else would. He began working for CDCR in 2007 and was promoted to senior psychologist specialist. One of Reininga's duties was to conduct "suicide reviews." These were audits to determine whether CDCR had extended appropriate mental health treatment to the inmate who had committed suicide. CDCR was under a court monitor for a lawsuit originally filed in 1990, which resulted in a finding that CDCR provided unconstitutionally inadequate mental healthcare. Commonly called the Coleman Action, it has resulted in a court-appointed monitor to ensure that CDCR meet mandated mental healthcare standards. Reininga's duties included reviewing reports prepared for Coleman monitors. His editing was overseen by individuals above him in the management chain as well as a deputy attorney general.

He alleges in his lawsuit that he was instructed to edit out anything that would look bad for the institution and, also, temper the descriptions of superlative performance by some institutions as to not "set the benchmark too high" for others. He believed that the culture of CDCR was similar to a "siege mentality" and included viewing Coleman monitors as enemies with the goal to hold back as much information as possible. He was concerned that psychologists' suicide reviews were heavily edited by managers and attorneys, changing the content, but leaving the psychologists' names on the reports.

In 2013, Reininga became familiar with the case of Joseph Damien Duran who had died in CDCR custody. Duran was afflicted with bipolar disorder, depression, psychotic disorder not otherwise specified (NOS), and antisocial personality disorder. He also suffered from hallucinations, had been hospitalized in psychiatric inpatient hospitals, and had attempted suicide. Duran had a tracheostomy tube through which he breathed. In September 2013, he was sent to

(continued)

Mule Creek State Prison (MCSP) where he was assigned to a Mental Health Crisis Bed in a single-occupant cell on suicide prevention watch. For some reason, his assigned psychiatrist retracted the suicide watch order and placed him on "violence precautions" that had no stated policy of supervision attached to it. On September 6, he refused to put his hands out to be handcuffed to be taken to a treatment group. What then happened is somewhat in dispute, but evidently correctional officers sprayed him in the face with a full can of pepper spray, which entered his throat through the tracheostomy tube. CDCR rules require that correctional staff allow inmates to decontaminate after the administration of pepper spray, yet Duran was not allowed out of his cell nor given medical assistance to alleviate the effects of the pepper spray. Reininga was told by some staff members that Duran coughed up blood and attempted to clean the tracheostomy tube by rinsing it in the toilet and rubbing the area. A nurse eventually called the doctor on call and she ordered Duran to be taken out of his cell to clean and reinsert the tube and monitor him for respiratory distress, but that order was never carried out. A call went to his assigned psychiatrist as well who also ordered that he be removed and cleaned and administered an antipsychotic medication, but that order was never carried out. Correctional staff then observed Duran taking out his tube and putting in foreign matter (spaghetti and feces) into his stoma (the incised opening in throat). A nurse called the doctor again to tell her that the order to decontaminate was not carried out and the patient was in distress, but the doctor told the nurse not to call again unless it was important. By the next morning, Duran was found unresponsive on the floor of his cell and died.

Duran's death coincided with a federal court hearing on the Coleman case where CDCR's use-of-force policies were under review, including the use of pepper spray. Also under review were suicide prevention policies. Reininga believes that this was the reason that false information was given to the coroner who classified the death as a suicide. The CDCR Death Review Committee at CDCR indicated the death was an accidental death. Reininga became

aware that the senior psychologist specialist assigned as a suicide reviewer in the Duran case was obstructed in the review, but nevertheless concluded that the negligence of the MCSP staff was the proximate cause of death. This reviewer and others were pressured to change portions of the suicide review to decrease the appearance of negligence. The court-appointed special master (monitor) was informed of Duran's death, but not told the circumstances surrounding it. The monitor was supposed to receive suicide reports within 60 days of a death, but did not receive Duran's report until January 2014.

In December, Reininga determined that no one in the chain of command was going to inform the monitor of what happened in the Duran case. He believed that the matter was in the public interest and that the wrongdoing of staff members should be exposed and reviewed. He believed that everyone in the chain of command and individuals in the state Attorney General's office were complicit in keeping this negative information about CDCR from the court-appointed monitor and the public. Therefore, he provided the original suicide review report and other information about the Duran death to a *Sacramento Bee* reporter in December 2013. The original suicide report was different from the final one provided to the court monitors in several ways, with the "official" report excluding the custodial actions and the impact of the pepper spray on Duran.

The newspaper published a series of articles about the Duran death. When a reporter contacted his parents, they learned for the first time that their son had died because prison officials had not informed them. Evidently, officials had tried one old address and did not attempt any further to notify Duran's relatives of his death. Because of the articles, the federal hearings were reopened. CDCR officials began to investigate who leaked the report to the newspaper. After a year, they focused on Reininga. In February 2015, Reininga was accused, subjected to an administrative review, and fired. Evidently, he and another whistleblower in the case were the only ones fired as a result of Duran's death. Reininga is in private practice now and says even though he lost his job, he would do it again.

Sources: Stanton and Walsh, 2016; *Eric Reininga v. Timothy Belavich, Jeffrey Beard and Gary Viegas*. Complaint for Damages. U.S. District Court, Eastern Dist. California.

Another area that must be considered under the general heading of treatment is that of medical services. Recall that in *Brown v. Plata* (2011) the Supreme Court ordered California to release prisoners if they could not bring the level of medical care up to a constitutional standard. The record indicated that 34 inmates died because of lack of medical care. Court cases and exposés have documented the deadly consequences that can occur when the medical needs of inmates are ignored or not met.

One medical professional (Dubler, 2014) explains that healthcare providers must constantly negotiate with prison officials to provide adequate care because the Supreme Court standard of "deliberate indifference" stated in *Estelle v. Gamble*, 429 U.S. 97, 1976, has no parallel in civilian standards of care. While inmates do have the right to access medical care, the right to care that is ordered, and the right to a professional medical judgment; there is only the right to "some" medical care and medical malpractice standards do not apply. While medical providers are socialized to meet the needs of their patients, issues of cost and security override these concerns in a correctional environment. Medically proscribed diets and follow-up visits interfere with the smooth running of the facility and are accommodated only grudgingly. Some inmates do manipulate healthcare staff or utilize medical services for purposes other than honest need, although it may be understandable as to why inmates in the negative environment of a prison may invent reasons to see a more sympathetic authority figure. Neglected problems become major issues in confinement, for example, hypertension, tooth decay, and diabetes are common ailments. Issues are exacerbated in private prisons where cost is the overriding factor rather than need.

Specific areas of ethical concern for medical professionals are the independence of the doctor–patient relationship, informed consent, and right of refusal to care. While the ideal doctor–patient relationship is one of informed consent, this ideal is quite incongruent with the reality of prisons and jails where doctors have few choices available to them in a care regimen and patients have virtually no power. Confidentiality is another major ethical issue as the typical doctor–patient confidential relationship cannot exist—the prison is too small (inmates who go to HIV/AIDS clinics become known) and medical staff have dual loyalties. Another ethical area of concern is end-of-life care as the correctional population grows increasingly older and hospice units increase. What level of care is owed to a dying inmate? Finally, there are unique ethical dilemmas presented to correctional healthcare professionals, such as their duty to participate in strip and cavity searches, witnessing uses of force, approving unpalatable but minimally sufficient diets, and certifying inmates for solitary confinement punishment. These duties are inconsistent with the profession, yet the mandate for medical staff to be involved is not negotiable (Dubler, 2014).

A study of burnout and ethical challenges for healthcare workers in the New York jail healthcare system discovered that about a quarter of respondents believed their ethics were regularly compromised by their work. The ethical challenges came from "dual loyalties" where they were treatment professionals, but also correctional employees. So, for instance, they would be called upon to "clear" patients for placement into solitary confinement (essentially certifying that the mental health of the inmate is sufficient to withstand isolation), eroding the relationship with the client. Three common ethical challenges mentioned were violations of patient confidentiality, a focus on quantity of care versus quality of care, and poor treatment of patients by COs (Kalra, et al., 2016).

Unfortunately, because of the culture of corrections, medical professionals may not uphold standards of care or the principles inherent in their ethics codes. In one case, for instance, a mentally ill young man was arrested in Virginia for shoplifting a soda. A judge ordered him to be transferred to a psychiatric hospital, but several orders from the judge were ignored and the man remained in jail for months. The man's psychiatric state deteriorated and he refused to eat. His weight dropped by 35 pounds, evidently without any red flags raised by a mental health worker or jail nurses employed by a private, for-profit firm. Three months later, he was sent to a local emergency room, where he refused treatment. He died several days later (Editorial Board, Washington Post, 2016). How someone can die, literally of starvation, in a controlled environment such as a jail with mental health and medical staff on-site is an issue that is probably due, to some extent, to the culture of corrections.

Vaughn and Smith (1999) described several different ways in which medical services—or more specifically, the lack of such services—created pain and suffering for inmates. Sometimes, poor medical care is a result of neglect or lack of resources, but sometimes the medical staff simply did not care, believed that prisoners should suffer, and/or did not believe that inmates were sick or injured. The authors suggest that the medical staff sometimes furthers penal harm by withholding medical services and justifies such actions by a type of ethical relativism in which inmates aren't seen as deserving the same type of care as others.

Various international bodies have promulgated ethics or values statements concerning the ethics of medical professionals involved in corrections, including the United Nations (UN), the Council of Europe, the World Medical Association, the International Council of Nurses, Physicians for Human Rights, and Penal Reform International. These ethical statements consistently identify important principles of medical care for prisoners, including free access to medical care, equal healthcare to what would be available in the community, confidentiality, patients' consent, preventive healthcare, humanitarian assistance, complete professional independence, and competence. However, according to Pont, Stover, and Wolff (2012), these principles continue to be ignored across the world. The most overriding problem is dual loyalties where the healthcare professional is also an employee of the correctional agency and owes a duty to that agency as his or her employer. These dual loyalties are in contravention to the principles of independent and objective medical treatment.

There have also been some cases where medical professionals tasked with providing medical care for prisoners have involved themselves in activities arguably against ethical principles, including forensic assessments, disclosure of patient-related medical data to others without consent of the patient, assisting in body searches or obtaining blood or urine for analyses for safety and security reasons, providing medical expertise for the application of disciplinary measures, and assisting or being complicit in physical or capital punishment. The reason that these ethical violations continue is that there is virtually no ethics training in correctional medical-care training, there are no sanctions for medical professionals who violate the ethical codes, and professional organizations have not directed any attention to the topic. Assisting in body-cavity searches and testing for drugs are two activities that have been raised as ethically questionable in American prisons. These control activities are not a part of the helping profession of medicine and may interfere with the medical professional–client relationship (Kipnis, 2001).

Recommendations to remove medical care from the direct authority of the correctional agency are proposed to eliminate dual loyalty pressures (Pont, Stover, and Wolff, 2012). However, there have been recurrent issues of poor medical services by contracted providers as well who absorb the "penal harm" culture of a prison or jail and/or have profit motives that conflict with a high level of service delivery.

Community Corrections

Community corrections has a more positive and helpful image than does institutional corrections. However, even in this subsystem of the criminal justice system, the ideals of justice and care become diluted by bureaucratic mismanagement and personal agendas. The Bureau of Justice Statistics reports that there were about 870,500 parolees in 2015 (compared to 3,789,800 probationers). This, combined with those in prisons or jails, equates to about 1 in 37 people being on some sort of correctional supervision (Kaeble and Glaze, 2016: 2). Professionals in community corrections do not have the same power as police or correctional officers to use physical force, but they do have a great deal of nonphysical power over the clients they control. Like other treatment personnel, ethical dilemmas for probation and parole officials often revolve around the dual goals of promoting rehabilitation for the client and safety and security for the community.

Discretion in probation exists at the point of sentencing: probation officers make recommendations to judges concerning whether the offender should be sent to prison or be monitored on probation and the number of years to be served. Discretion also exists during supervision in the following ways:

- Probation officers decide when to file violation reports.
- They decide what recommendation to make to the judge during revocation hearings.
- They make numerous decisions along the way regarding the people on their caseload.

Parole board members or their designees make decisions regarding release, and parole officers have the same discretion in managing their caseload that probation officers do. What criteria are used for these decisions? Usually, the risk to the public is the primary factor for decision making on the part of probation and parole officials, but other considerations also intrude. Some of these other considerations are ethical; some might not be, such as race, type of crime, family ties, crowding in institutions, who the victim was, what the judge wants, and publicity concerning the crime. As noted in the last chapter, increasingly the offender's ability to pay supervision fees is used to determine the punishment.

Probation and parole officers have been described as adopting different roles on the job. Recall the typologies offered to describe how police officers approached their role and how their "type" might affect their decisions; the same discussion can be applied to probation and parole officers. They have also been described by their orientation to the job and individual adaptation to organizational goals. For instance, Souryal (1992) summarizes other literature in his description of the following types:

- The punitive law enforcer
- The welfare/therapeutic practitioner
- The passive time server
- The combined model

Different ethical issues can be discussed in relation to each of these types. For instance, the **punitive law enforcer** may need to examine his or her use of authority. This officer may tend to use illegal threats and violate the due-process protections that

Community corrections
A term that encompasses halfway houses, work release centers, probation, parole, and any other intermediate sanctions, such as electronic monitoring, either as a condition of probation or as a sentence in itself that takes place in the community rather than prison.

punitive law enforcer
The type of officer who perceives the role as one of enforcer, enforces every rule, and goes "by the book."

welfare/ therapeutic worker
The type of officer who perceives the role as one of counselor to the offender and who helps to effect rehabilitative change.

passive time server
The type of officer who does the bare minimum on the job to stay out of trouble.

each client deserves. The **welfare/therapeutic worker** may need to think about natural law rights of privacy and autonomy. These officers tend to infringe on clients' privacy because of their mindset that they are helping the client (and, indeed, they might be), but the client may prefer less help and more privacy. The **passive time server** may violate professional ethics in not performing duties associated with the role.

All of us may have some tendency to be a time server in our respective professions. It is important to continue to take personal inventories and ask whether we are still putting in a "day's work for a day's pay." As is the case for many of the other criminal justice professionals we have discussed in this book, parole and probation officers often have a great deal of flexibility in their day. They leave the office to make field contacts, and they often trade weekdays for weekend days because weekends are more conducive to home visits. This flexibility is necessary if they are to do the job, but some abuse it and use the freedom to accomplish personal tasks or spend time at home. Some offices have attempted to prevent this behavior by instituting measures such as time clocks and strict controls on movements, but these controls are inconsistent with professionalism and not conducive to the nature of the task.

Caseload Supervision

Discretion exists not only at the recommendation-to-release stage but also throughout supervision. Officers do not make the decision to revoke, but they do make the decision to file a violation report and make a recommendation to the judge or the parole hearing examiner to continue with supervision status (perhaps with new conditions), or recommend revocation and prison. Many do not submit violation reports automatically upon discovery of every offender infraction. In this way, they are like police officers, who practice selective enforcement of the laws. Like police officers, some of their criteria for decision making are ethical and some are not. Also like police officers, the individual officer may face ethical dilemmas when the law doesn't seem to consider social realities, such as poverty.

The discretion to decide when to write a violation report is a powerful element in the control the officer has over the offender, but this can obviously be a difficult decision to make at times. If the officer excuses serious violations (e.g., possessing a firearm or continuing drug use) and the decision to do so is based on personal favoritism, fear, or bribery, that officer is putting the community at risk and is unethical in making the decision to do so. Situations in which the officer sincerely believes the offender made a mistake, has extraordinary excuses for such misbehavior, and is a good risk still present a danger to the community. Is the decision any more ethical because of the officer's belief in the offender? Would it be more ethical to conduct oneself "by the book" and always submit violation reports when the offender commits any violation, including a purely technical one?

Probation and parole officers are presented with other dilemmas in their supervision of offenders. For instance, the offender often acquires a job without the employer's knowledge of his or her previous criminality. Is it the duty of the officer to inform the employer and thereby imperil the continued employment of the offender? What about offenders becoming personally involved with others and refusing to tell them about their history? Does the probation or parole officer have a duty to the unwary party, especially if the offender is on probation or parole for an assaultive offense? If the probation or parole officer knows or suspects that the offender is HIV positive and the offender begins an intimate relationship with someone, does the officer have a duty to warn the other party? Most states protect the confidentiality of victims of AIDS, and in these cases the officer has a legal duty *not* to disclose.

What is the probation or parole officer's responsibility to the offender's family? If family members are unwilling to help the offender and perhaps fear his or her presence, should the officer find a reason for revocation? Again, these questions revolve around competing loyalties to the public and client. The correctional professional must balance these interests in every decision, and the decisions are often not easy to make.

Like the police officer, at times the probation officer's role as a family member or friend conflicts with the professional role. Family members and/or friends may expect special treatment or expect that the officer will use his or her powers for unethical purposes, such as using official records to find out information about someone. These are always difficult dilemmas because family and friends may not be sympathetic to the individual's ethical responsibilities to the organization and to society at large. Probation and parole officers are likely to have overlapping circles of acquaintances and family connections with those on their caseloads, especially in small towns. Confidentiality and favoritism are issues that come up frequently.

The officer also must contend with the issue of gratuities. Again, like the police officer, probation or parole officers may be offered special treatment, material goods, or other items of value because of their profession. In most cases, the situation is even more clearly unethical for probation and parole officers because the gift is offered by a client over whom decisions are made, as opposed to police officers who may or may not ever be able to make a decision regarding a restaurant or convenience store manager.

Probation departments have clear rules against any "business relationships" with probationers, and this makes sense, but probation officers in small towns ask, "How can I avoid a business relationship with a client when the only coffee shop in town is run by one of my clients? Am I never to go there during the years he is on probation?" In the same manner as police, probation and parole officers may believe that some gifts offered are given in the spirit of gratitude or generosity and not to influence decision making.

Some probation or parole officers encounter ethical conflicts when they seek part-time employment at counseling centers. They may have counseling or drug treatment licenses that allow them to run groups and engage in individual counseling to earn extra income. This becomes an ethical issue when their part-time employment may involve working with correctional clients. Because their role as private counselor would conflict with their role as professional correctional supervisor, ethics boards have ruled that such employment is acceptable only when counselors do not interact with their own clients.

Because some probationers may appear to be like the probation or parole officer in socioeconomic status, family background, lifestyle, or personal value systems, they have a greater tendency to feel affinity and friendship for some clients. Some probation officers have been known to have clients babysit for them, to rent a room in their house, or to socialize with them and their families. Obviously, these personal relationships hinder the ability to perform one's official function as a protector of the community and enforcer for the legal system. Personal relationships of any type—romantic, platonic, or financial—are simply not appropriate or ethical for the probation and parole professional.

Parole Officers

We have been discussing probation and parole officers simultaneously earlier, but there are some important distinctions between the two. First, parolees are perceived to be more of a threat to the community, so the supervision role of parole officers is emphasized much more strongly than in probation, where supervision is balanced with a service/counseling emphasis. Further, paroled offenders are usually older and have a longer criminal record, so the relationship between supervisor and client might be different. The problems faced by parolees are quite different from those faced by probationers.

Because of the drastic increase in the number of those incarcerated during the 1980s even though the use of parole decreased, the sheer number of those eligible has been swelling the ranks of parole caseloads. Most have the same low levels of education and vocational skills that they had going into prison and have not had access to many, if any, rehabilitative programs in prison. Further, many of those newly released will be those who *maxed out*—meaning that they completed their entire sentence with no requirements to be supervised.

Many of those released from prison return. A BJS study tracked 404,638 prisoners in 30 states after their release from prison in 2005. The researchers found that about two-thirds (67.8 percent) of released prisoners were rearrested within three years (not necessarily convicted); 76.6 percent were rearrested within five years of release. More than half (56.7 percent) were arrested by the end of the first year. About 82.1 percent of released property offenders were arrested for a new crime compared with 76.9 percent of drug offenders, 73.6 percent of public-order offenders, and 71.3 percent of violent offenders (Ducrose, Cooper, and Snyder, 2014). Given these dismal results, what is the ethical duty of the parole officer—to file a violation report when necessary, or to take proactive steps to assist the inmate to succeed?

Our incarceration rate—currently one of the highest in the world—has had a tremendously negative impact on communities. Entire neighborhoods are affected when a large percentage of their population is sent away for years at a time. Generational effects are obvious; children of inmates are six times as likely to be delinquent (Mauer, Chesney-Lind, and Clear, 2002). More subtle effects exist as well. The economy and the social fabric of a community are also affected when large numbers of young people are removed. Community corrections professionals have some power in this scenario. They make release recommendations and affect revocation rates. They can help offenders with reentry problems, or they can stringently enforce every bureaucratic rule.

Recall that under ethical formalism, to be an ethical professional, one must do one's duty. Some officers believe that they have met their ethical duty by explaining the rules to a parolee and then catching the person if he or she "messes up." Others see a more expanded role wherein the officer has some duty to help the offender readjust to society. This may involve taking some responsibility for counseling the offender, referring him or her to services, acting as a troubleshooter or mediator in conflict with family or others, and acting as an advocate in obtaining help. In other words, this officer takes a proactive approach to the parolee's success. Is filing a violation report a success (because the offender was caught) or a failure (because the offender failed)? How an officer feels about the answer to that question may indicate how they view their role.

Halfway Houses

The ethical issues concerning halfway houses are a combination of those that confront institutional corrections and those seen in community corrections. Halfway houses can be large institutions and staff may feel like correctional officers, in which case there are concerns that they will abuse their positions by exploiting the residents. However, halfway houses are in the community, and halfway house staff members have similar concerns to those of probation and parole officers, balancing the rights of offenders against the safety concerns of the community in their use of discretion in allowing furloughs, disciplining offenders for infractions, or deciding to send the offender back to the prison. Other potential ethical issues arise from the profits to be made by providing housing and services.

Because there has been a strong financial pressure to reduce the prison population in every state, there are increasing numbers of halfway houses, most are privately owned. In 2012, the *New York Times* conducted an eight-week investigation into the use of halfway houses in New Jersey. The impetus for the investigation was the number of escapes from halfway houses, but the investigation also uncovered some troubling facts. Community Education Centers is a for-profit agency that owned most halfway houses in New Jersey and other states, receiving $71 million out of the total $105 million New Jersey allocated for halfway houses annually. The large number of escapes prompted the investigation, but after the news articles, the state revised its escape numbers down, explaining that some were technical escapes only. In addition to escapes, evidence indicated that there was an unacceptable level of drugs, gang activity, violence, and even sexual assault in these facilities. Further, there were virtually no true treatment programs offered (Dolnick, 2012a).

The investigation also uncovered troubling relationships between the governor of New Jersey, Chris Christie, who supported the company receiving the lion's share of public funding, and the vice president of Community Education Centers (Dolnick, 2012b). After the investigative series of articles was published, William J. Palatucci, a close friend and political advisor of Gov. Chris Christie's, stepped down as a senior executive at Community Education Centers. The governor announced stronger oversight of halfway houses (Dolnick, 2012c).

There are ethical and legal issues with the relationship between nonprofit programs and for-profit companies that are owned by the same people. The New Jersey investigative series described how, even though only nonprofit companies can receive government contracts for halfway house services, the largest (Community Education Centers) and second largest (The Kintock Group) each had a second for-profit-related company. The nonprofit "hired" the second company and money flowed straight through one to the other (Dolnick, 2012d). David Fawkner, founder of The Kintock Group, reportedly received an annual salary and benefits as high as $805,000. His daughter, brother-in-law, and son-in-law all worked for the for-profit company, and some worked for both, earning two salaries (Dolnick, 2012d). The other major nonprofit operator, Education and Health Centers of America, was essentially a nonprofit arm of Community Education Centers. Both were controlled by John J. Clancy and carried about $35 million in contracts. Critics contended that the relationship between the nonprofit and for-profit subsidiary violated IRS rules (Dolnick, 2012d).

Money was also at the center of a scandal involving New York City's "three quarter" houses and a drug treatment program, Narco Freedom, one of the largest drug treatment providers in the northeast. Three-quarter houses are unregulated housing for individuals who would otherwise be on the street. A $200 per month subsidy is available from the city and that's what these houses charge per month, unless the person also receives some type of disability check in which case they are charged more. Individuals exiting prison or the homeless have literally no choices for affordable housing; thus, they are dependent on the three-quarter houses, or sober houses, as they are sometimes called. Some are run well and present a lifeline to those on the margins, but others were decrepit and dangerous (Seville and Gates, 2013).

The investigation revealed that in some three-quarter houses, residents would be squeezed together in dilapidated houses, sometimes with rats, bedbugs, and cockroaches. Heat and water would be chronically broken, tenants died of overdoses, and individuals were evicted at a moment's notice if they argued or complained. For just $200 per month, those who owned the three-quarter houses could not make a profit; however, if they insisted the residents go to drug treatment as a condition to stay in the facility, the drug treatment program would receive Medicaid dollars and the three-quarter house owners would receive a kickback fee for each person in treatment. Medicaid was being billed millions, making these schemes profitable for the treatment provider and the three-quarter house owners, especially if they put the bare minimum amount of funds into the houses themselves (Barker, 2015a). One of the largest operators of these homes was a Russian man with felony indictments pending against him related to a Medicaid and insurance fraud scheme. Ex-residents allege he would tell them to start using drugs again if they wanted to stay in the house because, otherwise, they weren't eligible for treatment, he wouldn't get the kickback, and he would evict them.

Narco Freedom cut out the middle person by running both treatment programs and houses. Being in treatment was a condition of having a bed in one of the houses, yet the houses themselves were not regulated because they were considered a housing program not a treatment program, but tenants were perceived to have no rights vis-à-vis landlords because the houses were considered a treatment program, not a normal apartment house or rental dwelling (Barker, 2015a, 2015b).

After the series ran, the Russian operator and his wife were indicted on Medicaid fraud (Barker, 2017). In 2017, the New York City Council passed five bills that are intended to improve the three-quarter houses. One bill would prohibit landlords from interfering with tenants' medical treatment, meaning they couldn't force residents to go to specific providers; and, it allowed tenants to take landlords who violated the rule to Housing Court. Another bill would create emergency relocation services, making it easier for residents to relocate if they are living in dangerous homes. Another bill would require all people on public assistance to be informed of their housing rights, including the right not to be summarily evicted, even from a three-quarter house. Finally, a bill required public reports every three months on inspections of three-quarter homes (Barker, 2017).

Executives at Narco Freedom were indicted and charged with money laundering, insurance fraud, commercial bribe receiving, and two counts of grand larceny. Charging documents indicated that Narco Freedom received nearly $40 million annually in Medicaid funds and about $27 million of it was "stolen" by the individuals involved through a variety of schemes, including excessive services and kickbacks. The stolen money financed a lavish lifestyle of Florida condos, luxury cars and mansions (Kates, 2014, 2015; Seville and Kates, 2015). In May 2017, a federal bankruptcy judge approved a $118.4 million settlement to the federal government and state of New York for claims against Narco Freedom, and the bank-appointed trustee pleaded guilty, on behalf of the corporation, to charges of enterprise corruption, grand larceny and filing false paperwork. The criminal charges against the executives are still pending (Reuters, 2017).

In a more recent, almost identical, news investigation into similar schemes in Philadelphia, "recovery houses" (like three-quarter houses) were described as sending drug addicts to treatment centers who then paid the house owners fees for the addicts; this practice was called "pimping out" addicts. Fees range from $100 to $400 per month for each person. If the addicts didn't go, they were evicted. Supporters of some of these recovery houses say they save lives and keep people off the street. Critics say most benefits accrue only to the owners of the houses and treatment centers who reap inflated profits from a perpetual supply of addicts and government money. Treatment might be 60 people in a room for so-called group therapy, each person represents a billing of $75 per session and $800 per month in reimbursements. Federal statutes prohibit treatment centers from paying for clients; violators face prison or fines. It is also a violation of Medicaid rules for a house operator to force residents to go to a specific treatment program. However, because the recovery houses are private homes that receive no housing allowance payments from the city, they are unregulated and much of this activity goes undetected (Fairbanks, 2009; Lubrano, 2017).

The privatization of corrections is a problematic issue because, as discussed in the last chapter, profit motives are always present. Advocating for more releases to halfway houses and three-quarter houses may be the right thing to do, but when there are profits to be made, some individuals will inevitably learn how to manipulate the system. Drug addicts and the homeless are victimized by such schemes, but so, too, are the taxpayers.

Caution must be taken when interpreting the results of these journalistic investigations. They clearly focus on the most egregious cases and we can assume that other for-profit companies stay within the law; however, clearly legitimate concerns have been raised and responded to by the states involved. One wonders, in fact, what is going on in states that have not been the target of these investigative reports. It is important that community corrections, including halfway houses, play a role in every state's correctional system, but, obviously, it is also important to address problems in their implementation. An important element of any well-run halfway house is obviously staff who are trained in and committed to an ethical code.

Conclusion

In this chapter, we touched on some of the ethical issues that correctional personnel face in institutional corrections and in the community. Discretion exists at each stage of the criminal justice system, and each of the correctional professionals we have introduced in these chapters has discretion in different ways. The difficult decisions for correctional officers arise from the personal relationships that develop with inmates, the trust that is sometimes betrayed, the favors that seem harmless, and the coercive environment that makes violence normal and caring abnormal. Correctional treatment personnel have their own problems in resolving conflicts between loyalty toward clients and toward the system. Community correctional professionals also must balance public safety with client interests. They often, especially in small towns, have difficulty in their supervisor role when it overlaps with other community relationships.

To be in a helping profession in a system geared for punishment is a difficult challenge for anyone, and the temptation to retreat into bureaucratic compliance or, worse, egoistic relativism is always present. Arguably, the criminal justice system operates as well as it does only because of the caring, committed, honest people who choose it as a career.

Chapter Review

1. **Describe the role conflict of correctional officers.**

    Prisons experienced changing goals (from custody to rehabilitation) in the 1970s and 1980s, and this created role conflict and ambiguity for the correctional officer. Also in the 1970s, federal courts recognized an expanding number of prisoner rights, including the rights to exercise religious beliefs, obtain medical care, and enjoy some due process. The disruption in the old way of doing things created real chaos, and the 1970s and 1980s brought danger, loss of control, and stress for officers.

2. **List and describe some ethical issues for correctional officers.**

    Officers' uniforms bestow authority and some officers abuse their position. Reciprocity and personal relationships with inmates are potential problem for officers; officers may like an inmate too much and compromise security, or utilize their position to coerce or harass an inmate. Correctional officers report that they sometimes experience a great deal of stress from their role. They are generally disliked by inmates and scorned by society. Some lose their morality in the negative environment of a prison.

3. **Compare the challenges that face jail officers as compared to correctional officers in prisons.**

    Jail officers have become more professional in recent years, but the position is still sometimes used as a dreaded rite-of-passage assignment, a punishment, or a steppingstone to deputy status. The jail officer deals with a transient population that includes juveniles, the mentally ill or intoxicated, and those with other health problems. There is more interaction with relatives of offenders because the jail is in the community; this also means the jail officers may know or be neighbors of offenders or relatives of offenders. Contraband is a major problem in jails and sometimes officers facilitate smuggling.

4. **Explain the role conflict of treatment professionals and provide examples.**

    Correctional treatment professionals have the dual goals of treating the individual and protecting the safety and security of the institution and/or the community. Sometimes this creates conflict—for instance, prison psychologists may be privy to information or confessions that they feel bound to hold in confidence, even though this may jeopardize the security of the prison. Medical professionals are subject to the penal harm culture and allocating resources is also an issue, especially if medical services are provided by a for-profit company.

5.   **List and describe the ethical issues of probation and parole officers.**

Ethical issues arise in the probation or parole officers' ability to file violation reports or (for probation officers) recommend sentencing in that there are ethical and unethical criteria for such decisions. There is also discretion in managing the caseload, including issues of gratuities, relationships with clients, and when family or friends expect special favors or treatment.

Study Questions

1.   How is the discretion of CO's like police officers and court personnel's discretion?
2.   Describe the role ambiguity that COs faced in the 1970s and 1980s.
3.   What are the ethical issues for treatment professionals in corrections?
4.   Explain the two areas where probation and parole officers have discretion.
5.   What are the role types of probation and parole officers? Describe them.

Writing/Discussion Exercises

1.   Write an essay on (or discuss) the range of legal rights that you believe prisoners should have. Look at international treaties on human rights, the ACA standards, and other sources before you write your essay.
2.   Write an essay on (or discuss) how you would put together a policy manual for treatment professionals who work in a prison or jail. Evaluate the professional codes and identify problematic controversies, and then create a policy that can accommodate a conflict (such as confidentiality).
3.   Write an essay on (or discuss) whether probation and parole officers should have the power to carry weapons (in some states they are required to, in others they are prohibited from doing so).

Key Terms

community corrections	punitive law enforcer	"tune-ups"
correctional officer	reciprocity	welfare/therapeutic
passive time server	Tucker telephone	worker

ETHICAL DILEMMAS

Situation 1
You are a prison guard supervising a tier. One of the inmates comes to you and asks a favor. He wants you to check to see why he hasn't been called down to the admin building to see a counselor, because he put in a slip to see his counselor that morning. You know that it is likely he won't be called out today, and you could tell him that, or you could make a call, or you could do neither. Which would you do? Why?

Situation 2
As a new CO, you soon realize that a great deal of corruption and graft are taking place in the prison. Guards routinely bring in contraband for inmates in return for

money, food bought for the inmates' mess hall finds its way into the trunks of staff cars, and money is being siphoned from inmate accounts. You are not sure how far up the corruption goes. Would you keep your mouth shut? Would you go to your supervisors? What if, in exposing the corruption, you implicate yourself? What if you implicate a friend?

Situation 3

You are a prison psychologist, and during your counseling session with one drug offender, he confesses that he has been using drugs. Obviously, this is a serious violation of prison rules. Should you report him? What if he tells you of an impending escape plan?

Situation 4

You are a parole officer whose caseload includes a single mother with three hyperactive, attention-deficit-disordered young children. She receives no support from her ex-husband. Her own mother wants nothing to do with her or the children, believing that "God is punishing her." The parolee works as a topless dancer but hates it. She continues dancing because it pays the bills so well. You know that she smokes marijuana on a regular basis in an effort to deal with stress. Obviously, this is a violation of probation. However, if you file a violation report on her, she will go back to prison. You know she is doing the best she can with her kids, she is heavily involved with their school, and they are strongly bonded to her. You worry about what will happen to the kids. What would you do?

Situation 5

You are a prison counselor and have a good relationship with the other counselors. You all go out drinking after work sometimes, and in general you like and respect everyone. Recently you've noticed that something seems to be going on with one of the other counselors. Stella is usually outgoing and cheerful, but lately she seems distracted and upset. You see her in the parking lot one evening and ask her what is wrong. She confides to you that she is in love with an inmate. She knows it is wrong, but she says that they had an instant chemistry and that he is like no man she has ever known. She has been slipping him love notes, and he has also been writing her. You tell her that she has to stop it or else quit her job. She tearfully tells you that she can't let him go, she needs her job, and you've got to keep quiet or you'll get her fired. What would you do?

Correctional Professionals: Misconduct and Responses

13

Joyce Mitchell, a prison worker who helped two inmates escape from a prison in New York, was sentenced to prison for her actions.

Learning Objectives

1. Explain the Zimbardo experiment and what it might imply for correctional professionals.

2. Describe types of misconduct by correctional officers, including the typologies of misconduct by Souryal and McCarthy.

3. Describe types of misconduct by community corrections professionals.

4. Provide explanations for misconduct.

5. Present some suggestions to decrease misconduct by correctional professionals.

In 1971, Dr. Phillip Zimbardo conducted an infamous experiment on the grounds of Stanford University designed to explore the effects of power. In this experiment, college men were arbitrarily assigned to be correctional officers or inmates, and a mock prison was set up in the basement of a building on the grounds of Stanford University. The changes in both groups were so profound that the experiment was cancelled after six days. Zimbardo (1982; http://www.prisonexp.org/) noted that about one-third of the correctional officers became brutal and authoritarian, and prisoners became manipulative and exhibited signs of emotional distress and mental breakdown. Zimbardo realized even he had been corrupted by the experience of being "warden" and his decision making began to be based on that power. What was even more shocking than the brutality exhibited by some "guards" was that others, clearly uncomfortable with the gratuitous cruelty, did nothing to stop them. If college men who knew the experiment was artificial succumbed to the temptation to inflict their will on the powerless, the inescapable conclusion is that the environment itself causes people to act in ways that they would not otherwise.

399

Periodic scandals in prisons reinforce the findings of the Zimbardo experiment. The nature of the prison and characteristics of prisoners seem to lead to small groups of officers in some prisons exhibiting a pattern of abuse against inmates. For instance, a group of correctional officers (COs), known as the Cowboys, worked the Special Housing Unit (SHU) of the Bureau of Prison's supermax prison in Florence, Colorado. In the mid-1990s, the group retaliated against defiant, violent inmates by routinely beating them and then fabricating a story about why they had to use force. The group eventually attacked not just violent inmates, but troublesome inmates who were verbally defiant as well. The Cowboys also threatened other officers, at one point promising that any officer who snitched would be taken out to the parking lot and beaten.

The group's alleged themes were: "Lie 'til you die" and "What happens in SHU stays in SHU." Years after the group broke up and were transferred to other prisons, they were investigated. The ensuing FBI and Department of Justice investigation described 55 acts of beatings, intimidations, and lies. At trial, despite several of the correctional officers' admitting their activities and testifying for the prosecution, the jury acquitted four officers of all charges and convicted three others of only some of the charges (Prendergast, 2003).

This pattern of a small group of officers who use violence as retaliation and to control inmates is repeated in several other prison and jail scandals across the country over the last several decades. The practices are not pervasive and the number of officers involved is small; however, the practices emerge periodically when conditions are optimal, for example, a wave of inmate violence against officers and administrative support or tolerance. More importantly, the culture of the prison tends to protect and support this illegal violence and juries are not inclined to find guilt, setting the stage for the next scandal.

Misconduct and Corruption

McCarthy (1991, 1995) and Souryal (2009) discuss the major types of corruption by correctional officers and other officials in institutional corrections. Under misuse of authority, McCarthy (1991) details the following:

- Accepting gratuities for special consideration during legitimate activities
- Accepting gratuities for protection of illicit activities
- Mistreatment/harassment or extortion of inmates
- Mismanagement (e.g., prison industries)
- Miscellaneous abuses

misfeasance
Illegitimate acts done for personal gain.

malfeasance
Acts that violate authority.

nonfeasance
Acts of omission.

Souryal (2009: 28–29) describes acts of **misfeasance** (illegitimate acts done for personal gain), acts of **malfeasance** (acts that violate authority), and acts of **nonfeasance** (acts of omission such as ignoring rule violations).

Bomse (2001) identifies different types of prisoner abuse as follows:

- *Malicious or purposeful abuse.* This is the type of abuse inflicted by individual officers intentionally, including excessive use of force, rape and sexual harassment, theft and destruction of personal property, false disciplinary charges, intentional denial of medical care, failure to protect, racial abuse and harassment, and excessive and humiliating strip searches.

- *Negligent abuse.* This type of abuse is also inflicted by individual officers, but not intentionally, and includes negligent denial of medical care, failure to protect, lack of responsiveness, and negligent loss of property or mail.

- *Systemic or budgetary abuse.* This type of abuse is systemwide and refers to policies, including overcrowding, inadequate medical care (systematic budget cutting), failure to protect, elimination of visits or other programs, co-payments and surcharges, and use of isolation units.

Although there is no research that supports this premise, a reading of a wide range of news reports, both current and historical, of corruption in corrections indicates that corruption tends to occur in patterns. That is, if there is sexual misconduct, there is also smuggling. If there is physical abuse of inmates, there are also other forms of mistreatment. It also appears that corruption tends to permeate levels of supervisors who protect the corrupt activities. Cover-ups at the highest levels also occur, arguably not because the highest level administrators are involved directly, but more so because of long-term friendships between those involved and those who can protect them and/or a desire to keep the illegal activities from being exposed to the public. Patterns of corruption also seem to occur when there is a deficit of resources, including understaffing, deferred maintenance leading to decrepit facilities, and a seeming lack of care and attention from the top management. In a way, one might describe it as the "broken windows" theory of corrections in that when policies and procedures are ignored, when buildings fall into disrepair, when relationships between inmates and correctional officers drift into unprofessional familiarity or animosity, then corruption/crime seems to be present as well.

Sexual abuse of inmates, brutality, bribery at the highest levels, and drug smuggling all are reported with depressing regularity. Some scandals live in infamy, such as the gladiator fights that were orchestrated by correctional officers in Corcoran prison in California where correctional officers coerced inmates to fight in the prison yard and then used shotguns from the towers to stop them. Despite the litigation and criminal prosecutions that followed from the California scandal, correctional

⬛ 🗩 IN THE NEWS | *Correctional Crimes*

In 2016, an FBI undercover investigation called Operation Ghost Guard, resulted in the arrests of 130 current and former Georgia prison guards, civilian staff, and inmates. The correctional officers thought they were being paid thousands of dollars to protect drug smuggling operations for a high-level trafficker, using their status as correctional officers to protect them from a vehicle search if they were stopped by police. The investigation also uncovered contraband smuggling and criminal activity in the prisons. Officials began the investigation after discovering a telephone scam—people received phone calls saying they had missed jury duty and they could either pay a fine or be arrested—traced to Georgia prison inmates using cellphones. When agents investigated how the phones got into the prison, they identified guards in nine different prisons. When these corrupt guards were given an opportunity to protect a purported drug trafficker, they agreed to wear their uniforms to transport the drugs. Ironically, some of the correctional officers arrested were on the Department of Corrections' COBRA tactical team which investigates drug trafficking inside the prison.

Source: Brumback, 2016.

officer–coerced "gladiator fights" have been alleged more recently in the Denver jail, in juvenile detention facilities in Texas, and other locations. Other scandals, such as smuggling rings where correctional officers bring in cellphones, drugs, and other contraband for inmates, are so similar when they appear in various states, that it seems only the names of the individuals and prison gangs involved are different. Officers are often tempted by the large sums of money or coerced by inmates who tell the officers they know where they live or where their kids go to school.

In the sections that follow, we focus on a few states (California, Florida, and New York). This is not to portray these states as worse than others, or indicate that there is no corruption in states that aren't represented here. Indeed, it is noteworthy how similar scandals are across the country: drug and cellphone smuggling rings, "beat-up" squads, and sexual exploitation seem to occur with remarkable similarity across many states.

California

California's Department of Corrections has been, in the past, described as corrupt "from the top down" because investigations of wrongdoing seemed to be thwarted by powerful union leaders. The 1990s gladiator fights and shootings of inmates in the yard at Corcoran led to federal indictments, and several officers were tried for a killing, but they were acquitted. Some argue that the officer union "tainted" the jury pool by running television ads before the jury selection, showing officers as tough, brave, and underappreciated (Arax, 1999; Lewis, 1999).

During legislative hearings about a Folsom riot that was said by some to have originated through correctional officers conspiring with one of the gangs, one legislator received death threats, and witnesses were put under protective custody (Thompson, 2004). The riot and its cover-up evidently led directly to the suicide of an officer who attempted to thwart the riot but was stopped by a supervisor. He left a message: "My job killed me" (Warren, 2004a). Several wardens and assistant wardens resigned, took early retirement, or were fired over the Folsom Prison riot scandal, and dozens of correctional officers were fired for wrongdoing (Warren, 2004b).

Donald Vodicka, a 15-year correctional officer veteran in California, testified in a criminal case about the "Green Wall" and the code of silence. His story is described in the Walking the Walk box.

WALKING THE WALK

D. J. Vodicka looks like someone you wouldn't want to anger. At six feet, six inches tall and 300 pounds, with a shaved head and an inscrutable look honed by a hitch in the military and 16 years as a correctional officer, he is not the picture of a liberal do-gooder. Yet Vodicka gave up his career, and even some friends, and risked his safety when he broke rank with other correctional officers and exposed "the Green Wall" for their abuse of inmates. The phrase was

adopted by a group of officers at the Salinas Valley State Prison in California after a prison disturbance on Thanksgiving Day in 1998; more than a dozen officers were injured in the melee. The prison suffered from the effects of understaffing and too many inexperienced officers combined with some of the worst offenders in the California prison system. The desire to teach the inmates a lesson and keep control of a dangerously unstable institution allegedly led

(continued)

to officers using illegal force, planting evidence on inmates, and utilizing a pattern of intimidation and threats on inmates. Even other officers were threatened to keep their activities under the radar of prison officials.

When he was asked by his superior to write a report on the activities of the Green Wall, Vodicka followed orders, as he had always done in his military career and his years with the California Department of Corrections. He wrote a report that detailed the green armbands, lapel pins, and ink pens used by members; the incident where one member received an engraved green-handled knife upon his promotion; the graffiti scrawled on walls and desks proclaiming the group; and the evidence that indicated that Green Wall members were well known in the institution and even tacitly supported by the warden. Instead of dealing with the situation through proper disciplinary channels, the lieutenant who asked for the report was summarily transferred and the report was leaked to other correctional officers, leading to a situation where Vodicka was transferred for his own safety. The news that he was a "rat" traveled with him to the new prison. He encountered hostile remarks and ostracism there until the day he ran to respond to an emergency

alarm, turned around and found that the officers behind him had stopped behind a gate, leaving him alone in a yard full of brawling, violent inmates. Their excuse was that they were waiting for a sergeant. Realizing his vulnerability, Vodicka left the prison that day, never to return.

In 2004, he testified before a California State Senate Committee about the Green Wall and how prison administrators did little or nothing to stop the illegal activities, nor did they punish those who were retaliating against him for speaking out. The hearings led to the resignation of some officials and a broad effort by the Department of Corrections to "clean house" at Salinas Valley. Eventually, Vodicka won a whistleblower lawsuit against the Department of Corrections, but he continues to live in an undisclosed location because his safety is still compromised by his decision to stand up against the Green Wall. He continues to be perceived by many correctional officers in the system as disloyal. Others argue that Vodicka displays the right kind of loyalty—loyalty to the law, to the truth, and to the citizens of the state who employed him, rather than the criminals in green uniforms who forgot what it meant to be public servants.

Sources: Arax, 2004; Vodicka, 2009.

CDCR has a centralized internal affairs office that investigates allegations of wrongdoing, but there is also a state Office of the Inspector General that performs reviews of CDCR investigations and prepares reviews at the request of the legislature. One 2015 review of High Desert State Prison in Susanville provides an example of how an isolated prison can develop a culture that is resistant to change. The report details problems going back to 2007 when advocates, journalists, and inmates reported systematic abuses. Inmates reportedly were strip searched and made to stand for hours in the snow, and correctional officers allegedly tried to provoke attacks between inmates, spread feces on cell doors, and used excessive force. Inmates who filed grievances against officers were allegedly retaliated against and threatened. Internal affairs investigators sent to the prison to investigate abuses concluded that correctional officers believed they could carry out extreme forms of punishment against inmates because it was a behavioral modification unit for inmates who had been identified as disruptive in other prisons (Piller, 2010). News articles at that time led to a Senate investigation.

In 2012, the Office of Inspector General (OIG) conducted another review of the prison due to complaints, and in 2015, the most recent major OIG review was undertaken, prompted by news articles describing how a correctional officer killed himself, allegedly because of events that were occurring in the prison. That review provided a history of the previous problems and reports, reviewed the news articles, and concluded with a detailed review of some of the entrenched problems of the prison. In the report, it was stated that there was a perception of insularity and indifference to inmates exacerbated by the prison's isolation, the high stress environment, and a union that actively discouraged correctional officers from cooperating with the inspectors. The result was an entrenched culture of self-protection and loyalty to the prison. Inmates told investigators that appeals were destroyed by officers, and that officers used profane and derogatory language toward inmates. California separates inmates who are considered high risk for victimization and in these "sensitive need yards" (SNY) at High Desert, evidently there was just as much violence as in regular housing units, with gangs, gambling debts, and extortion. The staff complaint system was not performing adequately because very few complaints were referred for investigation. The unit did not have a system for addressing officers who had numerous complaints against them. The investigators found that the CDCR Office of Internal Affairs agents were based at the prison (rather than Sacramento), causing issues in that the agents were perhaps too close to the officers being investigated. The report presented a long list of recommendations designed to address the entrenched culture, the problematic appeal and staff complaint systems, and the lack of follow-up on abuse complaints. For instance, one recommendation was to install more security cameras and utilize body-cameras for some officers; also, to stop the use of place-based internal affairs agents (California Office of the Inspector General, 2015). The correctional union is suing the OIG for the investigation at High Desert, alleging that investigators had no authority to require COs to talk to them without union representatives present (Thompson, 2016).

The OIG also publishes summary reports of internal affairs investigations, suicides, critical incidents, and employee discipline cases. Incidents are reviewed to determine whether the investigation procedures and discipline followed proper procedures (see, https://oig.ca.gov/). The practice of having an outside agency (OIG) conduct periodic audits of the discipline process of a corrections department no doubt helps to improve procedures and identify problem areas. In other states, these outside investigative agencies also play a role in exposing corruption with corrections.

The current head of CDCR, Scott Kernan, appointed in 2015, has stated publicly that he would like to see a cultural change at CDCR and to have correctional officers become engaged in rehabilitative efforts. Kernan came up through the ranks, starting as a guard in the early 1980s. He pledged to work more cooperatively with the OIG's office and inmates' attorneys and to continue the new training on diversity and stress management that was instituted at High Desert after the OIG report (Thompson, 2016).

As described earlier, California has drastically reduced its prison population due to the court holding in *Brown v. Plata*, and the Realignment Act resulted in many more inmates in county jails rather than prisons. The Los Angeles County Jail has been cited in past years by advocates, inmates, attorneys, and staff members as a place where widespread abuse of inmates occurred. Years ago, the Department of Justice was asked to investigate the jail in a letter signed by former California attorney general John Van de Kamp, two former U.S. attorneys, three former assistant U.S. attorneys, the Los Angeles County public defender, the former head of the Civil Rights Division of the Department of Justice, several law school deans, and numerous attorneys and religious leaders (Faturechi, 2011). The American Civil Liberties Union (ACLU) published a report detailing incidents where deputies slammed inmates' heads into walls, kicked them when they were on the floor unresisting, used Tasers on unresisting inmates, and allowed other inmates to brutalize and sexually assault victims. Documented injuries include a fractured jaw, broken collarbone, eye damage, and numerous other injuries—all received, according to deputy reports, while the inmate was "resisting." The ACLU collected 70 sworn statements by prisoners, chaplains, teachers, civilian staff, and deputies and submitted them to the court in *Rutherford v. Baca* (begun as *Rutherford v. Block*, 2006 WL 3065781 [C.D. Cal. Oct 27, 2006]).

Some of the abuse was witnessed by civilians (chaplains and attorneys) who alleged being threatened by correctional officers if they reported what they saw. Even when the abuse was reported to administrators, nothing was done about it. A chaplain, despite being threatened, did report an incident where an unresisting inmate was being beaten and some deputies called the chaplain a "rat" and "motherf****r" when he passed them in the hallway in the days that followed (Faturechi, 2011).

Most of the abuse took place on the third floor of the jail, and this group was described as "gang-like" who used gang hand signs and called themselves the 3,000 Boys (for the third floor); in later court filings, they were described as having tattoos on the back of their necks and awarding one another points for breaking prisoners' bones (Williams, 2014). The jail has had gang-like groups of officers before with names such as the Grim Reapers, Vikings, and Little Devils (Faturechi and Blankstein, 2011; Liebowitz, Eliasberg, Winter, and Lim, 2011).

The LA jail had already been under a federal monitor for 12 years for its treatment of mentally ill inmates (Chang, 2013). A county blue ribbon panel, created after the ACLU report was published, issued a report in 2012 that said Sheriff Baca and his assistants had created an environment where deputies believed it was acceptable to use physical beatings and humiliation to control inmates and to cover up such abuse. The Department of Justice opened a civil rights investigation (similar to those conducted in cities where there are problems with police departments) (Williams, 2014). In two separate civil lawsuits filed by inmates who had been injured in the jail, two juries found Sheriff Baca personally liable for incidents of abuse. In one of those cases the plaintiff was a man awaiting trial in 2009 in the jail when deputies severely beat him; he was punched and kicked repeatedly, shot with a Taser multiple times and struck "numerous times" in the ankle with a heavy metal flashlight, causing fractures and head injuries. The jury found in favor of the plaintiff against the deputies involved, their supervisors, and Sheriff Baca who, it was determined, failed to control violence in the jail. The jury awarded $165,000 in punitive damages to the plaintiff and the defendants agreed that Baca would pay $100,000 of it (Medina, 2013; Sewell and Faturechi, 2013).

The most bizarre chapter in the saga of the LA County jail occurred in 2011 when the FBI engineered an undercover operation by paying a corrupt correctional officer to smuggle in a cellphone to a prisoner-informant, who was supposed to collect evidence of the brutality in the jail with the phone. When the cellphone was discovered and the prisoner-informant told deputies he was working for the FBI, he was prevented from communicating with his FBI handlers. The FBI filed a writ in court to produce him, but the court order "got lost" at the sheriff's department. He was successfully hidden for several weeks by deputies moving him around to different facilities under false names, until the sheriff's department was finally forced to produce him in response to a judge's order. Their explanation for secreting the inmate from his FBI handlers was that they were only trying to keep him safe. Recorded interviews between the informant and deputies, however, made it clear that they were upset about the FBI investigating "their house" and that they were attempting to persuade the informant not to tell the FBI agents anything. Two deputies also conducted surveillance on and accosted an FBI agent in her driveway and told her there was going to be a warrant for her arrest to coerce her to tell them what the FBI knew about what was going on in the jail (Kim and Chang, 2014).

The investigation resulted, in late 2013, in 18 deputies and supervisors arrested under four different grand jury indictments on an array of charges, including civil rights violations and obstruction charges (Hews, 2013). In 2014, federal prosecutors won guilty verdicts against six of these sheriff's deputies for their roles in the scheme to obstruct the federal investigation, including the two who threatened the FBI agent with arrest. The deputies were sentenced to prison terms from 21 to 41 months for their actions. The federal judge found that there was routine cover-up of inmate abuse, and an "unwritten code" taught to new jail deputies that any inmate who fought a guard should end up in the hospital (Kim, 2014). The defendants insisted they were merely following orders from Sheriff Lee Baca and Undersheriff Paul Tanaka. Sheriff Baca resigned abruptly in January 2014, and one of those who ran for the sheriff's position was Undersheriff Paul Tanaka. He denied any wrongdoing (Kim and Chang, 2014; Medina, 2013). Tanaka lost the election to Jim McDonnell, who had been on the Citizens' Commission on Jail Violence, the blue ribbon panel formed after the ACLU report that had issued the highly critical report in 2012. Tanaka left the Los Angeles County Jail after losing the election (Chang and Winton, 2015).

Tanaka was indicted in 2015, convicted, and sentenced to five years in prison. His case is on appeal. Former Sheriff Lee Baca was tried and the first trial resulted in a hung jury. His defense was that he did not know what had been happening and had no role in the obstruction of the FBI investigation. He proposed that Tanaka was responsible for everything. In a second trial, prosecutors convinced jurors that he did know, partly because of testimony that proved his participation in a conversation regarding how they would threaten the FBI agent with arrest. The judge sentenced the 74-year-old to three years in prison despite the fact he was in the early stages of Alzheimer's and hundreds of letters of support, including from former Gov. Arnold Schwarzenegger, had been submitted to plead for leniency. The judge excoriated the former sheriff for his betrayal of the public trust. He stated that Baca was more concerned for his reputation than for justice and that his actions "embarrass[ed] the thousands of men and women [in the department] who put their lives on the line every day." The prison term was to serve as a deterrent to other public servants to show that "Blind obedience to a corrupt culture has serious consequences," and that, "No person, no matter how powerful, no matter his or her title, is above the law." He is expected to begin his sentence by August 2017, but may be allowed to remain free while his case is on appeal (Rubin, 2017).

In 2014, the ACLU lawsuit was settled when the Los Angeles County Board of Supervisors agreed to a federal consent decree. The agreement involved neither financial damages nor an admission of wrongdoing by the Sheriff's Department, but a three-person panel, appointed by a federal judge, would oversee the implementation of sweeping new policy changes. A new assistant sheriff was brought in from the state corrections system and outside experts were consulted to assist in numerous changes (Chang, 2016; Williams, 2014). Jail suicides have declined from 10 in 2013 to 1 in 2015. Uses of force have declined from a high

QUOTE & **QUERY**

You don't serve the public by using your position to conceal wrongdoing in the jails. You don't serve the public by hiding witnesses. You don't serve the public by tampering with witnesses, and you don't serve the public by threatening to arrest an FBI agent in some misguided effort to get her to reveal the details of her investigation.

The court hopes that if and when other deputies are faced with decisions similar to those you face, they will remember what happened here today. They will not look the other way or obstruct an investigation; that they will recognize that blind obedience to a corrupt culture has serious consequences, that they will enforce the law rather than conspire to commit crimes, that they will do what is right rather than what is easy.

Judge Percy Anderson (sentencing the six deputies in the FBI obstruction case).

Source: Quoted in Bartley, 2014.

 What ethical system would provide a justification for the deputies who kept the informant from his FBI handlers and threatened the FBI agent with arrest?

of 763 in 2009 to 216 in 2014, but increased to 302 in 2015. The ACLU was involved in helping to write use-of-force policies when dealing with the mentally ill. Other changes included better training for guards, providing basic equipment, reducing overcrowding, cleaning crews to reduce unpleasant smells, changing the color of the paint from dark green to light blue, and bolting bunk beds to the floor. Deputies are encouraged to take pride in working the jails, which had been considered a second-class assignment. However, deputies have resisted changes in the rules on uses of force and argue that they have led to increased assaults on deputies; assaults by inmates on jail staff increased from 190 in 2013 to 380 in 2015. One challenge has been an increase in mentally ill inmates: from 2,500 in 2011 to nearly 4,000 in 2015 (Chang, 2016).

Florida

With 20,000 employees and more than 100,000 inmates, Florida's prison system is the third largest in the country, after California and Texas, with one of the highest rates of imprisonment. Florida has also seen its share of scandals. The federal courts, citing the Eighth Amendment violations, oversaw the state's prisons for more than two decades starting in the mid-1970s, ordering legislators to relieve overcrowding and to provide adequate medical and healthcare.

James Crosby, appointed secretary of the corrections system by Governor Jeb Bush, was forced to resign in 2006 after stories of alcohol-fueled parties and cozy relationships with prison vendors circulated. Crosby ended up in a federal prison himself for bribery. The investigation led to criminal charges against more than two dozen other employees (Morgan, 2010; York, 2012).

In 2014 and 2015, a *Miami Herald*'s investigative series of Florida's prison system by reporter Julie Brown exposed a seemingly corrupt system that was chronically underfunded and rife with abusive staff and cover-ups. In 2014, the Department of Justice indicated they would be investigating the prison system for civil rights violations. Inmate deaths that may have been covered up were the most serious allegations (Brown, 2014a). Several suspicious deaths of inmates were reviewed in various news stories and investigations. Bernadette Gregory was found dead in her cell in 2009, supposedly she hung herself in 11 minutes, between observations, despite being handcuffed and in a wheelchair. A few days before her death, she reported abuse and a threat by a correctional officer (Brown, 2014a). Darren Rainey, a mentally ill inmate, was found dead in a shower in 2012. Inmates stated that he had been screaming to get out for two hours, that the shower was set at a high temperature, and was used as punishment. Reports indicate that his skin sloughed off his body and his body temperature was unreadably high (Brown, 2014d). After the *Miami Herald* series reported on the death three years later, police detectives finally interviewed witnesses. In 2016, a 101-page report of an investigation by Miami-Dade State Attorney Katherine Fernández Rundle said the death was an accident, the result of complications from his mental illness, a heart condition, and "confinement in a shower." Inmate accounts were considered not credible. Critics argue the investigation was flawed because several employees were not interviewed and there are inconsistencies between the official autopsy used in the report and a preliminary autopsy at the time of death that seemingly showed different findings. His family filed a federal civil rights lawsuit in 2016 (Brown, 2017).

Randall Jordan-Aparo's death occurred after he was gassed with chemical agents so severely that the pictures show an outline of his body with the yellow chemical agent covering the wall behind the spot where his body lay. Reports written by the officers after the death falsely claimed that he had been involved in a prison disturbance. Four investigators with the Florida Department of Corrections' Inspector General's office subsequently filed a whistleblower lawsuit against the chief inspector general, Linda Miguel, claiming there was a cover-up to thwart their efforts to expose and punish the officers in 2013 (Brown, 2014f; Brown and Bousquet, 2014).

Latandra Ellington's death is also suspicious. She was found dead in October 2014, supposedly of natural causes, after she sent a letter to her family saying that a sergeant at Lowell Correctional Institution was threatening to kill her. Her family hired an attorney and paid for a private autopsy, which showed she suffered blunt-force trauma to her stomach consistent with being punched or kicked (Brown, 2014b).

After the *Miami Herald* series in 2014, 32 correctional officers were fired (Associated Press, 2014). Mike Crews, the head of the Department of Corrections at the time, also fired or forced into retirement several wardens and deputy wardens and attempted a series of reforms. He also asked that the Florida Department of Law Enforcement (FDLE), a separate independent investigative body that answered to the governor, take on the duty of investigating inmate deaths and correctional officer abuse (Associated Press, 2014; Brown, 2014c). Crews also created an ombudsman to monitor the care of inmates with mental illnesses and warned the healthcare provider Corizon that it must rectify serious deficiencies in its medical care (Brown and Bousquet, 2014).

One of the wardens forced to retire said that his attempts to improve the prison were thwarted and said that "the biggest challenge a warden has is to change the culture of an institution." When he made surprise visits to the prison at 2 a.m., he would see doors wide open, unstaffed stations, and sleeping guards. He described a maintenance worker that was so involved in smuggling drugs and cigarettes that he never had time to do his job. Cummings said, "It is, by far, the most dangerous prison I've ever worked in." He also said that the inmates weren't treated like human beings. A major problem was understaffing, so much so that there was "ghost rostering"—in which guards listed as working at a post were not there. He described the mental health unit where Rainey died: "There was no air conditioning. The doors to the control rooms were broken. The plumbing was bad, bad, bad. Water was leaking everywhere. All you could smell was urine and feces. The inmates were all in soiled clothing. . . I would walk in there and they would beg for food, for soap, for a toothbrush. . . The officers held all the power and if they didn't want to feed them, they wouldn't feed them." Cummings said he tried to fire officers, but was ordered not to do so (Brown, 2014e).

In 2014, a Florida State University group called The Project on Accountable Justice, a think tank made up of academics, judges, and law enforcement and corrections professionals, urged the legislature to conduct a complete overhaul of the prison system because of what they called mismanagement from the highest level. The report concluded with a series of recommendations, including the following:

- Create a public safety oversight commission that would set policy and standards for prisons.
- Raise the minimum standard for hiring corrections officers and set up educational incentives.
- Separate the terms of the secretaries of the department of corrections from the governors who appoint them and have the legislature involved in the vetting and evaluation to improve independence (Brown, 2014c).

The Miami Herald reporters also looked at the problems of medical care, or lack of it. Investigators reviewed five years of medical complaints, audits, surveys, and facility inspections at Lowell Women's Prison. Inmates provided medical records, e-mails, and other documents. The news reports described a system whereby there was understaffing and a lack of care toward inmates. Corizon, a private company, had taken over medical care for the state prison system in 2013. Spending on health-care in the prisons dropped. An audit revealed chronic conditions neglected, colonoscopies not ordered that should have been; vaccinations and immunizations for hepatitis never initiated; follow-up appointments that didn't happen; post-partum exams that occurred four weeks late; ultrasound for a head trauma that was ordered but not given; HIV patients not given treatment; breast cancer patients deprived of their medication; and many other issues. The response from Corizon was that inmates always complain about healthcare, but they are getting adequate treatment (Brown, 2015b).

In January 2015, Julie Jones, who had been a state law enforcement officer for 30 years, and most recently the director of the Department of Highway Safety and Motor Vehicles, was appointed as secretary of the Corrections Department (Brown and Bousquet, 2014; Brown and Klas, 2015). She fired 44 correctional officers and supervisors in her first year (Brown, 2015b). One firing was of an assistant warden who was allegedly sexually involved with several female inmates and protected them from discipline. A correctional officer who worked for the assistant warden filed a police report after he was threatened by him with a beating because he searched a female inmate's cell who was a favorite of the assistant warden (Brown, 2015a).

In testimony to the state legislature in early 2015, current and former prison inspectors testified that they were repeatedly ordered to ignore evidence of crimes committed by corrupt officials because doing so would give the Department of Corrections a "black eye." Three inspectors and one former inspector cited cases where they were told to withhold information from prosecutors, to close investigations into staffers who were politically connected and to avoid bringing criminal charges no matter how much evidence they had. They said they were threatened or retaliated against by their boss Jeffrey Beasley in the Inspector General's (IG) Office, especially after they spoke with *Miami Herald* reporters in the story series about mysterious inmate deaths (Klas and Brown 2015a, 2015b). Jeffery Beasley has since stepped down from that position (Brown, 2017). Legislative hearings in 2015 led to a prison-reform bill that would have created a joint committee to oversee the DOC and a list of reforms, including an overhaul of the IG's investigative function of the prisons. The bill died when the Senate refused to pass it (Klas, 2015a, 2015b).

By March of 2016, Jones had fired or forced 1,080 people to resign. She vowed that the department would not tolerate the kind of abuse that has been part of the prisons' culture for decades. She stated that the problems of the prison system are at least partially due to 700 correctional officer positions cut during the recession. The understaffing has led to dangerous conditions in many prisons. Officers also haven't had a pay raise in a decade and their average salary is low. Since she's been the head of the corrections department, she has overseen changes in the use-of-force policy, centralized the inmate grievance system, renegotiated the healthcare contract, had surveillance cameras put in prisons, and piloted a body camera program (Brown and Klas, 2016). However, the problems in the Florida Department of Corrections continue.

Several Florida correctional officers, reputedly members of the Ku Klux Klan, were arrested in 2015 for conspiring to kill a released inmate for assaulting one of them (Robles, 2015). At least six correctional officers were arrested in 2016 from the women's prison the Miami Herald series targeted in the exposure of sexual exploitation (Brown, 2016a). In 2017, a Florida legislator wrote the governor an open letter pleading for a new warden and resources to respond to what he described as a "loss of institutional control" in the state's largest women's prison. During surprise inspections with investigators from the Department of Corrections and the state's Office of Chief Inspector General, he found numerous conditions at the Gadsden prison that posed significant health concerns, including 55 degree temperatures in the cells, no hot water, medical care being withheld, a tooth extraction without sedation, guards who impregnated inmates allowed to remain on the job, and other issues. The prison is run by a private corrections company, and after a surprise visit in February with the head of the Department of Management Services that oversees private prisons, the state's on-site monitor was fired (Klas, 2017).

The changes needed in the Florida prison must be navigated through the influence of the powerful correctional officers' union, which has strong supporters in the legislature, a seemingly chronically underfunded corrections system, and the politicization of employee discipline. An entrenched culture and code of silence is very difficult to change, but it is even harder to gain success when there is a lack of commitment from state legislature to fund at a level that provides programming and safety for both inmates and officers.

New York

The New York Department of Corrections and Community Services (DOCCS) has had a series of scandals in recent years, not the least of which was the escape from Clinton (Dannemora) prison in 2015 by two prisoners, aided by staff members and the negligence of others. A 150-page scathing report by the state Inspector General uncovered a series of lapses, including the well-known habit of Officer Ronald Blair to never make late-night rounds as he was supposed to. This allowed the two escapees several hours out of the prison before the alarm was sounded. Investigators discovered that guards routinely would falsify records to make it appear as if they were conducting late-night rounds when they did not. One of the inmates who escaped spent 85 nights outside his cell exploring the tunnels beneath the prison in search of an escape route—only possible because of 400 compulsory bed checks that should have been done but were not. Investigators noted that "just one" bed-check during the six months they planned the escape would have foiled the escape. Joyce E. Mitchell, a civilian supervisor of the prison tailor shop, believed herself to be in a romantic relationship with one of the prisoners, and brought in contraband and tools that facilitated their escape. She also hid two chisels, a steel punch, two concrete drill bits, and two hacksaw blades in frozen ground beef that she gave to a correctional officer who delivered them to the inmates. In response to the escape, the DOCCS installed new security cameras, disciplined employees involved, and appointed a new superintendent (Schwirtz and Winerip, 2016).

In January 2016, James Ferro, the former second-in-command of the corrections department's internal affairs unit pleaded guilty to a misdemeanor coercion charge immediately before his trial was about to begin. Ferro was indicted on misdemeanor charges of sexually harassing a male subordinate during a four-year period and threatening the employee if he reported the incidents. He was sentenced to 120 hours of community service and a $1,000 fine. The charges were the result of an investigation by the state Inspector General's office into allegations that the DOCCS inspector general's office was mismanaged and that supervisors covered up or ignored complaints about workplace harassment. Ferro, like nearly all investigators in the DOCCS internal affairs office who investigate allegations of misconduct at state correctional facilities, is a former corrections officer. He was accused by a female employee of grabbing her and allegedly threatening that it would be a "bad career move" if she filed a harassment complaint against him. The criminal case he pleaded guilty to was related to a male employee's allegations that Ferro kissed and hugged him, touched his genitals, struck him on the knee with a small bat, and other inappropriate behavior. Ferro retired with an annual pension of $66,384 (Lyons, 2016).

After Ferro and his unit was investigated by the state Inspector General's office and the head of the internal affairs unit (who had laughed when he heard that Ferro had kissed his subordinate) retired, DOCCS renamed it the Office of Special Investigations and appointed a new director, Stephen J. Maher, who was previously a deputy bureau chief with the state attorney general's Criminal Enforcement and Financial Crimes Bureau (Winerip, Schwirtz, and Robbins, 2016). This office investigates any excessive force allegations and suspicious deaths. New York, like other states, has had a series of deaths and horrific beatings, including the following cases.

Leonard Strickland (2010)—At Clinton Correctional Facility, Strickland, a schizophrenic, had an argument with a guard, and was beaten by up to a dozen guards resulting in his death. Security video footage shows Strickland, in handcuffs, barely conscious and being dragged along the floor by officers to the prison medical office. He lies face down on the floor, not moving, while guards can be heard shouting, "Stop resisting." He is motionless for 11 minutes before someone begins CPR. Medical experts reviewing the video were scathing in their criticism of the prison nurse who did little to help Strickland even after he was unresponsive. When ambulance staff arrived, 30 minutes later, they reported his body was cold to the touch and covered in cuts and bruises, with blood flowing from his ears. The coroner's report said he died of cardiac ischemia. The police and the district attorney concluded there had been no criminal wrongdoing, though two state prison watchdog agencies, the State Commission of Correction, and the Commission on Quality Care and Advocacy for Persons with Disabilities, issued highly critical reports documenting numerous misleading and false statements by officers (Winerip and Schwirtz, 2015a).

George Williams (2011): Williams was believed to have cursed at a guard (he said it was a case of mistaken identity). He was removed from his cell by three guards and taken to a day room where he was kicked and beaten with fists and batons. Inmates two floors below reported they heard Mr. Williams pleading for his life. Inmates saw Williams dragged out of the day room, covered in blood. Officers dragged him to the solitary unit, but the sergeant on duty ordered them to take him to the infirmary and, there, a nurse insisted he be taken to an outside hospital. Doctors inserted a plate and six screws in one of his legs. The three officers were charged with assault and each received a one-year conditional discharge after pleading guilty to a single charge of official misconduct. They will be allowed to keep their pensions (Robbins, 2015a; Robbins and D'Avolio, 2015).

Kevin Moore (2013)—Moore received five broken ribs, a collapsed lung, and shattered facial bones in an incident with five correctional officers who said that he had attacked them. Moore's dreadlocks were ripped out and one of the officers kept them as a "trophy." Then they placed him in solitary confinement instead of allowing him to received medical assistance. When he was transported to Rikers Island the next day for a court appearance, jail staff refused to accept him because of his condition and he was transported to a hospital where he spent 17 days. In 2016, federal prosecutors charged the officers involved with civil rights violations and fraud. Prosecutors alleged that one of the officers hit another to create an injury to justify the beating. Two officers pleaded guilty and three officers pleaded not guilty (Winerip and Schwirtz, 2016).

Ramon Fabian (2014)—Fabian lost part of his right testicle after a prison guard punished him for talking during count by having him face the wall, spread his legs, and then kicked him in his testicles. He was taken to the hospital and underwent surgery. The guard denied kicking him and was still on duty a year later despite facing criminal assault charges (Robbins, 2015b).

Samuel Harrell (2015)—Harrell died after an incident involving more than a dozen officers who were known in the prison as the "Beat-up Squad" at Fishkill Prison. He was beaten and allegedly thrown down stairs. Inmates who saw the incident were told to keep their mouths shut or they would be next. The officers were observed to have punched, kicked, stomped, and jumped on his face, head, neck, back, and legs. He was evidently already unconscious when he went down the stairs. A criminal investigation is being conducted by the U.S. Attorney's office for the Southern District of New York and the Dutchess County District Attorney's office (Winerip and Schwirtz, 2015b, 2016).

The 20,000-member union (the New York State Correctional Officers & Police Benevolent Association) has formidable political power. The union has negotiated favorable labor contracts giving them more control over personnel decisions than the prison superintendents or even the corrections department's commissioner. Superintendents have practically no power to transfer problem officers. Disciplinary rules give final say on firing to an arbitrator, not the commissioner. Many argue that union protection has allowed a "culture of brutality" in that a few rogue guards engage in excessive force, but are not disciplined, and most officers simply look the other way believing it to be impossible to come forward when they see misconduct or change the culture (Winerip, Schwirtz, and Robbins, 2016).

Stephen Maher, the new head of the DOCCS Inspector General's office, and Daniel F. Martuscello III, the department's deputy commissioner, reportedly declared their willingness to stand up to the correctional officers' union who tend to support and protect all officers, even those who brutalize and sexually exploit inmates. They have hired new internal affairs investigators and some of them are from law enforcement agencies rather than former correctional officers who sometimes transfer back to their prisons as officers after a time in the Inspectors' General office.

In the meantime, the incidents continue. A lawsuit by female inmates alleges that sex abuse is rampant and, even if the inmate complains, nothing is done and the inmate is retaliated against. The lawsuit details allegations of forcible sexual intercourse, other forms of sexual misconduct, verbal threats, harassment and voyeurism in Bedford Hills, and Taconic and Albion correctional facilities. The lawsuit does not seek monetary damages, but demands court oversight to put in place policies to address sexual misconduct, including changes in the investigation and discipline process (Weiser, 2016b).

The difficulty in removing problematic officers is exemplified by one officer in a woman's prison who was investigated by the internal affairs unit four times between 2008 and 2012 on suspicion of sexual assault yet remained in his job. Surveillance video recorded him having sex with an inmate and, in one episode, the video showed him tipping his hat to the camera. The 65-year-old officer impregnated the 24-year-old inmate, but union contract protections prohibited the Superintendent from removing him. He was finally convicted of rape and the state settled a civil suit in the case for $895,000. Between 2010 and 2015, attempts to fire 30 prison guards accused of abusing inmates have resulted in only 8 losing their jobs because arbitrators generally rule against the state. Another 80 cases didn't even reach arbitration and were settled with lesser punishments, such as suspension (Winerip and Schwirtz, 2016).

Since Maher has headed the Inspector General's office for DOCCS, he has fired 10 percent of the investigators as unqualified, hired a nurse to assess injuries in brutality cases, started a pilot program to equip officers with body cameras, and increased the number of disciplinary actions against guards. Unit investigators are also increasingly willing to refer cases for criminal prosecution. Investigators report that when investigating allegations of officer misconduct, they have faced guards being slow to produce inmate witnesses, conferring to get their stories straight, being blocked from entering prisons, and a "culture of silence" among guards. Officers who come forward and speak out when they see other guards abuse inmates face retaliation and harassment. One such guard, who was fired after she reported a fellow CO for using excessive force, won a $200,000 settlement against the DOCCS and identified two union officials as leading the campaign of harassment against her that included threats to her and her family (Winerip and Schwirtz, 2016). Only with strong oversight and discipline does a department have any chance of changing a culture where abuse of inmates is accepted. However, if strong union contracts prohibit administrators from firing abusive officers, and if arbitration is set up to "split the baby" and moderate any punishment meted out by administrators, it makes change very difficult.

Treatment Professionals

Most news items and academic articles describe misconduct in prisons in terms of correctional officers, but there are instances where counselors and other treatment professionals also engage in misconduct. Sometimes, they smuggle in contraband; sometimes, they coerce inmates or engage in consensual sex with inmates (Colarossi, 2009; York, 2012).

Probably the most common issue for treatment and medical personnel is not providing the services that inmates are legally entitled to. As discussed in the last chapter, medical personnel sometimes adopt the "penal harm" philosophy of corrections and deprive inmates of services because of a belief that they don't deserve treatment. It is very difficult to maintain a helping profession orientation in a correctional environment. Inmates are often unpleasant individuals and sometimes violent as well. Like law enforcement's attitude toward certain segments of society, treatment personnel in corrections sometimes develop an attitude that all inmates are liars, crooks, and addicts and don't deserve even basic services. The trouble with this line of reasoning, besides the fact that it is contrary to professional duties, is that once some are perceived as outside the bounds of professional duties, it is easier to ignore duties and respect for all.

Community Corrections

While most news items describe misconduct in prisons, there are also examples of ethical misconduct and criminal acts by community corrections professionals. Peter Maas's (1983) book *Marie* details a scheme in Tennessee that involved selling paroles to convicts. In the early 1990s, ex-parole board members in Texas were found to have sold their services as "parole consultants" to inmates and inmates' families to help them obtain a favorable release decision (Ward, 2006). A 2013 *Denver Post* review of parole records discovered "fundamental errors" in 60 percent of the cases. The review showed that parole officers left parolees on their caseload even after repeated failures to appear. In one case a parolee had missed therapy sessions or failed drug tests 49 times and was arrested twice and the parole officer still had not filed a violation report. This offender ended up sexually assaulting a six-year-old and was sent back to prison. In another case, an offender tested positive for drugs 12 times and the parole officer did nothing, not even a home visit of the parolee, as required, for over a year. In another case, despite a string of well-publicized arrests for robberies, one parolee's supervision report included nothing about the arrests. Auditors concluded that parole officers did not respond appropriately to violations or complete required visits in about a third of the cases. The head of the parole division was fired after a parolee murdered Tom Clements, the head of corrections in March 2013 (Osher and Olinger, 2013).

Also in 2013, four Texas parole officers were arrested after a year-long investigation into parole officers taking bribes to ignore drug trafficking and other illegal activity by parolees. Federal indictments allege that the four arrested parole officers took

IN THE NEWS | *Parole Performance*

The governor of Utah announced a comprehensive review of Utah's probation and parole system in 2016 and two top officials quit their jobs, including the head of the agency. The shake-up occurred after a parolee (Cory Lee Henderson) absconded from a halfway house and shot and killed a police officer. Another parolee also escaped from the same halfway house and stole a car and rammed a police cruiser and was later shot by police. Other incidents, including inaccurate information about a parolee during a parole hearing and parolees not being revoked even after arrest, led to the overhaul of the department. The governor promised that those who were found to be in dereliction of their duties would be fired. A full-scale review of the halfway house will also occur and will cover the procedures for sharing data between state and local agencies. In the initial stages of the overhaul, 29 people in halfway houses were returned to prison for drug use, supervision has increased, a fugitive response team has begun to pursue absconders who walked away, and fugitive warrants are being enforced.

In Missouri, a parole board member and an employee were chastised publicly for playing word games during parole hearings. A Department of Corrections Inspector General's report described how a member of the parole board and an employee allegedly played a word game using chosen words or song titles of the day, such as "platypus" and "Hound Dog." If one of them said the word, they would earn one point and if the inmate repeated it, they would earn two points. While prisoners pleaded for their freedom, the two giggled and kept score. Critics of the parole board have described board membership as a "plum place" for former lawmakers; the member involved in the word game was a former state representative and earned over $85,000 for his position on the board. Many have no correctional or law enforcement experience at all. Several other employees knew of the game and did nothing. The parole board member resigned, but the parole employee was not named in any of the reports.

Source: Bogan, 2017; Gehrke, 2016.

bribes averaging $1,000, although one payoff was $3,000. Federal authorities said the four officers worked at two Houston parole offices, where allegations of bribery and exchanges of sexual favors had been the target of investigation for some time. The inspector general's office of the Texas Department of Corrections, the FBI, the Houston Police, and the Texas Rangers were involved in the investigation, which started when an inmate reported to a state legislator's office that he or she had been "shaken down" for money and sex (Ward, 2013). The In the News box describes more recent cases.

In other states, there have been scandals regarding probation departments. In Massachusetts, probation officials were accused of giving jobs to relatives and friends of state legislators (Levenson, 2010). In Cook County (Chicago), the head of probation was removed after a newspaper investigation series that exposed the fact that the office had lost track of hundreds of offenders and overlooked new crimes (Dizikes and Lighty, 2014). There was also an investigation of the practice of probation officers working with police officers to conduct illegal searches of probationers' homes. Some offenders alleged that contraband was planted and they were coerced to become informants for the FBI and law enforcement (Dizikes and Lighty, 2014). In response, there has been a proposal to fund body cameras for probation officers to protect them from allegations that they plant evidence or steal items from probationers' homes. Initially the program will equip 64 probation officers. The largest proposed use of body cameras for probation officers will occur in Georgia where all the officers in the state are expected to wear them once the program is fully implemented (Lighty, 2016). The ethical issue box below explores the question of whether probation officers should use their powers of search to help law enforcement avoid the need for warrants.

ETHICAL ISSUE

Should Probation Officers Partner with Law Enforcement to Search Probationers' Homes?

Law

In *Griffin v. Wisconsin*, 483 U.S. 868, 1987, the Supreme Court upheld warrantless searches of probationers' homes under a special needs analysis. Specifically, the Court held that probationers were under a restricted form of liberty and that probation officers had special duties of supervision that justified the intrusion of privacy. Most state corrections probation orders moot the issue anyway by requiring, as a condition of probation, that the offender allow probation officers into their home at any hour of the day or night. Some states may give probationers (or parolees) more comprehensive rights, such as requiring a probation officer to have reasonable suspicion, but there is no Fourth Amendment right recognized that a probation officer must have a warrant, even if accompanied by a law enforcement officer. Generally, bringing law enforcement officers is reasonable because of safety concerns for the probation officer who may or may not, depending on the state, carry a weapon.

Policy

The policies of offices may require home visits and searches periodically to supervise offenders on caseloads. Probation officers may be asked to perform searches by law enforcement specifically because of suspicions that do not give rise to probable cause, and to do a search based solely on a request from law enforcement to avoid the need for a warrant may violate policy.

Ethics

As with all ethical issues, we begin by examining the issue considering law, policy, and then ethics. If there is no law that prohibits the practice, and the policy of the agency allows it, then we look at the inherent "right or wrongness" of the action. Searches are an invasion of privacy of the offender but also the offender's family members. If he or she lives with a relative or friend, those individuals have less Fourth Amendment protections than other citizens

(continued)

merely because of their association with an offender. On the other hand, searches by probation officers may uncover contraband, including weapons, so one might imagine that they may prevent serious violent crimes. As we have discussed many times previously in this text, utilitarianism would weigh the costs and benefits of the practice. In this case, it seems as if the benefit of probation (over prison) for the offender outweighs the invasion of privacy. The disutility for others requires, however, that the searches are done with some form of protections, for example, only with reasonable suspicion, only with supervisor approval, only with the minimal amount of disruption (e.g., the search doesn't extend to rooms lived in exclusively by those other than the offender). While partnering with law enforcement might be perceived as skirting the Fourth Amendment requirements of a warrant, probationers are on a restricted liberty status.

They have different legal protections than others in the community and, thus, just as prisoners in a prison cannot expect warrants before searches of their cell, neither can probationers expect the same degree of liberty as those who have not been convicted of crimes.

If such searches are done for other, ulterior motives, however, then their ethical justification is more suspect. If law enforcement officers use probation officers to coerce probationers to be informants, that would be using both parties and is a violation of the categorical imperative (do not treat others as a means . . .). The duty of a probation officer is to supervise and file violation reports when necessary, but it is not to help create informants for the FBI or local law enforcement. That would be using the powers invested in the role in a way that exceeds and is contrary to the duties of the role.

A Dallas (Texas) County audit revealed that officers mishandled 70 percent of cases, not following departmental procedures when handling technical violations. Like the Colorado audit, probation officers did not file violation reports when offenders had positive drug tests or did not pay their fees. Staff members from the probation department argue that strict policies regarding violations apply only to certain categories of offenders and that technical violations must be responded to using discretion and common sense, typically with additional conditions, not violation and revocation. The audit was requested by a judge who had not been informed of violations, such as repeated DWIs. The judge stated that if she couldn't trust that probation officers were enforcing conditions, she would disband the special DWI court. The auditors' recommendations included the following:

- Add pertinent e-mails about cases into the probationer's main file.
- Document all appearances by a probationer before a judge.
- Better inform the judges about the policies for sanctioning probationers with technical violations.
- Develop standard auditing forms and follow up with another audit when problems are found.
- Eliminate a policy that allows probation officers to work from home.
- Update probation department manual.
- Ensure probation officers' ongoing policy training is more timely (Emily, 2014).

The *New York Times* investigation of New Jersey halfway houses, described more fully in Chapter 12, detailed numerous instances of staff misconduct, including drinking on duty, notifying residents of "surprise" drug tests or forging test results completely, dealing drugs to residents, engaging in sexual relationships with residents, reading self-help books to inattentive residents instead of conducting actual group therapy, and making up case progress reports or cutting and pasting the same report in numerous case files (in one case, 30 case files had exactly the same progress report entered with just the name changed) (Dolnick, 2012b).

The unfortunate reality is that a few people can taint the entire agency or program and, even though community correctional alternatives are sorely needed, programs will be eliminated if perceived as allowing violence, drug use, or other forms of misconduct to occur. Staff members cannot be held responsible for parolees or probationers who commit new crimes if the employee has been completing their duties of supervision. A probation or parole officer or a halfway house employee can only do the supervision and programmatic tasks assigned to them; offenders still ultimately decide to commit a new crime and some of them cannot be deterred regardless of the actions of correctional employees. However, misconduct in the form of negligence can clearly contribute to new crimes by not removing the offender from the street after warning signs are clear. Other forms of misconduct, such as selling drugs to residents or sexually assaulting them, are not excusable no matter how understaffed or undertrained staff members are. Chief executive officers (CEOs) and administrators of private and public community correction facilities have ethical obligations to not accept more residents than the facility can safely accommodate and to maintain proper staffing levels and programming opportunities. To do less is to ignore one's ethical obligations, not to mention contractual obligations.

Explanations for Misconduct

The explanations for correctional misconduct can be described in similar ways to those in the law enforcement chapters, where they were divided into individual explanations, organizational explanations, and societal explanations.

Individual Explanations

Correctional managers attribute misconduct to low pay and poor screening during hiring (Mesloh, Wolf, and Henych, 2003). Law enforcement has made great strides in developing tools to help hire the most qualified individuals; however, corrections is decades behind in the research into and use of assessment tools. It may be that corrections will never catch up because the low pay and low status attached to the job discourage many from applying. Only in times of high unemployment do correctional agencies have no trouble finding qualified applicants. More often, they struggle to fill positions. There is no doubt that personality tests, more detailed background checks, and a stronger interview process would screen out some individuals unsuitable for the job. Some individuals simply cannot be trusted with the power and some COs seek the position in a long-term plan to smuggle drugs. One assumes that a more stringent background investigation would expose these individuals.

Another individual explanation of misconduct is posttraumatic stress disorder (PTSD). Like law enforcement, there is a growing recognition that some misconduct of correctional officers may be due to chronic or traumatic stress. As described earlier, correctional officers are often the victims of serious assaults by inmates; they have also been spat on, had body waste thrown on them, and sometimes subjected to horrible working conditions. It is important to remember that when there is no air conditioning, correctional officers are also spending their day in buildings that top 100 degrees. When toilets back up, correctional officers also must put up with the stench. When inmates are screaming for hours at a time because of mental illness or just because they feel like it, correctional officers must listen. When an inmate stabs their cellmate in the eyeball with a pencil, or disembowels a rival, or brutally rapes a snitch, correctional officers are the first on the scene. They also see their peers assaulted and suffer injuries themselves. There is virtually no research on the issue, but it is not hard to imagine that exposure to the incidents that occur in prison may create PTSD symptoms of flashbacks, hypervigilance, insomnia, alcohol or drug abuse, depression, and anger issues. It is reported that the suicide rate for correctional officers is twice as high as police officers or the general public. It is possible that some of the brutality by correctional officers is due, not to sadistic people being attracted to the job, but the job changing individuals and creating symptomatology that includes brutal behavior toward inmates. As in law enforcement, admitting the need for help goes against the macho culture, and for correctional officers, there is even less awareness of the problem than in law enforcement (Lisitsina, 2015; Spinaris, Denhof, and Kellaway, 2012).

As in law enforcement, a few correctional professionals will be crooks first and officers second; they use the job to pursue their deviant interests. Many others, however, probably slide into corruption because of a lack of organizational support for ethical behavior. Also, as in law enforcement, officers who are stressed and burned out may be the most vulnerable to ethical relativism and bad decisions. If the organization does not support and nurture ethical workers, there will inevitably be those who slide down the slippery slope.

A prison is an interesting place in that individuals work together over long periods of time, and often they live in small towns where acquaintances and family members also work at the prison. Male and female officers work in close proximity for long hours, sometimes they engage in sexual relationships, sometimes they marry, sometimes they divorce, and sometimes they have affairs with other staff members (or even inmates) while they are married. In some prison towns, everyone seems to be related to or have some type of relationship with a prison employee. While people's personal lives are their own, sometimes the personal lives of correctional officers, like police officers, influence their professional ethics. For instance, if a disciplinary sergeant is married to a CO who has written a ticket on an inmate, can that sergeant truly be objective when determining punishment? What happens when an inmate accuses an officer of sexual harassment and the grievance officer is the wife of the accused officer? Sometimes male and female COs allow a sexually charged atmosphere to develop where sexual joking and innuendos are rampant, and the atmosphere encourages officers to engage in the same type of behavior with inmates—obviously an inappropriate and unprofessional interaction. Correctional officers practically live with the inmates. If they pull double shifts, they may spend up to 16 or even 20 hours at a time with inmates. This familiarity with inmates sometimes tempts officers to engage in unethical behaviors.

The discretion and authority inherent in the role of correctional, probation, or parole officer takes maturity to handle as well as a strong internal ethical code. Other individual characteristics associated with misconduct have not been identified by research.

Organizational Explanations

When the abuse in Iraq's Abu Ghraib prison was exposed, many made comparisons between the behaviors of military prison correctional officers and those of

ETHICAL DILEMMA

You are a correctional sergeant who is assigned as disciplinary sergeant. You process disciplinary "tickets" written by COs against inmates and determine the punishment. If the inmate appeals your decision, it goes to a lieutenant, but the vast number of cases are dealt with at your level. The disciplinary case before you is one where an inmate has been accused of having contraband in his cell, in this case a knife. This is a very serious charge and the punishment should be loss of good time and segregation. The inmate swears that the knife isn't his and it has been planted by other inmates to get him in trouble. He is a "jailhouse lawyer" who files a steady stream of lawsuits against officers and the state. You also consider the officer involved, who has stated in front of other officers that the inmate deserves to get taught a lesson and that he should be sent "down" (to segregation). The other wrinkle is this officer is your brother. You have a gut feeling that the inmate is telling the truth, but the only evidence is that the knife was found in his cell—pretty strong evidence that it was his.

Law

The Supreme Court has held that inmates must have some form of due process before a neutral hearing body before having good time taken away. The disciplinary process in place today typically utilizes correctional sergeants or lieutenants and this has been accepted as neutral even though the hearing officer may have ties to the officers who write the tickets. There is a law that makes having a knife in prison a felony, which may subject the inmate to additional charges if you find him guilty. There is also a law against correctional officers or anyone else from lying on the official documents involved in filing a disciplinary charge; however, it is extremely rare, if ever, that someone is prosecuted, even if they are found to be lying.

Policy

The formal policies of a prison are that the inmates should be given due process before being punished. The informal policies of some prisons are that the disciplinary proceedings are merely pro forma exercises to meet court requirements, and inmates' appearances in front of these disciplinary boards are always exercises in futility.

Ethics

In this case, the disciplinary sergeant has the duty to evaluate the facts, decide, and assess punishment if necessary. The weight to assign to the credibility of the inmate, the officer, and/or other inmates is discretionary. The sergeant in this case would certainly be well within the norm if he found the inmate guilty and took away good time. Under ethical formalism, however, it would be his or her ethical duty to investigate if there was any doubt, even if it meant going against one's brother. How likely this is to occur is another matter. Some disciplinary officers split the difference by finding guilt but assessing a lesser punishment. This may be personally more palatable, but doesn't meet the necessity of doing one's duty as a fact finder. Arguably it also doesn't stop the process of using the disciplinary system to informally punish certain inmates who engage in legal, but unwanted, activity by staff members. Utilitarianism would evaluate the greater good. Does it result in a greater good to ensure that the jailhouse lawyer who takes up state resources gets punished, regardless of whether he had a knife, or is the greater good to protect the integrity of the disciplinary process? Egoism would also be concerned with how the decision would affect the relationship with one's brother. Most ethical systems would support investigating to see if there were any credible witnesses to the charge of possessing contraband.

correctional officers in U.S. prisons. The comparisons were hard to ignore because several of the worst abusers were correctional officers in civilian life, and the person who helped set up the Abu Ghraib prison was Lane McCotter, an ex-head of the Texas, New Mexico, and Utah prison systems (Ward, 2004). Allegations of misconduct in prisons and jails in the United States that were like what took place in Abu Ghraib include (Butterfield, 2004)

- male inmates being forced to wear pink underwear as punishment (Arizona),
- inmates being stripped as punishment (Pennsylvania),

- inmates being made to wear black hoods (Virginia), and
- using dogs to attack inmates (Texas).

The Commission on Safety and Abuse in America's Prisons (2006) was created after the scandal at Abu Ghraib. This national commission was tasked to examine U.S. prison conditions and chaired by a former U.S. attorney general and a chief judge of the Third Circuit. The commission spent several years holding hearings and obtained testimony from researchers, experts, prison staff members, and family members concerning the state of prisons in this country. (The entire report or an executive summary can be accessed by going to www.vera.org/project/commission-safety-and-abuse-americas-prisons). The commission concluded that violence in prisons was partially caused by inactive and unproductive inmates and an overuse of force by officers. They also found that medical services were inadequate, and the use of high-tech segregation (supermax prisons) was counterproductive and needed to be reduced.

The commission went on to conclude that the culture in prison was also due to underqualified and underpaid staff and that to reduce violence, steps needed to be taken to reduce crowding; promote productive programming; improve classification; reduce the use of pepper spray, Tasers, and other uses of force; and support community and family bonds of inmates. Their major finding was that a culture of violence needed to be replaced with a culture of mutual respect. This was necessary not only because it would make the prison a better place to live for inmates—it would also improve the working conditions of correctional staff members. As stated by a correctional official giving testimony, "When you go to work in a place that has a tendency to be condescending, negative, vulgar, that can show up in your life" (Commission..., 2006: 67).

It cannot be denied that the very environment of an incarceration facility sometimes brings out the worst in people. Many people have described the culture of prison as a "jungle" where inmates and officers are affected by pervasive hopelessness and negativity. While, typically, very few officers engage in serious abuse, the culture of the institution protects them because officers are always right and inmates are always wrong.

The informal culture of a prison is created by administrators and staff. If administrators turn a blind eye to misconduct and excessive force, then COs will feel free to engage in such activity, and ethical officers will quit or succumb to temptation. If the administration of an institution pays only lip service to rehabilitation for inmates, then it should be no surprise when officers became lethargic and negative. Worse, if leaders are unethical, then it is unlikely that ethics will flourish in the organization. In many of the case studies and news stories presented in these chapters, top leaders exhibited the worst models of leadership. They were exposed for their bribery and economic corruption, but it isn't hard to imagine that they exhibited poor ethics in other ways as well. Also, top administrators often seem to focus on suppressing investigations of wrongdoing and thwart employee discipline rather than provide clear direction for those employees who tried to do their job ethically.

Unions have been seen by researchers as a force resistant to rehabilitation, concerned only with individual benefits for members rather than the mission or goal of corrections. Unions provide legal assistance to officers accused of wrongdoing and support officers who, many would argue, have no business working in corrections. This is like police unions that defend police officers who are guilty of using excessive force. Union representatives would argue that they only ensure that the accused receive their rightful due process after being accused, and it is certainly true that accused employees deserve due process just like everyone else. However, what has happened in some instances is that when some correctional officers come forward to testify against the accused, they are vilified and treated as enemies of the union. This one-sided position that officers can do no wrong—except for the wrong of speaking out against other officers—is problematic and a disservice to those officers who try to do the right thing.

Stohr et al. (2000) developed a survey instrument to measure the ethics of correctional workers. In their study, they could find few significant individual correlates that predicted ethical beliefs or behavior, but they did find that the type of institution affected officers' attitudes. Mesloh, Wolf, and Henych (2003) found that the existence of a deviant subculture among correctional officers affected misconduct. These two academic studies place the responsibility of running an ethical organization on the shoulders of leaders who set the culture.

In cases of abuse in prison, the reasons seem to be a failure of leadership and lack of discipline, training, and supervision. When prison leaders ignore violations on the part of staff and do not clearly convey that the mission is to run a safe and secure prison without the corrupting presence of extra-legal force, the result is more likely to be a spiral of violence where hatred grows on each side.

Another useful way to understand prison corruption by staff members is to consider the procedural justice research. Tyler's (2006) original work on the importance of believing in the legitimacy of the law has been applied to various elements of the criminal justice system, including corrections. As discussed in prior chapters, the concept of **procedural justice** (Tyler, 2006, 2010/2011) includes the idea that the perception of legitimacy (of legal authorities) comes about when the elements of procedural justice are present and treatment is fair; specifically: participation (letting people speak), neutrality (governing by rules neutrally and consistently), dignity and respect, and illustrate trustworthiness (authorities are sincerely concerned with well-being) (Jackson, Tyler, Bradford, Taylor, and Shiner, 2010; Rottman, 2007). Research has shown that if legal authorities are perceived as legitimate, this leads to people following the law, even without monitoring, and encourages rule following.

Several studies have explored procedural justice principles in corrections, and findings indicate that inmates' perceptions of procedural justice lead to a belief in the legitimacy of correctional authorities, while feelings of injustice seem to affect recidivism (Jackson et al., 2010; Rottman, 2007). In another study, prisoners who believed in a "just world" expressed less anger, reported greater well-being, and were less likely to have problem behaviors even after controlling for criminal and personal backgrounds (Dalbert and Filke, 2007). A Dutch study found that inmates perceived more procedural justice was present in units where correctional officers were more likely to be

QUOTE & **QUERY**

Security and control—given necessities in a prison environment—only become a reality when dignity and respect are inherent in the process.

Source: A prison warden, cited in Commission on Safety and Abuse in America's Prisons, 2006: 15.

? Why is it so hard to run a prison where dignity and respect toward inmates exist?

procedural justice
The idea that the perception of legitimacy of legal authorities comes about when legal authorities practice fairness, participation, neutrality, respect, and illustrate trustworthiness.

female, had more favorable attitudes toward rehabilitation, and where there was a higher officer-to-inmate ratio (Beijersbergen, 2015).

Just as with police organizations, correctional officers also perceive varying levels of procedural justice in their organizations relative to how they are treated by management. Baker, Gordon, and Taxman (2015) found that correctional officers who had a say in decisions, a sense that institutional rules were impartial, and the perception that management utilized motivation and encouragement had significantly higher perceptions of procedural justice. Findings indicate that workers who have higher levels of belief in the procedural justice of their agency and believe they are being treated fairly are probably more likely to behave ethically (Lambert, 2003; Lambert, Hogan, and Allen, 2006; Lambert, Hogan, and Griffin, 2007; Pollock et al., 2012). Lambert (2003) found that procedural justice perceptions had a significant positive effect on organizational commitment. Lambert, Hogan, and Allen (2006) found that both "outcome" and procedural justice were related to job stress, but procedural justice was the strongest predictor (in a negative direction) for job stress. Lambert, Hogan, and Griffin (2007), in another study, found that both outcome and procedural justice had negative relationships with job stress and organizational commitment. However, only procedural justice influenced job satisfaction (Lambert, Hogan, and Griffin, 2007).

The previously mentioned studies do not prove that officers who perceive procedural justice is high in their organization are more likely to treat inmates ethically; however, the "trickle down" theory of ethical management is that officers will treat inmates the way they perceive they are being treated by management—with fairness, compassion, and respect, or with less than fairness, compassion, and respect. It becomes easier to justify unethical actions if one feels victimized. Obviously, if employees are expected to be responsible, loyal, and treat each other and inmates with respect, administrators should practice these same behaviors (Houston, 1999; Souryal, 1999; Wright, 2001). Furthermore, staff members who are coerced by management to do unethical or illegal actions are more likely to behave in unethical and illegal ways by their own initiative.

Societal Explanations

As mentioned earlier, the community helps to create the correctional environment by their tacit or direct endorsement of the informal subcultural norm that inmates deserve less due process and legal protection than the rest of us. When juries acquit correctional officers solely because the victim of a brutal beating was an inmate, this endorsement reinforces unethical subcultural norms. When criminal correctional officers are not prosecuted and simply fired or allowed to retire and collect their pensions, this provides a message that there are few costs involved in such misconduct. If the state doesn't care enough about corrections to allocate enough funding to provide decent programming, training, or hiring of qualified staff, it sends a message that the prison (or community correctional program) houses throw-away people who fall outside legal protection. Once a group is removed from the envelope of protection of civil society, then there are no limits to the abuses that might be visited upon them, and the attitude that such conduct lies outside the bounds of law inevitably, it seems, transcends to abuses against others. If groups of correctional officers can inflict physical beatings on prisoners, often these officers also threaten physical retaliation against other correctional officers for perceived disloyalty. If no one stops widespread sexual innuendos directed to and exploitation of female inmates, then female correctional officers sometimes find themselves the victims of the same type of behavior. If inmate accounts and property are considered fair game to steal from, then it becomes more likely that state monies are also embezzled. The point is that there can be no dividing line between those whom one should treat ethically and those who do not "deserve" ethical treatment. One's behavior is either ethical or not, legal or not, without regard to the target of it. If society wants an ethical correctional system, then we must demand it and expect that even murderers will be treated according to the law.

Recall that in Chapter 7 we made the argument that the community helps to create a corrupt police department if they allow or encourage illegal sanctions to take place against those they don't like (e.g., the homeless or rowdy youth) because once the bonds of legality are removed, the same treatment may be directed to anyone. The guardian style of policing reflects the idea that the primary goal of law enforcement should be to enforce the law; any other goal (such as "catching bad guys") runs the risk of utilizing utilitarian thinking that may subvert law to another end. The same is true with corrections. There is no ethical or legal justification for punishment that is not the product of formal due process and restrained by legal guidelines, regardless of what the inmate has done. No ethical system supports such conduct; even under utilitarianism, the cost to justice and due process is just too high. In the news account below, the quote from the district attorney echoes these sentiments.

▐▐ IN THE NEWS | *Punishing Crimes Against Criminals*

Six former NYC jail officers were sentenced in 2016 to terms of 4.5–6.5 years in prison for a brutal beating of an inmate in 2012. The Bronx District attorney, after the guilty verdict was announced, was reported to have said: "A Bronx jury has sent a clear message that a uniform and a badge does not absolve anyone from committing a crime, and that even a criminal behind bars deserves to be treated like a human being."

The trial, which lasted two months, involved an assistant chief for security and two captains. The prosecution showed that a former assistant chief for security, and a former captain, ordered five members of an elite correction squad to beat Jamal Lightfoot, an inmate at Rikers. Allegedly, Hunter was perceived to be an inmate with an attitude and the assistant chief of security told officers to "kick his teeth in." Lightfoot testified that he was pummeled with fists and boots even as he lay in a fetal position. He suffered fractures to both eye sockets,

among other injuries, and still suffers from blurry vision and headaches. The defense rested their case without calling a single witness. The jury returned guilty verdicts in a range of charges, including attempted assault in the first degree, assault in the second degree, falsifying business records, and official misconduct. The head of the correctional union called the jury verdict a travesty.

Between 2012 and 2016, 26 other correctional officers had been prosecuted in cases of excessive force and/or cover-ups. Of the 15 closed cases, 9 were convicted and 6 were acquitted. Prosecutors and others noted how difficult it was to obtain guilty verdicts against correctional officers because of jury members' lack of sympathy for inmates and tendency not to believe them. Given that reality, perhaps the defense chose not to present any evidence to counteract the state's case because they assumed they didn't have to. It is likely that there will be an appeal.

Source: Hu, 2016; Hu and Pastor, 2016.

■ Responses to Corruption

Correctional managers can and should generate a strong anti-corruption policy (obviously, managers should not be engaging in corrupt practices themselves). Such a policy would include (McCarthy, 1991)

- proactive measures such as mechanisms to investigate and detect wrongdoing,
- reduced opportunities for corruption,
- screening of employees using state-of-the-art psychological tools,
- improved working conditions, and
- providing good role models in the form of supervisors and administrators who follow the appropriate code of ethics.

The Commission on Safety and Abuse in American Prisons (2006) developed a comprehensive list of recommendations to reduce the "culture of violence," including the following:

- Improve staffing levels, hiring, and training
- Provide independent oversight for complaints and investigations of misconduct
- Create a national database of violent incidents and misconduct
- Increase access to the courts by repealing or amending the Prison Litigation Reform Act
- Increase the level of criminal prosecution of wrongdoers (perhaps using federal prosecutions)
- Strengthen professional standards

Souryal (2009: 33) discusses the "civility" of a correctional institution as being influenced by the level of education required for hire, the amount of in-service training officers receive, the policies regarding employees who act in unethical ways, and the presence of a professional association or union that can effectively monitor the agency's practices. He also discusses the importance of integrated thinking (use of reasoning and wisdom) and moral agility (distinguishing between moral choices). To improve the ethical climate of an agency, he advocates upgrading the quality of personnel, establishing quality-based supervisory techniques, strengthening fiscal controls, and emphasizing true ethical training.

Wright (2001) offers seven principles as a guide for how administrators and supervisors should treat employees:

1. Safety
2. Fair treatment
3. Due process
4. Freedom of expression
5. Privacy
6. Participation in decision making
7. Information

Burrell (2000) directs attention to probation and proposes that to prevent stress and burnout, probation (and parole) organizations should provide clear direction, manage proactively, establish priorities if there are high workloads, ensure stability and constancy, be consistent in expectations, manage with fairness, enforce accountability, delegate authority, provide proper resources, maintain communication, and allow participative decision making.

Barrier et al. (1999) discussed an ethics training program with correctional officers in which part of the training involved having the officers identify important elements of an ethics code. Many of the elements the officers described had to do with the practices of management rather than officers:

- Treating all staff fairly and impartially
- Promoting based on true merit
- Showing no prejudice
- Leading by example
- Developing a clear mission statement
- Creating a positive code of ethics (a list of dos, rather than don'ts)
- Creating a culture that promotes performance, not seniority
- Soliciting staff input on new policies
- Being respectful
- Getting the word out that upper management cares about ethics

As discussed earlier, correctional administrators in the 1970s and 1980s had to deal with court decisions that were decided in favor of prisoners. In response, correctional administrators sometimes barely complied with the letter of a court ruling, much less the spirit of the ruling. The career path of an administrator, with its investment of time and energy and the mandate to be a "company man," often creates an immersion in bureaucratic thinking to the point that an individual loses sight of ethical issues. For instance, protecting the department or the director from scandal or litigation becomes more important than analyzing the behavior that created the potential for scandal in the first place. If decision making becomes influenced solely by short-term gains or by avoiding scandal, decisions may be unsupported by any ethical system.

Administrators are responsible for what happens in their facility, and training, supervision, and careful attention to assignments can avoid many problems. It should go without saying that administrators and managers should take pains to avoid illegal or unethical behavior themselves. Administrators should act as role models and never engage in behavior that may be misconstrued as sexual coercion or be perceived by their employees as offensive. Supervisors have a higher duty than coworkers to set a tone for an office free from sexual innuendo that may lead to a description of the workplace as a hostile work environment. Supervisors have an ethical and legal duty to stop sexual humor, inappropriate touching, disparaging and unprofessional remarks about inmates, racial jokes, and inappropriate behavior before there is a complaint. Top administrators often have an outward orientation because their role is to communicate with legislators, the central office, and the community; however, a good administrator does not ignore his or her own backyard. Management by walking around (MBWA) and having a good sense of what is happening in the institution have always been the marks of a good administrator and are also the best defense against having the institution ending up on the front page of the newspaper.

In community corrections, there seems to be the same management tendency to hide or ignore wrongdoing on the part of individual officers. This may be a misguided utilitarianism in managers who are attempting to protect the organization from public scandal, or it may be simply self-interested egoism from managers who fear that the blame will be directed at them. For whatever reason, there seems to be a tendency to ignore officers who are obviously unable or unwilling to do the job. If this is true, it's not surprising that some probation and parole officers seem to have little moral authority over the clients they supervise.

Another way to respond to misconduct and corruption in corrections is to shift the orientation away from punishment and retribution. The high incarceration rate in the United States has led to the prison–industrial complex, which has provided jobs and profits to legions of companies and people. The penal harm movement discussed in Chapter 11 has generated a cultural message that inmates and offenders are worthless, deserving of whatever harm befalls them in the corrections systems. Unfortunately, some offenders are violent and manipulative and so all get treated as if they were. Violence in prison is often a spiral, where correctional officers (as in ADX in Florence, Colorado; the California prison where the Green Wall correctional officers operated; and the Los Angeles jail) decide to inflict illegal punishment after inmates have assaulted correctional officers. The reaction is understandable, but illegal. It is also the case that once such illegal violence begins, it tends to spread to target inmates who are not violent, and, more tellingly, such violence has a way of targeting even other correctional officers, who are threatened or sometimes even assaulted when they are perceived as rats or traitors. At that point, there truly is no difference between those who wear the correctional officer uniform and those who wear the prisoner uniform. Once one is outside the law and knows it, subsequent illegalities to cover up and protect oneself become almost inevitable.

A New Era? Procedural Justice/Restorative Justice

Recall from Chapter 11 that there seems to be a new vision of corrections that is permeating legislatures, advocates, and governmental agencies. There is a growing realization that this country incarcerates too many people and that the prisons are warehouses, not places of reform. If such a shift is strong enough to permeate the culture of corrections, then we may see fundamental changes in the ethics and expectations for correctional officers and other correctional professionals. Once again, it is important to note that most professionals perform their jobs ethically and with integrity. What might be the result of a cultural shift is that they will feel more supported in their adherence to ethical standards of behavior.

The principles of procedural justice seem to show the most promise in reforming the prison culture. If correctional officers are managed under the principles of fairness, voice, respect, neutrality, and trustworthiness as described in an earlier section, then they will be more likely to treat prisoners in the same way. This approach can be described as evidence-based in that there are research findings that show supervising people under these principles does achieve behavioral change.

A major shift in the ideology of punishment may have been spurred by the economic burden that the penal harm era has generated; the cost of imprisoning so many people simply cannot be sustained. However, there is also a moral element in that many advocates consider that the pendulum has swung too far toward severe prison terms, especially for drug offenders. There are alternative approaches that are not based on a punishment ideology. The restorative justice movement was mentioned briefly in Chapter 3. It is an approach that seeks to provide reparation rather than retribution.

The historical origins of and analogies to restorative justice can be found throughout recorded history. Early laws demanded victim compensation, and reparation has a much longer history than penal servitude. Many advocates now believe that restorative justice appropriately places the emphasis back onto the victims and can be life-affirming and positive for the offender as well (Perry, 2002). The key is to find a method of restoration that is meaningful and somehow related to the offense instead of merely punitive labor—such as the infamous rock pile, which is devoid of worth to the victim, the offender, or society. The Quote and Query box is Braithwaite's summary of restorative justice.

Peacemaking corrections also offers an approach of care and of *wholesight*, or looking at what needs to be done with both the heart and the head (Braswell and Gold, 2002). Both restorative justice and peacemaking corrections are consistent with the ethics of care and might be considered "feminine" models of justice because of the emphasis on needs rather than retribution. It is said that a retributive, punitive orientation results in an offender's perception of unfairness (through denial of victim, denial of injury, or a belief that a more serious victimization was visited upon the offender). A different model may reduce those feelings and force the offender to squarely face his or her own responsibility. Arguably, a restorative justice program directs attention to the injuries of the victim and does not involve stigma, banishment, or exclusion for the offender. The offender then would have more difficulty generating rationalizations and excuses for his or her behavior.

Programs under the rubric of restorative justice include sentencing circles, family group counseling, victim–offender mediation, community reparation boards, and victim education programs (Umbreit, Coates, and Vos, 2002). Such programs instill a strong dose of morality and redemption, and the public seems to respond favorably to that.

Dzur and Wertheimer (2002) discuss how restorative justice can further forgiveness, but they ask the question "Is forgiveness a social good?" They argue against the idea that what is good for the individual victim is also good for everyone else. They point out that forgiving offenders may be good for the individual victim but may not be good for the "class of victims" who have yet to be victimized. They argue that utilitarianism might support punishment even if the individual victim forgives the offender because the greater good will accrue to society from deterrence. Of course, there is no empirical approach that could determine (or has yet determined) whether punishment deters more offenders than forgiveness.

Restorative justice programs are looked upon with favor by some victims' rights groups because of the idea of restoration and restitution for victims. However, the approach is oriented to meeting the needs of both victims and offenders, and in some cases it may be that the offender is needier. Would a victim reject such an approach? Should the victim be able to veto this approach and demand traditional punishment? Is it possible for a victim to be too vindictive? Other victims' rights groups tend to

QUOTE & QUERY

Key values of restorative justice are healing rather than hurting, respectful dialogue, making amends, caring and participatory community, taking responsibility, remorse, apology, and forgiveness.

Source: Braithwaite, 2000: 300.

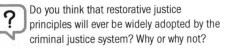 Do you think that restorative justice principles will ever be widely adopted by the criminal justice system? Why or why not?

peacemaking corrections An approach to corrections that depends on care and wholesight, or looking at what needs to be done with both the heart and the head.

be cautious about restorative justice programs in general because of the focus on offenders. The anger that victims feel toward offenders and the system that ignores their needs leaves little room for forgiveness. Most groups advocate harsher punishments, not restorative justice; they discuss "rights" rather than "needs" and thus draw their moral legitimacy from retribution rather than the ethics of care. However, other sources also argue that forgiveness and restorative justice are just as beneficial to the victim as the offender (Morris, 2000).

Restorative justice programs may lead to a greater sense of mission for correctional professionals and, therefore, decrease burnout and misconduct. However, there are ethical issues with such programs. First, because such interventions are benign, they have the potential to create net widening, further enlarging the scope of corrections over the citizenry. There are also questions of due process and whether restorative justice meets the traditional goals of crime prevention (Dzur and Wertheimer, 2002). Another issue is the potential privacy issues of the offender and other members who are involved. One of the strengths of restorative justice interventions is the inclusion of many parties, including the offender's family, coworkers, and friends, as well as the victim and the victim's support group. But what if some individuals important to the process choose not to participate? If even schools have trouble getting some parents to involve themselves in their children's progress, it is entirely possible that a juvenile who is otherwise qualified for a program would not be able to participate because of unwillingness of family members. Also, even when the process is perceived as a positive intervention, whenever state actors are involved, there is a potential for coercion, and some people react strongly to that idea.

Restorative justice programs would not be appropriate for all offenders; there will always be a need for incarceration facilities for the violent, recidivistic offenders who need to be incapacitated. It does, however, offer an approach that seems to be more positive for offenders and personnel alike. It provides a more optimistic vision and mission and, one assumes, creates better relationships between correctional professionals and offenders. Thus, it might be an approach where there is less burnout, cynicism, and unethical behavior.

The idea of having a prosocial, ethical correctional institution where inmates are not coddled, but neither are they abused, seems to be a difficult goal to achieve. Scandinavian countries have long been known for humane prisons. Of course, these countries have very few prisoners, compared to the United States. For instance, Norway's rate of incarceration (70 per 100,000) is about a tenth of the rate found in the United States. Experts point out that Norway and other Scandinavian countries enjoy very low crime rates, possibly because they invest much more in social welfare programs. The horrific massacre by Anders Behring Breivik in July 2011 has challenged the Scandinavian model of corrections. Breivik set off a car bomb in downtown Oslo, killing eight people, and then went to a holiday island where a group of teenagers were at a Labor party camp for young people. He shot and killed 69 people and wounded scores more. Still, according to Norwegian law, he was sentenced to only 21 years in prison. One of the important elements of Norway's prisons is that officers have an elevated status as compared to the United States. They go through one year of theoretical training and then a year of practical training at an academy (Adams, 2010).

It seems the concepts of individual respect, rehabilitation, and integration with the community were prevalent in American corrections in the 1970s, but fell by the wayside during the ramping up of the incarceration binge in the 1980s and the punitive era of the 1990s–2000s. As the saying goes, everything old is new again, and perhaps, that will be true in corrections as well if the principles of respect and rehabilitation are regenerated in the years to come. If so, the shift in mission will affect the duties and expectations of correctional professionals.

Conclusion

In this chapter, we examined various forms of misconduct by correctional professionals. Research has indicated that the very nature of a prison may encourage an abuse of power. It was also noted that much of the misconduct may occur because of the informal subculture and a loss of a sense of mission by professionals, as well as poor management. Responses to ethical misconduct and corruption in corrections lag behind the efforts previously reported in law enforcement. Suggestions include ethics training and improving management. Procedural justice research shows that if authorities practice fairness, neutrality, and the other elements of procedural justice, there is more faith in and compliance with rules. This concept applies to prisoners and correctional officers equally. Restorative justice principles may help to improve the sense of mission and commitment to ethical behavior by correctional workers, but legality should be the overriding theme of corrections as well as law enforcement. Regardless of what offenders have done, they are still protected by the law. Correctional professionals who agree with that premise are more likely to conduct themselves in an ethical manner.

Chapter Review

1. **Explain the Zimbardo experiment and what it might imply for correctional professionals.**

   The Zimbardo experiment of the 1970s put college men into an artificial prison as correctional officers or inmates. About one-third of the correctional officers became brutal and authoritarian, and prisoners became manipulative and exhibited signs of emotional distress and mental breakdown. It is widely used as evidence that placing people in absolute power over others breeds corruption.

2. **Describe types of misconduct by correctional officers, including the typology of misconduct by Souryal and McCarthy.**

   McCarthy's categories of misconduct include theft, trafficking, embezzlement, and misuse of authority. Under misuse of authority, he includes the following: gratuities (as bribes for legitimate or illegitimate activities), mistreatment/harassment or extortion, mismanagement, and miscellaneous abuses. Souryal's categories of corruption are malfeasance, misfeasance, and nonfeasance.

3. **Describe types of misconduct by community corrections professionals.**

   There are not as many news stories of corruption, but there have been instances of inappropriate influences and errors in parole release decisions, nepotism in awarding jobs in probation departments, and accepting bribes from offenders to get out of community service obligations or drug testing.

4. **Provide explanations for misconduct.**

   Similar individual, organization, and societal explanations for misconduct exist as were described in Chapter 7. Some reasons for misconduct involve hiring those who should not be in corrections. As in law enforcement, officers who are stressed and burned out may be the most vulnerable to ethical relativism and bad decisions. Organizational explanations include a failure of leadership and lack of discipline, training, and supervision. Management practices that do not provide the direction, mission, oversight, and training needed contribute to misconduct. Society is also at fault in that if we allow inmates to be mistreated because they are inmates, then that lawlessness tends to spread.

5. **Present some suggestions to decrease misconduct by correctional professionals.**

   McCarthy's suggestions are largely directed to management practices, including proactive measures such as mechanisms to investigate and detect wrongdoing, reduced opportunities for corruption, screening of employees using state-of-the-art psychological tools, improved working conditions, and providing good role models in the form of supervisors and administrators. Ethics training is also suggested. Finally, restorative justice is offered as a different approach to respond to criminal offenders that is more positive and less conducive to the creation of a subculture that supports mistreatment.

Study Questions

1. Describe Bomse's categories of misconduct.
2. Describe some of the reported instances of misconduct and corruption in prisons.
3. Describe some of the reported instances of misconduct in probation or parole.
4. What management practices were identified as contributing to an ethical workplace?
5. What are the principles of restorative justice? Contrast these with traditional models of justice.

Writing/Discussion Exercises

1. Write an essay on (or discuss) how you would implement an anti-corruption strategy in a prison known for brutality and other forms of corruption.
2. Write an essay on (or discuss) forgiveness. Would you want to meet with the murderer of a loved one? What would you want to ask him or her? Would you be able to forgive?
3. Write an essay on (or discuss) restorative justice. Find examples in your state. Do you agree or disagree with the philosophy of restorative justice? Why?

Key Terms

malfeasance	nonfeasance	procedural justice
misfeasance	peacemaking corrections	

ETHICAL DILEMMAS

Situation 1

You are a probation officer and have a specialized sex-offender caseload. The judge disagrees with a recommendation for a prison sentence and places an offender on probation. This man was convicted of molesting his four-year-old niece. One of the conditions of his probation is that he notifies you whenever he is around children. He becomes engaged to and moves in with a woman who has three children under the age of 12. You believe that the man is not repentant and that there is a good chance he will molest these children. Although the woman knows his criminal history, she does not seem to care and even allows him to babysit the young girls. The judge has indicated that he will not entertain new conditions or a revocation unless there is evidence of a crime, but you understand from the offender's counselor that the offender continues to be sexually aroused by children. What can you do? What should you do?

Situation 2

You are a probation officer with a DWI probationer who has not been reporting for any of the court-sanctioned programs, and a motion to revoke (MTR) was supposed to be filed. However, a high-ranking administrator in your office tells you not to file the MTR or take any other negative actions because the probationer is a personal friend and, anyway, he isn't a "serious criminal." What would you do?

Situation 3

You are the director of a restorative justice program in your community. It is set up for juvenile offenders and involves circle sentencing, in which the offender meets with family members, school officials, and the victim and the victim's relatives and friends. The circle comes up with what should be done, and often there is no punishment per se. Rather, the juvenile is connected with programs that can help him or her get back to school, get a job, or receive vocational training. In the case you are reviewing, you suspect that there are real questions as to whether the juvenile actually committed the burglary he is accused of. There is no evidence to link the juvenile with the crime, and he and his court-appointed attorney have claimed innocence. They then changed their plea and agreed to the restorative justice program, perhaps because if it is completed successfully, the juvenile will have no criminal record. Should you care whether the juvenile is innocent or not, given that the program is restorative, not punitive?

Situation 4

You are a prison warden, and a new CO comes to you and says she has been sexually harassed by the captain. You know that the captain has been with the prison for 20 years and has not had any negative reports in his record. On the one hand, you like him and think he is an excellent captain. On the other hand, this CO seems earnest and believable and is quite upset, so you believe something must have happened. What is the ethical course of action? What is the legal course of action?

Situation 5

You are a prison counselor in a co-ed prison and have some real concerns about your coworker's treatment of offenders. You hear him screaming obscenities at them in his office, and one time you saw him pat a female prisoner on the rear end and say, "Be sweet to me and I'll get you out of here." No one else seems to notice that anything is wrong. Could you have misinterpreted the exchange with the prisoner? Might it have been simply bad taste rather than sexual harassment? Should you do anything?

CAMP DELTA
JTF GUANTANAMO

Joe Raedle/Getty Images

There are now only 41 detainees at Guantanamo Bay compared to 800 or more when "enemy combatants" were held with no due process.

Learning Objectives

1. Identify the basic themes of the book.

2. Describe the basic elements of the "just war" debate and the "just means" discussion.

3. Describe the responses to 9/11.

4. Explain the human rights model of policing.

5. Present a method to resolve ethical dilemmas.

In this book, we have explored ethical issues in each of the subsystems of the criminal justice system. We have discovered certain themes that run through each of the subsystems:

- The presence of authority, power, force, and discretion
- Informal subcultures that sometimes are contrary to formal codes of ethics
- The importance of ethical leadership
- Tension between deontological ethical systems and teleological or "means–end" ethical analysis

In this final chapter, we will reiterate some of these themes and conclude with some last thoughts regarding how to behave in an ethical manner as a justice professional. We will review the basic themes of the book and the path to ethical decision making within a discussion of one of the most important ethical issues of our time—the response to terrorism.

Just Wars and Just Means

On September 11, 2001, the United States was changed forever. The terrorist attack on the World Trade Center was the single most devastating terrorist attack in this country and, indeed, the world with almost 3,000 deaths and the complete destruction of two buildings that stood as icons of Western capitalism. Although we had experienced earlier incidents—the 1993 bombing of the World Trade Center, the Oklahoma City bombing in 1995, and the bombing of the U.S.S. Cole in 2000—nothing prepared the country for the severity of the attack. The event traumatized a city, affected the American psyche, led to U.S. military engagement on foreign soil in two countries, and spurred the dramatic restructuring of federal agencies with the creation of the Department of Homeland Security. We have also seen pervasive changes in law enforcement at both the federal and the local levels, and the country is still mired in controversy over the responses taken in the "war on terror." In addition to governmental responses that took place immediately after 9/11, Edward Snowden's June 2013 exposure of NSA's domestic surveillance activities showed that the war on terror affected us in ways seen and unseen.

The threat of terrorism continues and it seems as if there has been an uptick in lone-wolf attacks in this country and worldwide. Law enforcement is the first responder to these incidents, and sometimes the target. In 2015, the San Bernardino attack killed 14 people and the Paris multiple attacks killed 130. In 2016, the Belgium airport and subway attacks killed 32 people, the Orlando shooting killed 50, the truck attack in Nice, France, killed 77, and an attack in a German Christmas market killed 12. In 2017, two truck attacks in London killed 7 people, 22 were killed at the Ariana Grande concert in Manchester, 5 people were killed in a truck attack in Stockholm, and 14 were killed in a bombing in the St. Petersburg, Russia, subway station. In addition to these incidents, there have been numerous others. It seems as if a week does not go by without some loss of life in this country or Europe from terrorist events. We should also be aware that the loss of life from terrorism in Europe and the United States pales in comparison to the rest of the world. For instance, between 2015 and July 2016, 658 deaths were due to terrorism in Western Europe and the United States; however, there were 28,031 deaths in the Middle East, Africa, and Asia. These deaths do not receive as much attention in the western media (Gamio and Meko, 2016).

The controversy over what means are acceptable responses to terrorism is related to criminal justice ethics because the war on terror involves not only military and federal agencies, but also every law enforcement and justice agency in the land may have occasion to be involved. Targets of terrorist activity include not only buildings and bridges in big cities but also dams, power plants, schools, and government buildings. In recent attacks, a hired van was used as a weapon to mow down civilians; a machete was used to hack victims; and easily obtained ingredients were used to make a bomb.

In response to terrorism, there is a prevalence of means–end thinking: the idea that what would usually be wrong can be justified to achieve a good end. We see this argument repeatedly in the war on terror and, surprisingly, some people seem to think it is a new argument. It isn't. Nor is terrorism a new threat.

Terrorism has been defined as the "deliberate, negligent, or reckless use of force against noncombatants, by state or non-state actors for ideological ends and in the absence of a substantively just legal process" (Rodin, 2004: 755). Terrorism has led to questions about what is appropriate or ethical in investigative techniques, individual privacy rights vis-à-vis the government, and what is legal and ethical in the detention

terrorism The deliberate, negligent, or reckless use of force against noncombatants, by state or non-state actors for ideological ends.

and treatment of prisoners. However, it is important to note that these are not new questions. From the very earliest philosophers, there has been a struggle to define and agree upon when it is right to wage war and what means are acceptable to secure victory. There is no coincidence in why we use the term *war* to denote a national challenge. We can see the same argument played out whether we are talking about the war on terror, the war on drugs, the war on illegal immigrants, or the war on crime. War implies that the normal rules don't apply and, arguably, justifies extreme methods (e.g., "All is fair in love and war."). Interestingly, however, philosophers have concluded that rules should apply and not everything is fair—even in war.

The traditional justification for war comes from natural law, and the second comes from positivist law. Classical "just war" theorists such as Hugo Grotius (1583–1645) have held that natural law gives sovereigns the right to use force when it is necessary:

- To uphold the good of the community

- When unjust injuries are inflicted on others

- To protect the state (Bellamy, 2004; Grotius, 1625/2005)

States are justified to engage in war when any of these events exist; otherwise, the war is unjust and immoral. However, natural law as a justification for war has been criticized because of the likelihood that leaders will use moral arguments to justify wars that are initiated for other means. For instance, some people criticized the U.S. invasion of Iraq. President Bush justified it under self-defense (because of the alleged presence of weapons of mass destruction) or protection (protecting the Iraqi people from Saddam Hussein), but some believed it was only to protect American interests in the oilfields. The problem with the natural law justification for armed conflict is that there are no bright lines to distinguish when the self-defense or protection justifications become "ripe." That is, there are incipient enemies around the globe and there are dictators who oppress their people—when does it become acceptable to go to war against them?

positivist law
Human-made law.

The second, more recent, justification for war comes from **positivist law**, which is man-made law. Increasingly, this is used as the only legitimate justification for war; legal incursions into the sovereignty of other nations are justified only under the auspices of international law as provided through the United Nations and other multilateral treaties and organizations (e.g., NATO). The problem with positivist law as the basis for justifying war is that no single authoritative legal body in international relations sits above all sovereigns, and international legal bodies do not include all countries and cover all circumstances (Bellamy, 2004).

Because of the lack of complete coverage of positivist law, natural law justifications continue to be used when military action is not mandated by the United Nations. There are always questions as to whether to intervene in internal conflicts within states when gross humanitarian violations have occurred, such as the ethnic cleansing campaigns in Rwanda in 1994 (the United States did not intervene), or the Bosnia conflict occurring between 1992 and 1995 (the United States eventually did intervene).

Discussions occurred over whether the United States should have intervened in countries involved in the Arab Spring in 2012 when citizen-led uprisings in Tunisia, Egypt, Libya, Yemen, Bahrain, Syria, and Algeria occurred with brutal repressive countermeasures taken by some respective governments. There is tension weighing whether to protect a people from violent actions from their government and respecting a sovereign state's autonomy. Some argued the United States should have become involved in the Ukraine after Russia took over Crimea in March 2014 by military force, while others argue the United States has no business being in Afghanistan, Iraq, or any country that does not pose a direct and immediate threat.

In 2017, President Trump's order to fire missiles at the Syrian airbase that delivered poison gas to a Syrian village was widely hailed as a humanitarian censure to a horrific and immoral assault; in this discussion, *natural law* would be used as the justification. In contrast, many fear that the United States would not honor the *positive law* obligations of NATO given President Trump's criticism of the agreement. While positive law does not provide comprehensive protections against unjust acts of war, using natural law or moral imperative justifications to engage in war can be misused. Therefore, limits on the moral justifications for war have been proposed, including the following (Bellamy, 2004):

- The violations must be knowable to all.
- The violations must be widespread and systematic.
- The force used must save more lives than it injures.

These are not too different from other justifications that have been offered by other writers. For instance, Crank and Gregor (2005: 230) and Hicks (2004) have offered the following justifications for any war:

- The threat must be grave, lasting, and certain.
- There are no other means to avert the threat.
- There must be a good probability of success.
- The means must not create a greater evil than the threat responded to.

These justifications seem to be consistent with a utilitarian system of ethics and are not inconsistent with ethical formalism because of the principle of forfeiture, which states that someone who impinges on others' rights forfeits his or her rights to the same degree.

Even if a military action can be justified by natural or positivist law, the second question is: what means are acceptable in fighting the war? Under utilitarianism, in determining "just means," the extent of the harm is weighed against the end or injury averted, just as when one asks if the war itself is justified. Ethical formalism does not look at the consequences of an action to justify it; however, the **principle of double effect** states that if one undertakes an action that is a good, but that also results in a negative end, if the negative end was not the intent of the actor, the good action and the good end can be considered a good. For instance, if one bombs a military target and innocents are harmed during the bombing, the act, if otherwise considered ethical, does not become unethical because of the death of civilians. However, if one intends to bomb a civilian target and does so to instill fear and psychological advantage over the enemy, then that would be immoral because it would be violating the categorical imperative.

principle of double effect The concept that a means taken for a good end that results in the good end but also in an inevitable, but unintended, bad effect is still considered ethical.

Today the more amorphous war on terror continues to spur discussions about acceptable means. There has been a good deal of argument and analysis over whether traditional "just war" arguments can be applied to the fight against terrorists (Crank and Gregor, 2005; Zohar, 2004). Smilansky (2004) argues that terrorists have no moral justification, and they attack democracies partially because the ethos and values of such countries prohibit taking an "any means necessary" response. However, the fact is that democratic governments have resorted to a variety of means in response to terrorist attacks that are arguably inconsistent with democratic values and the United States has undertaken acts that many consider illegal, immoral, and contrary to our ideals. Even though some of these acts occurred over 15 years ago, it is important to be aware of and continue to analyze them because the spectre of terrorism continues, as do the arguments about what is legal and/or moral in the fight against terrorism.

The Response to 9/11

Since 9/11, we have seen a fundamental shift in the goals and mission of law enforcement and public safety. This shift has included an expansion of the number of law enforcement agencies and personnel, a nationalization and/or militarization of law enforcement, a reduction of civil liberties, and a merging of immigration control and traditional law enforcement. One of the most dramatic changes after 9/11 has been the creation of the Department of Homeland Security, an umbrella federal agency that has incorporated many federal law enforcement functions. Many observers note that the creation of this mammoth federal agency indicates a move toward the nationalization of our police force. Historically, a national police force has been resisted because of the origins of this country and the legacy of distrust of centralized power. The Department of Homeland Security has absorbed agencies such as Immigration and Naturalization Service and Customs, and the director is the central coordinator of all information regarding counterterrorism, even though the FBI and the CIA are not formally under the organization chart of the DHS.

Community policing, popular before 9/11, was an approach that sought to forge links between law enforcement and the community it served by having police officers take on expanded duties in helping improve quality of life for residents. Community policing faded as a law enforcement priority after 9/11, and federal financial support was drastically reduced. We have seen federal money directed instead to training law enforcement officers to act as "first responders" to critical events such as terrorist attacks and active shooter scenarios. There has also been more federal money available for hardware purchases and the creation of fusion centers where intelligence analysts receive and analyze information from an array of law enforcement agencies as well as open sources (e.g., newspapers). Beyond policing, since 9/11, the nation has been involved in moral debates over such responses as the following:

- Detainments
- Renditions and secret prisons
- Guantanamo and the military commissions
- The use of torture
- Governmental secrecy
- Wiretapping and threats to privacy
- Undercover operations

Detainments

Immediately after 9/11, hundreds of noncitizens were detained on either immigration charges or material witness warrants. The Patriot Act required that all individuals on visas report to immigration offices, and once there, many were detained for minor violations of their visa. Hundreds were held for months in federal facilities and county jails without hearings. Despite civil liberties groups pressing for the names of the detainees, it took months for the federal government to release even the numbers of individuals detained, much less their names.

The deportation hearings that were held were closed to the public and to the media, despite legal suits to open them. Individuals were deported for extremely minor immigration violations, some of whom had lived in the United States for 30 years or more. The detainment of individuals on material witness warrants seemed to be based on rumor, innuendo, and a level of proof that did not even meet reasonable suspicion (Kreimer, 2007).

While some individuals believe that nothing like the Japanese internment during World War II could happen again in this country, pundits and some politicians advocated just such a response in the fearful days following 9/11 against those of Middle Eastern descent, especially those who practiced the Muslim faith (Harris, 2006). Legal experts point out that the Supreme Court case that upheld the internment of 110,000 Japanese, *Korematsu v. U.S.*, 323 U.S. 214, 1944, has never been overturned, even though Congress has issued an official apology and voted to make reparations to internees (Harris, 2006).

Renditions and Secret Prisons

Other actions that the United States has taken in response to 9/11 have occurred overseas. Officials in Canada, Sweden, Germany, and Italy have declared that the CIA kidnapped individuals in those countries and subjected them to torture to discover what they knew about terrorist activities. The practice, called rendition, is usually done with the host country's knowledge, but in some cases no notice was given or permission granted. Several countries' leaders have objected to the U.S. practice of ignoring the sovereignty of the country and its laws (Weinstein, 2007; Whitlock, 2005).

In Italy, CIA operatives kidnapped a radical Egyptian cleric in February 2003 and smuggled him out on a U.S. military airplane. Italy prosecuted *in absentia* 26 American officials, including CIA agents and the bureau chief, in 2008. Testimony showed that Osama Moustafa Hassan Nasr was kidnapped, taken to an Egyptian prison, beaten, shocked over all parts of his body including his genitals, and tortured in other ways. After 14 months, he was released with no explanation of why he had been taken in the first place (Associated Press, 2008). After years of appeals, Italy's highest court upheld the convictions. In 2012, one of the CIA agents, Sabrina De Sousa, sued to force the U.S. government to grant her diplomatic immunity to protect her from the Italian conviction and prison sentence. The federal judge dismissed the lawsuit (Associated Press, 2012c). Recently, she was held in Portugal where she had travelled to visit relatives for extradition to Italy. Before the extradition was carried out, it was reported that the Trump administration obtained a partial commutation for her, reducing a four-year sentence to three that she does not have to serve in prison. She will not be extradited to Italy (Nelson, 2017). Ironically, it appears that those who played a more central role in the kidnapping received full pardons years ago (Shapira, 2016).

In another rendition case, Maher Arar, a Syrian-born Canadian, was seized in an American airport after officials received information from Canada that he was involved in terrorist activities. He was taken to Syria and tortured, then released because, as it turned out, the information was incorrect. Canada has reputedly offered him $10 million in damages, but his U.S. lawsuit in the Second Circuit of Appeals was dismissed based on the threat to state secrets. Also, news reports indicated that German authorities issued arrest warrants for the CIA agents believed to be responsible for a 2003 kidnapping of Khaled El-Masri, a German citizen believed to be a terrorist. He was allegedly kidnapped by U.S. agents, sent to Afghanistan, tortured, and then released. News reports indicate he was confused with a different man who was an al-Qaeda operative because they had a similar name. The United States exerted political pressure through diplomatic cables (later exposed by WikiLeaks) to get the legal action quashed, urging the German government to think about the foreign relation implications of pursuing prosecution (Slackman, 2010). The movie *Rendition* is a fictionalized account of El-Masri's story.

In some of the cases, the kidnapped suspects were sent to secret prisons run by the CIA in Eastern European countries. The existence of secret prisons run by the United States in formerly Soviet countries is an ironic and sad commentary on recent history. After the existence of such prisons was exposed in 2006, they were allegedly closed, with some of the detainees sent to Guantanamo (Whitlock, 2007). The Walking the Walk box describes how the secret prisons may have been exposed.

WALKING THE WALK

Mary McCarthy was born in 1945. She received a Ph.D. in history from the University of Minnesota. In 1984, she began working for the CIA as an intelligence analyst. Her specialty was Africa, and she was known as an independent-minded analyst. She was promoted to director of intelligence programs on the National Security Council staff and was appointed as special assistant to the president and senior director for intelligence programs under President Clinton. In this position, she reviewed all clandestine operations. After President George W. Bush was elected, she left that position in 2001, took a sabbatical, and obtained a J.D. In 2005, she was working for the CIA again, but in the Office of the Inspector General. That office investigates complaints about unethical or illegal actions by federal employees, and McCarthy's position involved investigating detainee treatment in Iraq and Afghanistan.

In 2006, she was castigated and fired over revealing governmental secrets. Although the whole affair continues to be murky, it seems that, weeks away from retirement, she spoke with Dana Priest, a *Washington Post* reporter who wrote a series of Pulitzer Prize-winning articles on the U.S. practice of rendition and operating "black sites," which were secret prisons in Eastern European countries. These were the places where enemy combatants picked up in Iraq,

Afghanistan, and in countries all over the world were taken for interrogation.

The Bush administration and CIA director Porter Goss launched an intensive investigation concerning the leak. McCarthy reportedly failed a polygraph and then admitted she talked to the reporter, according to CIA sources. McCarthy and her lawyer deny that she gave information to Priest about the black sites, and the reporter will only say that her information came from "multiple sources." McCarthy was fired 10 days before her planned retirement. Her colleagues were surprised since she was a veteran employee with decades of service. McCarthy has been described as "engaging, charming, persistent, loud, and aggressive." She evidently could not be "snowed easily" and was, by nature, a skeptic. The reason she spoke with the reporter seemed to be, according to news stories citing her friends and colleagues, that she was disturbed that senior officials were not telling the truth to the Senate and House committees investigating CIA activities regarding interrogation. She and other CIA staff members were convinced that the interrogation tactics approved by the White House violated international treaties. Worse, congressional committees were not aware of the extent of the interrogation tactics used, at least from her perspective.

(continued)

The news stories led to the decision to shut down the secret prisons and move the detainees (who were also known as "ghost detainees" since they never appeared on official lists provided to the International Red Cross) to Guantanamo. Whether Mary McCarthy is a hero or a traitor depends on one's perspective. It is still unclear if she was the source for the reporter's story about the secret prisons. Some argue that her position at the Inspector General's Office would not have given her access to such information. Others argue that she would have had access to the information only if there had been internal complaints from other CIA employees that laws were being broken. To some, she betrayed the secrets of her employer and country. Most CIA agents and other observers condemned her actions, arguing that you never leak secrets, no matter what the reason. To others, once McCarthy saw that the internal processes were not going to stop what she believed was unlawful and wrong, she did something that was much more effective—bringing the white light of public scrutiny to the activities. As the events such as Abu Ghraib, the secret prisons, and Guantanamo fade into memory, it is important to understand the dilemmas faced by those who saw wrong and tried to right it. They changed the pages of history.

Sources: Smith, 2006; Smith and Linzer, 2006: A01.

Guantanamo and the Military Commissions Act

Soon after the U.S. military initiated hostilities in Afghanistan, "enemy combatants" were captured and sent to Guantanamo Bay in Cuba, a military installation that is considered American territory. Suspected terrorists were also picked up in other countries and sent to Guantanamo or to the secret prisons. Then the Iraq War began, and enemy combatants from Iraq were also sent there.

The federal government argued that the individuals did not deserve the due-process rights granted by the American Constitution because they were not Americans and were not on American soil, and they did not deserve the due-process rights granted by the Geneva Conventions (the agreements made by all the major world powers after World War II on how to treat war prisoners) because they were defined as enemy combatants, not soldiers. This left the detainees in legal limbo where they had no legal protections or due process to determine if they were truly enemies or posed a danger to anyone.

In a series of court cases, the Supreme Court rejected the Bush administration's position regarding the detainees' legal rights. In *Hamdi v. Rumsfeld*, 542 U.S. 507, 2004, the Supreme Court held that U.S. citizens could not be held indefinitely without charges even if they were labeled enemy combatants. In *Rasul v. Bush*, 542 U.S. 466, 2004, the Supreme Court held that detainees, even if not U.S. citizens, in Guantanamo could challenge their detention in U.S. federal courts. A related case was *Clark v. Martinez*, 543 U.S. 371, 2005, which involved Cubans held for years in federal penitentiaries after illegally entering the United States. In this case, the Court held that the government may not indefinitely detain even illegal immigrants without some due process. In *Hamdan v. Rumsfeld*, 548 U.S. 557, 2006, the Supreme Court held that the military commissions, set up as a type of due process for the detainees, were outside the president's power to create (the power belonged to Congress) and were, therefore, invalid.

Congress then passed the Military Commissions Act, which set up the military commissions using procedures like those the Bush administration had created. The commissions were a poor example of due process because defendants had extremely limited ability to confront accusers or present evidence. In *Boumediene v. Bush*, 553 U.S. 723, 2008, the Supreme Court rejected the military commissions as a due-process substitute for federal courts and habeas corpus, and it further held that the Detainee

Treatment Act with the provision of some form of appeal over the "enemy combatant" status was also not an adequate substitute for habeas corpus rights. The Court's rationale was that Guantanamo is a legal territory of the United States and, therefore, is subject to U.S. law. Dissents by Chief Justice Roberts and Justices Scalia, Thomas, and Alito vigorously opposed the Court's rationale and predicted "devastating" consequences (Greenhouse, 2008; Savage, 2008).

The Obama administration refined the military commissions to respond to the due-process concerns raised by the Court and now there are more due-process elements than earlier versions. The Military Commissions Act of 2009 incorporates the presumption of innocence, requires proof beyond a reasonable doubt, provides for a right to counsel and a right to present evidence and crossexamine witnesses, prohibits the use of statements obtained through torture or cruel and inhuman treatment, states that hearsay can be used by both sides if it is deemed reliable and relevant, and provides for a right to appeal to Article III judges. The current military commissions also allow for the protection of sensitive sources in that defense attorneys must have secret-level security clearances. There are also no requirements for *Miranda* warnings, and interrogations must be interpreted considering "wartime realities." The commissions can only be used for al-Qaeda-affiliated cases and cannot be used for American citizens, and for only specified offenses (violations of laws of war).

There were close to 800 detainees at one point in Guantanamo. According to a website devoted to closing Guantanamo, there are now only 41 detainees still there (http://www.closeguantanamo.org/Prisoners). The remainder have been repatriated to their own countries or sent to other countries after a determination that they were no longer a danger or a finding of guilt with a determination that enough punishment had been served. The military commission for Hamdan (of *Hamdan v. Rumsfeld*) ended with a sentence of 66 months, but with credit for the 61 months he had already served. He was transferred to serve the rest of his sentence in Yemen. Reports indicate that some of the released detainees have joined terrorist organizations.

The prosecution of Khalid Sheikh Mohammed, the alleged mastermind of 9/11, has been criticized as rife with legal and ethical misconduct, including the release of a half-million defense attorney e-mails to prosecutors, the discovery of hidden microphones placed by the FBI in attorney–client conference rooms, and allegations that FBI agents have been spying on defense teams. One of the Judge Advocate General (JAG) officers (Major Jason Wright) assigned to Mohammed's defense was summarily reassigned. Instead of abandoning the case, which he viewed as a violation of his ethical duty as an attorney, he resigned from the army (Urza, 2014). As of July 2017, Khalid Sheikh Mohammed's military commission proceeding still had not begun because of continuing legal issues.

Evidently, some who were sent to Guantanamo were innocent and either accused by others who gave names because they were being tortured, or were accused by bounty hunters simply because they received money for identifying supposed terrorists (Selksky, 2009). Some of the detainees were captured as youngsters 14- or 15-years-old, sparking international outrage since treaties mandate that juveniles are not to be treated as war criminals (Williams, 2008).

Torture

After World War II, commanders of the Japanese and German armies were tried for war crimes that included unnecessary killings of civilians, mistreatment of civilians, and the use of torture against captured soldiers. One of the forms of interrogation used by the Japanese that was later the basis for convictions was the "water cure." We know it today as waterboarding. In the 1940s, judicial officials assessing guilt in war crime trials called it torture and convicted the military officers who ordered it or allowed it to happen; however, because of 9/11, President Bush called waterboarding legal and necessary. President Obama said that the enhanced interrogation techniques used, including waterboarding, was torture. He banned their use the second day in office. President Trump said during his campaign that he was in favor of waterboarding and, if he won, interrogation tactics would be "a hell of a lot worse" (Johnson, 2017). It remains to be seen, however, if that promise could be carried out since Congress voted to ban torture and the Uniform Code of Military Justice (UCMJ) specifically prohibits it as well.

Torture is defined as the deliberate infliction of violence and, through violence, severe mental and/or physical suffering upon individuals. Others describe it as any intentional act that causes severe physical or mental pain or suffering. Amnesty International considers all forms of corporal punishment as falling within the definition of torture and prohibited by the United Nations Convention against Torture (McCready, 2007).

We now know that immediately after 9/11, certain individuals suspected of being involved in the planning of the attacks or of being members of al-Qaeda were seized wherever they happened to be and taken to secret locations. First, they were sent to countries such as Egypt and Syria that used torture in interrogation. Later they were taken to secret prisons run by the CIA in Eastern Europe. Finally, some were moved to Guantanamo. Evidently, by 2002, various forms of coercive interrogation techniques were being used at Guantanamo, as well as at Bagram prison in Afghanistan and Abu Ghraib in Iraq. At these locations, suspects were subjected to extreme forms of coercive interrogations, including the following (Massimino, 2004: 74):

- Subjected to loud noises and extreme heat and cold
- Deprived of sleep, light, food, and water
- Bound or forced to stand in painful positions for long periods of time
- Kept naked and hooded
- Thrown into walls and slapped
- Sexually humiliated
- Threatened with attack dogs
- Shackled to the ceiling or kept in small containers

Military interrogators in Guantanamo were trained in the techniques of coercive interrogation techniques with material that was originally from a 1957 Air Force study of Chinese Communist techniques used during the Korean War. The original source detailed a continuum of coercive techniques that were used to obtain false confessions from U.S. soldiers, including practices such as semi-starvation, filthy surroundings, extreme cold, and stress positions. The techniques that could "brainwash" American soldiers into falsely confessing war crimes became included in military training on how to withstand such pressures. Survival–evasion–resistance–escape (SERE) training was designed and administered by the military with the assistance of civilian psychologist contractors. While the country was still in the grip of fear expecting another attack, officials sought advice on how to obtain information from the suspected terrorists they had captured and turned to these psychologists.

What seems unbelievable now is why psychologists who had no familiarity at all with interrogation were consulted instead of intelligence and interrogation experts in the military, FBI, or other federal agencies. The psychologists from the SERE training program, James Mitchell and Bruce Jessen, began to train military and CIA interrogators on the techniques used in SERE training, including waterboarding. These techniques, used on American soldiers to expose them to what they might experience while in enemy hands, were supposed to "break" detainees to get them to talk (Eban, 2007; Shane, 2008b; Shane and Mazzetti, 2009). Reports also indicate that Mitchell was there at the first waterboarding, reportedly of Abu Zubaida (also spelled Zubahday or Zubaidah, and Zayn al-Abidin Muhammad Hussein) and that the waterboarding took place before the 2002 memo that defined it as legal (Warrick and Finn, 2009). It was the videotapes of the waterboarding and interrogation of Zubaida that the CIA destroyed in 2005. Expert interrogators argued the methods were ineffective and unnecessary, and no one seemed to know or care that the methods, especially waterboarding, had been defined as war crimes after WWII. It was reported that veteran interrogators referred to these two psychologists as the "poster boys" because it was believed that they would eventually end up on the FBI's "most wanted" list for what they were doing (Eban, 2007).

The role of these psychologists is especially controversial and has sparked disciplinary action in their respective licensing agencies. Mitchell, Jessen, and other psychologists who were present during the enhanced interrogations at Guantanamo have been the subject of lawsuits and disciplinary actions because, it has been alleged, they have violated their professional ethical code in participating in what amounts to torture. There was an action filed in Texas, for instance, since Jim Mitchell is licensed there; another psychologist was licensed in New York and a Human Rights organization filed a lawsuit against him there. It appears that the psychologists will escape any sanctions, however, since the organization's disciplinary body decided that what they were doing was not part of professional psychological services; therefore, the professional rules would not apply and the professional body had no power to discipline (Eligon, 2011).

More recently, it has been revealed that there was coordination between officials at the American Psychological Association (APA) and CIA employees in that the APA standards covering psychologists involved in interrogations were written with the help of CIA employees, and the APA officials involved in writing the standards became consultants for the CIA. Even internal CIA psychologists who opposed the interrogation techniques were overruled because these outside experts maintained that it was ethically acceptable for psychologists to be involved, and that the interrogation techniques would not lead to long-term injury for the detainees (Risen, 2015a; 2015b).

An independent investigation determined that APA officials sought to "curry favor" and "colluded" with Pentagon officials by supporting the Pentagon's interrogation efforts, and lent credibility to the interrogation program of the CIA. At least one APA official was a partial owner of Mitchell and Jessen's company and two former APA presidents were on the CIA advisory board. The report also showed that other CIA contractors, who were psychologists or psychiatrists, opposed the techniques promoted by Mitchell and Jessen and argued that they did not lead to accurate information, but were overruled by the APA-affiliated outsiders. Mitchell and Jessen eventually earned about $80 million for their role in the "enhanced interrogation" program (Kitfield, 2017; Risen, 2015b).

In 2002, George Tenet, then director of the CIA, and his chief deputy described in detail the techniques they sought approval for to the Principals Committee of the National Security Council. This group included George W. Bush, Condoleezza Rice,

Dick Cheney, John Ashcroft, and Donald Rumsfeld. The techniques were also described to the top leaders of the Senate and House Intelligence Committees (although conflicting memories seem to exist as to what they were told). CIA memos that were written around this same time graphically described the techniques used. They were clinically specific, including how hard to slap a detainee's face, the total number of times a person could be slammed into a wall (30), and how many times someone could be waterboarded (six times within two hours). The memos also discuss Zubaida's fear of insects and how that could be used to torture him; in a scenario taken straight from George Orwell's *1984*, where the interrogators determined the greatest fear of the protagonist was rats and used this fear to torture him (Miller and Meyer, 2009).

These interrogation techniques were contrary to the military field manual and believed by many to be against American law. FBI agents who were at Guantanamo to assist in interrogations wrote memoranda to their superiors objecting to what they saw, as did some military lawyers and other officers. FBI officials instructed agents to leave the room when such interrogations were carried out. However, we now know that a legal memorandum authored by lawyers, John Yoo and Robert Delahunty, from the Office of Legal Counsel had provided a 2002 opinion that the president had legal authority to authorize waterboarding and other forms of torture based on the Authorization to Use Military Force passed by Congress and the executive power of the presidency. Yoo also wrote a 2003 memorandum with Jay Bybee that basically reiterated the justification that the president had the legal right to order torture if it did not result in organ failure or death. Steven Bradbury wrote a series of memos in 2005 basically endorsing the earlier memo's reasoning (Shane, 2008a).

Critics argue that these legal memoranda ignored other sources of law, specifically, international treaties that bar such acts, including the Convention against Torture, which the United States ratified in 1994 (Gillers, 2004). Years later, the authors, Bybee, Yoo, and Bradbury, faced an investigation from the Department of Justice's Office of Professional Responsibility and possible sanctions from their respective bar associations. However, the final report concluded that they exercised flawed legal reasoning but were not guilty of professional misconduct, and recommended that they not be referred to their state bar associations for discipline. Bybee is now a federal appeals court judge, and Yoo is a law professor (Lichtblau and Shane, 2010).

In December 2014, the Senate Select Committee on Intelligence released a summary report of an investigation into the activities of the CIA during the time after 9/11, including the enhanced interrogation techniques. Most of the information in the report was already known—at least to those paying attention. The report was widely condemned by Republicans as politically motivated, except for Senator John McCain, who had been tortured as a Vietnamese prisoner of war. Findings included the following:

1. *The CIA's interrogation techniques were more brutal and employed more extensively than the agency portrayed.* The waterboardings were described as "near drownings" and there were more subjected to it than the three acknowledged at the time by CIA officials. Descriptions of other techniques included sleep deprivation for up to a week, "rectal feedings," and death threats. Detainees experienced hallucinations, paranoia, insomnia, and attempts at self-harm and self-mutilation.

2. *The CIA interrogation program was mismanaged and was not subject to adequate oversight.* Insiders opposed the outside psychologists and their lack of experience in interrogation. CIA officials actively impeded congressional oversight.

3. *The CIA misled members of Congress and the White House about the effectiveness and extent of its brutal interrogation techniques.* The report details examples of where the CIA misled members of Congress and the White House regarding the actionable intelligence that was supposed to have been derived from interrogation. For example, the CIA Director told the Senate Select Committee on Intelligence in 2007 that Abu Zubaydah was subjected to enhanced interrogation with the result that they obtained important information. The records showed that Zubaydah had cooperated with FBI interrogators and provided information before, not after, the enhanced interrogation techniques were used.

4. *Interrogators in the field who tried to stop the brutal techniques were repeatedly overruled by senior CIA officials.* CIA officials reportedly assured personnel that the techniques had been approved at the highest levels.

5. *The CIA repeatedly underreported the number of people it detained and subjected to harsh interrogation techniques under the program.* The report indicates that about 119 people were detained in the secret prisons.

6. *At least 26 detainees were wrongfully held and did not meet the government's standard for detention.* These individuals were held as "leverage" to extract information from family members, or held despite not having the appropriate level of proof.

7. *The CIA leaked classified information to journalists, exaggerating the success of interrogation methods to gain public support* (Ashkenas, Fairfield, Keller, and Volpe, 2014).

A group of former senior CIA officers published a book disagreeing with the findings and the report was condemned by Republicans as shoddily done and partisan. The news box below describes what has happened to the full report.

▌📱 IN THE NEWS | *Legal Limbo*

The 500-page summary of the investigation into the CIA enhanced interrogation program and use of secret prisons was followed by the full report. News reports in 2015 discussed how a disk containing the full 6,700-page report on the CIA enhanced torture activities was delivered to the Pentagon, the CIA, the State Department, and the Justice Department in December 2014. A letter from Senator Dianne Feinstein urged officials to read the report to learn about the mistakes made to ensure it didn't happen again. The other intent in sending it to these agencies was that they were subject to open records requests while Congress was not. Reportedly, the report offers great detail when explaining the origins of the program of enhanced interrogation and the secret prisons, and names the officials involved.

The fate of the full report entered legal limbo because the Justice Department prohibited anyone from opening it, arguing that it was classified. Once the Senate reverted to Republican control, Senator Feinstein had no leverage to declassify the full report; in fact, Senator Richard Burr, who replaced her, demanded that every copy of the report be returned. Legal wrangling ensued over who owned the document and who could declassify it.

In June of 2017, the Trump administration ordered all copies of the report held by executive agencies be returned to Senator Burr's committee. Critics object that once the report is locked in the Senate vaults, not subject to open records requests, it will be hidden forever.

Source: Mazzetti and Apuzzo, 2015; Mazzetti and Rosenberg, 2017.

Ali Soufan, an FBI interrogator, has publicly stated that he had been successful in initial interrogations of Ali Zubaida, a Yemeni thought to be a high-ranking al-Qaeda official but eventually discovered to be more of a travel agent for the terrorist organization (Finn and Warrick, 2009). He practiced standard interrogation techniques that involved developing rapport; in Zubaida's case, he provided medical care and called him a nickname only used by his mother. Soufan has stated that it was he who obtained information about José Padilla (the "shoe bomber") from Zubaida, not the CIA agents who later claimed credit (Eban, 2007). It was when CIA interrogators and contractors arrived and began using the enhanced interrogation techniques that Zubaida began to provide information that was later determined to be useless or inaccurate, although others insist that he provided hundreds of names of al-Qaeda's agents (Finn and Warrick, 2009). Eventually Zubaida was waterboarded 83 times. Khalid Sheikh Mohammed was waterboarded 183 times.

Soufan and other interrogators have insisted that traditional techniques and old-fashioned "cop tricks" are effective and would have been effective in the interrogation of terrorist suspects without resorting to "enhanced" techniques (Margasak, 2009). Torture victims are unlikely to offer additional information and they are more likely to lie to stop the torture (Finn and Warrick, 2009; Ghosh, 2009). Furthermore, any information that is obtained through torture cannot be used to convict terrorist agents in military commissions or federal courts. If the only information that supports their guilt was obtained through torture, they can't be convicted and punished. The CIA and military have now attempted to reinterrogate men like Zubaida with "clean teams" (interrogators who did not participate in waterboarding or other questionable interrogation techniques), but, not surprisingly, the detainees are not very cooperative (Finn and Warrick, 2009).

By the time the Abu Ghraib prison scandal erupted in 2004, such techniques had been used in Guantanamo and in Bagram prison in Afghanistan. The pictures that Sergeant Joseph Darby provided to army CID showed prisoners being subjected to a range of physically painful and psychological traumatizing behaviors. Later investigations documented that the following acts occurred:

- Forcing naked prisoners to pose in humiliating, sexually oriented poses
- Forcing hooded prisoners to stand on a box and be attached to electric wires
- Threatening male detainees with rape
- Sodomizing a male detainee with a broomstick
- Threatening detainees with attack dogs
- Pouring chemicals from broken light bulbs onto detainees (Massimino, 2004)

Some bitterly criticized the fact that no higher-ranking military officers were ever punished for the Abu Ghraib incident, such as Brigadier General Janis Karpinski or Lt. Colonel Ricardo Sanchez. They argue that under the doctrine of "command responsibility" superiors are responsible for the war crimes committed by their soldiers when they either knew what was happening or should have known. Even though the United States and Allied Forces utilized the concept of command responsibility in war crimes trials after WWII to hold Japanese and German commanders responsible for the acts of others, the Uniform Code of Military Justice does not have a parallel responsibility of American commanders (Smith, 2006). General Taguba's report of Abu Ghraib indicated that the reserve soldiers assigned to be guards in the prison did not have training in the Geneva Conventions, nor were there clear directions from the commanding officers as to what was acceptable or not in the treatment of prisoners. The soldiers, such as Charles Graner, testified that they were never told not to engage in the abusive acts portrayed in the pictures and, in fact, Graner was complimented on his ability to "soften up" the prisoners for interrogation. However, when the soldiers tried to use a "superior orders defense" (which basically states that they were not guilty because they were following orders) in their court martials, the defense was rejected (Smith, 2006).

Others argue that military commanders over Abu Ghraib and other prisons may deserve some blame, but their position was tenuous since the questioning was often done by the CIA or other contractors. Military investigations and prosecutions have exposed the fact that paramilitary units called Scorpions, which included CIA operatives, Special Forces, and civilians, used tactics in Afghanistan and Iraq that included beating prisoners (White, 2005). In fact, the blurred lines of authority, not to mention conflicting legal opinions from the Justice Department and the Pentagon, led to a situation where abuse was probably not only possible, but, in fact, probable.

In Bagram prison in Afghanistan, similar practices occurred and included the following:

- Stepping on the neck of a detainee and kicking him in the genitals
- Forcing a detainee to roll on the floor of a cell and kiss the feet of the interrogators
- Forcing a detainee to pick plastic bottle caps out of a drum mixed with excrement and water (Golden, 2005)

QUOTE & QUERY

It became a kind of running joke, and people kept showing up to give this detainee a common peroneal strike just to hear him scream out "Allah." It went on over a 24-hour period, and I would think that it was over 100 strikes.

Source: Statement by military guard. Quoted in Golden, 2005: A16.

? Why did no one stop this abuse?

In one case, a detainee was stuffed in a sleeping bag, wrapped in electrical cord, and beaten to death (White, 2005). Also at Bagram, a young taxi driver was killed by interrogators who suspended him from the ceiling and beat his legs so badly that an autopsy revealed his leg bones were pulverized (see the Quote and Query box). It was discovered that Dilawar, the taxi driver, had no association at all with insurgents and that his taxi and the passengers in it had been picked at random by an Afghan guerrilla commander who told the Americans that they were responsible for bombing a U.S. camp. Later it was discovered that the commander himself was responsible for the bombing (Golden, 2005).

It seems that the worst forms of interrogation techniques were not used after 2005 although President Bush publicly continued to support waterboarding through 2008 and in his memoirs insists it was legal. In 2006, a new army field manual specified new rules of interrogation consistent with the Geneva Conventions' Article 3 (outlawing forced nudity, hooding, dogs, waterboarding, stress positions, and sleep deprivation). The military manual asks the soldier to question a method in a way reminiscent of ethical formalism and universalism: "If the proposed approach technique were used by the enemy against one of your fellow soldiers, would you believe the soldier had been abused?"

Today, there continues to be support for torture. One report indicated that nearly two-thirds of Americans agreed that torture of terrorism subjects could be justified (Kitfield, 2017). We know that, despite protestations to the contrary, the torture endured permanently damaged the minds and bodies of those victimized, some of whom were innocent, some of whom had already shared everything they knew to interrogators before the enhanced techniques were used. Reports indicate that at least half of the torture victims are still experiencing permanent headaches, disturbed sleep, feelings of suffocation, depression, psychosis, paranoia, amnesia, difficulty in decision making, and other symptoms, although it is possible that some had mental health issues before they were held and interrogated by Americans. Not surprisingly, the symptoms are like those experienced by the U.S. military members who became prisoners of war in Korea and Vietnam and were subject to brutality (Apuzzo, Fink, and Risen, 2016).

Part of the reason that the enhanced interrogation techniques, such as waterboarding, sleep deprivation, enforced nudity, and the like, were not defined as torture by the Justice Department memorandums was because they were presumed not to result in long-term damage to the detainees. There was remarkably little attention to that potential partially because the psychologists assured CIA officials that military trainees were not harmed by the SERE experience. The false equivalency between the controlled environment of the SERE training and torture inflicted on detainees is obvious (Apuzzo, Fink, and Risen, 2016).

Their torture has prevented prosecution in some cases because they either are too mentally ill to be tried, there is suspected brain damage, or the only information against them was obtained through torture. Others were taken back to their countries and released from Guantanamo, after being subjected to enhanced interrogation techniques, with no explanation of why they were taken. Their experience left them traumatized and deeply distrustful of the United States. Reportedly one explained how being tortured by agents of the United States was like being mugged by a trusted friend. He said that being tortured by a country that doesn't believe in torture made one lose faith in everything (Apuzzo, Fink, and Risen, 2016).

The argument that we should not use torture because our enemies then will feel free to use torture against American soldiers is a utilitarian argument (greatest benefit), but it also has elements of the categorical imperative (act in such a way that you will it to be a universal law) and the religious imperative (do unto others as you would have them do unto you). Kleinig (2001a) and others, even before the worst abuses were revealed, examined the weak justification for torture and abusive practices during interrogation and pointed out that they have been used in Northern Ireland, Israel, South Africa, and South America, among many other countries. The so-called doctrine of necessity is purely utilitarian, as is the argument of some that there must be secrecy concerning interrogation tactics so they can be more effective. To the contrary, Kleinig (2001a: 116) points out that torture dehumanizes both victim and oppressor: "There is a loss of the moral high ground, a compromising of values that supposedly distinguish a society as civilized and worth belonging to."

The national argument as to whether torture is legally or ethically justified is no different from Klockars' (1983)

QUOTE & **QUERY**

We take this moral high ground to make sure that if our people fall into enemy hands, we'll have the moral force to say, "You have got to treat them right." If you don't practice what you preach, nobody listens.

Source: Senator Lindsey Graham, in support of an amendment banning torture to military prisoners, quoted in Galloway and Kuhnhenn, 2005: A4.

 Is this argument against torture a utilitarian argument or an ethical formalist argument?

PART IV   *Corrections*

Dirty Harry problem The question of whether police should use immoral means to reach a desired moral end (taken from the Clint Eastwood movie *Dirty Harry*).

Dirty Harry problem. This dilemma originated in a situation from the *Dirty Harry* movie where a captured criminal refuses to tell the location of a kidnapped victim. Because the victim is sure to die without help, the police officer (played by Clint Eastwood) tortured the criminal by stepping on his injured leg until he admitted the location. Klockars' point was that the situation has no good solution. If the police officer behaved in a professional manner, the victim would be sure to die. If the officer behaved in an immoral manner, there was a chance he could save a life. Klockars' conclusion was that, by engaging in dirty means for good ends, the officer tainted his innocence and must be punished, for there is always a danger that dirty means will be redefined as neutral or even good by those who use them. Klockars also inferred that we all are guilty in a sense by expecting certain ones among us to do the dirty work and then condemning them for their actions. In effect, police (and others such as the CIA and Special Forces) become our *sin eaters* of early folklore; they are the shady characters on the fringe of society who absorb evil so the rest of us may remain pure. These persons are depended upon to protect us, but shunned and avoided when their actions see the light of day.

The post-9/11 Harry Callahan was Jack Bauer, the hero from the television show *24, w*hich began in 2001 and ran for eight seasons. Every season he was confronted with a variation of the "the ticking bomb scenario," specifically, whether one should use torture to find the location of a bomb that is about to go off and kill many people. While the stakes were higher, this is the same dilemma that faced the fictional Harry Callahan, and, one might add, the same analysis may be applied: are bad means ever justified by a good end? In the television drama, Bauer never hesitated and the show's villains were treated to a wide array of beating, cutting, burning, electrocuting, and other forms of psychological and physical torture. A group opposed to violence on television called it the worst show on the air and noted that depictions of torture in other programs increased fivefold after it began airing (Mayer, 2007).

The television show was entertainment, but also a powerful argument that enhanced interrogation was the right thing to do, supporting the Bush administration's position. The show's producer was a conservative, counting Rush Limbaugh as a good friend, and President Bush, Vice President Cheney, and Homeland Security Secretary Michael Chertoff were reportedly huge fans. Even Justice Scalia made a controversial public reference to the fact that Jack Bauer was a hero who shouldn't be prosecuted. Others, however, criticized the series in that it promoted the message that torture was effective and encouraged the viewer to root for the hero who illegally tortured. In 2006, U.S. Army Brigadier General Patrick Finnegan, dean of the United States Military Academy at West Point, led a delegation of expert interrogators from the army and FBI to Hollywood to meet with producers of the show to get them to change the message that torture was good. They noted that the show was being referenced by their students at West Point as justification for why they should not have to stay within legal guidelines. The producers and actor Kiefer Sutherland insisted the show was just entertainment and no one should take it seriously, but evidently Michael Chertoff, the head of Homeland Security and part of the group that approved enhanced interrogation techniques, said about the show at a public debate, "Frankly, it reflects real life." The real-life interrogators, however, as opposed to Washington bureaucrats, called the show immoral and said, "Only a psychopath can torture and be unaffected. You don't want people like that in your organization" (Mayer, 2007).

Whether torture is effective or not is a utilitarian argument. Some argue that it is not effective because people will say anything to stop the torture, and interrogators can't tell when someone is lying (Rejali, 2007). Others argue that torture does work in getting information out of individuals. Even those people, however, admit that using torture to interrogate may damage the interrogator as well as the detainee.

Individuals may find the dark corners of their soul when they realize that they get some form of excitement from inflicting pain on others. They may suffer guilt that destroys their peace of mind and affects them long after the detainee's wounds have healed. It has been reported that some interrogators are suffering posttraumatic stress syndrome (Blumenfeld, 2007). Eric Fair was an interrogator working for a private contractor. He has written a book (*Consequence*) about his experiences and explains how he has never overcome the guilt of what he did during those interrogations. He describes the situation at Abu Ghraib as chaotic, with no clear standards for who got security clearances. Perhaps up to 70 percent of the inmates were picked up in error, yet the interrogators were urged to "get creative" when inflicting pain to make them talk. Now, he suffers from nightmares about pools of blood that move as if alive. He still hears the cries of those he slammed into walls (Kakutani, 2016).

There is a tempting logic to the use of torture in a ticking time bomb scenario in which one knows that the person being tortured has information about a bomb that is going to go off soon, killing many people. Even Alan Dershowitz (2004), a renowned liberal defense attorney, offered a utilitarian argument as a rationale—he wrote that sometimes the greatest benefit for the majority is derived from torture, but that it should be limited to situations in which the benefit is so great that it overwhelms the harm to the individual. He also proposes, however, that any torture should be done under the auspices of a court or objective hearing body that issues a type of "torture warrant." Others (e.g., McCready, 2007) dispute the feasibility of this proposal, arguing that any need for torture would be immediate and, if there was time to pursue a warrant, there probably would be other ways to get that information.

Whether one accepts the utilitarian equation for the ticking bomb scenario does not necessarily justify the actual incidents of torture that have taken place. There is a world of difference between the ticking bomb scenario that appears in a hypothetical or in a television show where viewers already know that the interrogation target knows something, and the real-life situations that occurred in Guantanamo and Bagram. In these places, people were subjected to pain because they *might* have known something about al-Qaeda, or because someone else who was tortured cried out their name. The only calculus that supports a utilitarian rationale for torture is when the person being tortured does know something, that knowledge will avert a catastrophe, and the information cannot be discovered by other means. In real life, torture occurred against innocents, like Dilawar, the taxi driver, who suffered unimaginable pain and terror because he did not know anything about the bombing he was accused of. As discussed throughout the text, utilitarianism depends on an ability to know the consequences of one's actions because only then can one calculate whether the negative "means" outweighs the negative "end." Torture targets who are the victims of mistaken identity, or bad tips, end up suffering the most. There is no utilitarian calculus that can justify this negative effect. The other miscalculation is ignoring the long-term effects of torture on the United States. The actions of the interrogators may have saved lives (although even that is doubtful), but another possible consequence might lie in the horrifying spectre of the rise of ISIS in the Middle East, seemingly a group so lacking in humane sympathy that they are denounced even by al-Qaeda and Hamas. The United States has lost its moral high ground because of the actions taken in Guantanamo, Abu Ghraib, and other locations; knowledge that the United States employed the same tactics as the worst dictatorships in history has made it harder to practice diplomacy and destroyed the ability of this country to push for human rights around the world.

In 2009, Attorney General Holder appointed John Durham to investigate whether criminal charges should be brought against any CIA agents or other officials for their role in the enhanced interrogations that occurred, but President Obama also said they would not prosecute anyone who operated in good faith that they were following U.S. law. In 2011, the Justice Department dropped 99 of the 101 cases of alleged torture, reporting there was not enough evidence to pursue an investigation. The remaining cases concerned Manadel al-Jamadi, who died in 2003 in Abu Ghraib (he was the plastic-wrapped corpse soldiers posed next to in the Abu Ghraib pictures), and Gul Rahman, who died of hypothermia in Afghanistan shackled to a wall. In 2012, Eric Holder announced that there would be no prosecutions in these two cases either (Dilanian, 2012). This may not be the end of the story, however, since numerous legal actions are occurring around the world against American officials who are believed to have violated human rights and international law. *The New York Times* posted video depositions of Mitchell and Jessen from a lawsuit brought by former detainees who were subject to the enhanced interrogation techniques advocated by the two. You can watch them here: https://www.nytimes.com/interactive/2017/06/21/us/cia-torture.html?emc=edit_ta_20170621&nl=top-stories&nlid=66242298&ref=cta&_r=0.

Governmental Secrecy

The responses to 9/11 described earlier are now part of history and the government no longer engages in wholesale roundups of visa holders, renditions, or torture (as far as we know). There are other governmental responses to 9/11 that are continuing to play out and are very much part of current national discussions about "just means" in the war on terror. Perhaps as a response to 9/11, there is less openness in governmental activities, a trend begun in the Bush administration, but continuing through the Obama administration and into the Trump administration. President Obama campaigned on a promise to roll back the pattern of secrecy, but, instead, he accelerated the use of executive privilege and the classification of state secrets. A state secrets justification has also been used for dismissing lawsuits brought by victims of torture and wiretapping.

The Justice Department, under President Obama, prioritized finding and punishing whistleblowers who exposed governmental wrongdoing, such as John Kiriakou, an ex-CIA analyst who discussed waterboarding with journalists and served a 30-month prison sentence for revealing a CIA agent's name to a journalist even though the name was never published. The Kiriakou case is described in the documentary "*Silenced.*" In fact, Kiriakou's prosecution—along with the prosecutions of two other whistleblowers—Thomas Drake and William Binney—was mentioned by Edward Snowden as a reason for his decision to go public with the data he stole from the NSA. Drake came forward with information about wasteful spending and Binney was threatened with, but ultimately not prosecuted for, leaking classified information about the extent of the government's surveillance capability. Snowden reported to journalists in 2013 that the government's harsh treatment of these whistleblowers indicated to him that he would be unfairly treated if he tried to work within the system or stayed within legal reach of the justice system (Savage and Shane, 2013).

Today, we see the same zeal for identifying governmental whistleblowers, such as Reality Winner, the 25-year-old security analyst who leaked classified documents about the hacking attempts of the Russians during the last election. She was charged and faces 10 years of prison (Park, 2017). Critics point to a double standard when some "leakers," who are not trying to expose wrongdoing but still violate the law, are given a slap on the wrist. For instance, General Petraeus, a former CIA director, was found to have shared secret information with his biographer-lover but was charged with only a misdemeanor of mishandling classified information.

Government secrecy has other effects besides harsher sanctions against whistleblowers. Kauffman and Toomey (2015) argue that in earlier decades, Fourth Amendment law was developed because government agents gave notice to defendants of the type of surveillance that was used against them. For instance, the Supreme Court in *Katz v. United States,* 389 U.S. 347, 1967, concluded that the government required a warrant before wiretapping when the target had an expectation of privacy, and, in *Kyllo v. United States,* 533 U.S. 27, 2001, a warrant was deemed necessary before heat measuring devices were used to detect indoor marijuana cultivation. The resulting legal challenges to the government action were possible only because defendants *were told* that these devices had been used against them. The so-called sneak and peek provision of the Patriot Act means that the government does not have to give targets notice that they have been the object of secret surveillance, and government agents are taught "parallel construction," which means that they create a parallel track of evidence to be used in prosecution so that the secret surveillance will not be revealed (Kauffman and Toomey, 2015). What this means is that secret governmental activities that spy on citizens do not bear the light of day and, thus, escape legal analysis.

Others argue that opponents of secrecy are naïve and that the published reports of U.S. activities against terrorists provided by WikiLeaks and other anonymous sources make it more difficult to protect America. For instance, publishing the plans leading up to the killing of Osama bin Laden has resulted in a long prison term for the Pakistani doctor who assisted the American effort, and publishing the details of a foiled terrorist plot using a double agent in May 2012 endangered that man's life and led to a reduced probability of assistance by other countries. The release of the wiretapped private conversations of political leaders in our ally countries makes it more difficult to count on their support in times of need. It is hard to conclude that the benefit of such leaks outweighs the harm.

The Trump administration has reportedly experienced more leaks of classified information than any in recent history, including classified information about the investigation regarding Michael Flynn's connections with Russian officials, testimony from closed congressional hearings, and other secret information. It is a difficult and controversial question as to what should be public knowledge and what should not be. Edward Snowden's release of a massive treasure trove of governmental secrets to journalists at the *Washington Post* and *Guardian* newspapers exposed the activities of the NSA and spurred legislators to reexamine their powers. At the same time, it has created the debate as to whether Snowden is a hero or a traitor for exposing America's secrets for all to read about. One thing is certain, it has made Snowden a man without a country, and his residence in Russia is an ironic consequence for someone who violated the law to protect what he considered to be Americans' civil liberties.

Wiretapping and Threats to Privacy

In 1978, in response to governmental invasions of privacy during the 1960s and 1970s, the Foreign Intelligence Surveillance Act (FISA) was passed, which created the Foreign Intelligence Surveillance Court (FISC), consisting of seven federal district court judges appointed by the Supreme Court's chief justice. Federal agents who wanted to wiretap in this country had to go to this court and show that their target was an agent of a foreign power and that the information sought was in furtherance of counterintelligence. The FISA legislation originally approved only electronic eavesdropping and wiretapping, but was amended in 1994 to include covert physical entries and, in 1998, to permit pen/trap orders (which record telephone numbers) and business records. If the target is a U.S. citizen, there must be probable cause that his or her activities may involve espionage, and a warrant requested and obtained from the FISC was required.

The Patriot Act created expanded powers for federal agents in search and seizure, including provisions that allowed federal agents to "sneak and peek," and to utilize national security letters instead of warrants in cases "relevant" to national security investigations. **National security letters** are subpoenas issued by the Federal Bureau of Investigation (FBI) to access private information. They are not warrants and do not require a magistrate's signature; typically, they demand phone records or financial records. Recipients of such a letter, until later modifications of the Patriot Act, could not ever tell anyone of the letter. Thus, a librarian who received a letter demanding all Internet records for a particular patron, or a telecommunications agency that received a similar request, could not tell the target of the letter or even discuss the letter with their lawyers. Now recipients are at least allowed to confer with a lawyer.

National security letters Letters issued by the FBI to access private information without a warrant.

Freedom of Information Act requests showed that after the Patriot Act created the authority to circumvent warrant requirements, the FBI was issuing over 30,000 letters a year, and, in 2004, the actual number was closer to 65,000. It has also come to light that the FBI's use of such letters often broke the law by what was asked for or the level of proof they had to justify the letter. FBI agents invoked terrorism emergencies to obtain approval when they did not exist and it was revealed that call records obtained with national security letters included telephones belonging to the *Washington Post* and *New York Times*. In one random audit of 77 letters, 22 had possible violations of law or policy (Kreimer, 2007: 1185; Solomon and Johnson, 2010). The use of national security letters has been the subject of several conflicting lower federal appellate level lawsuits, but are still widely used today.

After 9/11, President Bush authorized secret wiretapping of American citizens by the National Security Agency without going through the FISC to obtain a warrant. Evidently, only a few people knew of the wiretapping, and warrantless wiretapping of American citizens had not received the formal approval of the Justice Department or Attorney General Ashcroft (Lichtblau, 2008). This led to the infamous hospital room showdown where Bush officials attempted to get Attorney General Ashcroft, sick and in his hospital bed, to sign off on the wiretapping as legal. James Comey rushed to the hospital and barred them from entering the room. There was evidently also a gap in what President Bush had authorized and what the NSA was collecting, which included purely domestic transactions, not just transactions which involved foreign targets. This required Bush officials to redraft the legal authorization to collect metadata only if at least one party was a foreigner and to search the database only for records related to terrorism (Savage, 2015).

After the wiretapping was exposed, civil libertarian groups tried to sue, but the Supreme Court refused to hear the case, deciding that they had no standing to sue and that the state secrets act barred the release of information on any wiretapping that might have been done (Savage, 2008). In August 2007, the Protect America Act was passed, which, in effect, gave approval to the secret wiretapping program after the fact. The Protect America Act expired in 2008, but its provisions were included in the FISA Amendments Act of 2008. Legal immunity for telecommunications companies that cooperated with warrantless wiretapping was also provided. The bill also changed some elements of the FISC by expanding government's powers to invoke emergency wiretapping before approval is granted, but affirming the position that the FISC is the only legal authority to grant wiretaps; specifically opposing any presidential power in that regard (Lichtblau, 2008).

Congress passed the FISA Amendments Reauthorization Act of 2012 that extended the provisions for five more years. Basically, the government now has the power to wiretap when it is for foreign intelligence collecting and at least one party is outside the United States. Further, even if both parties are in the United States, agents can begin a wiretap if they seek a warrant within 72 hours.

Targets of wiretapping have little recourse in the courts since they may not know they have been the object of wiretapping—or if they do know, courts defer to national security. In 2013, the Supreme Court held that a group of lawyers, journalists, and organizations couldn't sue to challenge the expansion of the FISA because they couldn't prove they were being monitored and, therefore, had no standing (*Clapper, Director of National Intelligence, et al. v. Amnesty International USA, et al.*, February 26, 2013).

The Quote and Query box illustrates the concerns of many.

The Bush administration had pushed for several data mining programs that basically sift through large amounts of information, tagging key words for further scrutiny. What we now know is that the NSA began to acquire massive amounts of electronic data and saved it for data mining. A semi-secret facility that could hold massive amounts (the equivalent of 500 quintillion pages of text) of metadata was built in Utah. According to reports, data are diverted to the facility from 10 to 20 data switching stations throughout the United States and satellite monitoring stations (Bamford, 2012). In June 2013, Edward Snowden revealed the extent of the NSA's surveillance activities.

> ## QUOTE & **QUERY**
>
> We're protecting freedom and democracy, but unfortunately freedom and democracy have to be sacrificed.
>
> *Source: Jethro Eisenstein, New York lawyer, quoted in Moss and Fessenden, 2002: A18.*
>
> **?** Is this claim overstating the issue?

Edward Snowden, a young cyber-security contractor for the NSA, flew to Hong Kong and then released a huge trove of secrets to journalists at major newspapers. He said he did it because he was increasingly concerned about the extent of NSA's spying on Americans and lying to Congress about the extent of their capabilities and activities. He was accused of being a spy for the Chinese and then for Russia when he ended up in that country to stay out of the reach of extradition. His revelations led to embarrassment and apologies from U.S. officials to world leaders like German Chancellor

Angela Merkel whose cellphone was evidently tapped with her private conversations stored in the NSA data banks and revealed, along with others, by Snowden.

Now, from Snowden's disclosures, we know that the NSA did collect all electronic transmissions and stored them to analyze "metadata." PRISM is the intelligence-gathering program disclosed by Snowden. The NSA collects e-mail, instant-message chats, and videos from major tech companies, including Google, Yahoo, Microsoft, Facebook, and Apple. The targets are foreigners overseas, although communications with Americans are collected also and sometimes shared with the CIA and the FBI. Snowden has told journalists that NSA analysts also monitor content and even pull nude pictures from private cellphone transmissions to share with each other. No independent corroboration exists for that allegation, but the fact that NSA officials say they do not monitor phone conversations or e-mail transmissions without court orders does not, by itself, mean that it does not happen since they also had previously testified in Congressional hearings that they did not collect metadata and that was not true.

Some individuals knowledgeable about NSA's activities reported that there could have been ways to limit the collection of data, but the decision was made to capture all communications, arguably because the vast trove of information was being used to develop encryption-breaking software and, also, storing older data allowed them to retrieve it and break the encryption as their tools improved (Bamford, 2012).

Interestingly, the American public seemingly quickly lost interest in the fact that their private communications may be monitored by the government, and, by 2015, less than 40 percent of respondents in one survey was concerned about the government spying on them (Raine and Madden, 2015). Legislators seem to be more concerned, than the general public, however, and they probably should be since anyone with the political power to control and utilize the governmental spying apparatus would conceivably be able to use it against their political enemies.

In May 2015, the House passed the USA Freedom Act that supposedly ends the NSA's storage of metadata, but still allows the NSA to request records from telecommunications companies with a court order. The provision of the Patriot Act (Section 215) that the NSA interpreted to give them the broad power to collect data expired June 1, 2015 without a Senate vote on the bill, but on June 2, 2015, the Senate passed the USA Freedom Act (which stands for "Uniting and Strengthening America by Fulfilling Rights and Ending Eavesdropping, Dragnet-collection and Online Monitoring Act"), and it was signed into law by the president. Proponents say it has ended the mass storage of American's data, critics say that such activities can still take place (and probably are) under Executive Order 12333 and/or FISA Court judges' generous interpretation of Section 702 of the FISA Amendments Act. These powers include the collection of the actual content of internet communications and phone calls, not just metadata.

Privacy advocates challenged the use of PRISM information in domestic crime prosecutions; however, the FISA court disagreed that it was unconstitutional if the collection was originally for foreign intelligence (Nakashima, 2016).

In 2017, the NSA said it would no longer collect Americans' e-mails and texts exchanged with people overseas that simply mention flagged terms or e-mail addresses unless the e-mail is to or from identified suspects. It was discovered that NSA analysts had violated rules imposed by the FISC by collecting such "mention only" or "about" e-mail. In a news article about the change, the various methods of collecting data are described, including "upstream" collection that is when telecommunications

▤ IN THE NEWS | *Smart TVs and Spying*

Government officials have fought with technology companies to prevent them from developing and marketing encrypted messaging systems because it will interfere with their ability to identify terrorists. A new study finds, however, that new technologies—such as television sets with microphones and web-connected cars—create new ways to spy on people. The argument against creating a backdoor for government into any encryption system is that it also would be available to hackers, and would also hasten the pattern of authoritarian governments insisting on similar access if the American technology companies operated in their countries. However, devices such as cellphones and EZ passes are already being used to determine location. Microphones on smart TV's or even some dolls that send the verbal message through the Internet may be exploited by government agents for surveillance by reverse commands that would make the microphones into listening devices.

Source: Sanger, 2016.

companies give the NSA copies of Internet communications that cross the border and contain search terms provided by the NSA (names or e-mail addresses of suspects). This is the type of communication that the NSA says it will no longer collect. So-called downstream communications originate with foreign targets and are collected under the Prism program through Internet providers. Even if they are to American residents, they will be collected. The FISA Amendments Act that authorizes NSA activities will expire at the end of 2017, although a judge's order of extension may allow it to operate until 2018, even without Congressional approval (Savage, 2017).

A range of surveillance technology is being used by domestic law enforcement that citizens are only dimly aware of. Recall that the national security letters are used liberally by the FBI. Most cases are not or only marginally related to any threat of terrorism, and, typically, are for drug investigations.

Other means of surveillance, typically originating with the military or counterintelligence, have migrated to local law enforcement. A "stingray" is a cell tower simulator that hijacks all cellphone transmissions in an area. About the size of a suitcase, it can be used to track a cellphone to within a few feet because it "tricks" all surrounding devices to see it as a cellphone tower. Critics allege it is extremely invasive because it picks up or disrupts all cellphones in the area, not just the suspect's. It was engineered for federal use, but has been shared with local law enforcement, although the law enforcement agencies that were given the stingray to use, had to sign nondisclosure agreements to keep it secret. This has led to dropping criminal cases or plea bargaining out cases if prosecution required exposure of the use of the device. It has been used to locate kidnappers and murderers, but it has also been used by some departments to track stolen cellphones and in other petty theft cases. The device has been used since at least 2007, but it has only been recently that its use has become general knowledge. At this point, there is no Fourth Amendment law that is related specifically to the use of the device, primarily because no appeal challenging its use can take place from convictions that are obtained without mentioning the use of the device (Heath, 2015; Nakashima, 2015). Interestingly, the federal agencies that use stingrays must obtain a warrant per agency policy, but local law enforcement agencies that have been given the device do not (Zetter, 2015). Some states have now passed laws to require law enforcement agencies to obtain warrants (Heath, 2015).

IN THE NEWS | Convictions in Jeopardy

In Maryland, hundreds of convictions are in jeopardy because of the use of stingrays, which were used, perhaps, illegally. Maryland's second-highest court held that Baltimore police violated the Fourth Amendment when they used a stingray device to find a suspect without a search warrant. The court held that users have a reasonable expectation that their phone will not be used to track them. Nearly 2,000 cases in Baltimore alone may be in jeopardy. The decision will be appealed.

Source: Heath, 2016b.

Other surveillance tools used by local law enforcement include cameras on a manned civilian aircraft for wide-scale surveillance, military-grade facial recognition software, license-plate scanners, streetlights with recording capabilities, behavioral recognition software (using camera footage, the software detects suspicious activity), and intelligence analysis software partially funded by the CIA (Chen, 2014). The problematic nature of these types of surveillance and analysis technology is not so much that law enforcement is using them, but that the public is not aware of the use, nor are there good checks and balances in place to make sure the use stays within the bounds of legality. For instance, one company, Geofeedia, developed a tool that used text, photos, and videos obtained through Facebook, Twitter, Instagram, and other social media sources to help law enforcement conduct surveillance of protests and identify protesters. Law enforcement, using the software, could locate an individual based on data gleaned from social media. Reportedly they had 500 law enforcement clients before they were challenged by the ACLU. The social media companies did not give Geofeedia the right to use the information to develop the tool and barred them from using the sites after the challenge (Bromwich, Victor, and Isaacoct, 2016).

License plate readers have been an important tool for law enforcement. Basically, the device picks up license plates, feeds the plate number into a computer, and the law enforcement officer gets a notice back if there are outstanding warrants. There was little to no challenge to this technology by privacy advocates. However, the new chapter in license plate readers is a partnership with a private for-profit company. A private company called Digital Recognition Network contracts with private cars equipped with high-speed cameras that drive around and snap license plates. Nationally, about 2,300 photos per minute flow into a massive database of license plate photos maintained by the Fort Worth company. This data is shared with law enforcement; in return, law enforcement shares data of outstanding warrants, typically for traffic tickets. Now the law enforcement agency receives a read-out of defendant's name, a picture of his vehicle, and an aerial photograph of the exact location of the car only hours earlier. Law enforcement officers can more easily find the person and, in the jurisdictions in Texas where this is being used, are even provided credit card readers so the person can pay the deputy or constable the outstanding fine right away. Of course, the company that processes the payments, which is affiliated with the camera reader company, gets a 25 percent fee tacked onto the fine. Some argue that paying the fines directly to police saves time and keeps the offender out of jail. Critics argue that the arrangement has turned cops into debt collectors, police energies have now been diverted to tracking down 10-year-old warrants for traffic violators instead of crime prevention tasks, and the technology allows police to conduct "virtual stakeouts" of individuals raising privacy concerns. Courts thus far have concluded that taking pictures of license plates is legal, but the hundreds of millions of license-plate pictures, stored into a searchable database that can potentially be combined with other personal information, raises alarms. For instance, a license plate could be entered into the system and a record of where the car goes daily could be obtained; a query of an address would result in the license plates of cars that could be found at that address over time. It is not only law enforcement that purchases the data, but banks and lenders are also customers. The company has stated that it could merge facial recognition technology with license plate cameras. Some states have limited the use of these devices or at least the storage of information from them. As of 2016, only Arkansas had an outright ban on private companies utilizing and storing information from license plate cameras (Dexheimer and Plohetski, 2016; Maass, 2016).

Finally, facial recognition technology is the stuff of television, but, increasingly it has become a viable tool for law enforcement, raising privacy concerns. Software programs can identify 16,000 points on a person's face and compare them, at a rate of more than one million faces a second, with a photo database. Reports indicate that law enforcement agencies are using facial recognition software more frequently with little oversight, guidelines, or public disclosure. Individuals are reporting that police officers are taking their picture without their permission (permission may not be needed in public places), even if they were not put under arrest, in some jurisdictions. The picture is used to confirm identity, but then also stored in the database so that the number of pictures in the database continues to increase. In the jurisdictions where this is happening, for example, San Diego, there may not even be records of the stops if there is no arrest. Other cities, like New York and Chicago, use facial recognition technology linked to 25,000 surveillance cameras. Boston discarded the idea of using facial recognition technology in 2013 to scan faces of thousands of people in outdoor concerts because of a belief that it crossed an ethical line (Williams, 2015d).

Perhaps even more troubling are the attempts to link data sources for more comprehensive monitoring. The FBI has undertaken a $1 billion "Next Generation Identification" program that will gather fingerprints, iris scans, and photographs for a broader than just facial recognition software. The system will eventually be made accessible to all local, state, federal, and international law enforcement agencies (Williams, 2015b). New York City uses stingrays, military-grade X-ray vans to see through walls, and is perfecting a "Domain Awareness System" that will combine data from license plate readers, MetroCards, and public and private security cameras. Using these sources, facial recognition technology is used to scan for offenders. Privacy advocates worry that the trove of information about identities will be scooped up by the federal government for immigration raids or other purposes (Patel and Price, 2017).

Undercover Operations

There were close to 500 prosecutions for terrorist-related activities between 9/11 and 2012 (Human Rights Watch, 2014). Most of these prosecutions have been for "material support" and conspiracy. Generally, a target is identified in a chat room or through contacts and evaluated as to their likely involvement. An informant or governmental agent will then develop a relationship with the person. When there has been sufficient preparatory activity for criminal liability, the plot is exposed and the would-be terrorists are arrested. Critics argue, however, that many would-be terrorists would never have been able to accomplish the tasks without the involvement of the government agent. In some cases, the targets were juveniles, still living at home. In another case, the target was mentally disturbed and was in a downward mental spiral even as the plot unfolded. In still others, informants offered the targets money to participate, therefore, making it unclear if they were motivated by jihad or purely money. These cases, which result in very long prison sentences, have enraged some in Muslim communities who wonder why the targets were selected and encouraged by government agents to participate in the plot (Human Rights Watch, 2014).

Sting operations have long been used in drug and other criminal investigations and the legal test is whether the target has a predisposition to commit the crime. Supporters of such sting operations argue that identification of the would-be terrorists in jihad chat rooms shows evidence of predisposition; therefore, no entrapment has occurred and none of the accused has been successful in an entrapment defense (Wheeler, 2012). The April 2013 Boston bombing by Chechen brothers Dzhokhar Tsarnaev and Tamerlan Tsarnaev show that young malcontents are very capable of harming large numbers of people without government help. Discovering these potential bombers in a chat room and targeting them for an undercover operation might have saved lives.

Not only federal agents are involved in undercover operations to combat terrorism. The New York City Police Department (NYPD) evidently had an intelligence division of about 1,000 individuals, led from 2003 to 2014 by an ex-CIA agent. The unit included two dozen civilian experts, lawyers, academics, linguists, and other specialists in addition to law enforcement investigators. Later it was revealed that at least four CIA agents were "embedded" in the NYPD; in some cases, taking unpaid leave from the CIA and being paid by the NYPD. In other cases, NYPD officers went to Langley for training. Privacy advocates are concerned with this overlap and merging of domestic law enforcement and a spy agency that was created and continues to have a mission to protect the nation against external threats (Savage, 2013).

The NYPD unit, called the Demographic Unit and then the Zone Assessment unit, monitored jihad websites, gathered tips regarding terrorist activity, and monitored mosques with "mosque crawlers" (agents who infiltrated mosques and neighborhoods to collect information) and surveillance (Feuer, 2010; Wasikowska, 2013). Critics point out that such surveillance, if conducted solely because of one's ethnicity, race, religion, or legal activities may be against the law. One informant reported that he attended and took notes on the people attending a Muslim Student Group at John Jay College. This type of focus on perfectly legal groups with no suspicion attached to them is like the overreach that occurred in the 1970s that led to the Church Committee, which investigated governmental surveillance abuse, and the creation of the FISA court (Wasikowska, 2013).

One such surveillance operation in Newark, New Jersey, was exposed when Newark police were called to investigate the suspicious activities of NYPD operatives. The NYPD officers were "staking out" the local mosque taking pictures of car licenses and people who attended. Citizens called police to report the suspicious activity of the officers and Newark politicians were understandably concerned to find NYPD officers conducting such an operation in their city (Apuzzo and Goldman, 2011; Associated Press, 2012b).

In 2014, Bill Bratton, Commissioner of NYPD again, disbanded the unit and reassigned the officers (Apuzzo and Goldstein, 2014), although obviously the NYPD's activities involving terrorism investigations have not ended. Two lawsuits arising from NYPD surveillance were settled in 2016. The settlement agreement changed the guidelines and procedures in investigations and surveillance that involves political or religious groups. One of the lawsuits, *Handschu v. Special Services Division*, 349 F.Supp. 766, 1972, was brought decades ago, due to alleged privacy abuses by the department's "Red Squad" back in the 1960s. That lawsuit led to court monitoring and the "Handschu Guidelines" that were supposed to restrict the NYPD's surveillance of political groups unless they had specific information about criminal conduct. In 2003, because of terrorism concerns, these rules were loosened. Now the settlement will bring back strict rules about when surveillance can take place and mandates a monitoring committee that will review all ongoing investigations involving political and religious groups or individuals. The committee includes one member from outside the NYPD, appointed by the mayor who has the authority to report to a federal judge if he or she feels that civil liberties are being violated by police activity. Under the settlement agreement, authorization for use of an undercover or confidential informant lasts only 90 days. Rules also require the NYPD to consider whether the investigative techniques employed have a deleterious effect on the community. Suspicion must be based on facts, not simply belonging to a religion or other protected group (Apuzzo and Baker, 2016; Patel and Price, 2016).

The New York City Police Department is obviously not the only police department that has increased its activities in domestic surveillance. In fact, there has been a sea change within law enforcement that has been described as a move toward "intelligence-led" policing. Part of the emphasis on collection and analysis of "pre-reasonable suspicion" data has been the creation of "fusion centers" and joint terrorism task forces, funded by the federal government, to help local police develop the capability of identifying potential threats. A national information sharing network connecting police departments and federal agencies, known as the Information Sharing Environment (ISE), has developed the ability to coordinate and share information. In 2013, approximately 14,600 different sub-federal law enforcement agencies, 78 regional and state-run fusion centers, and 103 Joint Terrorism Task Forces (JTTFs) existed in an overlapping and patchwork network of information gathering (Price, 2013: 3). It is not known how many exist today. This intelligence sharing may be helpful in improving the ability to protect national security, but it also raises important questions about what information local police collect, how long do they keep it, and who do they share it with.

Various legal and privacy advocates have concerns that the fusion centers are either violative of individual privacy in collecting information about private citizens, ineffective in the types of information it collects, or both. The federal government spends well over a billion dollars on the fusion centers, but in the only governmental audit of the centers, there was little evidence that they had helped uncover any terrorist plots and they had a troubling pattern of violating Constitutional provisions regarding privacy. A lot of the money, for instance, was used to buy laptops and flat-screen televisions to monitor "open source" information, otherwise known as cable news. In a review of fusion centers and local law enforcement's role in intelligence gathering, investigators from the Brennan Center (a law school-affiliated think tank focusing on civil liberties) reported that individuals who worked in such centers and task forces received inadequate training and oversight regarding privacy protections (Price, 2013). One can go to the Department of Homeland Security website and find the location of fusion centers (see: https://www.dhs.gov/fusion-center-locations-and-contact-information). Whether they are a useful tool or a waste of money is not clear.

Critics allege that, just as in the 1960s and 1970s, unfettered power to spy has been misused today in the indiscriminate use of national security letters and spying on groups that have no possible connection to terrorism but are merely left-leaning or are groups that disagree with the administration's actions (Harris, 2006). For instance, it has been reported that the Department of Homeland Security issued a "threat assessment" of pro-choice and antiabortion groups for a local police department, and issued a report on a Muslim conference held in Georgia. These investigations of American citizens are outside the scope of the investigative powers created to protect us against espionage and terrorism and cause concern for civil libertarians even though the reports were destroyed after concerns were raised (Savage and Shane, 2009). The Office of the Inspector General (2010) issued a report that described FBI investigations of groups that could not reasonably be considered terrorist organizations, such as the Thomas Merton Center of Pittsburgh, the People for the Ethical Treatment of Animals, Greenpeace, the *Catholic Worker*, and the Religious Society of Friends. The report concluded that the FBI activities potentially implicated First Amendment rights even though the reports were destroyed. There is no current report indicating whether such investigations have occurred since then.

Thus far, the Supreme Court has either refused to hear cases concerning governmental surveillance and undercover operations or ruled in the government's favor, meaning that, legally, there seems to be great power invested in government operatives to intrude into Americans' privacy. This greater power requires greater self-control to stay within legal and ethical boundaries. Even more troubling than mission creep and use of surveillance tools against suspected domestic criminals is the documented abuse of such power by NSA analysts and others. Top secret reports were released by the NSA in response to a records request by the American Civil Liberties Union that showed dozens of NSA agents and others misused their great powers of surveillance to spy on girlfriends, spouses, and others. Workers were fired or allowed to retire rather than face criminal charges (Hensley, 2014; Walker, 2014). When the barrier between federal powers designed to protect against external threats and law enforcement's domestic powers used against citizens no longer exists, we have much less legal protection against unethical abuses of such power.

Utilitarianism versus Human Rights-Based Policing

human rights-based policing The policing approach that recognizes the police as servants of the public good; although crime control is important, protection of civil liberties is the fundamental mission.

Utilitarianism is the ethical justification offered for the counterterrorism measures we've discussed, but utilitarianism is a faulty ethical justification for what has been done in the name of security. The internationally recognized **human rights-based policing** is more firmly grounded in ethical principles.

Our discussions since 9/11 have always been about a forced choice between safety and liberty. More surveillance, more intrusions on privacy, and more law enforcement are supposed to make us safe, so we should not complain. Some argue, however, that it is a false argument to weigh privacy or any civil liberty against security. Writing before

9/11, Alderson (1998: 23) presented a prescient argument against the "end" of security as a justification for taking away liberties:

> *I acknowledge that liberty is diminished when people feel afraid to exercise it, but to stress security to unnecessary extremes at the price of fundamental freedoms plays into the hands of would-be high police despots. Such despots are quick to exploit fear in order to secure unlimited power.*

Alderson also addressed terrorism directly: "It is important for police to maintain their high ethical standards when facing terrorism, and for their leaders to inspire resistance to any degeneration into counter-terrorism terror" (1998: 71).

The major problem of utilitarianism or means–end thinking is that we are unable to know the outcome of our actions. Justifying otherwise unethical means by arguing that these means will lead to a good end depends on the ability to know that the means will result in the desired outcome. Unfortunately, this is not possible. For instance, not respecting the rights of Muslims in this country may backfire in that the Muslim community can be a great ally to police in preventing or investigating terrorist activity. If the Muslim community is cooperative with preventive efforts, it is because the community believes in the legal system and the integrity of those within it. In 2012, the Muslim community in New York City marched against the police department in opposition to what they considered illegal surveillance of their community. It is possible, then, that police actions in this country, justified as leading to a good end, have made it *less* likely that a good end will result because they will receive less help from the community against potential terror threats.

According to Cherney and Hartley (2015), three challenges for law enforcement when interacting with Muslim communities (or any communities likely to be the site of terrorists) is (1) overcoming distrust, (2) balancing the need for intelligence gathering and community engagement, and (3) distinguishing friendly partners in community. They note that one of the platforms of counterterrorism efforts in the United Kingdom is partnership with Muslim communities to generate communication, trust, and, also, assist the community in creating avenues of opportunity for youth to divert them from radicalism. Challenges to these efforts are politicians who malign whole groups or communities, and police tactics that target the community such as wholesale raids, stops, or curfews. Community leaders must be careful when interacting with authorities because if their cooperation is viewed as harming the community, they will lose legitimacy. Law enforcement tends to underestimate the fractured nature of these communities and competing leaders. If law enforcement involvement is primarily intelligence gathering it will backfire, so efforts must be genuinely focused on community engagement and support to be successful.

In our utilitarian measures to protect ourselves from terrorists, it is at least conceivable that we may create more terrorists. The current generation of Middle Eastern children may identify the United States only as an aggressor. Children have grown into adults in the Middle East hearing about Bagram and Abu Ghraib, and been exposed to accidents where U.S. bombs have hit civilian targets like hospitals. How do they feel about the United States? By engaging in renditions, operating secret prisons, and defending the right to torture, we have lost allies and gained enemies around the world and, in the process, have threatened our future security. By engaging in acts that are associated with oppressive countries, such as torture and secret prisons, we make it easier for radical clerics and others to convince adherents that this country is evil and deserves to be a victim of terroristic acts. By deciding that human rights exist for some and not for others, we weaken civil liberties for all citizens. Once we start parceling out human rights and justice differentially, it opens the door to those who look for an excuse to abuse and victimize.

Human rights-based law enforcement is not utilitarian. There is recognition that some acts are never justified. No end is so important that governments can stoop to slavery, genocide, or torture. No situation ever justifies sexism, racism, murder, rape, or intimidation. There is a suspicion of state power in rights-based law enforcement and a fear that police will be used to oppress the powerless. The way to avoid this is to place the protection of rights, rather than crime control (or terrorism), as the central theme of policing, because the definition of crime and the identification of who is a criminal may be subverted for political ends. The United Nations' *Code of Conduct for Law Enforcement Officials* illustrates the values and premise of the rights-based approach: "In the performance of their duty, law enforcement officials shall respect and protect human dignity and maintain and uphold the human rights of all persons" (Article 2, reported in Kleinig, 1999).

Neyroud and Beckley (2001: 62) have described the police standards of the United Kingdom as reflecting an emphasis on human rights. Standards include the following provisions:

- To fulfill the duties imposed on them by the law
- To respect human dignity and uphold human rights
- To act with integrity, dignity, and impartiality
- To use force only when strictly necessary, and then proportionately
- To maintain confidentiality
- Not to use torture or use ill-treatment
- To protect the health of those in their custody
- Not to commit any act of corruption
- To respect the law and the code of conduct and oppose violations of them
- To be personally liable for their acts

Bayley (2014) reviewed human rights policing across the world and observed that the incredibly expensive attempt to bring policing in Afghanistan and Iraq into conformance with democratic ideals has been largely regarded as a failure. Despite major efforts from the United Nations and other bilateral organizations, police reform across the world has not been extremely successful. He argues that the principles of human rights policing, including humane treatment, due process, and justice-based interactions with the public have been disseminated widely across the world; however, the implementation of actual practices is much less successful. As to dissemination, Bayley reports that the United Nations' *Universal Declaration of Human Rights* (1948) is the most translated document in history. The United Nations has several documents that present standards for human rights policing, including the *Human Rights Standards for Law Enforcement* in 1996, and the Council of Europe has published the *European Code of Police Ethics* in 2001. The United Nations also has a police unit that deploys police officers worldwide to provide technical assistance and mentoring as well as monitor international agreements. The Quote and Query box indicates that Bayley is quite optimistic about the success of promoting the ideals of human rights and the role of police in protecting them.

As to implementation of democratic ideals, Bayley (2014), after conducting a small survey of international police experts is less optimistic. He found that experts cited only three countries that had undertaken substantial reforms: Northern Ireland, El Salvador, and South Africa. Others mentioned by some, but not most experts included: Croatia, Bosnia-Herzegovina, Kosovo, East Germany, Poland, the Czech Republic, and Slovenia. Across the world, police departments continue to reflect the problems of their respective countries. Police departments in problematic, corrupt regimes share these same qualities. Democratic policing and the rule of law are associated with higher education and higher socioeconomic standing of the citizenry. Human rights-based policing comes along with broader political reform. In his presentation of proposals to advance human-rights policing, Bayley mentions the commitment of political leaders and external accountability measures for policing. Ironically, recall that external accountability measures (e.g., civilian review boards) create raging controversy whenever they are proposed even in the United States.

In Chapter 10, we discussed the importance of an independent judiciary. This concept is an essential element of the discussion here as well. It is no coincidence that the United Nations and the European Union both mandate that a country have an independent judiciary for that nation to be considered protective of human rights and thus eligible to join the European Union. The way to freedom and democracy is through the recognition of human rights, and the way to protect human rights is through an independent judiciary (Keith, 2002: 196–197).

The increased militarization of the police since 9/11 may not be consistent with the human rights approach described here. Police departments have increasingly taken on military characteristics, buying armored vehicles and normalizing the use of military style tactics in mainstream policing. SWAT officers wear military uniforms and use flash-bang grenades and entry explosives exactly like military commando squads. The overlap between police and the military is understandable—military veterans are physically fit, respond to authority, are trained in weapons, understand hierarchy of command, and are familiar with dangerous conditions. In other ways, however, policing and military service are not similar at all and should not be. The war analogy is especially inappropriate when dealing with citizens, and police are much more likely to violate citizens' rights when they view them as the enemy. The Quote and Query box encapsulates this view.

Human rights-based policing is consistent with procedural justice research and guardian policing. There are good reasons for protecting rights for everyone. Criminals can be considered our "canaries in the coal mine." What this means is, like the canaries that were used to detect whether dangerous levels of methane or carbon monoxide existed in mines before the invention of electronic detectors, the way criminals are treated may be a harbinger of things to come for us all. The Supreme Court Justices may be reflecting this in their ruling that the information we keep on our cellphones is personal and police

QUOTE & QUERY

More has been done in the past 25 years internationally to advance the cause of human rights than in the 400 years since Hugo Grotius first began to write about the necessity for international law.

Professor David Bayley.

Source: Bayley, 2014: 3.

? What role do police have in promoting human rights across the world?

QUOTE & QUERY

Since 9/11, America has experienced an arguably dangerous weakening of the traditional separation between these two occupations, a blurring of the boundary lines separating the military and the police, and a move toward rather than away from, a more authoritarian dispensation.

Source: Brown, 2011: 670.

? Do you agree that law enforcement is becoming more militarized? Give examples if so.

officers must obtain a warrant to access it (*Riley v. California*, 573 U.S. __, 2014). The surprising unanimous decision in this case may indicate that even the most conservative Supreme Court justices are troubled by the reach of government and, at least in this case, were not persuaded by the utilitarian argument that the end of crime control justifies incursions into the liberties that all Americans should cherish and protect.

▮ Ethical Dilemmas and Decisions

This last chapter has focused on the war on terror because it is the greatest challenge facing this country today, but it also illustrates in dramatic ways how ethics and morals permeates national discussions. The deliberations over what was done and is being done to prevent the scourge of terrorism utilize legal analyses, but morality and ethics are also part of the discussion.

    This last section reiterates the idea that ultimately ethics is about making decisions. Like police officers, CIA and FBI agents may be tempted to use illegal and unethical means to accomplish their mission. Like prosecutors, lawyers in the Justice Department and the military justice system have been pressured to skirt the law to pursue a good end. Like correctional officers, personnel who worked in Guantanamo and Bagram were exposed to a subculture where prisoners were considered not worthy of basic respect and humane treatment. Like any of us who are faced with a moral or ethical dilemma, how these individuals resolved their dilemma speaks to their character and conscience.

    The My Lai incident in Vietnam has almost passed out of this nation's consciousness, but at the time, there was great debate over whether soldiers should follow their superiors' orders blindly or make an independent assessment of the morality of the action. In this case, several officers were prosecuted by a military court for killing women and children in a village during the Vietnam War without any evidence that they were a threat to the unit's safety. The officers' defense was that their superiors gave the orders to take the village without regard to whether the inhabitants were civilians or guerrillas. The rationale was that often there wasn't time to establish whether a civilian was friendly or not, and that, in any event, civilians often carried grenades or otherwise harmed U.S. troops. There was heated public discussion in support of and against the soldiers' actions. Is an individual excused from moral culpability when following orders, or should one disobey orders that one believes to be illegal or immoral? Generally, military justice does not allow a defense of "following orders" if the order is against a treaty or law.

    In the Abu Ghraib prison scandal, while soldiers argued that they were only following orders when they abused the detainees, Joseph Darby was so distressed by the pictures showing various types of abuse that he turned them in to the army's CID, and the resulting investigation led to indictments and resignations. Some, however, condemned Darby as a traitor to his country, and he and his family received death threats and were not able to return to their hometown to live because of the town's hostility to him.

    A soldier's dilemma is not all that different from a police officer's dilemma in that both organizations place a great emphasis on chain of command and loyalty. It is possible that police officers may receive orders that they know to be illegal and/or unethical from their field training officer (FTO) or supervisor. Do police officers or other criminal justice professionals have a duty to substitute their personal moral judgments when presented with an unlawful or unethical order, or is obedience to superiors mandatory? In these circumstances, one must depend on the law rather than the chain of command. If the action is clearly illegal, there will be no defense if the individual officer follows orders; he or she will still be legally culpable. If the action is not against the law but is against policy, departmental sanctions may be applied. If the action is not against the law and not against departmental policy, does any ethical system support going against one's superior? Following appropriate grievance procedures if something seems to be wrong may be a more supportable avenue unless there is immediate harm to an innocent or a pattern of wrongful action including the chain of command.

Some of the hardest decisions one will be faced with during a career involve going against superiors or colleagues. Even if the troubling behavior is obviously illegal, it is difficult to challenge authority. **Whistleblowers** are those who risk their career to expose wrongdoing in their organization. Of course, some may have purely egocentric reasons for exposing wrongdoing, but many whistleblowers do so because their principles and individual ethical system will not allow them to stand quiet when others in the organization are committing unethical and/or illegal acts. In most cases, whistleblowers face retaliation even when everyone agrees that the wrong exposed should have been dealt with. Governmental agencies, seemingly, are no different than for-profit businesses when employees expose wrongdoing and are retaliated against. This has resulted in whistleblower protection laws that utilize the protections of the First Amendment.

> **whistleblowers**
> Individuals, usually employees, who find it impossible to live with knowledge of corruption or illegality within a government or organization and expose it, usually creating a scandal.

In one Supreme Court case, a youth worker testified that a legislator was being paid from public funds but not actually working. The legislator was convicted of bribery, but the worker who testified against her was fired. He filed a whistleblower protection suit and the state's position was that it was his duty to report, therefore, it was not First Amendment speech and unprotected. If so, his firing would not be able to be challenged. The Supreme Court held that he had testified as a citizen and his testimony was on a matter of public concern, thus it was First Amendment speech and protected (*Lane v. Franks*, 134 S.Ct. 2369, 2014). This case should provide some degree of comfort to whistleblowers in public agencies, although the extent of the ruling remains to be seen.

There were many individuals who faced difficult decisions in the aftermath of 9/11. For most of them, their decisions had devastating effects on their careers:

- Charles Swift, a navy attorney who defended Salim Ahmed Hamdan against the president and the Pentagon and had to leave the navy because he upheld his oath to provide a zealous defense.

- Mary McCarthy, the CIA analyst who was alleged to have exposed the secret prisons and was forced to retire.

- James Yee, who defended the rights of the detainees in Guantanamo and was labeled a traitor as a result and had his reputation destroyed.

- Sergeant Joe Darby, who revealed the abuses occurring at Abu Ghraib and had to move with his family into hiding because of death threats from other military members.

- Babak Pasdar, a computer security expert, who found the "Quantico circuit," (used to collect communications from and to Americans) and testified before Congress about what he witnessed (Devine, 2008).

- Lieutenant Commander Matthew Diaz, a Judge Advocate General lawyer for the joint military task force at Guantanamo, who sent a list of detainees to the Center for Constitutional Rights in New York and was prosecuted, sentenced to six months imprisonment, and given a dishonourable discharge, even though a federal court declared the information was public, not classified (Wiltrout, 2007).

- Coleen Rowley, an FBI lawyer who publicly reported that officials in Washington ignored reports from the field about Zacarias Moussaoui, and who exposed the practice of punishing those who criticized superiors who were not doing their job in sharing and analyzing important information (Carr, 2005).

- General Antonio Taguba, who conducted the investigation of Abu Ghraib and found his career was derailed, evidently because of the comprehensiveness of the report, his strong condemnation of the practices he found there, and his documentation of the lack of leadership.

In 2014, an editorial in the *New York Times* called for "positive accountability." Noting that there were not going to be any prosecutions for torture, illegal wiretapping, or other potential illegalities that took place in the governmental response to 9/11, the writer called for publicly celebrating those who "kept their moral clarity intact" and objected to what they knew to be wrong; in some cases, at great personal cost. In addition to those already mentioned earlier, they included:

> *Alberto Mora, former general counsel of the Navy, who fought against the vicious new protocols [of enhanced interrogation]; Philip Zelikow, an adviser to Condoleezza Rice who wrote an "anti-torture memo" that the White House attempted to destroy; and Ian Fishback, an infantry captain who reported widespread prisoner abuses by his own unit. Getting no clear response from his chain of command, Fishback wrote an open letter to Senator John McCain. Fishback asked: "Do we sacrifice our ideals in order to preserve security?" His answer: "I would rather die fighting than give up even the smallest part of the idea that is 'America'"* (Luban, 2014).

The author called for President Obama to praise these people, and even award some Presidential Medals of Freedom. It didn't happen. There are many others—some known, many more unknown—who faced difficult decisions about what was right in the days, months, and years after 9/11. In the face of continued acts of terror is this country and across the world, there will continue to be temptation to subvert law and morality to do what seems necessary, and, there will continue to be individuals who will stand against illegal and unethical means, despite the justification of a good end.

How we face and resolve dilemmas is influenced by our ethical systems and understanding that doing the right thing is not always easy, nor is it necessarily easy to determine what is right. Some of the individuals mentioned earlier were and still are criticized bitterly over their decisions. While some consider them heroes, others consider them traitors. One might agree with their goals and disagree with their actions. We cannot deny, however, that they faced their dilemma and chose to do what they considered was right, knowing they would face consequences for doing so.

In the final analysis, the approach we have taken throughout this book is perhaps the best one when faced with any type of ethical dilemma. To review, when faced with a dilemma, one should consider law, policy, and then, if necessary, apply several ethical systems such as utilitarianism and ethical formalism to determine the right course of action:

- Is there relevant law? Are you being asked to do something or observe something that is contrary to state, national, international, or military law?

- Is there relevant policy? Does the action violate company or agency policy? If you feel the policy is wrong, can you use official channels to object?
- Finally, what do ethical systems tell you is the right thing to do?

Utilitarianism may be the most pervasive ethical system used in the war on terror. Even under utilitarianism, however, there must be limits to what can be done for a "good end." Too often, the worst abuses are justified by perpetrators using a faulty utilitarian justification. Utilitarianism cannot provide a justification when there is no proof that the bad "means" was the only way to get to the good "end." More importantly, it is impossible to know the outcome of one's actions, therefore, the argument of greater good cannot be supported in many cases. Expediency and fear often are the enemies of coherent ethical analysis. It is always best to also consider ethical formalism or ethics of care when considering the right course of action along with utilitarianism, or, even the simpler "front page test," which basically just asks you to consider how you would feel if your action was described on the front page of a newspaper. If you would not want your actions exposed, there may be problems with your ethical analysis.

For the criminal justice professional who must uphold and enforce the law, the discussion of morality, justice, and law is not just academic. Line officers often face questions of individual morality versus obedience and loyalty to one's superiors or the organization. One thing that every professional must understand is that they alone are morally and ethically responsible for their own decisions and actions. It is for this reason that the study of ethics is so important. Although professionals and practitioners may get bogged down with day-to-day problems, and bureaucratic agendas may cause them to lose sight of larger goals, foremost in their minds should always be the true scope and meaning of the power inherent in the criminal justice system. It is people who make a *justice* system *just* (or corrupt). To protect the citizenry from misuse and abuse of power, personnel in the criminal justice system must have a strong professional identity. Their power must be recognized for what it is and held as a sacred trust.

Criminal justice professionals are public servants and, as such, should aspire to a higher standard of behavior. They have a duty to the citizenry they serve, but even more than that, they must possess the moral and ethical sense to prevent the power inherent in their positions from being used for tyranny. Education isn't enough. Learning a body of knowledge and acquiring essential skills do not give individuals the moral sense necessary to use those skills wisely. Witness the recurring scandals involving lawyers and business professionals. A highly educated group is not necessarily free from corruption.

Criminal justice practitioners find themselves faced with a wide spectrum of ethical choices, including the following:

- Balancing friendship against institutional integrity—that is, when friends and colleagues engage in inappropriate or illegal behavior or rule breaking
- Balancing community and/or client (or offender) needs against bureaucratic efficiency and institutional goals
- Balancing personal goals or biases that conflict with fair and impartial treatment of the public and the clients served

Most people in the criminal justice field (or, indeed, any profession) have basically good characters. However, it can be argued that in some situations even those who have formed habits of honesty, truthfulness, and integrity are sincerely perplexed as to the correct course of behavior. These situations arise because the behavior choice seems so innocuous or trivial (e.g., whether to accept free coffee) or so difficult (e.g., a partner or friend wants you to cover up something she did wrong). In these instances, where basically good people have trouble deciding what to do, the ethical systems might help them analyze their choices.

It must also be accepted that in some dilemmas there are going to be costs involved in making the right decision. For instance, an officer who knows it is his duty to provide evidence against his brother-in-law, who is a major drug dealer, may lose his wife's and children's love. There is no assurance that doing the right thing will not come at a high cost. The ethical person may not necessarily be honored; some have been heavily punished for taking an ethical stand. However, those who do not expose wrongdoing and/or go along with it in an effort not to "rock the boat" often find that their long-term peace of mind pays the price for their silence.

Conclusion

The 9/11 attack created a sense of vulnerability and fear. Recently, an uptick in terrorist acts in this country and in Europe has reignited that fear. The risk that officials may resort to some of the tactics described earlier is high. The "end justifies the means" thinking is insidious and pervasive. If utilitarianism is used as a justification for wiretapping, detainments, governmental secrecy, and other actions, then one must also have facts to prove that the desired end will be brought about and that negative side effects do not outweigh the good that one seeks. This step seems to be missing in most justifications of what governments do when faced with threats. Ethical formalism and other systems would conclude that, even if one could prove the good end outweighs the bad means, some acts cannot ever be justified. Certain human rights belong to everyone—even criminals, even terrorists. In the crime war, drug war, or war on terror, the most important element of making ethical decisions is to apply ethical reasoning and not succumb to fear. Our final Quote and Query box makes a case for political liberty.

Most of us are lucky in that we will never have to decide whether to participate in torture, violate laws against wiretapping, or expose secrets in a way that could be considered a threat to national security. Criminal justice professionals, however, will probably encounter at least some of the dilemmas that have been described in previous chapters. The power of discretion, authority, and the duty of protecting public safety create dilemmas for these professionals that are quite different from those that most citizens encounter. Ultimately, for criminal justice professionals, as well as everyone else, the

QUOTE & QUERY

Political liberty, which is one of the greatest gifts people can acquire, is threatened when social order is threatened. It is dismaying to see how ready many people are to turn to strong leaders in hopes that they will end, by adopting strong measures, the disorder that has been the product of failed or fragile commitments. Drug abuse, street crime, and political corruption are the expression of unfettered choices. To end them, rulers, with the warm support of the people, will often adopt measures that threaten true political freedom. The kind of culture that can maintain reasonable human commitments takes centuries to create but only a few generations to destroy.

Source: James Q. Wilson, cited in Cole, 2002: 234.

? Although Wilson's statement is discussing the sacrifice of due process in the drug war and crime control, it has incredible relevance to the issues of terrorism. Interestingly, it was made by a noted conservative. How do we meet the threat of terrorists?

way you resolve dilemmas throughout the course of your career will constitute, in no small measure, the person you are.

Chapter Review

1. **Identify the basic themes of the book.**

   The presence of authority, power, force, and discretion exists in each of the subsystems of the criminal justice system. Informal practices and value systems among criminal justice actors may vary from formal codes of ethics. The importance of ethical leadership exists in each area of the system. The tension between deontological ethical systems and teleological or "means–end" ethical analysis also exists in each area of the system, as well as in the war on terror.

2. **Describe the basic elements of the "just war" debate and the "just means" discussion.**

   The traditional justification for war comes from natural law, and the second justification comes from positivist law. Natural law gives sovereigns the right to use force to uphold the good of the community, when unjust injuries are inflicted on others, and to protect the state. Positivist law justifies war when agreed upon by international bodies such as the United Nations. Once a war can be justified, there is a second determination over means. Not all means, even in war, are morally acceptable.

3. **Describe the responses to 9/11.**

   Since 9/11, the nation has been involved in moral debates over such responses as detainments, renditions and secret prisons, Guantanamo and the military commissions, the use of torture, governmental secrecy, wiretapping, and threats to privacy through undercover operations.

4. **Explain the human rights-based model of policing.**

   Human rights-based policing is not utilitarian. In the human rights model, values, and ethics focus on human rights, including the right to due process, and the fundamental duty of all public servants is to protect those rights. In this approach, the protection of rights is more important than the end of crime control.

5. **Present a method to resolve ethical dilemmas.**

   The method used throughout the book has been to evaluate the choices of action based on relevant law, policy, and ethics. If law and policy do not resolve the dilemma, then ethical systems, such as ethics of care, ethical formalism, and/or utilitarianism can help us resolve the dilemma. A short and simple ethical test is the "front-page test."

Study Questions

1. What are some actions the federal government has taken in response to terrorism?
2. What are the arguments in support of torture? What are the arguments against torture?
3. What are some rights recognized by the United Nations and the European Union?
4. Explain why "means–end" thinking leads to criminal actions.
5. What are the two justifications for a just war?

Writing/Discussion Exercises

1. Write an essay on (or discuss) the most difficult ethical dilemma in this chapter, and try to answer it by considering law, policy, and ethics. Also, use the "front-page test." This is a quick ethics test that asks if you would feel comfortable if your action were published on the front page of the newspaper. If you would not want it to be, there may be an ethical problem with your action.

2. Write an essay on (or discuss) an ethical or moral dilemma from your own life. Try to solve it by using any guidelines derived from this book. Be explicit about the procedure you used to arrive at a decision and about the decision itself.

3. Write a code of ethics for yourself.

Key Terms

Dirty Harry problem
human rights-based
    policing model

national security letters
positivist law
principle of double effect

terrorism
whistleblowers

ETHICAL DILEMMAS

Situation 1
You are a member of Congress, and the President is asking for a law that would allow "enhanced interrogation techniques," including waterboarding. Would you vote yes?

Situation 2
As a soldier in Afghanistan, you have pictures of fellow soldiers engaging in various acts of abuse and torture. What, if anything, would you do with the pictures?

Situation 3
You are a new police officer and are talking with other officers before roll call. The group is loudly and energetically proposing various gruesome torture techniques to get al-Qaeda operatives to talk. There is some hyperbole in the discussion, but also the sincere belief that torture is justified by the circumstances. What do you think about this position? If you object to torture, would you make your position known?

Situation 4
You live next door to an Arab family, and you hear the husband talking negatively about the United States. Your friends at work tell you that you should report him to the police because he might be a terrorist. What would you do? Why?

Situation 5
You are the president of the United States, and there has been another terrorist attack using passenger airplanes. One has crashed into the Pentagon, and another is heading for the White House. You have deployed fighter jets to surround the plane, and whoever is flying it refuses to acknowledge the command to turn around. Your military commanders are advising you to shoot down the plane—an act that would kill the 353 people aboard. What would you do? Would your answer be any different if it were heading toward the Statue of Liberty? Toward a crowded athletic stadium?

Bibliography

Abbey-Lambertz, J. 2015. "Charges Dismissed Against Joseph Weekley, Cop Who Fatally Shot Sleeping 7-Year-Old." *Huffington Post.com*, January 28. Retrieved from http://www.huffingtonpost.com/2015/01/28/joseph-weekley-charges-dismissed-aiyana-stanley-jones_n_6566032.html.

ABC News. 2016. "Dallas Police Chief David Brown Retiring After 33 Years." *ABC News*, September 1. Retrieved from http://abcnews.go.com/US/dallas-police-chief-david-brown-retiring-33-years/story?id=41804711.

Acker, J. and A. Redlich. 2011. *Wrongful Convictions: Law, Science, and Policy*. Durham, NC: Carolina Academic Press.

Adams, S. 2014. "The Highest Paid CEOs Are the Worst Performers, Study Says." *Forbes.com*, June 18. Retrieved from http://www.forbes.com/sites/susanadams/2014/06/16/the-highest-paid-ceos-are-the-worst-performers-new-study-says/.

Adams, V. 1981. "How to Keep 'Em Honest." *Psychology Today*, November: 52–53.

Adams, W. 2010. "Sentenced to Serving the Good Life in Norway." *Time*. Retrieved from www.time.com/time/magazine/article/0,9171,2000920,00.html.

Akers, R. L. 1998. *Social Learning and Social Structure: A General Theory of Crime and Deviance*. Boston, MA: Northeastern University Press.

Albarazi, H. 2015. "DA Launches Probe into Law Enforcement Misconduct." *SF Bay.com*, March 30, 2015. Retrieved from http://sfbay.ca/2015/03/30/da-launches-probe-into-law-enforcement-misconduct.

Alderson, J. 1998. *Principled Policing: Protecting the Public with Integrity*. Winchester, MA: Waterside.

Aleixo, P. and C. Norris. 2000. "Personality and Moral Reasoning in Young Offenders." *Personality and Individual Differences* 28(3): 609–623.

Alexander, A. 2017a. "Inmates Say Officers Handcuffed Them, Then Broke Their Bones." *Charlotte Observer*, May 31. Retrieved from http://www.charlotteobserver.com/news/local/article152335532.html.

Alexander, A. 2017b. "Officers Called It the 'Boom-Boom' Room. Inmates Found Out Why." *Charlotte Observer*, May 31. Retrieved from http://www.charlotteobserver.com/news/local/article152335532.html.

Alexander, M. 2010. *The New Jim Crow: Mass Imprisonment in the Age of Colorblindness*. New York: The New Press.

Alexander, M. 2013. "Why Police Lie Under Oath." *New York Times*, February 3: SR4.

Allgov.com. 2015. "58 California Cities Have Anti-Homeless Laws." *Allgov.com*, February 23. Retrieved from http://www.allgov.com/news/controversies/58-california-cities-have-anti-homeless-laws-150223?news=855748.

Allyn, B. 2015. "Philadelphia Spends Millions Every Year to Settle Claims of Police Misconduct." *NewsWorks*, July 17. Retrieved from http://www.newsworks.org/index.php/local/philadelphia/84249-philadelphia-spends-millions-every-year-to-settle-claims-of-police-misconduct.

Alpert, G. and R. Dunham. 2004. *Understanding Police Use of Force*. New York: Cambridge University Press.

Alpert, G. and J. MacDonald. 2001. "Police Use of Force: An Analysis of Organizational Characteristics." *Justice Quarterly* 18(2): 393–409.

Alpert, G. and J. Noble. 2009. "Lies, True Lies, and Conscious Deception: Police Officers and the Truth." *Police Quarterly* 12(2): 237–254.

American Bar Association. 2017. *Model Code of Judicial Conduct*. Retrieved from www.americanbar.org/groups/professional_responsibility/publications/model_code_of_judicial_conduct.html.

American Bar Association. 2015a. *Model Rules of Professional Responsibility*. Retrieved from www.americanbar.org/groups/professional_responsibility/publications/model_rules_of_professional_conduct.html.

American Bar Association. 2015b. *Standards for Criminal Justice*, 4th ed. Retrieved from http://www.americanbar.org/groups/criminal_justice/standards/ProsecutionFunctionFourthEdition.html.

American Civil Liberties Union. 2011. *Banking on Bondage: Private Prisons and Mass Incarceration*. New York: ACLU.

Amnesty International. 2007. *Amnesty International's Concerns About TASER Use: Statement to the U.S. Justice Department Inquiry into Deaths in Custody*. London: Amnesty International.

Anderson, C. 2010. "John Connolly Gets 40 Years in Prison." *WBZ38.com*, January 15. Retrieved from http://wbtv.com/local/john.connolly.sentence.2.909001.html.

Anderson, J. 2017. "How Wisconsin Is Weeding Out Bad Cops." *Daily Herald Network*, April 14. Retrieved from http://www.wausaudailyherald.com/story/news/2017/04/14/how-wisconsin-weeding-out-bad-cops/98867530/.

Anderson, P. and L. T. Winfree. 1987. *Expert Witnesses: Criminologists in the Courtroom*. Albany, NY: SUNY Press.

Antes, A., S. Murphy, E. Waples, M. Mumford, R. Brown, S. Connelly, and L. Devenport. 2009. "A Meta-Analysis of Ethics Instruction Effectiveness in the Sciences." *Ethics and Behavior* 19(5): 379–402.

Apuzzo, M. 2014. "Local Police Gearing Up with Tools of Combat." *The Seattle Times*, June 9: A4.

Apuzzo, M. 2015. "Police Rethink Long Tradition on Using Force." *New York Times*, May 5: A1.

Apuzzo, M. and A. Baker. 2016. "New York to Appoint Monitor to Review Police's Counterterrorism Activity." January 7. Retrieved from http://www.nytimes.com/2016/01/08/nyregion/new-york-to-appoint-monitor-to-review-polices-counterterrorism-activity.html?emc=edit_na_20160107&nlid=66242298&ref=cta&_r=0.

Apuzzo, M., S. Fink, and J. Risen. 2016. "U.S. Torture Leaves a Legacy of Detainees with Damaged Minds." *New York Times*, October 9: A1.

Apuzzo, M. and A. Goldman. 2011. "New York Police, CIA Team Up for Secret Anti-Terror Unit." *Austin American-Statesman*, August 25, 2011: A5.

Apuzzo, M. and J. Goldstein. 2014. "New York Drops Unit that Spied Among Muslims." *New York Times*, April 16: A1.

Apuzzo, M., M. Schmidt, A. Goldman, and E. Lichtblau. 2017. "In Trying to Avoid Politics, Comey Shaped an Election." *New York Times*, April 23: A1.

Arax, M. 1999. "Ex-Guard Says 4 Men Set Up Rape of Inmate." *Los Angeles Times*, October 14, 1999: A3.

Arax, M. 2004. "Guard Challenges Code of Silence." *Los Angeles Times*, January 20. Retrieved from http://articles.latimes.com/2004/jan/20/local/me-guard20.

Ariens, M. 2008. "American Legal Ethics in an Age of Anxiety." *St. Mary's Law Journal* 40: 343–452.

Ariens, M. 2009. "Playing Chicken: An Instant History of the Battle Over Exceptions to Client Confidences." *Journal of the Legal Profession* 33: 239–300.

Aristotle. 2012. *Nicomachean Ethics*. Retrieved 7/30/2012 from www.cwu.edu/~warren/Unit1/aristotles_virtues_and_vices.htm.

Armstrong, K. and M. Possley. 2002. "The Verdict: Dishonor." *Chicago Tribune Reports*, November 11. Retrieved from www.chicagotribune.com/news/watchdog/chi-020103trial1,0,479347.story.

Aronson, R. and J. McMurtrie. 2007. "The Use and Misuse of High-Tech Evidence by Prosecutors: Ethical and Evidentiary Issues." *Fordham Law Review* 76: 1453–1538.

Arrigo, B. and N. Claussen. 2003. "Police Corruption and Psychological Testing: A Strategy for Reemployment Screening." *International Journal of Offender Therapy and Comparative Criminology* 47: 272–290.

Arthur, R. 2017. "Will Trump Reverse Obama's Push for Greater Police Oversight?" *FiveThirtyEight*, March 25. Retrieved from https://fivethirtyeight.com/features/will-trump-reverse-obamas-push-for-greater-police-oversight/.

Ashkanasy, N., C. Windsor, and L. Trevino. 2006. "Bad Apples in Bad Barrels Revisited: Cognitive Moral Development, Just World Beliefs, Rewards, and Ethical Decision-Making." *Business Ethics Quarterly* 16(4): 449–473.

Ashkenas, J., H. Fairfield, J. Keller, and P. Volpe. 2014. "7 Key Points from the C.I.A. Torture Report." *New York Times*, December 9: A1.

Associated Press. 2004. "FBI Apologizes to Lawyer Held in Madrid Bombings." *MSNBC.com*, May 25. Retrieved from www.msnbc.msn.com/id/5053007/.

Associated Press. 2008. "Wife Says Cleric Tortured After CIA Captured Him." *Austin American-Statesman*, May 15: A4.

Associated Press. 2012a. "Port Angeles: Death Penalty Option for Sex Offender Killer." *The Olympian*, June 8. Retrieved from www.theolympian.com/2012/06/08/2133098/port-angeles-death-penalty-option.html.

Associated Press. 2012b. "Records Detail Mosque Spying, NYPD Defends Tactics." *USA Today*, February 24. Retrieved from www.usatoday.com/news/nation/story/2012-02-22/newark-nypd-muslim-spying/53212918/1.

Associated Press. 2012c. "Judge Dismisses Former State Department Official's Lawsuit in Italian Kidnapping Case." *Washington Post*, January 5. Retrieved from www.washingtonpost.com/politics/courts-law/judge-dismisses-former-state-department-officials-lawsuit-in-italian-kidnapping-case/2012/01/05/gIQAMnuodP_story.html.

Associated Press. 2014. "Florida Fires 32 Prison Guards After Inmate Deaths." *Associated Press*, September 21. Retrieved from http://www.tallahassee.com/story/news/2014/09/21/florida-fires-prison-guards-inmate-deaths/15999207/Florida fires 32 prison guards after inmate deaths.

Associated Press. 2015. "A Look inside AP's Investigation on Officer Sex Misconduct." *ABC News*, November 1. Retrieved from http://abcnews.go.com/US/wireStory/inside-aps-investigation-officer-sex-misconduct-34885624.

Associated Press. 2016. "Texas 1st State to Recommend Court Ban on Bite Mark Evidence." *FOXNews.com*, February 12. Retrieved from http://www.foxnews.com/us/2016/02/12/texas-1st-state-to-recommend-court-ban-on-bite-mark-evidence.html.

Atherley, L. and M. Hickman. 2013. "Officer Decertification and the National Decertification Index." *Police Quarterly* 16: 420–437.

Attard, B. 2010. "Oversight of Law Enforcement Is Beneficial and Needed—Both Inside and Out." *Pace Law Review* 30: 1548–1561.

Auerhahn, K. 1999. "Selective Incapacitation and the Problem of Prediction." *Criminology* 37(4): 705–734.

Axtman, K. 2003. "Bungles in Texas Crime Lab Stir Doubt Over DNA." *Christian Science Monitor*, April 18. Retrieved from www.csmonitor.com/2003/0418/p03s01-usgn.html.

Baelz, P. 1977. *Ethics and Beliefs*. New York: Seabury.

Baker, A. 2012. "Independent Agency Gets New Powers to Prosecute New York Police Officers." *New York Times*, March 28: A20.

Baker, A. 2015a. "19 Bronx Officers Distorted Crime Data, Police Say." *New York Times*, July 18: A17.

Baker, A. 2015b. "Prosecutor Tries to Ease a Backlog of Warrants." *New York Times*, October 8: A24.

Baker, A. 2016. "Police Leaders Urge New Set of Standards." *New York Times*, January 30: A10.

Baker, A. 2017a. "Updated N.Y.P.D. Anti-Crime System to Ask: 'How We Doing?'" *New York Times*, May 8. Retrieved from https://www.nytimes.com/2017/05/08/nyregion/nypd-compstat-crime-mapping.html?_r=0.

Baker, A. 2017b. "Street Stops by New York City Police Have Plummeted, Federal Monitor Finds." *New York Times*, May 31: A17.

Baker, T., J. Gordon, and F. Taxman. 2015. "A Hierarchical Analysis of Correctional Officers' Procedural Justice Judgments of Correctional Institutions: Examining the Influence of Transformational Leadership." *Justice Quarterly* 32(6): 1037–1063.

Balcerzak, A. 2015. "Md. Gov. Larry Hogan Signs Bill Limiting Civil Asset Forfeiture." *Washington Post*, May 19. Retrieved from https://www.washingtonpost.com/politics/in-a-reversal-md-gov-larry-hogan-signs-bill-limiting-civil-asset-forfeiture/2016/05/19/c2b960e4-1df2-11e6-9c81-4be1c14fb8c8_story.html.

Balko, R. 2009. "Report: New York State Crime Lab Tainted by Incompetence, Corruption, Indifference." *Reason.com blog,* December 18. Retrieved from http://reason.com/blog/2009/12/18/report-new-york-state-crime-la.

Balko, R. 2011a. "Take the Money and Run." *Slate,* February 4. Retrieved from www.slate.com/articles/news_and_politics/jurisprudence/2010/02/take_the_money_and_run.html.

Balko, R. 2011b. "Private Crime Labs Could Prevent Errors, Analyst Bias: Report." *Huffington Post,* June 14. Retrieved from http://www.huffingtonpost.com/2011/06/14/the-case-for-private-crime-labs_n_876963.html.

Balko, S. 2013a. *Rise of the Warrior Cop.* New York City: Public Affairs.

Balko, S. 2013b. "Rise of the Warrior Cop." *Wall Street Journal,* July 19: C1.

Balko, R. 2014. "A (Sort Of) Defense of South Carolina State Trooper Sean Groubert." *Washington Post,* September 26. Retrieved from http://www.washingtonpost.com/news/the-watch/wp/2014/09/ 26/a-sort-of-defense-of-south-carolina-state-trooper-sean-groubert.

Balko, R. 2016. "Cleveland's Vile, Embarrassing Scheme to Avoid Paying Victims of Police Abuse." *Washington Post,* January 20. Retrieved from https://www.washingtonpost.com/news/the-watch/wp/2016/01/20/clevelands-vile-embarrassing-scheme-to-avoid-paying-victims-of-police-abuse/.

Bamford, J. 2012. "The NSA Is Building the Country's Biggest Spy Center (Watch What You Say)." *Wired.com,* March 15. Retrieved from www.wired.com/2012/03/ff_nsadatacenter.

Bandura, A. 1964. *Principles of Behavior Modification.* New York: Holt, Rinehart and Winston.

Bandura, A. 1969. "Social Learning of Moral Judgments." *Journal of Personality and Social Psychology* 11: 275–279.

Bandura, A. 1971. *Social Learning Theory.* New York: General Learning Press.

Bandura, A. 1990. "Mechanisms of Moral Disengagement in Terrorism." In *Origins of Terrorism: Psychologies, Ideologies, Theologies, States of Mind,* ed. W. Reich, 161–191. Cambridge, England: Cambridge University Press.

Bandura, A. 1991. "Social Cognitive Theory of Moral Thought and Action." In *Handbook of Moral Behavior and Development,* ed. W. Kurtines and J. Gewirtz, 44–103. Hillsdale, NJ: Lawrence Erlbaum.

Bandura, A. 2002. "Selective Moral Disengagement in the Exercise of Moral Agency." *Journal of Moral Education* 31(2): 101–119.

Banks, C. 2014. "Implementing Law Enforcement Ethics Democratic Policing Reform: Challenges and Constraints in Three Developing Countries." In *Law Enforcement Ethics,* ed. B. Fitch, 347–385. Thousand Oaks, CA: Sage

Banks, D., J. Hendrix, M. Hickman, and T. Kyckelhahn. 2016. *National Sources of Law Enforcement Employment Data.* Washington, DC: Bureau of Justice Statistics, U.S. Department of Justice.

Bannon, A., E. Velasco, L. Casey, and L. Reagan. 2013. *The New Politics of Judicial Elections, 2011–2012.* Washington, DC: Brennan Center. Retrieved from http://www.brennancenter.org/publication/new-politics-judicial-elections-2011-12.

Barber, E. 2014. "Dallas Targets Wrongful Convictions, and Revolution Starts to Spread." *Christian Science Monitor,* May 25. Retrieved from http://www.csmonitor.com/USA/Justice/2014/0525/Dallas-targets-wrongful-convictions-and-revolution-starts-to-spread.

Barchenger, S. and D. Boucher. 2016. "Ex-Nashville Judge Casey Moreland Indicted on Federal Bribery, Tampering Charges." *The Tennessean,* April 26. Retrieved from http://www.tennessean.com/story/news/crime/2017/04/26/casey-moreland-indicted-five-federal-felonies/100395790/.

Barker, K. 2015a. "Choice for Addicts: Use Again, or Lose Home." *New York Times,* May 31: A1.

Barker, K. 2015b. "Stringer Zeros in on 'Three-Quarter' Homes, Urging an End to City Referrals." *New York Times,* June 16: A20.

Barker, K. 2017. "Bills Passed to Help Tenants of New York 'Three-Quarter Homes.'" *New York Times,* February 1. Retrieved from https://www.nytimes.com/2017/02/01/nyregion/bills-tenants-protection-three-quarter-homes-new-york.html.

Barker, T. 2002. "Ethical Police Behavior." In *Policing and Misconduct,* ed. K. Lersch, 1–25. Upper Saddle River, NJ: Prentice-Hall.

Barker, T. and D. Carter. 1991. "Police Lies and Perjury: A Motivation-Based Taxonomy." In *Police Deviance,* 2nd ed., ed. T. Barker and D. Carter. Cincinnati, OH: Anderson.

Barker, T. and D. Carter, eds. 1994. *Police Deviance,* 3rd ed. Cincinnati, OH: Anderson.

Barling, J., A. Christie, and N. Turner. 2008. "Pseudo-Transformational Leadership: Towards the Development and Test of a Model." *Journal of Business Ethics* 81: 851–861.

Barrier, G., M. Stohr, C. Hemmens, and R. Marsh. 1999. "A Practical User's Guide: Idaho's Method for Implementing Ethical Behavior in a Correctional Setting." *Corrections Compendium* 24(4): 1–3.

Barry, V. 1985. *Applying Ethics: A Text with Readings.* Belmont, CA: Wadsworth.

Bartley, L. 2014. "ABC7 Eyewitness News Obtains Evidence Against Los Angeles County Sheriff's Department Defendants." *ABC7 Eyewitness News,* October 14. Retrieved 8/3/2015 from http://abc7.com/news/exclusive-abc7-eyewitness-news-obtains-lasd-trial-evidence/350453.

Barton, G. 2014. "Officers Investigated for Hampering Strip Search Inquiry Not Charged." *Milwaukee Journal Sentinel,* September 13. Retrieved from www.jsonline.com/watchdog/watchdogreports/officers-investigated-for-hampering-strip-search-inquiry-not-charged-b99345460z1-275030441.html.

Barton, G. and A. Luthern. 2017. "ACLU Sues Milwaukee Police Over Profiling, Stop-and-Frisk." *Milwaukee Journal Sentinel,* February 22. Retrieved from http://www.jsonline.com/story/news/crime/2017/02/22/aclu-sues-milwaukee-police-over-profiling-stop-and-frisk/98155822/.

Bateman, T. S. and D. W. Organ. 1983. "Job Satisfaction and the Good Soldier: The Relationship Between Affect and Employee 'Citizenship.'" *Academy of Management Journal* 26(4): 587–595.

Bauer, S. 2016. "My Four Months as a Private Prison Guard." *MotherJones Magazine.* Retrieved from http://www.motherjones.com/politics/2016/06/cca-private-prisons-corrections-corporation-inmates-investigation-bauer/.

Baumgartner, F., L. Christiani, D. Epp, K. Roach, and K. Shoub. 2017. "Racial Disparities in Traffic Stop Outcomes." *Duke Forum for Law and Social Change.* Retrieved from http://www.unc.edu/~fbaum/articles/BaumgartnerEtAl-2017-DukeForum-RacialDisparitiesInTrafficStops.pdf.

Bay City News. 2007. "Three Oakland 'Riders' Still Seeking Arbitration." *East Bay Daily News*, February 6. Retrieved from www.ebdailynews.com/article/2007-2-6-02-06-07-bcn89.

Bay City News. 2016. "San Francisco Panel Report Calls for Increased Transparency, Accountability at Police Department." *Mercury News*, July 12. Retrieved from http://www.mercurynews.com/breaking-news/ci_30117965/san-francisco-panel-report-calls-increased-transparency-accountability.

Bayley, D. 2014. "Human Rights in Policing: A Global Assessment." *Policing and Society: An International Journal of Research and Policy*. DOI: 10.1080/10439463.2014.895352.

Bayley, D. and R. Perito. 2011. *Police Corruption, What Past Scandals Teach About Current Challenges*. U.S. Institute for Peace. Retrieved from www.usip.org.

Bazelon, L. 2015. "Scalia's Embarrassing Question: Innocence Is Not Enough to Get You Out of Prison." *Slate*, March 11. Retrieved from www.slate.com/articles/news_and_politics/jurisprudence/2015/03/innocence_is_not_cause_for_exoneration_scalia_s_embarrassing_question_is.single.html.

Bazerman, M. and M. Tenbrunsel. 2011. *Blind Spots: Why We Fail to Do What's Right and What to Do About It*. Princeton, NJ: Princeton University Press.

Bazley, T., T. Mieczkowski, and K. Lersch. 2009. "Early Intervention Program Criteria: Evaluating Officer Use of Force." *Justice Quarterly* 26(1): 107–124.

Beauchamp, T. 1982. *Philosophical Ethics*. New York: McGraw-Hill.

Beccaria, C. 1764/1977. *On Crimes and Punishment*, 6th ed., trans. Henry Paolucci. Indianapolis, IN: Bobbs-Merrill.

Beck, C. 2016. "Police Shooting in Alabama Highlights Challenge of Policing Mentally Ill." *Christian Science Monitor*, April 5. Retrieved from http://www.csmonitor.com/USA/Justice/2016/0405/Police-shooting-in-Alabama-highlights-challenge-of-policing-mentally-ill.

Beck, A., P. Guerino, and P. Harrison. 2010. *Sexual Victimization in Juvenile Facilities Reported by Youth, 2008–2009*. Washington, DC: Bureau of Justice Statistics, U.S. Deptartment of Justice.

Beck, A. and C. Johnson. 2012. *Sexual Victimization Reported by Former State Prisoners, 2008*. Washington, DC: Bureau of Justice Statistics, U.S. Deptartment of Justice.

Beck, A., M. Berzofsky, R. Caspar, and C. Krebs. 2013. *Sexual Victimization in Prisons and Jails Reported by Inmates*. Washington, DC: Bureau of Justice Statistics, U.S. Department of Justice.

Bedau, H. 1982. "Prisoners' Rights." *Criminal Justice Ethics* 1(1): 26–41.

Beecher-Monas, E. 2009. "Reality Bites: The Illusion of Science in Bite-Mark Evidence." *Cardozo Law Review* 30: 1369–1410.

Beijersbergen, K., A. Dirkzwager, T. Molleman, P. van der Laan, and P. Nieuwbeerta. 2015. "Procedural Justice in Prison: The Importance of Staff Characteristics." *International Journal of Offender Therapy and Comparative Criminology* 59(4): 337–358.

Beijersbergen, K., A. Dirkzwager, and P. Nieuwbeerta. 2016. "Reoffending After Release: Does Procedural Justice During Imprisonment Matter?" *Criminal Justice and Behavior* 43(1): 63–82.

Bellafante, G. 2016. "Bratton Says He Has 'Strong Concerns' About the Arrest of a Brooklyn Mailman." *New York Times*, March 30: A17.

Bellamy, A. 2004. "Ethics and Intervention: 'The Humanitarian Exception' and the Problem of Abuse in the Case of Iraq." *Journal of Peace Research* 41: 131–145.

Bentham, J. 1843. "The Rationale of Punishment." In *Ethical Choice: A Case Study Approach*, ed. R. Beck and J. Orr. New York: Free Press, 1970.

Berman, M. 2015. "After the Justice Department Report, What's Next for Ferguson?" *Washington Post*, March 8. Retrieved from www.washingtonpost.com/news/post-nation/wp/2015/03/06/after-the-justice-department-report-whats-next-for-ferguson/.

Bernstein, M. 2017. "Portland Police Not Meeting Obligation to Report Compromised Officers, Study Finds." *OregonLive.com*. Retrieved from http://www.oregonlive.com/portland/index.ssf/2017/04/portland_police_lack_policy_tr.html.

Better Government Association. 2015. "BGA Launches Police Accountability Portal." *Better Government Association Website*. Retrieved from http://www.bettergov.org/news/bga-launches-police-accountability-portal.

Billeaud, J. 2015. "Arpaio Immigration Unit Tarnished by Misconduct Allegations." *Associated Press*, April 19. Retrieved from www.nytimes.com/aponline/2015/04/19/us/ap-us-arizona-sheriff-smuggling-squad.html.

Binder, A., M. Fernandez, and B. Mueller. 2015. "Use of Tasers Is Scrutinized After Walter Scott Shooting." *New York Times*, June 1: A1.

Binelli, M. 2015. "Inside America's Toughest Federal Prison." *New York Times*, March 29: MM37.

Black, C. 2015. "Convictions Tied to Disgraced Detective Demand Closer Look." *Chicago Reporter*, October 22. Retrieved from http://chicagoreporter.com/convictions-tied-to-disgraced-detective-demand-closer-look/.

Blinder, A. 2016. "Mine Chief Is Sentenced in Conspiracy Over Safety." *New York Times*, April 7: A12.

Blinder, A. and C. Robertson. 2014. "Judge Pressed to Resign After Abuse Charges." *New York Times*, September 19: A21.

Blumberg, A. 1969. "The Practice of Law as a Confidence Game." In *Sociology of Law*, ed. V. Aubert, 321–331. London: Penguin.

Blumenfeld, L. 2007. "The Tortured Lives of Interrogators." *Washington Post*, June 4: A01.

Bogan, J. 2017. "Missouri Parole Board Played Word Games During Hearings with Inmates." *St. Louis Post-Dispatch*, June 9. Retrieved from http://www.stltoday.com/news/local/crime-and-courts/missouri-parole-board-played-word-games-during-hearings-with-inmates/article_ce6cba9b-5932-52a4-899a-f7644ec4d7d8.html.

Boghani, P. 2017. "'Norfolk Four' Pardoned 20 Years After False Confessions." *Frontline*, March 22. Retrieved from http://www.pbs.org/wgbh/frontline/article/norfolk-four-pardoned-20-years-after-false-confessions/.

Bommer, W., G. Rich, and R. Rubin. 2005. "Changing Attitudes About Change: Longitudinal Effects of Transformational Leader Behavior on Employee Cynicism About Organizational Change." *Journal of Organizational Behavior* 26: 733–753.

Bomse, A. 2001. "Prison Abuse: Prisoner-Staff Relations." In *Discretion, Community and Correctional Ethics*, ed. J. Kleinig and M. Smith, 79–104. Oxford, England: Rowman and Littlefield.

Bonner, R. and L. Vandecreek. 2006. "Ethical Decision Making for Correctional Mental Health Providers." *Criminal Justice and Behavior* 33: 542–578.

Borchert, D. and D. Stewart. 1986. *Exploring Ethics*. New York: Macmillan.

Boss, J. 2001. *Ethics for Life*, 2nd ed. Mountain View, CA: Mayfield Publishing.

Bossard, A. 1981. "Police Ethics and International Police Cooperation." In *The Social Basis of Criminal Justice: Ethical Issues for the 80's*, ed. F. Schamalleger and R. Gustafson, 23–38. Washington, DC: University Press.

Bott, C. 2017. "Missouri Hit with Lawsuit Over 'Shockingly Inadequate' Funding for Public Defenders." *St. Louis Post-Dispatch*, March 9. Retrieved from http://www.stltoday.com/news/local/crime-and-courts/missouri-hit-with-lawsuit-over-shockingly-inadequate-funding-for-public/article_5971fea2-d3ff-5c6e-8ac3-99f6c0f2f5a4.html.

Bouie, J. 2014. "Black and Blue: Why More Diverse Police Departments Won't Put an End to Police Misconduct." *Slate Magazine*, October 13. Retrieved from http://www.slate.com/articles/news_and_politics/politics/2014/10/diversity_won_t_solve_police_misconduct_black_cops_don_t_reduce_violence.html.

Bouie, J. 2015. "Broken Taillight Policing." *Slate Magazine*, April 8. Retrieved from www.slate.com/articles/news_and_politics/politics/2015/04/north_charleston_shooting_how_investigatory_traffic_stops_unfairly_affect.single.html.

Bourge, C. 2002. "Sparks Fly Over Private vs. Public Prisons." *UPI*. Retrieved from www.upi./com/view.cfm?storyID=20022002-064851-U221.

Bowes, M. 2015. "Blacks Disproportionately Killed by Police, Assault Police in Va." *Richmond Times-Dispatch*, January 24. Retrieved from www.richmond.com/news/article_364d9fc4-e56a-58c2-baf9-53c8b6e6f328.html.

Bowie, N. 1985. *Making Ethical Decisions*. New York: McGraw-Hill.

Bowling, B. and A. Conte. 2016. "Trib Investigation: Cops Often Let Off Hook for Civil Rights Complaints." *Tribune*, March 12. Retrieved from http://triblive.com/usworld/nation/9939487-74/police-rights-civil.

Boyce, W. and L. Jensen. 1978. *Moral Reasoning: A Psychological-Philosophical Integration*. Lincoln: University of Nebraska Press.

Boyer, P. 2001. "Bad Cops." *New Yorker*, May 21. Retrieved from www.newyorker.com/archive/2001/05/21/010521fa_FACT.

Braithwaite, J. 2000. "Shame and Criminal Justice." *Canadian Journal of Criminology* 42(3): 281–301.

Braithwaite, J. 2002. "Linking Crime Prevention to Restorative Justice." In *Repairing Communities Through Restorative Justice*, ed. J. Perry, 67–83. Lanham, MD: American Correctional Association.

Braswell, M. and J. Gold. 2002. "Peacemaking, Justice, and Ethics." In *Justice, Crime, and Ethics*, ed. M. Braswell, B. McCarthy, and B. McCarthy, 13–25. Cincinnati, OH: Anderson.

Braswell, M., B. McCarthy, and B. McCarthy. 2002/2007. *Justice, Crime, and Ethics*, 3rd ed. Cincinnati, OH: Anderson.

Braswell, M., L. Miller, and D. Cabana. 2006. *Human Relations and Corrections*, 6th ed. Prospect Heights, IL: Waveland Press.

Breitenbach, S. 2016. "Right to an Attorney? Not Always in Some States." *The Pew Charitable Trusts*, April 11. Retrieved from http://www.pewtrusts.org/en/research-and-analysis/blogs/stateline/2016/04/11/right-to-an-attorney-not-always-in-some-states.

Brennan Center. 2016. *Police Body-Worn Camera Policies*. Brennan Center. Retrieved from https://www.brennancenter.org/body-cam-city-map?splash.

Bright, J. 2017. "Bharara Blames 'Helter-Skelter Incompetence' for His Surprise Firing." *The New York Times*, April 7: A24.

Broadwater, L. 2016. "Baltimore to Pay $42K to Whistle-Blower Former Officer Who Found Rat on Car." *The Baltimore Sun*, June 1. Retrieved from http://www.baltimoresun.com/news/maryland/baltimore-city/bs-md-ci-crystal-settlement-20160601-story.html.

Bromwich, J., D. Victor, and M. Isaacoct. 2016. "Police Use Scanner of Social Networks to Monitor Protests." *New York Times*, October 12: B1.

Brown, B. 2007. "Community Policing in Post-September 11 America: A Comment on the Concept of Community-Oriented Counterterrorism." *Police Practice and Research* 8(3): 239–251.

Brown, C. 2011. "Divided Loyalties: Ethical Challenges for America's Law Enforcement in Post 9/11 America." *Case Western Reserve Journal of International Law* 43(3): 651–675.

Brown, J. 2014a. "After Inmate Deaths, Department of Justice to Probe Florida Prison System." *Miami Herald*, December 13. Retrieved from http://www.miamiherald.com/news/special-reports/florida prisons/article4457578.html.

Brown, J. 2014b. "After Inmate's Death, Sergeant to Be Questioned." *Miami Herald*, October 8. Retrieved from www.miamiherald.com/news/state/florida/article2628799.html#storylink=cpy.

Brown, J. 2014c. "Group Calls for Overhaul of Florida Prisons." *Miami Herald*, November 14. Retrieved from www.miamiherald.com/news/local/community/miami-dade/article3916342.html#storylink=cpy.

Brown, J. 2014d, "2 Years Later, Florida Keeps Lid on Prison Death Details." *Miami Herald*, June 11. Retrieved from www.miamiherald.com/2014/06/11/4172535/2-years-later-florida-keeps-lid.html#storylink=cpy.

Brown, J. 2014e. "Deposed Warden Says Dade Correctional Was a Dysfunctional Mess." *Miami Herald*, November 2. Retrieved from www.miamiherald.com/news/state/florida/article3527395.html#storylink=cpy.

Brown, J. 2014f. "Inmate's Gassing Death Detailed in Florida DOC Whistle-Blower Complaint." *Miami Herald*, July 7. Retrieved from www.miamiherald.com/news/local/community/miami-dade/article1974526.html.

Brown, J. 2015a. "'Daddy,' Womanizing Assistant Warden, Fired from Troubled Prison." *Miami Herald*, January 22. Retrieved from www.miamiherald.com/news/special-reports/florida-prisons/article7943703.html#storylink=cpy.

Brown, J. 2015b. "Beyond Punishment. (How the Series Was Reported)." *Miami Herald* (multiple dates). Retrieved from http://media.miamiherald.com/static/media/projects/2015/beyond-punishment/index.html.

Brown, J. 2016. "Male Officer at Florida's Prison for Women Faces Sex Charge."

Orlando Sentinel, June 2. Retrieved from http://www.orlandosentinel.com/news/breaking-news/os-sex-attacks-florida-womens-prison-20160602-story.html.

Brown, J. 2017. "Prosecutors Find No Wrongdoing in Shower Death at Dade Correctional Mental Health Unit." *Miami Herald*, March 20. Retrieved from http://www.miamiherald.com/news/local/community/miami-dade/article139206653.html.

Brown, J. and S. Bousquet. 2014. "Amid Turmoil, Florida Prisons Boss Exits." *Miami Herald*, November 24. Retrieved from www.miamiherald.com/news/local/community/miami-dade/article4122143.html#storylink=cpy.

Brown, J. and M. Klas. 2015. "Former Florida Prisons Chief Says Gov. Rick Scott Ignored Crisis in Corrections System." *Miami Herald*, January 31. Retrieved from www.miamiherald.com/news/local/community/miami-dade/article8875121.html#storylink=cpy.

Brown, J. and M. Klas. 2016. "The Education of Julie Jones, Florida's Prisons Chief." *Miami Herald*, March 18. Retrieved from http://www.miamiherald.com/news/special-reports/florida-prisons/article66868842.html.

Brown, M. 1981. *Working the Street*. New York: Russell Sage Foundation.

Brown, S. 2015. "Hospital Defends NYPD Cop's Forced Stay in Psych Ward." *New York Daily News*, February 3. Retrieved from /www.nydailynews.com/new-york/exclusive-hospital-defends-nypd-psych-hold-article-1.2101357.

Brumback, K. 2016. "Feds Accuse Prison Guards of Taking Bribes, Drug Trafficking." *Washington Times*, February 11. Retrieved from http://www.washingtontimes.com/news/2016/feb/11/feds-accuse-prison-guards-of-taking-bribes-drug-tr/.

Bryan, A. 2016. "Ethical Dilemmas in the Prison Setting." *British Journal of Psychotherapy* 32(2): 256–273.

Bryson, D. 2010. "South Africa: Mandela Marks 20 Years of Freedom." *Associated Press*, February 11. Retrieved from www.guardian.co.uk/world/feedarticle/8941298.

Buckle, S. 1993. "Natural Law." In *A Companion to Ethics*, ed. P. Singer, 161–175. London: Blackwell Publishing.

Bureau of Justice Statistics. 2015. "Corrections Statistical Analysis Tool." Retrieved 6/24/2015 from http://www.bjs.gov/index.cfm?ty=tp&tid=13.

Burgess, R. L. and R. L. Akers. 1966. "A Differential Association-Reinforcement Theory of Criminal Behavior." *Social Problems* 14(2): 128–147.

Burrell, W. 2000. "How to Prevent PPO Stress and Burnout." *Community Corrections Report* 8(1): 1–2, 13–14.

Butterfield, F. 2004. "Mistreatment of Prisoners Is Called Routine in U.S." *New York Times*, May 8. Retrieved from www.nytimes.com/2004/05/08/national/08PRIS.html.

Caldero, M. and A. Larose. 2001. "Value Consistency Within the Police: The Lack of a Gap." *Policing* 24: 2162–2180.

California District Attorneys Association (CDAA). 2012. *The California Prosecutor: Integrity, Independence and Leadership*. Retrieved from http://digitalcommons.law.ggu.edu/cgi/viewcontent.cgi?article=1227&context=caldocs_agencies.

California Office of the Inspector General. 2015. *Special Review: High Desert State Prison. Susanville*. Retrieved from http://www.oig.ca.gov/media/reports/Reports/Reviews/2015_Special_Review_-_High_Desert_State_Prison.pdf.

Callahan, D. 1982. "Applied Ethics in Criminal Justice." *Criminal Justice Ethics* 1(1): 1–64.

Carmichael, D., G. Naufal, S. Wood, H. Caspers, and M. Marchbanks. 2017. *Liberty and Justice: Pretrial Practices in Texas*. Austin, TX: Texas Public Policy Institute. Retrieved from https://tinyurl.com/Texas-Bond-Study.

Carr, R. 2005. "In Federal Job: Blow Whistle, Get Boot." *Austin American-Statesman*, December 11: A1, A6.

Carr, R. and H. Herman. 2007. "Attorney General Apologizes for Handling of Firings But Says He Can Do Job." *Austin American-Statesman*, April 14: A1, A7.

Carrega, C., R. Parascandola, and R. Greene. 2017. "NYPD Officers Accused of Beating Queens Postal Worker Who Gave Directions to Cop Killer See Charges Cleared." *New York Daily News*, March 17. Retrieved from http://www.nydailynews.com/new-york/nypd-cops-accused-beating-postal-worker-charges-cleared-article-1.3000248.

Carroll. D. 2015. *How Public Defenders Struggle with Ethical Blindness*. Sixth Amendement Center, February 4. Retrieved from http://sixthamendment.org/how-public-defenders-struggle-with-ethical-blindness.

Carroll, L. 1998. *Lawful Order: A Case Study of Correctional Crisis and Reform*. New York: Garland.

Carroll, R. 2017. "One Prison, Two Realities: Detainees Suffer, But Locals Say It Keeps a Poor Town Afloat." *The Guardian*, June 6. Retrieved from https://www.theguardian.com/us-news/2017/jun/06/eloy-prison-arizona-detention-deportation-trump.

Carson, E. and E. Anderson. 2016. *Prisoners in 2015*. Washington, DC: Bureau of Justice Statistics, U.S. Department of Justice.

Carter, D. 1999. "Drug Use and Drug-Related Corruption of Police Officers." In *Policing Perspectives*, ed. L. Gaines and G. Cordner, 311–324. Los Angeles: Roxbury.

Carter, J. and S. Phillips. 2013. "Intelligence-Led Policing and Forces of Organizational Change in the USA." *Policing and Society: An International Journal of Research and Policy*. DOI: 10.1080/10439463.2013.865738.

Cassidy, M. 2017. "Prosecution, Defense Rest in Joe Arpaio's Criminal-Contempt Trial." *USA Today*, June 30. Retrieved from https://www.usatoday.com/story/news/nation-now/2017/06/30/attorneys-rest-joe-arpaios-criminal-contempt-trial/443026001/.

Cassidy, R. 2006. "Character and Context: What Virtue Theory Can Teach Us About a Prosecutor's Ethical Duty to 'Seek Justice.'" *Notre Dame Law Review* 82(2): 635–697.

Cathcart, R. 2010. "Wrongly Convicted Man Gets $7.95 Million." *New York Times*, August 13: A14.

CBSDC.com. 2015. "Detainees from Closed Baltimore Jail Have Moved, But Not Far." *CBSDC.com*, August 27. Retrieved from http://washington.cbslocal.com/2015/08/27/detainees-closed-baltimore-jail-have-moved-not-far/.

CBSDFW.com. 2012. "Irving Women Claim Assault, Humiliation After Roadside Cavity Search." *CBS News*, December 18. Retrieved from http://dfw.cbslocal.com/2012/12/18/irving-women-claim-assault-humiliation-after-roadside-cavity-search-by-troopers/.

Chang, C. 2013. "L.A. County Unable to Avert Federal Oversight of Jails." *Los Angeles Times*, October 3. Retrieved from www.latimes.com/local/countygovernment/la-me-1003-sheriff-consent-decree-20141003-story.html.

Chang, C. 2016. "Assistant Sheriff Credited with Curtailing the Worst Abuses in L.A. County Jails is Leaving." *Los Angeles Times*, April 26. Retrieved from http://www.latimes.com/local/california/la-me-jails-abuse-reformer-20160426-story.html.

Chang, C. and R. Winton. 2015. "Paul Tanaka Indicted, Accused of Obstructing Federal Jail Abuse Probe." *Los Angeles Times*, May 14. Retrieved from http://touch.latimes.com/#section/-1/article/p2p-83538720/.

Chappell, A. and A. Piquero. 2004. "Applying Social Learning Theory to Police Misconduct." *Deviant Behavior* 25: 89–108.

Cheever, J. 2015. "Suhr: Convicted Officers Betrayed Public Trust." *Bay City News*, January 22. Retrieved from http://sfbay.ca/2015/01/22/suhr-convicted-officers-betrayed-public-trust.

Chen, K. 2014. "7 Mass Surveillance Tools Your Local Police Might Be Using." *Beacon Reader*, July 29. Retrieved from https://www.beaconreader.com/the-center-for-investigative-reporting/7-mass-surveillance-tools-your-local-police-might-be-using.

Cherney, A. and J. Hartley. 2015. "Community Engagement to Tackle Terrorism and Violent Extremism: Challenges, Tensions and Pitfalls." *Policing and Society*. Retrieved from http://dx.doi.org/10.1080/10439463.2015.1089871.

Childress, S. 2016. "How States Are Moving to Police Bad Cops." *Frontline (PBS)*, April 8. Retrieved from http://www.pbs.org/wgbh/frontline/article/how-states-are-moving-to-police-bad-cops/.

Christensen, D. 2012. "TV Show Case Leads to Disclosure of Broward Cops in Trouble with the Law." *Sun-Sentinel.com*, January 3. Retrieved from http://articles.sun-sentinel.com/2012-01-03/news/fl-cops-suspect-testimony-bulldog-20120103_1_officers-and-deputies-prosecutors-tv-show.

Christianson, S. 2004. *Innocent: Inside Wrongful Conviction Cases*. New York: New York University Press.

Churchland, P. 2011. *Braintrust: What NeuroScience Tell Us About Morality*. Princeton, NJ: Princeton University Press.

Clarke, M. 2010. "Celebrity Justice: Prison Lifestyles of the Rich and Famous." *Prison Legal News*, July 15. Retrieved from https://www.prisonlegalnews.org/news/2010/jul/15/celebrity-justice-prison-lifestyles-of-the-rich-and-famous/.

Clarridge, C. and J. Sullivan. 2013. "$1.1M Verdict for Victim's Family Upheld by State Supreme Court." *Seattle Times*, October 17, 2013. Retrieved from http://www.seattletimes.com/seattle-news/11m-verdict-for-victimrsquos-family-upheld-by-state-supreme-court.

Claussen-Rogers, N. and B. Arrigo. 2005. *Police Corruption and Psychological Testing*. Durham, NC: Carolina Academic Press.

Clear, T. 1996. *Harm in American Penology: Offenders, Victims, and Their Communities*. Albany, NY: SUNY Albany Press.

Clement, S. and W. Lowery. 2017. "Survey Reveals Disconnect Between Police and Public Attitudes." *Washington Post*, January 11. Retrieved from https://www.washingtonpost.com/investigations/survey-reveals-disconnect-between-police-and-public-attitudes/2017/01/10/65b24f3a-d550-11e6-a783-cd3fa950f2fd_story.html?hpid=hp_rhp-more-top-stories_no-name%3Ahomepage%2Fstory&utm_term=.f5689a755a66.

Clifford, S. 2014. "14 More Brooklyn Convictions Examined." *New York Times*, July 31: A20.

Clifford, S. 2015. "Any Sexual Abuse by Guards May Violate Inmates' Rights, U.S. Appeals Court Says." *New York Times*, August 12: A15.

Close, D. and N. Meier. 1995. *Morality in Criminal Justice*. Belmont, CA: Wadsworth.

CNN.com. 2010. "Oil Inspectors Took Company Gifts, Watchdog Group Finds." *CNN.com*, May 25. Retrieved from www.cnn.com/2010/US/05/25/oil.spill.interior/.

CNN.com. 2011. "Baltimore Police Officers Arrested in Repair Shop Extortion Scheme." *CNN.com*, February 23. Retrieved from www.cnn.com/2011/CRIME/2/23/maryland.police.arrests/index.html.

CNN.com. 2015. "Same-Sex Marriage in the U.S." *CNN.com*, April 3. Retrieved from www.cnn.com/interactive/us/map-same-sex-marriage.

Cohen, E. 1991. "Pure Legal Advocates and Moral Agents: Two Concepts of a Lawyer in an Adversary System." In *Justice, Crime, and Ethics*, ed. M. Braswell, B. McCarthy, and B. McCarthy, 123–163. Cincinnati, OH: Anderson.

Cohen, E. 2002. "Pure Legal Advocates and Moral Agents Revisited: A Reply to Memory and Rose." *Criminal Justice Ethics* 21(1): 39–55.

Cohen, H. 1986. "Exploiting Police Authority." *Criminal Justice Ethics* 5(2): 23–31.

Cohen, H. and M. Feldberg. 1991. *Power and Restraint: The Moral Dimension of Police Work*. New York: Praeger.

Cohen, L. and M. Felson, 1979. "Social Change and Crime Rate Trends: A Routine Activity Theory Approach." *American Sociological Review* 44(4): 588–608.

Cohen, M. 2015. "How For-Profit Prisons Have Become the Biggest Lobby No One Is Talking About." *Washington Post*, April 28. Retrieved from http://www.washingtonpost.com/posteverything/wp/2015/04/28/how-for-profit-prisons-have-become-the-biggest-lobby-no-one-is-talking-about.

Cohen, P. 2015. "Owner of a Credit Card Processor Is Setting a New Minimum Wage: $70,000 a Year." *New York Times*, April 14: B3.

Cohen, R. 2001. "How They Sleep at Night: DAs Turned Defenders Talk About Their Work." *American Lawyer: The Legal Intelligence*, April 9.

Cohen, T. 2011. "Who's Better at Defending Criminals? Does Type of Defense Attorney Matter in Terms of Producing Favorable Case Outcomes?" *Social Science Research Working Paper Series*. Retrieved from https://nationalcdp.org/docs/defense-counsel-and-ajudication.pdf.

Coherty, J., J. Levine, and P. Thomas, 2014. "Alabama Prison Was House of Horrors for Female Inmates, Feds Say." *ABCNews.com*, January 22. Retrieved from http://abcnews.go.com/US/women-universally-fear-safety-alabama-prison-feds/story?id=21627510.

Colarossi, A. 2009. "Lake County Prison Official Arrested on Drug Charge." *Orlando Sentinel*, September 4. Retrieved from www.orlandosentinel.com/news/local/breakingnews/orl-bk-prison-worker-arrest-090409,0,980900.story.

Cole, D. 1999. *No Equal Justice*. New York: Free Press.

Cole, G. 1970. "The Decision to Prosecute." *Law and Society Review* 4, February: 313–343.

Coleman, S. 2004a. "Police, Gratuities, and Professionalism: A Response to Kania." *Criminal Justice Ethics* 23(1): 63–65.

Coleman, S. 2004b. "When Police Should Say 'No!' to Gratuities." *Criminal Justice Ethics* 23(1): 33–14.

Colloff, P. 2011. "Innocence Found." *Texas Monthly*, January 2011. Retrieved from www.texasmonthly.com/2011-01-01/feature2.php.

Colloff, P. 2013. "Jail Time May Be the Least of Ken Anderson's Problems." *Texas Monthly*, November 14. Retrieved from www.texasmonthly.com/story/jail-time-may-be-least-ken-anderson%E2%80%99s-problems.

Columbia Law School. 2002. "A Broken System, Part II: Why There Is So Much Error in Capital Cases, and What Can Be Done About It." *Columbia Law School Publications*. Retrieved from www2.law.columbia.edu/brokensystem2/report.pdf.

Colvin, G. 2017. "The Wells Fargo Scandal Is Now Reaching VW Proportions." *Fortune*, January 25. Retrieved from http://fortune.com/2017/01/25/the-wells-fargo-scandal-is-now-reaching-vw-proportions/.

Commission on Safety and Abuse in America's Prisons. 2006. *Confronting Confinement*. Washington, DC: Commission on Safety and Abuse in America's Prisons.

Community Tool Box. 2012. *Ethical Issues in Community Interventions*. Retrieved 7/30/2012 from http://ctb.ku.edu/en/tablecontents/sub_main_1165.aspx.

Conlon, E. 2004. *Blue Blood*. New York: Riverhead.

Conti, N. 2006. "Role Call: Preprofessional Socialization into Police Culture." *Policing and Society* 16(3): 221–242.

Conti, N. and J. Nolan. 2005. "Policing the Platonic Cave: Ethics and Efficacy in Police Training." *Policing and Society* 15(2): 166–186.

Cook, R. 2014. "Family Files Lawsuit Against East Point in Taser Death." *The Atlanta Journal-Constitution*, August 28. Retrieved from http://www.ajc.com/news/news/breaking-news/family-files-lawsuit-against-east-point-in-taser-d/nhBKk.

Cooper, C. 2009. "Yes Virginia, There Is a Police Code of Silence: Prosecuting Police Officers and Police Subculture." *Criminal Law Bulletin* 45(2): 277–293.

Cooper, J. 2012. "Noble Cause Corruption as a Consequence of Role Conflict in the Police Organization." *Policing and Society: An International Journal in Research and Policing* 22(2): 169–184.

Corey, G., M. Corey, and P. Callanan. 1988. *Issues and Ethics in Helping Professions*. Pacific Grove, CA: Brooks/Cole.

Correll, J., S. Hudson, S. Guillermo, and D. Ma. 2014. "The Police Officer's Dilemma: A Decade of Research on Racial Bias in the Decision to Shoot." *Social and Personality Psychology Compass* 8: 201–213.

Cotton, A. 2014. "Denver Releases 40 Draft Recommendations for Sheriff Department Reform." *Denver Post*, August 21. Retrieved from www.denverpost.com/news/ci_26383613/denver-releases-40-draft-recommendations-sheriff-dept-reform.

Cowell, B. and A. Kringen. 2016. *Engaging Communities One Step at a Time*. Washington, DC: Police Foundation. Retrieved from https://www.policefoundation.org/publication/engaging-communities-one-step-at-a-time/.

Cox, E. 2016. "Maryland Task Force Recommends 22 Police Reforms." *The Baltimore Sun*, January 11. Retrieved from http://www.baltimoresun.com/news/maryland/politics/bs-md-policing-group-20160111-story.html.

Cox, T. 2016. *Prosecutor Misconduct and Good Faith Error: A Reanalysis of Current Studies in California and Texas* (Unpublished dissertation). Texas State University.

Cox, T., S. Cunningham, and J. Pollock. 2017. "A Closer Look at Prosecutor Misconduct and Good Faith Error." *Criminal Law Bulletin*. 53(1): 61–74.

Crank, J. 1998. *Understanding Police Culture*. Cincinnati, OH: Anderson.

Crank, J. 2003. *Imagining Justice*. Cincinnati, OH: Anderson.

Crank, J. and M. Caldero. 2000/2005. *Police Ethics: The Corruption of Noble Cause*. Cincinnati, OH: Anderson.

Crank, J. and P. Gregor. 2005. *Counter Terrorism After 9/11: Justice, Security and Ethics Reconsidered*. Cincinnati, OH: Lexis/Nexis Publishing.

Crank, J., D. Flaherty, and A. Giacomazzi. 2007. "The Noble Cause: An Empirical Assessment." *Journal of Criminal Justice* 35(1): 103–116.

Craven, J. 2015. "Baltimore Buys Victims' Silence with Settlements for Police Misconduct." *The Huffington Post*, November 7. Retrieved from http://www.huffingtonpost.com/entry/baltimore-police-misconduct-settlements_563bc4b2e4b0411d30703ca2

(The) Crime Report. 2017. "Implicit Bias Influences Cops Involved in Deadly Force Incidents: Study." *The Crime Report*, February 2. Retrieved from https://thecrimereport.org/2017/02/08/implicit-bias-influences-cops-involved-in-deadly-force-incidents-study-finds/.

Crockett, M., L. Clark, M. Hauser, and T. Robbins. 2010. "Serotonin Selectively Influences Moral Judgment and Behavior Through Effects on Harm Aversion." *Proceedings of the National Academy of Science* 107: 17433–17438.

Crouch, B. 1980. *Keepers: Prison Guards and Contemporary Corrections*. Springfield, IL: Charles C Thomas.

Crouch, B. 1986. "Guard Work in Transition." In *The Dilemmas of Corrections*, 3rd ed., ed. K. Haas and G. Alpert, 183–203. Prospect Heights, IL: Waveland.

Crouch, B. and J. Marquart. 1989. *An Appeal to Justice: Litigated Reform in Texas Prisons*. Austin: University of Texas Press.

Cullen, F. 1995. "Assessing the Penal Harm Movement." *Journal of Research in Crime and Delinquency* 32(3): 338–358.

Cummings, L. 2010. "Can an Ethical Person Be an Ethical Prosecutor? A Social Cognitive Approach to Systemic Reform." *Cardozo Law Review* 31(6): 2139–2159.

Cunningham, L. 1999. "Taking on Testilying: The Prosecutor's Response to In-Court Police Deception." *Criminal Justice Ethics* 18(1): 26–40.

Cunningham, S. 2016. *Defense Attorney's Perceptions of Prosecutorial Misconduct* (Unpublished dissertation). Texas State University.

Curry, M. 2002. "Faulty Drug Cases Draw Police Inquiry." *Dallas Morning News*, February 21: 25A.

Dalbert, C. and E. Filke. 2007. "The Belief in a Personal Just World, Justice Judgments, and Their Function for Prisoners." *Criminal Justice and Behavior* 34(1): 1516–1527.

Daly, K. 1989. "Criminal Justice Ideologies and Practices in Different Voices: Some Feminist Questions About Justice." *International Journal of the Sociology of Law* 17: 1–18.

Dantzker, M. and J. H. McCoy. 2006. "Psychological Screening of Police Recruits: A Texas Perspective." *Journal of Police and Criminal Psychology* 21(1): 23–32.

Dardick, H. 2010. "Police Missed Early Clues in Riley Fox's Slaying." *Chicago Tribune*, June 16. Retrieved from http://articles.chicagotribune.com/2010-06-16/news/ct-met-0616-riley-fox-clues-20100616_1_riley-fox-partial-dna-sample-deputy-scott-swearengen.

Dardick, H. 2013. "City Council Approves $4.1 Million Settlement of Chicago Police Misconduct Case." *Chicago Tribune.com*, February 13. Retrieved from http://articles.chicagotribune.com/2013-02-13/news/chi-city-council-approves-41-million-settlement-of-chicago-police-misconduct-case-20130213_1_police-mi.

Dart, B. 2004. "Police Use Taser Guns 'Excessively,' Rights Group Asserts." *Austin American-Statesman*, November 30: A14.

Davey, M. and M. Smith. 2017. "3 Officers Are Charged in Aftermath of Shooting." *New York Times*, June 28: A14.

Davies, N. 1991. *White Lies*. London: Chatto and Windus.

Davis, A. 2016. "'YouTube Effect' Has Left Police Officers Under Siege, Law Enforcement Leaders Say." *Washington Post*, October 8. Retrieved from https://www.washingtonpost.com/news/post-nation/wp/2015/10/08/youtube-effect-has-left-police-officers-under-siege-law-enforcement-leaders-say/?utm_term=.4d019673b64c.

Davis, K. 2014. "SDPD Seeks Audit on Misconduct Cases." *San Diego Union-Tribune*, February 16. Retrieved from http://www.sandiegouniontribune.com/news/2014/feb/16/police-audit-misconduct-hays-lansdowne/.

De Angelis, J. and A. Kupchik, A. 2007. "Citizen Oversight, Procedural Justice, and Officer Perceptions of the Complaint Investigation Process." *Policing: An International Journal of Police Strategies & Management* 30(4): 651–671.

De Angelis, J., R. Rosenthal, and B. Buchner. 2017. *Civilian Oversight of Law Enforcement: A Review of the Strengths and Weaknesses of Various Models*. Washington, DC: Office of Justice Programs Diagnostic Center.

De Angelis, J. and B. Wolf. 2016. "Perceived Accountability and Public Attitudes Toward Local Police." *Criminal Justice Studies*. DOI: http://dx.doi.org/10.1080/1478601X2016.1158177.

Death Penalty Information Center. 2017. *Execution List*. Retrieved from https://deathpenaltyinfo.org/execution-list-2016.

Dejarnette, B. 2015. "Five Studies: Why Kids Who Kill Are Getting a Second Chance." *Pacific Standard Magazine*, November 11. Retrieved from http://www.psmag.com/politics-and-law/five-studies-debunking-the-superpredator-myth.

Delattre, E. 1989a. *Character and Cops: Ethics in Policing*. Washington, DC: American Enterprise Institute for Public Policy Research.

Delattre, E. 1989b. "Ethics in Public Service: Higher Standards and Double Standards." *Criminal Justice Ethics* 8(2): 79–83.

DeLeon-Granados, W. and W. Wells. 1998. "Do You Want Extra Police Coverage with Those Fries?" *Police Quarterly* 1(2): 71–85.

Denvir, D. 2015. "How Philadelphia Prosecutors Protect Police Misconduct: Cops Get Caught Lying—And Then Get Off the Hook." *Salon*, December 28. http://www.salon.com/2015/12/28/how_philadelphia_prosecutors_protect_police_misconduct_cops_get_caught_lying_and_then_get_off_the_hook/.

Department of Justice. 2012. *Consent Decrees*. Retrieved from http://www.justice.gov/opa/pr/2012/July/12-ag-917.html.

Dershowitz, A. 1982. *The Best Defense*. New York: Vintage.

Dershowitz, A. 2004. *Rights from Wrongs: A Secular Theory of the Origins of Rights*. New York: Basic Books.

Deutsch, L. 2001. "L.A. Police Corruption Probe Set to Wrap Up." *San Jose Mercury News*. Retrieved 11/12/2001 from www.mercurycenter.com/premium/local/docs/rampart08.htm.

Devine, T. 2008. "The Need for Privacy." *San Marcos Daily Record*, March 28: 4A.

Dewan, S. 2015. "Company Extorts Poor on Probation, Lawsuit Says." *New York Times*, October 2: A15.

Dewan, S. and A. Lehren. 2016. "After a Crime, the Price of a Second Chance." *New York Times*, December 12. Retrieved from https://www.nytimes.com/2016/12/12/us/crime-criminal-justice-reform-diversion.html?_r=0.

Dewan, S. and R. Oppel. 2017. "Efforts to Curb Police Abuses Have Mixed Record, and Uncertain Future." *New York Times*, January 14. Retrieved from https://www.nytimes.

com/2017/01/14/us/chicago-police-consent-decree.html?_r=0.

Dexheimer, E. and T. Plohetski. 2016. "Local Police Use of Vast License Plate Database Raises Privacy Concern." *Austin American Statesman*, February 1. Retrieved from http://www.mystatesman.com/news/local-police-use-vast-license-plate-database-raises-privacy-concern/HXB5UL1BYyUlUOyhnFalOI/.

Dial, K. and R. Worley 2008. "A Quantitative Analysis of Inmate Boundary Violators in a Southern Prison System." *American Journal of Criminal Justice* 33: 69–84.

Dilanian, K. 2012. "Investigations of CIA End Without Criminal Charges." *Austin American Statesman*, August 31, 2012: A3.

Dills, A., S. Goffard, and J. Miron. 2016. *Dose of Reality: The Effects of State Marijuana Legalization: Policy Analysis*. Cato Institute, September 16. Retrieved from https://object.cato.org/sites/cato.org/files/pubs/pdf/pa799.pdf.

Dilulio, J. 1987. *Governing Prisons: A Comparative Study of Correctional Management*. New York: Free Press.

Dizikes, C. and T. Lighty. 2014. "Watchdog Update: Head of Cook Co. Adult Probation Removed." *Chicago Tribune*, March 17. Retrieved from www.chicagotribune.com/news/local/breaking/chi-watchdog-update-head-of-cook-co-adult-probation-removed-20140317-story.html.

Dodge, M., D. Starr-Gimeno, and T. Williams. 2005. "Puttin' on the Sting: Women Police Officers' Perspectives on Reverse Prostitution Assignments." *International Journal of Police Science and Management* 7(2): 71–85.

Dolliver, R. H. 1981. "Reflections on Fritz Perls's Gestalt Prayer." *Personnel and Guidance Journal* 59(5): 311–313.

Dolnick, S. 2012a. "As Escapes Stream Out, a Business System Thrives." *New York Times*, June 17: A1.

Dolnick, S. 2012b. "Poorly Staffed: A Halfway House in New Jersey Is Mired in Chaos." *New York Times*, June 18: A1.

Dolnick, S. 2012c. "Executive at Company Tied to New Jersey's Halfway Houses Is Leaving." *New York Times*, November 9: A23.

Dolnick, S. 2012d. "Halfway Houses Prove Lucrative to Those at Top." *New York Times*, December 30: A1

Donner, F. 1992. *Protectors of Privilege.* Berkeley, CA: University of California Press.

Donovan, D. 2017. "Baltimore Police Cut Taser Use by Nearly Half in 2016." *Baltimore Sun,* January 19. Retrieved from http://www.baltimoresun.com/ news/maryland/baltimore-city/bs-md-ci-tasers-20170119-story.html.

Dorschner, J. 1989. "The Dark Side of the Force." In *Critical Issues in Policing,* 2nd ed., ed. R. Dunham and G. Alpert, 254–274. Prospect Heights, IL: Waveland.

Doyle, M. 2014. "Data on Police Shootings Is Hard to Find." *McClatchy Washington Bureau,* August 20. Retrieved from http://www.mcclatchydc. com/2014/08/20/237137_data-on-police-shootings-is-hard. html?sp=/99/200/365/&rh=1 #storylink=cpy.

Drew, J. 2015. "After 37 Years in Prison, Innocent Man Goes Free." *Austin American Statesman,* January 24: A6.

Dubler, N. 2014. "Ethical Dilemmas in Prison and Jail Health Care." *Health Affairs,* March 10. Retrieved from http:// healthaffairs.org/blog/2014/03/10/ ethical-dilemmas-in-prison-and-jail-health-care/.

Ducrose, M., A. Cooper, and H. Snyder. 2014. *Recidivism of Prisoners Released in 30 States in 2005: Patterns from 2005 to 2010.* Bureau of Justice Statistics Special Report. Washington, DC: Bureau of Justice Statistics, U.S. Department of Justice.

Ducrose, M., P. Langan, and E. Smith. 2007. *Contacts Between Police and the Public, 2005.* Bureau of Justice Statistics Report, April 29. Retrieved 7/30/2012 from http://bjs.ojp.usdoj.gov/index. cfm?ty=pbdetailandiid=653.

Duncan, I. 2013. "Federal Authorities Ensnare Criminals in 'Reverse Stings.'" *The Baltimore Sun,* July 28. Retrieved from www.baltimoresun.com/news/ maryland/baltimore-city/bs-md-ci-atf-dea-stings-20130727,0,6298276. story#ixzz2b1i1g8Bl.

Dunningham, C. and C. Norris. 1999. "The Detective, the Snout, and the Audit Commission: The Real Costs in Using Informants." *Howard Journal of Criminal Justice* 38(1): 67–87.

Durkheim, E. 1969. "Types of Law in Relation to Types of Social Solidarity." In *Sociology of Law,* ed. V. Aubert, 17–29. London: Penguin.

Dwyer, J. 2007. "New York Police Spied on Protesters." *Austin American-Statesman,* March 25: A11.

Dzur, A. and A. Wertheimer. 2002. "Forgiveness and Public Deliberation: The Practice of Restorative Justice." *Criminal Justice Ethics* 21(1): 3–20.

Eban, K. 2007. "Rorschach and Awe." *Vanity Fair,* July 17. Retrieved from www. vanityfair.com/politics/features/2007/07/ torture200707.

Eckholm, E. 2014. "More Judges Question Use of Fake Drugs in Sting Cases." *New York Times,* November 21: A16.

Eckholm, E. 2015a. "Prosecutor Drops Toughest Charges in Chicago Stings that Used Fake Drugs." *New York Times,* January 31: A14.

Eckholm, E. 2015b. "Court Ruling May Clarify the Rights of Suspects." *New York Times,* November 11: A16.

Editorial Board (New York Times). 2016. "Ken Thompson: The Death of a Visionary Prosecutor." *New York Times,* October 12: A22.

Editorial Board (Washington Post). 2016. "Hospital and Jail Staff Looked the Other Way as a Young Man Starved to Death in Va." *Washington Post,* April 3. Retrieved from https://www. washingtonpost.com/opinions/death-by-incompetence/2016/04/03/e03a727c-f83e-11e5-8b23-538270a1ca31_story. html?wpisrc=nl_rainbow.

Editorial Board. 2017. "Plenty More Villains at Wells Fargo." *New York Times,* April 12: A22.

Egan, P. 2016. "Michigan to Clamp Down on Privatized Prison Deals." *Detroit Free Press,* January 7. Retrieved from http://www.freep.com/story/ news/politics/2016/01/07/prison-department-sets-up-unit-monitor-contractors/75949704/.

Ehrenfreund, M. 2017. "The Alarming Numbers on Race and Police Misconduct in Chicago." *Washington Post,* November 25. Retrieved from https://www.washingtonpost.com/ news/wonk/wp/2015/11/25/the-alarming-numbers-on-race-and-police-misconduct-in-chicago/?utm_ term=.10d4d621fdec.

Eldred, T. 2013. "Prescriptions for Ethical Blindness: Improving Advocacy for Indigent Defendants in Criminal Cases." *Rutgers Law Review* 65: 333–379.

Eligon, J. 2011. "Advisors on Interrogation Face Legal Action by Critics." *New York Times,* April 27: A21.

Elinson, Z. 2013. "False Confessions Dog Teens: Protocols Proposed to Protect Youth Who Admit to Crimes They Didn't Commit." *Wall Street Journal,* September 8, 2013.

Elliott, A. and B. Weiser. 2004. "When Prosecutors Err, Others Pay the Price." *New York Times.* Retrieved from www.nytimes.com/2004/03/21/ nyregion/21prosecute.html.

Ellis, L. and A. Pontius. 1989. *The Frontal-Limbic-Reticular Network and Variations in Pro-Antisociality: A Neurological Based Model of Moral Reasoning and Criminality.* Paper presented at 1989 ASC conference, Reno, NV.

Emerson, T. and J. McKinney. 2010. "Importance of Religious Beliefs to Ethical Attitudes in Business." *Journal of Religion and Business Ethics* 1(2): 1–15.

Emett, A. 2016. "Texas 'Cop of the Year' Exposed as Member of Mexico's Most Dangerous Cartel." *Rawstory.com,* January 1. Retrieved from http://www. rawstory.com/2016/01/texas-cop-of-the-year-exposed-as-member-of-mexicos-most-dangerous-cartel/.

Emily, J. 2014. "Dallas County Officers Mishandled 70% of Probation Violations, Initial State Audit Finds." *DallasNews.com,* May 18. Retrieved from www.dallasnews.com/news/crime/ headlines/20140518-dallas-county-officers-mishandled-70-of-probation-violations-initial-state-audit-finds.ece.

Engel, R. S., J. Calnon, and T. Bernard. 2002. "Theory and Racial Profiling: Shortcomings and Future Directions in Research." *Justice Quarterly* 19(2): 249–273.

Engel, R., R. Tillyer, C. Klahm, and J. Frank. 2011. "From the Officer's Perspective: A Multilevel Examination of Citizens' Demeanor During Traffic Stops." *Justice Quarterly* 29(5): 574–643.

Epp, C., S. Maynard-Moody, and D. Haider-Markel. 2014. *Pulled Over: How Police Stops Define Race and Citizenship.* Chicago, IL: University of Chicago Press.

Equilar.com. 2017. "200 Highest Paid Executives." *Equilar.com,* April 2. Retrieved from http://www.equilar. com/reports/38-2-new-york-times-200-highest-paid-ceos-2016.html.

Eterno, J., A. Verma, and E. Silverman. 2014. "Police Manipulations of Crime Reporting: Insiders' Revelations." *Justice Quarterly.* DOI: 10.1080/07418825.2014.980838.

Etter, L. 2015. "How Local Governments Got Burned by Private Prison Investments." *Bloomberg News*, October 1. Retrieved from http://www.bloomberg.com/news/articles/2015-10-02/how-local-governments-got-burned-by-private-prison-investments.

Evans, N. 2017. "Speaker Urges Governor to Suspend Orlando Area Prosecutor that Refuses to Seek Death Penalty." *WLRN Miami*, March 23. Retrieved from http://wusfnews.wusf.usf.edu/post/speaker-urges-governor-suspend-orlando-area-prosecutor#stream/0.

Ewin, R. 1990. "Loyalty and the Police." *Criminal Justice Ethics* 9(2): 3–15.

Fachner, G. and S. Carter. 2015. *An Assessment of Deadly Force in the Philadelphia Police Department.* Collaborative Reform Initiative. Washington, DC: Office of Community Oriented Policing Services, U.S. Office of Justice Programs.

Fahrenthold, D. 2006. "Online Registry or Target List?" *Washington Post*, April 20: A03.

Fahrenthold, D. and J. O'Connell. 2017. "What Is the 'Emoluments Clause'? Does It Apply to President Trump?" *Washington Post*, January 23. https://www.washingtonpost.com/politics/what-is-the-emoluments-clause-does-it-apply-to-president-trump/2017/01/23/12aa7808-e185-11e6-a547-5fb9411d332c_story.html?utm_term=.bf786096db89.

Fairbanks, R. 2009. *How It Works: Recovering Citizens in Post Welfare Philadelphia.* Chicago, IL: University of Chicago Press.

Farmer, S., T. Beehr, and K. Love. 2003. "Becoming an Undercover Police Officer: A Note on Fairness Perceptions, Behavior, and Attitudes." *Journal of Organizational Behavior* 24: 373–387.

Farrar, T. 2013. "Self-Awareness to Being Watched and Socially Desirable Behavior: A Field Experiment on the Effect of Body Worn Cameras on Police Use of Force." *Police Foundation.* Retrieved from http://www.policefoundation.org/content/body-worn-camera.

Faturechi, R. 2011. "L.A. County Sheriff's Department to Dismiss 6 Deputies Involved in Montebello Assault." *New York Times*, March 23. Retrieved 7/30/2012 from http://articles.latimes.com/2011/mar/23/local/la-me-deputies-fired-20110323.

Faturechi, R. and A. Blankstein. 2011. "L.A. County Sheriff's Department Fosters 'Gang-Like Activity' Among Jail Deputies, Suit Alleges." May 5. Retrieved 7/30/2012 from http://articles.latimes.com/2011/may/05/local/la-me-deputies-lawsuit-20110505.

Fausset, R. 2014. "Indictment of Ex-Official Raises Questions on Mississippi's Private Prisons." *New York Times*, November 16. Retrieved 8/3/2015 from http://www.nytimes.com/2014/11/17/us/indictment-of-ex-official-raises-questions-on-mississippis-private-prisons.html?_r=0.

Fausset, R., A. Blinder, and M. Fernandez. 2016. "Dallas Police Chief, David O. Brown, Is Calm at Center of Crisis." *New York Times*, July 11. Retrieved from https://www.nytimes.com/2016/07/12/us/dallas-police-chief-brown-protests.html.

Fazlollah, M., J. Slobodzian, and A. Steele. 2012. "21 Suits Settled in Narcotics Unit Case." *Philly.com*, May 21. Retrieved from http://articles.philly.com/2012-05-21/news/31788992_1_security-cameras-surveillance-cameras-officers.

Fazlollah, M. and Whelan, A. 2015. "Officer Acquitted in Corruption Case Gets Promotion." *Philly.com*, November 14. Retrieved from http://www.philly.com/philly/news/20151114_Officer_acquitted_in_federal_corruption_case_gets_promotion.html#BlPmcUuyuLhfr0Dq.99.

Federal Bureau of Investigation (FBI). 2017. *The Assailant Study.* FBI Office of Partner Engagement. Retrieved from http://lawofficer.com/wp-content/uploads/2017/05/MindsetReport.pdf.

Feeney, J. 2005. "The Wisdom and Morality of Present-Day Criminal Sentencing." *Akron Law Review* 38: 853–867.

Feibleman, J. 1985. *Justice, Law and Culture.* Boston, MA: Martinus Nijhoff.

Feinberg, J. and H. Gross. 1977. *Justice: Selected Readings.* Princeton, NJ: Princeton University Press.

Felkenes, G. 1987. "Ethics in the Graduate Criminal Justice Curriculum." *Teaching Philosophy* 10(1): 23–36.

Fenton, J. 2010. "Raid on Corrections Officer's Home Shows Links to Criminals." *Baltimore Sun*, July 9. Retrieved 7/30/2012 from http://articles.baltimoresun.com/2010-07-09/news/bs-md-bgf-search-warrant-20100709_1_corrections-officer-gang-members-criminals.

Fenton, J. 2017. "Baltimore Attorney Arrested for Allegedly Offering Rape Victim $3K to Not Testify, Saying Trump Will Deport Her." *Baltimore Sun*, May 24. Retrieved from http://www.baltimoresun.com/news/maryland/crime/bs-md-ci-attorney-rape-deportation-20170524-story.html.

Ferdik, F., J. Rojek, and G. Alpert. 2013. "Citizen Oversight in the U.S. and Canada: An Overview." *Police Practice and Research* 14(2): 104–116.

Ferner, M. 2016. "Cheating California Prosecutors Face Prison Under New Law." *Huffington Post*, October 1. Retrieved from http://www.huffingtonpost.com/entry/california-prosecutor-misconduct-felony_us_57eff9b7e4b024a52d2f4d65.

Ferrandino, J. 2016. "The Effectiveness and Equity of NYPD Stop and Frisk Policy, 2003–2014." *Journal of Crime and Justice.* DOI: 10.1080/0735648X.2016.1249385.

Feuer, A. 2010. "The Terror Translators." *New York Times*, September 19: MB1.

Feuer, A. 2017a. "Candidates Line Up Behind Legacy of Former Brooklyn District Attorney." *New York Times*, April 9: A21.

Feuer, A. 2017b. "Civil Rights Law Shields Police Personnel Files, Court Finds." *New York Times*, March 30. Retrieved from https://www.nytimes.com/2017/03/30/nyregion/civil-rights-law-section-50-a-police-disciplinary-records.html?emc=edit_th_20170331&nl=todaysheadlines&nlid=66242298&_r=0.

Fink, P. 1977. *Moral Philosophy.* Encino, CA: Dickinson.

Finn, M. and L. Stalans. 2002. "Police Handling of the Mentally Ill in Domestic Violence Situations." *Criminal Justice and Behavior* 29: 278–289.

Finn, P. and J. Warrick. 2009. "Detainee's Harsh Treatment Foiled No Plots." *Washington Post*, March 29. Retrieved from www.washingtonpost.com/wp-dyn/content/article/2009/03/28/AR2009032802066.html.

Fishbein, D. 2000. *Biobehavioral Perspectives on Criminology.* Belmont, CA: Wadsworth.

Fisher, A. 2016. "Why It's So Hard to Stop Bad Cops from Getting New Police Jobs." *Reason.com*, September 30. Retrieved from http://reason.com/archives/2016/09/30/why-its-so-hard-to-stop-bad-cops-from-ge.

Fisher, J. 2008. *Forensics Under Fire: Are Bad Science and Dueling Experts Corrupting Criminal Justice?* New Brunswick, NJ: Rutgers University Press.

Fisher, M., S. Higham, and D. Hawkins. 2015. "Uneven Justice." *Washington Post*, November 3. Retrieved from http://www.washingtonpost.com/sf/investigative/2015/11/03/uneven-justice/?hpid=hp_rhp-top-table-main_copsettlement-1010pm%3Ahomepage%2Fstory.

Fitzgerald, D. 2009. "Wrong-Door Raids, Phantom Informants, and the Controlled Buy." *The Champion*, November. Retrieved from www.NACDL.org.

Fitzgerald, P. 2009. "Thoughts on the Ethical Culture of a Prosecutor's Office." *Washington Law Review* 84: 11–35.

Flanagan, D. and K. Jackson. 1987. "Justice, Care, and Gender: The Kohlberg-Gilligan Debate Revisited." *Ethics* 97: 622–637.

Fletcher, G. 1993. *Loyalty: An Essay on the Morality of Relationships*. New York: Oxford University Press.

Fogel, D. 1975. *We Are the Living Proof*. Cincinnati, OH: Anderson.

Fogelson, R. 1977. *Big City Police*. Cambridge, MA: Harvard University Press.

Foot, P. 1982. "Moral Relativism." In *Relativism: Cognitive and Moral*, ed. J. Meiland and M. Krausz, 152–167. Notre Dame, IN: University of Notre Dame Press.

Ford, D. 2015. "Man Jailed as Teen Without Conviction Commits Suicide." *CNN.com*, June 8. Retrieved from www.cnn.com/2015/06/07/us/kalief-browder-dead/.

Forrest, K. and W. Woody. 2010. "Police Deception During Interrogation and Its Surprising Influence on Jurors' Perceptions of Confession Evidence." *Trial*, November: 9–19.

Fraternal Order of Police. 2017. *The Trump Administration: The First 100 Days*. Retrieved from https://fop.net/CmsDocument/Doc/TrumpFirst100Days.pdf.

Frederick, B. and D. Stemen. 2012. *The Anatomy of Discretion: An Analysis of Prosecutorial Decisionmaking*. NIJ Doc. #240334. Washington, DC: National Institute of Justice.

Freedman, M. 1986. "Professional Responsibility of the Criminal Defense Lawyer: The Three Hardest Questions."

In *Ethics and the Legal Profession*, ed. M. Davis and F. Elliston, 328–339. Buffalo, NY: Prometheus.

Friedersdorf, C. 2015. "The Number of Cops Indicted for Murder Spikes Upward." *The Atlantic*, August 19. Retrieved from https://www.theatlantic.com/politics/archive/2015/08/the-shocking-number-of-cops-recently-indicted-for-murder/401732/.

Friedman, B. 2015. "America's Most Heinous Judge Resigns." *Salon*, June 1. Retrieved from www.salon.com/2015/06/01/americas_most_heinous_judge_resigns_wife_beater_mark_fuller_leaves_the_bench_finally_but_not_easily.

Fritzsche, D. 1995. "Personal Values: Potential Keys to Ethical Decision-Making." *Journal of Business Ethics* 14: 909–922.

Fryer, R. 2016. *An Empirical Analysis of Racial Differences in Police Use of Force*. Cambridge, MA: National Bureau of Economic Research.

Fuller, L. 1969. *The Morality of Law*. New Haven, CT: Yale University Press.

Fyfe, J. and R. Kane. 2006. *Bad Cops: A Study of Career-Ending Misconduct Among New York City Police Officers* (Document #215795). Washington, DC: U.S. Department of Justice.

Galloway, J. and J. Kuhnhenn. 2005. "Senators Add Anti-Torture Words to Bill." Austin American-Statesman, October 6: A4.

Gallup Poll. 2017a. "Americans' Respect for Police Surges." *Gallup*. Retrieved from http://www.gallup.com/poll/196610/americans-respect-police-surges.aspx.

Gallup Poll. 2017b. "Honesty/Ethics in Professions." *Gallup*. Retrieved from http://www.gallup.com/poll/1654/Honesty-Ethics-Professions.aspx.

Galston, W. 1980. *Justice and the Human Good*. Chicago, IL: University of Chicago Press.

Gamio, L. and T. Meko. 2016. "How Terrorism in the West Compares to Terrorism Everywhere Else." *Washington Post*, July 16. Retrieved from https://www.washingtonpost.com/graphics/world/the-scale-of-terrorist-attacks-around-the-world/.

Garay, A. 2007. "Man's Innocence in Gang Rape Affirmed." *Austin American-Statesman*, April 10: B5.

Gardner, H. 2007. *Five Minds for the Future*. Boston, MA: Harvard Business School.

Garland, D. 1990. *Punishment and Modern Society*. Chicago, IL: University of Chicago Press.

Garner, J., C. Maxwell, and C. Heraux. 2002. "Characteristics Associated with the Prevalence and Severity of Force Used by the Police." *Justice Quarterly* 19(4): 705–745.

Garrett, B. 2011. *Convicting the Innocent: Where Criminal Prosecutions Go Wrong*. Cambridge, MA: Harvard University Press.

Garrett, B. 2014. *Too Big to Fail*. New York: Belknap Press.

Garrett, B. and P. Neufeld. 2009. "Invalid Forensic Science Testimony and Wrongful Convictions." *Virginia Law Review* 95(1): 72–93.

Garrick, B. 2017. "San Diego Police Body Cameras Reducing Misconduct, Aggressive Use of Force, Report Says." *Los Angeles Times*, February 10. Retrieved from http://www.sandiegouniontribune.com/news/politics/sd-me-body-cameras-20170209-story.html.

Gass, H. 2015a. "When Expert Testimony Isn't." *Christian Science Monitor*, May 26. Retrieved from www.csmonitor.com/USA/Justice/2015/0526/When-expert-testimony-isn-t-Tainted-evidence-wreaks-havoc-in-courts-lives-video.

Gass, H. 2015b. "The Freddie Gray $6.4 Million Settlement Is Big, But Will It Send Right Message?" *Christian Science Monitor*, September 9. Retrieved from http://www.csmonitor.com/USA/Justice/2015/0909/The-Freddie-Gray-6.4-million-settlement-is-big-but-will-it-send-right-message.

Gates, J. 2017. "Chris Epps Sentenced to Almost 20 Years." *The Clarion-Ledger*, May 24. Retrieved from http://www.clarionledger.com/story/news/2017/05/24/chris-epps-sentencing/341916001/.

Gau, J. 2014. "Procedural Justice and Police Legitimacy: A Test of Measurement and Structure." *American Journal of Criminal Justice* 39: 187–205.

Gavaghan, M., K. Alex, and J. Gibbs. 1983. "Moral Judgment in Delinquents and Nondelinquents: Recognition Versus Production Measures." *Journal of Psychology* 114: 267–274.

Gehrke, R. 2016. "Two Top Parole Officials Resign as Utah Guv Launches Review of State's Parole System." *The Salt Lake Tribune*, February 11. Retrieved from http://www.sltrib.com/news/3527750-

155/after-inmates-disappear-utah-gov-launches.

Geis, G., A. Mobley, and D. Shichor. 1999. "Private Prisons, Criminological Research and Conflict of Interest." *Crime and Delinquency* 45(3): 372–388.

George, J. 2017. "Can Bipartisan Criminal Justice Reform Survive in the Trump Era." *The New Yorker*, June 6. Retrieved from http://www.newyorker.com/news/news-desk/can-bipartisan-criminal-justice-reform-survive-in-the-trump-era.

Gerda, N. 2017. "Santa Ana Will Appeal Decision to Reinstate Officer Fired After Pot Shop Raid." *Voice of OC.com*, February 8. http://voiceofoc.org/2017/02/santa-ana-will-appeal-decision-to-reinstate-officer-fired-after-pot-shop-raid/.

Gershman, B. 1991. "Why Prosecutors Misbehave." In *Justice, Crime, and Ethics*, ed. M. Braswell, B. McCarthy, and B. McCarthy, 163–177. Cincinnati, OH: Anderson.

Gershman, B. 2003. "Misuse of Scientific Evidence by Prosecutors." *Oklahoma City University Law Review* 28: 17–41.

Getlin, J. 2002. "DA Suggests Overturning Convictions in Jogger Case." *Austin American-Statesman*, December 6: A16.

Ghosh, B. 2009. "After Waterboarding: How to Make Terrorists Talk?" *Time.com*, May 29. Retrieved from www.time.com/time/magazine/article/0,9171,1901491,00.html.

Giannelli, P. 2012. "The North Carolina Crime Lab Scandal." *Criminal Justice* 27(1): 1–10.

Giannelli, P. and K. McMunigal. 2007. "Prosecutors, Ethics, and Expert Witnesses." *Fordham Law Review* 76(3): 1493–1537.

Gillers, S. 2004. "Tortured Reasoning." *American Lawyer*, July: 65–66.

Gilligan, C. 1982. *In a Different Voice: Psychological Theory and Women's Development*. Cambridge, MA: Harvard University Press.

Gilligan, C. 1987. "Moral Orientation and Moral Development." In *Women and Moral Theory*, ed. E. F. Kittay and D. Meyers, 19–37. Totowa, NJ: Rowman and Littlefield.

Gilmartin, K. and J. Harris. 1998. "Law Enforcement Ethics: The Continuum of Compromise." *Police Chief*, January 1998. Retrieved from www.rcmp-learning.org/docs/ecddl 222.htm.

Giradeaux, J. 1949. *The Madwoman of Chaillot*, adapted by Maurice Valency. New York: Random House.

Glaun, D. 2016. "New Training Teaches Springfield Officers to Police Each Other." *Mass.Live*, November 2. Retrieved from http://www.masslive.com/news/index.ssf/2016/11/new_training_teaches_springfie.html.

Glendon, M. 1994. *A Nation Under Lawyers*. New York: Farrar, Straus and Giroux.

Glenn, L. 2001. *Texas Prisons: The Largest Hotel Chain in Texas*. Austin, TX: Eakin.

Glover, S. and M. Lait. 2000. "71 More Cases May Be Voided Due to Rampart." *Los Angeles Times*. Retrieved from www.latimes.rampart/lat_ rampart000418.html.

Goffard, C. 2016. "Prosecutors Who Withhold or Tamper with Evidence Now Face Felony Charges." *Los Angeles Times*, October 6. Retrieved from http://www.latimes.com/local/lanow/la-me-prosecutor-misconduct-20161003-snap-story.html.

Golab, J. 2000. "L.A. Confidential." *Salon.com*. Retrieved from http://dir.salon.com/news/feature/2000/24/rampart/index.html.

Golden, T. 2005. "Cruel and Unusual Punishment." *Austin American-Statesman*, May 21: A16.

Gonnerman, J. 2013. "Before the Law." *The New Yorker*, October 6. Retrieved from www.newyorker.com/magazine/2014/10/06/before-the-law.

Gonnerman, J. 2015. "Kalief Browder, 1993–2015." *The New Yorker*, June 7. Retrieved from www.newyorker.com/news/news-desk/kalief-browder-1993-2015.

Goode, E. 2012. "Average Prison Stay Grew 30 Percent in Two Decades." *New York Times*, June 6: A12.

Goode, E. 2013. "Some Chiefs Chafing as Justice Department Keeps Closer Eye on Policing." *New York Times*, July 27: A14.

Goodman, J. 2015. "Officer Settles Suit Over Whistleblowing." *New York Times*, September 30: A22.

Gordon, M. 2015. "Racial Disparity in Charlotte Traffic Stops Grows, Study Finds." *Charlotte Observer*, April 11. Retrieved from www.charlotteobserver.com/news/local/crime/article18289739.html#storylink=cpy.

Gorta, A. 2008. "Illegal Drug Use by Police Officers: Using Research and Investigations to Inform Prevention Strategies." *International Journal of Police Science and Management* 11(1): 85–96.

Gottschalk, P. and S. Holgersson. 2011. "Whistleblowing in the Police." *Police Practice and Research* 12(5): 397–409.

Gould, J., J. Carrano, R. Leo, and K. Hail-Jares. 2014. "Predicting Erroneous Convictions." *Iowa Law Review* 99(1): 471–522.

Gould, J., J. Carrano, R. Leo, and J. Young. 2012. *Predicting Erroneous Convictions: A Social Sciences Approach to Miscarriages of Justice*. National Institute of Justice Report. Retrieved from https://www.ncjrs.gov/pdffiles1/nij/grants/241389.pdf.

Gourarie, C. 2016. "Inside the Invisible Institute's Fight for Police Accountability." *The Criminal Justice Report*, January 29. Retrieved from http://www.cjr.org/united_states_project/inside_the_invisible_institutes_fight_for_police_accountability.php.

Gourevitch, P. and E. Morris. 2008. "Exposed: The Woman Behind the Pictures at Abu Ghraib." *New Yorker* (March). Retrieved from www.newyorker.com/reporting/2008/03/24/080324fa_fact_gourevitch.

Governing.com. 2017. *State Marijuana Laws in 2017*. Website. Retrieved from http://www.governing.com/gov-data/state-marijuana-laws-map-medical-recreational.html.

Government Security News. 2017. "Former Dallas Police Chief Named as a Managing Director for Kroll." *Government Security News*, April 13. Retrieved from http://gsnmagazine.com/article/48196/former_dallas_police_chief_named_managing_director.

Graham, T. and L. Gormisky. 2010. "Two Philadelphia Cops Charged with Robbing Undercover Investigator." *Philadelphia Inquirer*, October 5: A1.

Grasmick, H. and R. Bursik. 1990. "Conscience, Significant Others, and Rational Choice: Extending the Deterrence Model." *Law and Society Review* 24: 837–899.

Gray, M. 2014. "Racketeering, Smuggling, Sex with Guards: 25 Indicted in Massive Baltimore Prison Scandal." *Time*, April 24, 2013. Retrieved from http://nation.time.com/2013/04/24/sex-with-guards-in-baltimore-prison-scandal.

Green, E. 2015. "African Americans Cited for Resisting Arrest at High Rate in S.F." *S.F.Gate.com*, April 29. Retrieved from www.sfgate.com/bayarea/article/African-Americans-cited-for-resisting-arrest-at-6229946.php.

Green, E., B. Egelko, J. Lyons, and E. Allday. "SFPD 2016. Chief Greg Suhr Resigns After Police Killing of Woman." *SFGate.com*, May 20. Retrieved from http://www.sfgate.com/bayarea/article/Police-Chief-Greg-Suhr-resigns-after-killing-of-7758122.php.

Green, F. 2010. "Williamsburg DNA Case Raises Question of Effort." *Richmond Times-Dispatch*, February 5. Retrieved from www2.timesdispatch.com/member-center/share-this/print/?content=ar1665060.

Greene, J., A. Piquero, M. Hickman, and B. Lawton. 2004. *Police Integrity and Accountability in Philadelphia: Predicting and Assessing Police Misconduct.* Washington, DC: U.S. Department of Justice, NCJRS. Retrieved from www.ncjrs.gov.

Greenberg, J. 2002. "Who Stole the Money and When? Individual and Situational Determinants of Employee Theft." *Organizational Behavior and Human Decision Processes* 89: 985–1003.

Greenhouse, L. 2007. "Supreme Court Took Big, Small Steps to Right." *Austin American-Statesman*, July 1. A15.

Greenhouse, L. 2008. "Justices, 5–4, Back Detainee Appeals for Guantanamo." *New York Times*, June 13: A1.

Greenhut, S. 2015. "The Sweeping Impact of Copley Decision: 2006 Decision Shielded Police Disciplinary Hearings from Public." *San Diego Union Tribune*, May 30. Retrieved from www.utsandiego.com/news/2015/may/30/sweeping-impact-copley-decision-significance.

Grimm, A. 2017. "Rate of Suicides Among Chicago Police a Badge of High-Stress Job." *Chicago Sun-Times*, February 1. Retrieved from http://chicago.suntimes.com/politics/rate-of-suicides-among-chicago-police-a-badge-of-high-stress-job/.

Grissom, B. 2010. "Too Many Laws, Too Many Prisoners." *The Economist*, July 22. Retrieved from www.economist.com/node/16636027.

Grometstein, R. 2007. "Prosecutorial Misconduct and Noble Cause Corruption." *Criminal Law Bulletin* 43(1): 1–22.

Gross, N. 2016. "Is There a 'Ferguson Effect'?" *New York Times*, October 2: SR9.

Gross, S., M. Possley, and K. Stephens. 2017. *Race and Wrongful Convictions in the United States.* National Registry of Exonerations. Retrieved from https://www.law.umich.edu/special/exoneration/Documents/Race_and_Wrongful_Convictions.pdf.

Grossi, E. and B. Berg. 1991. "Stress and Job Dissatisfaction Among Correctional Officers: An Unexpected Finding." *International Journal of Offender Therapy and Comparative Criminology* 35(1): 79–110.

Grotius, H. 1625/2005. *The Rights of War and Peace.* Book 1, ed. Richard Tuck. Indianapolis, IN: Liberty Fund.

Grovum, J. 2015. "Can States Slow the Flow of Military Equipment to Police?" *Stateline*, March 24. Retrieved from www.pewtrusts.org/en/research-and-analysis/blogs/stateline/2015/3/24/can-states-slow-the-flow-of-military-equipment-to-police.

Guilfoil, J. 2010. "Ex-Officer Admits to Obstruction of Justice." *Boston.com*, February 17. Retrieved from www.boston.com/news/local/massachusetts/article.

Guo, J. 2016. "Researchers Have Discovered a New and Surprising Racial Bias in the Criminal Justice System." *Washington Post*, February 24. Retrieved from https://www.washingtonpost.com/news/wonk/wp/2016/02/24/researchers-have-discovered-a-surprising-racial-bias-in-the-criminal-justice-system/.

Gurman, S. 2017a. "Justice Department Wants Pause in Consent-Decree Cases." *Seattle Times* (AP), April 6: A8.

Gurman, S. 2017b. "Federal Overhauls of Police Departments Bring Mixed Results." *US News.com*, April 5. Retrieved from https://www.usnews.com/news/politics/articles/2017-04-05/cities-say-federal-overhauls-of-police-bring-mixed-results.

Gutierrez, M. and K. Minugh. 2013. "California Police Unions Fight Discipline of Officers Under Prosecutors' Lists." *Sacramento Bee*, September 12. Retrieved from www.sacbee.com/2013/09/12/5728305/california-police-unions-fight.html#storylink=cpy.

Haag, A. 2006. "Ethical Dilemmas Faced by Correctional Psychologists in Canada." *Criminal Justice and Behavior* 33: 93–109.

Haake, K. 2014. "Missoula County, State, DOJ Sign Agreements to Improve Handling of Sexual Assault Cases." *The Missoulian*, June 10. Retrieved from http://missoulian.com/news/local/missoula-county-state-doj-sign-agreements-to-improve-handling-of/article_bb8c665a-f0c1-11e3-8689-0019bb2963f4.html.

Haederle, M. 2010. "The Best Fiscal Stimulus: Trust." *Miller-McCune Magazine*, September/October: 42–49.

Hagan, R. 2012. "SCOTUS Denies Prosecutorial Misconduct Appeal." *FindLaw.com*, November 16. Retrieved from http://blogs.findlaw.com/eleventh_circuit/2012/11/scotus-denies-prosecutorial-misconduct-appeal.html.

Hager, E. 2017. *The Seismic Change in Police Interrogations.* The Marshall Project, March 7. Retrieved from https://www.themarshallproject.org/2017/03/07/the-seismic-change-in-police-interrogations#.zxEFRRfxp.

Haidt, J. 2001. "The Emotional Dog and Its Rational Tail: A Social Intuitionist Approach to Moral Judgment." *Psychological Review* 108(4): 814–834.

Hall, C. and L. Brasier. 2015. "Michigan Cops Fume Over Loss of U.S. Military Vehicles." *Detroit Free Press*, December 3. Retrieved from http://www.freep.com/story/news/local/michigan/2015/12/02/federal-military-surplus-return/76605640/.

Hall, M. 2002. "Death Isn't Fair." *Texas Monthly*, December: 124–167.

Hall, M. 2010. "Trial and Error." *Texas Monthly*, September: 82–97.

Hamidi, A. and P. Koga. 2014. "Neuropsychological Correlates of Misconduct in Law Enforcement Officers with Subclinical Post-Traumatic Stress Disorder." In *Law Enforcement Ethics*, ed. B. Fitch, 209–227. Thousand Oaks, CA: Sage.

Hamilton, M. and J. Queally. 2016. "Failure of Leadership at the Orange County DA's Office Led to Informant Issues, Report Says." *Los Angeles Times*, January 4. Retrieved from http://www.latimes.com/local/lanow/la-me-ln-orange-county-jailhouse-informant-scandal-20160104-story.html.

Haney, C. 2008. "A Culture of Harm: Taming the Dynamics of Cruelty in Supermax Prisons." *Criminal Justice and Behavior* 35: 956–984.

Hansen, M. 2007. "The Toughest Call." *ABA Journal*, August: 28–29.

Harbison, R. 2015. "Traffic Fines Forgiven: Why California Is Offering Amnesty for Poor?" *The Christian Science Monitor*, September 30. Retrieved from http://www.csmonitor.com/USA/

Justice/2015/0930/Traffic-fines-forgiven-Why-California-is-offering-amnesty-for-poor.

Hardy, M. 2017. "In Fight Over Bail's Fairness, a Sheriff Joins the Critics." *New York Times*, March 9. Retrieved from https://www.nytimes.com/2017/03/09/us/houston-bail-reform-sheriff-gonzalez.html.

Harmon, R. 2017. "Evaluating and Improving Structural Reform in Police Departments." *Criminology and Public Policy* 16(2): 617–627.

Harms, W. 2012. "Moral Evaluations of Harm Are Instant and Emotional." *Science Daily*, November 28. Retrieved from https://www.sciencedaily.com/releases/2012/11/121128182725.htm?utm_source=TrendMD&utm_medium=cpc&utm_campaign=ScienceDaily_TrendMD_1.

Harris Poll. 2008. "Support for Capital Punishment." *Harris Opinion Poll*. Retrieved from www.pollingreport.com/crime.htm.

Harris, C. 1986. *Applying Moral Theories*. Belmont, CA: Wadsworth.

Harris, C. 2010a. *Pathways of Police Misconduct*. Durham, NC: Carolina Academic Press.

Harris, C. 2010b. "Problem Officers: Analyzing Problem Behavior Patterns from a Large Cohort." *Journal of Criminal Justice* 38: 216–225.

Harris, C. 2012. "Longitudinal Patterns of Internally Generated Complaints Filed Against a Large Cohort of Police Officers." *Policing and Society: An International Journal of Research and Policy* 20(4): 401–415.

Harris, C. and R. Worden. 2014. "The Effect of Sanctions on Police Misconduct." *Crime & Delinquency* 60(8): 1258–1288.

Harris, D. 2004. "Review Essay/Profiling: Theory and Practice." *Criminal Justice Ethics* 23(2): 51–57.

Harris, D. 2005. *Good Cops: The Case for Preventive Policing*. New York: The New Press.

Harris, D. 2006. "Do Something Before the Next Attack, But Not This." *Criminal Justice Ethics* 25(2): 46–54.

Harris, W. 2011. *Badge of Honor: Blowing the Whistle*. Shelbyville, KY: Wasteland Press.

Harrison, S. 2016. "For Small Amounts of Marijuana, Blacks Are Far More Likely Than Whites to Go to Jail in Charlotte." *Charlotte Observer*, February 12. Retrieved from http://www.charlotteobserver.com/news/local/crime/article60170981.html#storylink=cpy.

Harshman, C. and E. Harshman. 2008. "The Gordian Knot of Ethics: Understanding Leadership Effectiveness and Ethical Behavior." *Journal of Business Ethics* 78(1/2): 175–192.

Hart, S. 2017. "Cops in Cook County Among Worst, Huge Study of Traffic Stops Across U.S. Finds." *Injustice Watch*, February 28. Retrieved from http://www.injusticewatch.org/news/2017/cook-county-cops-among-worst-huge-study-of-traffic-stops-across-u-s-finds/.

Hashimoto, E. 2008. "Toward Ethical Plea Bargaining." *Cardozo Law Review* 30: 949–963.

Hassell, K. and C. Archbold. 2009. "Widening the Scope on Complaints of Police Misconduct." *Policing: An International Journal of Police Strategies and Management* 33(3): 473–489.

Hassine, V. 1996. *Life Without Parole: Living in Prison Today*. Los Angeles, CA: Roxbury.

Hatamyar, P. and K. Simmons. 2002. "Are Women More Ethical Lawyers? An Empirical Study." *Florida State University Law Review* 31: 785–857.

Hauser, C. 2009. "Few Results for Reports of Police Misconduct." *New York Times*, October 5. Retrieved from www.nytimes.com/2009/10/05/nyregion/05ccrb.html.

Hays, K. 2005. "Report: Houston Crime Lab Was Long Neglected." *Austin American-Statesman*, July 1: B7.

Heath, B. 2013. Exclusive: FBI *Allowed Informants to Commit 5,600 Crimes*. *USA Today*, August 4. Retrieved from www.usatoday.com/story/news/nation/2013/08/04/fbi-informant-crimes-report/2613305/.

Heath, B. 2015. "Police Secretly Track Cellphones to Solve Routine Crimes." *USA Today*, August 24. Retrieved from http://www.usatoday.com/story/news/2015/08/23/baltimore police stingray cell surveillance/31994181/.

Heath, B. 2016a. "ATF Drug Stings Targeted Minorities, Report Finds." *USA Today*, September 24. Retrieved from http://www.usatoday.com/story/news/2016/09/23/atf-stash-house-stings-minorities/90950474/.

Heath, B. 2016b. "200 Imprisoned Based on Illegal Cellphone Tracking, Review Finds." *USA Today*, March 31. Retrieved from https://www.usatoday.com/story/news/2016/03/31/200-imprisoned-based-illegal-cellphone-tracking-review-finds/82489300/.

Heffernan, E. 2014. "Police Fill a Need with 'Beds for Kids'." *The Seattle Times*, June 26: B1.

Heffernan, W. and J. Kleinig. 2000. *From Social Justice to Criminal Justice: Poverty and the Administration of Criminal Law*. New York: Oxford University Press.

Heidensohn, F. 1986. "Models of Justice: Portia or Persephone? Some Thoughts on Equality, Fairness and Gender in the Field of Criminal Justice." *International Journal of the Sociology of Law* 14: 287–298.

Helfgott, J., Atherley, L., Pollock, J., Vinson, J., Conn-Johnson, C., Strah, B., Neidhart, E., Hickman, M., and Wood, N. 2015. *Evaluation of the Washington State Criminal Justice Training Commission's "Warriors to Guardians" Cultural Shift and Crisis Intervention Team (CIT) Training*. Seattle, WA: Seattle University. (Available from author).

Hennelly, R. 2015. "Poisonous Cops, Total Immunity: Why an Epidemic of Police Abuse Is Actually Going Unpunished." *Salon.com*, May 13. Retrieved from http://www.salon.com/2015/05/13/poisonous_cops_total_immunity_why_an_epidemic_of_police_abuse_is_actually_going_unpunished/.

Henriques, Z. 2001. "The Path of Least Resistance: Sexual Exploitation of Female Offenders as an Unethical Corollary to Retributive Ideology and Correctional Practice." In *Discretion, Community and Correctional Ethics*, ed. J. Kleinig and M. Smith, 192–201. Oxford, England: Rowman and Littlefield.

Hensley, N. 2014. "NSA Analysts Spied on Spouses, Girlfriends: Documents." *New York Daily News*, December 27. Retrieved from www.nydailynews.com/news/politics/nsa-analysts-spied-spouses-girlfriends-documents-article-1.2058282.

Hentoff, N. 1999. "Serpico: Nothing Has Changed." *Village Voice*, November 4. Retrieved from http://www.villagevoice.com/issues/9944/hentoff.shtml.

Herbert, B. 2002. "In Tulia, Justice Has Gone into Hiding." *Austin American-Statesman*, August 13: A9.

Herbert, B. 2003. "Truth Has Been Told About Tulia, But Story Isn't Over Yet." *Austin American-Statesman*, April 29: A9.

Herbert, S. 1996. "Morality in Law Enforcement: Chasing 'Bad Guys' with the Los Angeles Police Department." *Law and Society Review* 30(4): 799–818.

Hermann, P. 2009. "The Murky World of Informants." *Baltimore Sun*, October 4. Retrieved from http://articles.baltimoresun.com/2009-10-04/news/0910030041_1_informants-fbi-agent-cops-and-crooks/3.

Hersh, F. 1979. *Developing Moral Growth: From Piaget to Kohlberg*. New York: Longman.

Hews, B. 2013. "18 Los Angeles County Sheriff Officials Indicted in Massive Corruption, Civil Rights Case." *Los Cerritos News*, December 9. Retrieved from www.loscerritosnews.net/2013/12/09/18-los-angeles-county-sheriff-officials-indicted-in-massive-corruptioncivil-rights-case.

Hickey, J. and P. Scharf. 1980. *Toward a Just Correctional System*. San Francisco, CA: Jossey-Bass.

Hickman, M., A. Piquero, and J. Garner. 2008. "Toward a National Estimate of Police Use of Nonlethal Force." *Criminology & Public Policy* 7: 563–604.

Hickman, M., A. Piquero, B. Lawton, and J. Greene. 2001. "Applying Tittle's Control Balance Theory to Police Deviance." *Policing* 24(4): 497–519.

Hicks, W. 2004. "Constraints in the Police Use of Force: Implications of the Just War Tradition." *American Journal of Criminal Justice* 28(2): 254–270.

Hight, B. 2005. "In Atoning for Tragedy, a Former Navy Captain Finds His Voice." *Austin American-Statesman*, March 11: A11.

Hinman, L. 1998. *Ethics: A Pluralistic Approach to Moral Theory*, 2nd ed. Ft. Worth, TX: Harcourt Brace.

Hirschi, T. 1969. *Causes of Delinquency*. Berkeley, CA: University of California Press.

Hobbes, T. 1651. *Leviathan*. New York: Penguin Classics, 1982.

Hofer, P., K. Blackwell, and R. B. Ruback. 1999. "The Effect of Federal Sentencing Guidelines on Inter-judge Sentencing Disparity." *Journal of Criminal Law and Criminology* 90(1): 239–321.

Holmes, M. 2000. "Minority Threat and Police Brutality: Determinants of Civil Rights Criminal Complaints in U.S. Municipalities." *Criminology* 38(2): 336–343.

Hopfe, L. 1983. *Religions of the World*. New York: Macmillan.

Hopkins, S. 2013. "How Effective Are Ethics Codes and Programs?" *Financial Executives*, March: 43–45.

Horn, D. 2009. "Fired to Rehired." *Cincinnati.com*, August 25. Retrieved from www.cincinnati.com/apps/pbcs.dll/article?Dato=20080629&Kategori=NEWS01&Lopenr=108250002.

Horswell, C. 2013. "Judge Accused of Texting Prosecution from Bench to Sway Case." *Houston Chronicle*, July 14, 2013: A1.

Houston, J. 1999. *Correctional Management: Functions, Skills, and Systems*. Chicago, IL: Nelson-Hall.

Hsu, S. 2014. "Federal Review Stalled After Finding Forensic Errors by FBI Lab Unit Spanned Two Decades." *Washington Post*, July 29, 2014.

Hsu, S. 2015. "FBI Admits Flaws in Hair Analysis Over Decades." *Washington Post*, April 18. Retrieved from www.washingtonpost.com/local/crime/fbi-overstated-forensic-hair-matches-in-nearly-all-criminal-trials-for-decades/2015/04/18/39c8d8c6-e515-11c4 b510-962fcfabc310_story.html.

Hsu, S. 2016. "Town Near Ferguson, Mo., Agrees to Pay $4.7 Million to Settle 'Debtors Prison' Case." *Washington Post*, July 14. Retrieved from https://www.washingtonpost.com/local/public-safety/town-near-ferguson-mo-agrees-to-pay-47-million-to-settle-debtors-prison-case/2016/07/14/37b42078-49db-11e6-acbc-4d4870a079da_story.html.

Hu, W. 2014. "Ex-Lieutenant Gets Community Service in Ticket-Fixing Case." *New York Times*, December 19: A27.

Hu, W. 2016. "Judge Sentences 6 Former Guards to Prison for Attack on Rikers Inmate." *New York Times*, September 17: A13

Hu, W. and K. Pastor. 2016. "5 Rikers Officers Convicted in 2012 Beating of Inmate." *New York Times*, June 7: A16.

Huberts, L., M. Kaptein, and K. Lasthuizen. 2007. "A Study of the Impact of Three Leadership Styles on Integrity Violations Committed by Police Officers." *Policing* 30(4): 587–607.

Human Rights Watch. 2011. *Getting Away with Torture: The Bush Administration and Mistreatment of Detainees*. New York: Human Rights Watch.

Human Rights Watch. 2014. *Illusion of Justice: Human Rights Abuses in US Terrorism Prosecutions*. Retrieved from www.hrw.org/reports/2014/07/21/illusion-justice-0.

Hume, D. 1739. *A Treatise of Human Nature*. Retrieved from https://www.gutenberg.org/files/4705/4705-h/4705-h.htm.

Hunter, G. 2017. "Cop Misconduct Suits Drop After Reforms." *The Detroit News*, February 24. Retrieved from http://www.detroitnews.com/story/news/local/detroit-city/2017/02/24/detroit-police-reforms/98372122/.

Huspek, M., R. Martinez, and L. Jiminez. 2001. "Violations of Human Civil Rights on the U.S.-Mexico Border, 1997–1997: A Report." In *Notable Selections in Criminal Criminology and Criminal Justice*, ed. D. Baker and R. Davin, 183–202. Guilford, CT: McGraw-Hill/Dushkin.

Ingraham, C. 2016a. "The Feds Have Resumed a Controversial Program that Lets Cops Take Stuff and Keep It." *Washington Post*, March 28. Retrieved from https://www.washingtonpost.com/news/wonk/wp/2016/03/28/the-feds-have-resumed-a-controversial-program-that-lets-cops-take-stuff-and-keep-it.

Ingraham, C. 2016b. "New Report: In Tough Times, Police Start Seizing a Lot More Stuff from People." *Washington Post*, November 10. https://www.washingtonpost.com/news/wonk/wp/2015/11/10/report-in-lean-times-police-start-taking-a-lot-more-stuff-from-people/?utm_term=.f99c336f6903.

Institute for Justice. 2017. *Policing for Profit*, 2nd ed. Retrieved from http://ij.org/report/policing-for-profit.

Institute for Law Enforcement Administration. 2008. *Ethical Courage Awards*. Retrieved from www.cailaw.org/ilea/pastwinners.html.

International Association of Chiefs of Police (IACP). 2008. *Ethics Training in Law Enforcement*. Retrieved from www.theiacp.org.

Iris, M. 1998. "Police Discipline in Chicago: Arbitration or Arbitrary?" *Journal of Criminal Law and Criminology* 89: 215–244.

Iris, M. 2002. "Police Discipline in Houston: The Arbitration Experience." *Police Quarterly* 5:132–151.

Jablon, R. 2000. "L.A. Confronts Police Scandal that May Cost Tens of Millions." *Austin American-Statesman*, February 19: A18.

Jackman, T. 2016. "Protocol for Reducing Police Shootings Draws Backlash from Unions, Chiefs Group." *Washington Post*, March 31. Retrieved from https://www.washingtonpost.com/local/public-safety/move-to-reduce-police-shootings-draws-sharp-backlash-from-unions-chiefs-group/2016/03/30/03c81e6a-ec55-11e5-bc08-3e03a5b41910_story.html?utm_term=.3347e1adc95d.

Jackman, T. 2017. "Mass. Crime Chemist Admits Daily Drug Use in Lab, Sparking a Second Scandal." *Washington Post*, May 5. Retrieved from https://www.washingtonpost.com/news/true-crime/wp/2016/05/05/mass-crime-chemist-admits-daily-drug-use-in-lab-sparking-a-second-scandal/?utm_term=.7961045190d0.

Jackson, J., T. Tyler, B. Bradford, D. Taylor, and M. Shiner. 2010. "Legitimacy and Procedural Justice in Prisons." *Prison Service Journal* 19(1): 4–6.

Jacoby, J., L. Mellon, and W. Smith. 1980. *Policy and Prosecution*. Washington, DC: Bureau of Social Science Research.

Jaffee, S. and J. Hyde. 2000. "Gender Differences in Moral Orientation: A Meta-Analysis." *Psychological Bulletin* 126(5): 703–726.

James, L., B. Vila, and K. Daratha. 2014. "Results from Experimental Trials Testing Participant Responses to White, Hispanic and Black Suspects in High-Fidelity Deadly Force Judgment and Decision-Making Simulations." *Journal of Experimental Criminology*. DOI: 10.1007/s11292-012-9163-y.

Jeffrey, D. 2007. "How Prosecutors Go Bad." *Legal Times*, August 6: 1–2.

Johanek, M. 2008. "Justice Department Scandal Almost Buried by Financial Crisis." *Toledo Blade*, October 10. Retrieved from www.toledoblade.com/MarilouJohanek/2008/10/10/Justice-Department-scandal-almost-buried-by-financial-crisis.html.

Johnson, C. 2009. "Justice Department Aims to Prevent Another Stevens Fiasco." *Washington Post*, October 15. Retrieved from www.washingtonpost.com/wp-dyn/content/article/2009/10/14/AR2009101403771.html.

Johnson, J. 2017. "Trump Says 'Torture Works,' Backs Waterboarding and 'Much Worse'." *Washington Post*, February 17. Retrieved from https://www.washingtonpost.com/politics/trump-says-torture-works-backs-waterboarding-and-much-worse/2016/02/17/4c9277be-d59c-11e5-b195-2e29a4e13425_story.html?utm_term=.f0d419125085.

Johnson, K. 2014. "Police Killings Highest in Two Decades." *USA Today*, November 11. Retrieved from www.usatoday.com/story/news/nation/2014/11/11/police-killings-hundreds/18818663/.

Johnson, K. 2015. "DEA Chief Resigns Amid Reports of Agents' Misconduct." *USA Today*, April 21. Retrieved from www.usatoday.com/story/news/nation/2015/04/21/dea-chief-leaving-sex-parties/26129977/.

Johnson, R. 1996/2002/2006. *Hard Time: Understanding and Reforming the Prison*. Belmont, CA: Wadsworth.

Jonathan-Zamir, T., B. Hasisi, and Y. Margalioth. 2016. "Is It the What or the How? The Roles of High-Policing Tactics and Procedural Justice in Predicting Perceptions of Hostile Treatment: The Case of Security Checks at Ben-Gurion Airport, Israel." *Law & Society Review* 50(3): 608–636.

Jondle, D., A. Ardichvili, and A. Mitchell. 2014. "Modeling Ethical Business Culture: Development of the Ethical Business Culture Survey and Its Use to Validate the CEBC Model of Ethical Business Culture." *Journal of Business Ethics* 119: 29–43.

Jones, D. A. 2009. "A Novel Approach to Business Ethics Training: Improving Moral Reasoning in Just a Few Weeks." *Journal of Business Ethics* 88: 367–379.

Jones, J. 2010. "Nurses Top Honesty and Ethics List for 11th Straight Year." *Gallup Economy*, December 3. Retrieved from www.gallup.com/poll/145043/Nurses-Top-Honesty-Ethics-List-11-Year.aspx#2.

Jones, J. 2016. "U.S. Death Penalty Support at 60%." *Gallup Poll*, October 25. Retrieved from http://www.gallup.com/poll/1606/death-penalty.aspx.

Jones, T., M. Niquette, and J. Nash. 2016. "As the Cost of Police Misconduct Grows, So Do Taxes." *Boston Globe*, February 23. Retrieved from https://www.bostonglobe.com/news/nation/2016/02/23/cost-police-misconduct-grows-taxes/zC1oqf9icMxTE14ZyVVt8J/story.html.

Jonsson, P. 2014. "Darren Wilson Testimony Raises Fresh Questions About Racial Perceptions." *Christian Science Monitor*, November 25. Retrieved from www.csmonitor.com/USA/Justice/2014/1125/Darren-Wilson-testimony-raises-fresh-questions-about-racial-perceptions-video.

Jonsson, P. 2016. "Slam Dunk Video by Florida Cop: Can Positive Images of Police Change Minds?" *Christian Science Monitor*, January 23. Retrieved from http://www.csmonitor.com/USA/Justice/2016/0123/Slam-dunk-video-by-Florida-cop-Can-positive-images-of-police-change-minds.

Joseph, G. 2016. "Leaked Police Files Contain Guarantees Disciplinary Records Will Be Kept Secret." *The Guardian*, February 7. Retrieved from http://www.theguardian.com/us-news/2016/feb/07/leaked-police-files-contain-guarantees-disciplinary-records-will-be-kept-secret.

Josephson Institute of Ethics. 2005. *Preserving the Public Trust*. Retrieved from www.josephsoninstitute.org.

Josephson Institute of Ethics. 2008. *The Six Pillars of Character*. Retrieved from http://josephsoninstitute.org/MED/MED-2sixpillars.html.

Joy, P. 2016. "Lawyers Serving as Judges, Prosecutors, and Defense Lawyers at the Same Time: Legal Ethics and Municipal Courts." *Washington University Journal of Law & Policy* 51. Retrieved from http://openscholarship.wustl.edu/cgi/viewcontent.cgi?article=1925&context=law_journal_law_policy.

Joy, P. and K. McMunigal. 2016. "Different Rules for Prosecutors?" *Criminal Justice* 31: 3. Retrieved from https://papers.ssrn.com/sol3/cf_dev/AbsByAuth.cfm?per_id=624590.

Kaeble, D. and L. Glaze. 2016. *Correctional Populations in the United States, 2015*. Washington, DC: Bureau of Justice Statistics, U.S. Department of Justice.

Kakutani, M. 2016. A Penitent Stalked by Abu Ghraib. *New York Times*, April 5: C1.

Kalra, R., S. Kollisch, R. MacDonald, N. Dickey, Z. Rosner, and H. Venters. 2016. "Staff Satisfaction, Ethical Concerns, and Burnout in the New York City Jail Health System." *Journal of Correctional Health Care* 22(4): 383–392.

Kalshoven, K., D. Den Hartog, and A. De Hoogh. 2013. "Courtesy: Moral Awareness and Empathic Concern as Moderators." *Applied Psychology: An International Review* 62(2): 211–235.

Kamisar, Y., W. LeFave, and J. Israel. 1980. *Modern Criminal Procedure: Cases, Comments, and Questions*. St. Paul, MN: West.

Kane, R. and M. White. 2009. "Bad Cops: A Study of Career-Ending Misconduct Among New York City Police Officers." *Criminology and Public Policy* 8(4): 737–769.

Kania, R. 1988. "Police Acceptance of Gratuities." *Criminal Justice Ethics* 7(2): 37–49.

Kania, R. 1999. "The Ethics of the Death Penalty." *The Justice Professional* 12: 145–157.

Kania, R. 2004. "The Ethical Acceptability of Gratuities: Still Saying 'Yes' After All These Years." *Criminal Justice Ethics* 23(1): 54–63.

Kant, I. 1981. "Ethical Duties to Others: Truthfulness." In *Lectures on Ethics*, ed. L. Infield, 224–232. Indianapolis, IN: Hackett.

Kant, I. 1788/1949. *Critique of Practical Reason*, trans. Lewis White Beck. Chicago, IL: University of Chicago Press, 1949.

Kaplan, M. 1976. *Justice, Human Nature and Political Obligation*. New York: Free Press.

Kaplan, S. 2015. "Chicago Police Officer Charged in Deadly Shooting Has a History of Misconduct Complaints." *Washington Post*, November 25. Retrieved from https://www.washingtonpost.com/news/morning-mix/wp/2015/11/25/chicago-cop-charged-in-deadly-shooting-has-a-history-of-misconduct-complaints/?hpid=hp_hp-top-table-main_mm-chicagocop-355am%3Ahomepage%2FstoryChicago.

Kappeler, V. and P. Kraska. 2013 "Normalizing Police Militarization, Living in Denial." *Policing and Society: An International Journal of Research and Policy*. DOI: 10.1080/10439463.2013.

Kappeler, V., R. Sluder, and G. Alpert. 1984/1994. *Forces of Deviance: Understanding the Dark Side of Policing*. Prospect Heights, IL: Waveland.

Kassin, S. 2015. "The Social Psychology of False Confessions." *Social Issues and Policy Review* 9(1): 25–51.

Kassin, S., S. Drizin, T. Grisso, G. Gudjonsson, and R. Leo. 2010. "Police-Induced Confessions: Risk Factors and Recommendations." *Law and Human Behavior* 34: 3–38.

Kates, G. 2014. "NYC 'Sober Homes' Operators Accused of Fraud." *The Crime Report*, October 23. Retrieved from. http://www.thecrimereport.org/news/articles/2014-10-nyc-sober-homes-operators-accused-of-fraud.

Kates, G. 2015. "New Indictments in Narco Freedom Case." *The Crime Report*, March 2. Retrieved from www.thecrimereport.org/news/inside-criminal-justice/2015-03-new-indictments-in-narco-freedom-case.

Katz, D. 1964. "The Motivational Basis of Organizational Behavior." *Behavioral Sciences* 9: 462–466.

Kauffman, B. and P. Toomey. 2015. "The Notice Paradox: Secret Surveillance, Criminal Defendants and the Right to Notice." *Santa Clara Law Review* 54: 843–900.

Kauffman, K. 1988. *Prison Officers and Their World*. Cambridge, MA: Harvard University Press.

Kauffman, M. 2015. "Data: Minority Motorists Still Pulled Over, Ticketed At Higher Rates Than Whites." *The Hartford (CT) Courant*, September 22. Retrieved from http://www.courant.com/news/connecticut/hc-racial-profiling-0923-20150922-story.html.

Keith, L. 2002. "Judicial Independence and Human Rights Protection Around the World." *Judicature* 84(4): 195–200.

Kelly, K. 2016. "Can Big Data Stop Bad Cops?" *Washington Post*, August 21. Retrieved from https://www.washingtonpost.com/investigations/can-big-data-stop-bad-cops/2016/08/21/12db0728-3fb6-11e6-a66f-aa6c1883b6b1_story.html.

Kelly, K., S. Childress, and S. Rich. 2015. "Forced Reforms, Mixed Results." *Washington Post*, November 13. Retrieved from http://www.washingtonpost.com/sf/investigative/2015/11/13/forced-reforms-mixed-results/?hpid=hp_rhp-banner-low_cop-reforms-615pm%3Ahomepage%2Fstory.

Kessler, G. 1992. *Voices of Wisdom: A Multicultural Philosophy Reader*. Belmont, CA: Wadsworth.

Kiefer, M. 2016. "Defense Attorney File Complaints Against Arias Prosecutor Juan Martinez." *AZ Central*, January 7. Retrieved from http://www.azcentral.com/story/news/local/arizona/2016/01/07/juan-martinez-arizona-state-bar-complaints-aacj-jodi-arias/78320668/.

Kim, V. 2014. "Six L.A. County Sheriff Workers Get Prison for Obstructing Jail Probe." *Los Angeles Times*, September 24. Retrieved from www.latimes.com/local/countygovernment/la-me-deputy-corruption-20140924-story.html.

Kim, V. and C. Chang. 2014. "L.A. County Jail Verdicts Don't Let Sheriff Leaders Off the Hook." *Los Angeles Times*, July 14. Retrieved from www.latimes.com/local/countygovernment/la-me-deputies-verdict-20140703-story.html.

Kindy, K. 2015. "Fatal Police Shootings in 2015 Approaching 400 Nationwide." *Washington Post*, May 30. Retrieved from www.washingtonpost.com/national/fatal-police-shootings-in-2015-approaching-400-nationwide/2015/05/30/d322256a-058e-11e5-a428-c984eb077d4e_story.html.

Kindy, K., W. Lowery, S. Rich, and J. Tate. 2016. "Fatal Shootings by Police Are Up in the First Six Months of 2016, Post Analysis Finds." *Washington Post*, July 7. Retrieved from https://www.washingtonpost.com/national/fatal-shootings-by-police-surpass-2015s-rate/2016/07/07/81b708f2-3d42-11e6-84e8-1580c7db5275_story.html?utm_term=.24ec5e74b779.

King, R. and M. Mauer. 2001. *Aging Behind Bars: Three Strikes Seven Years Later*. Washington, DC: The Sentencing Project.

King, S. 2015. "Overlooking Police Misconduct Doesn't Start with Lt. Joe Gliniewicz, Life-Long Wash. Cop Is Now a Murder Suspect." *New York Daily News*, November 10. Retrieved from http://www.nydailynews.com/news/national/king-police-misconduct-lt-joe-gliniewicz-article-1.2429641.

Kipnis, K. 2001. "Health Care in the Corrections Setting: An Ethical Analysis." In *Discretion, Community and Correctional Ethics*, ed. J. Kleinig and M. Smith, 113–124. Lanham, MD: Rowman and Littlefield.

Kirchmeier, J., S. Greenwald, H. Reynolds, and J. Sussman. 2009. "Vigilante Justice: Prosecutor Misconduct in Capital Cases." *Wayne Law Review* 55: 1327–1385.

Kirka, D. 2016. "Police Using Body Cameras See Huge Drop in Complaints, Study Says." *Las Vegas Review Journal*, September 29. Retrieved from http://www.reviewjournal.com/news/nation-and-world/police-using-body-cameras-see-huge-drop-complaints-study-says.

Kitfield, J. 2017. "The Lingering Stench of Torture." *New York Times*, January 13.

Retrieved from https://www.nytimes.com/2017/01/13/opinion/the-lingering-stench-of-torture.html.

Klas, M. 2015a. "Major Florida Prison Reform Bill Dies in Wake of House, Senate Feud." *Herald Times Tallahassee*, April 25. Retrieved from http://www.tampabay.com/news/politics/stateroundup/major-florida-prison-reform-bill-dies-in-wake-of-house-senate-feud/2227625.

Klas, M. 2015b. "Senate Committee Starts Effort to Fix Abusive Prison System." *Tampa Bay Times*, April 29. Retrieved from http://www.miamiherald.com/news/state/florida/article5472549.html.

Klas, M. 2017. "Florida's Largest Privately-Operated Women's Prison Is in Danger Zone. Lawmaker Wants Gov. Scott to Act." *Miami Herald*, March 23. Retrieved from http://www.miamiherald.com/news/politics-government/state-politics/article140446938.html#storylink=cpy.

Klas, M. and J. Brown. 2015a. "Florida Prisons Riddled with Corruption, Staffers Tell Senators." *Miami Herald*, March 10. Retrieved from www.miamiherald.com/news/special-reports/florida-prisons/article13200422.html#storylink=cpy.

Klas, M. and J. Brown. 2015b. "New Prison Policy Punishes Investigators Who Speak Out." *Miami Herald*, February 5. Retrieved from www.miamiherald.com/news/special-reports/florida-prisons/article9371633.html#storylink=cpy.

Klaver, J. 2014. "Research on Ethics Codes." In *Law Enforcement Ethics*, ed. Brian Fitch, 3–29. Thousand Oaks, CA: Sage.

Kleinig, J. 1986. "The Conscientious Advocate and Client Perjury." *Criminal Justice Ethics* 5(2): 3–15.

Kleinig, J. 1999. "Human Dignity and Human Rights: An Emerging Concern in Police Practice." In *Human Dignity and Police: Ethics and Integrity in Police Work*, ed. G. Lynch, 8–40. Springfield, IL: Charles C Thomas.

Kleinig, J. 2001a. "National Security and Police Interrogations: Some Ethical Considerations." In *Policing, Security and Democracy: Special Aspects of Democratic Policing*, ed. S. Einstein and M. Amir, 105–127. Huntsville, TX: Office of International Criminal Justice (OICJ), Sam Houston State University.

Kleinig, J. 2001b. "Professionalizing Incarceration." In *Discretion, Community and Correctional Ethics*, ed.

J. Kleinig and M. Smith, 1–17. Oxford, England. Rowman and Littlefield.

Klinger, D. 2012. "On the Problems and Promise of Research on Lethal Police Violence: A Research Note." *Homicide Studies* 16(1): 78–96.

Klockars, C. 1983. "The Dirty Harry Problem." In *Thinking About Police: Contemporary Readings*, ed. C. Klockars and S. Mastrofski, 428–438. New York: McGraw-Hill.

Klockars, C. 1984. "Blue Lies and Police Placebos." *American Behavioral Scientist* 27(4): 529–544.

Klockars, C., S. Ivkovic, and M. Haberfeld. 2004. *The Contours of Police Integrity*. Thousand Oaks, CA: Sage.

Knudten, M. 1978. "The Prosecutor's Role in Plea Bargaining: Reasons Related to Actions." In *Essays on the Theory and Practice of Criminal Justice*, ed. R. Rich, 275–295. Washington, DC: University Press.

Koenigs, M., L. Young, R. Adolphs, D. Tranel, F. Cushman, M. Hauser, and A. Damasio. 2007. "Damage to the Prefrontal Cortex Increases Utilitarian Moral Judgements." *Nature* 446: 908–911.

Kohlberg, L. 1976. "Moral Stages and Moralization." In *Moral Development and Behavior: Theory, Research and Social Issues*, ed. T. Lickona, 31–53. New York: Holt, Rinehart and Winston.

Kohlberg, L. 1983. *Essays in Moral Development, Vol. 2. The Psychology of Moral Development*. New York: Harper and Row.

Kohlberg, L. 1984. *The Psychology of Moral Development*. San Francisco, CA: Harper and Row.

Kohler, J. 2017. "Municipal Court Business Is Way Down After Ferguson Unrest." *St. Louis Today.com.*, February 5. Retrieved from http://www.stltoday.com/news/local/crime-and-courts/municipal-court-business-is-way-down-after-ferguson-unrest/article_6c541acb-a28d-524b-ba83-c0238af72ce7.html.

Kopan, T. 2017. "What Are Sanctuary Cities, and Can They Be Defunded?" *CNN*, January 25. Retrieved from http://www.cnn.com/2017/01/25/politics/sanctuary-cities-explained/index.html.

Korecki, N. 2014. "Illinois Supreme Court Ruling Means Burge Can Keep His Pension." *Chicago Sun-Times*, July 3. Retrieved from http://politics.suntimes.com/article/chicago/illinois-supreme-

court-ruling-means-burge-can-keep-his-pension/thu-07032014-808am.

Kottak, C. 1974. *Anthropology: The Exploration of Human Diversity*. New York: Random House.

Krajicek, D. 2015. "A Freakishly Rare Anamoly: America's Awkward Relationship with Wrongful Convictions." *The Crime Report*, February 9. Retrieved from www.thecrimereport.org/news/inside-criminal-justice/2015-02-a-freakishly-rare-anomaly.

Kraska, P. B. 1999. "Questioning the Militarization of US Police: Critical Versus Advocacy Scholarship." *Policing and Society* 9(2): 141–155.

Kraska, P. B. 2001. *Militarizing the American Justice System: The Changing Roles of the Armed Forces and the Police*. Boston, MA: Northeastern University Press.

Kraska, P. B. 2007. "Militarization and Policing—Its Relevance to 21st Century Police." *Policing* 1(4): 501–513.

Kraska, P B. and L. J. Cubellis. 1997. "Militarizing Mayberry and Beyond: Making Sense of American Paramilitary Policing." *Justice Quarterly* 14(4): 607–629.

Kraska, P. B. and V. E. Kappeler. 1995. "To Serve and Pursue: Exploring Police Sexual Violence Against Women." *Justice Quarterly* 12(1): 85–111.

Kraska, P. B. and V. E. Kappeler. 1997. "Militarizing American Police: The Rise and Normalization of Paramilitary Units." *Social Problems* 44(1): 1–18.

Krayewski, E. 2014. "Ex-Baltimore Cop Alleges Retaliation for Reporting Police Brutality." *Reason Magazine*, December 26. Retrieved from http://reason.com/blog/2014/12/26/ex-baltimore-cop-alleges-retaliation-for.

Kreiger, M. 2009. "A Twenty-First Century Ethos for the Legal Profession: Why Bother?" *Denver University Law Review* 86: 865–900.

Kreimer, S. 2007. "Rays of Sunlight in a Shadow 'War': FOIA, the Abuses of Anti-Terrorism, and the Strategy of Transparency." *Lewis and Clark Law Review* 11(4): 1141–1220.

Kringen, A. L. 2014. *Understanding Barriers that Affect Recruiting and Retaining Female Police Officers: A Mixed Method Approach* (Doctoral dissertation). Retrieved from ProQuest Dissertations & Theses Global. (3681033).

Kristian, B. 2014. "7 Reasons Police Brutality Is Systemic Not Anecdotal." *The American Conservative*,

July 2. Retrieved from http:// www.theamericanconservative. com/2014/07/02/seven-reasons-police-brutality-is-systematic-not-anecdotal/.

Krogstand, J. and J. Robertson. 1979. "Moral Principles for Ethical Conduct." *Management Horizons* 10(1): 13–24.

Kroneberg, C., I. Heintze, and G. Mehlkop. 2010. "The Interplay of Moral Norms and Instrumental Incentives in Crime Causation." *Criminology* 48(1): 259–294.

Kronenwerter, M. 1993. *Capital Punishment: A Reference Handbook*. Santa Barbara, CA: ABC-CLIO.

KTRK. 2009. "Man Walks Free After 22 Years." *KTRK News*, April 30. Retrieved from http://abclocal. go.com/ktrk/story?section=news/ localandid=6789190.

Kunzelman, M. and K. McGill. 2016. "5 Ex-Cops Plead Guilty in Bridge Shootings After Katrina." *Associatated Press/CBS News*, April 20. Retrieved from http:// www.cbsnews.com/news/5-ex-cops-plead-guilty-in-new-orleans-danziger-bridge-shootings-after-katrina/.

KUSA. 2016. "Coverage of Black Female Victims of Police Brutality Falls Short." *KUSA.9news.com*, April 22. Retrieved from http://www.9news.com/news/ nation-now/coverage-of-black-female-victims-of-police-brutality-falls-short-column/150152172.

Kutateladze, B. and N. Andiloro. 2014. *Prosecution and Racial Justice in New York County—Technical Report*. Vera Institute of Justice. Retrieved from https://www.ncjrs.gov/pdffiles1/nij/ grants/247227.pdf.

Kutner, M. 2016. "The New American Cop: Smarter, More Diverse, Better Equipped and Scared." *Newsweek*, August 11. Retrieved from http://www.newsweek. com/2016/08/19/police-officers-training-black-lives-matter-489228. html.

LaFraniere, S. and A. Lehren. 2015. "The Disproportionate Risk of Driving While Black." *New York Times*, October 25: A1.

Laird, L. 2016. "Court Systems Rethink the Use of Financial Bail, Which Some Say Penalizes the Poor." *ABA Journal*, April 1. Retrieved from http://www. abajournal.com/magazine/article/ courts_are_rethinking_bail.

Lait, M. and S. Glover. 2000. "LAPD Chief Calls for Mass Dismissal of Tainted Cases." *Los Angeles Times*. Retrieved from http://articles.latimes.com/2000/ jan/27/news/mn-58195.

Lamb, J. 2015. "Gascon Draws SF Police Union Rebuke Over Officer Misconduct Investigation." *SF Examiner.com*, April 6. Retrieved from www.sfexaminer.com/ sanfrancisco/gascon-draws-sf-police-union-rebuke-over-officer-misconduct-investigation/Content?oid=2925769.

Lambert, E. 2003. "Justice in Corrections: An Exploratory Study of the Impact of Organizational Justice on Correctional Staff." *Journal of Criminal Justice* 31: 155–168.

Lambert, E., N. Hogan, and R. Allen. 2006. "Correlates of Correctional Officer Job Stress: The Impact of Organizational Structure." *American Journal of Criminal Justice* 30: 227–246.

Lambert, E. G., N. Hogan, and M. Griffin. 2007. "The Impact of Distributive and Procedural Justice on Correctional Staff Job Stress, Job Satisfaction, and Organizational Commitment." *Journal of Criminal Justice* 35: 644–656.

Land, K., R. Teske, and H. Zheng. 2009. "The Short Term Effects of Execution on Homicides: Deterrence, Displacement or Both?" *Criminology* 47(4): 1009–1039.

Lane, C. 2006. "Scalia's Recusal Sought in Key Detainee Case." *Washington Post*, March 28: A06.

Langton, L. and M. Durose. 2013. *Police Behavior During Traffic and Street Stops, 2011*. Washington, DC: Bureau of Justice Statistics, DOJ.

Lantigua-Williams, J. 2016. "Police Brutality Leads to Thousands Fewer Calls to 911." *The Atlantic*, September 28. Retrieved from http://www.theatlantic. com/politics/archive/2016/09/police-violence-lowers-911-calls-in-black-neighborhoods/501908/.

Larrabee, M. 1993. *An Ethics of Care: Feminist and Interdisciplinary Perspectives*. New York: Routledge.

Lau, L. and J. Haug. 2011. "The Impact of Sex, College, Major, and Student Classification on Students' Perception of Ethics." *Mustang Journal of Business Ethics* 1: 92–105.

Lau, M. 2017. "A Court Is Blocking L.A. County Sheriff from Handing Over a List of 300 Problem Deputies." *Los Angeles Times*, February 19. Retrieved from http://www.latimes.com/local/ california/la-me-sheriff-deputies-misconduct-list-20170219-story.html.

Lauer, C. 2016. "Arkansas Judge Is Investigated for Sex Abuse, Misconduct." *St. Louis Tribune*, June 6. Retrieved from http://www.sltrib.com/home/3974553-

155/arkansas-judge-is-investigated-for-sex.

Laughland, O., J. Lartey, and C. McCarthy. 2015. "Bolts from the Blue." *Guardian*, November 5. Retrieved from https:// www.theguardian.com/us-news/2015/ nov/05/police-tasers-deaths-the-counted.

Lavelle, J., D. Rupp, and J. Brockner. 2007. "Taking a Multifoci Approach to the Study of Justice, Social Exchange, and Citizenship Behavior: The Target Similarity Model." *Journal of Management* 33(6): 841–866.

LeBlanc, C. 2015. "SC Officers Exonerated in More Than 200 Shootings." *The State. com*, March 21. Retrieved from http:// www.thestate.com/news/local/crime/ article15654974.html#storylink=cpy.

Lee, H. 2004. "Oakland 'Riders' Lied, Brutalized Man, Ex-Rookie Testifies." *SFGate.com*, December 14. Retrieved from www.sfgate.com/bayarea/article/ OAKLAND-Riders-lied-brutalized-man-2629441.php.

Lee, H., H. Lim, D. Moore, and J. Kim. 2011. "How Police Organizational Structure Correlates with Frontline Officers' Attitudes Toward Corruption: A Multilevel Model." *Police Practice and Research* 1: 1–16.

Lee, L. 2016. "How Science Could Help Prevent Police Shootings." *Mother Jones*, May/June. Retrieved from http://www. motherjones.com/politics/2016/04/ data-prediction-police-misconduct-shootings.

Lefstein, N. 2011. *Securing Reasonable Caseloads: Ethics and Law in Public Defense*. Washington, DC: ABA, Standing Committee on Legal Aid and Indigent Defense.

Leighton, P. 2014. "'A Model Prison for the Next 50 Years:' The High Tech Public Private Shimane Asahi Rehabilitation Center." *Justice Policy Journal* 11(1): np.

Leiser, B. 1986. *Liberty, Justice and Morals*. New York: Macmillan.

Leonard, J. 2009. "Law Students Help Free Three-Strikes Offenders." *Los Angeles Times*, May 13. Retrieved from http:// articles.latimes.com/2009/may/13/local/ me-threestrikes13.

Leonard, J. 2013. "District Attorney Revises Policy on Police Misconduct Disclosure." *Los Angeles Times*, June 11, 2013.

Leonard, J., J. Rabin, and A. Blankstein. 2013. "Dorner's LAPD Firing Hinged on Credibility." *Los Angeles Times*, February 10. Retrieved from http://articles.

latimes.com/2013/feb/10/local/la-me-lapd-dorner-20130211.

Leonnig, C. and D. Nakamaura. 2014. "Whistleblowers Tell Senate Panel of Alleged Sexual Misconduct by Secret Service Agents." *Washington Post*, November 14. Retrieved from www.washingtonpost.com/politics/secret-service-agents-and-managers-accused-of-sexual-misconduct-by-whistleblowers/2013/ 11/14/8d1c4750-4d6e-11e3-9890-a1e0997fb0c0_story.html.

Levenson, M. 2010. "Probation Uproar Fuels State Campaigns." *Boston.com*, May 20. Retrieved from www.boston.com/news/local/massachusetts/articles/2010/05/29/probation_department_scandal_puts_incumbents_on_defensive.

Levine, C., L. Kohlberg, and A. Hewer. 1985. "The Current Formulation of Kohlberg's Theory and Response to Critics." *Human Development* 28: 94–100.

Lewis, M. 1999. "Corcoran Guards Launch Ads." *Fresno Bee*, September 17: A1.

Lewis, R., X. Landen, and N. Veltman. 2015. "New York Leads in Shielding Police Misconduct." *WNYC.com*, October 15. Retrieved from http://www.wnyc.org/story/new-york-leads-shielding-police-misconduct/.

Lewis, R. and N. Veltman. 2015. "The Hard Truth About Cops Who Lie." *WNYC.com*, October 13. Retrieved from http://www.wnyc.org/story/hard-truth-about-cops-who-lie/.

Lichtblau, E. 2008. "Senate Approves Bill to Broaden Wiretap Powers." *New York Times*, July 10. Retrieved from www.nytimes.com/2008/07/10/washington/10fisa.html.

Lichtblau, E. and S. Shane. 2010. "Report Faults 2 Authors of Bush Memos." *New York Times*, February 19. Retrieved from www.nytimes.com/2010/02/20/us/politics/20justice.html.

Liebowitz, S., P. Eliasberg, M. Winter, and E. Lim. 2011. *Cruel and Unusual Punishment: How a Savage Gang of Deputies Controls LA County Jails*. Los Angeles, CA: ACLU National Prison Project.

Lighty, T. 2016. "Probation Officers to Wear Body Cameras." *Chicago Tribune*, December 7. Retrieved from http://www.chicagotribune.com/news/local/breaking/ct-probation-body-cameras-20161207-story.html.

Lindell, C. 2006a. "When $25,000 Is the Limit on a Life." *Austin American-Statesman*, October 30: A1.

Lindell, C. 2006b. "Sloppy Lawyers Failing Clients on Death Row." *Austin American-Statesman*, October 29: A1, A8.

Lindell, C. 2006c. "Lawyer's Writs Come Up Short." *Austin American-Statesman*, October 30: A11.

Lindell, C. 2007. "Criticism Grows for Judge Over Execution." *Austin American-Statesman*, October 11: B1.

Lindell, C. 2009. "Man Executed Over Arson that Wasn't, Scientist Says." *Austin American-Statesman*, August 26: A1, A5.

Lindell, C. 2010a. "Ex-Deputy, Dogs Facing Court Test Over Scent Evidence in Murder Case." *Austin American-Statesman*, April 11: A1, A8.

Lindell, C. 2010b. "Panel Hits Judge with $100,000 Ethics Fine." *Austin American-Statesman*, May 1: A1.

Lindell, C. 2010c. "Judges Find Scent Evidence Unreliable." *Austin American-Statesman*, September 23: A1, A4.

Lindell, C. 2012. "State Bar Dismisses Bradley Complaint." *Austin American-Statesman*, January 4: B1.

Lindell, C. and J. Embry 2009. "Governor Shakes Up Forensic Agency." *Austin American-Statesman*, October 1: A1, A8.

Linderman, J. 2013. "Judge Grants New Trial for Ex-New Orleans Police Officers Convicted in Notorious Danziger Bridge Slayings After Hurricane Katrina." *NOLA.com*, September 17. Retrieved from http://www.nola.com/crime/index.ssf/2013/09/judge_grants_new_trial_for_ex-.html.

Lindquist, C. 1994. "Criminalistics in the Curriculum: Some Views from the Forensic Science Community." *Journal of Criminal Justice Education* 5(1): 59–68.

Lipinski, J. 2016. "NOPD Sex Crimes Unit Making Progress Under Federal Consent Decree, Monitors Say." *Nola.com*, August 22. Retrieved from http://www.nola.com/crime/index.ssf/2016/08/consent_decree_sexual_assault.html.

Liptak, A. 2003. "Houston DNA Lab Worst in Country, Experts Say." *Austin American-Statesman*, March 11: B1.

Liptak, A. 2004. "Study Suspects Thousands of False Convictions." *New York Times*, April 19. Retrieved from www.nytimes.com/2004/04/19/national/19DNA.html.

Liptak, A. 2007. "Study Reveals Gap in Performance of Public Defenders." *Austin American-Statesman*, July 14: A7.

Liptak, A. 2016. "Charged a Fee for Getting Arrested, Whether Guilty or Not." *New York Times*, December 26. Retrieved from https://www.nytimes.com/2016/12/26/us/politics/charged-a-fee-for-getting-arrested-whether-guilty-or-not.html.

Lisitsina, D. 2015. "'Prison Guards Can Never Be Weak': The Hidden PTSD Crisis in America's Jails." *The Guardian*, May 20. Retrieved from http://www.theguardian.com/us-news/2015/may/20/corrections-officers-ptsd-american-prisons.

Lithwick, D. 2015a. "Revenge, Not Justice." *Slate*, March 12. Retrieved from www.slate.com/articles/news_and_politics/jurisprudence/2015/03/david_dow_suspended_by_texas_court_death_penalty_defense_lawyer_s_conflicts.html.

Lithwick, D. 2015b. "You're All Out: California Prosecutors and Police Engaged in Massive Misconduct—And Finally Got Caught." *Slate*, May 28. Retrieved from www.slate.com/articles/news_and_politics/jurisprudence/2015/05/orange_county_prosecutor_misconduct_judge_goethals_takes_district_attorney.html.

Loftus, B. 2010. "Police Occupational Culture: Classic Themes, Altered Times." *Policing and Society: An International Journal of Research and Policy* 20(1): 1–20.

Lombardo, L. 1981/1989. *Guards Imprisoned: Correctional Officers at Work*. New York: Anderson (Elsevier).

Loo, R. 2003. "Are Women More Ethical Than Men? Findings from Three Independent Studies." *Women in Management Review* 18(4): 169–181.

Lord, R. 2014. "Confidential Informants Are an Integral But Problematic Part of Federal Law Enforcement." *Pittsburg Post Gazette*, October 19. Retrieved from www.post-gazette.com/local/region/2014/10/19/Confidential-informants-are-an-integral-but-problematic-part-of-federal-law-enforcement/stories/201410190076.

Lord, V. and B. Bjerregaard. 2003. "Ethics Courses: Their Impact on the Values and Ethical Decisions of Criminal Justice Students." *Journal of Criminal Justice Education* 14(2): 191–211.

Lowery, W. 2015. "A Disproportionate Number of Black Victims in Fatal Traffic Stops." *Washington Post*, December 24. Retrieved from https://www.washingtonpost.com/national/a-disproportionate-number-of-black-victims-in-fatal-traffic-stops/2015/12/24/c29717e2-a344-11e5-9c4e-be37f66848bb_story.html?utm_term=.cc85cca03414.

Luban, D. 2014. "Celebrate the Ones Who Stood Up for What Was Right." *New York Times,* December 10. Retrieved from http://www.nytimes.com/roomfordebate/2014/12/09/a-tortured-accounting/celebrate-the-ones-who-stood-up-for-what-was-right.

Lubrano, A. 2017. "'Pimping Out' Drug Addicts For Cash." *Philly.com,* June 1. Retrieved from http://www.philly.com/philly/health/addiction/Philadelphia_exploited_heroin_addicts_recovery_houses_treatment_centers_kickbacks_Medicaid.html.

Lucas, J. 1980. *On Justice.* Oxford, England: Oxford University Press.

Lundahl, B. 2007. *Prison Privatization: A Meta-Analys Is of Cost Effectiveness and Quality of Confinement Indicators.* Salt Lake City: Utah Criminal Justice Center.

Lush, T. 2007. "The G-Man and the Snitch." *MiamiNewTimes.com,* February 8. Retrieved from www.miaminewtimes.com/2007-02-08/news/the-g-man-and-the-snitch/print.

Lutwak, N. and J. Hennessy. 1985. "Interpreting Measures of Moral Development to Individuals." *Measurement and Evaluation in Counseling and Development* 18(1): 26–31.

Lyons, B. 2016. "Former New York Prison Internal Affairs Chief Pleads Guilty to Coercion." *Albany Times-Union,* January 6. Retrieved from http://www.timesunion.com/local/article/Former-prison-internal-affairs-chief-pleads-6738650.php.

Maas, D. 2016. "'No Cost' License Plate Readers Are Turning Texas Police into Mobile Debt Collectors and Data Miners." *Electronic Frontier Foundation,* January 26. Retrieved from https://www.eff.org/deeplinks/2016/01/no-cost-license-plate-readers-are-turning-texas-police-mobile-debt-collectors-and.

Maas, P. 1973. *Serpico.* New York: Viking.

Maas, P. 1983. *Marie.* New York: Random House.

MacDonald, H. 2015. "The New Nationwide Crime Wave." *The Wall Street Journal,* May 29. Retrieved from http://www.wsj.com/articles/the-new-nationwide-crime-wave-1432938425.

MacIntyre, A. 1991. *After Virtue.* South Bend, IN: University of Notre Dame Press.

MacIntyre, A. 1999. *Dependent Rational Animals: Why Human Beings Need the Virtues.* Chicago, IL: Open Ct.

MacIntyre, S. and T. Prenzler. 1999. "The Influence of Gratuities and Personal Relationships on Police Use of Discretion." *Policing and Society* 9: 181–201.

Mackie, J. L. 1977. *Ethics: Inventing Right and Wrong.* New York: Penguin.

Mackie, J. L. 1982. "Morality and the Retributive Emotions." *Criminal Justice Ethics* 1(1): 3–10.

Maddaus, G. 2016. "Should Misbehaving Cops Be Shielded from Public Scrutiny?" *LAWeekly,* April 28. Retrieved from http://www.laweekly.com/news/should-misbehaving-cops-be-shielded-from-public-scrutiny-6832927.

Mador, C. 2014. "Why It's Impossible to Indict a Cop: It's Not Just Ferguson—Here's How the System Protects Police." *The Nation,* November 25. Retrieved from www.thenation.com/article/190937/why-its-impossible-indict-cop.

Maestri, W. 1982. *Basic Ethics for the Health Care Professional.* Washington, DC: University Press.

Magid, L. 2001. "Article: Deceptive Police Interrogation Practices: How Far Is Too Far." *Michigan Law Review* 99(5): 1168–1210.

Maguire, E., J. Nix, and B. Campbell. 2016. "A War on Cops? The Effects of Ferguson on the Number of U.S. Police Officers Murdered in the Line of Duty." *Justice Quarterly.* DOI: 10.1080/07418825.2016.1236205.

Maguire, M. and T. Nolan. 2011. "Faux Hos: Women Police Attitudes About Decoy Sex Work." *Police Practice and Research: An International Journal* 12(3): 209–222.

Maher, T. 2010. "Police Sexual Misconduct: Female Police Officers' Views Regarding Its Nature and Extent." *Women and Criminal Justice* 20: 263–282.

Malloy, E. 1982. *The Ethics of Law Enforcement and Criminal Punishment.* Lanham, NY: University Press.

Manning, P. 2009. "Bad Cops." *Criminology and Public Policy* 8(4): 787–794.

Margasak, L. 2009. "Harsh Methods Useless, Ex-Interrogator Says." *Austin American-Statesman,* May 14: A4.

Mariano, N. 2015. "Justice Denied: The High Price of Justice." *The Southern.com,* April 19. Retrieved from http://thesouthern.com/news/local/justice-denied/the-high-price-of-

justice-sixth-amendment-guarantee-deteriorating-under/article_2992e476-c4ca-5124-a433-23a025a26bf8.html.

Mark, M. 2017. "Sessions Criticizes Police Reform Efforts for Depleting Resources: 'These Decrees Are Not a Silver Bullet.'" *Business Insider,* April 11. Retrieved from http://www.businessinsider.com/sessions-consent-decrees-police-reform-efforts-for-depleting-resources-2017-4.

Markowitz, P. 2011. *Accessing Justice: The Availability and Adequacy of Counsel in Immigration Proceedings.* Available through Cardozo Law School. Retrieved from www.cardozolawreview.com/content/33-2/NYIRS%20Report.33-2.pdf.

Marks, F., F. Raymond, and D. Cathcart. 1986. "Discipline Within the Legal Profession." In *Ethics and the Legal Profession,* ed. M. Davis and F. Elliston, 62–105. Buffalo, NY: Prometheus.

Marquart, J., M. Barnhill, and K. Balshaw-Biddle. 2001. "Fatal Attraction: An Analysis of Employee Boundary Violations in a Southern Prison System, 1995–1998." *Justice Quarterly* 18(4): 877–911.

Marquart, J. and J. Roebuck. 1986. "Prison Guards and Snitches." In *The Dilemmas of Corrections: Contemporary Readings,* ed. K. Haus and G. Alpert, 158–176. Prospect Heights, IL: Waveland.

Martelle, S. 2017. "When Wrongful Convictions Affect Blacks More Than Whites, Can We Call It a Justice System?" *Los AngelesTimes,* March 7. Retrieved from http://www.latimes.com/opinion/opinion-la/la-ol-wrongful-convictions-race-20170307-story.html.

Martin, D. 1993. *Committing Journalism: The Writings of Red Hog.* New York: Norton.

Martin, N. 2014. "Allegations of Bungled Rape, Child Abuse Cases Latest for Troubled NOPD Unit." *The Times-Picayune,* November 12. Retrieved from www.nola.com/crime/index.ssf/2014/11/nopd_rape_problems.html#incart_m-rpt-2.

Martin, R. 2015. "For Undercover Agents, On-The-Job Adrenaline Can Be Addictive." *National Public Radio Website,* March 29. Retrieved from http://www.npr.org/2015/03/29/396071802/for-undercover-agents-on-the-job-adrenaline-can-be-addictive.

Martinez, M. 2011. "Calif. Study: Prosecutors' Misconduct Reverses

18 Convictions in 2010." *CNN.com.* Retrieved from www.cnn.com/2011/CRIME/03/30/california.prosecutors.misconduct/.

Martinez, P. and J. Pollock. 2008. "The Impact of Type of Attorney on Criminal Sentencing." *Criminal Law Bulletin* 5(44): 1–22.

Martyn, S., L. Fox, and W. Wendel. 2008. *The Law Governing Lawyers: 2007–2008 Edition.* New York: Aspen Publishers.

Marx, G. 1985a. "Police Undercover Work: Ethical Deception or Deceptive Ethics?" In *Police Ethics: Hard Choices in Law Enforcement,* ed. W. Heffernan and T. Stroup, 83–117. New York: John Jay Press.

Marx, G. 1985b. "Who Really Gets Stung? Some Issues Raised by the New Police Undercover Work." In *Moral Issues in Police Work,* ed. F. Elliston and M. Feldberg, 99–129. Totawa, NJ: Rowman and Allanheld.

Marx, G. 1991. "The New Police Undercover Work." In *Thinking About Police: Contemporary Readings,* ed. C. Klockars and S. Mastrofski, 240–258. New York: McGraw-Hill.

Marzulli, J. 2015. "Brooklyn Prosecutor Loses Warrant to Arrest Witness in Murder Case, Finds It 7 Years Later." *New York Daily News,* May 11. Retrieved from www.nydailynews.com/new-york/nyc-crime/exclusive-da-finds-warrant-murder-case-7-years-article-1.2217479.

Marzulli, J. and D. Gregorian. 2014. "In 179 Fatalities Involving On-Duty NYPD Cops in 15 years, Only 3 Just 1 Conviction." *New York Daily News,* December 8. Retrieved from http://www.nydailynews.com/new-york/nyc-crime/179-nypd-involved-deaths-3-indicted-exclusive-article-1.2037357.

Massimino, E. 2004. "Leading by Example? U.S. Interrogation of Prisoners in the War on Terror." *Criminal Justice Ethics* 23(1): 2, 74–76.

Mastrofski, S., M. Reisig, and J. McCluskey. 2002. "Police Disrespect Toward the Public: An Encounter-Based Analysis." *Criminology* 40(3): 519–551.

Mather, L. 2003. "Ethics Symposium: What Do Clients Want? What Do Lawyers Do?" *Emory Law Journal* 52: 1065–1088.

Mauer, M., M. Chesney-Lind, and T. Clear. 2002. *Invisible Punishment: The Collateral Consequences of Mass Imprisonment.* New York: The Sentencing Project.

Mayer, J. 2007. "Whatever It Takes: The Politics of the Man Behind 24." *New Yorker,* February. Retrieved from www.newyorker.com/reporting/2007/02/19/070219fa_fact_mayer.

Mazerolle, L., S. Bennett, J. Davis, E. Sargeant, and M. Manning, 2013. "Procedural Justice and Police Legitimacy: A Systematic Review of Research Evidence." *Journal of Experimental Criminology* 9: 245–274.

Mazzetti, M. and M. Apuzzo. 2015. "Classified Report on the C.I.A.'s Secret Prisons Is Caught in Limbo." *New York Times,* November 10: A1.

Mazzetti, M. and M. Rosenberg. 2017. "Trump Administration Starts Returning Copies of C.I.A. Torture Report to Congress." *New York Times,* June 2. Retrieved from https://www.nytimes.com/2017/06/02/us/politics/cia-torture-report-trump.html?emc=edit_na_20170602&nl=breaking-news&nlid=66242298&ref=cta.

McCarthy, B. 1991. "Keeping an Eye on the Keeper: Prison Corruption and Its Control." In *Justice, Crime, and Ethics,* ed. M. Braswell, B. McCarthy, and B. McCarthy, 239–253. Cincinnati, OH: Anderson.

McCarthy, B. 1995. "Patterns of Prison Corruption." In *Morality in Criminal Justice,* ed. D. Close and N. Meier, 280–285. Belmont, CA: Wadsworth.

McCoy, C. and D. Purcell. 2014. "In Stepping Down, McCaffery Moved to Save Pension, Avoid Ethics Inquiry." *Philly.com,* October 28. Retrieved from http://www.philly.com/philly/news/politics/20141028_In_stepping_down__McCaffery_moved_to_save_pension__avoid_ethics_inquiry.html.

McCoy, T. 2016. "This Officer Accidentally Shot and Killed His Best Friend and Partner 27 Years Ago. What He Did Next Was Remarkable." *Washington Post,* March 17. Retrieved from https://www.washingtonpost.com/local/social-issues/prince-georges-officer-in-friendly-fire-death-gets-help-from-someone-who-knows/2016/03/17/82f4900c-ec31-11e5-bc08-3e03a5b41910_story.html?hpid=hp_rhp-top-table-main_friendlyfire-7pm%3Ahomepage%2Fstory.

McCready, D. 2007. "When Is Torture Right?" *Studies in Christian Ethics* 20: 393–398.

McDonald, W. 2000. *Testilying: The Psychological and Sociological Determinants of Police Testimonial Deception* (Dissertation). City University of New York, Ann Arbor, MI: University of Michigan Dissertation Abstracts.

McGurrin, D. and V. Kappeler. 2002. "Media Accounts of Police Sexual Violence." In *Policing and Misconduct,* ed. K. Lersch, 121–142. Upper Saddle River, NJ: Prentice Hall.

McKelway, D. 2013. "Win at All Costs? Suicide of Computer Whiz Prompts Look at Federal Prosecutors' Tactics." *FoxNews.com,* February 15. Retrieved from www.foxnews.com/politics/2013/02/15/win-at-all-costs-suicide-computer-whiz-prompts-look-at-federal-prosecutors.

McKeown, M. 2011. "To Judge or Not to Judge: Transparency and Recusal in the Federal System." *Review of Litigation* 30(4): 653–669.

McKinney, M. 2015. "Minneapolis Police Officer with Two Costly Lawsuits Has Record of Complaints." *Minneapolis Star Tribune,* May 15. Retrieved from www.startribune.com/minneapolis-police-officer-with-two-costly-lawsuits-has-record-of-complaints/258717081/.

McKoski, R. 2008. "Charitable Fundraising by Judges: The Give and Take of the 2007 ABA Model Code of Judicial Conduct." *Michigan State Law Review:* 769–841.

McMahon, P. 2013. "Caravella Case Not Deputy's First Link to Wrongful Convictions." *Sun-Sentinel,* March 14. Retrieved from http://articles.sun-sentinel.com/2013-03-14/news/fl-tony-fantigrassi-bso-sued-20130314_1_anthony-caravella-caravella-case-lie-detector-test.

McNally, J. 2014. "A Big Boot Drops on Police Misconduct." *Express Milwaukee,* August 12. Retrieved from http://expressmilwaukee.com/article-permalink-23799.html.

McRoberts, F. and S. Mills. 2004. "From the Start, a Faulty Science." *Chicago Tribune,* October 19. Retrieved from http://www.chicagotribune.com/news/watchdog/chi-041019forensics-story.html.

McRoberts, F., S. Mills, and M. Possley. 2004. "Forensics Under the Microscope." *Chicago Tribune,* October 17. Retrieved from http://articles.chicagotribune.com/2004-10-17/news/0410170393_1_bite-mark-comparison-forensic-lip-prints.

Medina, J. 2013. "Arrests Challenge Los Angeles County Sheriff's 4-Term

Tenure." *New York Times*, December 15: A24.

Medwed, D. 2009. "The Prosecutor as Minister of Justice: Preaching to the Unconverted from the Post-Conviction Pulpit." *Washington Law Review* 84: 35–66.

Meekins, T. 2007. "Risky Business: Criminal Specialty Courts and the Ethical Obligations of the Zealous Criminal Defender." *Berkeley Journal of Criminal Law* 12: 75–135.

Meisner, J. 2013. "City OKs $10 Million Payment Over Coerced Guilty Plea." *Chicago Tribune*, July 24. Retrieved from http://articles.chicagotribune.com/2013-07-25/news/ct-met-chicago-police-brutality-burge-20130725_1_eric-caine-city-oks-police-misconduct.

Memory, J. and C. Rose. 2002. "The Attorney as Moral Agent: A Critique of Cohen." *Criminal Justice Ethics* 21(1): 28–39.

Mendoza, J. 2016. "San Francisco Lesson: to Help Police Departments, Less Could Be More." *Christian Science Monitor*, February 3. Retrieved from http://www.csmonitor.com/USA/Justice/2016/0203/San-Francisco-lesson-to-help-police-departments-less-could-be-more.

Merchant, N. 2016. "Database of Problem Police May Get Test in Ferguson." *Boston Globe*, March 9. Retrieved from https://www.bostonglobe.com/news/nation/2016/03/09/database-problem-police-officers-may-get-test-ferguson/CCIOA2xFitchMEkYFXZKsM/story.html.

Merchant, N. and M. Sedensky. 2015. "Broken System Lets Problem Officers Jump from Job to Job." *Associated Press*, November 3. Retrieved from http://bigstory.ap.org/article/4e3d597c0b7849a1a59fb4ad90b1cb75/ap-broken-system-lets-problem-officers-jump-job-job.

Mesloh, C., R. Wolf, and M. Henych. 2003. "Perceptions of Misconduct: An Examination of Ethics at One Correctional Institution." *Corrections Compendium* 28(5): 1–19.

Metz, H. 1990. "An Ethical Model for Law Enforcement Administrators." In *Ethics in Criminal Justice*, ed. F. Schmalleger, 95–103. Bristol, IN: Wyndam Hall.

Micucci, A. and I. Gomme. 2005. "American Police and Subcultural Support for the Use of Excessive Force." *Journal of Criminal Justice* 33: 487–500.

Mieczkowski, T. 2002. "Drug Abuse, Corruption, and Officer Drug Testing." In *Policing and Misconduct*, ed. K. Lersch, 157–192. Upper Saddle River, NJ: Prentice Hall.

Milgram, S. 1963. "Behavioral Study of Obedience." *Journal of Abnormal and Social Psychology* 67: 371–378.

Miller, G. and J. Meyer. 2009. "Obama Discloses Memos Outlining CIA Torture Tactics." *Austin American-Statesman*, April 17: A3.

Miller, J. M. 2011. "Becoming an Informant." *Justice Quarterly* 28: 203–220.

Miller, J. and R. Davis. 2007. "Unpacking Public Attitudes to the Police: Contrasting Perceptions of Misconduct with Traditional Measures of Satisfaction." *International Journal of Police Science and Management* 10(1): 9–22.

Milligan, S. 2015. "Police Settlement Cases Rare—And Rarely Deter Misconduct." *U.S.News.com*, September 9. Retrieved from http://www.usnews.com/news/articles/2015/09/09/police-settlement-cases-rare-and-rarely-deter-misconduct.

Mills, S. 2005. "Texas May Have Put Innocent Man to Death." *Chicago Tribune*, April 20: A7.

Mills, S. 2015. "Burge Reparations Deal a Product of Long Negotiations." *Chicago Tribune*, May 6. Retrieved from http://my.chicagotribune.com/#section/-1/article/p2p-83469100.

Mills, S. and F. McRoberts. 2004. "Critics Tell Experts: Show Us the Science." *Chicago Tribune*, October 17: A18.

Mitchell, J. 2014. "Private Prisons Face Suits, Federal Probes." *The Clarion-Ledger*, October 15. Retrieved from http://www.clarionledger.com/story/news/2014/10/11/private-prisons-face-suits-federal-probes/17122977.

Moll, J., R. Zahn, R. de Oliveira-Souza, F. Krueger, and J. Grafman. 2005. "The Neural Basis of Human Moral Cognition." *Nature* 6: 799–809.

Mondics, C. 2014. "Court Restricts City's Ability to Seize Homes Used by Drug Dealers." *The Philadelphia Inquirer*, December 29. Retrieved from www.philly.com/philly/business/20141230_Appeals_court_restricts_use_of_civil_forfeiture_to_seize_homes_used_by_drug_dealers_.html#31JFZbubbeEKAP1F.99.

Montemayor, S. 2016. "Are Tasers the Way to Reduce Fatal Shootings by Police?" *Star Tribune*, January 10.

Retrieved from http://www.startribune.com/tasers-examined-as-option-for-police/364750781/.

Moore, T. 2014. "NYPD Commissioner Bill Bratton Disbands Unit Responsible for Spying on Muslim Communities." *NY Daily News.com*, April 16. Retrieved from www.nydailynews.com/new-york/bratton-disbands-nypd-muslim-spying-unit-article-1.1757446.

Moran, J. 2005. "'Blue Walls,' 'Grey Areas' and 'Cleanups': Issues in the Control of Police Corruption in England and Wales." *Crime, Law and Social Change* 43: 57–79.

Morelli, K. 2016. "Fla. Deputy Acted as 'Human Shield' for Another Car in Wrong-Way Collision." *Tampa Tribune*, March 15. Retrieved from http://www.policeone.com/police-heroes/articles/162381006-Fla-deputy-acted-as-human-shield-for-another-car-in-wrong-way-collision?nlid=162530044&utm_source=iContact&utm_medium=email&utm_content=TopNewsRelated1Image&utm_campaign=P1Member&cub_id=usr_mUsnBiv9F7lRI7Ff.

Morgan, L. 2010. "Two Florida Businessmen Indicted in Prison Kickback Case." *Tampa Bay Times*, July 16. Retrieved from www.tampabay.com/news/politics/two-florida-businessmen-indicted-in-prison-kickback-case/1109244.

Morgenson, G. 2015. "Comparing Paychecks with C.E.O.s." *New York Times*, April 12: BU1.

Morin, R. and R. Stepler. 2016. *The Racial Confidence Gap in Police Performance.* Pew Research Center. Retrieved from http://www.pewsocialtrends.org/2016/09/29/the-racial-confidence-gap-in-police-performance/.

Morris, R. 2000. *Stories of Transformative Justice.* Toronto, ON: Canadian Scholars Press.

Moskos, P. 2009. *Cop in the Hood: My Year Policing Baltimore's Eastern District.* Princeton, NJ: Princeton University Press.

Moss, M. and F. Fessenden. 2002. "War Against Terrorism Stirs a Battle Over Privacy." *Austin American-Statesman*, December 11: A17–A19.

Muir, W. 1977. *Police: Streetcorner Politicians.* Chicago, IL: University of Chicago Press.

Mulgan, R. and J. Wanna, 2011. "Developing Cultures of Integrity in the Public and

Private Sectors." In *Handbook of Global Research and Practice in Corruption*, Vol. 1, ed. A. Graycar and R. G. Smith, 416–429. Northampton, MD: Edward Elgar Publishing, Inc.

Mulhausen, M. 2010. "A Second Chance at Justice: Why States Should Adopt ABA Model Rules of Professional Conduct 3.8(g) and (h)." *University of Colorado Law Review* 81(1): 309–341.

Muoio, D. 2017. "Volkswagen Just Made a Big Move to Regain Customers' Trust After the Emissions' Scandal." *Business Insider*, April 12. Retrieved from http://www.businessinsider.com/volkswagen-big-move-regain-trust-after-fuel-emissions-scandal-2017-4.

Murphy, C. 2002. "Monitor Gives DC Police Mixed Review." *Washington Post*, August 6. Retrieved from www.washingtonpost.com/ac2/wp-dyn?pagename=article&contentId=A52807-2002Aug6.

Murphy, J. 1985/1995. *Punishment and Rehabilitation*. Belmont, CA: Wadsworth.

Murphy, M. 2012. "Crime Lab Scandal Puts 34,000 Cases Under Review." *Statehouse News.com*, September 6. Retrieved from www.com/dpp/news/massachusetts/crime-lab-scandal-puts-34000-cases-under-review.

Murphy, P. and D. Caplan. 1989. "Conditions that Breed Corruption." In *Critical Issues in Policing*, ed. R. Dunham and G. Alpert, 304–324. Prospect Heights, IL: Waveland.

Murphy, P. and K. Moran. 1981. "The Continuing Cycle of Systemic Police Corruption." In *The Social Basis of Criminal Justice: Ethical Issues for the 80's*, ed. F. Schmalleger and R. Gustafson, 87–101. Washington, DC: University Press.

Murray, J. 2005. "Policing Terrorism: A Threat to Community Policing or Just a Shift in Priorities?" *Police Practice and Research* 6(4): 347–361.

Murray, J. 2009. "Ex-Drug Cop's 25-Year Sentence Among Longest for Local Police." *Indystar.com*, September 24. Retrieved from www.indystar.com/article/20090924/NEWS02/909240450/Ex-drug-cop-s-25-year-sentence-among-longest-local-police.

Murray, J. 2014. "Denver Pays Millions to Settle Abuse Claims Against Police and Sheriff." *Denver Post*, August 3. Retrieved 8/3/2015 from www.denverpost.com/politics/ci_26266070/denver-pays-millions-settle-abuse-claims-against-police.

Murray, R. 2016. "Gravity Payments' $70K Minimum Salary: CEO Dan Price Shares Result Over a Year Later." *Today.com*, August 11. Retrieved from http://www.today.com/money/gravity-payments-70k-minimum-salary-ceo-dan-price-shares-results-t101678.

Murrie, D., D. Boccaccini, L. Guarnera, and K. Rufino. 2013. "Are Forensic Experts Biased by the Side that Retained Them?" *Psychological Science*. DOI: 10.1177/0956797613481812.

Murton, T. 1976. *The Dilemma of Prison Reform*. New York: Irvington.

Murton, T. and J. Hyams. 1969. *Accomplices to the Crime: The Arkansas Prison Scandal*. New York: Grove.

Nakashima, E. 2015. "Secrecy Around Police Surveillance Equipment Proves a Case's Undoing." *Washington Post*, February 22. Retrieved from www.washingtonpost.com/world/national-security/secrecy-around-police-surveillance-equipment-proves-a-cases-undoing/2015/02/22/ce72308a-b7ac-11e4-aa05-1ce812b3fdd2_story.html.

Nakashima, E. 2016. "Public Advocate: FBI's Use of PRISM Surveillance Data Is Unconstitutional." *Washington Post*, April 20. Retrieved from https://www.washingtonpost.com/world/national-security/public-advocate-fbis-use-of-prism-surveillance-data-is-un constitutional/2016/04/20/0282ed52-0693-11e6-b283-e79d81c63c1b_story.html?wpisrc=nl_rainbow.

National Center for State Courts. 2017. *Judicial Selection*. Retrieved from http://www.judicialselection.us/judicial_selection/methods/selection_of_judges.cfm?state=.

National Institute of Justice. 1992. "Community Policing in the 1990s." *National Institute of Justice Research Bulletin*, August: 2–9.

National Institute of Justice. 2008. *Study of Deaths Following Electro Muscular Disruption*. Washington, DC: Office of Justice Programs.

National Law Enforcement Officers Memorial Fund. 2016. *2016 Preliminary End-of-Year Law Enforcement Officer Fatalities Report*. Retrieved from http://www.nleomf.org/facts/research-bulletins/.

National Police Research Platform. 2017. Retrieved from http://www.nationalpoliceresearch.org/.

National Registry of Exonerations. 2017. *Interactive Map of Exonerations*. Retrieved from https://www.law.umich.edu/special/exoneration/Pages/Exonerations-in-the-United-States-Map.aspx.

NBC.com. 2013. "Houston Women Sue DPS for Intrusive Cavity Search." *NBC.com*, October 29. Retrieved from www.nbcdfw.com/news/local/Houston-Woman-Sues-DPS-for-Intrusive-Cavity-Search-214326731.html.

Nelson, K. 2017. "Sabrina De Sousa: Ex-CIA Agent Avoids Extradition Thanks to Trump." *Newsmax*, March 1. Retrieved from http://www.newsmax.com/TheWire/sabrina-de-sousa-cia-extradition-trump/2017/03/01/id/776333/.

Neuschatz, J., M. Wilkinson, C. Goodsell, S. Wetmore, D. Quinlivan, and N. Jones, 2012. "Secondary Confessions, Expert Testimony, and Unreliable Testimony." *Journal of Police and Criminal Psychology* 27: 179–192.

New York Times. 2010. "Justice in the Jury Box." June 4. Retrieved from www.nytimes.com/2010/06/06/opinion/06sun2.html.

Newport, F. 2014. "Gallup Review: Black and White Attitudes Toward Police." *Gallup.com*. Retrieved from www.gallup.com/poll/175088/gallup-review-black-white-attitudes-toward-police.aspx.

Newport, F. 2016. "Public Opinion Context: Americans, Race and Police." *Gallup.com*. Retrieved from http://www.gallup.com/opinion/polling-matters/193586/public-opinion-context-americans-race-police.aspx.

Neyfakh, L. 2015. "The Bad Cop Database: A Radical New Idea for Keeping Tabs on Police Misconduct." *Slate.com*, February 13. Retrieved from www.slate.com/articles/news_and_politics/crime/2015/02/bad_cops_a_new_database_collects_information_about_cop_misconduct_and_provides.html.

Neyroud, P. and A. Beckley. 2001. *Policing, Ethics and Human Rights*. Devon, England: Willan.

Nix, J., B. Campbell, E. Byers, and G. Alpert. 2017. "A Bird's Eye View of Civilians Killed by Police in 2015." *Criminology and Public Policy* 16: 309–340.

Nix, J. and S. Wolfe. 2015. "The Impact of Negative Publicity on Police Self-Legitimacy." *Justice Quarterly*. DOI: 10.1080/07418825.2015.1102954.

Noddings, N. 1986. *Caring: A Feminine Approach to Ethics and Moral Education*. Berkeley, CA: University of California Press.

Nolan, T. 2001. "Galateas in Blue: Women Police as Decoy Sex Workers." *Criminal Justice Ethics* 20(2): 2–67.

Norfleet, N. 2015. "Community Advocates Call for Dissolution of Minneapolis Police Review Board." *Minneapolis Star Tribune*, July 17. Retrieved from http://www.startribune.com/community advocates call for dissolution of minneapolis police review board/315955151.

North Carolina Innocence Commission. 2017. Retrieved from http://www.innocencecommission-nc.gov/stats.html.

O'Brien, J. 2013. "Centro Bus Video Shows Syracuse Police Tasering Disabled Man." *Syracuse.com*, August 5. Retrieved from http://www.syracuse.com/news/index.ssf/2013/08/disabled_man_plans_to_sue_syracuse_police_over_tasering_for_standing_on_a_bus.html.

O'Brien, R., K. Weir, and C. Young. 2014. "Federal Judges Plead Guilty." *Public Integrity.org*, Retrieved from www.publicintegrity.org/2014/04/28/14630/federal-judges-plead-guilty.

O'Connell, K. 2016. "Law Enforcement Lobby Succeeds in Killing California Transparency Bill." *Mint Press News*, June 6. Retrieved from http://www.mintpressnews.com/law-enforcement-lobby-succeeds-killing-cal/216959/.

Office of the Inspector General. 2010. *A Review of the FBI's Investigations of Certain Domestic Advocacy Groups*. Washington, DC: Office of the Inspector General.

O'Harrow, R. 2015. "Lawmakers Urge End to Program Sharing Forfeited Assets with State and Local Police." *Washington Post*, January 9. Retrieved from www.washingtonpost.com/investigations/lawmakers-urge-end-to-program-sharing-forfeited-assets-with-state-and-local-police/2015/01/09/8843a43c-982f-11e4-8005-1924ede3e54a_story.html.

O'Harrow, R., S. Horwitz, and S. Rich. 2015. "Holder Limits Seized-Asset Sharing Process that Split Billions with Local, State Police." *Washington Post*, January 18. Retrieved from www.washingtonpost.com/investigations/holder-ends-seized-asset-sharing-process-that-split-billions-with-local-state-police/

2015/01/16/0e7ca058-99d4-11e4-bcfb-059ec7a93ddc_story.html.

Onorato, M. and J. Zhu. 2015. "The Relationship Between Authentic Leadership and Employee Job Satisfaction: A Cross Industry-Sector Empirical Study." *International Leadership Journal* 7(2): 81–103.

Oppel, R. 2017. "States Trim Penalties and Prison Rolls, Even as Sessions Gets Tough." *New York Times*, May 18. Retrieved from https://www.nytimes.com/2017/05/18/us/states-prisons-crime-sentences-jeff-sessions.html?emc=edit_th_20170519&nl=todaysheadlines&nlid=66242298.

Orlov, R. 2013. "Chris Dorner Firing Review Officially Complete, LAPD Defends Termination." *Huffington Post*, June 22. Retrieved from www.huffingtonpost.com/2013/06/22/christopher-dorners-firi_n_3483056.html.

Osher, C. and D. Olinger. 2013. "Colorado Parole Audits Find Fundamental Errors 60 Percent of Cases." *Denver Post*, November 17. Retrieved from www.denverpost.com/news/ci_24539737/colorado-parole-audits-find-fundamental-errors-60-percent#ixzz2lDL53VUV.

Owen, B., J. Wells, J. Pollock, B. Muscat, and S. Torres. 2008. *Gendered Violence and Safety: A Contextual Approach to Improving Security in Women's Facilities*. Washington, DC: National Institute of Justice.

Packer, H. 1968. *The Limits of the Criminal Sanction*. Stanford, CA: Stanford University Press.

Packman, D. 2011. *2010 NPMSRP Police Misconduct Statistical Report*. Cato Institute. Retrieved from http://www.policemisconduct.net/2010-npmsrp-police-misconduct-statistical-report.

Paoline, E. 2003. "Taking Stock: Toward a Richer Understanding of Police Culture." *Journal of Criminal Justice* 31: 199–214.

Paoline, E., S. Myers, and R. Worden. 2000. "Police Culture, Individualism, and Community Policing: Evidence from Two Police Departments." *Justice Quarterly* 17(3): 575–605.

Papke, D. 1986. "The Legal Profession and Its Ethical Responsibilities: A History." In *Ethics and the Legal Profession*, ed. M. Davis and F. Elliston, 29–49. Buffalo, NY: Prometheus.

Parascandola, R. 2012. "NYPD Report Supports Claims by Adrian Schoolcraft, Cop Whistleblower." *New York Daily*

News, March 7. Retrieved from http://articles.nydailynews.com/2012-03-07/news/31134075_1_officer-adrian-schoolcraft-deputy-inspector-steven-mauriello-jon-norinsberg.

Park, M. 2017. "What We Know About Reality Winner." *CNN.com*, June 6. Retrieved from http://www.cnn.com/2017/06/06/politics/reality-winner-who-is-accused-leaker/index.html.

Parvini, S. 2015. "Sheriff Arpaio Admits Violating Court Order in Profiling Suit." *Los Angeles Times*, March 18. Retrieved from http://touch.latimes.com/#section/-1/article/p2p-83093795.

Patel, F. and M. Price. 2016. "Settlement of NYPD Muslim Surveillance Lawsuits: A Platform for Better Oversight." *JustSecurity.org*, January 15. Retrieved from http://www.brennancenter.org/blog/settlement-nypd-muslim-surveillance-lawsuits-platform-better-oversight.

Patel, F. and M. Price. 2017. "Keeping Eyes on NYPD Surveillance." *Brennan Center*, March 1. Retrieved from https://www.brennancenter.org/blog/ny-city-council-needs-increase-scrutiny-nypd's-surveillance-arsenal.

Paul, R. and L. Elder. 2003. *The Miniature Guide to Critical Thinking: Concepts and Tools*. Dillon Beach, CA: The Foundation for Critical Thinking.

Pavelka, S. 2016. "Restorative Justice in the States: An Analysis of Statutory Legislation and Policy." *Justice Policy Journal* 2(13): 1–24.

Payne, D. 2002. *Police Liability: Lawsuits Against the Police*. Durham, NC: Carolina Academic Press.

Payscale. 2017. "Prosecutor Salary." *Payscale*. Retrieved from http://www.payscale.com/research/US/Job=Prosecutor/Salary.

Pellicotti, J. 1990. "Ethics and the Criminal Defense: A Client's Desire to Testify Untruthfully." In *Ethics and Criminal Justice*, ed. F. Schmalleger, 67–78. Bristol, IN: Wyndam Hall.

Peralta, E. and D. Eads. 2015. "White House Ban on Militarized Gear for Police May Mean Little." *National Public Radio*, May 21. Retrieved from www.npr.org/sections/thetwo-way/2015/05/21/407958035/white-house-ban-on-militarized-gear-for-police-may-mean-little.

Perez, N. 2015. "Former Bexar County Judge Expected to Plead Guilty in Court

Today." *KSAT12.com*, April 10. Retrieved from www.ksat.com/content/pns/ksat/news/2015/04/10/former-bexar-county-judge-expected-to-plead-guilty-to-bribery-ch.html.

Perksy, A. 2009. "A Cautionary Tale: The Ted Stevens Prosecution." *Alaska Bar Rag* 33: 1–8.

Perry, J. (Ed.). 2002. *Repairing Communities Through Restorative Justice*. Lanham, MD: American Correctional Association.

Perry, S. 2011. *Prosecutors in State Courts, 2007. Statistical Tables*. Washington, DC: Bureau of Justice Statistics, U.S. Department of Justice.

Perry, T. 2015. "San Diego Police Body Camera Report: Fewer Complaints, Less Use of Force." *Los Angeles Times*, March 18. Retrieved from http://touch.latimes.com/#section/-1/article/p2p-83088560.

Peterson, R. 2012. "The Central Place of Race in Crime and Justice." *Criminology* 50(2): 303–327.

Pew Research Center. 2015. *American Support for Death Penalty Declining*. Retrieved from www.people-press.org/2015/04/16/less-support-for-death-penalty-especially-among-democrats.

Pew Research Center. 2016. *National Imprisonment and Crime Rates Continue to Fall*, March 8. Retrieved from http://www.pewtrusts.org/en/research-and-analysis/fact-sheets/2016/12/national-imprisonment-and-crime-rates-continue-to-fall.

Pew Research Center. 2017. *Behind the Badge*. Retrieved from http://www.pewsocialtrends.org/2017/01/11/behind-the-badge/.

Piquero, N., M. Meitl, E. Brank, J. Woolard, L. Lanza-Kaduse, and A. Piquero. 2016. "Exploring Lawyer Misconduct: An Examination of the Self-Regulation Process." *Deviant Behavior*. DOI: 10.1080/01639625.2015.1060795.

Pfaff, J. 2011. "The Micro and Macro Causes of Prison Growth." *Georgia State University Law Review* 28(4): 1237–1272.

Pfaff, J. 2016. "A Mockery of Justice for the Poor." *New York Times*, April 29. Retrieved from https://www.nytimes.com/2016/04/30/opinion/a-mockery-of-justice-for-the-poor.html?_r=0.

Phillips, N. 2015. "Consultants Uncover Deep Problems Within Denver Sheriff Department." *Denver Post*, May 21. Retrieved from www.denverpost.com/news/ci_28159042/consultants-uncover-deep-problems-within-denver-sheriff-department.

Phillips, N. 2017. "Denver Sheriff Department Selects Its Citizens Advisory Board." *Denver Post*, May 14. Retrieved from http://www.denverpost.com/2017/05/14/denver-sheriff-department-citizens-advisory-board/.

Phillips, S. 2013. "Police Recruit Attitudes Toward the Use of Unnecessary Force." *Police Practice and Research: An International Journal*. DOI: 10.1080/15614263.2013.845942.

Philly.com. 2014. "Report: Police Gun Deaths Up, Still Below Average." *Philly.com*, December 30. Retrieved from http://www.philly.com/philly/news/nation_world/20141230_ap_3ed514f2eb674d2fab8a6c4d14d62481.html#6HXcZiHeE1lrlGTL.99.

PICO. 2011. "Unholy Alliance: How the Private Prison Industry Is Corrupting Our Democracy and Promoting Mass Incarceration." Retrieved from http://publicampaign.org/reports/unholyalliance.

Piller, C. 2010. "Prison Officials Open 'Full Investigation' into Abuse Claims." *Sacramento Bee*, May 10: 1A.

Piller, C. and R. Mejia. 2003. "FBI's Bullet Analysis Method Is Flawed, Studies Suggest." *Austin American-Statesman*, February 4: A8.

Pimentel, D. 2009. "The Reluctant Tattletale: Closing the Gaps in Federal Judicial Discipline." *Tennessee Law Review* 76: 909–957.

Pinker, S. 2002. *The Blank Slate: The Modern Denial of Human Nature*. New York: Viking.

Pino, N. W. and M. D. Wiatrowski. 2006. "Implementing Democratic Policing and Related Initiatives." In *Democratic Policing in Transitional and Developing Countries*, ed. N. W. Pino and M. D. Wiatrowski, 99–128. Burlington, MA: Ashgate Publishing.

Planas, R. 2015. "Poll Reveals Widespread Fear of Police among Latinos." *Huffington Post*, November 12. Retrieved from www.huffingtonpost.com/2014/11/12/poll-police-brutality-latinos_n_6147162.html.

Plog, K. 2014. "Two Fife Corrections Officers Resigned—Weeks Apart—Amid Claims of Sexual Misconduct, Records Show." *The News Tribune*, December 6. Retrieved from www.thenewstribune.com/news/local/crime/article25901554.html.

Plohetski, T. 2012. "Police Use of Doctored DNA Report Prompts Legal Questions." *Austin American-Statesman*, January 29: A1.

Plohetski, T. and E. Dexheimer. 2012. "Austin's Taser Policy Is Less Restrictive Than Others." March 11: A4.

Podsakoff, P., S. MacKenzie, and W. Bommer. 1996. "Transformational Leader Behaviors and Substitutes for Leadership as Determinants of Employee Satisfaction, Commitment, Trust, and Organizational Citizenship Behaviors." *Journal of Management* 22: 259–298.

Pogarsky, G. and A. Piquero. 2004. "Studying the Reach of Deterrence: Can Deterrence Theory Help Explain Police Misconduct?" *Journal of Criminal Justice* 32: 371–386.

Pollock, J. 2004/2013a. *Prisons and Prison Life: Costs and Consequences*. Los Angeles, CA: Roxbury (Oxford University Press).

Pollock, J. 2013b. *Criminal Law*. Cincinnati, OH: Anderson Publishing Company.

Pollock, J. 2014. *Women's Crimes, Criminology and Corrections*. Prospect Heights, IL: Waveland Press.

Pollock, J. 2016. *Crime and Criminal Justice in America*, 3rd ed. New York: Routledge.

Pollock, J., N. Hogan, E. Lambert, J. I. Ross, and J. Sundt. 2012. "A Utopian Prison: Contradiction in Terms?" *Journal of Contemporary Criminal Justice* 28: 60–76.

Pollock, J. and B. Strah. 2016. *A Qualitative Study of Academy Graduates and their Use of Communication Techniques*. Unpublished report for Washington State Law Enforcement Training Commission. Available from the author.

Pont, J., H. Stover, and H. Wolff. 2012. "Health Policy and Ethics." *American Journal of Public Health* 102(3): 475–480.

Possley, M. 2014. *The Prosecutor and the Snitch*. The Marshall Project, August 3. Retrieved from www.themarshallproject.org/2014/08/03/did-texas-execute-an-innocent-man-willingham.

Possley, S., S. Mills, and F. McRoberts. 2004. "Scandal Touches Even Elite Labs." *Chicago Tribune*, October 21. Retrieved from www.chicagotribune.com/news/watchdog/chi-041021forensics,0,3075697.story.

Post, L. 2005. "FBI Bullet Test Misses Target: Court Rejects Test." *Whistleblowers.org*.

Retrieved from www.whistleblowers. org/storage/whistleblowers/documents/ fbi_bullet_test_misses_target.pdf.

Postema, G. 1986. "Moral Responsibility in Professional Ethics." In *Ethics and the Legal Profession*, ed. M. Davis and F. Elliston, 158–179. Buffalo, NY: Prometheus.

Poveda, T. 2001. "Estimating Wrongful Convictions." *Justice Quarterly* 18(3): 689–708.

Powell, M. 2014. "Takeover of Hotel: Informer Recalls His Complicity." *New York Times*, July 3: A19.

Powell, Z., M. Meitl, and J. Worrall. 2017. "Police Consent Decrees and Section 1983 Civil Rights Litigation." *Criminology & Public Policy* 16(2): 575–605.

Power, C. and L. Kohlberg. 1980. "Faith, Morality, and Ego Development." In *Toward Moral and Religious Maturity*, ed. J. Fowler and C. Bursselmans, 311–372. Morristown, NJ: Silver Burdett.

Prendergast, A. 2003. "Cowboy Justice." *Denver Westword*, June 26. Retrieved from www.westword.com/2003-06-26/ news/cowboy-justice/4.

Prenzler, T. 1995. "Police Gratuities: What the Public Thinks." *Criminal Justice Ethics* 14(1): 15–26.

Prenzler, T. 2000. "Civilian Oversight of Police: A Test of Capture Theory." *British Journal of Criminology* 40: 659–674.

Prenzler, T. 2006. "Senior Police Managers' Views on Integrity Testing, and Drug and Alcohol Testing." *Policing: An International Journal of Police Strategies and Management* 29(3): 394–407.

Prenzler, T. and J. Ransley. 2002. *Police Reform: Building Integrity*. Sydney, Australia: Hawkins.

Prenzler, T. and C. Ronken. 2001a. "Police Integrity Testing in Australia." *Criminal Justice* 1(2): 319–342.

Prenzler, T. and C. Ronken. 2001b. "Models of Police Oversight: A Critique." *Policing and Society* 11: 151–180.

President's Task Force on 21st Century Policing. 2015. *Final Report*. Retrieved from https://cops.usdoj.gov/pdf/ taskforce/TaskForce_FinalReport.pdf.

Price, M. 2013. *National Security and Local Police*. New York: Brennan Center.

Prior, W. 1991. "Aristotle's Nicomachean Ethics." In *From Virtue and Knowledge: An Introduction to Ancient Greek Ethics*, ed. W. Prior, 144–193. New York: Routledge, Kegan Paul.

Putman, Y. 2008. "Retired Navy Officer Reflects on Honesty, Responsibility." *Chattanooga Times Free Press*, February 27. Retrieved from www.timesfreepress. com/news/2008/feb/27/retired-navy- officer-reflects-honesty-responsibili.

Queally, J. and J. Mozingo. 2016. "Feds Fault San Francisco Police for Violence Against Minorities and Recommend 272 Reforms." *Los Angeles Times*, October 12. Retrieved from http://www. latimes.com/local/lanow/la-me-ln-san- francisco-police-bias-20161012-snap- story.html.

Quinn, M. 2005. *Walking with the Devil*. Minneapolis, MN: BooksbyQuinn.

Quinney, R. 1974. *Critique of the Legal Order*. New York: Little, Brown.

Radelet, M., H. Bedau, and C. Putnam. 1992. *In Spite of Innocence: Erroneous Convictions in Capital Cases*. Boston, MA: Northeastern University Press.

Raeder, M. 2007. "See No Evil: Wrongful Convictions and the Prosecutorial Ethics of Offering Testimony by Jailhouse Informants and Dishonest Experts." *Fordham Law Review* 76: 1413–1452.

Rahr, S. and S. Rice. 2015. "From Warriors to Guardians: Recommitting American Police Culture to Democratic Ideals." (New Perspectives in Policing Series). Washington, DC: U.S. Department of Justice, National Institute of Justice, 2015. NCJ 248654.

Raine, L. and M. Madden. 2015. "Americans' Views on Government Surveillance Programs." *Pew Research Center*. Retrieved from http://www.pewinternet. org/2015/03/16/americans-views-on- government-surveillance-programs.

Ramsey, R. 2007. "Perceptions of Criminal Justice Professionals Regarding the Frequency of Wrongful Conviction and the Extent of System Errors." *Crime and Delinquency* 53(3): 436–470.

Rantala, R. J. Rexroat, and A. Beck. 2014. *Sexual Victimization Reported by Adult Correctional Authorities, 2009–11* (NCJ 243904). Washington, DC: Bureau of Justice Statistics, U.S. Department of Justice.

Raphael, D. 1980. *Justice and Liberty*. London: Athlone.

Raphael, S. and M. Stoll. 2008. *Do Prisons Make Us Safer? The Benefits and Costs of the Prison Boom*. New York: Russell Sage Foundation.

Rashbaum, W. and T. Kaplan. 2015. "U.S. Says Assembly Speaker Sheldon Silver Took Millions in Payoffs, Abusing Office." *New York Times*, January 23: A1.

Rashbaum, W. and M. Schwirtz. 2017. "Chaos at Rikers, But City Jails Chief Was Gone for 90 Days." *New York Times*, April 28. Retrieved from https://www. nytimes.com/2017/04/28/nyregion/new- york-correction-commissioner-joseph- ponte-reprimand.html.

Ratcliffe, J. 2008. *Intelligence Led Policing*. Cullompton, Devon: Willan Publishing.

Ratcliffe, R. 2017. "Abbott Wants to ICE Sheriffs Over Sanctuary Cities." *Texas Monthly*, February 2. Retrieved from http://www.texasmonthly.com/ burka-blog/abbott-wants-ice-sheriffs- sanctuary-cities/.

Rawls, J. 1971. *A Theory of Justice*. Cambridge, MA: Belknap.

Reasons, C. 1973. "The Politicalization of Crime, the Criminal and the Criminologist." *Journal of Criminal Law, Criminology and Police Science* 64(March): 471–477.

Reeves, B. 2015. *Local Police Departments, 2013: Personnel, Policies, and Practices*. Washington, DC: Bureau of Justice Statistics, U.S. Department of Justice.

Reilly, R. 2016. "Obama Commutes 153 Sentences, Pardons 78, In Clemency Push." *Huffington Post*, December 19. Retrieved from http://www. huffingtonpost.com/entry/obama- commutation-pardon-clemency_ us_58581b72e4b0b3ddfd8db881.

Reiman, J. 1984/2005/2007. *The Rich Get Richer and the Poor Get Prison: Ideology, Class, and Criminal Justice*. Boston, MA: Allyn & Bacon.

Reiman, J. 1990/2004. *Justice and Modern Moral Philosophy*. New Haven, CT: Yale University Press.

Reimer, N. 2015. "Flawed Forensics: The Story Behind an Historic FBI Review." *The Crime Report*, April 30. Retrieved from www.thecrimereport.org/ viewpoints/2015-04-flawed-forensics- the-story-behind-an-historic-fbi-re.

Reisig, M. and R. Parks. 2000. "Experience, Quality of Life, and Neighborhood Context: A Hierarchical Analysis of Satisfaction with Police." *Justice Quarterly* 17(3): 607–630.

Reisig, M., J. McCluskey, S. Mastrofski, and W. Terrill. 2004. "Suspect Disrespect Toward the Police." *Justice Quarterly* 21(2): 241–268.

Rejali, D. 2007. "What Torture Tells Us (And What It Doesn't)." *Washington*

Post. Reprinted in *Austin American-Statesman*, December 23: Gl, G4.

Reuss-Ianni, E. 1983. *Two Cultures of Policing: Street Cops and Management Cops.* New Brunswick, NJ: Transaction.

Reuters. 2011. "Settlement Reached in Massey Mining Disaster." *Reuters News. online.* Retrieved 7/30/2012 from www.reuters.com/article/2011/12/06/us-masseyenergy-mineaccident-idUSTRE7B507V20111206.

Reuters. 2017. "NYC Rehab Chain Narco Freedom Pleads Guilty to Corruption." *Reuters*, May 31. Retrieved from http://www.reuters.com/article/us-usa-crime-narcofreedom-idUSKBN18R3AX.

Reynolds, P. 2015. *The Impact of Fairness, Organizational Trust, and Perceived Organizational Support on Police Officer Performance* (Unpublished doctoral dissertation). Texas State University.

Reynolds, P. and J. Hicks 2014. "There Is No Justice in a Police Department: A Phenomenological Study of Police Experiences." *Police Practice and Research: An International Journal.* DOI: 10.1080/15614263.2014.931229.

Rezendes, M. 2014. "Feds Probe Use of Informants in Lowell." *The Boston Globe*, September 19, 2014.

Richards, N. 2010. "Police Loyalty Redux." *Criminal Justice Ethics* 29(3): 221–240.

Ridolfi, K. and M. Possley. 2010. *Preventable Error: A Report on Prosecutorial Misconduct in California 1997–2009.* Santa Clara, CA: Northern California Innocence Project. Retrieved from http://law.scu.edu/ncip.

Rimer, S. 2000. "Lawyer Sabotaged Case of a Client on Death Row." *New York Times*, November 24. Retrieved from www.nytimes.com/2000/11/24/us/lawyer-sabotaged-case-of-a-client-on-death-row.html.

Risen, J. 2015a. "Report Finds Collaboration Over Torture." *New York Times*, May 1: A1.

Risen, J. 2015b. "Torture Efforts Were Protested by Psychologists." *New York Times*, July 11: A1.

Ritter, N. 2013. "Predicting Recidivism Risk: New Tool in Philadelphia Shows Great Promise." *NIJ Journal (February).* Retrieved from http://www.nij.gov/journals/271/pages/predicting-recidivism.aspx.

Robbins, T. 2015a. "A Brutal Beating Wakes Attica's Ghosts." *New York Times*, March 1: A1.

Robbins, T. 2015b. "Abused Inmates, Strong Unions and Hard to Fire Prison Guards." *New York Times*, September 28: A1.

Robbins, T. and L. D'Avolio. 2015. "3 Attica Guards Resign in Deal to Avoid Jail." *New York Times*, March 2. Retrieved from https://www.nytimes.com/2015/03/03/nyregion/attica-prison-guards-plead-guilty-in-2011-inmate-beating-case.html.

Robertson, C. 2015. "Court Penalties for Poor Inspire New Orleans Suit." *New York Times*, September 18: A14.

Robertson, C. 2016a. "With Eye on Reform, New Orleans Is Training Officers to Police One Another." *New York Times*, August 29: A9.

Robertson, C. 2016b. "New Orleans Officers Plead Guilty in Civilian Shootings After Hurricane." *New York Times*, April 21: A13

Robertson, C. 2016c. "New Orleans Settles Katrina-Era Police Brutality Cases for $13.3 Million." *New York Times*, December 20: A12.

Robles, F. 2013a. "Scrutiny of Prosecutors After Questions About Brooklyn Detective." *New York Times*, May 2: A3.

Robles, F. 2013b. "In Review of Brooklyn Cases, So Many Obstacles." *New York Times*, May 24: A1.

Robles, F. 2015a. "Racist Police Emails Put Florida Cases in Doubt." *New York Times*, May 16: A10.

Robles, F. 2015b. "Florida Officials Say Guards Who Are in Klan Plotted to Kill an Ex-Inmate." *New York Times*, April 3: A13

Rocha, V. 2016. "Judicial Panel Clears California Judge Who Gave Lenient Sentence in Stanford Sexual Assault." *Los Angeles Times*, December 19. Retrieved from http://www.latimes.com/local/lanow/la-me-ln-judge-aaron-persky-no-judicial-misconduct-20161219-story.html.

Rodd, S. 2017. *Should Police Be Allowed to Keep Property Without a Criminal Conviction?* Pew Research Center, February 8. Retrieved from http://www.pewtrusts.org/en/research-and-analysis/blogs/stateline/2017/02/08/should-police-be-allowed-to-keep-property-without-a-criminal-conviction.

Rodin, D. 2004. "Terrorism Without Intention." *Ethics* 114: 752–771.

Roebuck, J. 2015. "Acquitted Narcotics Officers Sue City's Top Brass for Defamation." *The Inquirer*, July 27.

Retrieved from http://www.philly.com/philly/news/local/20150728_Acquitted_narcotics_cops_sue_city_s_top_brass_for_defamation.html#qMWBqbyD4a7LMdDi.99.

Roebuck, J. 2017. "Philly DA Seth Williams Pleads Guilty, Goes to Prison." *www.philly.com*, June 29. Retrieved from http://www.philly.com/philly/news/crime/philly-da-seth-williams-xxxxxxxx-20170629.html.

Roebuck, R. and C. Brennan. 2017. "Philly DA Seth Williams: Brought 'Shame' to Office, Won't Run for Reelection." *The Philadelphia Inquirer*, February 10. Retrieved from http://www.philly.com/philly/blogs/real-time/Philadelphia-District-Attorney-Seth-Williams-announcement-Feb-10-2017.html.

Roebuck, J., D. Gambacorta, and C. Brennan. 2017. "D.A. Seth Williams Indicted on Corruption, Bribery-Related Charges." *Phillynews.com*, March 21. Retrieved from http://www.philly.com/philly/news/DA-Seth-Williams-federal-charges-Philadelphia.html.

Roeder, O., L. Eisen, and J. Bowling. 2015. *What Caused the Crime Decline?* Washington, DC: Brennan Center for Justice.

Rohrer, G., R. Stutzman, and G. Lotan. 2017. "Gov. Rick Scott Reassigns 21 Murder Cases, Citing Aramis Ayala's Death Penalty Stance." *Orlando Sentinel*, June 26. Retrieved from http://www.orlandosentinel.com/news/politics/political-pulse/os-rick-scott-ayala-death-penalty-20170403-story.html.

Rojas, R. and S. Schmid. 2016. "Latinos Seek More Public Scrutiny of Their Encounters with the Police." *New York Times*, July 14: A12.

Rokeach, M. 1973. *The Nature of Human Values.* New York: Free Press.

Romero, M. 2006. "Racial Profiling and Immigration Law Enforcement: Rounding Up the Usual Suspects in the Latino Community." *Critical Sociology* 32(2/3): 447–473.

Romney, L. 2017. "Private Diversion Programs Are Failing Those Who Need Help the Most." *RevealNews.com*, May 31. Retrieved from https://www.revealnews.org/article/private-diversion-programs-are-failing-those-who-need-help-the-most/.

Rosenbaum, D. and D. Lawrence. 2012. *Teaching Respectful Police-Citizen Encounters and Good Decision-Making:*

Results of a Randomized Control Trial with Police Recruits. National Police Research Platform Report. Washington, DC: National Institute of Justice.

Rosenfeld, R. 2015. *Was There a Ferguson Effect on Crime in St. Louis?* Washington, DC: Sentencing Project, 2015. Retrieved from http://sentencingproject.org/doc/publications/inc_Ferguson_Effect.pdf.

Rosenfeld, R. 2016. *Documenting and Explaining the 2015 Homicide Rise: Research Directions*. Washington, DC: National Institute of Justice, U.S. Department of Justice.

Rosenfeld, R. and R. Fornango. 2017. "The Relationship Between Crime and Stop, Question, and Frisk Rates in New York City Neighborhoods." *Justice Quarterly*. DOI: 10.1080/07418825.2016.1275748.

Ross, D. and P. Parker. 2009. "Policing by Consent Decree: An Analysis of 42 U.S.C. §14141 and the New Model for Police Accountability." *Police Practice and Research* 19(3): 199–208.

Rossmo, K. 2008. *Criminal Investigative Failures*. Boca Raton, FL: Taylor and Francis.

Roth, A. and J. Roth. 1989. *Devil's Advocates: The Unnatural History of Lawyers*. Berkeley, CA: Nolo.

Rothbart, M., D. Hanley, and M. Albert. 1986. "Differences in Moral Reasoning." *Sex Roles* 15(11/12): 645–653.

Rothlein, S. 1999. "Policy Agency Efforts to Prevent Abuses." In *Human Dignity and the Police: Ethics and Integrity in Police Work*, ed. G. Lynch, 15–27. Springfield, IL: Charles C Thomas.

Rothwell, G. and J. Baldwin. 2007a. "Ethical Climate Theory, Whistle-Blowing, and the Code of Silence in Police Agencies in the State of Georgia." *Journal of Business Ethics* 70: 341–361.

Rothwell, G. and J. Baldwin. 2007b. "Whistle-Blowing and the Code of Silence in Police Agencies: Policy and Structural Predictors." *Crime and Delinquency* 53(4): 605–632.

Rottman, D. J. 2007. "Adhere to Procedural Fairness in the Justice System." *Criminology and Public Policy* 6: 835–842.

Rubin, J. 2017. "Ex-L.A. County Sheriff Lee Baca Sentenced to Three Years in Prison in Jail Corruption Scandal." *Los Angeles Times*, May 12. Retrieved from http://www.latimes.com/local/lanow/la-me-baca-sentenced-jail-sheriff-corruption-20170512-story.html.

Ruggiero, V. 2001. *Thinking Critically About Ethical Issues*, 5th ed. New York: McGraw-Hill.

Ruiz, J. and C. Bono. 2004. "At What Price a 'Freebie'? The Real Cost of Police Gratuities." *Criminal Justice Ethics* 23(1): 44–54.

Ryan, H. 2015. *Unequal Treatment: Mobilizing the Private Bar to Fight Mass Incarceration*. New York: Lawyers Committee for Civil Rights Under the Law.

Sallah, M. and J. Bernstein. 2015. "How 2 Police Agencies Built a Money-Laundering Machine." *Miami Herald*, June 19. Retrieved from http://www.miamiherald.com/news/local/community/miami-dade/article24903394.html.

Saltzburg, S. 2008. "Changes to Model Rules Impact Prosecutors." *Criminal Justice* 23: 1–36.

Saltzman, J. 2010. "Former Stoughton Detective Pleads Guilty to Lying to FBI Agents." *Boston.com*, January 6. Retrieved from www.boston.com/news/local/breaking_news/2010/01/former_stoughto_2.html.

San Antonio Express News. 2002. "Lawyers Should Not Aid, Abet Wrongdoers." December 29: 2H.

Sandel, M. 2009. *Justice: What's the Right Thing to Do?* New York: Farrar, Straus and Giroux.

Sanders, B. 2008. "Using Personality Traits to Predict Police Officer Performance." *Policing: An International Journal of Police Strategies and Management* 31(1): 129–147.

Sanger, D. 2016. "New Technologies Give Government Ample Means to Track Suspects, Study Finds." *New York Times*, February 1: A6.

Santana, R. 2017. "Groups Slam Louisiana's Public Defender System in Lawsuit." *Associated Press*, February 6. Retrieved from https://www.yahoo.com/news/groups-slam-louisianas-public-defender-system-lawsuit-180340534.html.

Santo, A. 2015. *Preying on Prisoners*. The Marshall Project, June 17. Retrieved from www.themarshallproject.org/2015/06/17/preying-on-prisoners?utm_medium=email&utm_campaign=newsletter&utm_source=opening-statement&utm_term=newsletter-20150617-203.

Santo, A., V. Kim, and A. Flagg. 2017. "Upgrade Your Jail Cell—For a Price."

Los Angeles Times, March 9. Retrieved from http://www.latimes.com/projects/la-me-pay-to-stay-jails/.

Sapien, J. and S. Hernandez. 2013. "Who Polices Prosecutors Who Abuse Their Authority? Usually Nobody." *Propublica*, April 3. Retrieved from www.propublica.org/article/who-polices-prosecutors-who-abuse-their-authority-usually-nobody.

Sapp, A. 1994. "Sexual Misconduct by Police Officers." In *Police Deviance*, 3rd ed., ed. T. Barker and D. Carter, 187–200. Cincinnati, OH: Anderson.

Saul, J. 2014. "DA Planning to Overturn Another of Scarcella's Murder Convictions." *New York Post*, November 5. Retrieved from http://nypost.com/2014/11/15/da-planning-to-overturn-another-of-scarcellas-murder-convictions.

Savage, D. 2008. "High Court Won't Hear Surveillance Program Challenge." *Austin American-Statesman*, February 20: A10.

Savage, C. 2013. "C.I.A. Report Finds Concerns with Ties to New York Police." *New York Times*, June 26: A1.

Savage, C. 2015. "George W. Bush Made Retroactive N.S.A. 'Fix' After Hospital Room Showdown." *New York Times*, September 20. Retrieved from https://www.nytimes.com/2015/09/21/us/politics/george-w-bush-made-retroactive-nsa-fix-after-hospital-room-showdown.html?_r=0.

Savage, C. 2017. "N.S.A. Halts Collection of Americans' Emails About Foreign Targets." *New York Times*, April 28. Retrieved from https://www.nytimes.com/2017/04/28/us/politics/nsa-surveillance-terrorism-privacy.html?emc=edit_th_20170429&nl=today sheadlines&nlid=66242298&_r=0.

Savage, C. and S. Shane, 2009. "Intelligence Improperly Collected on U.S. Citizens." *New York Times*, December 16. Retrieved from www.nytimes.com/2009/12/17/us/17disclose.html.

Savage, C. and S. Shane. 2013. "N.S.A. Leaker Denies Giving Secrets to China." *New York Times*, June 17: A1.

Sawyer, W. 2017. "The Steep Cost of Medical Co-Pays in Prison Puts Health at Risk." *Prison Policy Initiative*, April 19. Retrieved from https://www.prisonpolicy.org/blog/2017/04/19/copays/.

Schafer, J. 2002. "Community Policing and Police Corruption." In *Policing and*

Misconduct, ed. K. Lersch, 193–217. Upper Saddle River, NJ: Prentice Hall.

Schafer, J. 2010a. "The Ineffective Police Leader: Acts of Commission and Omission." *Journal of Criminal Justice* 38: 737–746.

Schafer, J. 2010b. "Effective Leaders and Leadership in Policing: Traits, Assessment, Development, and Expansion." *Policing: An International Journal of Police Strategies and Management* 33(4): 644–663.

Scheck, B. 2010. "Professional and Conviction Integrity Programs: Why We Need Them, Why They Will Work, and Models for Creating Them." *Cardozo Law Review* 31(6): 225–256.

Schehr, R. and J. Sears. 2005. "Innocence Commissions: Due Process Remedies and Protection for the Innocent." *Critical Criminology* 13(2): 181–209.

Scheiber, N. 2017. "How a Rising Minimum Wage Affects Jobs in Seattle." *New York Times*, June 26. Retrieved from https://www.nytimes.com/2017/06/26/business/economy/seattle-minimum-wage.html?_r=0

Scheingold, S. 1984. *The Politics of Law and Order*. New York: Longman.

Schmadeke, S. 2015. "Inmates Who Allege Police Abuse by Burge May Get Hearing on Innocence Claims." *Chicago Tribune*, March 26. Retrieved from http://my.chicagotribune.com/#section/-1/article/p2p-83148566.

Schmidt, M. 2015. "Scant Data Frustrates Efforts to Assess Number of Shootings by Police." *New York Times*, April 9: A16.

Schmidt, M. 2017. "Comey Wanted President Kept at a Distance." *New York Times*, May 19: A1.

Schoeman, F. 1982. "Friendship and Testimonial Privileges." In *Ethics, Public Policy and Criminal Justice*, ed. F. Elliston and N. Bowie, 257–272. Cambridge, MA: Oelgeschlager, Gunn and Hain.

Schoeman, F. 1985. "Privacy and Police Undercover Work." In *Police Ethics: Hard Choices in Law Enforcement*, ed. W. Heffernan and T. Stroup, 133–153. New York: John Jay Press.

Schuck, A. and D. Rosenbaum. 2011. *The Chicago Quality Interaction Training Program: A Randomized Control Trial of Police Innovation*. National Police Research Platform Topical Report. Washington, DC: National Institute of Justice.

Schuppe, J. 2016. "Dallas Police Chief David Brown Faces Toughest Challenge of Difficult Career." *NBC News*, July 12. Retrieved from http://www.nbcnews.com/storyline/dallas-police-ambush/dallas-police-chief-david-brown-faces-toughest-challenge-difficult-career-n607266.

Schuppe, J. 2017. "Rogue East Cleveland Cops Framed Dozens of Drug Suspects." *NBC News*, March 27. Retrieved from http://www.nbcnews.com/news/us-news/rogue-east-cleveland-cops-framed-dozens-drug-suspects-n736671.

Schwartz, J. 2010. "Myths and Mechanics of Deterrence: The Role of Lawsuits in Law Enforcement Decisionmaking." *U.C.L.A. Law Review* 57:1023–1070.

Schweigert, F. 2002. "Moral and Philosophical Foundations of Restorative Justice." In *Repairing Communities Through Restorative Justice*, ed. J. Perry, 19–37. Lanham, MD: American Correctional Association.

Schwirtz, M. and W. Rashbaum. 2017. "Joseph Ponte to Resign as New York City Jails Chief." *New York Times*, May 11. Retrieved from https://www.nytimes.com/2017/05/11/nyregion/bill-de-blasio-joseph-ponte-correction-commissioner.html.

Schwirtz, M. and M. Winerip. 2015a. "Correction Commissioner Calls Overhauling Rikers a 'Long, Heavy Lift'." *New York Times*, June 5: A19.

Schwirtz, M. and M. Winerip. 2015b. "De Blasio, at Rikers, Unveils a Plan to Reduce Violence and Smuggling." *New York Times*, March 13: A22.

Schwirtz, M. and M. Winerip. 2016. "Major Lapses Let Killers Flee New York Jail." *New York Times*, June 7: A1.

Seiler, S., A. Fischer, and Y. Ooi. 2010. "An Interactional Dual-Process Model of Moral Decision Making to Guide Military Training." *Military Psychology* 22: 490–509.

Sekerka, L. 2009. "Organizational Ethics Education and Training: A Review of Best Practices and Their Application." *International Journal of Training and Development* 13(2): 77–95.

Selksky, A. 2009. "Many Guantanamo Detainees Innocent, Ex-Bush Official Says." *Austin American-Statesman*, March 20: A5.

Selman, D. and P. Leighton. 2010. *Punishment for Sale: Private Prisons, Big Business, and the Incarceration Binge*. Boston, MA: Rowman & Littlefield Publ.

Semukhina, O. and K. M. Reynolds. 2013. "Russian Citizens' Perceptions of Corruption and Trust of the Police." *Policing and Society: An International Journal of Research and Policy*. DOI: 10.1080/10439463.2013.784290.

Sentencing Project. 2012. *Too Good to Be True: Private Prisons in America*. Washington, DC: Sentencing Project.

Serpas, R. and D. Brown. 2017. *Fighting Crime and Strengthening Criminal Justice. Law Enforcement Leaders*. Retrieved from www.lawenforcementleaders.org.

Serrano, R. and R. Ostrow. 2000. "Probe of FBI Lab Reviews 3,000 Cases, Affects None." *Los Angeles Times*, August 17. Retrieved from http://articles.latimes.com/2000/aug/17/news/mn-5863.

Seville, L. and G. Kates. 2013. "A Home of Their Own." *The Crime Report*, July 8, 2013. Retrieved from www.thecrimereport.org/news/inside-criminal-justice/2013-07-a-home-of-their-own.

Seville, L. and G. Kates. 2015. "The Narco Freedom Case: Who's Watching the Caregivers?" *The Crime Report*, January 5. Retrieved from www.thecrimereport.org/news/inside-criminal-justice/2015-01-the-narco-freedom-case-whos-watching-the-caregivers.

Sewell, A. and R. Faturechi. 2013. "L.A. Sheriff Baca Held Liable for $100,000 in Inmate Abuse Case." *Los Angeles Times*, October 17. Retrieved from www.latimes.com/local/lanow/la-me-ln-baca-inmate-abuse-damages-20131017,0,2160426.story.

Shackford, S. 2017. "When Even Prosecutors Can't Be Informed About Corrupt Cops, We've Got a Problem." *Reason.com*, February 22. Retrieved from http://reason.com/blog/2017/02/22/when-even-prosecutors-cant-be-informed-a.

Shaffer, T. and R. Cochran. 2007. "'Technical' Defenses: Ethics, Morals, and the Lawyer as Friend." *Clinical Law Review* 14: 337–353.

Shafroth, A. and L. Schwartzol. 2017. *Confronting Criminal Justice Debt: The Urgent Need for Comprehensive Reform*. Criminal Justice Policy Program, Harvard University. Retrieved from http://cjpp.law.harvard.edu/assets/Confronting-Crim-Justice-Debt-Guide-to-Policy-Reform-FINAL.pdf.

Shakespeare, W. *The Merchant of Venice*, Act 4, Scene 1.

Shane, J. M. 2012. "Police Employee Disciplinary Matrix: An Emerging Concept." *Police Quarterly* 15(1): 62–91.

Shane, S. 2008a. "Waterboarding Inquiry Focuses on Legal Advice." *Austin American-Statesman*, February 23: A10.

Shane, S. 2008b. "China Inspired Interrogations at Guantanamo." *New York Times*, July 2. Retrieved from www.nytimes.com/2008/07/02/us/02detain.html.

Shane, S. and S. LaFraniere. 2016. "Comey Role Recalls Hoover's F.B.I., Fairly or Not." *New York Times*, November 1: A1.

Shane, S. and S. Mazzetti. 2009. "In Adopting Harsh Tactics, No Look at Past Use." *New York Times*, April 22. Retrieved from www.nytimes.com/2009/04/22/us/politics/22detain.html.

Shapira, I. 2016. "Ex-CIA Officer Faces Extradition from Portugal to Italy for Alleged Role in Cleric's Rendition." *Washington Post,* April 21. Retrieved from https://www.washingtonpost.com/local/ex-cia-officer-faces-extradition-from-portugal-to-italy-for-her-alleged-role-in-clerics-rendition/2016/04/21/b8b08b22-0727-11e6-bdcb-0133da18418d_story.html?utm_term=.be592fe35228.

Shapiro, J. 2015. "Lawsuits Target 'Debtors' Prisons' Across the Country." *National Public Radio (NPR)*, October 21. Retrieved from http://www.npr.org/2015/10/21/450546542/lawsuits-target-debtors-prisons-across-the-country.

Shapiro, J. 2017. "National Panel Advises Judges on People Who Can't Pay Court Fees." *NPR*, February 3. Retrieved from http://www.npr.org/sections/thetwo-way/2017/02/03/513338061/national-panel-advises-judges-on-people-who-cant-pay-court-fees.

Sharp, E. and P. Johnson. 2009. "Accounting for Variations in Distrust of Local Police." *Justice Quarterly* 26(1): 157–182.

Shaw, A. 2014. "City Pays Heavy Price for Police Brutality." *Chicago Sun-Times*, April 13. Retrieved 8/3/2015 from http://chicago.suntimes.com/chicago-politics/7/71/167182/city-pays-heavy-price-for-police-brutality.

Sheley, J. 1985. *Exploring Crime*. Belmont, CA: Wadsworth.

Shelton, L. 2013. "Exonerated Man Sues Burge, Others Over Police Beating, Wrongful Conviction." *Chicago Tribune*, May 30, 2013: A1.

Shepherd, J. 2013. *Justice at Risk: An Empirical Analysis of Campaign Contributions and Judicial Decisions.* Washington, DC: American Constitution Society.

Sherman, L. 1981. *The Teaching of Ethics in Criminology and Criminal Justice.* Washington, DC: Joint Commission on Criminology and Criminal Justice Education and Standards, Law Enforcement Assistance Administration.

Sherman, L. 1982. "Learning Police Ethics." *Criminal Justice Ethics* 1(1): 10–19.

Sherman, L. 1985a. "Becoming Bent: Moral Careers of Corrupt Policemen." In *Moral Issues in Police Work*, ed. F. Elliston and M. Feldberg, 253–273. Totawa, NJ: Rowman and Allanheld.

Sherman, L. 1985b. "Equity Against Truth: Value Choices in Deceptive Investigations." In *Police Ethics: Hard Choices in Law Enforcement*, ed. W. Heffernan and T. Stroup, 117–133. New York: John Jay Press.

Shermer, M. 2004. *The Science of Good and Evil: Why People Cheat, Gossip, Care, Share, and Follow the Golden Rule.* New York: Times Books, Holt and Co.

Silberman, M. 1995. *A World of Violence: Corrections in America.* Belmont, CA: Wadsworth.

Simon, J. 2014. *On Trial: A Remarkable Court Decision and the Future of Prisons in America.* New York: The Free Press.

Simpson, I. 2015. "Prosecution of U.S. Police for Killings Surges to Highest in Decade." *Reuters*, October 25. Retrieved from http://www.reuters.com/article/2015/10/26/us-usa-police-idUSKCN0SK17L20151026.

Skelton, A. 2014. "ACLU Report Criticizes Nebraska Law Enforcement's Citizen Complaint Procedures." *Omaha.com*, August 13. Retrieved from www.omaha.com/news/nebraska/aclu-report-criticizes-nebraska-law-enforcement-s-citizen-complaint-procedures/article_8fa0f534-40cf-5984-9c71-ce9fefa8acd4.html.

Skutch, J. 2014. "Former Savannah-Chatham Police Chief Fall Mirrors Department Ills." *Savannahnow.com*, November 29. Retrieved from http://savannahnow.com/news/2014-11-29/lovetts-fall-mirrors-department-ills-shame.

Skogan, W., M. Van Craen, and C. Hennessy. 2014. "Training Police for Procedural Justice." *Journal of Experimental Criminology*, December 2014. DOI: 10.1007/s11292-014-9223-6.

Skogan, W. and M. Wycoff. 1986. "Storefront Police Officers: The Houston Field Test." In *Community Crime Prevention: Does It Work?* ed. D. Rosenbaum, 122–126. Beverly Hills, CA: Sage.

Skolnick, J. 1982. "Deception by Police." *Criminal Justice Ethics* 1(2): 40–54.

Skolnick, J. 2001. "Corruption and the Blue Code of Silence." *Police Practice and Research* 3(1): 7–19.

Skolnick, J. and R. Leo. 1992. "Ideology and the Ethics of Crime Control." *Criminal Justice Ethics* 11(1): 3–13.

Slackman, M. 2010. "Officials Pressed Germans on Kidnapping by C.I.A." *New York Times*, December 8. Retrieved from http://www.nytimes.com/2010/12/09/world/europe/09wikileaks-elmasri.html?_r=0.

Slobodzian, J. 2009. "FBI Report Finds Pattern of Police Misdeeds." *Philly.com*, April 25. Retrieved from www.philly.lcom/philly/news/homepage/20090425_FBI_report_finds_pattern_of_police_misdeeds.html.

Slobodzian, J. and M. Fazlollah. 2015. "Phila. Judge Overturns 158 Convictions Tied to Rogue Narcotics Cops." *Philly.com*, August 9. Retrieved from http://articles.philly.com/2015-08-09/news/65354633_1_narcotics-officers-perry-betts-convictions.

Smart, C. 2017. "Obama Granted Clemency Unlike Any Other President in History." *FiveThirtyEight.com*, January 19. Retrieved from https://fivethirtyeight.com/features/obama-granted-clemency-unlike-any-other-president-in-history/.

Smilansky, S. 2004. "Terrorism, Justification and Illusion." *Ethics* 114: 790–805.

Smith, M. and G. Alpert. 2002. "Searching for Direction: Courts, Social Science, and the Adjudication of Racial Profiling Claims." *Justice Quarterly* 19(4): 673–703.

Smith, R. 2006. "Fired Officer Believed CIA Lied to Congress." *Washington Post*, May 14. Retrieved from www.washingtonpost.com/wp-dyn/content/article/2006/05/13/AR2006051301311.html.

Smith, R. and D. Linzer. 2006. "CIA Officer's Job Made Any Leaks More Delicate." *Washington Post*, April 23: A01.

Smith, S. and R. Meyer. 1987. *Law, Behavior, and Mental Health*. New York: New York University Press.

Smith, V. 2014. "Whistle-Blowing Former Baltimore Police Detective Sues Department for Retaliation." *City Paper*, December 30. Retrieved from www.citypaper.com/news/mobtownbeat/bcp-whistleblowing-former-baltimore-police-detective-sues-department-for-retaliation-20141230,0,7758822.story#sthash.cy3Bp3uR.dpuf.

Snyder, L., P. McQuillan, W. Murphy, and R. Joselson. 2007. *Report on the Conviction of Jeffrey Deskovic*. Retrieved from http://www.westchesterda.net/Jeffrey%20Deskovic%20Comm%20Rpt.pdf.

Solomon, J. 2007. "Former N.C. Chief Justice Takes up Prisoner's Case." *Washington Post*, November 28: A07.

Solomon, J. and C. Johnson. 2010. "FBI Broke Law for Years in Phone Record Searches." *Washington Post*, January 19. Retrieved from www.washingtonpost.com/wp-dyn/content/article/2010/01/18/AR2010011803982.html.

Sontag, D. 2015a. "Push to End Prison Rapes Loses Earlier Momentum." *New York Times*, May 13: A1.

Sontag, D. 2015b. "Every Day I Struggle: Transgender Woman Cites Attacks and Abuse in Men's Prison." *New York Times*, April 6: A1.

Souryal, S. 1992/2007. *Ethics in Criminal Justice: In Search of the Truth*. Cincinnati, OH: Anderson.

Souryal, S. 1996. "Personal Loyalty to Superiors in Public Service." *Criminal Justice Ethics*, Summer/Fall: 44–62.

Souryal, S. 1999. "Corruption of Prison Personnel." In *Prison and Jail Administration: Practice and Theory*, ed. P. Carlson and J. Garrett, 171–177. Gaithersburg, MD: Aspen.

Souryal, S. 2009. "Deterring Corruption by Prison Personnel: A Principle-Based Perspective." *Prison Journal* 89: 21–45.

South, N. 2001. "Police, Security and Information: The Use of Informants and Agents in a Liberal Democracy." In *Policing, Security and Democracy: Special Aspects of Democratic Policing*, ed. S. Einstein and M. Amir, 87–105. Huntsville, TX: Office of International Criminal Justice (OICJ), Sam Houston State University.

Southall, A. 2016a. "2 Detectives Are Indicted in Beating of Mailman." *New York Times*, April 21: A24.

Southall, A. 2016b. "Police Officer Is Reassigned After Arrest of a Mailman." *New York Times*, April 2: A13.

Spence, G. 1989. *With Justice for None*. New York: Penguin.

Spielman, F. 2013a. "City Council OKs $10 Million Settlement in Burge Case." *Chicago Sun-Times*, July 24. Retrieved from http://articles.chicagotribune.com/2013-07-25/news/ct-met-chicago-police-brutality-burge-20130725_1_eric-caine-city-oks-police-misconduct.

Spielman, F. 2013b. "$12.3 Million Settlement in Police Torture Case Spares Daley from Testifying." *Chicago Sun-Times*, September 5. Retrieved from www.suntimes.com/22374750-761/123-million-settlement-in-police-torture-case-spares-daley-from-testifying.html.

Spielman, F., 2016. "Chicago Pays $5.5M in Reparations to 57 Burge Torture Victims." *Chicago Sun-Times*, January 4. Retrieved from http://chicago.suntimes.com/news/7/71/1225034/city-attorney-under-fire-in-police-shooting-case-resigns.

Spina, M. 2015. "When a Protector Becomes a Predator." *Buffalo News*, November 22. Retrieved from http://projects.buffalonews.com/abusing-the-law/index.html.

Spinaris, C., M. Denhof, and J. Kellaway. 2012. *Posttraumatic Stress Disorder in United States Correctional Professionals: Prevalence and Impact on Health and Functioning*. Florence, CO: Desert Waters Correctional Outreach. Retrieved from http://www.correctionsfatigue.com/images/PTSD_Prevalence_in_ Corrections_2012.pdf.

Staats, C., K. Capatosto, R. Wright, and D. Contractor. 2015. *State of the Science: Implicit Bias Review, 2015*. Kirwin Institute for the Study of Race and Ethnicity. Retrieved from http://kirwaninstitute.osu.edu/wp-content/uploads/2015/05/2015-kirwin-implicit-bias.pdf.

Stanton, S. and D. Walsh. 2016. "Lawsuit Says 'Code of Silence' Hid California Inmate's Death." *Sacramento Bee*, April 19. Retrieved from http://www.sacbee.com/news/local/crime/article72982367.html.

Starr, S. 2014. "Sentencing by the Numbers." *New York Times*, August 11: A17.

Stein, K. 2015. "8 Promises Alabama Just Made to Feds About Treatment of Female Inmates." *Al.com*, May 29. Retrieved from www.al.com/news/index.ssf/2015/05/8_promises_alabama_just_made_t.html#incart_river.

Stefanic, M. 1981. "Police Ethics in a Changing Society." *Police Chief*, May: 62–64.

Steffen, J. and C. Osher. 2015. "How Police Reliance on Confidential Informants in Colorado Carries Risk." *Denver Post*, April 17. Retrieved from www.denverpost.com/informants/ci_27937446/special-report-police-reliance-informants-colorado-brings-risks.

Stephens, D. 2011. *Police Discipline: A Case for Change*. (New Perspectives in Policing Series). Washington, DC: U.S. Department of Justice, National Institute of Justice.

Sterngold, J. 2000. "Los Angeles Police Admit a Vast Management Lapse." *New York Times*, March 2: A14.

Stevens, D. 1999. "Corruption Among Narcotics Officers: A Study of Innocence and Integrity." *Journal of Police and Criminal Psychology* 14(2): 1–11.

Stewart, J. 2015. "When the Buck Doesn't Stop: Individual Accountability Is Elusive." *New York Times*, February 20: B1.

Stewart, M. 2016. "Journalists Arrested in Ferguson Barred from Talking About Settlement." *Huffington Post*, May 16. Retrieved from http://www.huffingtonpost.com/entry/journalists-st-louis-county-police-settlement_us_573a18bee4b060aa781ae513.

Stillman, S. 2013. "Taken." *The New Yorker*, August 12. Retrieved from www.newyorker.com/magazine/2013/08/12/taken.

Stinson, P., S. Brewer, and B. Mathna. 2015. "Police Sexual Misconduct: Arrested Officers and Their Victims." *Victims and Offenders* 10: 117–151.

Stinson, P., J. Liederback, S. Lab, and S. Brewer. 2016. *Police Integrity Lost: A Study of Law Enforcement Officers Arrested*. Washington, DC: United States Department of Justice.

Stinson, P., N. Todak, and M. Dodge. 2013. "An Exploration of Crime by Policewomen." *Police Practice and Research: An International Journal*. DOI: 10.1080/15614263.2013.846222.

Stohr, M., C. Hemmens, R. March, G. Barrier, and D. Palhegyl. 2000. "Can't Scale This? The Ethical Parameters of Correctional Work." *Prison Journal* 80(1): 56–79.

Stolberg, S. 2017. "'It Did Not Stick': The First Federal Effort to Curb Police Abuse." *New York Times*, April 9, 2017.

Stroud, M. 2013. "Why Would a Prison Corporation Restructure as a Real Estate Company?" *Forbes*, January 31, 2013.

Sullivan, G. 2014. "Ex-Massey CEO Donald Blankenship Indicted for Coal Mine Disaster that Killed 29." *Washington Post*, November 14. Retrieved from www.washingtonpost.com/news/morning-mix/wp/2014/11/14/ex-massey-ceo-don-blankenship-indicted-for-coal-mine-disaster-than-killed-29.

Sullivan, T. and M. Possley. 2016. "The Chronic Failure to Discipline Prosecutors for Misconduct: Proposals for Reform." *The Journal of Criminal Law & Criminology* 105(4): 881–945.

Sunne, S. 2016. "When Cities Criminalize Small Offenses, Non-White People Suffer." *Washington Post*, September 8. https://www.washingtonpost.com/posteverything/wp/2016/09/08/i-got-arrested-for-putting-my-feet-up-on-the-subway-i-was-lucky-i-was-white/?utm_term=.e3d27b5e22cd.

Sunshine, J. and T. R. Tyler. 2003. "Moral Solidarity, Identification with the Community, and the Importance of Procedural Justice: The Police as Prototypical Representation of a Group's Moral Values." *Social Psychology Quarterly* 66: 153–165.

Sutherland, E. H. 1947. *Principles of Criminology*, 4th ed. Philadelphia, PA: J.B. Lippincott.

Swenson, A. 2016. "How the Most Disliked and Elected Profession Is Disappearing from Politics." *Washington Post*, January 19. Retrieved from https://www.washingtonpost.com/news/wonk/wp/2016/01/19/how-the-most-disliked-and-elected-profession-is-disappearing-from-politics/?utm_term=.0241a787baee.

Swift, A. 2017. "Support for Legal Marijuana Use Up to 60% in US." *Gallup.com*, October 19. Retrieved from http://www.gallup.com/poll/196550/support-legal-marijuana.aspx.

Swisher, K. 2009. "The Judicial Ethics of Criminal Law Adjudication." *Arizona State Law Journal* 41: 755–828.

Sykes, G. 1980. "The Defects of Total Power." In *Keepers: Prison Guards and Contemporary Corrections*, ed. B. Crouch. Springfield, IL: Charles C. Thomas.

Sykes, G. 1989. "The Functional Nature of Police Reform: The Myth of Controlling the Police." In *Critical Issues in Policing*, ed. R. Dunham and G. Alpert, 292–304. Prospect Heights, IL: Waveland.

Sykes, G. M. and D. Matza. 1957. "Techniques of Neutralization: A Theory of Deviance." *American Sociological Review* 22(6): 664–670.

Tabish, S. and K. N. Jha. 2012. "The Impact of Anti-Corruption Strategies on Corruption Free Performance in Public Construction Projects." *Construction Management & Economics* 30(1): 21–35.

Taggart, K. 2015. "In Texas It's a Crime to Be Poor." *BuzzFeed*, October 7. Retrieved from https://www.buzzfeed.com/kendalltaggart/in-texas-its-a-crime-to-be-poor?utm_term=.upKDeLw1b#.bt8Y50Pbw.

Tanay, E. 1982. "Psychiatry and the Prison System." *Journal of Forensic Sciences* 27(2): 385–392.

Tanner, R. 2002. "Central Park Case Puts Focus on Confessions." *Austin American-Statesman*, December 7: A9.

Tanner, R. 2006. "Bad Science May Taint Many Arson Convictions." *Austin American-Statesman*, May 3: A1, A5.

Tashea, J. 2017. "Courts Are Using AI to Sentence Criminals. That Must Stop Now." *Wired*, April 17. Retrieved from https://www.wired.com/2017/04/courts-using-ai-sentence-criminals-must-stop-now/.

Tau, B. 2014. "Curbing Police Militarization Would Be Uphill Battle." *Politico*, September 2014. Retrieved from www.politico.com/story/2014/09/police-militarization-110690_Page2.html#ixzz3ETGIi0nb.

Taylor, W. 1993. *Brokered Justice: Race Politics and Mississippi Prisons 1798–1992*. Columbus: Ohio State University Press.

Terrill, W. 2001. *Police Coercion: Application of the Force Continuum*. New York: LFB Scholarly Publishing.

Terrill, W. 2005. "Police Use of Force: A Transactional Approach." *Justice Quarterly* 22(1): 107–139.

Terrill, W. and S. Mastrofsky. 2002. "Situational and Officer-Based Determinants of Police Coercion." *Justice Quarterly* 19(2): 216–248.

Terrill, W. and E. Paoline. 2007. "Non-Arrest Decision Making in Police-Citizen Encounters." *Police Quarterly* 10: 308–331.

Terrill, W. and E. Paoline. 2011. "Conducted Energy Devices (CEDs) and Citizen Injuries: The Shocking Empirical Reality." *Justice Quarterly* 29(2): 153–182.

Terrill, W., E. Paoline, and P. Manning. 2003. "Police Culture and Coercion." *Criminology* 41(4): 1003–1034.

Texas Bar Association. 2000. *Muting Gideon's Trumpet: The Crisis in Indigent Defense*. Report by the Committee on Legal Services to the Poor in Criminal Matters, Texas State Bar. Retrieved from www.uta.edu/pols/moore/indigent/last.pdf.

Texas Civil Rights Project. 2011. *Police Misconduct in San Antonio*. Austin, TX: Texas Civil Rights Project. Retrieved from www.texascivilrightsproject.org.

Texas District & County Attorneys Association (TDCAA). 2012. *Setting the Record Straight on Prosecutorial Misconduct*. Retrieved 3/23/2014 from http://www.tdcaa.com/reports/setting-the-record-straight-on-prosecutorial-misconduct.

Thibaut, J. and L. Walker, L. 1975. *Procedural Justice*. Hillsdale, NJ: Erlbaum.

Thoma, S. 1986. "Estimating Gender Differences in the Comprehension and Preference of Moral Issues." *Developmental Review* 6: 165–180.

Thomas, E. 2001. "A Captain's Story." *Newsweek*, April 2. Retrieved from http://www.newsweek.com/captains-story-150105.

Thompson, C. 2015. "Dozens in D.C., Maryland Paid the Ultimate Price for Cooperating with Police." *Washington Post*, January 10. Retrieved from www.washingtonpost.com/local/dozens-in-dc-maryland-paid-the-ultimate-price-for-cooperating-with-police/2015/01/10/978b1a18-b5f6-11e3-b899-20667de76985_story.html.

Thompson, D. 1980. "Paternalism in Medicine, Law and Public Policy." In *Ethics Teaching in Higher Education*, ed. D. Callahan and S. Bok, 3–20. Hastings, NY: Hastings Center.

Thompson, D. 2004. "Prison System Blasted by Lawmakers, New Administration." *Sandiego.com*, January 20. Retrieved 7/30/2012 from http://signonsandiego.com/news/state/20040120-1658-ca-prisonhearings.html.

Thompson, D. 2016. "California Corrections Chief Aims to Change Prison Culture." *Sacramento Bee*, February 9. Retrieved from http://www.sacbee.com/news/state/california/article59502198.html.

Tobin, W. and C. Spiegleman. 2013. "Crime Labs Stained by 'Junk Science.'" *Austin*

American Statesman, October 13, 2013, E1, E3.

Toch, H. 1977. *Living in Prison*. New York: Free Press.

Tonry, M. 2005. "The Functions of Sentencing and Sentencing Reform." *Stanford Law Review* 58: 37–67.

Toobin, J. 2014 "This Is My Jail." *The New Yorker*, April 14, 2014.

Trager, R. 2014. "Hard Questions After Litany of Forensic Failures at US Labs." *Chemistryworld.com*, December 1. Retrieved from www.rsc.org/chemistryworld/2014/12/hard-questions-after-litany-forensic-failures-malpractice-labs-us.

Trainum, J. 2008. "The Case for Videotaping Interrogations." *Los Angeles Times*, October 24. Retrieved from www.latimes.com/news/opinion/commentary/la-oe-trainum24-2008oct24,0,7918545.story.

Transparency International. 2014. *Corruption Perceptions Index, 2013*. Retrieved from https://www.transparency.org/cpi2013/results.

Transparency International. 2017. *Corruption Perceptions Index, 2016*. Retrieved from http://www.transparency.org/news/feature/corruption_perceptions_index_2016.

Trautman, N. 2008. "The Ethics Continuum." Retrieved from www.ethicsinstitute.com/pdf/Corruption%20Continum.pdf.

Travis, J., B. Western, and S. Redburn. 2014. *The Growth of Incarceration in the United States: Exploring Causes and Consequences*. Washington, DC: National Research Council of the National Academies of Science.

Treatment Advocacy Center. 2014. *The Treatment of Persons with Mental Illness in Prisons and Jails: A State Survey*. Retrieved from www.tacreports.org/storage/documents/treatment-behind-bars/treatment-behind-bars.pdf.

Tullio, E. 2009. "Comment: Chemical Castration for Child Predators: Practical, Effective and Constitutional." *Chapman Law Review* 13: 191–219.

Turner, A. 2010. "Panel Cites 'Flawed Science' in Arson Case." *Houston Chronicle*, July 24. Retrieved from www.chron.com/disp/story.mpl/metropolitan/7122381.html.

Turner, C. 2007. "Ethical Issues in Criminal Justice Administration." *American Jails*, January/February: 49–53.

Tyler, T. 1990/2006. *Why People Obey the Law*. New Haven, CT: Yale University Press.

Tyler, T. 2003. "Procedural Justice, Legitimacy, and the Effective Rule of Law." In *Crime and Justice: A Review of Research*, Vol. 30, ed. M. Tonry. Chicago, IL: University of Chicago Press.

Tyler, T. 2010. "Legitimacy in Corrections." *Criminology and Public Policy* 9: 127–134.

Tyler, T. R. 2010/2011. *Why People Cooperate: The Role of Social Motivations*. Princeton, NJ: Princeton University Press.

Tyler, T. and J. Fagan 2008. "Legitimacy and Cooperation: Why Do People Help the Police Fight Crime in Their Communities?" *Ohio State Journal of Criminal Law* 6: 231–75.

Tyler, T., P. Goff, and R. MacCoun. 2015. "The Impact of Psychological Science on Policing in the United States: Procedural Justice, Legitimacy, and Effective Law Enforcement." *Psychological Science in the Public Interest* 16(3): 75–109.

Tyler, T. and Y. Huo. 2002. *Trust in the Law: Encouraging Public Cooperation in the Police and Courts*. New York: Russell Sage Foundation.

Tyler, T. and L. Wakslak. 2004. "Profiling and Police Legitimacy: Procedural Justice, Attributions of Motive, and Acceptance of Police Authority." *Criminology* 42(2): 253–281.

Umbreit, M., R. Coates, and B. Vos. 2002. "Peacemaking Circles in Minnesota: An Exploratory Study." *Crime Victims Report* 5(6): 81–82.

United States Department of Justice. 2014. *Justice Department Releases Findings Showing that the Alabama Department of Corrections Fails to Protect Prisoners from Sexual Abuse and Sexual Harassment at the Julia Tutwiler Prison for Women*. Retrieved from http://www.justice.gov/opa/pr/justice-department-releases-findings-showing-alabama-department-corrections-fails-protect.

United States Department of Justice. 2016. *Investigation of the Baltimore City Police Department*. Washington, DC: USDOJ, Civil Rights Division.

United States Department of Labor. 2017. *Wage and Hour Division*. Retrieved from https://www.dol.gov/whd/minwage/america.htm.

Urza, G. 2014. "Indefensible: Why Khalid Sheikh Mohammed's Lawyer Is Leaving the Defense Team—And the Army." *Slate*, August 26. Retrieved from http://www.slate.com/articles/news_and_politics/jurisprudence/2014/08/khalid_sheikh_mohammed_s_guantanamo_defense_lawyer_jason_wright_is_departing.html.

Van Craen, M. and W. Skogan. 2017. "Achieving Fairness in Policing: The Link Between Internal and External Procedural Justice." *Police Quarterly* 20(1): 3–23.

Van Maanen, J. 1978. "The Asshole." In *Policing: A View from the Street*, ed. P. Manning and J. van Maanen, 221–240. Santa Monica, CA: Goodyear.

Van Ness, D. and K. Heetderks Strong. 1997. *Restoring Justice*. Cincinnati, OH: Anderson.

Vargas, T. 2016. "Dallas Police Chief David Brown Lost His Son, Former Partner and Brother to Violence." *Washington Post*, July 8. Retrieved from https://www.washingtonpost.com/local/dallas-police-chief-david-brown-has-lost-his-son-former-partner-and-brother-to-violence/2016/07/08/01419ea8-451c-11e6-8856-f26de2537a9d_story.html?utm_term=.13880d6e64f4.

Vaughn, M. and L. Smith. 1999. "Practicing Penal Harm Medicine in U.S. Prisons." *Justice Quarterly* 16(1): 175–231.

Vedantam, S. 2007. "If It Feels Good to Be Good, It Might Be Only Natural." *WashingtonPost.com*. Retrieved from www.washingtonpost.com/wp-dyn/content/article/2007/05/27/AR2007052701056.html.

Vera Institute of Justice. 2017. *To Protect and Serve: New Trends in State-Level Policing Reform, 2015–2016*. (April). Retrieved from https://www.vera.org/publications/protect-and-serve-policing-trends-2015-2016.

Verdugo, E. 2017. "Trump's "Tough on Crime" Policies Won't Make Us Safer-They'll Make Corporations Richer." *American Friends Service Committee*, March 16. Retrieved from https://www.afsc.org/blogs/news-and-commentary/trumps-tough-crime-policies.

Verges, A. 2010. "Integrating Contextual Issues in Ethical Decision Making." *Ethics & Behavior* 20: 497–507.

Victor, B. and J. Cullen. 1987. "A Theory and Measure of Ethical Climate in

Organizations." *Research in Corporate Social Performance and Policy* 9: 51–71.

Victor, B. and J. Cullen. 1988. "The Organizational Bases of Ethical Work Climates." *Administrative Science Quarterly* 33: 101–125.

Vitiello, M. 2008. "Punishing Sex Offenders: When Good Intentions Go Bad." *Arizona State Law Review* 40: 651–689.

Vodicka, D. 2009. *The Green Wall.* Bloomington, IN: iUniverse Inc.

Vogelstein, R. 2003. "Confidentiality vs. Care: Re-Evaluating the Duty to Self, Client, and Others." *Georgetown Law Journal* 92: 153–171.

Voigt, R., N. Camp, V. Prabhakaran, W. Hamilton, R. Hetey, C. Griffiths, D. Jurgens, D. Jurafskya, and J. Eberhardt. 2017. "Language from Police Body Camera Footage Shows Racial Disparities in Officer Respect." *Proceedings of the National Academy of Sciences* 114(25): 6521–6526.

Von Hirsch, A. 1976. *Doing Justice.* New York: Hill and Wang.

Von Hirsch, A. 1985. *Past or Future Crimes.* New Brunswick, NJ: Rutgers University Press.

Von Hirsch, A. and L. Maher. 1992. "Should Penal Rehabilitationism Be Revived?" *Criminal Justice Ethics* 11(1): 25–30.

Wagner, P. and A. Walsh. 2016. *States of Incarceration: The Global Context 2016.* East Hampton, MA: Prison Policy Initiative. Retrieved from http://www.prisonpolicy.org/.

Walker, L. 1986. "Sex Difference in the Development of Moral Reasoning." *Child Development* 57: 522–526.

Walker, L. 2014. "Snowden Docs Lead to Discovery NSA Employees Spied on Spouses, Girlfriends." *Newsweek*, December 26. Retrieved from www.newsweek.com/snowden-docs-lead-discovery-nsa-employees-spied-spouses-girlfriends-294994.

Walker, S. 1985/2005. *Sense and Nonsense About Crime.* Monterey, CA: Brooks/Cole.

Walker, S. 2001. *Police Accountability: The Role of Citizen Oversight.* Belmont, CA: Wadsworth.

Walker, S. 2007. *Police Accountability: Current Issues and Research Needs.* Paper presented at National Institute of Justice, Policing Research Workshop: Planning for the Future, Washington, DC, November 28–29, 2006. (Available through National Institute of Justice, Washington, DC.)

Walker, S. 2015. "How Seattle Bridged the Community Police Divide." *The Crime Report*, August 27. Retrieved from https://thecrimereport.org/2015/08/27/2015-08-how-seattle-bridged-the-community-police-divide/.

Walker, S. 2017. "Twenty Years of DOJ "Pattern or Practice" Investigations of Local Police: Achievements, Limitations, and Questions." Retrieved from samuelwalker.net/wp-content/uploads/2017/02/DOJ-PP-Program-Feb24.pdf.

Walker, S. and G. Alpert. 2002. "Early Warning Systems as Risk Management for Police." In *Policing and Misconduct*, ed. K. Lersch, 219–230. Upper Saddle River, NJ: Prentice Hall.

Walker, S., G. Alpert, and D. Kenney. 2000. "Early Warning Systems for Police: Concept, History, and Issues." *Police Quarterly* 3: 132–152.

Wallack, T., J. Ransom, and T. Anderson. 2015. "Boston Paid $36m to Settle Police Lawsuits." *Boston Globe*, May 15. Retrieved from www.bostonglobe.com/metro/2015/05/14/boston-spends-million- resolve-claims-against-police/KZ1NKhzahIDG51568m5FLK/ story.html.

Walsh, D., M. Raju, and S. Collinson. 2017. "House Republicans Pull Plan to Gut Independent Ethics Committee After Trump Tweets." *CNN Politics*, January 3. Retrieved from http://www.cnn.com/2017/01/02/politics/office-of-congressional-ethics-oversight-of-ethics-committee-amendment/index.html.

Ward, M. 2004. "Echoes of Texas' Sordid Past in Iraq Prison Abuse." *Austin American-Statesman*, May 12: B4.

Ward, M. 2006. "Secrecy of Parole Files Opens Door for Abuses." *Austin American-Statesman*, March 18: A1, A11.

Ward, M. 2013. "Parole Officers, Youth-Prison Workers Busted in Separate Crackdowns." *American-Statesman*, July 1. Retrieved from www.statesman.com/news/news/parole-officers-youth-prison-workers-busted-in-sep/nYbXh/.

Ward, S. 2007. "Pulse of the Legal Profession." *ABA Journal*, October. Retrieved from www.abajournal.com/magazine/article/pulse_of_the_legal_profession.

Warren, J. 2004a. "Guards Tell of Retaliation for Informing." *Los Angeles Times*, January 21. Retrieved from http://articles.latimes.com/2004/jan/21/local/me-prison21.

Warren, J. 2004b. "State Penal System Is Hammered in Report." *Los Angeles Times.* Retrieved from http://articles.latimes.com/2004/jan/16/local/me-prisons16.

Warrick, J. and P. Finn. 2009. "Harsh Tactics Readied Before Their Approval." *Washington Post*, April 22. Retrieved from www.washingtonpost.com/wp-dyn/content/article/2009/04/21/AR2009042104055.html.

Wasikowska, M. 2013. "Spying on Law-Abiding Muslims." *New York Times,* February 10, 2013: SR10.

Weber, D. 1987. "Still in Good Standing. The Crisis in Attorney Discipline." *American Bar Association Journal*, November: 58–63.

Weichselbaum, S. and B. Schwartzapfel. 2017. "When Veterans Become Cops, Some Bring War Home." *USA Today*, March 30. Retrieved from https://www.usatoday.com/story/news/2017/03/30/when-veterans-become-cops-some-bring-war-home/99349228/.

Weinstein, H. 2007. "ACLU: Company Aiding Torture." *Los Angeles Times.* Reprinted in *Austin American-Statesman*, May 31: A8.

Weisburd, D. and R. Greenspan. 2000. *Police Attitudes Toward Abuse of Authority: Findings from a National Study (Research In Brief).* Washington, DC: U.S. Department of Justice.

Weiser, B. 2015. "Deal Is Near on Far-Reaching Reforms at Rikers, Including a Federal Monitor." *New York Times*, June 19: A1.

Weiser, B. 2016a. "No U.S. Charges Against Cuomo on Ethics Panel." *New York Times*, January 12: A1.

Weiser, B. 2016b. "Female Inmates' Suit Says Sex Abuse Is Persistent in State Prisons." *New York Times,* February 26: A24.

Weiss, D. 2014. "Lawyers in Prestige Positions Aren't as Happy as Those in Public Service Jobs, Study Finds." *ABA Journal*, March 14. Retrieved from http://www.abajournal.com/news/article/lawyers_in_prestige_positions_arent_as_happy_as_those_in_public_service-job/.

Weiser, B., M. Schwirtz, and M. Winerip. 2014. "U.S. Plans Suit Over Conditions at Rikers Island." *New York Times*, December 19: A1.

Weitekampa, E. and S. Parmentier. 2016. "Restorative Justice as Healing Justice: Looking Back to the Future of the Concept." *Restorative Justice: An International Journal* 4(2): 141–147.

Weitzer, R. 1999. "Citizens' Perceptions of Police Misconduct: Race and Neighborhood Context." *Justice Quarterly* 16(4): 819–846.

Weitzer, R. and S. Tuch. 2002. "Perceptions of Racial Profiling: Race, Class, and Personal Experience." *Criminology* 40(2): 435–456.

Weitzer, R. and S. Tuch. 2004. "Race and Perceptions of Police Misconduct." *Social Problems* 51(3): 305–325.

Wells, W. and J. Schafer. 2006. "Officer Perceptions of Police Responses to Persons with a Mental Illness." *Policing: An International Journal of Police Strategies and Management* 29(4): 578–601.

Wendle, J. 2009. "New Rules for Russia's Cops: No Bribes or Wild Sex." *Time.com*, April 15. Retrieved from www.time.com/time/printout/0,8816,1891215,00.html.

Westmarland, L. 2005. "Police Ethics and Integrity: Breaking the Blue Code of Silence." *Policing and Society* 15(2): 145–165.

Westneat, D. 2017a. "UW Leader's Perfect Timing on Free Speech." *Seattle Times*, February 1: B1.

Westneat, D. 2017b. "Oregon ACLU Test Backers' Principles." *Seattle Times*, May 31: B1.

WHAS. 2017. "Alabama Cop Buys Groceries for Mom Caught Stealing Food for Infant." *WHAS*, May 13. Retrieved from http://www.insideedition.com/headlines/23349-officer-buys-groceries-for-mom-caught-stealing-food-for-infant-i-felt-so-grateful.

Wheeler, B. 2012. "The Rise of the Undercover Sting." *BBC News Magazine*, February 28. Retrieved from www.bbc.co.uk/news/magazine-17160690.

White, J. 2005. "Documents Tell of Brutal Improvisation by GIs." *Washington Post*, August 3: A1.

White, M., P. Mulvey, and L. Dario. 2016. "Arrestees' Perceptions of the Police: Exploring Procedural Justice, Legitimacy, and Willingness to Cooperate with Police Across Offender Types." *Criminal Justice and Behavior* 43(3): 343–364.

White, M. and J. Ready. 2009. "Examining Fatal and Nonfatal Incidents Involving the TASER." *Criminology and Public Policy* 8(4): 865–891.

White, R. 1999. "Are Women More Ethical? Recent Findings on the Effects of Gender on Moral Development." *Journal of Public Administration Research and Theory* 9: 459–472.

Whitehead, S. 2015. "The Specter of Racism: Exploring White Racial Anxieties in the Context of Policing." *Contemporary Justice Review*. DOI: 10.1080/10282580.2015.1025622.

Whitlock, C. 2005. "CIA Role in Abductions Investigated." *Austin American-Statesman*, March 13: A5.

Whitman, J. 1998. "What Is Wrong with Inflicting Shame Sanctions?" *Yale Law Journal* 197(4): 1055–1092.

Wiggins, O., J. Hicks, and F. Nirappil. 2016. "Police and Sentencing Reform Pass, Tax-Relief Fails in Annapolis." *Washington Post*, April 11. Retrieved from https://www.washingtonpost.com/local/md-politics/in-annapolis-signs-that-noahs-law-paid-sick-leave-will-advance/2016/04/11/0605d974-ff24-11e5-9203-7b8670959b88_story.html?utm_term=.9c5c97d4e248.

Wilber, D. 2017. "Justice Department Watchdog Finds DEA Cash Seizure Program May Pose Risk to Civil Liberties." *Los Angeles Times*, March 30. Retrieved from http://www.latimes.com/politics/washington/la-na-essential-washington-updates-justice-department-watchdog-finds-that-1490800542-htmlstory.html.

Wilder, F. 2013. "Give Us Your Tired, Your Poor, Your Huddled Masses—We Have Private Prisons to Fill." *Texas Observer*, May 1. Retrieved from www.texasobserver.org/give-us-your-tired-your-poor-your-huddled-masses-we-have-private-prisons-to-fill/.

Wilder, F. and P. Mosqueda, 2014. "Immigrants in Federal Prisons 'Subjected to Shocking Abuse and Mistreatment.'" *ACLU/Texas*, June 9, 2014. Retrieved from www.prisonlegalnews.org/news/publications/aclu-warhoused-and-forgotten-immigrants-trapped-our-private-prison-system/.

Williams, C. 2008. "Prosecution of Youths at Guantanamo Spurs Outrage." *Los Angeles Times*, December 28: A1.

Williams, H. 2010. *Are the Recommendations of the Braidwood Commission on Conducted Energy Weapons Use Sound Public Policy?* Paper presented at the Academy of Criminal Justice Sciences Meeting, February, San Diego.

Williams, H. 2013. *Physiological Attributes of Arrest-Related Sudden Deaths Proximate to the Application of Taser Electronic Control Devices: An Evidence Based Study of the Theory of High Risk Groups* (Doctoral Dissertation). Texas State University.

Williams, M., J. Holcomb, T. Kovandzic, and S. Bullock. 2010. "Policing for Profit: The Abuse of Civil Asset Forfeiture." *Institute for Justice*. Retrieved from www.ij.org/images/pdf_folder/other_pubs/assetforfeituretoemail.pdf.

Williams, T. 2014. "Panel to Set Terms to End Abusive Reign at Jail System." *Los Angeles Times*, December 17: A18.

Williams, T. 2015a. "Inquiry to Examine the Extent of Racial Bias in the San Francisco Police." *New York Times*, May 8: A13.

Williams, T. 2015b. "Jails Have Become Warehouses for the Poor, Ill and Addicted, a Report Says." *New York Times*, February 11: A19.

Williams, T. 2015c. "Chicago Rarely Penalizes Officers for Complaints, Data Shows." *New York Times*, November 19, 2015: A19.

Williams, T. 2015d. "Police Depts. Using ID Tool Honed in War." *New York Times*, August 13: A1.

Williams, T. 2016a. "U.S. Taking Back Military Gear from Local Law Enforcement." *New York Times*, January 27: A1.

Williams, T. 2016b. "Officers with Troubled Pasts Often Wind Up Back in Blue." *New York Times*, September 11: A1.

Wilson, J. Q. 1976. *Varieties of Police Behavior*. New York: Atheneum.

Wilson, J. Q. 1993. *The Moral Sense*. New York: Free Press.

Wilson, R. 2015. "Police Accountability Measures Flood State Legislatures After Ferguson, Staten Island." *Washington Post*, February 4. Retrieved from www.washingtonpost.com/blogs/govbeat/wp/2015/02/04/police-accountability-measures-flood-state-legislatures-after-ferguson-staten-island/.

Wiltrout, K. 2007. "Naval Officer Sentenced to Six Months in Prison, Discharge."

McClatchy-Tribune Information Services, May 18. Retrieved from www.accessmylibrary.com/coms2/summary_0286-30808288_ITM.

Wiltz, T. 2017. "How 'Raise the Age' Laws Might Reduce Recidivism." *Stateline*, May 31. Retrieved from http://www.pewtrusts.org/en/research-and-analysis/blogs/stateline/2017/05/31/how-raise-the-age-laws-might-reduce-recidivism.

Wimbush, J., J. Shepard, and S. Markham. "An Empirical Examination of the Relationship Between Ethical Climate and Ethical Behavior from Multiple Levels of Analysis." *Journal of Business Ethics* 16(16): 1705–1716.

Winerip, M. and M. Schwirtz. 2014a. "In Rare Rebuke for Rikers Officers, Judge Urges Firing of 6 Who Beat Inmate." *New York Times*, September 30: A18.

Winerip, M. and M. Schwirtz, M. 2014b. "Rikers: Where Mental Illness Meets Brutality in Jail." *New York Times*, July 14: A1.

Winerip, M. and M. Schwirtz. 2015a. "An Inmate Dies, and No One Is Punished." *New York Times*, December 14: A1.

Winerip, M. and M. Schwirtz. 2015b. "Family Files Suit in Prison Homicide as an Ex Inmate Speaks Out." *New York Times*, September 10: A27.

Winerip, M. and M. Schwirtz. 2016. "Prison Guards Are Charged in '13 Beating of an Inmate." *New York Times*, September 21: A25.

Winerip, M., M. Schwirtz, and T. Robbins. 2016. "New York State Taking on Union of Prison Guards." *New York Times*, April 12: A1.

Wines, M. 2014. "Are Police Bigoted?" *New York Times*, August 31: SR1.

Wines, M. and S. Cohen. 2015. "Police Killings Rise Slightly." *New York Times*, May 1: A1

Wing, N. 2015. "16 Numbers that Explain Why Police Reform Became an Even Bigger Story in 2015." *Huffington Post*, December 29. Retrieved from http://www.huffingtonpost.com/entry/police-reform-numbers 2015_5672e150e4b0688701dc7a54.

Wise, R. and M. Safer. 2012. "A Method for Analyzing the Accuracy of Eyewitness Testimony in Criminal Cases." *Court Review* 48: 22–34.

Wisnieski, A. 2015. "Outrageous Government Conduct." *The Crime Report*, November 16. Retrieved from http://www.thecrimereport.org/news/inside-criminal-justice/2015-11-outrageous-government-conduct.

Wisnieski, A. 2016. "Your Assets Are Mine." *The Crime Report*, January 6. Retrieved from http://www.thecrimereport.org/news/articles/2016-01-your-assets-are-mine.

Witt, A. 2001. "Allegations of Abuses Mar Murder Cases." *Washington Post*, June 23: A01.

Wogan, J. 2017. "The New, More Powerful Wave of Civilian Oversight of Police." *Governing.gov*, February 27. Retrieved from http://www.governing.com/topics/public-justice-safety/gov-police-civilian-oversight-oakland-seattle.html.

Wolfe, C. 1991. *Judicial Activism*. Pacific Grove, CA: Brooks/Cole Publishing.

Wolfe, S. and A. Piquero. 2011. "Organizational Justice and Police Misconduct." *Criminal Justice and Behavior* 38(4): 332–353.

Wood, D. 2015. "San Francisco Police Texting Scandal: How Can Police Root Out Racism?" *Christian Science Monitor*, March 19. Retrieved from www.csmonitor.com/USA/Justice/2015/0319/San-Francisco-police-texting-scandal-How-can-police-root-out-racism.

Wood, J. 1997. *Royal Commission into the New South Wales Police Service, Final Report*. Sydney, Australia: Government of the State of N.S.W. (cited in Prenzler and Ronken, 2001b).

Worley, R. and V. Worley. 2011. "Guards Gone Wild: A Self Report Study of Correctional Officer Misconduct and the Effect of Institutional Deviance on 'Care' Within the Texas Prison System." *Deviant Behavior* 32: 293–319.

Worrall, J. and T. Kovandzi. 2008. "Is Policing for Profit? Answers from Asset Forfeiture." *Criminology and Public Policy* 7(2): 219–244.

Wren, T. 1985. "Whistle-Blowing and Loyalty to One's Friends." In *Police Ethics: Hard Choices in Law Enforcement*, ed. W. Heffernan and T. Stroup, 25–37. New York: John Jay Press.

Wright, K. 2001. "Management-Staff Relations: Issues in Leadership, Ethics, and Values." In *Discretion, Community and Correctional Ethics*, ed. J. Kleinig

and M. Smith, 203–218. Oxford, England: Rowman and Littlefield.

Wyatt-Nichol, H. and G. Franks. 2010. "Ethics Training in Law Enforcement Agencies." *Public Integrity* 12(1): 39–50.

Yakin, H. 2015. "Police Learn New Way of Dealing with the Mentally Ill." *Times Herald-Record*, September 26. Retrieved from http://www.recordonline.com/article/20150926/NEWS/150929449.

Yong, E. 2012. "One Molecule for Love, Morality, and Prosperity?" *Slate*, July 17. Retrieved from http://www.slate.com/articles/health_and_science/medical_examiner/2012/07/oxytocin_is_not_a_love_drug_don_t_give_it_to_kids_with_autism_.single.html.

Yong, E. 2014. "Oxytocin Boosts Dishonesty." *The Scientist*, March 31. Retrieved from http://www.the-scientist.com/?articles.view/articleNo/39595/title/Oxytocin-Boosts-Dishonesty/.

York, G. 2012. *Corruption Behind Bars: Stories of Crime and Corruption in Our American Prison System*. Seattle, WA: Amazon (Kindle EBooks).

York, G. 2013. *Inside the Inner Circle: More Stories of Crime and Corruption in Our American Prison System*. Bloomington, IN: iUniverse.

Yost, P. 2010. "FBI Looking into Deadly Coal Mine Explosion." *Austin American-Statesman*, May 1: A9.

Zacharias, F. and B. Green. 2009. "The Duty to Avoid Wrongful Convictions: A Thought Experiment in the Regulation of Prosecutors." *Boston University Law Review* 89: 1–59.

Zak, P. 2012. *The Moral Molecule*. New York: Dutton.

Zalman, M., B. Smith, and A. Kiger. 2008. "Officials' Estimates of the Incidence of 'Actual Innocence' Convictions." *Justice Quarterly* 25(1): 72–100.

Zamora, J., H. Lee, and J. van Derbeke. 2003. "Ex-Cops Cleared of 8 Counts." *SFGate.com*, October 1. Retrieved from www.sfgate.com/bayarea/article/Ex-cops-cleared-of-8-counts-mistrial-on-27-2555011.php.

Zetter, K. 2015. "The Feds Need a Warrant to Spy with Stingrays from Now On." *Wired*, September 3. Retrieved from http://www.wired.com/2015/09/feds need warrant spy stingrays now/.

Zhao, J., N. He, and N. Lovrich. 1998. "Individual Value Preferences Among American Police Officers." *Policing: An International Journal of Police Strategies and Management* 21(1): 22–37.

Zimbardo, P. 1982. "The Prison Game." In *Legal Process and Corrections*, ed.

N. Johnston and L. Savitz, 195–198. New York: Wiley.

Zimring, F., G. Hawkins, and S. Kamin. 2001. *Punishment and Democracy: Three Strikes and You're Out in California*. Oxford, England: Oxford University Press.

Zitrin, R. and C. Langford. 1999. *The Moral Compass of the American Lawyer*. New York: Ballantine Books.

Zohar, N. 2004. "Innocence and Complex Threats: Upholding the War Ethic and the Condemnation of Terrorism." *Ethics* 114: 734–751.

Author Index

Subject Index

Note: Page numbers followed by italic *f* or *b* refer to figures or boxes.

Table of Cases

523